S0-AIU-039

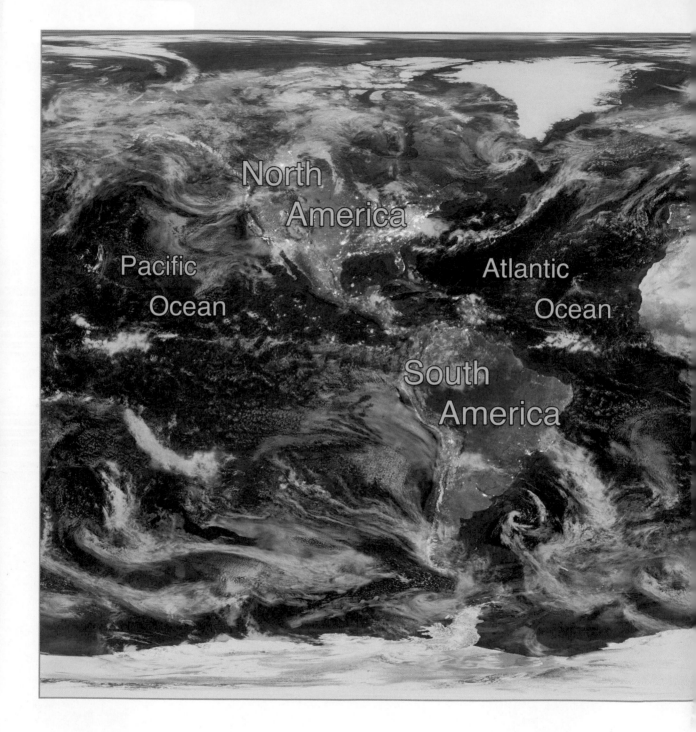

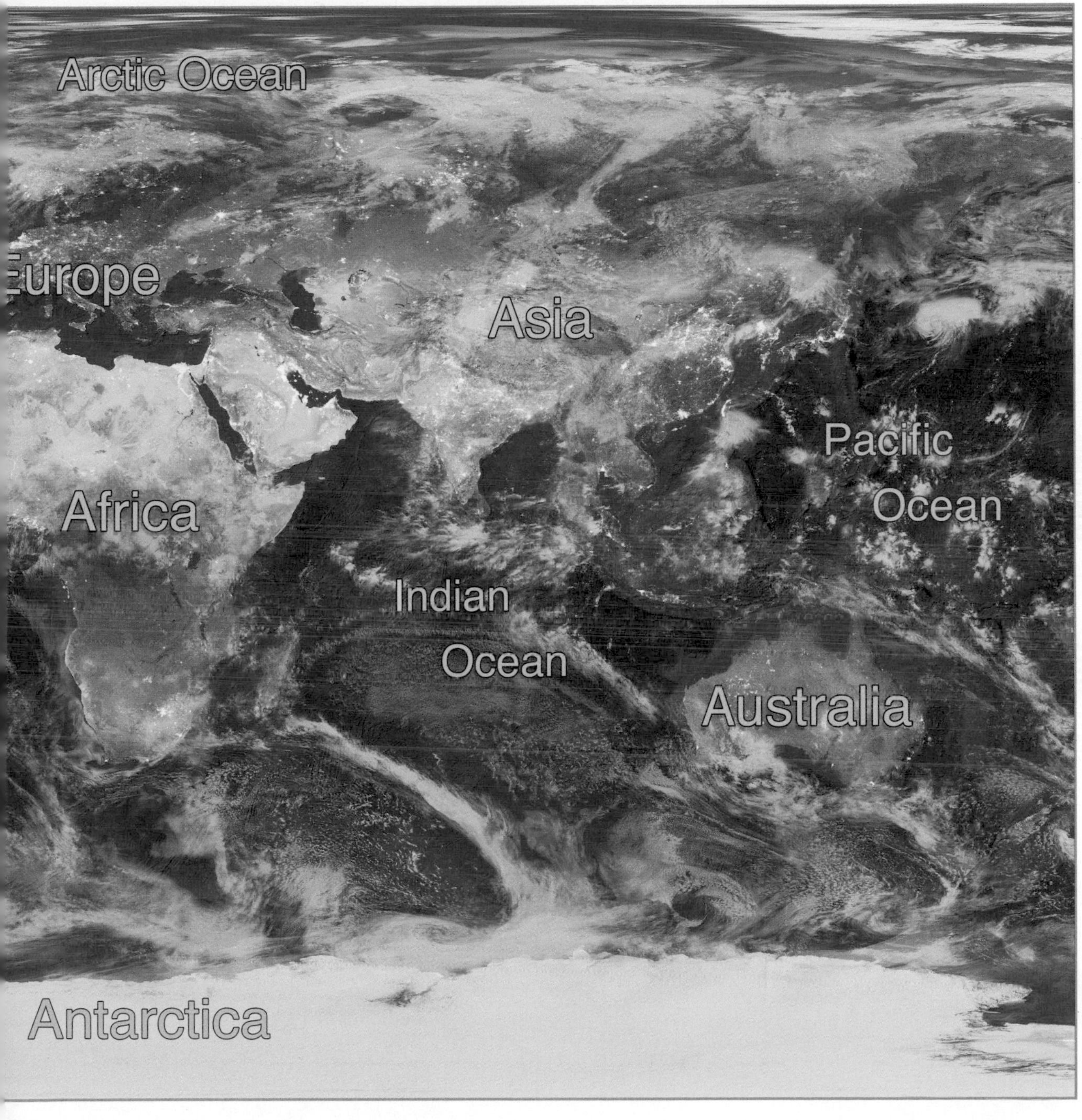

Arctic Ocean

Europe

Asia

Africa

Pacific Ocean

Indian Ocean

Australia

Antarctica

CONCISE THIRD EDITION

Worlds Together, Worlds Apart

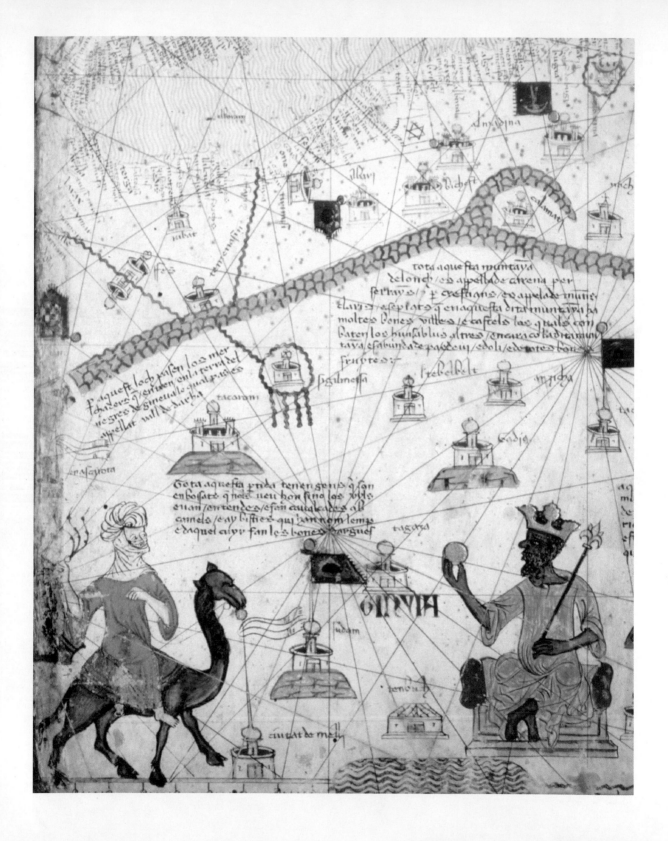

CONCISE THIRD EDITION

Worlds Together, Worlds Apart

VOLUME 1
Beginnings through the Fifteenth Century

Jeremy Adelman

Elizabeth Pollard

Clifford Rosenberg

Robert Tignor

W. W. NORTON & COMPANY
Independent Publishers Since 1923

W. W. Norton & Company has been independent since its founding in 1923, when William Warder Norton and Mary D. Herter Norton first published lectures delivered at the People's Institute, the adult education division of New York City's Cooper Union. The firm soon expanded its program beyond the Institute, publishing books by celebrated academics from America and abroad. By midcentury, the two major pillars of Norton's publishing program—trade books and college texts—were firmly established. In the 1950s, the Norton family transferred control of the company to its employees, and today—with a staff of five hundred and hundreds of trade, college, and professional titles published each year—W. W. Norton & Company stands as the largest and oldest publishing house owned wholly by its employees.

Copyright © 2021, 2019, 2015 by W. W. Norton & Company, Inc.
All rights reserved
Printed in Canada

Editor: Jon Durbin
Project Editor: David Bradley
Assistant Editor: Lily Gellman
Managing Editor, College: Marian Johnson
Managing Editor, College Digital Media: Kim Yi
Production Managers: Jane Searle and Benjamin Reynolds
Media Editor: Carson Russell
Media Project Editor: Rachel Mayer
Associate Media Editor: Alexander Lee
Assistant Media Editor: Alexandra Malakhoff
Marketing Manager, History: Sarah England Bartley
Design Director: Rubina Yeh
Designer: Lissi Sigillo
Director of College Permissions: Megan Schindel
Permissions Specialist: Elizabeth Trammell
Photo Editor: Mike Cullen
Composition: KnowledgeWorks Global Ltd.
Illustrations: Mapping Specialists, Ltd.
Manufacturing: Transcontinental Printing–Beauceville

Permission to use copyrighted material is included in the credits section of this book, which begins on page C-1.

ISBN: 978-0-393-44289-2

W. W. Norton & Company, Inc., 500 Fifth Avenue, New York, NY 10110-0017
wwnorton.com

W. W. Norton & Company Ltd., 15 Carlisle Street, London W1D 3BS

1 2 3 4 5 6 7 8 9 0

BRIEF CONTENTS

CONTENTS

1

Becoming Human   3

STORYLINE: Prehistory and the Peopling of the Earth

2

Rivers, Cities, and First States, 3500–2000 BCE   57

STORYLINE: Comparing First Cities

3

Nomads, Territorial States, and Microsocieties, 2000–1200 BCE　109

STORYLINE: Comparing First States

4

First Empires and Common Cultures in Afro-Eurasia, 1250–325 BCE 163

STORYLINE: Comparing First Empires and the Beginnings of Judaism

5

Worlds Turned Inside Out, 1000–350 BCE   213

STORYLINE: The Axial Age

6

Shrinking the Afro-Eurasian World, 350–100 BCE 263

STORYLINE: The Creation of the Silk Roads and the Beginnings of Buddhism

7

Han Dynasty China and Imperial Rome, 300 BCE–300 CE   315

STORYLINE: Comparing the Han and Roman Empires

8

The Rise of Universalizing Religions, 300–600 CE   365

STORYLINE: The Rise of Christianity, the Spread of Buddhism, and the Beginnings of Common Cultures

9

New Empires and Common Cultures, 600–1000 CE 421

STORYLINE: Religion and Empires: Islam, the Tang Dynasty, Christendom, and Common Cultures

10

Becoming "The World," 1000–1300 CE

473

STORYLINE: The Emergence of the World We Know Today

11

Crisis and Recovery in Afro-Eurasia, 1300–1500   531

STORYLINE: The Black Death, Recovery, and Conquest

CURRENT TRENDS IN WORLD HISTORY

GLOBAL THEMES AND SOURCES AND INTERPRETING VISUAL EVIDENCE

MAPS

PREFACE

Worlds Together, Worlds Apart sets the standard for those who want to teach a globally integrated and comparative world history survey course. Building on the success of the Concise Second Edition, co-authors Jeremy Adelman (Princeton University), Elizabeth Pollard (San Diego State University), Clifford Rosenberg (City University of New York), and Robert Tignor (Princeton University) have created this dynamic and highly accessible new Concise Third Edition of *Worlds Together, Worlds Apart*.

The new Concise Edition is written with clear, accessible prose and explanations, with a narrative that is twenty percent shorter than the Full Edition. It is a coherent, concise, cutting-edge survey of the field built around world history stories of significance, which we call **"Global Storylines."** These Global Storylines have the dual benefit of making the material more focused and more manageable for students. They also allow students to more readily make connections and comparisons across time and place since most, if not all, regions of the world are discussed in many of the chapters. Some of our favorite examples of Global Storylines include the creation of the Silk Roads and comparing the Han dynasty and the Roman Empire in the first volume and, in the second volume, the global impact of the Atlantic and industrial revolutions and the alternative visions for organizing societies in response to the rise of nineteenth-century capitalism and the impact of modern globalization today.

Worlds Together, Worlds Apart, **Concise Third Edition, provides a global history learning framework built around core objectives that is designed to guide students' reading, help students make the connections and comparisons that are a unique learning objective for world history, and improve their skills, overall knowledge, and performance.**

The core objective guided-reading pedagogy in each chapter helps students make global connections and comparisons as they read:

* The first four pages of each chapter provide a conceptual road map for the Global Storyline that the chapter features throughout. **Chapter Outlines** and **Core Objectives** appear on the first two pages and identify important global concepts and developments that relate to the Global Storyline. A **Global Storyline** feature on page three addresses the world history story of significance for that chapter and its underlying historical forces. And the **Big Picture** feature on the fourth page poses a question that highlights

the chapter's most important global core objective—the one that focuses on the Global Storyline.

- Throughout the chapter, **Key Term Marginal Definitions** expand on **Boldfaced Key Terms** in the text to make the narrative more accessible. And the **Marginal Core Objective flags** reference the Core Objectives throughout the chapter so that students know when to focus in on the most relevant material. The unique **The Global View** maps feature a two-page global map that provides a cartographic representation of each chapter's Global Storyline.

- End-of-chapter features include **Tracing the Global Storyline** summaries that remind students of the overarching global story introduced at the start of each chapter and show its impact on each world region, visual **Chronologies** that compare—region by region—the dates of key events covered in the chapter, and **Thinking about Global Connections** questions.

- *Worlds Together, Worlds Apart*'s unique **built-in reader** includes two skill-building features in the **Global Themes and Sources** and **Interpreting Visual Evidence** features. Global Themes and Sources provides comparative perspectives from around the world on each chapter's Global Storyline, while focusing on historical thinking skills like causation, continuity and change, context, and comparison. Interpreting Visual Evidence features focus on images and objects from around the word that connect back to each chapter's Global Storyline.

The New Concise Third Edition

New Authorial Leadership

The publication of the new editions of the *Worlds Together, Worlds Apart* book family (Concise Third, Seagull Third, and Full Sixth Editions) brings a number of significant changes, most visibly with the authorial team. Out of that initial team of authors, the authors of *Worlds Together, Worlds Apart* agreed to reconstitute into a smaller team of four. **Elizabeth Pollard,** a Roman historian at San Diego State University, becomes the lead author of the first volume, cutting across all versions. For nearly two decades, she has taught the pre-1500 CE world history survey to classes of 30 to 500 students both in person and remotely. **Jeremy Adelman,** a historian of Latin America and the Atlantic world and the director of the Global History Lab at Princeton University, becomes lead author of the second volume of the Full Edition. Adelman teaches a survey in global history from 1300 to the present both at Princeton and online. Tens of thousands of students worldwide have taken his course. **Clifford Rosenberg** (City University of New York), a distinguished historian of modern France and its empire, continues to bring his diverse teaching experiences and pedagogical insights to the modern volumes in the Concise and Seagull Editions. **Robert Tignor,** a distinguished Africanist and the original general editor and the soul behind this book, remains an author in both volumes of the Full Edition, bringing his experience and eye for the big picture to bear on the book's prose. The changes in our authorial team have also brought departures. We started *Worlds Together, Worlds Apart* in its first edition as a much larger group, which included Steve Aron, Peter Brown, Ben Elman, Steve Kotkin, Xinru Liu, Sue Marchand, Holly Pittman, Gyan Prakash, Brent Shaw, and Michael Tsin. They were vital to mobilizing the latest specialist scholarship and to integrating a wide range of perspectives into one narrative, and this edition is indebted to their contributions. Our team of four allows us to strengthen the core themes with a unity of voice while remaining committed to the original principles of diversity of perspective.

Authors with Diverse Classroom Experiences and a Strong Focus on Teaching with Primary Sources

From teaching a diverse array of students, we have learned about the challenge of teaching complex global processes—how societies converge, connect, and come together and how global orders fall apart. In addition to teaching a varied set of students, we have also taught world history in multiple formats and settings, including hybrid, fully online, and large lecture classes. In each of these modalities, we have developed extensive experience teaching with primary sources, which the Concise Third Edition of *Worlds Together, Worlds Apart* reflects in its unique built-in reader. The **Global Themes and Sources** and **Interpreting Visual Evidence** features that appear at the end of each chapter bring a global comparative approach, highlighting the Global Storyline in each chapter to help students learn how to analyze and interpret both textual and visual sources, while developing their historical thinking skills like causation, continuity and change, comparison, and contexts. These Primary Source features also bring a range of important themes to life, from gender to the environment. For example, the Global Themes and Sources for Chapter 9, "New Empires and Common Cultures, 600–1000 CE," has a number of sources on gender and new empires, and the new Chapter 22, "Twenty-First-Century Global Challenges, 2001–the Present," focuses on global climate change and features selections from Donald Trump and Greta Thunberg.

New Scholarship on Compelling Topics for Students

Our diverse teaching experience has also made us fully aware that most students taking world history survey courses come from majors cutting across the undergraduate curriculum. As a result, we have purposefully highlighted cutting-edge world history research on a wide range of topics that appeal highly to students, such as gender, race, migrations, the environment, trade, and technological changes. The Concise Third Edition pays considerable attention to looking at world history through the lens of gender. In Chapter 4, covering parts of the second and first millennia BCE, we encounter the brilliant leader and military strategist Sammuramat, who wore clothes that disguised her gender, built a massive city at Babylon, and undertook daring and far-reaching military campaigns stretching from Egypt to India. Al-Khayzurān Bint Atta and her daughter-in-law Zubaidah in the Abbasid court of the late eighth and early ninth centuries CE, not to mention the collection of sources at the end of Chapter 9, provide insight into exceptional women's power in increasingly patriarchal contexts. In Chapter 10, a fascinating discussion on Mongol women shows the powerful role that women could play in cultures regarded as male dominant. We see a similar phenomenon in the early modern period in West Africa in Chapter 13, where we highlight strong women leaders who fought for their visions for the Kongo kingdom as it endured civil wars and the future of its lucrative slave trade hung in the balance. In Chapter 18, as part of the discussions on cultural modernity, we provide insights into the global nature of the women's suffrage movement in the early part of the twentieth century. And in the era of decolonization, covered in Chapter 20, we draw attention to women's mobilization in struggles to decolonize colonial Africa, and to women's roles in decolonization movements all over the world.

A second major focus is climate and the role it has played in producing radical changes in the lives of humans and our environment. For example, a long-term warming of the globe facilitated the domestication of plants and animals and led to an agricultural revolution and the emergence of settled societies. In the seventeenth century, the dramatic drop in global temperatures, now known as the Little Ice Age, produced political and social havoc and led to civil wars, population decline, and regime change all around the globe. These are the new focuses of Chapters 1 and 13. Likewise, the rise of modern empires significantly altered the balance of commercial ties between societies, while the later turn to industrialism turned an interconnected world into an interdependent and even more fragile one. These are the subjects of major revisions in Chapters 12, 15, and 19. Indeed, all chapters have been substantially revised, and the new Chapter 22, "Twenty-First-Century Global Challenges, 2001–the Present," focuses on four major challenges of the twenty-first century—global terror, global inequality, global climate change, and pandemics—and provides major new discussions on the expansion of state violence, racial justice protests, and new LGBTQ rights.

New Media for In-Person, Hybrid, and Remote Learning Experiences

The Concise Third Edition is also the most innovative to date when it comes to learning with digital materials, exercises, and activities. **Lead media author Alan Karras** (University of California, Berkeley) has brought together an outstanding team of media authors to develop the comprehensive ancillary package for the Concise Third Edition, substantially increasing the learning and teaching support available to students and instructors for in-person, hybrid, remote, and "flipped classroom" learning modalities.

- **NEW online: Primary Source Exercises** and **Map Exercises** reengage students with important content from the chapter reading that they may have skipped. These exercises exist for each chapter in the book and draw directly from the book's maps and built-in text reader, which includes Global Themes and Sources and Interpreting Visual Evidence features at the end of the chapter. These assignable, interactive learning tools provide the opportunity for critical analysis practice every week of the semester. Either set of exercises can be integrated directly into an existing learning management system, making for easy assignability and easy student access.
- **InQuizitive**, Norton's award-winning adaptive learning tool, is constructed around the Core Objectives and global comparisons in each chapter. InQuizitive offers an interactive game-like platform that strengthens student comprehension, allowing students to arrive at class better prepared to engage in meaningful discussion.
- **History Skills Tutorials** give students the necessary framework to analyze primary source documents, images, and maps. Guided by videos with author Elizabeth Pollard and supported by interactive assessments, these tutorials help students learn and practice the ways historians think.

Worlds Together, Worlds Apart's Guiding Principles

Five principles inform this book, guiding its framework and the organization of its individual chapters. The first is that **world history is global history**. We have chosen not to deal with the great regions and cultures of the world as separate units, devoting individual chapters to East Asia, South Asia, Southwest Asia, Europe, Africa, and the Americas. Instead, our goal is to place each of these regions in its largest geographical context. Accordingly, we have written chapters that are truly global in that most major regions of the world are discussed in each chapter. We achieved these globally integrated chapters by building each around a significant world history story—a "Global Storyline." It would be misleading, of course, to assert that the context is always "the world," because none of these regions, even the most highly developed commercially, enjoyed prolonged commercial or cultural contact with peoples all over the globe before Columbus's voyage to the Americas and the later expeditions of the sixteenth century. Yet, surprisingly, a "global" story can be told even from the earliest history of humanity. Humans were on the move more than 100,000 years ago and migrated across the planet more than 10,000 years ago. Long after these initial large-scale migrations, the peoples living on the Afro-Eurasian landmass, an important building block for our study, deeply influenced one another, as did the more scattered peoples living in the Americas and in Africa below the Sahara. Products, ideas, and persons traveled widely across the large land units of Eurasia, Africa, and the Americas. Our Global Storylines—sometimes traced across connected regions and sometimes told as comparative narratives—give meaning to these exchanges of goods and ideas and movements of people.

The second principle informing this work is **the importance of chronology in framing world history**. We have framed the chapters around significant world history stories and periods that transcended regional and cultural boundaries—moments or periods of meaningful change in the way that human beings organized their lives. Some of these changes were dramatic and affected many people, sweeping across large landmasses. They affected peoples living in widely dispersed societies, and they often led to radically varied cultural responses in different regions of the world. In other cases, changes occurred in only one locality while other places retained their traditions or took alternative routes. Chronology helps us understand the ways in which the world has, and has not, shared a common history. It also provides a continual forward momentum toward the present for students and makes it easier for them to see connections and make comparisons.

The third principle is **historical and geographical balance**. Ours is not a history focused on the rise of the west. We pay attention to the histories of all peoples and take care not to privilege the developments that led directly into European history, as if the history of the rest of the world were but a prelude to the rise of the west. We engage peoples living outside Europe on their own terms and try to see world history from their perspectives. Our presentation of Europe in the period leading up to and including the founding of the Roman Empire is different from many of the standard treatments. The Europeans we describe are rather rough, wild-living, warring peoples living on the fringes of the settled parts of the world and looked down on by more politically stable communities. They hardly seem to be the ilk that will catapult Europeans to world leadership a millennium later—indeed, they were very different people from those who, as the result of myriad intervening and contingent events, founded the nineteenth- and twentieth-century empires whose ruins are still all around us.

Our fourth principle is **an emphasis on connections and disconnections across societal and cultural boundaries**. World history is the history of the connections among peoples often living at great distances from one another, and it is also the history of the resistance of peoples living within and outside societies to connections that threatened to rob them of their independence. A stress on connections inevitably foregrounds the elements within societies that promoted long-distance ties. *Worlds Together, Worlds Apart,* as a title, is not intended to convey the message that the history of the world is a story of increasing integration. What for one ruling group brought benefits in the form of increased workforces, material prosperity, and political stability often meant enslavement, political subordination, and loss of territory for other groups. The historian's task, then, is not only to represent the different experiences of increased connectedness, describing worlds that came together, but also to trace the opposite trends, describing peoples and communities that remained, or intentionally grew, apart.

The fifth and final principle is that **world history is a narrative of big stories and broad comparisons**. *Worlds Together, Worlds Apart* is not a book of record or a history of the world. Indeed, in a work that traces global storylines from the beginnings to the present, the notion that no event or individual worthy of attention would be excluded is folly. We have sought to offer clear stories and interpretations that synthesize the vast body of data that often overwhelms histories of the world. Our aspiration is to identify the main historical forces that have shaped human experience and to highlight the monumental innovations that have changed the way humans lived. Cross-cultural comparisons of developments, institutions, and even founding figures receive attention to make students aware that some common institutions, such as family or the economy, did not have the same features in every society. But conversely, the seemingly diverse terms that were used, say, to describe learned and religious people in different parts of the world—monastics in Europe, *ulama* in the Islamic world, Brahmans in India, and scholar-gentries in China—often meant much the same thing in very different settings. We have constructed *Worlds Together, Worlds Apart* around big ideas and stories rather than filling the book with names and dates that encourage students to memorize rather than understand world history concepts.

Overview of Volume One

Volume One of *Worlds Together, Worlds Apart* deals with the period from the beginnings of human history through the development of new political structures like cities, territorial states, and empires and the rise of the world's universalizing religions, all leading toward the emergence of the regions of the world that we recognize today, which then immediately face the major disruptions of the Mongol invasions of the thirteenth century and the spread and destruction of the Black Death across Afro-Eurasia in the fourteenth century. It is divided into eleven chronological chapters, each of which marks a distinct global historical period.

Chapter 1 Becoming Human

Global Storyline: Prehistory and the Peopling of the Earth

Chapter 2 Rivers, Cities, and First States, 3500–2000 BCE

Global Storyline: Comparing First Cities

Chapter 3 Nomads, Territorial States, and Microsocieties, 2000–1200 BCE

Global Storyline: Comparing First States

Overview of Volume Two

The chronological organizational structure for Volume Two reaffirms the commitment to write a decentered, global history of the world that is not moving inevitably toward a "rise of the west" story. Christopher Columbus is not the starting point, as he is in so many modern world histories. Rather, we begin in the eleventh and twelfth centuries with two major developments in world history: the Mongol invasions and the destruction and recovery from the Black Death. From there we describe how major historical processes changed the modern world in significant ways, including the rise of global exploration, the creation of global cultures, the expansion of global trade, alternative visions in the nineteenth century of western expansions, the transformation of nation-states into global empires, the uncertainty and disruption of modernism, World War I and the growth of mass societies, World War II and the emergence of a three-world order during the Cold War, and the emergence and impact of modern globalism today. We are excited that the epilogue from previous editions has now been rewritten and expanded to become the new standalone Chapter 22, "Twenty-First-Century Global Challenges, 2001–the Present."

Chapter 21 Globalization, 1970–2000

Global Storyline: The Emergence of Modern Globalization

Chapter 22 Twenty-First-Century Global Challenges, 2001–the Present

Global Storyline: The Impact of Modern Globalization Today

Media & Print Ancillaries

The Concise Third Edition of *Worlds Together, Worlds Apart* is supported by a collection of digital resources proven to help faculty meet their course goals—in the classroom and online—and activities for students to develop core skills in reading comprehension, critical thinking, and historical analysis.

For Students

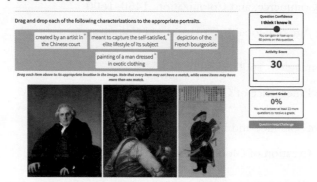

- To support the continued growth of students' historical skills, *Worlds Together, Worlds Apart* offers a series of brief, assignable **Primary Source Exercises** to accompany every chapter of the book. These exercises give students practice analyzing the primary source documents from the Global Themes and Sources section of the chapter and the primary source images from the Interpreting Visual Evidence section of the chapter, plus a few additional sources from outside the text. Students are asked a series of interactive questions through which they practice analyzing the building blocks of the world history course.

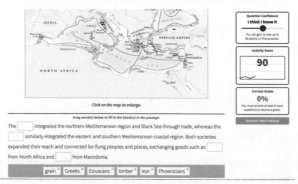

- To provide the opportunity for map-reading practice each week of the semester, *Worlds Together, Worlds Apart* offers stand-alone **Map Exercises** for every chapter of the book. Each exercise extracts the key maps from the chapter and presents students with interactive questions designed to assess their ability to read, dissect, interpret, and draw historical conclusions from the information depicted. Answer-specific feedback helps guide students through the maps, and connect the information back to the chapter reading.

- **InQuizitive** is Norton's award-winning, easy-to-use adaptive learning tool that personalizes the learning experience for students, helping them master—and retain—key learning objectives. Through a variety of question types, answer-specific feedback, and game-like elements such as the ability to wager points, students are motivated to keep working until they've mastered the concepts.

Framework for Analyzing Documents

Historians keep important questions in mind while analyzing documents for clues to the past. Watch author and historian Elizabeth Pollard demonstrate how she analyzes documents.

Watch the video featuring Elizabeth Pollard analyzing an excerpt from Rabban Bar Sâwmâ, *Pilgrimage to Jerusalem.*

- The **History Skills Tutorials** feature three online modules—"Analyzing Images," "Analyzing Primary Source Documents," and "Analyzing Maps"—to support students' development of the key skills needed for the history course. Each module features author videos modeling the analysis process, followed by interactive questions that will challenge students to apply what they have learned. The tutorials can be integrated directly into an existing learning management system, making for easy assignability and easy student access.

- The **student website** offers additional study and review materials for students to use outside class. The website is available via the *Worlds Together, Worlds Apart* digital landing page and includes author videos, interactive maps from the text, flashcards, detailed chapter outlines, and an online reader with dozens of additional primary source documents and images, each with a brief headnote and sample analysis questions.

- Included free with new copies of the text, the **Norton Ebook** offers an active reading experience, enabling students to take notes, bookmark, search, highlight, and even read offline. Instructors can add notes that students see when they read the text. Norton Ebooks can be viewed on—and synced among—all computers and mobile devices, and can be made available for offline reading. Author videos are embedded throughout to create an engaging reading environment.

For Instructors

- Easily add high-quality **Norton LMS digital resources** to your online, hybrid, or lecture courses. Get started building your course with our easy-to-use integrated resources; all activities can be accessed right within your existing learning management system. The downloadable file includes integration links to the following resources, organized by chapter: the Norton Ebook,

InQuizitive, History Skills Tutorials, Primary Source Exercises, Map Exercises, and student website resources.

- The **Instructor's Manual** has everything instructors need to prepare lectures and classroom activities: lecture outlines; lecture ideas; classroom activities; image activities; lists of recommended books, films, and websites; and more. All resources from the Instructor's Manual are also available online through Norton's **Interactive Instructor's Guide** (IIG). The IIG includes searchable, filterable Instructor's Manual content plus instructor-facing videos with the book authors—great source material for instructors embarking on their first world history course.

- The **Test Bank** contains well over 1,000 multiple-choice, true/false, and short-answer questions. Questions are classified according to level of difficulty and Bloom's Taxonomy, providing multiple avenues for comprehension and skill assessment, and making it easy to construct tests that are meaningful and diagnostic. The Test Bank is available through the new **Norton Testmaker**, which allows you to create assessments for your course from anywhere with an Internet connection, without downloading files or installing specialized software.

- **Lecture PowerPoints and Art PowerPoints** feature lecture outlines, key talking points, and the photographs and maps from the book to support in-class presentations. **StoryMaps PowerPoints** break complex maps from the text into a sequence of annotated slides that address topics such as the Silk Roads, the spread of the Black Death, and population growth and the economy.

Acknowledgments

Worlds Together, Worlds Apart got its start with financial support from Princeton University's 250th Anniversary Fund for undergraduate teaching and, as such, it drew heavily on the expertise of the Princeton history department, in particular, Mariana Candido, Robert Darnton, Natalie Z. Davis, Sheldon Garon, Anthony Grafton, Molly Greene, David Howell, Harold James, William Jordan, Emmanuel Kreike, Elizabeth Lunbeck, Michael Mahoney, Arno Mayer, Kenneth Mills, John Murrin, Susan Naquin, Willard Peterson, Theodore Rabb, Bhavani Raman, Stanley Stein, and Richard Turits. When necessary, the authors of the initial iterations of the book reached outside the history department, getting help from Michael L. Bender, L. Carl Brown, Michael Cook, Norman Itzkowitz, Martin Kern, Thomas Leisten, Heath Lowry, and Peter Schaefer. David Gordon and Shamil Jeppie, graduates of the Princeton history department, offered input as the early editions developed.

The early iterations of *Worlds Together, Worlds Apart* relied on the above-and-beyond administrative support of Judith Hanson, Pamela Long, and Eileen Kane, all at Princeton University. More recent editions owe a debt of gratitude to Emily Pace and Leah Gregory, graduate students at San Diego State University who helped track down sources, images, and permissions.

Beyond Princeton, the authorial team benefited from exceptionally gifted and giving colleagues who have assisted this book in many ways. Colleagues at Louisiana State University, the University of North Carolina, the University of Pennsylvania, and the University of California at Los Angeles, where Suzanne Marchand, Michael Tsin, Holly Pittman, and Stephen Aron, respectively, are now teaching, pitched in whenever we turned to them. Especially helpful have been the contributions of Joyce Appleby, James Gelvin, Naomi Lamoreaux, and Gary Nash at UCLA; Michael Bernstein at Tulane University; and Maribel Dietz, John Henderson, Christine Kooi, David Lindenfeld, Reza Pirbhai, and Victor Stater at Louisiana State University. It goes without saying that none of these individuals bear any responsibility for factual or interpretive errors that the text may contain. Xinru Liu would like to thank her Indian mentor, Romila Thapar, who changed the way we think about Indian history.

Reviewers

The quality and range of reviews on this project were truly exceptional. The final version of the manuscript and the media package were greatly influenced by the thoughts and ideas of numerous instructors, including

Saad Abi-Hamad, Florida International University
Hugh Agnew, Columbian College of Arts and Sciences
Andreas Agocs, University of the Pacific
Stewart Anderson, Brigham Young University
Anthony Barbieri-Low, University of California, Santa Barbara
Michelle Benson-Saxton, University at Buffalo
Brett Berliner, Morgan State University
Carolyn Noelle Biltoft, Georgia State University
Edward Bond, Alabama A&M University
Liam Brockey, Michigan State University
Spencer Brown, Sierra College
Gayle Brunelle, California State University, Fullerton
Kate Burlingham, California State University, Fullerton
Daniel Burton-Rose, Northern Arizona University
Grace Chee, West Los Angeles College
Stephen Colston, San Diego State University
Matthew Conn, Michigan State University
John Corbally, Diablo Valley College
Christian Davis, James Madison University
Paula Devos, San Diego State University
Robert Dietle, Western Kentucky University
Eric Dursteler, Brigham Young University
Beth Fickling, Coastal Carolina Community College
Gerleman, George Mason University

Norah Gharala, University of Houston
Julie Gibbings, University of Edinburgh
Laura Hilton, Muskingum University
Paul Hudson, Georgia Perimeter College
Holly Hulburt, Southern Illinois University
Bonny Ibhawoh, McMaster University
Stefan Kamola, Eastern Connecticut State University
Alan Karras, University of California, Berkeley
David Kiracofe, Tidewater Community College
Jeremy LaBuff, Northern Arizona University
Senya Lubisich, Citrus College
Elaine MacKinnon, University of West Georgia
Anthony Makowski, Delaware County Community College
Harold Marcuse, University of California, Santa Barbara
Lindsey B. Maxwell, Gulliver Preparatory School
Jamie McCandless, Kennesaw State University
Anthonette McDaniel, Pellissippi State Community College
Jeff McEwen, Chattanooga State Community College
Thomas McKenna, Concord University
Eva Moc, Modesto Junior College
April Najjaj, Texas A&M University
Alice Pate, Kennesaw State University
Chandrika Paul, Shippensburg University
Sandra Peterson, Durham Technical Community College
David Pigott, BYU Idaho
Jared Poley, Georgia State University
Sara Pulliam, United States Naval Academy
Dana Rabin, University of Illinois, Urbana-Champaign
Masako Racel, Kennesaw State University
Charles Reed, Elizabeth City State University
Alice Roberti, Santa Rosa Junior College
Steven Rowe, Chicago State University
Ariel Salzmann, Queen's University
Lynn Sargeant, California State University, Fullerton
Robert Saunders, Farmingdale State College
Sharlene Sayegh-Canada, California State University, Long Beach
Claire Schen, University at Buffalo
Ethan Segal, Michigan State University
Jason Sharples, Florida Atlantic University
Jeffrey Shumway, Brigham Young University
Greg Smay, University of California, Berkeley
Kristin Stapleton, University at Buffalo
Margaret Stevens, Essex County College

Pamela Stewart, Arizona State University
David Terry, Grand Valley State University
Lisa Tran, California State University, Fullerton
Michael Vann, California State University, Sacramento
Theodore Weeks, Southern Illinois University
Jason Wolfe, Louisiana State University
Reza Yeganehshakib, Saddleback College
Krzysztof Ziarek, University at Buffalo

Publishing a special book like *Worlds Together, Worlds Apart* involves many talented people. We feel the *Worlds Together, Worlds Apart* media package is the best in the marketplace. We'd particularly like to thank our team of media authors for their extraordinary efforts, including Alan Karras, the lead media author, and his terrific team of media authors—Shane Carter, Ryba Epstein, Andrew Hardy, Emily Gottreich, and Erik Vincent. We also want to thank our digital primary source exercise team: Annette Chamberlin, Stephanie Ballenger, and Derek O'Leary.

And an equally big thanks to our extraordinary book and media team partners at W. W. Norton: Jon Durbin, our print editor for all six editions; Carson Russell, our media editor; Rachel Mayer, Alexander Lee, and Lexi Malakhoff, our media team; Sarah England Bartley, Janise Turso, Courtney Brandt, and Lib Triplett, our marketing and sales specialist team; Harry Haskell, David Bradley, Jennifer Greenstein, Gerra Goff, and Lily Gellman, our manuscript and project editing teams; Ben Reynolds, Ashley Horna, and Jane Searle, our production team; Jillian Burr and Lissi Sigillo, the book's extraordinary designers; Mike Cullen, our terrific photo researcher; and Elizabeth Trammell, our diligent permissions manager.

While the Concise Third Edition of *Worlds Together, Worlds Apart* marks the handoff to a new leadership team, we want to pause for a moment and send special thanks to all our original co-authors for making this a wonderful journey. The journey began with a year of regular lunch and dinner meetings, with shared readings and fascinating debates about how to remap world history in what was then the dawning of a global age. We would not be where we are today without your amazing collaboration, creative insights, hard work, and collegiality. Thank you, thank you, thank you—Steve Aron, Peter Brown, Ben Elman, Steve Kotkin, Xinru Liu, Sue Marchand, Holly Pittman, Gyan Prakash, Brent Shaw, and Michael Tsin. Just as your voices have shaped the way we came to think about the global past, they live on in this book.

Finally, much of the new Concise Third Edition was written during the pandemic. We are grateful for the support and understanding of our family members, also working from home, in some cases in another room of the house, and in the case of a homeschooling third-grader, at a makeshift desk three feet away. As the world seemed to be coming apart, we took joy in working together with you nearby.

ABOUT THE AUTHORS

Jeremy Adelman (*D.Phil. Oxford University*) has lived and worked in seven countries and on four continents. A graduate of the University of Toronto, he earned a master's degree in economic history at the London School of Economics (1985) and a doctorate in modern history at Oxford University (1989). He is the author or editor of ten books, including *Sovereignty and Revolution in the Iberian Atlantic* (2006) and *Worldly Philosopher: The Odyssey of Albert O. Hirschman* (2013), a chronicle of one of the twentieth century's most original thinkers. He has been awarded fellowships by the British Council, the Social Science and Humanities Research Council of Canada, the Guggenheim Memorial Foundation, and the American Council of Learned Societies (the Frederick Burkhardt Fellowship). He is currently the Henry Charles Lea Professor of History and the director of the Global History Lab at Princeton University. His next book is called *Earth Hunger: Global Integration and the Need for Strangers*.

Elizabeth Pollard (*Ph.D. University of Pennsylvania*) is professor of history at San Diego State University. Her research investigates women accused of witchcraft in the Roman world and explores the exchange of goods and ideas between the Mediterranean and the Indian Ocean in the early centuries of the Common Era. Her pedagogical interests include digital humanities approaches to Roman history and witchcraft studies as well as the impact of global perspectives on teaching, learning, and writing about the ancient Mediterranean. Pollard was named SDSU Distinguished Professor for Teaching Excellence in 2013 and was awarded the Faculty Innovation and Leadership Award by the California State University chancellor in 2020. In summer 2020, she co-designed and led the training program that will enable nearly 1,000 SDSU faculty to teach their courses entirely online in 2020–2021.

Clifford Rosenberg (*Ph.D. Princeton University*) is associate professor of European history at City College and the Graduate Center, CUNY. He specializes in the history of modern France and its empire and is the author of *Policing Paris: The Origins of Modern Immigration Control between the Wars*. He is now working on a book about the spread of tuberculosis between France and Algeria since the mid-nineteenth century.

Robert Tignor (*Ph.D. Yale University*) is professor emeritus and the Rosengarten Professor of Modern and Contemporary History at Princeton University and the three-time chair of the history department. With Gyan Prakash, he introduced Princeton's first course in world history thirty years ago. Professor Tignor has taught graduate and undergraduate courses in African history and world history and has written extensively on the history of twentieth-century Egypt, Nigeria, and Kenya. Besides his many research trips to Africa, Professor Tignor has taught at the University of Ibadan in Nigeria and the University of Nairobi in Kenya.

Alan Karras (*Ph.D. University of Pennsylvania*) is the associate director of International & Area Studies at the University of California, Berkeley, and has previously served as chair of the College Board's test development committee for world history and as co-chair of the College Board's commission on AP history course revisions. The author and editor of several books, he has written about the eighteenth-century Atlantic world and, more broadly, global interactions that focus on illicit activities like smuggling and corruption. An advocate of linking the past to the present, he is now working on a history of corruption in empires, focusing on the East India Company.

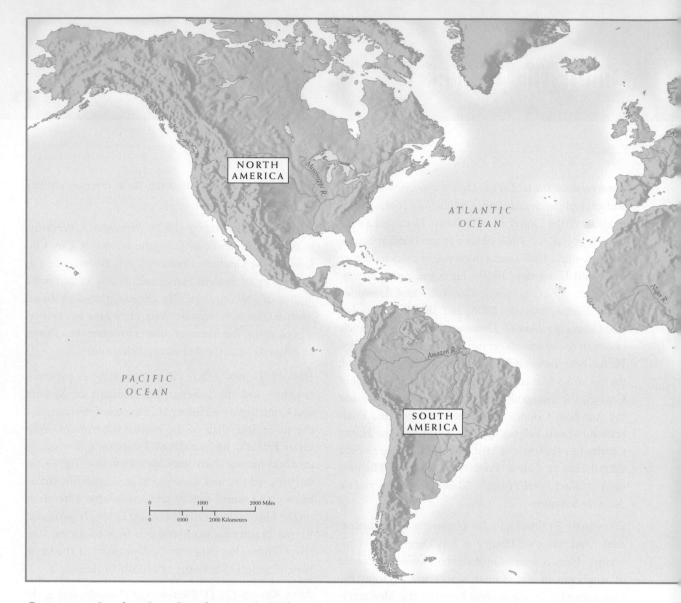

NORTH
AMERICA

Mississippi R.

ATLANTIC
OCEAN

Niger R.

PACIFIC
OCEAN

Amazon R.

SOUTH
AMERICA

| 0 | | 1000 | | 2000 Miles |
| 0 | 1000 | | 2000 Kilometers | |

Geography in the Ancient and Modern Worlds

Today, geographers usually identify six inhabited continents: Africa, Asia, Australia, Europe, North America, and South America. Inside these continents they locate a vast number of subcontinental units, such as East Asia, South Asia, Southeast Asia, the Middle East, North Africa, and sub-Saharan Africa. Yet this geographic understanding would have been alien to premodern people, who did not think of themselves as inhabiting continents bounded by large bodies of water. Lacking a firm command of the seas, they saw themselves as living on contiguous landmasses. Hence, in this textbook, we have chosen to use a set of geographic terms that more accurately reflect the world of the premoderns.

The most interconnected and populous landmass of premodern times was Afro-Eurasia. The term *Eurasia* is widely used in general histories, but we find it inadequate. The preferred term, from our perspective,

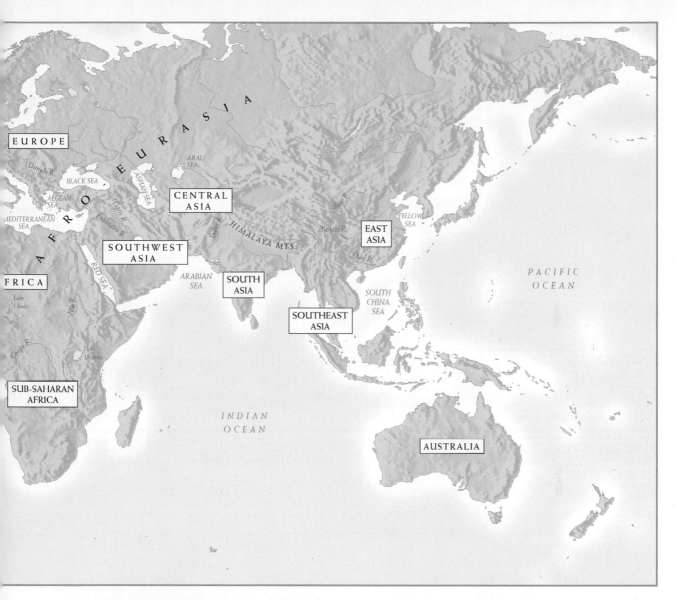

must be *Afro-Eurasia*, for the interconnected landmass of premodern—and, indeed, much of modern—times included large parts of Europe and Asia and significant regions in Africa—particularly Egypt, North Africa, and even parts of sub-Saharan Africa.

It was only in the period from 1000 to 1300 CE that the divisions of the world that we take for granted today began to take shape. The peoples of the northwestern part of Afro-Eurasia did not see themselves as European Christians, and hence as a distinct cultural entity, until the end of the Middle Ages. Islam did not

arise and extend its influence throughout the middle zone of Afro-Eurasia until the eighth and ninth centuries CE. Nor did the peoples living in what we today term the Indian subcontinent feel a strong sense of their own cultural and political unity until the Delhi Sultanate and the Mughal Empire brought political unity to that vast region. As a result, we use the terms *South Asia*, *Vedic society*, and *India* in place of *Indian subcontinent* for the premodern part of our narrative, and we use *Southwest Asia* and *North Africa* to refer to what today is designated as the *Middle East*.

CONCISE THIRD EDITION

Worlds Together, Worlds Apart

1

Becoming Human

In summer 2017, the story of human origins was rocked by findings that may well push back, and relocate to a different region of Africa, the earliest evidence for *Homo sapiens*. The new arguments about the time and place of our origins were grounded in the work of a team of paleoanthropologists who traveled to Jebel Irhoud in Morocco to establish a more precise date for hominin remains that had been uncarthed by miners in the 1960s. What the team found were stone tools and fossilized skull fragments (including a jaw) belonging to five individuals. Thermoluminescence dating of objects found with the bones, as well as uranium series dating of a tooth, showed that the possible *Homo sapiens* at Jebel Irhoud lived as early as 315,000 years ago—more than 100,000 years earlier than the previously accepted date of 200,000 years ago based on finds in East Africa.

Research on ancient DNA (aDNA) is also rewriting long-standing theories of human evolution and hominin migration out of Africa. For instance, DNA analysis of a 2,000-year-old skeleton from sub-Saharan Africa has pointed to a split in the branches of *Homo sapiens* lineage more than 250,000 years ago. And some paleogenomic researchers, using aDNA analyses together with statistical models, would push back the date for *Homo sapiens* long before that. As a result of these exciting new findings based on a diverse range of research methodologies, the genetic split indicated by the 2,000-year-old sub-Saharan skeleton supports the idea that the spread of *Homo sapiens* in Africa occurred longer ago and is more complicated than the 200,000-years-ago origin for *Homo sapiens* that scholars accepted just a decade ago. The modern scientific creation narrative evolves as new evidence unearthed through excavation adds more data to the story that scholars work to piece together.

Most of the common traits of human beings—the abilities to make tools, engage in family life, use language, and refine cognitive abilities—evolved over many millennia

Chapter Outline

- Creation Narratives
- Hominins to Modern Humans
- The Life of Early *Homo sapiens*
- The Global Agricultural Revolution
- Conclusion

Core Objectives

- **DESCRIBE** various creation narratives traced in this chapter, including the modern scientific narrative of human evolution, and **EXPLAIN** why they differ.

- **TRACE** the major developments in hominin evolution that resulted in the traits that make *Homo sapiens* "human."

- **DESCRIBE** human ways of life and cultural developments from 300,000 to 12,000 years ago.

- **COMPARE** the ways communities around the world shifted to settled agriculture, and **ANALYZE** the significance this shift had for social organization.

3

and crystallized around the time *Homo sapiens* migrated out of Africa more than 100,000 years ago. Only with the beginning of settled agriculture did significant cultural differences develop between groups of humans, as artifacts such as tools, cooking devices, and storage containers reveal. Put simply, the differences we think of as separating humankind's cultures today are less than 15,000 or 20,000 years old.

This chapter lays out the origins of humanity from its common source. It shows that many different hominins preceded modern humans and that humans came from a recent stock of migrants traveling out of Africa and across Eurasia in waves. Flowing across the world, our ancestors adapted to environmental constraints and opportunities. They created languages, families, and clan systems, often innovating to defend themselves against predators. One of the biggest breakthroughs was the domestication of plants and animals and the creation of settled agriculture. With this development, humans could stop following food and begin producing it where they desired.

Global Storyline

Prehistory and the Peopling of the Earth

- Communities, from long ago to today, produce varied creation narratives in order to make sense of how humans came into being.

- Hominin development across millions of years results in modern humans (*Homo sapiens*) and the traits that make us "human."

- During the period from 300,000 to 12,000 years ago, humans live as hunters and gatherers and achieve major breakthroughs in language and art.

- Global revolution in domesticating crops and animals leads to settled agriculture-based communities, while other communities develop pastoral ways of life.

Creation Narratives

For thousands of years, humans have constructed narratives of how the world, and humans, came to be. These **creation narratives** have varied over time and across cultures, depending on a society's values and the evidence available. To understand the origins of modern humans, we must come to terms with scales of time: the billions, millions, and hundreds of thousands of years through which the universe, earth, and life on it developed into what they are today. Though the hominin ancestors of modern humans lived millions of years ago, our tools for telling the modern creation narrative are relatively new.

Only 350 years ago, English clerics claimed on the basis of biblical calculations and Christian tradition that the first day of creation was Sunday, October 23, 4004 BCE. These seventeenth-century clerics were not the first to engage critically with the biblical story of creation. Rabbi Yose ben Halafta, a second-century CE rabbinic sage some 1,500 years earlier, used Genesis to calculate his own date for the beginning of creation (October 7, 3761 BCE). And the first-century CE writer Philo, an Alexandrian Jew who opined that "no one, whether poet or historian, could ever give expression in an adequate manner to the beauty of [Moses's] ideas respecting the creation of the world," wrote an extended philosophical treatise that set out to do just that.

Modern science, however, indicates that the origin of the universe dates back 13.8 billion years and that hominins began to separate from apes some 7 million years ago. These new discoveries have proved as mind-boggling to Hindus and Muslims as to Christians and Jews—all of whom believed, in different ways, that the universe was not so old and that divine beings had a role in creating it and all life, including the first humans. For millennia, human communities across the globe have constructed narratives that extend back differing lengths of time and suggest various roles for humans and gods in the process of universal creation. For instance, the Judeo-Christian narrative debated by English clerics and turn-of-the-first-millennium Jewish scholars portrays a single God creating a universe out of nothingness, populating it with plants, animals, and humans, in a span of six days. The centuries-old creation story of the Yoruba peoples of West Africa depicts a divine being descending from the heavens in human form and becoming the godlike king Oduduwa, who established the Yoruba kingdom and the rules by which his subjects were to live. The foundational texts of Hinduism, which date to the seventh or sixth century BCE, account that the world is millions, not billions, of years old. Chinese Han dynasty (206 BCE–220 CE) astronomers believed that at the world's beginning the planets were conjoined and that they would merge again at the end of time. The Buddhists' cosmos comprised millions of worlds, each consisting of a mountain encircled by four continents, its seas surrounded by a wall of iron.

Yet even the million-year time frames and multiple planetary systems that ancient Asian thinkers endorsed did not prepare their communities for the idea

THE BIG PICTURE

How did we become human? What are the defining characteristics of human beings?

Core Objectives

DESCRIBE the various creation narratives traced in this chapter, including the modern scientific narrative of human evolution, and **EXPLAIN** why they differ.

creation narratives
Narratives constructed by different cultures that draw on their belief systems and available evidence to explain the origins of the world and humanity.

that humans are related to apes. In all traditional cosmologies, humans came into existence fully formed, at a single moment, as did the other beings that populated the world. Modern discoveries about humanity's origins have challenged these traditions, because no tradition conceived that creatures evolved into new kinds of life; that apes, humans, and other hominins branched from one another in a long evolutionary process; and that all of humanity originated in Africa.

Hominins to Modern Humans

The modern scientific creation narrative of human evolution would have been unimaginable even just over a century ago, when Charles Darwin was formulating his ideas about human origins. As we will see in this section, scientific discoveries have shown that modern humans evolved from earlier hominins. Through adaptation to their environment, various species of hominins developed new physical characteristics and distinctive skills. Millions of years after the first hominins appeared, the first modern humans—*Homo sapiens*—emerged and spread out across the globe.

EVOLUTIONARY FINDINGS AND RESEARCH METHODS

New insights into the time frame of the universe and human existence have occurred over a long period of time. Geologists made early breakthroughs in the eighteenth century when their research into the layers of the earth's surface revealed a world much older than biblical time implied. Evolutionary biologists, most notably Charles Darwin (1809–1882), concluded that all life had evolved over long periods from simple forms of matter. In the twentieth century, astronomers, evolutionary biologists, and archaeologists developed sophisticated dating techniques to pinpoint the chronology of the universe's creation and the evolution of all forms of life on earth. And in the early twenty-first century, paleogenomic researchers are recovering full genomic sequences of extinct hominins (such as the Neanderthals) and using ancient DNA to reconstruct the full skeletons of human ancestors (such as the Denisovans) of whom only a few bones have survived. Their discoveries have radically transformed humanity's understanding of its own history (see Current Trends in World History: Using Big History and Science to Understand Human Origins). A mere century ago, who would have accepted the idea that the universe came into being 13.8 billion years ago, that the earth appeared about 4.5 billion years ago, and that the earliest life forms began to exist about 3.8 billion years ago?

Yet, modern science suggests that human beings are part of a long evolutionary chain stretching from microscopic bacteria to African apes that appeared about 23 million years ago, and that Africa's "Great Ape" population separated into several distinct groups of **hominids**: one becoming present-day

hominids
The family, in scientific classification, that includes gorillas, chimpanzees, and humans (that is, *Homo sapiens*, in addition to our now-extinct hominin ancestors such as the various australopithecines as well as *Homo habilis*, *Homo erectus*, and *Homo neanderthalensis*).

gorillas; the second becoming chimpanzees; and the third becoming modern humans only after following a long and complicated evolutionary process. Our focus will be on the third group of hominids, namely the **hominins** who became modern humans. A combination of traits, evolving over several million years, distinguished humans from other hominids, including (1) lifting the torso and walking on two legs (bipedalism), thereby freeing hands and arms to carry objects and hurl weapons; (2) controlling and then making fire; (3) fashioning and using tools; (4) developing cognitive skills and an enlarged brain and therefore the capacity for language; and (5) acquiring a consciousness of "self." All these traits were in place at least 150,000 years ago.

Two terms central to understanding any discussion of hominin development are *evolution* and *natural selection*. **Evolution** is the process by which species of plants and animals change and develop over generations, as certain traits are favored in reproduction. The process of evolution is driven by a mechanism called *natural selection*, in which members of a species with certain randomly occurring traits that are useful for environmental or other reasons survive and reproduce with greater success than those without the traits. Thus, biological evolution (human or otherwise) does not imply progress to higher forms of life, but instead implies successful adaptation to environmental surroundings.

EARLY HOMININS, ADAPTATION, AND CLIMATE CHANGE

It was once thought that evolution is a gradual and steady process. The consensus now is that evolutionary changes occur in punctuated bursts after long periods of stasis, or non-change. These transformative changes were often brought on, especially during early human development, by dramatic alterations in climate and by ruptures of the earth's crust caused by the movement of tectonic plates below the earth's surface. The heaving and decline of the earth's surface led to significant changes in climate and in animal and plant life. Also, across millions of years, the earth's climate was affected by slight variations in the earth's orbit, the tilt of the earth's axis, and the earth's wobbling on its axis.

Australopithecines As the earth experienced these immense changes, what was it like to be a hominin in the millions of years before the emergence of modern humans? An early clue came from a discovery made in 1924 at Taung, not far from the present-day city of Johannesburg, South Africa. A twenty-nine-year-old scientist named Raymond Dart identified the pint-sized skull and bones of a creature, nicknamed "Taung child," that had both ape-like and humanoid features. Dart officially labeled his bipedal find *Australopithecus africanus*. **Australopithecines** existed not only in southern Africa but in the north as well. In 1974, an archaeological

hominins
A scientific classification for modern humans and our now-extinct ancestors, including australopithecines and others in the genus *Homo*, such as *Homo habilis* and *Homo erectus*. Researchers once used the term *hominid* to refer to *Homo sapiens* and extinct hominin species, but the meaning of *hominid* has been expanded to include great apes (humans, gorillas, chimpanzees, and orangutans).

evolution
Process by which species of plants and animals change over time, as a result of the favoring, through reproduction, of certain traits that are useful in that species' environment.

australopithecines
Hominin species, including *anamensis, afarensis* (Lucy), and *africanus,* that appeared in Africa beginning around 4 million years ago and, unlike other animals, sometimes walked on two legs. Their brain capacity was a little less than one-third of a modern human's. Although not humans, they carried the genetic and biological material out of which modern humans would later emerge.

Core Objectives

TRACE the major developments in hominin evolution that resulted in the traits that make *Homo sapiens* "human."

Using Big History and Science to Understand Human Origins

The history profession has undergone transformative changes since the end of World War II. One of the most radical changes in historical narratives is what historian David Christian has called "Big History." Just what it is still remains a mystery for many historians, and few departments of history offer courses in Big History. But Big History presents a coherent narrative of the origins of the universe up to the present. Its influence on our sense of who we are and where we came from is impressive.

Big History covers the history of our universe from its creation 13.8 billion years ago to the present. (See Table 1.1.) Because it merges natural history with human history, its study requires knowledge of many fields of science. Big History's use of the sciences enables us to learn of the universe before our solar system (astrophysics), our planet before life (geology), life before humans (biology), and humans before written sources (paleoanthropology). At present, few historians feel comfortable using these findings or integrating these data into their own general history courses. Nevertheless, Big History provides another narrative of how and when our universe, and we as human beings, came into existence.

Most of this chapter deals with how our species, *Homo sapiens*, came into being, and here, too, scholars are dependent on a range of approaches, including the work of linguists, biologists, paleoanthropologists, archaeologists, geneticists, and many others.

The first major advance in the study of the time before written records occurred in the mid-twentieth century, and it involved the use of radiocarbon dating. All living things contain the radiocarbon isotope C^{14}, which plants acquire directly from the atmosphere and animals acquire indirectly when they consume plants or other animals. When these living things die, the C^{14} isotope begins to decay into a stable nonradioactive element, C^{12}. Because the rate of decay is regular and measurable, it is possible to determine the age of fossils that leave organic remains for up to 40,000 years.

The evidence for human evolution, discussed in this chapter, requires dating methods that can extend back much farther than radiocarbon dating. Using the *potassium-argon method*, scientists can calculate the age of nonliving objects by measuring the ratio of potassium to argon in them, since potassium decays into argon. This method allows scientists to calculate the age of objects up to a million years old. Likewise, scientists can use *uranium-thorium dating* to determine the date of objects (like shells, teeth, and bones) more closely linked to living beings. This uranium-series method permits scientists to date objects up to 500,000 years old. A similar date limit can be reached through *thermoluminescence methods* applied to soil deposits and objects with crystalline materials that have been exposed to sunlight or heat (as in the flames of a fire pit or the heat of a kiln). Even if a scientist cannot offer a direct date for an object—teeth, skull, or other bone—such methods offer a date for the sediments in which researchers find fossils, as a gauge of the age of the fossils themselves.

As this chapter demonstrates, the environment, especially climate, played a major role in the appearance of hominins and the eventual dominance of *Homo sapiens*. But how do we know so much about the world's climate so far back in time? This brings us to yet another scientific breakthrough, known as *marine isotope stages*. By exploring the marine life, mainly pollen and plankton, deposited in deep seabeds and measuring the levels of oxygen-16 and oxygen-18 isotopes in these life forms, oceanographers and climatologists are able to determine the temperature of the world hundreds of thousands and even millions of years ago and thus to chart the cooling and warming cycles of the earth's climate.

DNA (deoxyribonucleic acid) analysis is another crucial tool for unraveling the beginnings of modern humans. DNA, which determines biological inheritances, exists in two places within the cells of all living organisms—including the human body. *Nuclear DNA (nDNA)* and *mitochondrial DNA (mDNA)* exist in males and females, but only mitochondrial DNA from females passes to their offspring, as the females' egg cells carry their mitochondria with their DNA to the offspring. By examining mitochondrial DNA,

about 40,000 years ago. When the scientific journal *Nature* in 1987 published genetic-based findings about humans' spread across the planet, it inspired a groundswell of public interest—and a contentious scientific debate that continues today.

Botanical DNA Extraction A scientist at Senckenberg Research Institute and Natural History Museum in Frankfurt, Germany, prepares plant samples for DNA extraction.

Questions for Analysis

- How has the study of prehistory changed since the mid-twentieth century?
- Why are different dating methods appropriate for different kinds of artifacts?
- How does the study of climate and environment relate to the origins of humans?

Explore Further

Barham, Lawrence, and Peter Mitchell, Peter, *The First Africans: African Archaeology from the Earliest Toolmakers to Most Recent Foragers* (2008).

Barker, Graeme, *Agricultural Revolution in Prehistory: Why Did Foragers Become Farmers?* (2006).

Christian, David, *Maps of Time: An Introduction to Big History* (2004).

Lewis-Kraus, Gideon, "Is Ancient DNA Research Revealing New Truths—or Falling into Old Traps?" *New York Times Magazine*, January 17, 2019.

Reich, David, *Who We Are and How We Got Here: Ancient DNA and the New Science of the Human Past* (2018).

researchers can measure genetic relatedness and variation among living organisms—including human beings. Such analysis has enabled researchers to pinpoint human descent from an original African population and to determine various branches of *Homo sapiens* lineage.

Ancient DNA (aDNA) is opening up new avenues for research on early human ancestors. Paleogeneticists can use aDNA to reconstruct physical traits of long-extinct human ancestors for whom only a skull, or jaw, or finger bone may have been found. Teams of scientists, perhaps most notably the lab led by David Reich at Harvard, have developed methods for extracting aDNA and using computers and statistics to reconstruct a full genetic

sequence. aDNA findings by Reich, Johannes Krause at the Max Planck Institute, and others are challenging long-held assumptions about human origins hundreds of thousands of years ago and, more recently, human migrations such as those of Indo-Europeans and Pacific Islanders.

The genetic similarity of modern humans suggests that the population from which all *Homo sapiens* descended originated in Africa more than 250,000 years ago. When these humans began to move out of Africa as long as 180,000 years ago, they spread eastward into Southwest Asia and then throughout the rest of Afro-Eurasia. One group migrated to Australia about 50,000 years ago. Another group moved into Europe

Table 1.1 The Age of the Universe and Human Evolution

Development	Time
Big-bang moment in the creation of the universe	13.8 BILLION YEARS AGO (BYA)
Formation of the sun, earth, and solar system	4.5 BYA
Earliest life forms appear	3.8 BYA
Multicellular organisms appear	1.5 BYA
First hominids appear	7 MILLION YEARS AGO (MYA)
Australopithecus afarensis appear (including Lucy)	3.9 MYA
Homo habilis appear (including Dear Boy)	2.5 MYA
Homo erectus appear (including Java and Peking Man)	1.8 MYA
Homo erectus leave Africa	1.5 MYA
Neanderthals appear	400,000 YEARS AGO
Homo sapiens appear	300,000 YEARS AGO
Homo sapiens leave Africa	180,000 YEARS AGO
Homo sapiens migrate into Asia	120,000 YEARS AGO
Homo sapiens migrate into Australia	60,000 YEARS AGO
Homo sapiens migrate into Europe	50,000 YEARS AGO
Homo sapiens migrate into the Americas	16,000 YEARS AGO
Homo sapiens sapiens appear (modern humans)	35,000 YEARS AGO

(At right of table, spanning from "First hominids appear" through the end: <1% of Earth's Existence)

Before the agricultural revolution, dates are usually marked as BP, which counts the number of years before the present. These BP (or "before the present") dates might also be assigned units such as BYA (billions of years ago), MYA (millions of years ago), or KA (thousands of years ago), depending on what scale is most appropriate for the development being described. More recent dates, beginning around 12,000 years ago, are marked with BCE (before [the] Common Era) as the unit of time. To render a BP date into a BCE date, simply subtract 2,000 years to account for the 2,000 years of the Common Era (CE). So 12,000 BP = 10,000 BCE (plus the 2,000 years of the Common Era since the year 1).

team under the leadership of Donald Johanson unearthed a relatively intact skeleton of a young adult female australopithecine near the Awash River in present-day Ethiopia. While the technical name for the find became *Australopithecus afarensis*, the researchers who found the skeleton gave it the nickname Lucy, based on the then-popular Beatles song "Lucy in the Sky with Diamonds."

Lucy was remarkable. She stood a little over 3 feet tall, she walked upright, her skull contained a brain within the ape size range (that is, one-third human size), and her jaw and teeth were human-like. Her arms were long, hanging halfway from her hips to her knees—suggesting that she might not have been bipedal at all times and sometimes resorted to arms for locomotion, in the fashion of a modern baboon. Above all, Lucy's skeleton was relatively complete and showed us that hominins were walking around more than 3 million years ago. It is important to emphasize that australopithecines were not humans but they carried the genetic and biological material out of which modern humans would later emerge. These precursors to modern humans had a key trait for evolutionary survival: they were remarkably good adapters. They could deal with dynamic environmental shifts, and they were intelligent.

Adaptation For hominins, like the rest of the plant and animal world, survival required constant adaptation (the ability to alter behavior and to innovate, finding new ways of doing things). During the first millions of years of hominin existence, these slow changes involved primarily physical adaptations to the environment. The places where researchers have found early hominin remains in southern and eastern Africa had environments that changed from being heavily forested and well watered to being arid and desertlike, and then back again. (See Map 1.1.) Hominins had to keep pace with these changing physical environments or else risk extinction. In fact, many of the early hominin groups did die out.

In adapting, early hominins began to distinguish themselves from other mammals that were physically similar to themselves. It was not their hunting prowess that made the hominins stand out, because plenty of other species chased their prey with skill and dexterity. The single trait that gave early hominins a real advantage for survival was bipedalism: they became "two-footed" creatures that stood upright. At some point, the first hominins were able to remain upright and move about, leaving their arms and hands free for other useful tasks, like carrying food over long distances. Once they ventured into open savannas (grassy plains with a few scattered trees), about 1.7 million years ago, hominins had a tremendous advantage. They were the only primates (an order of mammals consisting of man, apes, and monkeys) to move consistently on two legs. Because they could move continuously and over great distances, they were able to migrate out of hostile environments and into more hospitable locations.

Table 1.2 Human Evolution	
Species	**Time***
Sahelanthropus tchadensis (including Toumai skull)	7 MILLION YEARS AGO (MYA)
Orrorin tugenensis	6 MYA
Ardipithecus ramidus (including Ardi)	4.4 MYA
Australopithecus anamensis	4.2 MYA
Australopithecus afarensis (including Lucy)	3.9 MYA
Australopithecus africanus (including Taung child)	3.0 MYA
Homo habilis (including Dear Boy)	2.5 MYA
Homo erectus and *Homo ergaster* (including Java and Peking Man)	1.8 MYA
Homo heidelbergensis (common ancestor of *Homo neanderthalensis* and *Homo sapiens*)	600,000 YEARS AGO
Homo neanderthalensis	400,000 YEARS AGO
Homo sapiens	300,000 YEARS AGO
Homo naledi	c. 280,000 YEARS AGO
Homo sapiens sapiens (modern humans)	35,000 YEARS AGO

*Dates are approximate (midpoint on a range), based on multiple finds. Some species are represented with hundreds of examples (more than 300 examples of *Australopithecus afarensis*, of which "Lucy" is the most famous, date across a span of almost 1 million years), while the evidence for other species is more limited (*Sahelanthropus tchadensis* is represented by a single skull).

Source: Smithsonian Institute Human Origins Program.

Climate Changes The climate in eastern and southern Africa, where hominin development began, was conducive to the development of diverse plant and animal species. When the world entered its fourth great ice age approximately 40 million years ago, the earth's temperatures dropped and its continental ice sheets, polar ice sheets, and mountain glaciers expanded. We know

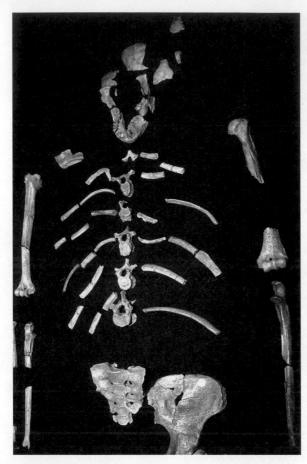

Fossil Bones of Lucy Archaeologist Donald Johanson discovered the fossilized bones of this young female in the Afar region of Ethiopia. Representative of *Australopithecus afarensis*, which lived from 3.9 to 2.9 million years ago, Lucy's bones are believed to date from approximately 3.2 million years ago and provide evidence of some of the first hominins to appear in Africa. This find was of great importance because the bones were so fully and completely preserved.

this because during the last several decades paleo-climatologists have used measurements of ice cores and oxygen isotopes in the ocean to chart the often-radical changes in the world's climate. The fourth great ice age lasted until 12,000 years ago. Like all ice ages, it had alternating warming and cooling phases that lasted between 40,000 and 100,000 years each. Between 10 and 12 million years ago, the climate in Africa went through one such cooling and drying phase. To the east of Africa's Rift Valley, stretching from South Africa north to the Ethiopian highlands, the cooling and drying forced forests to contract and savannas to spread. It was in this region that some apes left the shelter of the trees, stood up, and learned to walk, to run, and to live in savanna lands—thus becoming the precursors to humans and distinctive as a new species.

Using two feet for locomotion augmented the means for obtaining food and avoiding predators and improved the chances these creatures had to survive in constantly changing environments. In addition to being bipedal, hominins had opposable thumbs. This trait, shared with other primates, gave hominins great physical dexterity, enhancing their ability to explore and to alter materials found in nature. Manual dexterity and standing upright also enabled them to carry young family members if they needed to relocate, or to throw missiles (such as rocks and sticks) with deadly accuracy to protect themselves or to obtain food.

Hominins used their increased powers of observation and memory, what we call cognitive skills, to gather wild berries and grains and to scavenge the meat and marrow of animals that had died of natural causes or as the prey of predators. All primates are good at these activities, but hominins came to excel at them. Cognitive skills, which also included problem solving and—eventually—language, were destined to become the basis for further developments. Early hominins were highly social. They lived in bands of about twenty-five individuals, trying to survive by hunting small game and gathering wild plants. Not yet a match for large predators, they had to find safe hiding places. They thrived in places where a diverse supply of wild grains and fruits and abundant wildlife ensured a secure, comfortable existence. In such locations, small hunting bands of twenty-five could swell through alliances with others to as many as 500 individuals. Like other primates, hominins communicated through gestures, but they also may have developed a very basic

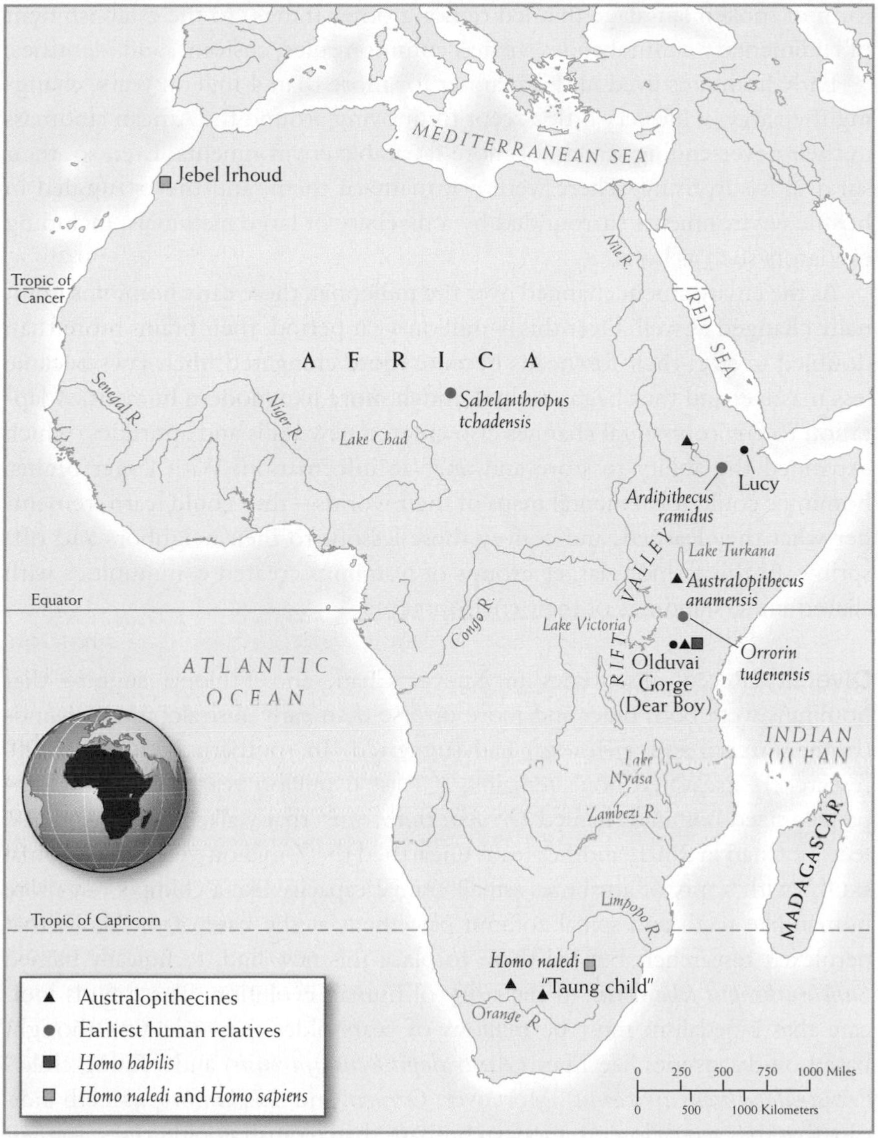

MEDITERRANEAN SEA
Jebel Irhoud
Nile R.
Tropic of Cancer
RED SEA
A F R I C A
Senegal R.
Niger R.
Sabelanthropus tchadensis
Lake Chad
Lucy
Ardipithecus ramidus
RIFT VALLEY
Lake Turkana
Australopithecus anamensis
Equator
Congo R.
Lake Victoria
Orrorin tugenensis
ATLANTIC OCEAN
Olduvai Gorge (Dear Boy)
INDIAN OCEAN
Lake Nyasa
Zambezi R.
MADAGASCAR
Limpopo R.
Tropic of Capricorn
Homo naledi
"Taung child"
Orange R.
Australopithecines
Earliest human relatives
Homo habilis
Homo naledi and Homo sapiens
0 250 500 750 1000 Miles
0 500 1000 Kilometers

Map 1.1 Early Hominins

The earliest hominin species evolved in Africa millions of years ago.

- Judging from this map, in which parts of Africa has evidence for hominin species been excavated?
- Use Table 1.2 to assign dates to these hominin finds. What, if any, hypotheses might you suggest to correlate the geographic spread of the finds with the evolution of hominin species over time?
- According to this chapter, how did the changing environment of eastern and southern Africa shape the evolution of these modern human ancestors?

form of spoken language that led (among other things) to the establishment of rudimentary cultural codes such as common rules, customs, and identities.

Early hominins lived in this manner for more than 4 million years, changing their way of life very little except for moving around the African landmass in their never-ending search for more favorable environments. Even so, their survival is surprising. There were not many of them, and they struggled in hostile environments surrounded by a diversity of large mammals, including predators such as lions.

As the environment changed over the millennia, these early hominins gradually changed as well. Over this 4-million-year period, their brains more than doubled in size; their foreheads became more elongated; their jaws became less massive; and they began to look much more like modern humans. Adaptation to environmental changes also created new skills and aptitudes, which expanded the ability to store and analyze information. With larger brains, hominins could form mental maps of their worlds—they could learn, remember what they learned, and convey these lessons to their neighbors and offspring. In this fashion, larger groups of hominins created communities with shared understandings of their environments.

Diversity Recent discoveries in Kenya, Chad, and Ethiopia suggest that hominins were both older and more diverse than early australopithecine finds (both *afarensis* and *africanus*) had suggested. In southern Kenya in 2000, researchers excavated bone remains, at least 6 million years old, of a chimpanzee-sized hominid (named *Orrorin tugenensis*) that walked upright on two feet. In Chad in 2001, another team unearthed the 7-million-year-old "Toumai skull," with a mix of attributes (small cranial capacity like a chimp's but more human-like teeth and spinal column placement at the base of the skull) that perplexed researchers but led them to place this new find, technically named *Sahelanthropus tchadensis*, in the story of human evolution. These finds indicate that bipedalism must be millions of years older than scientists thought based on discoveries like Lucy (*Australopithecus afarensis*) and "Taung child" (*Australopithecus africanus*). Moreover, *Orrorin* and *Sahelanthropus* teeth indicate that they were closer to modern humans than to australopithecines. In their arms and hands, though, which show characteristics needed for tree climbing, the *Orrorin* hominins seemed more ape-like than the australopithecines. So *Orrorin* hominins were still somewhat tied to an environment in the trees. Only the chimp-sized skull fragments of *Sahelanthropus* have been found, so no conclusions about their bodies, other than that they walked upright, can be drawn.

The story of hominin evolution continues to unfold and demonstrates that hominin diversity continued to thrive in Africa even as other hominins, like *Homo erectus*, migrated out of the continent. Far inside a cave near Johannesburg, South Africa, spelunkers recently made a discovery that led to the excavation of more than 1,550 fossil remains (now named *Homo naledi*, for the cave in which they were found). Researchers have been able to assemble a composite skeleton that revealed that the upper body parts resembled some of the much earlier pre-*Homo* finds, while the hands (both the palms and curved fingers), the wrists, the long legs, and the feet are close to those of modern humans. The males were around 5 feet tall and weighed 100 pounds, while the females were shorter and lighter. Recent publications have suggested a surprisingly late date range of 335,000 to 236,000 years ago, and therefore much research remains to be done to determine how these fossils fit the story of human evolution.

The fact that different kinds of early hominins were living in isolated societies and evolving separately, though in close proximity to one another, in eastern Africa between 4 and 3 million years ago until as recently as 300,000 years ago indicates much greater diversity among their populations than scholars previously imagined. The environment in eastern Africa generated a fair number of different hominin populations, a few of which would provide our genetic base, but most of which would not survive in the long run.

Tool Use by *Homo habilis*

One million years after Lucy, the first beings whom we assign to the genus *Homo*, or "true human," appeared. Like early hominins, *Homo habilis* was bipedal, possessing a smooth walk based on upright posture. *Homo habilis* had an even more important advantage over other hominins: brains that were growing larger. Big brains are the site of innovation: learning and storing lessons so that humans could pass those lessons on to later generations, especially in the making of tools and the efficient use of resources (and, we suspect, in defending themselves). Mary

The Leakeys Louis Leakey and his wife, Mary, were dedicated archaeologists whose work in East Africa established the area as one of the starting points of human development. Mary Leakey was among the most successful archaeologists studying hominins in Africa. Her finds, including the one in this photograph from Laetoli, Tanzania, highlight the activities of early men and women in Africa. The footprints, believed to be those of an *Australopithecus afarensis*, date from 3.7 to 3 million years ago.

and Louis Leakey, who made astonishing fossil discoveries in the 1950s at Olduvai Gorge in present-day northern Tanzania, identified these important traits. The Leakeys' finds included an intact skull that was 1.8 million years old. They nicknamed the creature whose skull they had unearthed Dear Boy.

Objects discovered with Dear Boy demonstrated that by this time early humans had begun to make tools for butchering animals and, possibly, for hunting and killing smaller animals. The tools were flaked stones with sharpened edges for cutting apart animal flesh and scooping out the marrow from bones. To mimic the slicing teeth of lions, leopards, and other carnivores, these early humans had devised these tools through careful chipping. Dear Boy and his companions had carried usable rocks to distant places, where they made their implements with special hammer stones—tools to make tools. Unlike other tool-using animals (for example, chimpanzees), early humans were now

Olduvai Gorge, Tanzania
Olduvai Gorge is probably the most famous archaeological site containing hominin finds. Mary and Louis Leakey, convinced that early humans originated in Africa, discovered the fossil remains of *Homo habilis* (skillful man) in this area between 1960 and 1963. They argued that these findings represent a direct link to *Homo erectus*.

Homo habilis
Species, confined to Africa, that emerged about 2.5 million years ago and whose toolmaking ability truly made it the forerunner, though a very distant one, of modern humans. *Homo habilis* means "skillful human."

Homo erectus
Species that emerged about 1.8 million years ago, had a large brain, walked truly upright, migrated out of Africa, and likely mastered fire. *Homo erectus* means "standing human."

intentionally fashioning implements, not simply finding them when needed. More important, they were passing on knowledge of these tools to their offspring and, in the process, gradually improving the tools. The Leakeys, believing that making and using tools represented a new stage in the evolution of human beings, gave Dear Boy and his companions the name **Homo habilis**, or "skillful human." While scholars today may debate whether toolmaking (rather than walking upright or having a large brain) is the key trait that distinguishes the first humans from earlier hominins, *Homo habilis*'s skills made them the forerunners, though very distant ones, of modern men and women.

MIGRATIONS OF *HOMO ERECTUS*

By 1 million years ago, many of the hominin species that flourished together in Africa had died out. One surviving species, which emerged about 1.8 million years ago, had a large brain capacity and walked truly upright; it therefore gained the name **Homo erectus**, or "standing human." Three important features distinguished *Homo erectus* from their competitors and made them more able to cope with environmental changes: their family dynamics, use of fire, and ability to travel long distances. Discoveries in Asia and Europe show that *Homo erectus* migrated out of Africa in some of the earliest waves of hominin migration around the globe.

Family Dynamics One of the traits that contributed to the survival of *Homo erectus* was the development of extended periods of caring for their young. Although their enlarged brain gave these hominins advantages over the rest of the animal world, it also brought one significant problem: their heads were too large to pass through the females' pelvises at birth. Their pelvises were only big enough to deliver an infant with a cranial capacity that was about a third an adult's size. As a result, offspring required a long period of protection by adults as they matured and their brain size tripled.

This difference from other species also affected family dynamics. For example, the long maturation process gave adult members of hunting and gathering bands time to train their children in those activities. In addition, maturation and brain growth required mothers to spend years breast-feeding and then preparing food for children after their weaning. In order to share the responsibilities of child-rearing, mothers relied on other women (their own mothers, sisters, and friends) and girls (often their own daughters) to help with nurturing and protecting, a process known as *allomothering* (literally, "other mothering").

Use of Fire *Homo erectus* began to make rudimentary attempts to control their environment by means of fire. It is hard to tell from fossils when hominins—*Homo erectus* or *Homo sapiens* (modern humans)—learned to use fire. The most reliable evidence comes from cave sites less than 250,000 years old, where early humans apparently cooked some of their food, but some archaeologists have suggested that hominin mastery of fire occurred as early as 500,000 years ago, by *Homo erectus*. Fire provided heat, protection, a gathering point for small communities, and a way to cook food. It was also symbolically powerful: here was a source of energy that humans could extinguish and revive at will. The uses of fire had enormous long-term effects on human evolution. Because they were able to boil, steam, and fry wild plants, as well as otherwise undigestible foods (especially raw muscle fiber), hominins who mastered this technology could expand their diets. Because cooked foods yield more energy than raw foods and because the brain, while only 2 percent of human body weight, uses between 20 and 25 percent of all the energy that humans take in, cooking was decisive in the evolution of brain size and functioning.

Early Migrations Being bipedal, *Homo erectus* could move with a smooth and rapid gait, so they could cover large distances quickly. They were the world's first long-distance travelers, forming the first mobile human communities. (See Table 1.3.) Around 1.5 million years ago, *Homo erectus* individuals began migrating out of Africa, first into the lands of Southwest Asia.

Table 1.3 Migrations of *Homo sapiens*	
Species	**Time**
Homo erectus leave Africa	c. 1.5 MILLION YEARS AGO
Homo sapiens leave Africa	c. 180,000 YEARS AGO
Homo sapiens migrate into Asia	c. 120,000 YEARS AGO
migrate into Australia	c. 60,000 YEARS AGO
migrate into Europe	c. 50,000 YEARS AGO
migrate into the Americas	c. 16,000 YEARS AGO

From there, they traveled along the Indian Ocean shoreline, moving into South Asia and Southeast Asia and later northward into what is now China. Their migration was a response in part to the environmental changes that were transforming the world. The Northern Hemisphere experienced thirty major cold phases during this period, marked by glaciers spreading over vast expanses of the northern parts of Eurasia and the Americas. The glaciers formed as a result of intense cold that froze much of the world's oceans, lowering them some 325 feet below present-day levels. These lower ocean levels made it possible for the migrants to travel across land bridges into Southeast Asia and from East Asia to Japan, as well as from New Guinea to Australia. The last parts of the Afro-Eurasian landmass to be occupied were in Europe.

Discoveries of the bone remains of "Java Man" and "Peking Man" (named according to the places where archaeologists first unearthed their remains) confirmed early settlements of *Homo erectus* in Southeast and East Asia. The remains of Java Man, found in 1891 on the island of Java, turned out to be those of an early *Homo erectus* that had dispersed into Asia nearly 2 million years ago. Peking Man, found near Beijing in the 1920s, was a cave dweller, toolmaker, and hunter and gatherer who settled in northern China. Originally believing that Peking Man dated to around 400,000 years ago, archaeologists thought that warmer climate might have made the region more hospitable to migrating *Homo erectus*. But recent application of the aluminum-beryllium technique to analyze the fossils has suggested they date to 770,000 years ago, a time when China's climate would have been much colder. Peking Man's brain was larger than that of his Javan cousins, and there is evidence that he controlled fire and cooked meat in addition to hunting large animals. He made tools of vein quartz, quartz crystals, flint, and sandstone. A major innovation was the double-faced axe, a stone instrument whittled down to sharp edges on both sides to serve as a hand axe, a cleaver,

Skulls of Ancestors of *Homo sapiens* Shown here are seven skulls of ancestors of modern-day men and women, arranged to highlight brain growth over time. The larger the brain, the more developed the regions of the brain that process vision, different kinds of cognition, and communication can be. The skulls represent (*left to right*): *Adapis*, a lemur-like animal that lived 50 million years ago; *Proconsul*, a primate that lived about 23 million years ago; *Australopithecus africanus*; *Homo habilis*; *Homo erectus*; *Homo sapiens* from the Qafzeh site in Israel, about 90,000 years old; and *Homo sapiens sapiens* from France, about 22,000 years old.

a pick, and probably a weapon to hurl against foes or animals. Even so, these early predecessors still lacked the intelligence, language skills, and ability to create culture that would distinguish the first modern humans from their hominin relatives.

HOMO SAPIENS: THE FIRST MODERN HUMANS

The first traces that we have of **Homo sapiens** come from modern-day Morocco and suggest that the first modern humans emerged sometime around 315,000 years ago. This bigger-brained, more dexterous, and more agile species of humans differed from their precursors, including *Homo habilis* and *Homo erectus*. Their distinctive traits, including greater cognitive skills, made *Homo sapiens* the first modern humans and enabled them to spread out from Africa by 100,000 years ago and flourish in even more diverse regions across the globe than *Homo erectus* did.

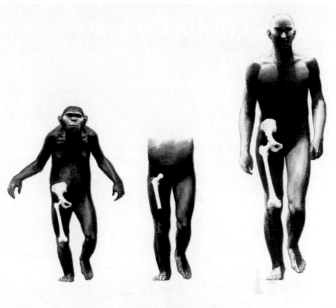

The Physical Evolution of Hominins These three figures show the femur bones of Lucy, *Orrorin tugenensis* (one of the earliest of the hominins, who may have existed around 6 million years ago), and *Homo sapiens*. *Homo sapiens* have a larger femur bone and were bigger than Lucy—a representative of the hominin species *Australopithecus afarensis*—but have the same bone structure. Particularly useful indicators for determining differences among human ancestors are skull size (which can indicate the size of the brain and thus cognitive ability), the position at the base of the skull where the spine enters the cranium (which can indicate bipedalism), jawbones and teeth (which can indicate the kind of food they could have chewed), femur bones (which can indicate overall size and manner of walking), and foot and hand structure (which can indicate the kind of activities they performed).

Large-scale shifts in Africa's climate and environment several hundred thousand years ago put huge pressures on all types of mammals, including hominins. In these extremely warm and dry environments, the smaller, quicker, and more adaptable mammals survived. What counted now was no longer large size and brute strength, but the ability to respond quickly, with agility, and with great speed. The eclipse of *Homo erectus* by *Homo sapiens* was not inevitable. After all, *Homo erectus* was already scattered around Africa and Eurasia by the time *Homo sapiens* emerged; in contrast, even as late as 100,000 years ago there were only about 10,000 *Homo sapiens* adults living primarily in a small part of the African landmass. When *Homo sapiens* began moving in large numbers out of Africa and the two species encountered each other in the same places across the globe, *Homo sapiens* individuals were better suited to survive—in part because of their greater cognitive and language skills.

The *Homo sapiens* newcomers followed the trails blazed by earlier migrants when they moved out of Africa. (See Map 1.2.) Evidence, including part of a fossilized jaw with teeth, from a cave on Mount Carmel in Israel indicates that *Homo sapiens* were living there as early as 180,000 years ago. Whether that evidence suggests significant migrations or more limited forays by *Homo sapiens* is still unclear. Nevertheless, it is clear that from 120,000 to 50,000 years ago, *Homo sapiens* were moving in ever increasing numbers into the same areas as their genetic cousins, reaching across Southwest Asia

The Global View

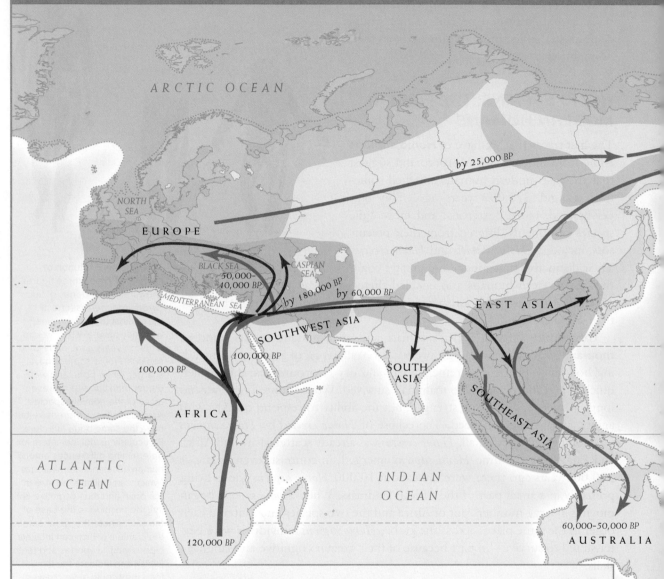

ARCTIC OCEAN

by 25,000 BP

NORTH
SEA

EUROPE

BLACK SEA
50,000–
40,000 BP

CASPIAN
SEA

MEDITERRANEAN SEA

by 180,000 BP

by 60,000 BP

EAST ASIA

SOUTHWEST ASIA

100,000 BP

SOUTH
ASIA

100,000 BP

AFRICA

SOUTHEAST ASIA

ATLANTIC
OCEAN

INDIAN
OCEAN

60,000–50,000 BP

AUSTRALIA

120,000 BP

Map 1.2 Early Migrations: Out of Africa

Hominin species, like *Homo erectus*, began migrating out of Africa hundreds of thousands of years before the present (BP), but only *Homo sapiens* went to all major inhabitable regions.

- According to this map, when and to what regions did *Homo erectus* migrate? *Homo neanderthalensis*? *Homo sapiens*? Compare the location, extent, and dates of each species' migration.

- Locate the extent of ice sheets and identify the differences in exposed landmasses, as compared to modern shorelines. How did ice sheets and exposed land shape each species' migration patterns?

- Examine the dates for human settlement of the Americas. What do these dates suggest about human migration in the Americas?

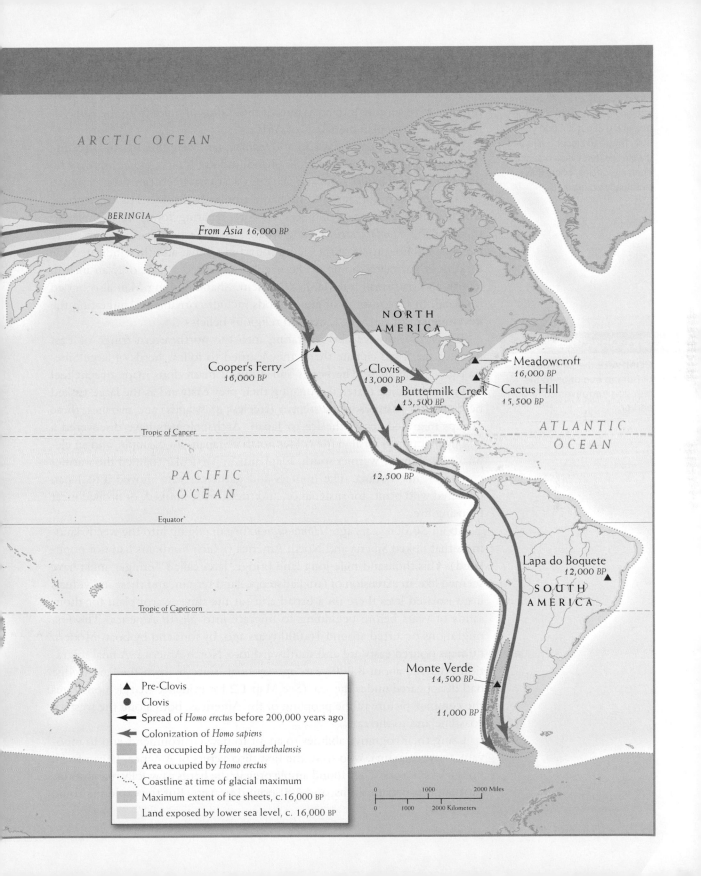

ARCTIC OCEAN

BERINGIA

From Asia 16,000 BP

NORTH
AMERICA

Cooper's Ferry
16,000 BP

Clovis
13,000 BP

Buttermilk Creek
15,500 BP

Meadowcroft
16,000 BP

Cactus Hill
15,500 BP

ATLANTIC
OCEAN

Tropic of Cancer

PACIFIC
OCEAN

12,500 BP

Equator

Lapa do Boquete
12,000 BP

SOUTH
AMERICA

Tropic of Capricorn

Monte Verde
14,500 BP

11,000 BP

▲ Pre-Clovis
● Clovis
→ Spread of *Homo erectus* before 200,000 years ago
→ Colonization of *Homo sapiens*
   Area occupied by *Homo neanderthalensis*
   Area occupied by *Homo erectus*
   Coastline at time of glacial maximum
   Maximum extent of ice sheets, c.16,000 BP
   Land exposed by lower sea level, c. 16,000 BP

0   1000   2000 Miles
0   1000   2000 Kilometers

The first humans; emerged in Africa as early as 315,000 years ago and migrated out of Africa beginning about 180,000 years ago. They had bigger brains and greater dexterity than previous hominin species, whom they eventually eclipsed.

Core Objectives

COMPARE the narrative of human evolution to the creation narratives covered earlier.

and from there into central Asia—but not into Europe. They flourished and reproduced. By 30,000 years ago, the population of *Homo sapiens* had grown to about 300,000. Between 60,000 and 12,000 years ago, these modern humans were surging into areas tens of thousands of miles from the Rift Valley and the Ethiopian highlands of Africa.

In the area of present-day China, *Homo sapiens* were thriving and creating distinct regional cultures. Consider Shandingdong Man, a *Homo sapiens* who dates to about 18,000 years ago. His physical characteristics were closer to those of modern humans, and he had a similar brain size. His stone tools, which included choppers and scrapers for preparing food, were similar to those of the *Homo erectus* Peking Man. His bone needles, however, were the first stitching tools of their kind found in China, and they indicated the making of garments. Some of the needles measured a little over an inch in length and had small holes drilled in them. Shandingdong Man also buried his dead. In fact, a tomb of grave goods includes ornaments suggesting the development of aesthetic tastes and religious beliefs.

Homo sapiens were also migrating into the northeastern fringe of East Asia. In the frigid climate there, they learned to follow herds of large Siberian grazing animals. The bones and dung of mastodons made decent fuel and good building material. Pursuing their prey eastward as the large-tusked herds sought pastures in the steppes (treeless grasslands) and marshes, these groups migrated across the ice to Japan. Archaeologists have discovered a woolly mammoth fossil in the colder north of Japan, for example, and an elephant fossil in the warmer south. Elephants in particular roamed the warmer parts of Inner Eurasia. The hunters and gatherers who moved into Japan gathered wild plants for sustenance, and they dried, smoked, or broiled meat by using fire.

About 30,000 years ago, *Homo sapiens* began edging into the weedy landmass that linked Siberia and North America (which hominins had not populated). This thousand-mile-long land bridge, later called Beringia, must have seemed like an extension of familiar steppe-land terrain, and these individuals lived isolated lives there on a broad and (at the time) warm plain for thousands of years before beginning to migrate into North America. The first migrations occurred around 16,000 years ago, by foot and by boat. Modern humans poured eastward and southward into North America. A final migration occurred about 8,000 years ago by boat, since by then the land bridge had disappeared under the sea. (See Map 1.2 for evidence that demonstrates the complex picture of the peopling of the Americas, both along the western coastline and to the east.)

Using their cognitive abilities to adapt to new environments and to innovate, these migrants, who were the first discoverers of America, began to fill up the landmasses. They found ample prey in the herds of woolly mammoths, caribou, 3-ton giant sloths, and 200-pound beavers. But the explorers could also themselves be prey—for they encountered saber-toothed tigers, long-legged eagles, and giant bears that moved faster than horses. The melting of the glaciers about 8,000 years ago and the resulting disappearance of the land bridge eventually cut off the first Americans from their Afro-Eurasian origins. Thereafter, the Americas became a world apart from Afro-Eurasia.

Although modern humans evolved from earlier hominins, no straight-line descent tree exists from the first hominins to *Homo sapiens*. Increasingly, scientists view our origins as shaped by a series of progressions and regressions as hominin species adapted or failed to adapt and died out. The remains of now-extinct hominin species, such as *Homo ergaster*, *Homo heidelbergensis*, *Homo neanderthalensis*, and now *Homo naledi* (see Table 1.2), offer intriguing glimpses of ultimately unsuccessful branches of the complex human evolutionary tree. Spreading into Europe and parts of Southwest Asia along with other hominins, Neanderthals, for example, had big brains, used tools, wore clothes, buried their dead, hunted, lived in rock shelters, and even interacted with *Homo sapiens*. Yet when faced with environmental challenges, *Homo sapiens* survived, while Neanderthals died out sometime between 45,000 and 35,000 years ago, although recent genetic evidence suggests that some interbreeding occurred between Neanderthals and *Homo sapiens*.

Indeed, several species could exist simultaneously, but some were more suited to changing environmental conditions—and thus more likely to survive—than others. Evidence that interbreeding between these different species may have given some *Homo sapiens* a survival advantage emerged in 2008, when Russian archaeologists dug up a pinky bone at the Denisova Cave in the Altai Mountains of southern Siberia and thereby discovered another hominin group that had many of the characteristics of *Homo sapiens*. These hominins, who looked different from *Homo sapiens*, had lived in this cave off and on from 287,000 years ago. They even shared a common ancestor with the Neanderthals about 400,000 years ago and interbred with the Neanderthals and our own species, as indicated by DNA drawn from living peoples in East Asia, Australia, the Pacific Islands, and the Americas. Some scientists have suggested that the interbreeding of *Homo sapiens* with the Denisovans enabled modern humans to survive in the Tibetan highlands at altitudes of close to 11,000 feet and as early as 15,000 years ago. Using aDNA drawn from Denisovan remains, scientists have reconstructed their body types, noting that they had massive brain cases and giant molars as well as larger neck vertebrae, thicker ribs, and a higher bone density than modern humans. They may have weighed well over 200 pounds and were robust and very large individuals. One investigator observed that they would have done well as modern-day football players. Advances in aDNA technology may allow researchers to identify previously unclassified remains as Denisovans. Scholars' understanding of this recent hominin relative, genetically distinct from Neanderthals and modern humans, is only beginning to take form.

Although the primary examples emphasized in this chapter—*Homo habilis* and *Homo erectus*—were among some of the world's first human-like inhabitants, they probably were not direct ancestors of modern men and women. By 25,000 years ago, DNA analysis reveals, nearly all genetic cousins to *Homo sapiens* had become extinct. *Homo sapiens*, with their physical agility and superior cognitive skills, were ready to populate the world.

The Life of Early *Homo sapiens*

Core Objectives

DESCRIBE human ways of life and cultural developments from 300,000 to 12,000 years ago.

In the period from 300,000 to around 12,000 years ago, early *Homo sapiens* were similar to other hominins in that they lived by hunting and gathering, but their use of language and new cultural forms represented an evolutionary breakthrough. Earlier hominins could not form large, lasting communities, as they had limited communication skills. While simple commands and hand signals developed over time, complex linguistic expression escaped them. This achievement was one of the last in the evolutionary process of becoming human; it did not occur until between 100,000 and 50,000 years ago. Many scholars view it as the critical ingredient in distinguishing human beings from other animals. It is this skill that made *Homo sapiens* "sapiens," which is to say "wise" or "intelligent"—humans who could create culture.

LANGUAGE

Few things set *Homo sapiens* off from the rest of the animal world more starkly than their use of language. Although the beginnings and development of language are controversial, scholars agree that the cognitive abilities involved in language development marked an evolutionary milestone. Some earlier hominins could express themselves by grunting, but natural language (the use of sounds to make words that convey meaning to others) is unique to modern humans. The development of language required a large brain and complex cognitive organization to create word groups that would convey symbolic meaning. Verbal communication required an ability to think abstractly and to communicate abstractions. Language was a huge breakthrough, because individuals could teach words and ideas to neighbors and offspring. Language thus enhanced the ability to accumulate knowledge that could be transmitted across both space and time.

Biological research has demonstrated that humans can make and process many more primary and distinctive sounds, called phonemes, than other animals can. Whereas a human being can utter fifty phonemes, an ape can form only twelve. Also, humans can process sounds more quickly than other primates can. With fifty phonemes it is possible to create more than 100,000 words; by arranging those words in different sequences and developing rules in language, individuals can express countless subtle and complex meanings. Recent research suggests that use of complex languages occurred about 100,000 years ago and that the nearest approximation to humanity's earliest language existing today belongs to two African peoples, the !Kung of southern Africa and the Hadza of Tanzania. These peoples make a clicking sound by dropping the tongue down from the roof of the mouth and exhaling. As humans moved out of Africa and spread around the globe, they expanded their original language into nineteen language families, from which all of the world's languages then evolved. (See Map 1.3.) It was the development of language and the cultural forms discussed later in this section that allowed *Homo sapiens* to engage dynamically with their environments.

Map 1.3 Original Language Family Groups

The use of complex language developed 100,000 years ago among **Homo sapiens** in Africa. As humans dispersed throughout the globe, nineteen language families evolved from which all modern languages originate.

- How many different landmasses did language evolve on? Which landmasses have a greater number of language families, and why might that be?
- On the basis of this map, what geographic features had an impact on the evolution of language groups?
- Why do you think separate languages emerged over time?

hunting and gathering
Lifestyle in which food is acquired through hunting animals, fishing, and foraging for wild berries, nuts, fruit, and grains, rather than planting crops, vines, or trees. As late as 1500 CE, as much as 15 percent of the world's population still lived by this method.

HUNTING AND GATHERING

Although these early humans were developing language skills that distinguished them from their hominin relatives, like their predecessors they remained hunters and gatherers until around 12,000 years ago (for almost 95 percent of our existence). As late as 1500 CE, as much as 15 percent of the world's population still lived by **hunting and gathering.** Early *Homo sapiens* hunted animals, fished, and foraged for wild berries, nuts, fruit, and grains, rather than planting crops, vines, or trees. Even today hunting and gathering societies endure, although only in the most marginal locations—often at the edge of deserts. Researchers consider the present-day San peoples of southern Africa as an isolated remnant continuing their traditional hunting and gathering modes of life. Modern scholars use the San to reveal how men and women must have lived hundreds of thousands of years ago. The fact that hominin men and women (going back to *Homo erectus* and *habilis* and beyond) survived as hunters and gatherers for millions of years, that early *Homo sapiens* also lived this way, and that a few contemporary communities still forage for food suggests the powerful attractions of this way of life. Hunters and gatherers could find enough food in about three hours of foraging each day, thus affording time for other pursuits such as relaxation, interaction, and friendly competitions with other members of their bands. Scholars believe that these small bands were relatively egalitarian compared with the more male-dominated societies that arose later. They speculate that men specialized in hunting and women specialized in gathering and child-rearing. Some scholars believe that women even made a larger contribution and had high status because the dietary staples of the community were cereals and fruits, whose harvesting and preparation were likely women's responsibility.

PAINTINGS, SCULPTURE, AND MUSIC

The ability to draw allowed *Homo sapiens* to understand their environment, to bond among their kin groups (groups related by blood ties), and to articulate important mythologies. Accomplished artwork from this era has been found across Afro-Eurasia. For instance, in a deep cave at Altamira in Spain more than two dozen life-size figures of bison, horses, and wild bulls, all painted in vivid red, black, yellow, and brown, are arranged across the ceiling of the huge chamber. More than 50,000 similarly stunning works of art have been found in caves across Europe and elsewhere. The images on cave walls accumulated in some instances over a period of 25,000 years, and they changed little in that time. The earliest figurative art now would appear to be found in a cave in Borneo. It features a spindly-legged, thick-bodied wild cow, drawn in reddish ocher, and is at least 40,000 years old. Like this wild cow, the subjects of most ancient art are large game—animals that early

Hadza of Modern Tanzania
Hunting and gathering was the way that most humans lived for hundreds of thousands of years. Although their way of life is dying out, modern hunters and gatherers offer useful ethnographic comparisons for understanding how humans lived in the millennia prior to sedentary agriculture. These Hadza, from modern Tanzania, dig up edible roots that offer a reliable and high-calorie food source for their community.

humans would have considered powerful symbols. The artists rendered these animals in such a way that the natural contours of the cave wall defined a bulging belly or an eye socket. Many images appear more than once, suggesting that they are works from several occasions or by several artists. And some, like the horses and lions of Chauvet cave in France from 35,000 years ago, appear in overlapping, layered images that might have evoked a sense of motion, especially when viewed by flickering torchlight in the dark of a cave. The remarkably few human images show hunters, naked females, or dancing males. There are also many handprints made by blowing paint around a hand placed on the cave wall, or by dipping hands in paint and then pressing them to the wall. There are even abstract symbols such as circles, wavy lines, and checkerboards; often these appear at places of transition in the caves.

Scholars have rejected an initial theory that these paintings were decorative, for the deep caves were not homes and had no natural light to render the images visible. Perhaps the images helped the early humans define themselves as separate from other parts of nature. Alternatively, they might have been the work of powerful shamans, individuals believed to hold special powers to understand and control the forces of the cosmos. The subjects and the style of the paintings are similar to images engraved or painted on rocks by some hunting and gathering societies living today, especially the San and the !Kung peoples of southern Africa. In those societies, paintings mark important places of ritual: shamans make them during trances while mediating with the spirit world on behalf of their communities.

Paintings were not the only form of artistic expression for early humans. Archaeologists also have unearthed small sculptures of animals shaped out of

Bone Flute Paleolithic flutes have been found at sites in Germany, France, and Slovenia. Made of animal bone (bird and bear) and mammoth ivory, these flutes date back to 35,000 years ago and perhaps even as long ago as 43,000 years ago.

bone and stone that are even older than the paintings. Most famous are figurines of rotund, and perhaps pregnant, females. Statuettes like the so-called Venus of Willendorf, found in Austria, demonstrate that successful reproduction was a very important theme. Other sculptures represent animals in postures of movement or at rest.

The caves of early men and women also resounded to the strains of music. In 2008, archaeologists working in southwestern Germany discovered a hollowed-out bone flute with five openings that they dated to approximately 35,000 years ago, roughly the same time that humans began to occupy this region. When researchers put the flute to musical tests, they also concluded that the instrument was capable of making harmonic sounds comparable to those of modern-day flutes.

Only *Homo sapiens* had the cognitive abilities to produce the abundant sculptures and drawings of this era, thus leaving a permanent mark on the symbolic landscape of human development. Such visual expressions marked the dawn of human culture and a consciousness of men's and women's place in the world. Symbolic activity of this sort enabled humans to make sense of themselves, nature, and the relationship between humanity and nature. That relationship with nature—which had remained static for hundreds of thousands of years of hunting and gathering—would change with the agricultural revolution.

Global Agricultural Revolution

About 12,000 years ago (around 10,000 BCE), a fundamental shift occurred in the way humans produced food for themselves—what some scholars have called an agricultural, or ecological, revolution. Around the same time, a significant warming trend that had begun around 11,000 BCE resulted in a profusion of plants and animals, large numbers of which began to exist closer to humans. In this era of major change, humans established greater control over nature. The transformation consisted of the **domestication** of wild plants and animals. Population pressure was one factor that triggered the move to settled agriculture, as hunting and gathering alone could not sustain the growth in numbers of people. A revolution in agriculture, in turn, led to

domestication
Bringing a wild animal or plant under human control.

a vast population expansion because men and women could now produce more calories per unit of land. As various plants and animals were domesticated around the world, people settled in villages and social relationships changed.

THE BEGINNINGS OF SETTLED AGRICULTURE AND PASTORALISM

Learning to control environments through the domestication of plants and animals was a gradual process. Communities shifted from a hunting and gathering lifestyle (which requires moving around in search of food) to one based on agriculture (which requires staying in one place until the soil has been exhausted). **Settled agriculture** refers to the application of human labor and tools to a fixed plot of land for more than one growing cycle. Alternatively, some people adopted a lifestyle based on **pastoralism** (the herding of domesticated animals), which complemented settled farming.

Early Domestication of Plants and Animals The formation of settled communities enabled humans to take advantage of favorable regions and to take risks, spurring agricultural innovation. In areas with abundant wild game and edible plants, people began to observe and experiment with the most adaptable plants. For ages, people gathered grains by collecting seeds that fell freely from their stalks. At some point, observant collectors perceived that they could obtain larger harvests if they pulled grain seeds directly from plants. The process of plant domestication probably began when people noticed that certain edible plants retained their nutritious grains longer than others, so they collected these seeds and scattered them across fertile soils. When ripe, these plants produced bigger and more concentrated crops. Plant domestication occurred when the plant retained its ripe, mature seeds, allowing an easy harvest. People used most seeds for food but saved some for planting in the next growing cycle, to ensure a food supply for the next year.

Dogs were the first animals to be domesticated (although in fact they may have adopted humans, rather than the other way around). At least 33,000 years ago in China and central Asia, including Mongolia and Nepal, humans first domesticated gray wolves and made them an essential part of human society. Dogs did more than comfort humans. They provided an example of how to achieve the domestication of other animals and, with their herding instincts, they helped humans control other domesticated animals, such as sheep. In the central Zagros Mountains region, where wild sheep and wild goats were abundant, they became the next animal domesticates. Perhaps hunters returned home with young wild sheep, which then reproduced, and their offspring never returned to the wild. The animals accepted

settled agriculture
Humans' use of tools, animals, and their own labor to work the same plot of land for more than one growing cycle. It involves switching from a hunting and gathering lifestyle to one based on farming.

pastoralism
A way of life in which humans herd domesticated animals and exploit their products (hides/fur, meat, and milk). Pastoralists include nomadic groups that range across vast distances, as well as transhumant herders who migrate seasonally in a more limited range.

Domestication This detail from a wall painting in the Tassili-n-Ajjer mountain range in modern Algeria depicts early domestication of cattle and other animals.

their dependence because the humans fed them. Since controlling animal reproduction was more reliable than hunting, domesticated herds became the primary source of protein in the early humans' diet.

When the number of animals under human control and living close to the settlement outstripped the supply of food needed to feed them, community members could move the animals to grassy steppes for grazing. These pastoralists herded domesticated animals, moving them to new pastures on a seasonal basis. Goats, the other main domesticated animal of Southwest Asia, are smarter than sheep but more difficult to control. The pastoralists may have introduced goats into herds of sheep to better control herd movement. Pigs and cattle also came under human control at this time.

Transhumant Herders and Nomadic Pastoralists Pastoralism appeared as a way of life around 5500 BCE, essentially at the same time that full-time farmers appeared (although the beginnings of plant and animal domestication had begun many millennia earlier). Over time, two different types of pastoralists with different relationships to settled populations developed: transhumant herders and nomadic pastoralists. Transhumant herders were closely affiliated with agricultural villages whose inhabitants grew grains, especially wheat and barley, which required large parcels of land. These herders produced both meat and dairy products, as well as wool for textiles, and exchanged these products with the agriculturalists for grain, pottery, and other staples. Extended families might farm and herd at the same time, growing crops on large estates and grazing their herds in the foothills and mountains nearby. They moved their livestock seasonally, pasturing their flocks in higher lands during summer and in valleys in winter. This movement over short distances is called *transhumance* and did not require herders to vacate their primary living locations, which were generally in the mountain valleys.

In contrast with transhumant pastoralism, *nomadic pastoralism* came to flourish especially in the steppe lands north of the agricultural zone of southern Eurasia. This way of life was characterized by horse-riding herders of cattle and other livestock. Because horses provided decisive advantages in transportation and warfare, they gained more value than other domesticated animals. Thus, horses soon became the measure of household wealth and prestige. Unlike the transhumant herders, the nomadic pastoralists often had no fixed home, though they often returned to their traditional locations. They moved across large distances in response to the size and needs of their herds. Beginning in the second millennium BCE, the northern areas of the Eurasian landmass, stretching from present-day Ukraine across Siberia and Mongolia to the Pacific Ocean, became the preserve of these horse-riding pastoral peoples, living as they did in a region unable to support the extensive agriculture necessary for large settled populations. Historians know much less about these horse-riding pastoral nomads than about the agriculturalists and the transhumant herders, as their numbers were small and they left fewer archaeological traces or historical records. Their role in world history, however, is as important as that of the settled societies. In Afro-Eurasia, they domesticated horses and developed weapons and techniques that at certain points in history enabled them to conquer sedentary societies. As we will see in the next section (and later chapters), they also transmitted ideas, products, and people across long distances, maintaining the linkages that connected east and west.

AGRICULTURAL INNOVATION: AFRO-EURASIA AND THE AMERICAS

The agricultural revolutions that occurred worldwide between 9000 and 2000 BCE had much in common: climatic change; increased knowledge about plants and animals; and the need for more efficient ways to feed, house, and promote the growth of a larger population. These concerns led peoples in Eurasia, the Americas, and Africa to see the advantages of cultivating plants and domesticating wildlife. (See Map 1.4.).

Some communities were independent innovators, developing agricultural techniques based on their specific environments. In Southwest Asia, East Asia, Africa, and the Americas, the distinctive crops and animals that humans first domesticated reflect independent innovation. As we will see in the following section, other communities (such as those in Europe) were borrowers

COMPARE the ways communities around the world shifted to settled agriculture.

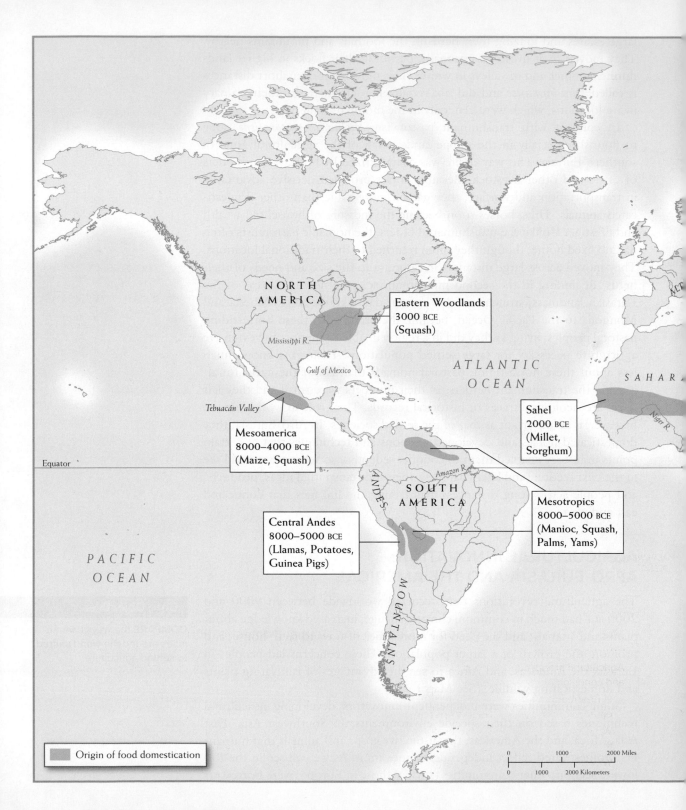

NORTH
AMERICA

Mississippi R.

Gulf of Mexico

Tehuacán Valley

Eastern Woodlands
3000 BCE
(Squash)

Mesoamerica
8000–4000 BCE
(Maize, Squash)

Equator

ATLANTIC
OCEAN

SAHAR

Sahel
2000 BCE
(Millet,
Sorghum)

Niger R.

Amazon R.

SOUTH
AMERICA

ANDES

Central Andes
8000–5000 BCE
(Llamas, Potatoes,
Guinea Pigs)

Mesotropics
8000–5000 BCE
(Manioc, Squash,
Palms, Yams)

PACIFIC
OCEAN

MOUNTAINS

Origin of food domestication

0   1000   2000 Miles

0   1000   2000 Kilometers

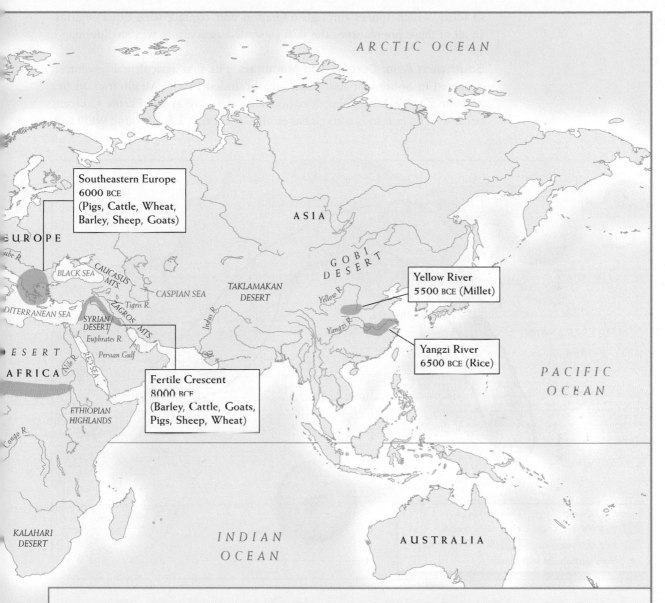

Southeastern Europe
6000 BCE
(Pigs, Cattle, Wheat,
Barley, Sheep, Goats)

Yellow River
5500 BCE (Millet)

Yangzi River
6500 BCE (Rice)

Fertile Crescent
8000 BCE
(Barley, Cattle, Goats,
Pigs, Sheep, Wheat)

Map 1.4 The Origins of Food Production and Animal Domestication

Agricultural production emerged in many regions at different times. The variety of patterns reflected local resources and conditions.

- In how many different locations, and at what different times, did agricultural production and animal domestication emerge? What is the range of crops and animals domesticated in each region?
- What specific geographic features (for instance, specific mountains, rivers, or latitudes) are common among these early food-producing areas? Do those geographic features appear to guarantee agricultural production?
- Why do you think agriculture emerged in certain areas and not in others?

of ideas, which spread through migration and contact with other regions. In all of these populations, the shift to settled agriculture was revolutionary.

Southwest Asia: Cereals and Mammals The first agricultural revolution occurred in Southwest Asia in an area bounded by the Mediterranean Sea and the Zagros Mountains, a region known today as the Fertile Crescent because of its rich soils and regular rainfall. (See Map 1.5.) Around 9000 BCE,

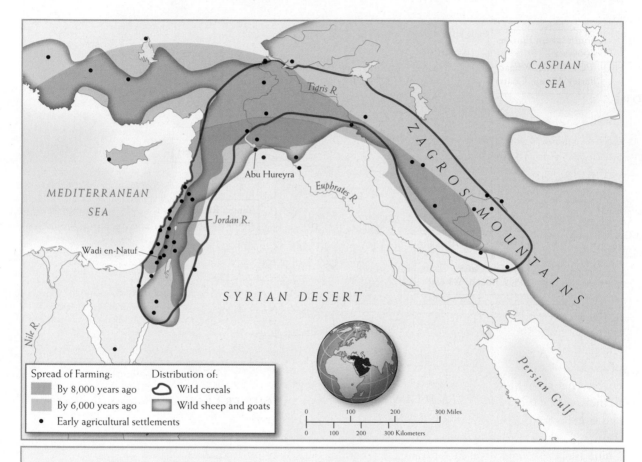

Map 1.5 The Birth of Farming in the Fertile Crescent

Agricultural production occurred in the Fertile Crescent starting roughly in 9000 BCE. Though the process was slow, farmers and herders domesticated a variety of plants and animals, which led to the rise of large-scale, permanent settlements.

- Trace the region where the wild cereals were domesticated as well as the density of agricultural settlements. How does the region you traced relate to the reason this area is called the "Fertile Crescent"?
- What topographical features appear to influence the location of agricultural settlements and farming?
- What relationship existed between cereal cultivators and herders of goats and sheep?

in the southern corridor of the Jordan River valley, humans began to domesticate the wild ancestors of barley and wheat, which were the easiest to adapt to settled agriculture and the easiest to transport. Although the changeover from gathering wild cereals to regular cultivation took several centuries and saw failures as well as successes, by 8000 BCE cultivators were selecting and storing seeds and then sowing them in prepared seedbeds. Moreover, in the valleys of the Zagros Mountains on the eastern side of the Fertile Crescent, similar experimentation was occurring with animals around the same time. Of the six large mammals—goats, sheep, pigs, cattle, camels, and horses—that have been vital for meat, milk, skins, and transportation, humans in Southwest Asia domesticated all except horses. With the presence of so many valuable plants and animals, Southwest Asia led the agricultural revolution and gave rise to many of the world's first major city-states (see Chapter 2).

Large Two-Handled Yangshao Pot In the village of Yangshao in Henan Province, remains were first found in 1921 of a people who lived more than 6,000 years ago. This pot comes from those people, who were named Yangshao after the modern village in which the evidence for their culture was first found. The ancient Yangshao lived in small, rammed-earth fortresses and, without the use of pottery wheels, created fine white, red, and black painted pottery with human and animal and geometric designs. This jar was found in Gansu Province and dates to around 2500 BCE.

East Asia: Water and Rice A revolution in food production also occurred among the coastal dwellers in East Asia, although under different circumstances. (See Map 1.6.) As the rising sea level created the Japanese islands, hunters in that area tracked a diminishing supply of large animals, such as giant deer. When big game became extinct, men and women sought other ways to support themselves, and before long they settled down and became cultivators of the soil. In this postglacial period, divergent human cultures flourished in northern and southern Japan. Hunters in the south created primitive pebble and flake tools, whereas those in the north used sharper blades about a third of an inch wide. Production of earthenware pottery—a breakthrough that enabled people to store food more easily—also may have begun in this period in the south. Throughout the rest of East Asia, the spread of lakes, marshes, and rivers created habitats for population concentrations and agricultural cultivation. Two newly formed river basins, along the Yellow River in northern China and the Yangzi River in central China, became densely populated areas that were focal points for intensive agricultural development.

What barley and wheat were for Southwest Asia, rice along the Yangzi River and millet along the Yellow River were for East Asia—staples adapted to local environments that humans could domesticate to support a large, sedentary population. Archaeologists have found evidence of rice cultivation in the Yangzi River valley in 6500 BCE, and of millet cultivation in the Yellow River valley in 5500 BCE. Innovations in grain production, including the introduction of a faster-ripening rice from Southeast Asia, spread through internal migration and wider contacts. Ox plows and water buffalo

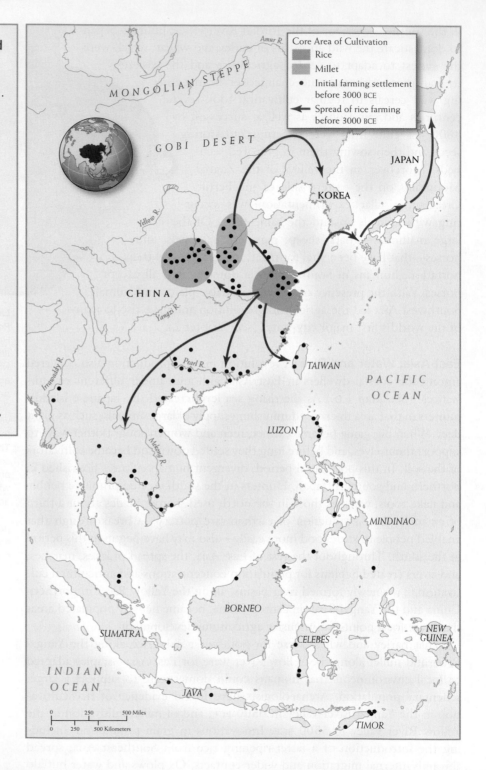

Map 1.6 The Spread of Farming in East Asia

....

Agricultural settlements appeared in East Asia between 6500 and 5500 BCE, several thousand years later than they did in the Fertile Crescent.

- According to this map, where did early agricultural settlements appear in East Asia?

- What two main crops were domesticated in East Asia? Where did each crop type originate, and to what regions did each spread?

- How did the physical features of these regions shape agricultural production?

Core Area of Cultivation
- Rice
- Millet
- • Initial farming settlement before 3000 BCE
- ← Spread of rice farming before 3000 BCE

plowshares were prerequisites for large-scale millet planting in the drier north and the rice-cultivated areas of the wetter south. By domesticating plants and animals, the East Asians, like the Southwest Asians, laid the foundations for more populous societies.

Africa: The Race with the Sahara The evidence for settled agriculture in the various regions of Africa is less clear. Most scholars think that the Sahel area (spanning the African landmass just south of the Sahara Desert) was likely where hunters and gatherers became settled farmers and herders without borrowing from other regions. In this area, an apparent move to settled agriculture, including the domestication of large herd animals, occurred two millennia before it did along the Mediterranean coast in North Africa. From this innovative heartland, Africans carried their agricultural breakthroughs across the landmass.

In the wetter and more temperate locations of the vast Sahel, particularly in mountainous areas and their foothills, villages and towns developed. These regions were lush with grassland vegetation and teeming with animals. Before long, the inhabitants had made sorghum, a cereal grass, their principal food crop. Residents constructed stone dwellings, underground wells, and grain storage areas. In one such population center, fourteen circular houses faced each other to form a main thoroughfare, or a street.

The Sahel was colder and moister in 8000 BCE than it is today. As the world became warmer and the Sahara Desert expanded, around 2000 BCE, this region's inhabitants had to disperse and take their agricultural and herding skills into other parts of Africa. (See Map 1.7.) Some went south to the tropical rain forests of West Africa, while others trekked eastward into the Ethiopian highlands. In their new environments, farmers searched for new crops to domesticate. The rain forests of West Africa yielded root crops, particularly the yam and cocoyam, both of which became the principal life-sustaining foodstuffs. The ensete plant, similar to the banana, played the same role in the Ethiopian highlands. Thus, the beginnings of agriculture in Africa involved both innovation and diffusion, as Africans applied the techniques that first emerged in the Sahel to new plants and animals.

The Americas: A Slower Transition to Agriculture The shift to settled agriculture occurred more slowly in the Americas. When people entered the Americas around 16,000 years ago (14,000 BCE), they set off an ecological transformation but also adapted to unfamiliar habitats. The flora and fauna of the Americas were different enough to induce the early settlers to devise ways of living that distinguished them from their ancestors in Afro-Eurasia. Then, when the glaciers began to melt around 12,500 BCE and water began to cover the land bridge between East Asia and America, the Americas and their peoples truly became a world apart.

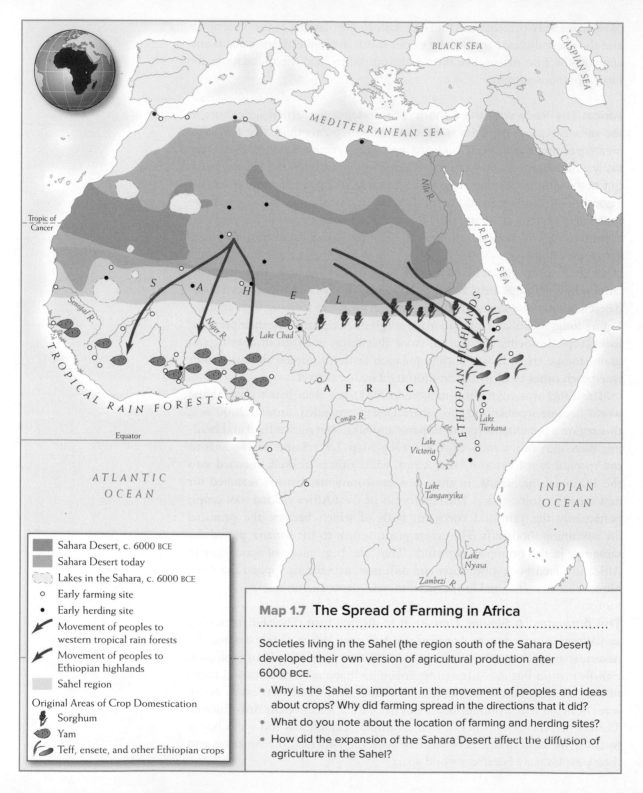

Map 1.7 The Spread of Farming in Africa

Societies living in the Sahel (the region south of the Sahara Desert) developed their own version of agricultural production after 6000 BCE.

- Why is the Sahel so important in the movement of peoples and ideas about crops? Why did farming spread in the directions that it did?
- What do you note about the location of farming and herding sites?
- How did the expansion of the Sahara Desert affect the diffusion of agriculture in the Sahel?

Legend:

- Sahara Desert, c. 6000 BCE
- Sahara Desert today
- Lakes in the Sahara, c. 6000 BCE
- ○ Early farming site
- ● Early herding site
- Movement of peoples to western tropical rain forests
- Movement of peoples to Ethiopian highlands
- Sahel region

Original Areas of Crop Domestication
- Sorghum
- Yam
- Teff, ensete, and other Ethiopian crops

Food-producing changes in the Americas were different from those in Afro-Eurasia because the Americas did not undergo the sudden cluster of innovations that revolutionized agriculture in Southwest Asia and elsewhere. Tools ground from stone, rather than chipped implements, appeared in the Tehuacán Valley in present-day eastern central Mexico by 6700 BCE, and evidence of plant domestication there dates back to 5000 BCE. But villages, pottery making, and sustained population growth came later. For many early American inhabitants, the life of hunting, trapping, and fishing went on as it had for millennia.

On the coast of what is now Peru, people found food by fishing and by gathering shellfish from the Pacific. Archaeological remains include the remnants of fishnets, bags, baskets, and textile implements; gourds for carrying water; stone knives, choppers, and scrapers; and bone awls (long, pointed spikes often used for piercing) and thorn needles. Thousands of villages likely dotted the seashores and riverbanks of the Americas. Some communities made breakthroughs in the management of fire, which enabled them to manufacture pottery; others devised irrigation and water sluices in floodplains; and some even began to send their fish catches inland in return for agricultural produce.

Maize (corn), squash, and beans (first found in what is now central Mexico) became dietary staples. The early settlers foraged small seeds of maize, peeled them from ears only a few inches long, and planted them. Maize offered real advantages because it was easy to store, relatively imperishable, nutritious, and easy to cultivate alongside other plants. Nonetheless, it took 5,000 years for farmers to complete its domestication. Over the years, farmers had to mix and breed different strains of maize for the crop to evolve from thin spikes of seeds to cobs rich with kernels, with a single plant yielding big, thick ears to feed a growing permanent population. Thus, the agricultural changes afoot in Mesoamerica were slow and late in maturing. The pace was even more gradual in South America, where early settlers clung to their hunting and gathering traditions.

Across the Americas, the settled, agrarian communities found that legumes (beans), grains (maize), and tubers (potatoes) complemented one another in keeping the soil fertile and offering a balanced diet. Unlike the Afro-Eurasians, however, the settlers did not use domesticated animals as an alternative source of protein. In only a few pockets of the Andean highlands is there evidence of the domestication of tiny guinea pigs, which may have been tasty but unfulfilling meals. Nor did people in the Americas tame animals that could protect villages (as dogs did in Afro-Eurasia) or carry heavy loads over long distances (as cattle and horses did in Afro-Eurasia). Although llamas could haul heavy loads, they were uncooperative and only partially domesticated, and thus mainly useful only for their fur, which was used for clothing.

Nonetheless, the domestication of plants and animals in the Americas, as well as the presence of villages and clans, suggests significant diversification and refinement of technique. At the same time, the centers of such activity were many, scattered, and more isolated than those in Afro-Eurasia—and thus more narrowly adapted to local geographical climatic conditions, with little exchange between communities. This fragmentation in migration and communication was a distinguishing force in the gradual pace of change in the Americas, and it contributed to their taking a path of development separate from Afro-Eurasia's.

BORROWING AGRICULTURAL IDEAS: EUROPE

In some places, agricultural revolution occurred through the borrowing of ideas from neighboring regions, rather than through innovation. Peoples living at the western fringe of Afro-Eurasia, in Europe, learned the techniques of settled agriculture through contact with other regions. By 7000 BCE, people in parts of Europe close to the societies of Southwest Asia, such as Greece and the Balkans, were abandoning their hunting and gathering way of life for an agricultural one. The Franchthi Cave in Greece, for instance, reveals that around 6000 BCE the inhabitants learned how to domesticate animals and plant wheat and barley, having borrowed that innovation from their neighbors in Southwest Asia.

The emergence of agriculture and village life occurred in Europe along two separate paths of borrowing. (See Map 1.8.) The first and most rapid trajectory followed the northern rim of the Mediterranean Sea: from what is now Turkey through the islands of the Aegean Sea to mainland Greece, and from there to southern and central Italy and Sicily. Whether the process involved the actual migration of individuals or, rather, the spread of ideas, connections by sea quickened the pace of the transition. Within a relatively short period of time, hunting and gathering gave way to domesticated agriculture and herding.

The second trajectory of borrowing took an overland route: from Anatolia, across northern Greece into the Balkans, then northwestward along the Danube River into the Hungarian plain, and from there farther north and west into the Rhine River valley in modern-day Germany. This route of agricultural development was slower than the Mediterranean route for two reasons. First, domesticated crops, or individuals who knew about them, had to travel by land, as there were few large rivers like the Danube. Second, it was necessary to find new groups of domesticated plants and animals that could flourish in the colder and more forested lands of central Europe, which meant planting crops in the spring and harvesting them in the autumn, rather than the other way around. Cattle rather than sheep became the dominant herd animals.

Map labels:
NORTH SEA
BALTIC SEA
ATLANTIC OCEAN
Land bridge
Elbe R.
Rhine R.
Dnieper R.
Loire R.
Seine R.
ALPS
Po R.
PYRENEES
ADRIATIC SEA
Danube R.
BLACK SEA
Franchthi Cave
Çatal Hüyük
MEDITERRANEAN SEA

Legend:
Spread of Farming Communities
Southeastern, 7000–5500 BCE
Mediterranean, 7000–4500 BCE
Central, 5500–4500 BCE
• Early farming communities
Regions of dense hunting and gathering settlements to 4500 BCE
Agricultural diffusion, continental
Agricultural diffusion, coastal

0   250   500 Miles
0   250   500 Kilometers

Map 1.8 The Spread of Agriculture in Europe

The spread of agricultural production into Europe after 7000 BCE represents geographic diffusion. Europeans borrowed agricultural techniques and technology from other groups, adapting those innovations to their own situations.

- Trace the two pathways by which agriculture spread across Europe. What shaped the routes by which agriculture diffused?
- How might scholars know that there were two routes of diffusion, and why would the existence of different diffusion routes matter?
- Identify the locations of the early farming communities. What geographical features seem to have influenced where these farming communities sprang up?

In Europe, the main cereal crops were wheat and barley (additional plants such as olives came later), and the main herd animals were sheep, goats, and cattle—all of which had been domesticated in Southwest Asia. Hunting, gathering, and fishing still supplemented the new settled agriculture and the herding of domesticated animals.

Thus, across Afro-Eurasia and the Americas, humans changed and were changed by their environments. While herding and gathering remained firmly entrenched as a way of life, certain areas with favorable climates and plants and animals that could be domesticated began to establish settled agricultural communities, which were able to support larger populations than hunting and gathering could sustain.

REVOLUTIONS IN SOCIAL ORGANIZATION

Core Objectives

ANALYZE the significance the shift to settled agriculture had for social organization across global regions.

In addition to creating agricultural villages, the domestication of plants and animals brought changes in social organization, notably changes in gender relationships.

Life in Villages In the many regions across the globe where domestication of plants and animals took hold, agricultural villages were established near fields for accessible sowing and cultivating, and near pastures for herding livestock. Villagers collaborated to clear fields, plant crops, and celebrate rituals in which they sang, danced, and sacrificed to nature and the spirit world for fertility, rain, and successful harvests. They also produced stone tools to work the fields, and clay and stone pots or woven baskets to collect and store the crops. The earliest dwelling places of the first settled communities were simple structures: circular pits with stones piled on top to form walls, with a cover stretched above that rested on poles. Social structures were equally simple, being clan-like and based on kinship networks. With time, however, population growth enabled clans to expand. As the use of natural resources intensified, specialized tasks evolved and divisions of labor arose. Some community members procured and prepared food; others built terraces and defended the settlement. Later, residents built walls with stones or mud bricks and clamped them together with wooden fittings. Some villagers became craftworkers, devoting their time to producing pottery, baskets, textiles, or tools, which they could trade to farmers and pastoralists for food. Craft specialization and the buildup of surpluses contributed to social stratification (the emergence of distinct and hierarchically arranged social classes), as some people accumulated more land and wealth while others led the rituals and sacrifices.

Archaeological sites in Southwest Asia have provided evidence of what life was like in some of the earliest villages. At Wadi en-Natuf, for example, located about 10 miles from present-day Jerusalem, a group of people known historically as Natufians began to dig sunken pit shelters and to chip stone tools around 12,500 BCE. In the highlands of eastern Anatolia, large settlements clustered around monumental public buildings with impressive stone carvings that reflect a complex social organization. In central Anatolia around 7500 BCE, at the site of Çatal Hüyük, a dense honeycomb settlement featured rooms with artwork of a high quality. The walls were covered with paintings, and sculptures of wild bulls, hunters, and pregnant women enlivened many rooms.

As people moved into the river valley in Mesopotamia (in present-day Iraq) along the Tigris and Euphrates Rivers, small villages began to appear after 5500 BCE. They collaborated to build simple irrigation systems to water their fields. Perhaps because of the increased demands for community work to maintain the irrigation systems, the communities in southern Mesopotamia became stratified, with some people having more power than others. We can see from the burial sites and myriad public buildings uncovered by archaeologists that, for the first time, some people had higher status derived from birth rather than from the merits of their work. A class of people who had access to more luxury goods, and who lived in bigger and better houses, now became part of the social organization.

Çatal Hüyük This artist's drawing depicts the settlement at Çatal Hüyük, which offers evidence of a Neolithic community's shift, over a 2,000-year span of time, to settled agriculture and more densely packed living. The one-room houses were entered from the roof (via ladders into the living areas) and included space for daily chores (like food preparation), storage, sleeping, and even the burial of the dead under the floor of the living area.

Men, Women, and Evolving Gender Relations

Gender roles became more pronounced during the gradual transition to agriculturally based ways of life. For millions of years, biological differences—the fact that females give birth to offspring and lactate to nourish them, and that males do neither of these—determined female and male behaviors and attitudes toward each other. One can speak of the emergence of gender relations and roles (as distinct from biological differences) only with the appearance of modern humans (*Homo sapiens*). Only when humans began to think in complex symbolic ways and give voice to these perceptions in a spoken language did well-defined gender categories of *man* and *woman* crystallize. At that point, around 150,000 years ago, culture joined biology in governing human interactions.

As human communities became larger, more hierarchical, and more powerful, the rough gender egalitarianism of hunting and gathering societies eroded. Because women had been the primary gatherers, their knowledge of wild plants had contributed to early settled agriculture, but they did not necessarily benefit from that transition. Advances in agrarian tools introduced a harsh working life that undermined women's earlier status as farmers. Men, no longer so involved in hunting and gathering, now took on the heavy work of yoking animals to plows. Women took on the backbreaking and repetitive tasks of planting, weeding, harvesting, and grinding the grain into flour. Thus, although agricultural innovations increased productivity, they also increased the drudgery of work, especially for women. Fossil evidence from Abu Hureyra, Syria, reveals damage to the vertebrae, osteoarthritis in the toes, and curved and arched femurs, all suggesting that the work of bending over and kneeling in the fields took its toll on female agriculturalists. The increasing differentiation of the roles of men and women also affected power relations within households and communities. The senior male figure became dominant in these households, and males dominated females in leadership positions.

The agricultural revolution marked a greater division among men, as well as between men and women. Where the agricultural transformation was most widespread, and where population densities began to grow, the social and political differences created inequalities. As these inequalities affected gender relations, patriarchy (the rule of senior males within households) began to spread around the globe.

Conclusion

Over thousands of generations, African hominins evolved from other primates, leading to new genera such as *Australopithecus* and *Homo*. The latter genus encompassed a range of now-extinct hominins, including the bipedal, toolmaking, fire-using *Homo erectus*, who migrated far from their native habitats to fill other landmasses. They did so in waves, often in response to worldwide cycles of climatic change. *Homo sapiens*, with bigger brains and consequently greater cognition, emerged in Africa about 300,000 years ago and migrated out of Africa beginning 180,000 years ago. With greater adaptive skills, they were better prepared to face the elements when a cooling cycle returned, and eventually they became the only surviving branch of the tree of human ancestors. *Homo sapiens* used language and art to engage in abstract, representational thought and to convey the lessons of experience to their neighbors and descendants. As modern humans stored and shared knowledge, their adaptive abilities increased.

Although modern men and women shared an African heritage, these individuals adapted over many millennia to the environments they encountered as they began to fill the earth's corners and practice hunting and gathering ways of life. Some settled near lakes and took to fishing, while others roamed the northern steppes hunting large mammals. No matter where they went, their dependence on nature yielded broadly similar social and cultural structures. It took another warming cycle for people ranging from Africa to the Americas to begin putting down their hunting weapons and start domesticating animals and plants.

The changeover to settled agriculture was not uniform worldwide. As communities became more settled, the world's regions began to vary as humans learned to modify nature to fit their needs. The varieties of animals that they could domesticate and the differing climatic conditions and topography that they encountered shaped the ways in which people drifted apart in spite of their common origins. What these settled communities shared, however, was increasing social hierarchy, including the unequal status of men and women.

TRACING THE GLOBAL STORYLINE

Focus On
Prehistory and the Peopling of the Earth

- ***Bipedalism:*** Hominins come down from the trees in Africa, become upright, and walk on two legs.
- ***Big brains:*** Ancestors to modern humans make tools and fire and acquire larger brains.
- ***Cognitive skills:*** *Homo sapiens* hominins develop the capacity for language and learn to communicate with one another, develop a sense of self, and produce art.
- ***Village life:*** People domesticate plants and animals and begin to live in more socially complex communities.

Key Terms

australopithecines p. 7
creation narratives p. 5
domestication p. 28
evolution p. 7
hominids p. 6
hominins p. 7
Homo erectus p. 16
Homo habilis p. 16
Homo sapiens p. 19
hunting and gathering p. 26
pastoralism p. 29
settled agriculture p. 29

CHRONOLOGY

5 MYA* — 1 MYA

Afro-Eurasia
- *Australopithecus africanus* hominid species appears 3 MYA
- *Homo habilis* appears 2.5 MYA
- *Homo erectus* appears and migrates 1.8 MYA
- Beginnings of Ice Age across the Northern Hemisphere 2.5–1 MYA

Africa

Europe and the Mediterranean

Southwest and Inner Asia

East Asia

The Americas

*millions of years ago

**years ago

- **Thinking about Exchange Networks and Human Evolution** Across several million years, the hominin ancestors of humans, especially *Homo erectus*, and then *Homo sapiens*, migrated out of Africa. What role did evolution play in making it possible for our hominin ancestors and then *Homo sapiens* to migrate across the globe?

- **Thinking about the Environment and Human Evolution** Climate change and environmental conditions have played a recurring role in the narrative recounted in this chapter. In what specific ways did the climate change, and in what specific ways did the environment help shape the evolution of humans and influence the shift from hunting and gathering to settled agriculture?

- **Thinking about Changing Gender Relationships and the Agricultural Revolution** Some scholars have argued that the hunting and gathering ways of life for both *Homo erectus* and *Homo sapiens* allowed women—biologically, through their lactation and child-rearing, and calorically, through their dominant role as gatherers—to make a larger and more significant contribution to their communities than their male counterparts did. In what ways might the development of settled agriculture have ushered in a shift in these gender roles?

 Go to **INQUIZITIVE** to see what you've learned—and learn what you've missed—with personalized feedback along the way.

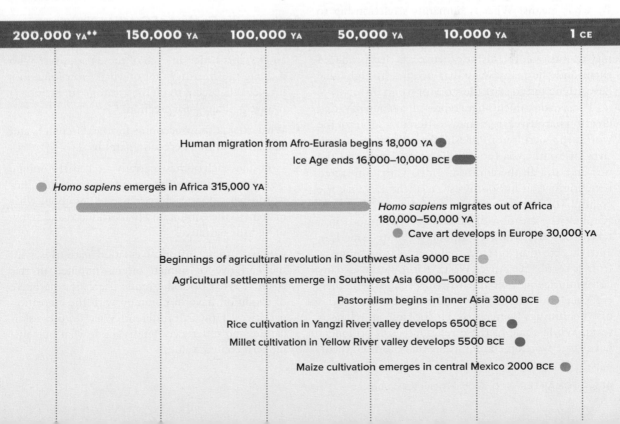

200,000 YA**	150,000 YA	100,000 YA	50,000 YA	10,000 YA	1 CE

Human migration from Afro-Eurasia begins 18,000 YA

Ice Age ends 16,000–10,000 BCE

Homo sapiens emerges in Africa 315,000 YA

Homo sapiens migrates out of Africa 180,000–50,000 YA

Cave art develops in Europe 30,000 YA

Beginnings of agricultural revolution in Southwest Asia 9000 BCE

Agricultural settlements emerge in Southwest Asia 6000–5000 BCE

Pastoralism begins in Inner Asia 3000 BCE

Rice cultivation in Yangzi River valley develops 6500 BCE

Millet cultivation in Yellow River valley develops 5500 BCE

Maize cultivation emerges in central Mexico 2000 BCE

Global Themes and Sources

Contextualizing Creation Narratives

Every story told needs a beginning. Where and how the story begins reveals a great deal about who is telling it and the context from which the storyteller comes. Finding a beginning for the narrative of world history is no different. Humans at many times and in many places have attempted to create all-encompassing narratives that explain their place in the world. And, to give those stories a beginning, communities have attempted to explain where they came from in the first place by constructing creation narratives. Creation narratives draw on a particular community's knowledge and beliefs to offer an account of human, and even universal, origins. These narratives reveal a great deal about the historical context from which they come by revealing the context into which they place humans and what makes up the natural world around them. Are humans the first or last thing to come into being? What else is created with them? By what means? What is humanity's relationship to the rest of creation? Analyzing these types of issues within texts that describe creation offers an opportunity to muse on the historical contexts that produced them and the many ways that people through time have attempted to start the story of world history.

The five documents here represent a range of varied creation narratives from many different regions of the world: the sacrifice of Purusha from the Vedic narratives of South Asia (now India); the creation of the universe and all therein from Judeo-Christian sacred text originating in Southwest Asia (the Levant); the creation of the universe in a text from East Asia (China); the creation of humanity by the gods in a text from Mesoamerica (modern Latin America); and the creation of land, palm trees, and humans from a Yoruba narrative (West Africa). Because many communities have credited divine action with their creation, an examination of the context for stories of "beginnings" often has us looking at religious texts. While some of these religious texts no longer have large worship communities that promote them,

many of these narratives—like the account of creation in Genesis or the sacrifice of Purusha in the Rig-Veda—are still important to communities of faith today. When historians examine creation narratives, the goal is not to decide which is "true" or to judge the rationality of the communities that produced or preserved them; rather, the goal is to analyze the narratives to understand what values and beliefs are encoded in these stories of beginnings and to get a sense of the historical context from which they came. In the chapters that follow, you will learn a great deal about the peoples of South Asia, Southwest Asia, East Asia, Mesoamerica, and Africa. The creation narratives excerpted here offer a chance to begin to explore these historical contexts and to think about how the context from which these narratives came shaped communities' understanding of where humans fit.

Analyzing the Context of Creation Narratives

- Compare the stories of creation. What is created, and in what order, in each of these narratives? Who is doing the creating? Out of what? How long does it take? What seem to be the creator's (or creators') motives—if any—for creation?

- What do you think accounts for the differences and similarities in these creation narratives?

- How does each of these narratives reflect the unique context from which the narrative comes? In other words, what does each narrative tell us about what matters to the community that produced and transmitted the narrative?

- Compare these historical creation narratives with the narrative of human origins outlined in this chapter. What does the modern creation narrative of evolution have in common with these creation narratives? How is it different? What do these similarities and differences tell us about what our own modern context values?

"The Sacrifice of Purusha" from the Rig-Veda (1500 BCE)

The Rig-Veda dates to around 1500 BCE, when Vedic peoples migrated into South Asia. These Vedic people sang hymns while making sacrifices to their gods, and the hymns were later collected in the Rig-Veda—the earliest Hindu sacred text. The portion of the hymn excerpted here describes the creation of the universe by the gods' sacrifice of a creature, Purusha, to create the various levels of society.

- How does the text describe Purusha? To what extent can you visualize this being?
- What exactly is produced through the sacrifice of Purusha by the gods?
- How might the product of the sacrifice of Purusha offer a mirror of the Vedic community that produced the text?

Thousand-headed Purusha, thousand eyed, thousand-footed—he, having pervaded the earth on all sides, extends ten fingers beyond it.

Purusha alone is all this—whatever has been and whatever is going to be. Further, he is the lord of immortality and also of what grows on account of food.

Such is his greatness; greater, indeed than this is Purusha. All creatures constitute but one-quarter of him, his three-quarters are the immortal in the heaven.

With his three-quarters did Purusha rise up; one-quarter of him again remains here. With it did he variously spread out on all sides over what eats and what eats not.

From him was Virāj born, from Virāj the evolved Purusha. He, being born, projected himself behind the earth as also before it. When the gods performed the sacrifice with Purusha as the oblation, then the spring was its clarified butter, the summer the sacrificial fuel, and the autumn the oblation.

The sacrificial victim, namely, Purusha born at the very beginning, they sprinkled with sacred water upon the sacrificial grass. With him as oblation, the gods performed the sacrifice, and also the Sādhyas [a class of semidivine beings] and the rishis [ancient seers].

From that wholly offered sacrificial oblation were born the verses and the sacred chants; from it were born the meters [*chandas*]; the sacrificial formula was born from it.

From it horses were born and also those animals who have double rows [i.e., upper and lower] of teeth; cows were born from it, from it were born goats and sheep.

When they divided Purusha, in how many different portions did they arrange him? What became of his mouth, what of his two arms? What were his two thighs and his two feet called?

His mouth became the brāhman; his two arms were made into the rājanya; his two thighs the vaishyas; from his two feet the shūdra was born.

The moon was born from the mind, from the eye the sun was born; from the mouth Indra and Agni, from the breath [*prāna*] the wind [*vāyu*] was born.

From the navel was the atmosphere created, from the head the heaven issued forth; from two feet was born the earth and the quarters (the cardinal directions) from the ear. Thus did they fashion the worlds.

Seven were the enclosing sticks in this sacrifice, thrice seven were the fire-sticks made when the gods, performing the sacrifice, bound down Purusha, the sacrificial victim.

With this sacrificial oblation did the gods offer the sacrifice. These were the first norms [*dharma*] of sacrifice. These greatnesses reached to the sky wherein live the ancient Sādhyas and gods.

Source: *Sources of Indian Tradition*, vol. 1, *From the Beginning to 1800*, 2nd ed., edited and revised by Ainslie T. Embree (New York: Columbia University Press, 1988), pp. 18–19.

Genesis 1:1–31 from the Bible

Genesis opens with an account of a singular God bringing order from chaos over the course of six days. According to the "documentary hypothesis" advanced by biblical scholars, the text of Genesis was collated by Jewish redactors, a specialized, scholarly type of editor, long ago from a range of sources with different emphases (including different Jewish understandings about God and priestly concerns) and likely reached its final form after the sixth century BCE. Genesis, the first book of the Hebrew Bible, was adopted as a part of authoritative scripture by the early Christian community, as well.

· **What is created in this text, and in what order?**

· **Who does the creating, and how exactly is creation achieved?**

· **What is the relationship between God and humans, and between humans and the rest of God's creation?**

¹In the beginning God created the heavens and the earth. ²The earth was without form and void, and darkness was upon the face of the deep; and the Spirit of God was moving over the face of the waters. ³And God said, "Let there be light"; and there was light. ⁴And God saw that the light was good; and God separated the light from the darkness. ⁵God called the light Day, and the darkness he called Night. And there was evening and there was morning, one day. ⁶And God said, "Let there be a firmament in the midst of the waters, and let it separate the waters from the waters." ⁷And God made the firmament and separated the waters which were under the firmament from the waters which were above the firmament. And it was so. ⁸And God called the firmament Heaven. And there was evening and there was morning, a second day.

⁹And God said, "Let the waters under the heavens be gathered together into one place, and let the dry land appear." And it was so. ¹⁰God called the dry land Earth, and the waters that were gathered together he called Seas. And God saw that it was good. ¹¹And God said, "Let the earth put forth vegetation, plants yielding seed, and fruit trees bearing fruit in which is their seed, each according to its kind, upon the earth." And it was so. ¹²The earth brought forth vegetation, plants yielding seed according to their own kinds, and trees bearing fruit in which is their seed, each according to its kind. And God saw that it was good. ¹³And there was evening and there was morning, a third day. ¹⁴And God said, "Let there be lights in the firmament of the heavens to separate the day from the night; and let them be for signs and for seasons and for days and years, ¹⁵and let them be lights in the firmament of the heavens to give light upon the earth." And it was so. ¹⁶And God made the two great lights, the greater light to rule the day, and the lesser light to rule the night; he made the stars also.

¹⁷And God set them in the firmament of the heavens to give light upon the earth, ¹⁸to rule over the day and over the night, and to separate the light from the darkness. And God saw that it was good. ¹⁹And there was evening and there was morning, a fourth day.

²⁰And God said, "Let the waters bring forth swarms of living creatures, and let birds fly above the earth across the firmament of the heavens." ²¹So God created the great sea monsters and every living creature that moves, with which the waters swarm, according to their kinds; and every winged bird according to its kind. And God saw that it was good. ²²And God blessed them, saying, "Be fruitful and multiply and fill the waters in the seas, and let birds multiply on the earth." ²³And there was evening and there was morning, a fifth day.

²⁴And God said, "Let the earth bring forth living creatures according to their kinds: cattle and creeping things and beasts of the earth according to their kinds." And it was so. ²⁵And God made the beasts of the earth according to their kinds and the cattle according to their kinds, and everything that creeps upon the ground according to its kind. And God saw that it was good.

²⁶Then God said, "Let us make man in our image, after our likeness; and let them have dominion over the fish of the sea, and over the birds of the air, and over the cattle, and over all the earth, and over every creeping thing that creeps upon the earth." ²⁷So God created man in his own image, in the image of God he created him; male and female he created them. ²⁸And God blessed them, and God said to them, "Be fruitful and multiply, and fill the earth and subdue it; and have dominion over the fish of the sea and over the birds of the air and over every living thing that moves upon the earth." ²⁹And God said, "Behold, I have given you every plant yielding seed which is upon the face of all the earth, and every tree with seed in its fruit; you shall have them for food. ³⁰And to every beast of the earth, and to every bird of the air, and to everything that creeps on the earth, everything that has the breath of life, I have given every green plant for food." And it was so. ³¹And God saw everything that he had made, and behold, it was very good. And there was evening and there was morning, a sixth day.

Source: *The New Oxford Annotated Bible: New Revised Standard Version with the Apocrypha*, 4th ed. (New York: Oxford University Press, 2010), pp. 11–13.

"The Creation of the Universe" from the *Huainanzi* (c. second century BCE)

The *Huainanzi*, from second-century BCE Han China, is a Confucian text that takes the form of dialogues between a prince and court scholars. It also reflects Daoist ideas, such as the role of the complementary forces of *yin* and *yang*. The *Huainanzi*'s creation story does not assign agency on the part of any god or gods and instead focuses on balance.

- By what means does creation take place in this narrative?
- What is created?
- What seems to matter to the community that valued this creation narrative?

Before Heaven and Earth had taken form all was vague and amorphous. Therefore it was called the Great Beginning. The Great Beginning produced emptiness, and emptiness produced the universe. The universe produced material-force, which had limits. That which was clear and light drifted up to become Heaven, while that which was heavy and turbid solidified to become Earth. It was very easy for the pure, fine material to come together but extremely difficult for the heavy, turbid material to solidify. Therefore Heaven was completed first and Earth assumed shape after. The combined essences of Heaven and Earth became the yin and yang; the concentrated essences of the yin and yang became the four seasons; and the scattered essences of the four seasons became the myriad creatures of the world. After a long time the hot Force of the accumulated yang produced fire, and the essence of the fire force became the sun; the cold force of the accumulated yin became water, and the essence of the water force became the moon. The essence of the excess force of the sun and moon became the stars, while Earth received water and soil. [3:1a]

When Heaven and Earth were joined in emptiness and all was unwrought simplicity, then, without having been created, things came into being. This was the Great Oneness. All things issued from this Oneness, but all became different, being divided into various species of fish, birds, and beasts. . . . Therefore while a thing moves it is called living, and when it dies it is said to be exhausted. All are creatures. They are not the uncreated creator of things, for the creator of things is not among things. If we examine the Great Beginning of antiquity we find that man was born out of nothing to assume form as something. Having form, he is governed by things. But he who can return to that from which he was born and become as though formless is called a "true man." The true man is one who has never become separated from the Great Oneness. [14:1a]

Source: *Sources of Chinese Tradition*, vol. 1, *From the Earliest Times to 1600*, 2nd ed., compiled by Wm. Theodore de Bary and Irene Bloom (New York: Columbia University Press, 1999), pp. 346–47.

Popul Vuh (date of origin unknown)

The Maya of Mesoamerica believed that humans were created by an assembly of divine beings, a story preserved in this excerpt from the *Popul Vuh*. Although many indigenous texts that had been passed down orally for centuries among Mesoamerican peoples were destroyed by Catholic priests when the Spanish entered the region, the copy of the *Popul Vuh* that has been passed down to the present was transcribed and translated by a Dominican friar in the early eighteenth century.

- Who creates humanity, and what is the process by which that creation takes place?
- From what substance are humans made? Why might that be significant in Mesoamerican creation?
- What is the relationship of humanity with the gods and with the rest of the world?

Here, then, is the beginning of when it was decided to make man, and when what must enter into the flesh of man was sought.

And the Forefathers, the Creators and Makers, who were called Tepeu and Gucumatz said: "The time of dawn has come, let the work be finished, and let those who are to nourish and sustain us appear, the noble sons, the civilized vassals: let man appear, humanity, on the face of the earth." Thus they spoke.

They assembled, came together and held council in the darkness and in the night; then they sought and discussed, and here they reflected and thought. In this way their decisions came clearly to light and they found and discovered what must enter into the flesh of man.

It was just before the sun, the moon, and the stars appeared over the Creators and Makers.

From Paxil, from Cayalá, as they were called, came the yellow ears of corn and the white ears of corn. These are the names of the animals which brought the food: *yac* [the mountain cat], *utiú* [the coyote], *quel* [a small parrot], and *hob* [the crow]. These four animals gave tidings of the yellow ears of corn and the white ears of corn, they told them that they should go to Paxil and they showed them the road to Paxil.

And thus they found the food, and this was what went into the flesh of created man, the made man; this was his blood; of this the blood of man was made. So the corn entered [into the formation of man] by the work of the Forefathers.

***

The animals showed them the road. And then grinding the yellow corn and the white corn, Xmucané made nine drinks, and from this food came the strength and the flesh, and with it they created the muscles and the strength of man. This the Forefathers did, Tepeu and Gucumatz, as they were called.

After that they began to talk about the creation and the making of our first mother and father; of yellow corn and of white corn they made their flesh; of corn meal dough they made the arms and the legs of man. Only dough of corn meal went into the flesh of our first fathers, the four men, who were created.

***

These are the names of the first men who were created and formed: the first man was Balam-Quitzé, the second, Balam-Acab, the third, Mahucutah, and the fourth was Iqui-Balam.

These are the names of our first mothers and fathers.

It is said that they only were made and formed, they had no mother, they had no father. They were only called men. They were not born of woman, nor were they begotten by the Creator nor by the Maker, nor by the Forefathers. Only by a miracle, by means of incantation were they created and made by the Creator, the Maker, the Forefathers, Tepeu and Gucumatz. And as they had the appearance of men, they were men; they talked, conversed, saw and heard, walked, grasped things; they were good and handsome men, and their figure was the figure of a man.

They were endowed with intelligence; they saw and instantly they could see far, they succeeded in seeing, they succeeded in knowing all that there is in the world. When they looked, instantly they saw all around them, and they contemplated in turn the arch of heaven and the round face of the earth.

The things hidden [in the distance] they saw all, without first having to move; at once they saw the world, and so, too, from where they were, they saw it.

Great was their wisdom; their sight reached to the forests, the rocks, the lakes, the seas, the mountains, and the valleys. In truth, they were admirable men, Balam-Quitzé, Balam-Acab, Mahucutah, and Iqui-Balam.

Then the Creator and the Maker asked them: "What do you think of your condition? Do you not see? Do you not hear? Are not your speech and manner of walking good? Look, then! Contemplate the world, look [and see] if the mountains and the valleys appear! Try, then, to see!" they said to [the four first men].

And immediately they [the four first men] began to see all that was in the world. Then they gave thanks to the Creator and the Maker: "We really give you thanks, two and three times! We have been created, we have been given a mouth and a face, we speak, we hear, we think, and walk; we feel perfectly, and we know what is far and what is near. We also see the large and the small in the sky and on earth. We give you thanks, then, for having created us, oh, Creator and Maker! for having given us being, oh, our grandmother! oh, our grandfather!" they said, giving thanks for their creation and formation.

Source: *Popol Vuh: The Sacred Book of the Ancient Quiché Maya*, translated into English by Delia Goetz and Sylvanus G. Morley from Spanish translation by Adrián Recinos (Norman: University of Oklahoma Press, 1950), pp. 165–68.

Yoruba Creation Narrative (date of origin unknown)

The Yoruba peoples of West Africa (modern-day Nigeria and Benin) preserve in songs and oral traditions their own creation narrative featuring a range of deities. The portion of the narrative excerpted here recounts how the god Obatala created and populated the land with palm trees and humans.

- How is the world created? Humanity?
- What reason does the story give for the creation of humanity?
- How do the various deities interact with one another? How would you describe the relationship between humans and the gods?

In the beginning was only the sky above, water and marshland below.

The chief god Olorun ruled the sky, and the goddess Olokun ruled what was below.

Obatala, another god, reflected upon this situation, then went to Olorun for permission to create dry land for all kinds of living creatures to inhabit. He was given permission, so he sought advice from Orunmila, oldest son of Olorun and the god of prophecy.

He was told he would need a gold chain long enough to reach below, a snail's shell filled with sand, a white hen, a black cat, and a palm nut, all of which he was to carry in a bag. All the gods contributed what gold they had, and Orunmila supplied the articles for the bag. When all was ready, Obatala hung the chain from a corner of the sky, placed the bag over his shoulder, and started the downward climb. When he reached the end of the chain he saw he still had some distance to go.

From above he heard Orunmila instruct him to pour the sand from the snail's shell, and to immediately release the white hen.

He did as he was told, whereupon the hen landing on the sand began scratching and scattering it about.

Wherever the sand landed it formed dry land, the bigger piles becoming hills and the smaller piles valleys. Obatala jumped to a hill and named the place Ife. The dry land now extended as far as he could see.

He dug a hole, planted the palm nut, and saw it grow to maturity in a flash. The mature palm tree dropped more palm nuts on the ground, each of which grew immediately to maturity and repeated the process. Obatala settled down with the cat for company.

Many months passed, and he grew bored with his routine.

He decided to create beings like himself to keep him company. He dug into the sand and soon found clay with which to mold figures like himself and started on his task, but he soon grew tired and decided to take a break.

He made wine from a nearby palm tree, and drank bowl after bowl. Not realizing he was drunk, Obatala returned to his task of fashioning the new beings; because of his condition he fashioned many imperfect figures.

Without realizing this, he called out to Olorun to breathe life into his creatures.

The next day he realized what he had done and swore never to drink again, and to take care of those who were deformed, thus becoming Protector of the Deformed.

The new people built huts as Obatala had done and soon Ife prospered and became a city.

When Obatala returned to his home in the sky for a visit, Olokun summoned the great waves of her vast oceans and sent them surging across the land. Wave after wave she unleashed, until much of the land was underwater and many of the people were drowned. Those that had fled to the highest land beseeched the god Eshu who had been visiting, to return to the sky and report what was happening to them. Eshu demanded sacrifice be made to Obatala and himself before he would deliver the message.

The people sacrificed some goats, and Eshu returned to the sky.

When Orunmila heard the news he climbed down the golden chain to the earth, and cast many spells which caused the flood waters to retreat and the dry land reappear.

So ended the great flood.

Source: "Yoruba Creation Narrative," translated by P. J. Criss, in Polat Kaya, "'Ak Tengiz': The Disappeared Ice Age Sea-Size Lake of Siberia," *Turk Dunyasi Arastirmalari*, no. 121 (August 1999): 38–39.

Interpreting Visual Evidence

Prehistoric Art

Prehistoric art provides some of the best direct evidence for the thoughts and experiences of humans who lived prior to the invention of writing (which, as we'll see in Chapter 2, has only been around for 5,000 years). Paintings showing the outlines of hands, images of animals, and even hunting scenes adorn the walls of caves across Afro-Eurasia, put there by humans over tens of thousands of years.

The artwork in Chauvet Cave in southwestern France may be the oldest in Europe, dating to about 35,000 years ago. In the two images below from Chauvet Cave, the repeated and overlapping images of horses and lions convey perspective, movement, and speed.

In central India, cave paintings at Bhimbetka date to as long as 30,000 years ago; the painting reproduced here includes several herds of different types of animals. Other images from this site painted over thousands of years include humans dancing and even having sex.

In a cave complex in Argentina, humans over generations used pipes fashioned from bone to blow black, white, red, yellow, and purple pigments at their hands pressed against the cave walls, leaving reverse-stenciled handprints that proclaimed "I was here" more than 7,000 years ago. Cave paintings from other areas like Lascaux in southeastern France (20,000 years old), Altamira in Spain (17,000 years old), and Tassili-n-Ajjer in North Africa (8,000 years old) provide similar insights into the artists' lives.

In addition to making paintings, early humans carved figurines. Small female figurines, often with emphasized breasts and genitalia, have been found at Willendorf in Austria, Dolni Vestonice in the Czech Republic, Cernavoda in Romania, and Malta in Siberian Russia. These figurines, carved from limestone, mammoth tusk, and reindeer horn, also range from about 35,000 to 8,000 years old. The figurine known as the Venus of Hohle Fels, found in Germany, dates to more than 35,000 years ago. This 2.4-inch carving may have been worn as an amulet. The 6-inch Venus of Willendorf from more than 25,000 years ago wears only a headdress (or braided hairstyle) and rests her arms across her breasts. The apparent continuity in both the cave art and figurines across thousands of years is striking.

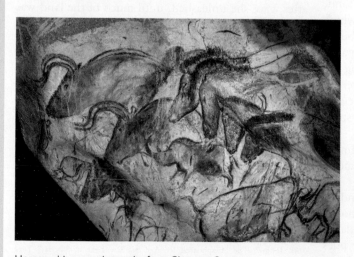

Horses, rhinos, and aurochs from Chauvet Cave.

Lions from Chauvet Cave.

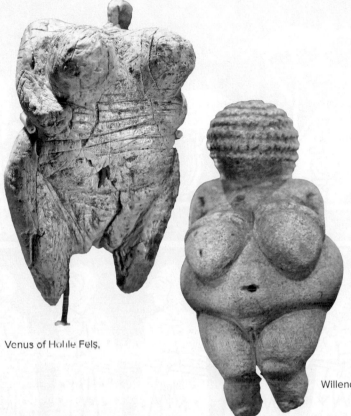

Venus of Hohle Fels,

Willendorf Venus.

Questions for Analysis

1. Based on these cave paintings and figurines, what types of subjects did humans in the prehistoric period depict in their art? Why do you think they chose those subjects?

2. Compare these paintings and figurines. Given that there was not likely any interaction between the communities that produced them, what do you think might account for the similarities and differences?

3. Imagine an artist in a dark cave, painting with plant-made pigments by the light of a flickering torch; or a man or woman spending a hundred hours to carve a figurine from limestone. What might spur the creation of such artworks? How does this art change your understanding of the hunting and gathering lifestyle?

Cave painting at Bhimbetka.

Stenciled hands from Cueva de las Manos (Cave of Hands) in Argentina.

2

Rivers, Cities, and First States

3500–2000 BCE

One of the first urban centers in the world was the ancient city of Uruk. Located in southern Mesopotamia on a branch of the Euphrates River, it was home to between 25,000 and 50,000 people by the late fourth millennium BCE and boasted many large public structures and temples. One temple, erected to house and honor the city's patron deity Inanna, had stood there since before 3000 BCE; with plastered mud-brick walls that formed stepped indentations, it perched high above the plain. In another area, administrative buildings and temples adorned with elaborate façades stood in courtyards defined by tall columns. Colored stone cones arranged in elaborate geometric patterns covered parts of these buildings. An epic poem devoted to its later king, Gilgamesh, described Uruk as the "shining city."

Over the years, Uruk became an immense commercial and administrative center. A huge wall with seven massive gates surrounded the metropolis, and down the middle ran a canal carrying water from the Euphrates. On one side of the city were gardens, kilns, and textile workshops. On the other was the temple quarter where priests lived, scribes kept records, and the *lugal* ("big man" in the Sumerian language) conferred with the elders. As Uruk grew, many small industries—including pottery crafting, metalworking, stone bowl making, and brickmaking—became centralized in response to the increasing sophistication of construction and manufacturing.

Chapter Outline

- Settlement and Pastoralism
- Between the Tigris and Euphrates Rivers: Mesopotamia
- "The Gift of the Nile": Egypt
- The Indus River Valley: A Parallel Culture
- The Yellow and Yangzi River Basins: East Asia
- Life Outside the River Basins
- Conclusion

Core Objectives

- **IDENTIFY** the earliest river-basin societies, and **ANALYZE** their shared and distinctive characteristics.
- **EXPLAIN** the religious, social, and political developments that accompany early urbanization in the river-basin societies from 3500 to 2000 BCE.
- **TRACE** and **EVALUATE** the influence of long-distance connections across Afro-Eurasia during this period.
- **COMPARE** early urbanization with the ways of life in small villages and among pastoralists.

Uruk Scholars from the Uruk visualization project drew on texts, excavation reports, and topographic data to produce this 2012 computer-generated reconstruction proposal of Uruk, King Gilgamesh's "shining city." The image includes more than 300 buildings and 4,000 human figures to visualize how the center of Uruk would have looked on the day of a religious festival.

Uruk was the first city of its kind in world history. Earlier humans had settled in small communities scattered over the landscape. As some communities gradually became focal points for trade, a few of these hubs grew into cities with large populations and institutions of economic, religious, and political power. Most inhabitants no longer produced their own food, working instead in specialized professions.

Between 3500 and 2000 BCE, a handful of remarkable societies clustered in a few river basins on the Afro-Eurasian landmass. These regions—in Mesopotamia (between the Tigris and Euphrates Rivers), in northwest India (on the Indus River), in Egypt (along the Nile), and in China (near the Yangzi and Yellow Rivers)—became the heartlands for densely populated settlements with complex cultures. Here the world saw the birth of the first large cities that exhausted surrounding regions of their resources. One of these settings (Mesopotamia) brought forth humankind's first writing system, and all laid the foundations for kingdoms radiating out of opulent cities. This chapter describes how each society evolved, and it explores their similarities and differences. It is important to note how exceptional these large city-states were, and we will see that many smaller societies prevailed elsewhere. The Aegean, Anatolia, western Europe, the Americas, and sub-Saharan Africa offer reminders that most of the world's people dwelt in small communities, far removed culturally from the monumental architecture and accomplishments of the big new states.

Comparing First Cities

- Complex societies form around five great river basins.

- Early urbanization brings changes, including new technologies, monumental building, new religions, writing, hierarchical social structures, and specialized labor.

- Long-distance trade connects many of the Afro-Eurasian societies.

- Despite impressive developments in urbanization, most people live in farming villages or in pastoralist communities.

Settlement and Pastoralism

Around 3500 BCE, cultural changes, population growth, and technological innovations gave rise to complex societies. Clustered in cities, these larger communities developed new institutions, and individuals took on a wide range of social roles and occupations, resulting in new hierarchies based on wealth and gender. At the same time, the number of small villages and pastoralist communities grew.

Water was the key to settlement, since predictable flows of water determined where humans settled. Reliable water supplies allowed communities to sow crops adequate to feed large populations. Abundant rainfall allowed the world's first villages to emerge, but the breakthroughs into big cities occurred in drier zones where large rivers formed beds of rich soils deposited by flooding rivers. With irrigation innovations, soils became arable. Equally important, a worldwide warming cycle expanded growing seasons. The **river basins**—with their fertile soil, irrigation, and available domesticated plants and animals—made possible the agricultural surpluses needed to support city dwellers.

EARLY CITIES ALONG RIVER BASINS

The material and social advances of the early cities occurred in a remarkably short period—from 3500 to 2000 BCE—in three locations: the basin of the Tigris and Euphrates Rivers in central Southwest Asia; the northern parts of the Nile River flowing toward the Mediterranean Sea; and the Indus River basin in northwestern South Asia. About a millennium later, a similar process began along the Yellow River and the Yangzi River in China. (See Map 2.1.)

THE BIG PICTURE

Identify the earliest river-basin societies. What are their shared characteristics?

river basin
Area drained by a river, including all its tributaries. River basins were rich in fertile soil, water for irrigation, and plant and animal life, which made them attractive for human habitation. Cultivators were able to produce surplus agriculture to support the first cities.

The Global View

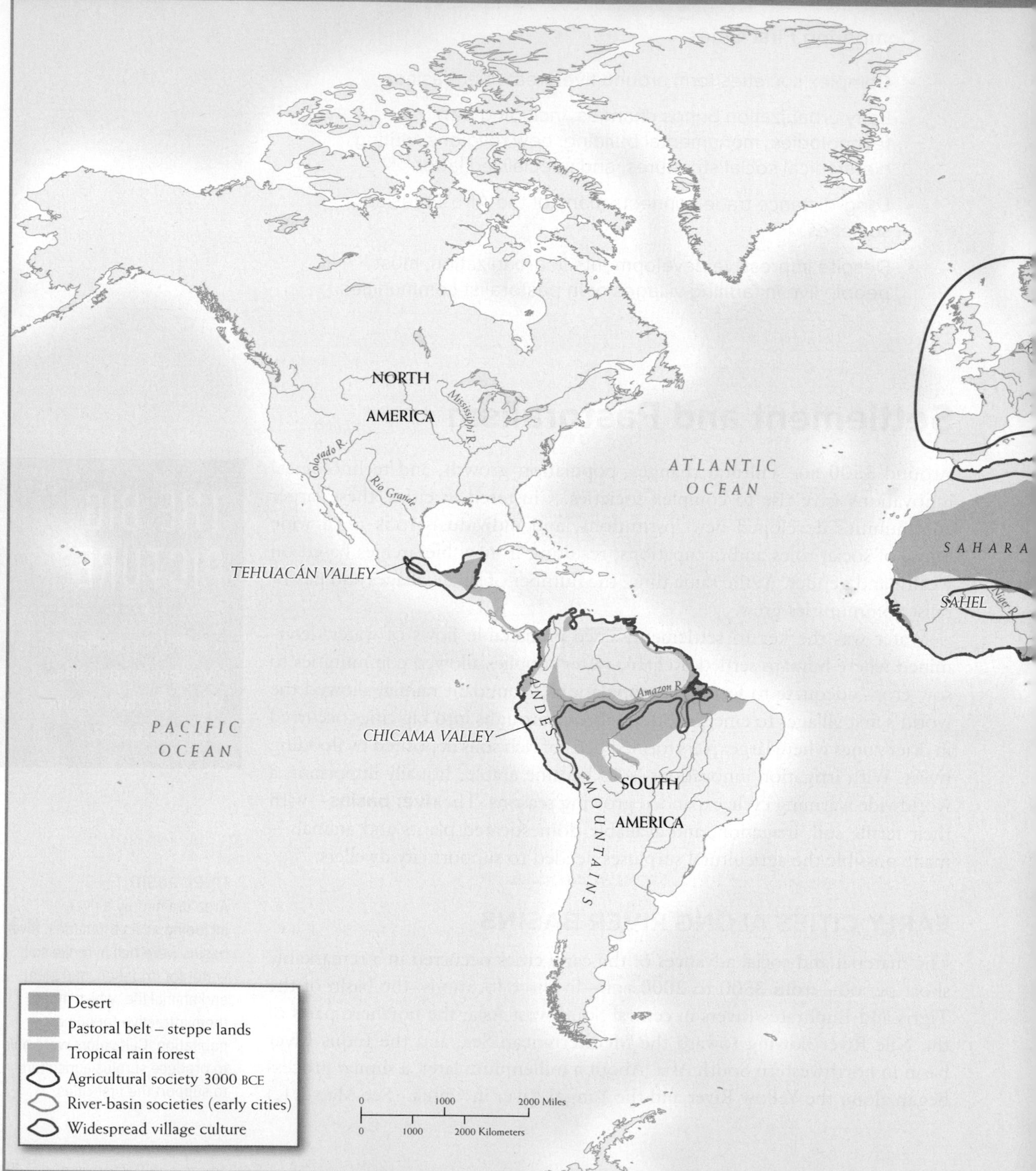
NORTH AMERICA
Mississippi R.
Colorado R.
Rio Grande
ATLANTIC OCEAN
SAHARA
SAHEL
Niger R.
TEHUACÁN VALLEY
Amazon R.
CHICAMA VALLEY
ANDES MOUNTAINS
PACIFIC OCEAN
SOUTH AMERICA
Desert
Pastoral belt – steppe lands
Tropical rain forest
Agricultural society 3000 BCE
River-basin societies (early cities)
Widespread village culture
0 1000 2000 Miles
0 1000 2000 Kilometers

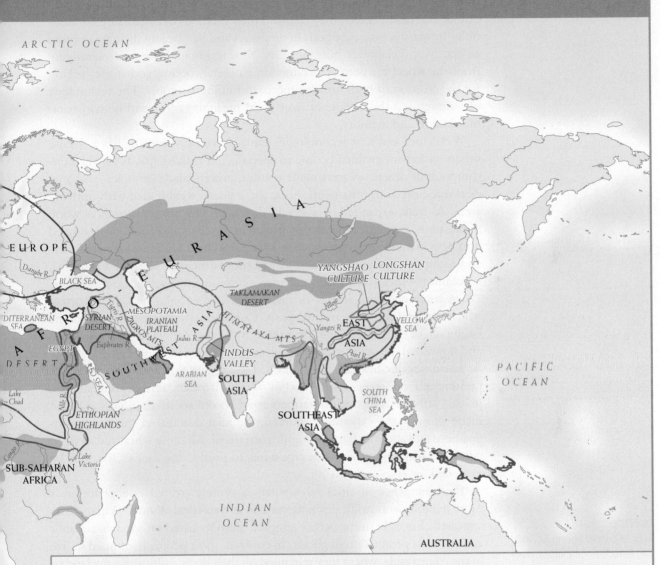

ARCTIC OCEAN

EUROPE

A F R O - E U R A S I A

Danube R.

BLACK SEA

MEDITERRANEAN SEA

SYRIAN DESERT

MESOPOTAMIA

IRANIAN PLATEAU

ZAGROS MTS

TAKLAMAKAN DESERT

YANGSHAO CULTURE

LONGSHAN CULTURE

Yellow R.

EAST ASIA

YELLOW SEA

EGYPT

Tigris R.

Euphrates R.

Indus R.

SOUTHWEST ASIA

HIMALAYA MTS

Yangzi R.

Pearl R.

DESERT

Lake Chad

Nile R.

Red Sea

ARABIAN SEA

INDUS VALLEY

SOUTH ASIA

SOUTHEAST ASIA

SOUTH CHINA SEA

PACIFIC OCEAN

ETHIOPIAN HIGHLANDS

Congo R.

Lake Victoria

SUB-SAHARAN AFRICA

INDIAN OCEAN

AUSTRALIA

Map 2.1 The World in the Third Millennium BCE

Human societies became increasingly diversified as agricultural, urban, and pastoralist communities expanded. While urban communities began to develop in several major river basins in the Eastern Hemisphere, not every river basin produced cities in the third millennium BCE. Pastoralism, village life, agricultural communities, and continued hunting and gathering were by far the norm for most of the peoples of the earth.

- In what different regions did pastoralism and river-basin societies emerge? Where did pastoralism and river-basin societies not emerge? What might account for where these ways of life developed and where they did not?
- Considering the geographic features highlighted on this map, why do you think cities appeared in the regions that they did? What might explain why cities did not appear elsewhere?
- How did geographic and environmental factors promote interaction between pastoralist and sedentary agricultural societies?

In these regions humans farmed and fed themselves by relying on intensive irrigation agriculture. Gathering in cities inhabited by rulers, administrators, priests, and craftworkers, they changed their methods of organizing communities by worshipping new gods in new ways and by obeying divinely inspired monarchs and elaborate bureaucracies. New technologies appeared, ranging from the wheel for pottery production to metalworking and stoneworking for the creation of both luxury objects and utilitarian tools. The technology of writing used the storage of words and meanings to extend human communication and memory.

With cities and new technologies came greater divisions of labor. Dense urban settlement enabled people to specialize in making goods for the consumption of others: weavers made textiles, potters made ceramics, and jewelers made precious ornaments. Soon these goods were traded with outlying areas. As trade expanded over longer distances, raw materials such as wool, metal, timber, and precious stones arrived in the cities and could be fashioned into new, manufactured goods. (See Map 2.2.) One of the most coveted metals was copper: easily smelted and shaped (not to mention shiny and alluring), it became the metal of choice for charms, sculptures, and valued commodities. When combined with arsenic or tin, copper hardens and becomes **bronze**, which is useful for tools and weapons. Consequently, this period marks the beginning of the Bronze Age, even though the use of this alloy extended into and flourished during the second millennium BCE (see Chapter 3).

The dawn of cities and city-states had drawbacks for those who had been hunters and gatherers or had lived in towns. As rulers, scribes, bureaucrats, priests, artisans, and wealthy farmers rose, so did social stratification. Men made gains at the expense of women, for men dominated the prestigious positions and societies became highly patriarchal. All those who lived close to cities had to fashion their own city-states to protect themselves lest they be exploited, or even enslaved.

The emergence of cities as population centers created one of history's most durable worldwide distinctions: the **urban-rural divide**. Where cities appeared alongside rivers, people adopted lifestyles based on specialized labor and the mass production of goods. In contrast, most people continued to live in the countryside, where they remained on their lands, cultivating the land or tending livestock, though they exchanged their grains and animal products for goods from the urban centers. The two ways of life were interdependent and both worlds remained linked through family ties, trade, politics, and religion.

PASTORALIST COMMUNITIES

The transhumant herder communities that had appeared in Southwest Asia around 5500 BCE (see Chapter 1) continued to be small and their settlements impermanent. They lacked substantial public buildings or infrastructure, but

bronze
Alloy of copper and tin brought into Europe from Anatolia; used to make hard-edged weapons.

urban-rural divide
Division between those living in cities and those living in rural areas. City dwellers had specialized jobs and mass-produced goods, while those in the countryside cultivated land and herded livestock.

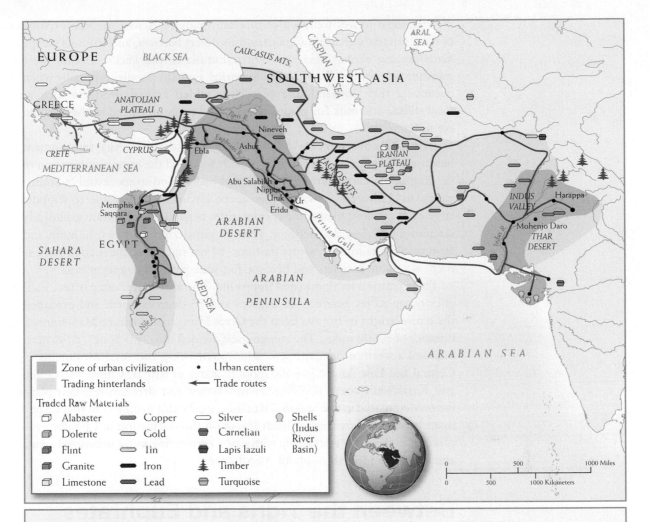

Map 2.2 Trade and Exchange in Southwest Asia and the Eastern Mediterranean, Third Millennium BCE

Extensive commercial networks linked the urban cores of Southwest Asia.

- Of the traded raw materials shown on the map, which ones were used for building materials, and which ones for luxury items?

- Which regions had timber, and which regions did not? How would the needs of river-basin societies have influenced trade with the regions that had timber?

- Using the map, describe the extent and likely routes of trade necessary for the creation of the treasures of Ur in Mesopotamia (with items fashioned from gold, lapis lazuli, and carnelian) and the wealth buried with kings of Egypt in their pyramids (silver, gold, lapis lazuli, and carnelian).

their seasonal moves followed a consistent pattern. Across the vast expanse of Afro-Eurasia's great mountains and its desert barriers, and from its steppe lands ranging across inner and central Eurasia to the Pacific Ocean, these transhumant herders lived alongside settled agrarian people, especially when occupying their lowland pastures. They traded animal products such as meat, hides, and milk for grains, pottery, and tools produced in the agrarian communities.

In the arid environments of Inner Mongolia and central Asia, transhumant herding and agrarian communities initially followed the same combination of herding animals and cultivating crops that had proved so successful in Southwest Asia. However, it was in this steppe environment, unable to support large-scale farming, that some communities began to concentrate exclusively on animal breeding and herding. Though some continued to fish, hunt, and farm small plots in their winter pastures, by the middle of the second millennium BCE many societies had become full-scale pastoral communities.

These pastoralists dominated steppe life. The area that these pastoral societies occupied lay between 40 degrees and 55 degrees north and extended the entire length of Eurasia from the Great Hungarian Plain to Manchuria, a distance of 5,600 miles. The steppe itself divided into two zones, an eastern one and a western one, the separation point being the Altai Mountains in Central and East Asia where the modern states of Russia, China, Mongolia, and Kazakhstan come together. Frost-tolerant and drought-resistant plant life predominated in the region. Over time, pastoralist groups—both transhumant herders and pastoral nomads (more on this distinction in Chapter 3)—played a vital role by interacting with cities, connecting more urbanized areas, and spreading ideas throughout Afro-Eurasia.

Between the Tigris and Euphrates Rivers: Mesopotamia

Core Objectives

EXPLAIN the religious, social, and political developments that accompany early urbanization in the river-basin societies from 3500 to 2000 BCE.

The world's first complex society arose in Mesopotamia. Here the river and the first cities changed how people lived. Mesopotamia, whose name is a Greek word meaning "[region] between two rivers," is a landmass including all of modern-day Iraq and parts of Syria and southeastern Turkey. From their headwaters in the mountains to the north and east to their destination in the Persian Gulf, the Tigris and Euphrates Rivers are wild and capricious. Unpredictable floodwaters could wipe out years of hard work, but when managed properly they could transform the landscape into verdant and productive fields. Both rivers provided water for irrigation and, although hardly navigable, were important routes for transportation and communication by pack animal and by foot. Mesopotamia's natural advantages—its rich agricultural land and water, combined with easy access to neighboring regions—favored the growth of cities and later territorial states (see Chapter 3). These cities and states became the sites of important cultural, political, and social innovations.

TAPPING THE WATERS

The first rudimentary advances in irrigation occurred in the foothills of the Zagros Mountains along the banks of the smaller rivers that feed the Tigris. Converting the floodplain—where the river overflows and deposits fertile soil—into a breadbasket required mastering the unpredictable waters. Both the Euphrates and the Tigris, unless controlled by waterworks, were unfavorable to cultivators because the annual floods occurred at the height of the growing season, when crops were most vulnerable. Low water levels occurred when crops required abundant irrigation. To prevent the river from overflowing during its flood stage, farmers built levees along the banks and dug ditches and canals to drain away the floodwaters. Engineers devised an irrigation system whereby the Euphrates, which has a higher riverbed than the Tigris, essentially served as the supply and the Tigris as the drain. Storing and channeling water year after year required constant maintenance and innovation by a corps of engineers.

Early Mesopotamian Waterworks From the sixth millennium BCE, irrigation was necessary for successful farming in southern Mesopotamia. By the first millennium BCE, sophisticated feats of engineering allowed the Assyrians to redirect water through constructed aqueducts, like the one illustrated here on a relief at Nineveh from the palace of the Assyrian king Sennacherib (who will be discussed in Chapter 4).

The Mesopotamians' technological breakthrough was in irrigation, not in agrarian methods. Because the soils were fine, rich, and constantly replenished by the floodwaters' silt, soil tillage was light work. Farmers sowed a combination of wheat, millet, sesame, and barley (the basis for beer, a staple of their diet).

CROSSROADS OF SOUTHWEST ASIA

Though its soil was rich and water was abundant, southern Mesopotamia had few other natural resources apart from the mud, marsh reeds, spindly trees, and low-quality limestone that served as basic building materials. To obtain high-quality stone, metal, dense wood, and other materials for constructing and embellishing their cities with their temples and palaces, Mesopotamians interacted with the inhabitants of surrounding regions. In return for their exports of textiles, oils, and other commodities, Mesopotamians imported cedar wood from Lebanon, copper and stones from Oman, more copper

from Turkey and Iran, and the precious blue gemstone called lapis lazuli, as well as ever-useful tin, from faraway Afghanistan. Maintaining trading contacts was easy, given Mesopotamia's open boundaries on all sides. The area became a crossroads for the peoples of Southwest Asia, including Sumerians, who concentrated in the south; Hurrians, who lived in the north; and Akkadians, who populated western and central Mesopotamia. Trade and migration contributed to the growth of cities throughout the river basin, beginning with the Sumerian cities of southern Mesopotamia.

THE WORLD'S FIRST CITIES

During the first half of the fourth millennium BCE, a demographic transformation occurred in the Tigris-Euphrates river basin, especially in the southern area called Sumer. The population expanded as a result of the region's agricultural bounty, and many Mesopotamians migrated from country villages to centers that eventually became cities. (A **city** is a large, well-defined urban area with a dense population.) The earliest Sumerian cities—Uruk, Eridu, and Nippur—developed over about 1,000 years, dominating the southern part of the floodplain by 3500 BCE. Buildings of mud brick show successive layers of urban development, as at Eridu, where more than twenty reconstructed temples were piled atop one another across four millennia, resulting in a final temple that rose from a platform like a mountain, visible for miles in all directions.

As the temple grew skyward, the village expanded outward and became a city. From their homes in temples located at the center of cities, the cities' gods broadcast their powers. In return, urbanites provided luxuries, fine clothes, and enhanced lodgings for the gods and their priests. In Sumerian cosmology, created by ruling elites, humans existed solely to serve the gods, so the urban landscape reflected this fact: a temple at the core, with goods and services flowing to the center and with divine protection and justice flowing outward.

Some thirty-five of these politically equal city-states with religious sanctuaries dotted the southern plain of Mesopotamia. Sumerian ideology glorified a way of life and a territory based on politically equal city-states, each with a guardian deity and sanctuary supported by its inhabitants. (A **city-state** is a political organization based on the authority of a single, large city that controls outlying territories.) Because early Mesopotamian cities served as meeting places for peoples and their deities, they gained status as religious and economic centers. Whether enormous (like Uruk and Nippur) or modest (like Ur and Abu Salabikh), all cities were spiritual, economic, and cultural homes for Mesopotamian subjects.

Simply making a city was therefore not enough: urban design reflected the city's role as a wondrous place to pay homage to the gods and their human

city
Highly populated concentration of economic, religious, and political power. The first cities appeared in river basins, which could produce a surplus of agriculture. The abundance of food freed most city inhabitants from the need to produce their own food, which allowed them to work in specialized professions.

city-state
Political organization based on the authority of a single, large city that controls outlying territories.

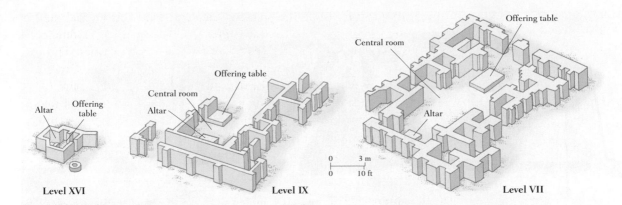

Level XVI

Central room

Offering table

Altar

Level IX

Offering table

Central room

Offering table

Altar

Level VII

Altar

Offering table

0   3 m
0   10 ft

intermediary, the king. Within their walls, early cities contained large houses separated by date palm plantations and extensive sheepfolds. As populations grew, the Mesopotamian cities became denser, houses became smaller, and new suburbs spilled out beyond the old walls. The typical layout of Mesopotamian cities reflected a common pattern: a central canal surrounded by neighborhoods of specialized occupational groups. The temple marked the city center, with the palace and other official buildings on the periphery. In separate quarters for craft production, families passed down their trades across generations. In this sense, the landscape of the city mirrored the growing **social hierarchies** (distinctions between the privileged and the less privileged).

GODS AND TEMPLES

The worldview of the Sumerians and, later, the Akkadians of Mesopotamia, included a belief in a group of gods that shaped their political institutions and controlled everything—including the weather, fertility, harvests, and the underworld. As depicted in the *Epic of Gilgamesh* (a second-millennium BCE composition based on oral tales about Gilgamesh, a historical but mythologized king of Uruk), the gods could give but could also take away—with droughts, floods, and death. Gods, and the natural forces they controlled, had to be revered and feared. Faithful subjects imagined their gods as immortal beings whose habits were capricious and who had contentious relationships and gloriously work-free lives.

Each major god of the Sumerian pantheon (an officially recognized group of gods and goddesses) dwelled in a lavish temple in a particular city that he or she had created; for instance, Enlil, god of air and storms, dwelled in Nippur; Enki (also called Ea), god of water, in Eridu; Nanna, god of the moon, in Ur; and Inanna (also called Ishtar), goddess of love, fertility, and war, in Uruk. These temples, and the patron deity housed within, gave rise to each city's character, institutions, and relationships with its urban neighbors.

Layout of Eridu Over several millennia, temples of increasing size and complexity were built atop each other at Eridu in southern Iraq. The culmination came with the elaborate structure of level VII.

social hierarchies
Distinctions between the privileged and the less privileged.

Ziggurat The first ziggurat of Mesopotamia, dedicated to the moon god Nanna, was built by the founder of the Neo-Sumerian dynasty, Ur-Nammu (2112–2095 BCE). Although temples had been raised on platforms since early times, the distinctive stepped form of the ziggurat was initially borrowed from the Iranian plateau. It became the most important sacred structure in Mesopotamia.

Inside these temples, benches lined the walls, with statues of humans standing in perpetual worship of the deity's images. By the end of the third millennium BCE, the temple's platform base had changed to a stepped platform called a *ziggurat*, with the main temple on top. Surrounding the ziggurat were buildings that housed priests, officials, laborers, and servants.

Temples functioned as the god's estate, engaging in all sorts of productive and commercial activities. Temple dependents cultivated cereals, fruits, and vegetables by using extensive irrigation and cared for flocks of livestock. Other temples operated workshops for manufacturing textiles and leather goods, employing craftworkers, metalworkers, masons, and stoneworkers. Enormous labor forces were involved in maintaining this high level of production.

ROYAL POWER, FAMILIES, AND SOCIAL HIERARCHY

Like the temples, royal palaces reflected the power of the ruling elite. Royal palaces appeared around 2500 BCE and served as the official residence of a ruler, his family, and his entourage. As access to palaces and temples over time became limited, gods and kings became inaccessible to all but the most elite. Although located at the edge of cities, palaces were the symbols of permanent secular, military, and administrative authority distinct from the temples' spiritual and economic power.

The Royal Cemetery at Ur shows how Mesopotamian rulers used elaborate burial arrangements to reinforce their religious and socioeconomic hierarchies. Housed in a mud-brick structure, the royal burials held not only the primary remains but also the bodies of more than eighty men and women who had been sacrificed. Huge vats for cooked food, bones of animals, drinking vessels, and musical instruments suggest the lifestyle of those who joined their masters in the graves. Honoring the royal dead by including their followers and possessions in their tombs underscored the social hierarchies—including the vertical ties between humans and gods—that were the cornerstone of these early city-states.

Social hierarchies were an important part of the fabric of Sumerian city-states. Ruling groups secured their privileged access to economic and political resources by erecting systems of bureaucracies, priesthoods, and laws. Priests and bureaucrats served their rulers well, championing rules and norms that legitimized the political leadership. Occupations within the cities were highly specialized, and a list of professions circulated across the land so that everyone could know his or her place in the social order. The king and priest in Sumer were at the top of the list, followed by bureaucrats (scribes and household accountants), supervisors, and craftworkers, such as cooks, jewelers, gardeners, potters, metalsmiths, and traders. There were also independent merchants who risked long-distance trading ventures, hoping for a generous return on their investment. The biggest group, which was at the bottom of the hierarchy, comprised workers who were not enslaved but were dependent on their employers' households. Movement among economic classes was not impossible but, as in many traditional societies, it was rare.

The family and the household provided the bedrock for Sumerian society, and its patriarchal organization, dominated by the senior male, reflected the balance between women and men, children and parents. The family consisted of the husband and wife bound by a contract: she would provide children, preferably male, while he provided support and protection. Monogamy was the norm unless there was no son, in which case a second wife or an enslaved woman would bear male children to serve as the married couple's offspring. Adoption was another way to gain a male heir. Sons would inherit the family's property in equal shares, while daughters would receive dowries necessary for successful marriage into other families. Some women joined the temple staff as priestesses and gained economic autonomy that included ownership of estates and productive enterprises, although their fathers and brothers remained responsible for their well-being.

DEATH-PIT PG. 1237

RAMP

ENTRANCE

Death Pit 1237 from the Royal Tombs of Ur The excavation team at Ur produced careful drawings and notes as they uncovered the Royal Tombs of Ur in 1927–28. Their drawing of Death Pit 1237 illustrates the rich grave offerings of gold, silver, lapis lazuli, and shell (including a lyre, on the left-hand side). It also shows the remains of six men (armed and lined up by the door, along the bottom) and sixty-seven well-dressed women who were likely buried alive as a funerary offering to honor and accompany the most elaborately decked-out female (Body 61, top right corner) in the afterlife.

FIRST WRITING AND EARLY TEXTS

scribes
Those who mastered writing and used it to document economic transactions, keep lists, and record religious and literary texts; from the very beginning, they were at the top of the social ladder, under the major power brokers.

Mesopotamia was the birthplace of the world's first writing system, inscribed to promote the economic power of the temples and kings. Those who wielded new writing tools were **scribes**; from the very beginning they were near the top of the social ladder, under the big man and the priests. As the writing of texts became more important to the social fabric of cities, and facilitated information sharing across wider spans of distance and time, scribes consolidated their elite status.

Mesopotamians were the world's first record keepers and readers. The precursors to writing appeared in Mesopotamian societies when farming peoples and officials who had been using clay tokens and images carved on stones to seal off storage areas began to use them to convey messages. These images, when combined with numbers drawn on clay tablets, could record the distribution of goods and services.

Around 3200 BCE, someone, probably in Uruk, understood that the marks (most were pictures of objects) could also represent words or sounds. Before long, scribes connected visual symbols with sounds, and sounds with meanings, and they discovered they could record messages by using abstract symbols or signs to denote concepts. Such signs later came to represent syllables, the building blocks of words. By impressing signs into wet clay with the cut end of a reed, scribes pioneered a form of wedge-shaped writing that we call *cuneiform*; it filled tablets with information that was intelligible to anyone who could decipher it, even in faraway locations or in future generations. Developing over 800 years, this Sumerian innovation enhanced the urban elites' ability to trade goods, to control property, and to transmit ideas through literature, historical records, and sacred texts. The result was a profound change in human experience, because representing symbols of spoken language facilitated an extension of communication and memory.

Much of what we know about Mesopotamia rests on scholars' ability to decipher cuneiform script. By around 2400 BCE, texts began to describe the political makeup of southern Mesopotamia, giving details of its history and economy. Adaptable to different languages, cuneiform script was borrowed by other peoples in Mesopotamia to write not only Semitic languages such as Akkadian and, much later, Old Persian, but also the languages of the Hurrians and the Hittites.

City life and literacy also gave rise to written narratives, the stories of a "people" and their origins. "The Temple Hymns," written around 2100 BCE, describe thirty-five divine sanctuaries. The Sumerian King List, known from texts written around 2000 BCE, recounts the reigns of kings by city and dynasty and narrates the long reigns of legendary kings before the so-called Great Flood. A crucial event in Sumerian identity, the Great Flood, a pastoral-focused version of which is also found in biblical narrative, explained

Changes in Cuneiform over Time The world's earliest script, cuneiform, changed over time and was used to write many different languages. The first image (*top left*) shows the earliest version of cuneiform being used to write in the Sumerian language (here, a c. 2500 BCE accounting text). The next image (*top right*) shows the more formalized cuneiform script used to write in the Akkadian language more than a millennium after its invention by the Sumerians. The third image (*bottom left*) shows the Hittites' use of cuneiform script to render their language (here, in a letter sealed in a clay envelope). The final image (*bottom right*) demonstrates the use of cuneiform more than 2,000 years after its invention, in this case to record in Assyrian the flood story from the *Epic of Gilgamesh*.

Uruk's demise as the gods' doing. Flooding was the most powerful natural force in the lives of those who lived by rivers, and it helped shape the foundations of Mesopotamian societies.

CITIES BEGIN TO UNIFY INTO "STATES"

No single city-state dominated the whole of Mesopotamia in the fourth and third millennia BCE, but the most powerful and influential were the Sumerian city-states (2850–2334 BCE) and their successor, the Akkadian territorial state (2334–2193 BCE). In the north, Hurrians urbanized their rich agricultural zone around 2600 BCE, including cities at Urkesh and Tell Brak. (See Map 2.3.)

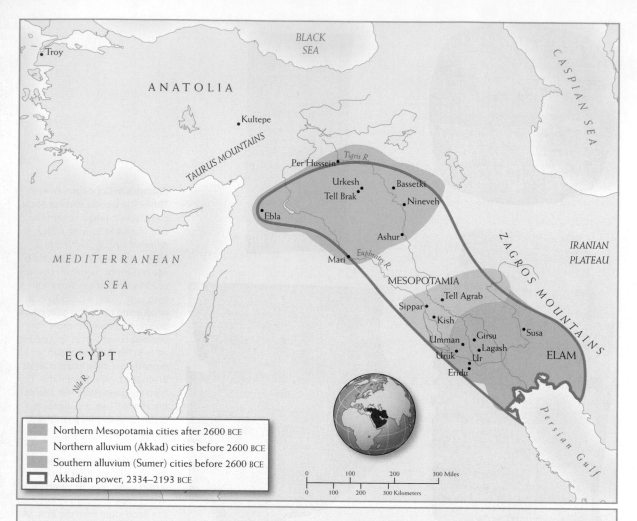

Map 2.3 **The Spread of Cities in Mesopotamia and the Akkadian State, 2600–2200 BCE**

Urbanization began in the southern river basin of Mesopotamia and spread northward. Eventually, the region achieved unification under Akkadian power.

- According to this map, what natural features influenced the location of Mesopotamian cities?
- Where were cities located before 2600 BCE, as opposed to afterward? What does the area under Akkadian power suggest that the Akkadian territorial state was able to do?
- How did the expansion northward reflect the continued influence of geographic and environmental factors on urbanization?

Sumerian city-states, with their expanding populations, soon found themselves competing for agrarian lands, scarce water, and lucrative trade routes. And as pastoralists far and wide learned of the region's bounty, they journeyed in greater numbers to the cities, fueling urbanization and competition. The world's first great conqueror—Sargon the Great (r. 2334–2279 BCE), king of Akkad—emerged from one of these cities. By the end of his reign, he had united (by force) the independent Mesopotamian cities south of modern-day Baghdad and brought the era of competitive independent city-states to an end. Sargon's unification of the southern cities by alliance, though relatively short-lived, created a territorial state. (A territorial state is a form of political organization that holds authority over a large population and landmass; its power extends over multiple cities.) Sargon's dynasty sponsored monumental architecture, artworks, and literary works, which in turn inspired generations of builders, architects, artists, and scribes. And by encouraging contact with distant neighbors, many of whom adopted aspects of Mesopotamian culture, the Akkadian kings increased the geographic reach of Mesopotamian influence. Just under a century after Sargon's death, foreign tribesmen from the Zagros Mountains conquered the capital city of Akkad around 2190 BCE, setting the beginning of a pattern that would fuel epic history writing, namely the struggles between city-state dwellers and those on the margins who lived a simpler way of life. The impressive state created by Sargon was made possible by Mesopotamia's early innovations in irrigation, urban development, and writing. While Mesopotamia led the way in creating city-states, Egypt went a step further, unifying a 600-mile-long region under a single ruler.

"The Gift of the Nile": Egypt

In Egypt, complex societies grew on the banks of the Nile River, and by the third millennium BCE their peoples created a distinctive culture and a powerful, prosperous state. The earliest inhabitants along the banks of the Nile were a mixed people. Some had migrated from the eastern and western deserts in Sinai and Libya as these areas grew barren from climate change. Others came from the Mediterranean. Equally important were peoples who trekked northward from Nubia and central Africa. Ancient Egypt was a melting pot where immigrants blended cultural practices and technologies.

Like Mesopotamia, Egypt had densely populated areas whose inhabitants depended on irrigation, built monumental architecture, gave their rulers immense authority, and created a complex social order based in commercial and devotional centers. Yet the ancient Egyptian culture was profoundly shaped by its geography. The environment and the natural boundaries of deserts, river rapids, and sea dominated the country and its inhabitants. Only about 3 percent of Egypt's land area was cultivable, and almost all of that cultivable land was in the Nile Delta—the rich alluvial land lying between the river's two main branches as it flows north of modern-day Cairo into the Mediterranean Sea. This environment shaped Egyptian society's unique culture.

THE NILE RIVER AND ITS FLOODWATERS

Knowing Egypt requires appreciating the pulses of the Nile. The world's longest river, it stretches 4,238 miles from its sources in the highlands of central Africa to its destination in the Mediterranean Sea. Egypt was deeply attached to sub-Saharan Africa; not only did its waters and rich silt deposits come from the African highlands, but much of its original population had migrated into the Nile Valley from the west and the south many millennia earlier.

The Upper Nile is a sluggish river that cuts through the Sahara Desert. Rising out of central Africa and Ethiopia, its two main branches—the White and Blue Niles—meet at present-day Khartoum and then scour out a single riverbed 1,500 miles long to the Mediterranean. The annual floods gave the basin regular moisture and enriched the soil. Although the Nile's floodwaters did not fertilize or irrigate fields as broad as those in Mesopotamia, they created green belts flanking the broad waterway. These gave rise to a society whose culture stretched along the navigable river and its carefully preserved banks. Away from the riverbanks, on both sides, lay a desert rich in raw materials but largely uninhabited. (See Map 2.4.) Egypt had no fertile hinterland like the sprawling plains of Mesopotamia. In this way, Egypt was arguably the most river focused of the river-basin cultures.

The Nile's predictability as the source of life and abundance shaped the character of the people and their culture. In contrast to the wild and uncertain Euphrates and Tigris Rivers, the Nile was gentle, bountiful, and reliable. During the summer, as the Nile swelled, local villagers built earthen walls that divided the floodplain into basins. By trapping the floodwaters, these basins captured the rich silt washing down from the Ethiopian highlands. Annual flooding meant that the land received a new layer of topsoil every year. The light, fertile soils made planting simple. Peasants cast seeds into the alluvial soil and then had their livestock trample them to the proper depth. The never-failing sun, which the Egyptians worshipped, ensured an abundant harvest. In the early spring, when the Nile's waters were at their lowest and no crops were under cultivation, the sun dried out the soil.

The peculiarities of the Nile region distinguished it from Mesopotamia. The Greek historian and geographer Herodotus noted 2,500 years ago that Egypt was the gift of the Nile and that the entire length of its basin was one of the world's most self-contained geographical entities. Bounded on the north by the Mediterranean Sea, on the east and west by deserts, and on the south by waterfalls, Egypt was destined to achieve a common culture. Due to

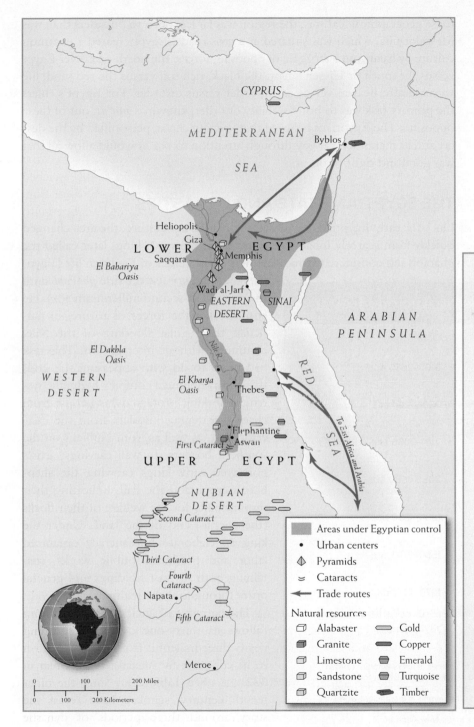

CYPRUS

MEDITERRANEAN

SEA

Byblos

Heliopolis
Giza
LOWER **EGYPT**
Saqqara Memphis
El Babariya
Oasis
Wadi al-Jarf
EASTERN *SINAI*
DESERT

ARABIAN
PENINSULA

El Dakhla
Oasis
WESTERN
DESERT

Nile R.

El Kharga
Oasis
Thebes

RED

To East Africa and Arabia

Elephantine
First Cataract Aswan

UPPER **EGYPT**

SEA

NUBIAN
DESERT

Second Cataract

Third Cataract

Fourth
Cataract
Napata

Fifth Cataract

Meroe

	Areas under Egyptian control
•	Urban centers
◊	Pyramids
≈	Cataracts
←	Trade routes

Natural resources

	Alabaster		Gold
	Granite		Copper
	Limestone		Emerald
	Sandstone		Turquoise
	Quartzite		Timber

0   100   200 Miles
0   100   200 Kilometers

Map 2.4 **Old Kingdom Egypt, 2686–2181 BCE**

Old Kingdom Egyptian society reflected a strong influence from its geographical location.

- What geographical features contributed to Egypt's isolation from the outside world and the people's sense of their unity?

- What natural resources enabled the Egyptians to build the Great Pyramids? What resources enabled the Egyptians to fill those pyramids with treasures?

- Based on the map, why do you think it was important to the people and their rulers for Upper and Lower Egypt to be united?

these geographical features, the region was far less open to outsiders than was Mesopotamia, which was situated at a crossroads. Egypt created a common culture by balancing a struggle of opposing forces: the north or Lower Egypt versus the south or Upper Egypt; the black, rich soil versus the red sand; life versus death; heaven versus earth; order versus disorder. For Egypt's rulers the primary task was to bring stability or order, known as *ma'at*, out of these opposites. The Egyptians believed that keeping chaos, personified by the desert and its marauders, at bay through attention to *ma'at* would allow all that was good and right to occur.

THE EGYPTIAN STATE AND DYNASTIES

Once the early Egyptians harnessed the Nile to agriculture, the area changed quickly from scarcely inhabited to socially complex. A king, later called the pharaoh and considered semidivine, was at the center of Egyptian life (Egyptian kings did not use the title *pharaoh* until the mid to late second millennium BCE). He ensured that the forces of nature, in particular the regular flooding of the Nile, continued without interruption. This task had more to do with appeasing the gods than with running a complex hydraulic system. The king protected his people from chaos-threatening invaders from the eastern desert, as well as from Nubians on the southern borders. In wall carvings, artists portrayed early kings carrying the shepherd's crook and the flail, indicating their responsibility for the welfare of their flocks (the people) and of the land. Under the king an elaborate bureaucracy organized labor and produced public works, sustaining both his vast holdings and general order throughout the realm.

The narrative of ancient Egypt's history follows its thirty-one dynasties, spanning nearly three millennia from 3100 BCE down to its conquest by Alexander the Great in 332 BCE. (See Table 2.1.) Since the nineteenth century, scholars have recast the story around three periods of dynastic achievement: the Old Kingdom, the Middle Kingdom, and the New Kingdom. At the

Table 2.1 Dynasties of Ancient Egypt

Dynasty*	Date
Predynastic Period dynasties I and II	3100–2686 BCE
Old Kingdom dynasties III–VI	2686–2181 BCE
First Intermediate Period dynasties VII–X	2181–2055 BCE
Middle Kingdom dynasties XI–XIII	2055–1650 BCE
Second Intermediate Period dynasties XIV–XVII	1650–1550 BCE
New Kingdom dynasties XVIII–XX	1550–1070 BCE
Third Intermediate Period dynasties XXI–XXV	1070–747 BCE
Late Period dynasties XXVI–XXXI	747–332 BCE

*The term *dynasty* generally refers to a series of rulers who are related to one another. Intermediate periods mark breaks between the kingdoms (Old, Middle, and New). While scholars make attempts to synchronize the dates with modern chronology and other events in the ancient world, the succession of rulers comes from Egyptian texts. The term *pharaoh*, as a title for the Egyptian king, came into use in the New Kingdom.

Source: Compiled from Ian Shaw and Paul Nicholson, eds., *The Dictionary of Ancient Egypt* (London: British Museum Press, 1995), pp. 310–11.

end of each era, cultural flourishing suffered a breakdown in central authority, known respectively as the First, Second, and Third Intermediate Periods.

KINGS, PYRAMIDS, AND COSMIC ORDER

The Third Dynasty (2686–2613 BCE) launched the foundational period known as the Old Kingdom, the golden age of ancient Egypt. By the time it began, the basic institutions of the Egyptian state were in place, as were the ideology and ritual life that legitimized the dynastic rulers.

The king presented himself to the population by means of impressive architectural spaces, and the priestly class performed rituals reinforcing his supreme status within the universe's natural order. One of the most important rituals was the Sed festival, which renewed the king's vitality after he had ruled for thirty years and sought to ensure the perpetual presence of water. King Djoser, from the Third Dynasty, celebrated the Sed festival at his tomb complex at Saqqara. This magnificent complex includes the world's oldest stone structure, dating to around 2650 BCE. Here Djoser's architect, Imhotep, designed a step pyramid that ultimately rose some 200 feet above the plain. The whole complex became a stage for state rituals that emphasized the divinity of kingship and the unity of Egypt.

The step pyramid at Djoser's tomb complex was a precursor to the grand pyramids of the Fourth Dynasty (2613–2494 BCE). These kings erected their monumental structures at Giza, just outside modern-day Cairo and not far from the early royal cemetery site of Saqqara, where Djoser's step pyramid stood. The pyramid of Khufu, rising 481 feet above the ground, is the largest stone structure in the world, and its corners are almost perfectly aligned to due north, west, south, and east. The oldest papyrus texts ever found—including a set of records kept by an official named Merer around 2550 BCE, which was excavated recently at the ancient port of Wadi al-Jarf—document a meticulous timetable for the gathering of stone for pyramid construction during Khufu's reign and tabulations of food to feed workers.

Construction of pyramids entailed the backbreaking work of quarrying the massive stones, digging a canal so barges could bring them from the Nile to the base of the Giza plateau, building a harbor there, and then constructing sturdy brick ramps that could withstand the stones' weight as workers hauled them ever higher along the pyramids' faces. Most likely a permanent workforce of up to 21,000 laborers endured 10-hour workdays, 300 days a year, for approximately 14 years just to complete the great pyramid of Khufu. The finished product was a miracle of engineering and planning. Khufu's great pyramid contained 21,300 blocks of stone with an average weight of 2½ tons, though some stones weighed up to 16 tons. Roughly speaking, one stone had to be put in place every 2 minutes during daylight. The stone blocks were planed so precisely that they required no mortar.

The Pyramids of Giza The Pyramid Fields of Giza lie on the western side of the Nile, with the bustling modern city of Cairo in the distance. Old Kingdom kings harnessed massive amounts of resources and human labor to complete these monumental structures over the course of several decades in the twenty-sixth century BCE. In the foreground stand three small pyramids of queens; the mostly collapsed structure belonged to Queen Hetepheres I (for her bracelets, see Interpreting Visual Evidence: Burials and Long-Distance Trade). Behind them is the pyramid of Menkaure, the penultimate king of the Fourth Dynasty. Beyond Menkaure's pyramid is that of Khafre, which retains some of its casing stones near the top. In the distance, behind Khafre's pyramid, is the pyramid of Khufu, the largest of the three (taller than Khafre's by just under 10 feet).

Surrounding these royal tombs at Giza were those of high officials, almost all members of the royal family. The enormous amount of labor involved in building these monuments came from peasant-workers as well as enslaved people captured and brought from Nubia and the Mediterranean. Filling these monuments with wealth for the occupants' afterlife similarly required a range of specialized labor (from jewelers to weavers to stone carvers to furniture makers). Long-distance trade was required to bring from far away not only the jewels and precious metals (like lapis lazuli, carnelian, and silver) required for such offerings, but also the materials to construct the ships that helped make that trade possible (like timber from Byblos). Through their majesty and complex construction, the Giza pyramids reflect the degree of centralization and the surpluses in Egyptian society at this time as well as the trade and specialized labor that fueled these undertakings.

Kings used their royal tombs, and the ritual of death leading to everlasting life, to embody the state's ideology and the principles of the Egyptian cosmos. They also employed symbols, throne names, and descriptive titles for themselves and their advisers to represent their own power and that of their administrators, the priests, and the landed elite. As in Mesopotamian city-states, the Egyptian cosmic order was one of inequality and stark hierarchy that did not seek balance among people (for it buttressed the inequalities and stark hierarchies of Egyptian society); rather, Egyptian religion sought balance between universal order (*ma'at*) and disorder. It was the job of the king to maintain this cosmic order for eternity.

GODS, PRIESTHOOD, AND MAGICAL POWER

Egyptians understood their world as inhabited by three groups: gods, kings, and the rest of humanity. Official records showed representations of only gods and kings. Yet the people did not confuse their kings with gods—at least during the kings' lifetimes. Mortality was the bar between rulers and deities; after death, kings joined the gods whom they had represented while alive.

As in Mesopotamia, every region in Egypt had its resident god. Some gods, such as Amun (believed to be physically present in Thebes, the political center of Upper Egypt), transcended regional status because of the importance of their hometown. Over the centuries the Egyptian gods evolved, combining often-contradictory aspects into single deities, including Horus, the sky god of kinship; Osiris, the god of regeneration and the underworld; Isis, who represented the ideals of sisterhood and motherhood; Hathor, the goddess of childbirth and love; Ra, the sun god; and Amun, a creator considered to be the hidden god.

Official religious practices took place in the main temples. The king and his agents offered respect, adoration, and thanks to the gods in their temples. In return, the gods maintained order and nurtured the king and—through him—all humanity. In this contractual relationship, the gods were passive while the kings were active, a difference that reflected their unequal relationship.

The tasks of regulating religious rituals and mediating among gods, kings, and society fell to one specialist class: the priesthood. Creating this class required elaborate rules for selecting and training the priests. Only priests could enter the temples' inner sanctuaries, and the gods' statues left the temples only for great festivals. Thus, priests monopolized communication between spiritual powers and their subjects.

Unofficial religion was also important. Ordinary Egyptians matched their elite rulers in faithfulness to the gods, but their distance from temple life caused them to find different ways to fulfill their religious needs and duties. They visited local shrines, where they prayed, made requests, and left offerings to the gods.

Unlike modern sensibilities that might see magic as opposed to, or different from, categories such as religion or medicine, Egyptians saw magic (personified by the god Heka) as a category closely intertwined with, if not indistinguishable from, the other two. Magic, or Heka, was a force that was present at creation and preexisted order and chaos. Magic had a special importance for commoners, who believed that amulets held extraordinary powers, such as preventing illness and guaranteeing safe childbirth. To deal with profound questions, commoners looked to omens and divination. Like the elites, commoners attributed supernatural powers to animals. Chosen animals received special treatment in life and after death: for example, the Egyptians adored cats, whom they kept as pets and whose image they used to represent certain deities. Apis bulls, sacred to the god Ptah, merited special cemeteries and mourning rituals. Ibises, dogs, jackals, baboons, lizards, fish, snakes, crocodiles, and other beasts associated with deities enjoyed similar privileges.

Egyptian Gods In this image from a thirteenth-century BCE copy of the *Book of the Dead* owned by a scribe named Huneter (on left, in white), falcon-headed Horus leads Hunefer to Osiris, who wears a white crown with plumes and holds a crook and flail across his chest. Behind Osiris stand Isis (left) and Nephthys (right).

Spiritual expression was central to Egyptian culture at all levels, and religion helped shape other cultural achievements, including the development of a written language.

WRITING AND SCRIBES

Egypt, like Mesopotamia, was a scribal culture. By the middle of the third millennium BCE, literacy was well established among small circles of scribes in Egypt and Mesopotamia. The fact that few individuals were literate heightened the scribes' social status. Most high-ranking Egyptians were also trained as scribes for the king's court, the army, or the priesthood. Some kings and members of the royal family learned to write as well. Although in both cultures writing may have emerged in response to economic needs, people in Egypt soon grasped its utility for commemorative and religious purposes.

Ancient Egyptians used two forms of writing. Elaborate *hieroglyphs* (from the Greek "sacred carving") served in formal temple, royal, or divine contexts. More common, however, was *hieratic* writing, a cursive script written with ink on papyrus or pottery. (*Demotic* writing, from the Greek *demotika*, meaning "popular" or "in common use," developed much later and became the vital transitional key on the Rosetta Stone that ultimately allowed the nineteenth-century

 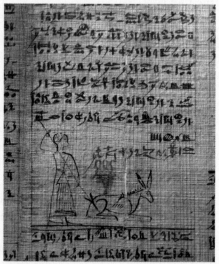

Egyptian Hieroglyphs and "Cursive Script" The Egyptians wrote in two distinctive types of script. The more formal is hieroglyphs, which are based on pictorial images that carry values of either ideas (logograms) or sounds (phonemes). All royal and funerary inscriptions, such as this funerary relief from the Old Kingdom (from the tomb of Nefertiabet, c. 2550 BCE), are rendered in hieroglyphic script. Nefertiabet's inscription describes, with a mixture of images and words, the funerary offerings, including food, fabric, and cosmetics. Daily documents, accountings, and literary texts—such as the fragment from the *Book of the Dead* (*top right*)—were most often written in a cursive script called hieratic, which was written with ink on papyrus. The form of the cursive signs is based on the hieroglyphs but is more abstract and can be formed more quickly.

decipherment of hieroglyphs.) Used for record keeping, hieratic writing also found uses in letters and works of literature—including narrative fiction, manuals of instruction and philosophy, cult and religious hymns, love poems, medical and mathematical texts, collections of rituals, and mortuary books.

Literacy spread first among upper-class families. Most students started training when they were young. After mastering the copying of standard texts in hieratic cursive or hieroglyphs, students moved on to literary works. The upper classes prized literacy as proof of high intellectual achievement. When elites died, they had their student textbooks placed alongside their corpses as evidence of their talents. The literati produced texts mainly in temples, where these works were also preserved. Writing in hieroglyphs and the composition of texts in hieratic, and later demotic, script continued without break in ancient Egypt for almost 3,000 years.

THE PROSPERITY AND DEMISE OF OLD KINGDOM EGYPT

Cultural achievements, agrarian surpluses, and urbanization ultimately led to higher standards of living and rising populations. Under pharaonic rule, Egypt enjoyed spectacular prosperity. Its population swelled from 350,000 in 4000 BCE to 1 million in 2500 BCE and nearly 5 million by 1500 BCE. However, expansion and decentralization eventually exposed the weaknesses of the Old and Middle Kingdom dynasties.

The state's success depended on administering resources skillfully, especially agricultural production and labor. Everyone, from the most powerful elite to the workers in the field, was part of the system. In principle, no one possessed private property; in practice, Egyptians treated land and tools as their own—but submitted to the intrusions of the state. The state's control over taxation, prices, and the distribution of goods required a large bureaucracy that maintained records, taxed the population, appeased the gods, organized a strong military, and aided local officials in regulating the Nile's floodwaters.

Royal power, along with the Old Kingdom, collapsed in the three years following the death of Pepy II in 2184 BCE. Local magnates assumed hereditary control of the government in the provinces and treated lands previously controlled by the royal family as their personal property. An extended drought strained Egypt's extensive irrigation system, which could no longer water the lands that fed the region's million inhabitants. (See Current Trends in World History: Climate Change at the End of the Third Millennium BCE in Egypt, Mesopotamia, and the Indus Valley.) In this so-called First Intermediate Period (2181–2055 BCE), local leaders plunged into bloody regional struggles to keep the irrigation works functioning for their own communities until the century-long drought ended. Although the Old Kingdom declined, it established institutions and beliefs that endured and were revived several centuries later.

Climate Change at the End of the Third Millennium BCE in Egypt, Mesopotamia, and the Indus Valley

During the long third millennium BCE, the first urban centers in Egypt, Mesopotamia, Iran, central Asia, and South Asia flourished and grew in complexity and wealth in a wet and cool climate. This smooth development was sharply if not universally interrupted beginning around 2200 BCE. Both archaeological and written records agree that across Afro-Eurasia most of the urban, rural, and pastoral societies underwent radical change. Those watered by major rivers were selectively destabilized, while the settled communities on the highland plateaus virtually disappeared. After a brief hiatus, some recovered, completely reorganized, and used new technologies to manage agriculture and water. The causes of this radical change have been the focus of much interest.

After four decades of research by climate specialists working together with archaeologists, a consensus has emerged that climate change toward a warmer and drier environment contributed to this disruption. Whether this disruption was caused solely by human activity, in particular agriculture

on a large scale, or was also related to cosmic causes such as the rotation of the earth's axis away from the sun, is still a hotly debated topic. It was likely a combination of factors.

The urban centers dependent on the three major river systems in Egypt, Mesopotamia, and the Indus Valley all experienced disruption. In Egypt, the hieroglyphic inscriptions tell us that the Nile no longer flooded over its banks to replenish the fields with fresh soil and with water for crops. Social and political chaos followed for more than a century. In southern Mesopotamia, the deeply downcut rivers changed course, disrupting settlement patterns and taking fields out of cultivation. Other fields were poisoned by salts brought on through overcultivation and irrigation without fallow periods. Fierce competition for water and land put pressure on the central authority. To the east and west, transhumant herders, faced with shrinking pasture for their flocks, pressed in on the river valleys, disrupting the already-challenged social and political structure of the densely urban centers.

In northern Mesopotamia, the responses to the challenges of aridity were more varied. Some centers were able to weather the crisis by changing strategies of food production and distribution. Some fell victim to intraregional warfare, while others, on the rainfall margin, were abandoned. When the region was settled again, society was differently organized. The population did not drastically decrease, but rather distributed itself across the landscape more evenly in smaller settlements that required less water and food. It appears that a similar solution was found by communities to the east on the Iranian plateau, where the inhabitants of the huge urban center of Shahr-i Sokhta abruptly left the city and settled in small communities across the oasis landscape.

The solutions found by people living in the cities of the Indus Valley also varied. Some cities, like Harappa, saw their population decrease rapidly. It seems that the bed of the river shifted, threatening the settlement and its hinterland. Mohenjo Daro, on the other hand, continued to be occupied for another several centuries, although the

The Indus River Valley: A Parallel Culture

Cities emerged in the Indus River valley in South Asia in the mid-third millennium BCE. The urban culture of the Indus area is called "Harappan" after the urban site of Harappa that arose on the banks of the Ravi River, a tributary large civic structures fell out of use, replaced by more modest structures. The Ghaggar-Hakra (as a year-round river) had dried up long before Harappan settlements of the third millennium BCE. The urban settlements along the course of its seasonal flow had already formed as an adaptation to an earlier climate change, since their inhabitants had likely clustered along the dried-up riverbed as a topographical feature that would focus monsoon flows even in the absence of a year-round river. And to the south, on the Gujarat Peninsula, population and the number of settlements increased. They abandoned wheat as a crop, instead cultivating a kind of drought-enduring millet that originated in West Africa. Apparently, conditions there became even more hospitable, allowing farming and fishing communities to flourish well into the second millennium BCE.

The evidence for this widespread phenomenon of climate change at the end of the third millennium BCE is complex and contradictory. This is not surprising, because every culture and each community naturally had an individual response to environmental and other challenges. Those with perennial sources of fresh water were less threatened than those in marginal zones where only a slight decrease in rainfall could mean failed crops and herds. Notably, certain types of social and political institutions were resilient and introduced innovations that allowed them to adapt, while others were too rigid or shortsighted to find local solutions. A feature of human culture is its remarkable ability to adapt rapidly. When people are faced with challenges, the traits of resilience, creativity, and ingenuity lead to cultural innovation and change. This is what we can see, even in our own times, during the period of environmental stress.

Millet This hardy grain, cultivated for its resistance to drought, persists in the desert environment of present-day western Pakistan.

Questions for Analysis

- How did the response to drought in the Indus Valley differ from the response in Mesopotamia?
- Imagine that the climate during the third millennium BCE had not changed. How do you think this might have affected the development of ancient Egypt?
- How has our understanding of global climate change affected the way we study prehistory?

Explore Further

Behringer, Wolfgang, *A Cultural History of Climate* (2010).

Bell, Barbara, "The Dark Ages in Ancient History. 1. The First Dark Age in Egypt," *American Journal of Archaeology* 75 (January 1971): 1–26.

Middleton, Guy D., *Understanding Collapse: Ancient History and Modern Myths* (2017).

Singh, Ajit, et al., "Counter-Intuitive Influence of Himalayan River Morphodynamics on Indus Civilisation Urban Settlements," *Nature Communications* 8, article no. 1617 (2017), doi:10.1038/s41467-017-01643-9.

Weiss, Max, et al., "The Genesis and Collapse of Third Millennium North Mesopotamian Civilization," *Science (New Series)* 261 (August 20, 1993): 995–1004.

of the Indus. Developments in the Indus basin reflected local tradition combined with strong influences from Iranian plateau peoples, as well as indirect influences from distant Mesopotamian cities. Villages appeared around 5000 BCE on the Iranian plateau along the Baluchistan Mountain foothills, to the west of the Indus. By the early third millennium BCE, frontier villages had spread eastward to the fertile banks of the Indus River and its tributaries. (See Map 2.5.) The river-basin settlements soon yielded agrarian surpluses

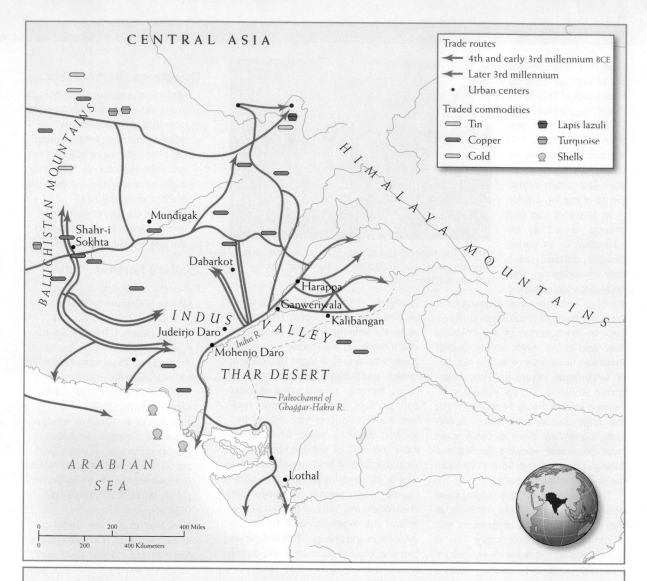

Map 2.5 The Indus River Valley in the Third Millennium BCE

Historians know less about the urban society of the Indus Valley in the third millennium BCE than they do about its contemporaries in Mesopotamia and Egypt, in part because of the absence of a written record. Recent scholarship has suggested the importance of a second seasonal flow (as opposed to a year-round river) in the channel of the long-dried-up Ghaggar-Hakra to the east of the Indus.

- Where were cities concentrated in the Indus Valley? Why do you think the cities were located where they were?
- How do the trade routes of the fourth and early third millennium BCE differ from those of the later third millennium BCE? What might account for those differences?
- What commodities appear on this map? What is their relationship to urban centers and trade routes?

that supported greater wealth, more trade with neighbors, and public works. Urbanites of the Indus region and the Harappan peoples began to fortify their cities and to undertake public works similar in scale to those in Mesopotamia, but strikingly different in function.

The Indus Valley ecology boasted many advantages—especially compared to the area near the Ganges River, the other great waterway of the South Asian landmass. The melting snows in the Himalayas watered the semitropical Indus Valley, ensuring flourishing vegetation, plus the region did not suffer the yearly monsoon downpours that flooded the Ganges plain. The expansion of agriculture in the Indus basin, as in Mesopotamia, Egypt, and China, depended on the Indus River's annual floods to replenish the soil and avert droughts. From June to September, the river inundated the plain. New evidence has suggested that the monsoons also brought seasonal flows of water into long-dried-up riverbeds (especially the so-called paleochannel of the Ghaggar-Hakra, a river that had dried up almost three thousand years before Harappan society began to thrive). This evidence poses a unique question about river-fueled society in the third millennium BCE: How did the Harappan settlements clustered along this paleochannel to the east of the Indus River harness a seasonal flow of water into an otherwise-dried-up riverbed, as compared with a year-round river?

Whether along the year-round-flowing Indus or the seasonal flows of water in the Ghaggar-Hakra paleochannel, farmers planted wheat and barley, harvesting the crops the next spring. Harappan villagers also improved their tools of cultivation. Researchers have found evidence of furrows, probably made by plowing, that date to around 2600 BCE. These developments suggest that, as in Mesopotamia and Egypt, farmers were cultivating harvests that yielded a surplus that allowed many inhabitants to specialize in other activities. In time, rural wealth produced urban splendor. More abundant harvests, now stored in large granaries, brought migrants into the area and supported expanding populations. By 2500 BCE cities began to replace villages throughout the Indus River valley, and within a few generations towering granaries marked the urban skyline. Harappa and Mohenjo Daro, the two largest cities, each covered a little less than half a square mile and may have housed 35,000 residents.

Harappan cities sprawled across a vast floodplain covering 500,000 square miles—two or three times the size of the Mesopotamian cultural zone. At the height of their development, the Harappan peoples reached the edge of the Indus ecological system and encountered the cultures of northern Afghanistan, the inhabitants of the desert frontier, the nomadic hunters and gatherers to the east, and the traders to the west. Scholars know less about Harappan society than about Mesopotamia or ancient Egypt, since many of the remains of Harappan culture lie buried under deep silt deposits accumulated over thousands of years of heavy flooding. But what they do know about Harappan urban culture and trade routes is impressive.

HARAPPAN CITY LIFE AND WRITING

The well-planned layout of Harappan cities and towns included a fortified citadel housing public facilities alongside a large residential area. The main street running through the city had covered drainage on both sides, with house gates and doors opening onto back alleys. Citadels were likely centers of political and ritual activities. At the center of the citadel of Mohenjo Daro was the famous great bath. The location, size, and quality of the bath's steps, mortar and bitumen sealing, and drainage channel all suggest that the structure was used for public bathing rituals.

The Harappans used brick extensively—in upper-class houses, city walls, and underground water drainage systems. Workers used large ovens to manufacture the durable construction materials, which the Harappans laid so skillfully that basic structures remain intact to this day. A well-built house of a wealthier family had private bathrooms, showers, and toilets that drained into municipal sewers, also made of bricks. Houses in small towns and villages were made of less durable and less costly sun-baked bricks.

Mohenjo Daro Mohenjo Daro, the "mound of dead," is a large urban site of the Harappan culture. The view of the city demonstrates a neat layout of houses and civic facilities such as sewer draining.

In terms of writing, the peoples of the Indus Valley developed a logographic system of writing made up of about 400 signs (far too many for an alphabetic system, which tends to have closer to thirty symbols). Without a bilingual or trilingual text, like the Behistun inscription for Sumerian cuneiform or the Rosetta Stone for Egyptian hieroglyphs, Indus Valley script has been impossible to decipher. Computer analysis, however, is helping researchers identify some features of the script and the pre-Indo-European language it might record. Even so, some scholars suggest that the signs might not represent spoken language, but rather might be a nonlinguistic symbol system. Although a ten-glyph-long public inscription has been found at the Harappan site of the ancient city of Dholavira, nearly all of what remains of the Indus Valley script is to be found on a thousand or more stamp seals and small plaques excavated from the region. These seals and plaques may represent the names and titles of individuals rather than complete sentences. As of yet, there is no evidence that the Harappans produced historical records such as the King Lists of Mesopotamia and Egypt, thus making it impossible to chart a history of the rise and fall of dynasties and kingdoms. Hence, our knowledge of

Harappa comes exclusively from archaeological reconstructions, reminding us that "history" is not what happened but only *what we know about what happened*.

TRADE

The Harappans engaged in trade along the Indus River, through the mountain passes to the Iranian plateau, and along the coast of the Arabian Sea as far as the Persian Gulf and Mesopotamia. They traded copper, flint, shells, and ivory, as well as pottery, flint blades, and jewelry created by their craftworkers, in exchange for gold, silver, gemstones, and textiles. Trade was facilitated by standardized sets of weights and measures. Carnelian, a precious red stone, was a local resource, but lapis lazuli had to come from what is now northern Afghanistan. Some of the Harappan trading towns nestled in remote but strategically important places. Consider Lothal, a well-fortified port at the head of the Gulf of Khambhat (Cambay). Although distant from the center of Harappan society, it provided vital access to the sea and to valuable raw materials. Its many workshops processed precious stones, both local and foreign. Because the demand for gemstones and metals was high on the Iranian plateau and in Mesopotamia, control of their extraction and trade was essential to maintaining the Harappans' economic power. So the Harappans built fortifications and settlements near sources of carnelian and copper mines.

Through a complex and vibrant trading system, the Harappans maintained access to mineral and agrarian resources. To facilitate trade, rulers relied not just on Harappan script but also on a system of weights and measures that they devised and standardized. Archaeologists have found Harappan seals, used to stamp commodities with the names of their owners or the nature of the goods, at sites as far away as the Persian Gulf, Mesopotamia, and the Iranian plateau.

The general uniformity in Harappan sites suggests a centralized and structured state. Unlike the Mesopotamians and the Egyptians, however, the Harappans apparently built neither palaces nor grand royal tombs. What the Indus River people show us is how much the urbanized parts of the world were diverging from one another, even as they borrowed from and imitated their neighbors.

Core Objectives

TRACE and **EVALUATE** the trade connections stretching from Mesopotamia to the Indus River valley societies.

The Yellow and Yangzi River Basins: East Asia

Like the Mesopotamians, Egyptians, and Harappans, East Asian peoples clustered in river basins. Their settlements along the Yellow River in the north and the Yangzi River to the south became the foundation of the future Chinese state. By 5000 BCE, both millet in the north and rice in the south were under widespread cultivation.

Yet in the following three millennia (when Mesopotamia, Egypt, and the Indus Valley were creating complex, city-based cultures), the Chinese moved slowly toward urbanization. (See Map 2.6.) Like the other regions' waterways, the Yellow and Yangzi Rivers had annual floods and extensive floodplains suitable for producing high agricultural yields and supporting dense populations. In China, however, the evolution of hydraulic works, big cities, priestly and bureaucratic classes, and a new writing system took longer. A lack of easily domesticated animals and plants contributed to the different developmental path in China, as did geographic barriers. The Himalaya Mountains and the Taklamakan and Gobi Deserts prevented large-scale migrations between East Asia and central Asia and hindered the diffusion of cultural breakthroughs occurring elsewhere in Afro-Eurasia.

FROM YANGSHAO TO LONGSHAN CULTURE

China's classical histories have claimed that China's cultural traditions originated in the Central Plains of the Yellow River basin and spread outward to less developed regions inside and even beyond mainland China. These histories place the beginnings of Chinese culture at the Xia dynasty, dating from 2200 BCE. Archaeological studies of river-basin environments in East Asia tell a different story, however. Whether or not the Xia existed as a historical dynasty, archaeological evidence suggests our study of the Yellow River basin and Yangzi delta should begin earlier—in the two millennia from 4000 to 2000 BCE.

China in 4000 BCE was very different geographically and culturally from what it is today. A warmer and moister climate divided its vast landmass into distinctive regions. Only after a long cycle of cooler and drier weather did these bodies of water dry up and the landmass become a single geographical unit. Recent archaeological research records that at least eight distinct regional cultures appeared between 4000 and 2000 BCE, and only as these communities interacted did their institutions and ways of life come together to create a unified Chinese culture.

Yet China was a land apart in the Afro-Eurasian landmass, isolated by the mountains of the Tibetan plateau in the west, the deserts of Inner Mongolia in the north, the tropical rain forests in the south, and the ocean in the east. China had only two difficult natural routes to the rest of Asia and Europe. One route led into central Asia by the narrow Gansu Corridor, running between the Qilian Mountains on the northern edge of the Tibetan plateau and the Gobi Desert. The other ran along a narrow band of the steppe north of the Yellow River and around the Gobi Desert, eventually ending up in the Mongolian steppe, the Altai Mountains, and the Kazakh steppe. Though trade with and migration into China were more limited than that which fused together Egypt, Mesopotamia, and the Indus Valley, nomadic cultures and technologies nevertheless filtered from the steppes to settled communities on the rivers.

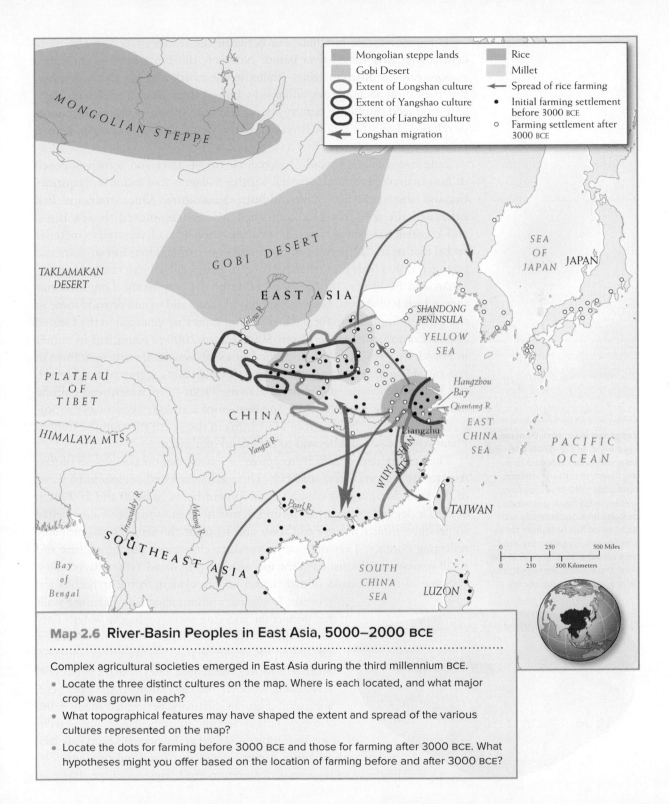

Map 2.6 River-Basin Peoples in East Asia, 5000–2000 BCE

Complex agricultural societies emerged in East Asia during the third millennium BCE.

- Locate the three distinct cultures on the map. Where is each located, and what major crop was grown in each?
- What topographical features may have shaped the extent and spread of the various cultures represented on the map?
- Locate the dots for farming before 3000 BCE and those for farming after 3000 BCE. What hypotheses might you offer based on the location of farming before and after 3000 BCE?

The major divide in China was between the northern Yellow and more centrally located Yangzi river basins. Not only did inhabitants of these two regions rely on different crops—millet in the north and rice in the south—but they built their houses differently, buried their dead in different ways, and produced distinctive pottery styles. The best known of the early cultures developed along the Yellow River and in the Central Plains area and is known as the Yangshao culture.

Yangshao villages typically covered 10 to 14 acres and were composed of houses erected around a central square. Villagers had to move frequently because they practiced slash-and-burn agriculture. Once residents had exhausted the soil, they picked up their belongings, moved to new lands, and constructed new villages. Their lives were hard. Excavated cemeteries reveal that nearly 20 percent of the burials were of children fifteen years and younger; only a little more than half of those buried lived past the age of forty.

Around 3000 BCE, the Yangshao culture gave way to the Longshan culture, which had an even larger geographical scope and would provide some of the cultural foundations for the first strong states that emerged in the Central Plains. Longshan flourished from 3000 BCE to 2000 BCE and had its center in Shandong Province. Although the Longshan way of life first took form in coastal and southern China, outside the Central Plains, it moved quickly into this hub of economic and political activity. Proof of its widespread cultural influence can be seen from the appearance of a unique style of black pottery, stretching all the way from Manchuria in the north through the Central Plains to the coast and beyond to the island of Taiwan.

The Longshan people likely migrated in waves from the peripheries of East Asia to the eastern China seashore. Their achievements, compared to those of the Yangshao, suggest marked development between 5000 and 2000 BCE. Several independent regional cultures in northern and southern China began to produce similar pottery and tools and to plant the same crops, probably reflecting contact. They did not yet produce city-states, but agriculture and small settlements flourished in the increasingly populated Yellow River valley.

Some of the hallmarks of early urban life are evident in the archaeological remains. Longshan communities built defensive walls for protection and dug wells to supply water. They buried their dead in cemeteries outside their villages. Of several thousand graves uncovered in southern Shanxi Province, the largest ones contain ritual pottery vessels, wooden musical instruments, copper bells, and painted murals. Shamans performed rituals using jade axes. Jade quarrying, in particular, indicated technical sophistication, as skilled craftworkers incised jade tablets with powerful expressions of ritual and military authority. The threat of organized violence among Longshan villages was real.

Yangshao Bowl with Dancing Figures, c. 5000–1700 BCE The Yangshao, also referred to as the "painted pottery" culture, produced gray or red pottery painted with black geometric designs and occasionally with pictures of fish or human faces and figures. Because the potter's wheel was unknown at the time, the vessels were probably fashioned with strips of clay.

Discoveries at one Longshan site revealed a household whose members were scalped. At this same site, attackers filled the water wells with five layers of human skeletons, some decapitated. Clearly, the villages' defensive walls were essential.

As communities became more centralized, contact between regions increased. Links between northern and southern China arose when Longshan peoples began to migrate along the East Asian coast to Taiwan and the Pearl River delta in the far south. Similarities in artifacts found along the coast and at Longshan sites in northern China, such as the form and decoration of pottery and jade items, also point to a shared sphere of culture and trade.

Archaeologists also have found evidence of short-lived political organizations. Although they were nothing like the dynastic systems in Egypt, Mesopotamia, and the Indus Valley, they were wealthy—if localized—polities. They constituted what scholars call the era of Ten Thousand States. One of them, the Liangzhu, has drawn particular interest for its remarkable jade objects and its sophisticated farming techniques. The Liangzhu grew rice and fruits and domesticated water buffalo, pigs, dogs, and sheep. Archaeologists have discovered the remains of net sinkers, wooden floats, and wooden paddles, which demonstrate a familiarity with watercraft and fishing. Artisans produced a black pottery from soft paste thrown on a wheel, and like the Longshan, they created ritual objects from several varieties of jade. Animal masks and bird designs adorned many pieces, revealing a shared cosmology that informed the rituals of the Liangzhu elite.

In the late third millennium BCE, a long drought hit China (as it did Egypt, Mesopotamia, and India). Although the climate change limited progress and forced migrations to more dependable habitats, the Chinese recovered early in the second millennium BCE. Now they created elaborate agrarian systems along the Yellow and Yangzi Rivers that were similar to earlier irrigation systems along the Euphrates, Indus, and Nile. Extensive trading networks and a stratified social hierarchy emerged; like the other river-basin complexes of Asia and North Africa, China became a centralized polity. Here, too, a powerful monarchy eventually united the independent communities. But what developed in China was a social and political system that emphasized an idealized past and a tradition represented by sage-kings, which later ages emulated. In this and other ways, China diverged from the rest of Afro-Eurasia.

Longshan Beaker, c. 2500 BCE Longshan has been called the "black pottery" culture, and its exquisite black pottery was not painted but rather decorated with rings, either raised or grooved. Longshan culture was more developed than the Yangshao culture, and its distinctive pottery was likely formed on a potter's wheel.

Life Outside the River Basins

In 3500 BCE, the vast majority of humans lived outside the complex cities that emerged in parts of Afro-Eurasia. At the other end of the spectrum, many peoples continued to live as hunters and gatherers, or in small agricultural villages, or as pastoralists tending flocks. In between were worlds such as those in the Aegean, Anatolia, Europe, and parts of China, where towns

Core Objectives

COMPARE early urbanization with the ways of life in small villages and among pastoralists.

emerged and agriculture advanced, but not with the leaps and bounds of the great river-basin societies.

Some cultures outside the river basins—in the Aegean, Anatolia, and Europe—had a distinctive warrior-based ethos, such that the top tiers of the social ladder held chiefs and military men instead of priests and scribes. In Europe and Anatolia especially, weaponry rather than writing, forts rather than palaces, and conquest rather than commerce dominated everyday life. Settlements in the Americas and sub-Saharan Africa were smaller and remained based on agriculture. Here, too, the inhabitants moved beyond stone implements and hunting and gathering, but they remained more egalitarian than river-basin peoples.

AEGEAN WORLDS

Contact with Egypt and Mesopotamia affected the worlds of the Aegean Sea (the part of the Mediterranean Sea between the Greek Peloponnese and Anatolia), but it did not transform them. Geography stood in the way of significant urban development on the mountainous islands of the Aegean, on the Anatolian plateau, and in Europe. Even though people from Anatolia, Greece, and the Levant had populated the Aegean islands in the sixth millennium BCE, their small villages, of 100 inhabitants or fewer, endured for 2,000 years before becoming more complex. On mainland Greece and on the Cycladic islands in the Aegean, fortified settlements housed local rulers who controlled a small area of agriculturally productive countryside.

Metallurgy developed both on the island of Crete and in the Cyclades. There is evidence of more formal administration and organizations in some communities by 2500 BCE, but the norm was scattered settlements separated by natural obstacles. One exciting recent find has been reported by scholars excavating a ritual center at Dhaskalio, a small islet off the coast of the Aegean island of Keros that was likely attached by land to Keros in the early Bronze Age. At this site, excavations have revealed mid-third-millennium BCE workshops for working imported metals like copper, as well as elaborate monumental engineering projects, including staircases and drainage tunnels, constructed with imported stone.

By the early third millennium BCE, the seafaring peoples of Crete had made occasional contact with Egypt and the coastal towns of the Levant, encountering new ideas, technologies, and materials as foreigners arrived on its shores. People coming by ship from the coasts of Anatolia and the Levant, as well as from Egypt, traded stone vessels and other luxury objects for the island's abundant copper. Graves of Aegean elites, such as those at Knossos on Crete, with their gold jewelry and other exotic objects, show that the elites did not reject the niceties of cultured life, but they knew that their power rested as much on their rugged landscape's resources as on self-defense and trade with others.

ANATOLIA

The highland plateau of Anatolia (in the region of modern-day Turkey) shows clear evidence of regional cultures focused on the control of trade routes and mining outposts. True cities did not develop here until the third millennium BCE, and even then they were not the sprawling population centers typical of the Mesopotamian plain. Instead, small communities emerged around fortified citadels housing local rulers who competed with one another. Two impressively fortified centers were Horoz Tepe and Alaça Hüyük, which have yielded more than a dozen graves—apparently royal—full of gold jewelry, ceremonial standards, and elaborate weapons. Similarly, the settlement at Troy—which would be the site of the Trojan War of the late second millennium BCE—was characterized by monumental stone gateways, stone-paved ramps, and high-status graves filled with gold and silver objects, vessels, jewelry, and other artifacts. Parallel grave finds on Crete, the Greek mainland, and as far away as Ur indicate that Troy participated in the trading system linking the Aegean and Southwest Asian worlds. At the same time, Troy faced predatory neighbors and pirates who attacked from the sea—an observation that explains its impressive fortifications.

EUROPE: THE WESTERN FRONTIER

At the western reaches of the Eurasian landmass was a region featuring cooler climates with smaller population densities. Its peoples—forerunners of present-day Europeans—began to make objects out of metal, formed permanent settlements, and started to create complex societies. Here, hierarchies began to undermine egalitarian ways. Yet, as in the Aegean worlds, population density and social complexity had limits.

More than in the Mediterranean or Anatolia, warfare dominated social development in Europe. Two contributing factors were the persistent fragmentation of the region's peoples and the type of agrarian development they pursued. (See Map 2.7.) The introduction of the plow and the clearing of woodlands expanded agriculture. Flint mining at an industrial level slashed the cost and increased the availability of raw materials needed to make tools for clearing forested lands and tilling them into arable fields. Compared to the river-basin societies, Europe was a wild frontier where violent conflicts over resources were common.

By 3500 BCE, the more developed agrarian peoples had combined into large communities, constructing impressive monuments that remain visible today. In western Europe, large ceremonial centers shared the same model: enormous shaped stones, some weighing several tons each, set in common patterns—in alleyways, troughs, or circles—known as *megalithic* ("great stone") constructions. These daunting projects required cooperative planning and

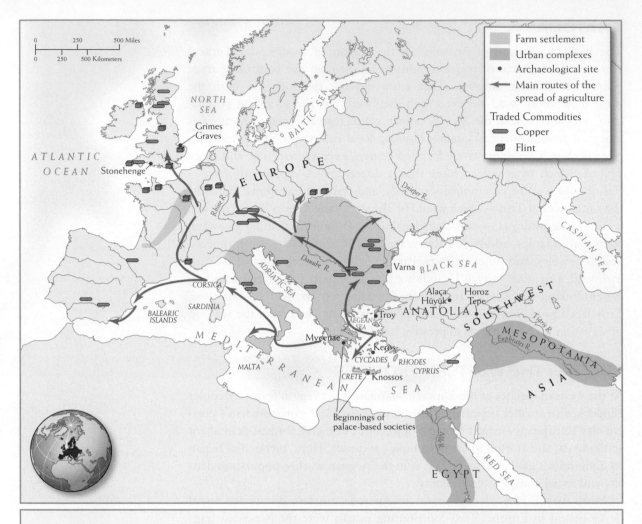

Map 2.7 Settlements outside the River Basins: The Eastern Mediterranean and Europe, 5000–2000 BCE

Urban societies in Southwest Asia, like those in Mesopotamia and the Nile Valley, had profound influences on societies in Anatolia, the Aegean, and western Europe.

- Trace the main routes for the spread of agriculture. Based on those routes, how did agriculture spread in this period?
- Locate the icons for copper and flint. Based on your reading of the chapter, how might these commodities have shaped the culture in the regions in which they were located?

work. In the British Isles, where such developments occurred later, the famous megalithic complexes at Avebury and Stonehenge probably reached their highest stages of development just before 2000 BCE.

By 2000 BCE, the whole of the northern European plain had come to share a common material culture based on agriculture, the herding of cattle for meat and milk, the use of the plough, and the use of wheeled vehicles and metal tools and weapons, mainly of copper. Increasing communication, exchange, and mobility among the European communities led to increasing wealth but also sparked organized warfare over frontier lands and valuable resources. In an ironic twist, the integration of local communities led to greater friction and produced regional social stratification. The violent men who now protected their communities received ceremonial burials complete with their own drinking cups and weapons. Archaeologists have found these warrior burials in a swath of European lands extending from present-day France and Switzerland to present-day central Russia. Because the agricultural communities now were producing surpluses that they could store, residents had to defend their land and resources from encroaching neighbors.

An aggressive culture was taking shape based on violent confrontations between adult males organized in "tribal" groups. War cultures arose in all western European societies. Armed groups carried bell-shaped drinking cups across Europe, using them to swig beer and mead distilled from grains, honey, herbs, and nuts.

Warfare had the effect of accentuating the borrowing among the region's competing peoples. The violent struggles and emerging kinship groups fueled a massive demand for weapons, alcohol, and horses. Warrior elites borrowed from Anatolia the technique of combining copper with tin to produce harder-edged weapons made of the alloy bronze. Soon smiths were producing them in bulk—as evidenced by hoards of copper and bronze tools and weapons from the period found in central Europe. Traders used the rivers of central and northern Europe to exchange their prized metal products, creating one of the first commercial networks that covered the landmass.

Stonehenge This spectacular site, located in the Salisbury Plain in Wiltshire in southwestern England, is one of several such megalithic structures found in the region. Constructed by many generations of builders, the arrangement of the large stone uprights enabled people to determine precise times in the year through the position of the sun. Events such as the spring and autumn equinoxes were connected with agricultural and religious activities.

THE AMERICAS

In the Americas, techniques of food production and storage, transportation, and communication restricted the surpluses for feeding those who did not work the land. Thus, these communities did not grow in size and complexity.

For example, in the Chicama Valley of Peru, which opens onto the Pacific Ocean, people still nestled in small coastal villages to fish, gather shellfish, hunt, and grow beans, chili peppers, and cotton (to make twined textiles, which they dyed with wild indigo). By around 3500 BCE, these fishermen abandoned their cane and adobe homes for sturdier houses, half underground, on streets lined with cobblestones.

Hundreds, if not thousands, of such villages dotted the seashores and riverbanks of the Americas. Some made the technological breakthroughs required to produce pottery; others devised irrigation systems and water sluices in areas where floods occurred. Some even began to send their fish catches inland in return for agricultural produce. Ceremonial structures highlighted communal devotion and homage to deities, as well as rituals to celebrate birth, death, and the memory of ancestors.

In the Americas, the largest population center was in the valley of Tehuacán (near modern-day Mexico City). Here the domestication of corn created a food source that enabled people to migrate from caves to a cluster of pit-house villages that supported a growing population. By 3500 BCE, the valley held nothing resembling a large city. People lived in clusters of interdependent villages, especially on the lakeshores: here was a case of high population density, but not urbanization.

SUB-SAHARAN AFRICA

The same pattern occurred in sub-Saharan Africa, where the population grew but did not concentrate in urban communities. About 12,000 years ago, when rainfall and temperatures increased, small encampments of hunting, gathering, and fishing communities congregated around the large lakes and rivers flowing through the region that would later become the Sahara Desert. Large game animals roamed, posing a threat but also providing a source of food. Over the millennia, in the wetter and more temperate locations of this vast region—particularly the upland mountains and their foothills—permanent villages emerged.

As the Sahara region became drier, people moved to the desert's edges, to areas along the Niger River and the Sudan. Here they grew yams, oil palms, and plantains. In the savanna lands that stretched all the way from the Atlantic Ocean in West Africa to the Nile River basin in present-day Sudan, settlers grew grains such as millet and sorghum, which spread from their places of origin to areas along the lands surrounding the Niger River basin. Residents constructed stone dwellings and dug underground wells and food storage areas. As an increasing population strained resources, groups migrated south toward the Congo River and east toward Lake Nyanza, where they established new farms and villages. Although population centers were often hundreds or thousands of miles apart and were smaller than the urban centers in

Egypt and Mesopotamia, the widespread use of the same pottery style, with rounded bottoms and wavy decoration, suggests that they maintained trading and cultural contacts. In these respects, sub-Saharan Africa matched the ways of life in Europe and the Americas.

Conclusion

Over the fourth and third millennia BCE, the world's social landscape changed in significant ways. In a few key locations, where giant rivers irrigated fertile lands, complex human cultures began to emerge. These areas experienced all the advantages and difficulties of expanding populations: occupational specialization; social hierarchy; rising standards of living; sophisticated systems of art and science; and centralized production and distribution of food, clothing, and other goods. Ceremonial sites and trading crossroads became cities that developed centralized religious and political systems. As scribes, priests, and rulers labored to keep complex societies together, social distinctions within the city (including the roles of men and women) and the differences between country folk and city dwellers sharpened.

Although river-basin cultures shared basic features, each one's evolution followed a distinctive path. Where there was a single river—the Nile or the Indus—the agrarian hinterlands that fed cities lay along the banks of the waterway. In these areas cities were small; thus, the Egyptian and Harappan worlds enjoyed more political stability and less rivalry. In contrast, cities in the immense floodplain of the Tigris and Euphrates needed large hinterlands to sustain their populations. Because of their growing power and need for resources, Mesopotamian cities vied for preeminence, and their competition often became violent.

In most areas of the world, however, people still lived in simple, egalitarian societies based on hunting, gathering, and basic agriculture—as in the Americas and sub-Saharan Africa. In Anatolia, Europe, and parts of China, regional cultures emerged as agriculture advanced and populations grew—but not with the leaps and bounds and fast-paced momentum of the river-basin cultures. Some of them, as in the Aegean and Europe, forged warrior societies. Beyond these frontiers, farmers and nomads survived as they had for many centuries. Thriving trading networks connected many, but not all, of these regions to one another.

Changes in climate affected everyone and could slow or even reverse development. How—and whether—cultures adapted depended on local circumstances. As the next chapter will show, the human agents of change often came from the fringes of larger settlements and urban areas.

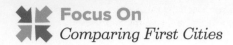

Focus On
Comparing First Cities

Mesopotamia

- Peoples living along the Tigris River and Euphrates River control floodwaters and refine irrigation techniques.

- Mesopotamians establish the world's first large cities, featuring powerful rulers, social hierarchies, and temples (ziggurats) for worship of their gods.

- Mesopotamia is the birthplace of writing.

Egypt

- Peoples of Egypt use Nile River waters to irrigate their lands and create a bountiful agriculture.

- Egyptian kings unify their territory, establish a powerful state, and develop a vibrant economy.

- Egyptians build magnificent burial chambers (pyramids), develop hieroglyphic writing, and worship a pantheon of gods.

Indus Valley

- South Asian peoples harness the Indus River and create cities (like Harappa and Mohenjo Daro), as well as a form of writing called Indus Valley script.

- Harappan cities include residential housing and public structures (like baths) with excellent drainage.

- Indus Valley peoples export copper, shells, and carnelian (as well as lapis lazuli and turquoise, from nearby sources) to peoples of Mesopotamia and Egypt.

East Asia

- Peoples dwelling in the basins of the Yellow River and the Yangzi River control the waters' flow and expand agriculture.

- These people develop elaborate cultures, which scholars later label Yangshao and Longshan.

- While agriculture in East Asia does not produce city-states in this period, Longshan peoples leave behind distinctive pottery and jade artifacts, suggesting evidence of regional trade.

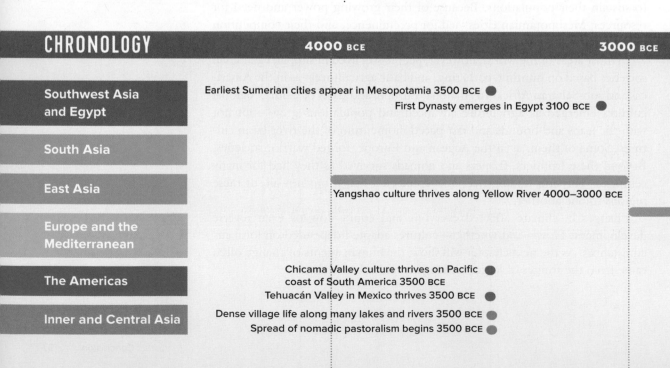

CHRONOLOGY

	4000 BCE	3000 BCE
Southwest Asia and Egypt	Earliest Sumerian cities appear in Mesopotamia 3500 BCE ●	First Dynasty emerges in Egypt 3100 BCE ●
South Asia		
East Asia	Yangshao culture thrives along Yellow River 4000–3000 BCE	
Europe and the Mediterranean		
The Americas	Chicama Valley culture thrives on Pacific coast of South America 3500 BCE ● Tehuacán Valley in Mexico thrives 3500 BCE ●	
Inner and Central Asia	Dense village life along many lakes and rivers 3500 BCE ● Spread of nomadic pastoralism begins 3500 BCE ●	

THINKING ABOUT GLOBAL CONNECTIONS

- **Thinking about River-Basin Societies and the Environment** Human interaction with the environment—including climate, geography, the characteristics of the rivers, and the continued cultivation of crops and herds—played a significant role in shaping each early river-basin community. Describe ways that these environmental factors influenced the unique characteristics of each river-basin society.

- **Thinking about Exchange Networks among Early River-Basin Societies** Carnelian from the Indus region buried in elite tombs of Egypt; lapis lazuli from the region of modern-day Afghanistan on necklaces adorning Harappan necks; shell from the Indus floodplain inlaid on Mesopotamian grave goods—these examples provide evidence of how trade in raw

materials bound river-basin societies together in the third millennium BCE. What routes might such goods have traveled? What does this exchange of commodities suggest about other types of exchange that may have been taking place between these river-basin societies?

- **Thinking about Changing Power Relationships in River-Basin Societies** From 3500 to 2000 BCE, as societies developed in the river basins of Mesopotamia, Egypt, South Asia, and East Asia, more intensive cultivation brought agricultural surpluses that ushered in a wide range of impacts. Explain, with examples from each of the river-basin societies, how food surpluses led to job specialization, wealth accumulation, and the resulting social hierarchies.

Key Terms

bronze p. 62	city-state p. 66	scribes p. 70	urban-rural divide p. 62
city p. 66	river basin p. 59	social hierarchies p. 67	

 Go to INQUIZITIVE to see what you've learned—and learn what you've missed—with personalized feedback along the way.

2000 BCE   **1000 BCE**

Old Kingdom Egypt 2686–2181 BCE

Sargon's Akkadian territorial state in Mesopotamia 2334–2200 BCE

Cities appear in Indus Valley 2500 BCE

Longshan culture flourishes in Yellow River valley 3000–2000 BCE

Fortified villages in the Aegean 2500 BCE

Stonehenge constructed 2000 BCE

Global Themes and Sources

Early Writing in Context

Agricultural surplus, and the urbanization and labor specialization that accompanied it, likely prompted the earliest development of writing and the profession of the scribes whose job it was to write. Early forms of writing were employed for a variety of purposes, such as keeping economic and administrative records, recording the reigns of rulers, and preserving religious events and practices (for calendars, rituals, and divinatory purposes). By the third millennium BCE, some early societies—Mesopotamia and Egypt, in particular—used writing to produce literature, religious texts, and historical documents.

Different types of writing developed in early societies at different times. Mesopotamians developed the world's first writing (a script called cuneiform) around 3200 BCE, but Egyptians were not far behind, developing their hieroglyphs within a century. Writing systems were not all the same. In some systems, symbols represented words or concepts. In other systems, symbols represented sounds, usually syllables. Some systems changed over time, beginning with symbols representing concepts, but then those symbols became simplified over time to represent the syllables that make up words. And in alphabetic systems, like the much later Phoenician and Greek, symbols are letters that are assembled to create words. Other record keeping did not use written symbols at all; for example, knotted cords formed a type of record keeping as early as 3000 BCE among the peoples of the Andean highlands of South America.

Unsurprisingly, scholars know more about early cultures whose writing has since been deciphered. This decipherment and the ancient texts that made it possible, however, are perhaps more recent than you might think. Cuneiform was cracked in the early nineteenth century (only 200 years ago), using a text written more than 2,000 years after cuneiform was invented, namely the multilingual Behistun inscription (written in Akkadian, Elamite, and Old Persian)

dating to 522 BCE. Hieroglyphs were also deciphered in the nineteenth century—almost 5,000 years after their inception—thanks to the trilingual Rosetta Stone (in Greek, demotic script, and hieroglyphs), which recorded a Hellenistic royal decree dating to 196 BCE, almost 3,000 years after hieroglyphs were invented. Some forms of writing, like the glyphs of the Maya of Mesoamerica beginning around 250 BCE, are still in the process of being deciphered. Undeciphered scripts, such as the Indus Valley script or Rongorongo of Pacific Islanders, offer intrigue and promise to those who would attempt their decipherment. Yet, even if the writing has been deciphered and the text can be translated by scholars, students encountering these translated texts must work through unfamiliar words, concepts, forms, and even gaps in the texts as preserved, in order to attempt to understand what that text can reveal about the context from which it comes.

Analyzing Early Writing in the Context of River-Basin Societies

- Looking at the examples, what differences or similarities do you notice in letter/symbol forms as well as the objects on which the writing was etched?

- What sorts of topics does each example of early writing address? What do the topics discussed in these texts suggest about the purpose and context for writing in their respective societies?

- To what extent does the type of society (river basin, seafaring, and so on), namely its context, seem to affect the development of writing in that region (date, type, purpose, and so on)?

- How does the fragmentary nature of the texts affect your ability to interpret them? How has the decipherment, or lack thereof, of these scripts affected scholars' understandings of the societies that produced them?

Items Needed to Build Boats

The text offered here was pressed into a clay tablet in cuneiform script during the late third millennium BCE. Found in southern Mesopotamia (Sumer), it describes the materials required to build "Magan boats." Magan was likely situated on the southern shores of the Arabian Peninsula, either in modern Yemen or Oman, although scholars are not certain of its location.

....

- **What sorts of materials are listed in this document, and how do you imagine they would be used for the construction of boats?**

- **What does the form of the document suggest about its context? What kind of document does this appear to be?**

- **What do the form and contents of the document suggest about the purpose of at least this example of Sumerian writing in cuneiform script?**

....

178 large palm trees
1400 large pine(?) trees
36 large tamarisk trees
32 large acacia(?)-trees
10 tamarisk trees, each 3 cubits
276 talents of palm fibre rope
34 talents of palm leaf rope
418 talents of reeds
207 talents of halfa-grass
753(?) ox hides
44 talents, 48 minas of goat hair
1695 litres of fish oil
. . .

4260 bundles of construction-reeds
12324 bundles of fuel(?)-reeds
3170 GUR-measures of purified bitumen

For making watertight the Magan-boats.
From the governor of Girsu.

10 shekels of oil
2 litres of dates
Magan-offerings

via Urabba, messenger

Expenditure
Month xii

Source: British Museum Collection Database. Reg no. 1895,0329.48; BM no. 18390. www.britishmuseum.org/collection. British Museum, Online. Accessed 12/2/2018.

Egyptian Mouth-Opening Ritual

Although writing appeared in Egypt just 100 years after it did in Mesopotamia, the hieroglyphs preserved in the pyramid of King Unis (r. 2375–2345 BCE) offer some of the earliest sustained religious writing from Egypt. These pyramid texts, such as the example included here, contain a range of rituals to facilitate the king's passage into the afterlife.

....

- **What gods are mentioned and for what purpose? What materials are mentioned in the text, and how are they used? What repetition do you see in this text?**

- **How are the gods, materials, and the repetition suggestive of a ritual, or religious, context for the writing?**

- **Why would ideas like these be inscribed on the walls inside a pyramid?**

....

Libation

Osiris, acquire for yourself all those who hate Unis and anyone who speaks bad of his name.
Thoth, go, acquire him for Osiris: get the one who speaks bad of Unis's name; put him in your hand.
Recitation 4 Times: Don't you let loose of him: beware that you not let loose of him.
Libation.

Censing

Someone has gone with his ka;
Horus has gone with his ka; Seth has gone with his ka;
Thoth has gone with his ka; the god has gone with his ka;
Osiris has gone with his ka; Eyes-Forward has gone with his ka;
you too have gone with your ka.
Ho, Unis! Your ka's arm is before you. Ho, Unis! Your ka's arm is after you.

Ho, Unis! Your ka's foot is before you. Ho, Unis! Your ka's foot is after you.

Osiris Unis, I have given you Horus's eye: provide your face with it. Let the scent of Horus's eye disseminate to you.

Recitation 4 times. Incense, fire.

Cleansing the Mouth with Salt Water

These your cool waters, Osiris—these your cool waters, oh Unis—have come from your son, have come from Horus.

I have come having gotten Horus's eye, that your heart may become cool with it; I have gotten it under your feet.

Accept the outflow that comes from you: your heart will not become weary with it.

Recitation 4 Times: Come, you have been invoked.

Cool Water; 2 pellets of natron.

Condensed milk, condensed milk, that parts your mouth, ho, Unis! may you taste its taste in front of those of the gods' booths: the spittle of Horus, condensed milk; the spittle of Seth, condensed milk; the reconciliation of the two gods' hearts, condensed milk.

Recitation 4 Times: Your natron-salt is among Horus's Followers.

5 pellets of Nile-Valley natron of Nekheb.

Your natron is Horus's natron;
  your natron is Seth's natron;
  your natron is Thoth's natron;
  your natron is the god's natron:
  your own natron is amongst them.

Your mouth is the mouth of a milk-calf on the day he is born.

5 Pellets of Delta natron of Shetpet.

Your natron is Horus's natron, your natron is Seth's natron, your natron is Thoth's natron, your natron is the god's natron; your natron is your ka's natron, your natron is your natron's natron: this your own natron is amongst your brothers, the gods.

Your natron is on your mouth: you should clean all your bones and end what is (bad) against you.

Osiris, I have given you Horus's eye: provide your face with it disseminated.

1 Pellet of natron.

The Mouth-Opening Ritual

Ho, Unis! I have fixed your jaws spread for you.
The flint spreader.

Osiris Unis, Let me part your mouth for you.
An ingot of Nile-Valley god's-metal; an ingot of Delta god's-metal.

Unis, accept Horus's eye, which went away: I have gotten it for you that I might put it in your mouth.
Nile-Valley Zrw-salt; Delta Zrw-salt.

Ho, Unis! Accept Osiris's *šjkw*-mineral.
Šjkw-mineral.

Here is the tip of the breast of Horus's own body: accept (it) to your mouth.
A jug of milk.

Here is the breast of your lactating sister Isis, which you should take to your mouth.
An empty jar.
Giving cool water; taking around.

Pyramid of Unis.

Here are Horus's two eyes, black and white: take them to your countenance, that they may brighten your face.
A white jar, a black jar; lifting up.

Source: James P. Allen, *Writings of the Ancient World: The Ancient Pyramid Texts* (Atlanta: Society of Biblical Literature, 2005), pp. 19–20.

PRIMARY SOURCE 2.3

Harappan Seals

As early as 2500 BCE, Indus Valley scribes made notations—usually pictorial emblems and five to six signs—on steatite seal stamps, pots, and even jewelry. The seal stamps shown here offer an example of this still-undeciphered script.

Harappan seal stamps.

- What figures can you make out on the seals? What other notations do you see that are suggestive of writing?

- How do you think scholars go about deciphering these figures and notations?

- The only evidence of writing in the mid-third-millennium BCE Indus Valley is these seal stamps and a few other short inscriptions (like the one at Dholavira). What does this fact suggest to you about their Harappan context?

Oracle bone.

Shang Dynasty Oracle Bone

While marks on pots produced by Yangshao peoples (c. 5000 BCE) may have been used for record keeping, the earliest full writing system did not appear in East Asia until the Shang dynasty (1600–1046 BCE). Shang kings used oracle bone predictions—etched on animal bones (like the one pictured here), which were heated until they cracked—to divine the answers to questions about the will of their ancestors and the weather.

- About what topic is this oracle bone attempting to divine an answer? How do you know?

- What is the ritual process of which this writing seems to be a part?

- What do the process of which this writing is a part and the topic about which it inquires suggest to you about the context for writing when it first appeared in East Asia, more than a millennium after its development in Mesopotamia and Egypt?

A partial translation of the left-hand side of this oracle bone reads:

[PREFACE:] Crack making on gui-si day, Que divined:
[CHARGE:] In the next ten days there will be no disaster.
[PROGNOSTICATION:] The king, reading the cracks, said, "There will be no harm; there will perhaps be the coming of alarming news."
[VERIFICATION:] When it came to the fifth day, ding-you, there really was the coming of alarming news from the west. Zhi Guo, reporting, said, "The Du Fang [a border people] are besieging in our eastern borders

and have harmed two settlements." The Gong-fang also raided the fields of our western borders.

Source: This translation follows (with slight modifications by Bryan W. Van Norden) David N. Keightley, *Sources of Shang History* (Berkeley: University of California Press, 1978), p. 44.

Early Greek Writing (Linear B)

The earliest deciphered Greek writing, known as Linear B, did not appear until around 1450 BCE among the Mycenaeans, although other forms of Greek writing developed several hundred years earlier on Crete among the Minoans. The example here comes from the Mycenaean palace at Pylos, on mainland Greece.

- Who and what are mentioned in this text, and what does this suggest about the text's purpose?

- What evidence for the economic context at Pylos in mainland Mycenaean Greece does the text offer?

- How does the fragmentary nature of the text affect your reading of it?

The plot of Qelequhontas: this much seed: 276 l. of wheat

R. slave of the god, holds a lease: so much seed: 12 l. of wheat

W. the priest holds a lease: so much seed: 12 l. of wheat

Thuriatis, female slave of the god, dependant of P. the old man: so much seed: 108 l. of wheat

The plot of Admaos, so much seed: 216 l. of wheat.
. . .
T. slave of the god, holds a lease: so much seed: 32 l. of wheat

The plot of A . . . eus, so much seed: 144 l. of wheat.
. . .
The plot of T. slave of the god, holds a lease: 18 l. of wheat

The plot of R., so much seed: 138 l. of wheat. . . .

The plot of Aktaios, so much seed: 384 l. of wheat.
. . .

Source: M. Ventris and J. Chadwick, *Documents in Mycenaean Greek*, 2nd ed. (Cambridge, England: Cambridge University Press, 1973), doc. 116.

Linear B from Pylos. From the excavated Mycenaean palace at Pylos, this is a typical Linear B document inscribed on clay with linear marks representing syllables and signs.

Interpreting Visual Evidence

Burials and Long-Distance Trade

One of the most intriguing types of evidence from the river-basin societies discussed in this chapter is the elaborate burials of the elite. These burials often contained tremendous wealth in the form of finely crafted items. A number of these items show not only highly specialized artisanship but also evidence of long-distance trade in raw materials among these third-millennium BCE societies.

Consider the types of objects pictured here and the materials used to make them. Queen Hetepheres I of the Fourth Dynasty of Egypt (c. 2550 BCE) was buried at Giza (near Memphis and Saqqara) with silver bracelets decorated with butterflies made of turquoise, lapis lazuli, and carnelian. In southern Mesopotamia, Pu-Abi was interred in the magnificent Royal Tombs of Ur (c. 2600–2400 BCE), which contained artifacts such as the Royal Standard of Ur pictured on the first page of this chapter. Among the many items found in Pu-Abi's tomb was a lyre made with lapis lazuli and shell set in bitumen, shown in the second image below. Excavation reports describe this lyre as being found in the arms of a female lyrist who may have been a sacrificial victim at the death of Pu-Abi. Harappan artisans in the Indus River valley used a bow drill to perforate tiny beads in order to craft the necklace shown here from lapis lazuli, carnelian, and other semiprecious stones. Much earlier, around 4000 BCE, at Varna on the coast of the Black Sea (see Map 2.7), an important person from a farming village was buried with 990 gold objects (mostly decorative pieces sewn onto his clothing), as well as flint daggers, axes, and spearheads; his burial is shown in the third image.

Bracelets of Queen Hetepheres I.

Harp, or "Queen's Lyre," from the Royal Tombs of Ur.

Male warrior burial at Varna.

Harappan gemstone necklace with lapis lazuli and carnelian.

Questions for Analysis

1. Looking at Map 2.2, where did the raw materials used to make each of the items here come from? Along what trade routes would these raw materials have traveled? What does that suggest about trade between river-basin societies in the third millennium BCE?

2. What does the presence of these highly crafted items in the graves of elite individuals suggest about river-basin societies, especially in terms of wealth accumulation, labor specialization, and the beginnings of social stratification?

3. What does the ability and willingness to bury so much wealth in the dirt suggest about these third-millennium BCE societies, especially as compared with earlier, more subsistence-based hunting and gathering communities?

3

Nomads, Territorial States, and Microsocieties

2000–1200 BCE

Around 2200 BCE, the Old Kingdom of Egypt collapsed. The collapse did not occur because of incompetent rulers, of which there were many, or a decline in the arts and sciences, which is evident in unfinished building projects; the Old Kingdom fell because of radical changes in climate—namely, a powerful warming and drying trend that blanketed Afro-Eurasia between 2200 and 2150 BCE. The Mesopotamians and Harappans were as hard hit as the Egyptians. (For more on the impact of climate change in the river-basin cultures, see Current Trends in World History: Climate Change at the End of the Third Millennium BCE in Egypt, Mesopotamia, and the Indus Valley, in Chapter 2, p. 82.)

In Egypt the environmental disaster yielded a series of low floods of the Nile because the usual monsoon rains did not arrive to feed the river's upper regions. With less water to irrigate crops, farmers could not grow enough food for the river basin's million inhabitants. Documents from this period reveal widespread suffering and despair. Consider the following tomb inscription: "All of Egypt was dying of hunger to such a degree that everyone had come to eating his children." Or another: "The tribes of the desert have become Egyptians everywhere. . . . The plunderer is everywhere, and the servant takes what he finds."

Chapter Outline

- Nomadic Movement, Climate Change, and the Emergence of Territorial States
- The Territorial State in Egypt
- Territorial States in Southwest Asia
- Nomads and the Indus River Valley
- The Shang Territorial State in East Asia
- Microsocieties in the South Pacific and in the Aegean
- Conclusion

Core Objectives

- **EXPLAIN** the relationship between climate change and human settlement patterns in the second millennium BCE.
- **DESCRIBE** the impact of trans-humant herders and pastoral nomads on settled communities.
- **COMPARE** the varied processes by which territorial states formed and interacted with each other across Afro-Eurasia.
- **EXAMINE** the development of microsocieties in the South Pacific and the Aegean, and **EXPLAIN** the role geography played in their development.

Herders and pastoral nomads also felt the pinch. As these outsiders pressed upon permanent settlements in search of food, the governing structures in Egypt—and elsewhere, in Mesopotamia and the Indus Valley—broke down. The pioneering city-states of the third millennium BCE may have created unprecedented differences between elites and commoners, between urbanites and rural folk, but everyone felt the effects of this disaster.

This chapter focuses on two related developments. The first focus is the impact of climate change on the peoples of Afro-Eurasia: famines occurred, followed by political and economic turmoil. The old order gave way as river-basin states in Egypt, Mesopotamia, and the Indus Valley collapsed. Herders and pastoral nomads, driven from grazing areas that were drying up, forced their way into the heartlands of these great states in pursuit of better-watered lands. Once there, they challenged the traditional ruling elites. The nomads also brought with them a new military weapon—the horse-drawn chariot. Nomads and their chariots form the second focus of this chapter, for chariots introduced a type of warfare that would dominate the plains of Afro-Eurasia for a half a millennium. The nomads' advantage proved only temporary, however. Soon the Egyptians, Mesopotamians, Chinese, and many others learned from their chariot-driving conquerors: they assimilated some of their foes into their own societies and drove others away, adopting the invaders' most useful techniques. This chapter also examines worlds apart from the expanding centers of population and politics, where climate change and chariot-driving nomads were shaping world history. The islanders of the Pacific and the Aegean did not interact with one another with such intensity—and therefore their political systems evolved differently. In these locales, microsocieties (small-scale, loosely interconnected communities) were the norm.

Global Storyline

Comparing First States

- Climate change and environmental degradation lead to the collapse of river-basin societies.

- Transhumant migrants (with their animal herds in need of pasturage) and pastoral nomads (with their horse-drawn chariots) interact, in both destructive and constructive ways, with settled agrarian societies.

- A fusion of migratory and settled agricultural peoples produce expanded territorial states—in Egypt, Southwest Asia, the Indus River valley, and Shang China—that supplant earlier river-basin societies.

- Microsocieties emerge in the eastern Mediterranean and South Pacific based on expanding populations and increased trade.

Nomadic Movement, Climate Change, and the Emergence of Territorial States

At the end of the third millennium BCE, a changing climate, drought, and food shortages led to the overthrow of ruling elites throughout central and western Afro-Eurasia. Walled cities could not defend their hinterlands. Trade routes lay open to predators, and pillaging became a lucrative enterprise. Clans of horse-riding **pastoral nomads**—from the relatively sparsely populated and isolated Inner Eurasian steppes—swept across vast distances, eventually threatening settled people in cities. **Transhumant herders**—who lived closer to agricultural settlements and migrated seasonally to pasture their livestock—also advanced on populated areas in search of food and resources. These migrations of pastoral nomads and transhumant herders occurred across Eurasia, in the Arabian Desert and Iranian plateau in the west, and in the Indus River valley and the Yellow River valley in the east. (See Map 3.1.) Many transhumant herders and nomadic pastoralists settled in the agrarian heartlands of Mesopotamia, the Indus River valley, the highlands of Anatolia, Iran, China, and Europe. After the first wave of newcomers, more migrants arrived by foot or in wagons pulled by draft animals. Some sought temporary work; others settled permanently. They brought horses and new technologies that were useful in warfare; religious practices and languages; and new pressures to feed, house, and clothe an ever-growing population. This millennia-long process is sometimes referred to as **Indo-European migrations**.

The term *Indo-European* was created by comparative linguists to trace and explain the similarities within the large language family that includes Sanskrit, Hindi, Persian, Greek, Latin, and what would become German and English. Words and concepts that appear in many languages, such as numbering systems and words like *mother*, *father*, and *god*, suggest these so-called Indo-European languages may have had a common origin. For instance, the number one is *eka* (in Sanskrit), *ek* (in Hindi), *hen* (in Greek), *unus* (in Latin), *un* (in French), and *ein* (in German). The word for mother is *mātṛ* (in Sanskrit), *mātā* (in Hindi), *mêter* (in Greek), *mater* (in Latin), *mère* (in French), and *mutter* (in German). A host of demographic, geographic, and other factors shape the movement and development of languages over time. Nonetheless, migrations of the earliest speakers of the Indo-European language group, who carried not only their language but also their technology and culture, are likely part of the story of the spread of pastoralists from the central Eurasian steppe into Europe, Anatolia, Southwest Asia, and South Asia.

Perhaps the most vital breakthroughs that nomadic pastoralists transmitted to settled societies were the harnessing of horses and the invention of the

THE BIG PICTURE

What was the relationship between climate change and human settlement patterns in the second millennium BCE?

pastoral nomads
Pastoral peoples who move with their herds in perpetual motion across large areas, like the steppe lands of Inner Eurasia, and facilitate long-distance trade.

transhumant herders
Pastoral peoples who move seasonally from lowlands to highlands, in proximity to city-states, with which they trade the products of their flocks (milk, fur, hides) for urban products (manufactured goods, such as metals).

Indo-European migrations
The migrations, tracked linguistically and culturally, of the peoples of a distinct language group (including Sanskrit, Persian, Greek, Latin, and German) from central Eurasian steppe lands into Europe, Southwest Asia, and South Asia.

The Global View

URAL MOUNTAINS

BALTIC SEA

EUROPE

Dnieper R.

Dniester R.

HUNGARIAN
PLAIN

Danube R.

Minoan
Mycenaean

BLACK SEA

Hittites

ANATOLIAN
PLATEAU

Volga R.

CASPIAN SEA

ARAL
SEA

Oxus R.

CENTRAL ASIA

Lake
Balkas

PAMIR MTS.

HINDU KUSH MTS.

HIM.

Tigris R.

Euphrates R.

MEDITERRANEAN SEA

Amorites
Hyksos

SOUTHWEST ASIA

ZAGROS MTS.

IRANIAN
PLATEAU

Indus R.

Nile R.

Persian Gulf

SOUT

ARABIAN
DESERT

RED SEA

ARABIAN SEA

← Transhumant migrations
← Spread of wheeled vehicles
← Spread of war chariots
← Dispersal of nomads
Pastoral nomads, c. 2000–1500 BCE

Southwest Asian Society
Zone of urban civilization

0   500   1000 Miles
0   500   1000 Kilometers

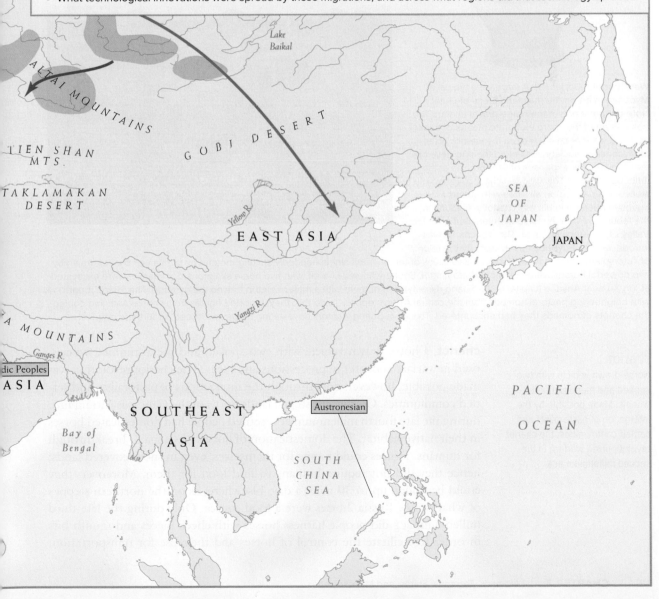

Map 3.1 Nomadic Migrations in Afro-Eurasia, 2000–1000 BCE

Many different groups of nomadic peoples were on the move in the second millennium BCE, migrating into many of the regions that had hosted the river-basin-fueled, city-state-filled cultures of the third millennium BCE.

- According to this map, from what specific parts of the world did pastoral peoples migrate? Into what specific areas did they move? What geographical features may have shaped the migrations in terms of the regions left behind, the routes traveled, and the locations traveled to?
- What regions did these migrations bring into closer connection?
- What technological innovations were spread by these migrations, and across what regions did that technology spread?

Lake
Baikal

ALTAI MOUNTAINS

TIEN SHAN
MTS.

GOBI DESERT

TAKLAMAKAN
DESERT

Yellow R.

EAST ASIA

SEA
OF
JAPAN

JAPAN

A MOUNTAINS

Ganges R.

dic Peoples

ASIA

Yangzi R.

SOUTHEAST
ASIA

Bay of
Bengal

Austronesian

SOUTH
CHINA
SEA

PACIFIC

OCEAN

War Chariots *Upper left:* A large vase typical of Mycenaean art on the mainland areas of Greece. Note the presence of the horse-drawn chariot. The possession of this more elaborate means of transport and warfare characterized the warrior elites of Mycenaean society and linked them to developments over wide expanses of Afro-Eurasia at the time. *Upper right:* This wooden chest covered with stucco and painted on all sides with images of the Egyptian pharaoh in his war chariot was found in the fabulously wealthy tomb of Tutankhamun in the Valley of the Kings in Egypt. The war chariot was introduced into Egypt by the Hyksos. By the reign of Tutankhamun in the New Kingdom, depictions of the pharaoh single-handedly smiting the enemy from a war chariot drawn by two powerful horses were common. *Bottom right:* Spoke-wheeled chariot, with two horse skeletons. Six chariots were excavated at Yin Xu near Anyang (capital of the Shang dynasty), five of them with a male skeleton behind the carriage. The Shang fought with neighboring pastoral nomads from the central Asian steppes. To do this, they imported horses from central Asia and copied the chariots of nomads they had encountered. This gave Shang warriors devastating range and speed for further conquest.

chariot

Horse-drawn vehicle with two spoked and metal-rimmed wheels. Made possible by the interaction of pastoralists and settled communities, the chariot revolutionized warfare in the second millennium BCE.

chariot, a horse-drawn vehicle with two spoked and metal-rimmed wheels, used in warfare and later in processions and races. The chariot revolution was made possible, however, only through the interactions of pastoralists and settled communities. On the vast steppe lands north of the Caucasus Mountains, during the late fourth millennium BCE, settled people had domesticated horses in their native habitat. The domestication of horses was a major breakthrough for humans. Horses could forage for themselves, even in snow-covered lands; hence they did not require humans to find food for them. Moreover, they could be ridden up to 30 miles a day. Elsewhere, as on the northern steppes of what is now Russia, horses were a food source. Only during the late third millennium BCE did people harness horses with cheek pieces and mouth bits in order to facilitate the control of horses and their use for transportation.

Parts of horse harnesses made from wood, bone, bronze, and iron, found in tombs scattered across the steppe, reveal the evolution of headgear from simple mouth bits to full bridles with headpiece, mouthpiece, and reins.

Sometime around 2000 BCE, pastoral nomads in the mountains of the Caucasus joined the bit-harnessed horse to the two-wheeled chariot. Various chariot innovations began to unfold: pastoralists lightened chariots so their warhorses could pull them faster; spoked wheels made of special wood bent into circular shapes replaced solid-wood wheels that were heavier and prone to shatter; wheel covers, axles, and bearings (all produced by settled people) were added to the chariots; and durable metal went into the chariot's moving parts. Hooped bronze and, later, iron rims reinforced the spoked wheels. Initially iron was a decorative and experimental metal, and all tools and weapons were bronze. Iron's hardness and flexibility, however, eventually made it more desirable for reinforcing moving parts and protecting wheels, like those on the chariot. Thus, the horse chariots combined innovations by both nomads and settled agriculturalists.

These innovations—combining engineering skills, metalworking, and animal domestication—revolutionized the way humans made war. The horse chariot slashed travel time between capitals. Slow-moving infantry now ceded to battalions of chariots. Each vehicle carried a driver and an archer and charged into battle with lethal precision and ravaging speed. The mobility, accuracy, and shooting power of warriors in horse-drawn chariots tilted the political balance. After the nomads perfected this type of warfare (by 1600 BCE), they challenged the political systems of Mesopotamia and Egypt, and chariots soon became central to the armies of Egypt, the Assyrians and Persians of Southwest Asia, the Vedic kings of South Asia, the later Zhou rulers in China, and local nobles as far west as Italy, Gaul, and Spain. Only with the development of cheaper armor made of iron (after 1000 BCE) did foot soldiers recover their military importance. And only after states developed cavalry units of horse-mounted warriors did chariots lose their decisive military advantage. For much of the second millennium BCE, then, charioteer elites prevailed in Afro-Eurasia.

For city dwellers in the river basins, the first sight of horse-drawn chariots must have been terrifying, but they quickly understood that war making had changed and they scrambled to adapt. The pharaohs in Egypt probably copied chariots from nomads or neighbors, and they came to value them highly. For example, the young pharaoh Tutankhamun (r. c. 1336–1327 BCE) was a chariot archer who made sure his war vehicle and other gear accompanied him in his tomb. A century later, the Shang kings of the Yellow River valley, in the heartland of agricultural China, likewise were entombed with their horse chariots.

While nomads and transhumant herders toppled the river-basin cities in Mesopotamia, Egypt, and China through innovations in warfare such as the chariot, the turmoil that ensued sowed seeds for a new type of regime: the territorial state. Even as Sargon and the Akkadians set up a short-lived territorial state in

territorial state
A kingdom made up of city-states and hinterlands joined together by a shared identity, controlled through the centralized rule of a charismatic leader, and supported by a large bureaucracy, legal codes, and military expansion.

earlier Mesopotamia (2334–2200 BCE) (see Chapter 2), the martial innovations and political and environmental crises of the early second millennium BCE helped spur more enduring development of territorial states elsewhere. The **territorial state** was a centralized kingdom organized around a charismatic ruler. The new rulers of these territorial states exerted power not only over localized city-states but also over distant hinterlands. They enhanced their stability through rituals for passing the torch of command from one generation to the next. People no longer identified themselves as residents of cities; instead, they felt allegiance to large territories, rulers, and broad linguistic and ethnic communities. These territories for the first time had identifiable borders, and their residents felt a shared identity. Territorial states differed from the city-states that preceded them in that the new territorial states in Egypt, Mesopotamia, and China based their authority on monarchs, widespread bureaucracies, elaborate legal codes, large territorial expanses, definable borders, and ambitions for continuous expansion.

The Territorial State in Egypt

The first of the great territorial states of this period arose from the ashes of chaos in Egypt. The long era of prosperity associated with Old Kingdom Egypt ended when drought brought catastrophe to the area. For several decades the Nile did not overflow its banks, and Egyptian harvests withered. (See Current Trends in World History: Climate Change and the Collapse of River-Basin Societies.) As the pharaohs lost legitimacy and fell prey to feuding among rivals for the throne, regional elites replaced the authority of the centralized state. Egypt, which had been one of the most stable corners of Afro-Eurasia, endured more than a century of tumult before a new order emerged. The pharaohs of the Middle Kingdom and, later, the New Kingdom reunified the river valley and expanded south and north.

RELIGION AND TRADE IN MIDDLE KINGDOM EGYPT (2055–1650 BCE)

Around 2050 BCE, after a century of drought, the Nile's floodwaters returned to normal and crops grew again. In the centuries that followed, pharaohs at Thebes consolidated power in Upper Egypt and began new state-building activity, ushering in a new phase of stability that historians call the Middle Kingdom. The rulers of this era developed Egypt's religious and political institutions in ways that increased state power, creating the conditions for greater prosperity and trade.

Religion and Rule Spiritual and worldly powers once again reinforced each other in Egypt. Gods and rulers together replaced the chaos that people believed had brought drought and despair. Amenemhet I (1985–1955 BCE), first pharaoh of the long-lasting Twelfth Dynasty (1985–1795 BCE), elevated a formerly less significant god, Amun, to prominence. The king capitalized on the god's name, which means "hidden," to convey a sense of his own invisible omnipresence throughout the realm. Because Amun's attributes of air and breath were largely intangible, believers in other gods were able to embrace his cult. Amun's cosmic power appealed to people in areas that had recently been impoverished.

The pharaoh's elevation of the cult of Amun unified the kingdom and brought even more power to Amun and the pharaoh. Consequently, Amun eclipsed all the other gods of Thebes. Merging with the formerly omnipotent sun god Re, the deity now was called Amun-Re: the king of the gods. Because the power of the gods and kings was intertwined, the pharaoh as Amun's earthly champion enjoyed enhanced legitimacy as the supreme ruler.

The massive temple complex dedicated to Amun-Re offers evidence of the gods' and the pharaoh's joint power. Middle Kingdom rulers tapped into their kingdom's renewed bounty, their subjects' loyalty, and the work of untold commoners and enslaved peoples to build Amun-Re's temple complex at Thebes (present-day Luxor). For more than 12,000 years, Egyptians and the people they enslaved toiled to erect monumental gates, enormous courtyards, and other structures in what was arguably the largest, longest-lasting public works project ever undertaken. Blending the pastoral ideals of herders into the institutions of their settled and hierarchical territorial state, Middle Kingdom rulers also nurtured a cult of the pharaoh as the good shepherd whose prime responsibility was to care for his human flock. In a building inscription at Heliopolis, a pharaoh named Senusret III from the nineteenth century BCE claims to have been appointed by Amun as "shepherd of the land." And 500 years later, in the fourteenth century BCE, Amenhotep III's building inscription at Karnak describes him as "the good shepherd for all people." By instituting charities, offering homage to gods at the palace to ensure regular floodwaters, and performing ceremonies to honor their own generosity, the pharaohs portrayed themselves as these shepherds. In these inscriptions and in imagery (recall the shepherd's crook as one of the pharaoh's symbols), pharaohs exploited distinctly pastoralist symbolism. As a result, the cult of Amun-Re was both a tool of political power and a source of spiritual meaning for the different peoples of the blended territorial state of Egypt.

Hypostyle Hall The precinct of Amun-Re in the Karnak temple complex (near modern-day Luxor) was made up of a series of gates, courts, and temples that were built over time by many pharaohs from the Middle and New Kingdoms. The lofty, inscribed columns of the Great Hypostyle Hall (pictured here), which was built by Ramses II in the thirteenth century BCE, offer stunning evidence of the construction projects that pharaohs built to underscore their power and their relationship to the divine.

Climate Change and the Collapse of River-Basin Societies

The three great river-basin societies discussed in Chapter 2—Egypt, Mesopotamia, and the Indus Valley—collapsed at around the same time. The collapse in Egypt and Mesopotamia was almost simultaneous (roughly between 2200 BCE and 2100 BCE). In contrast, while the collapse was delayed in the Indus Valley for approximately 200 years, when it came, it virtually wiped out the Harappan state and culture. At

River-Basin Society	Date of Collapse	Climatological Evidence	Archaeological Evidence	Literary Evidence
Egypt	The Old Kingdom collapsed and ushered in a period of notable political instability, the First Intermediate Period (2181–2055 BCE).	Sedimentation studies reveal markedly lower Nile floods and an invasion of sand dunes into cultivated areas.	Many of the sacred sites of the Old Kingdom and much of their artwork are believed to have been destroyed in this period due to political chaos.	An abundant literary record is full of tales of woe. Poetry and steles call attention to famine, starvation, low Nile floods, and even cannibalism.
Mesopotamia	The last effective ruler of the Kingdom of Akkad (2334–2193 BCE) was Naram Sin (r. 2254–2218 BCE).	Around 2100 BCE, inhabitants abruptly abandoned the Khabur drainage basin, whose soil samples reveal marked aridity as determined by the existence of fewer earthworm holes and wind-blown pellets.	Tell Leilan and other sites indicate that the large cities of this region began to shrink around 2200 BCE and were soon abandoned, and remained unoccupied for 300 years.	Later Ur III scribes described the influx of northern "barbarians" and noted the construction of a wall, known as the Repeller of the Amorites, to keep these northerners out.
Indus Valley and the Harappan society	Many of the Harappan peoples migrated eastward, beginning around 1900 BCE, leaving this region largely empty of people.	Hydroclimatic reconstructions show that precipitation began to decrease around 3000 BCE, reaching a low in 2000 BCE, at which point the Himalayan rivers stopped incising. Around 1700 BCE, the Ghaggar-Hakra rivers dried up.	Major Harappan urban sites began to shrink in size and lose their urban character between 1900 and 1700 BCE.	There is no literary source material because the Harappan script has still to be deciphered.

first, historians focused on political, economic, and social causes, stressing bad rulers, nomadic incursions, political infighting, population migrations, and the decline of long-distance trade. In more recent times, however, a group of scientists that included paleobiologists, climatologists, sedimentationists, and archaeologists has studied these societies and found convincing evidence that a truly radical change in the climate—a 200-year-long drought spreading across the Afro-Eurasian landmass—was a powerful factor in the collapse of these cultures. But how can these researchers know so much about the climate 4,000 years ago? The following table assembles the evidence for their assertions, drawing on their scholarly studies of Egypt, Mesopotamia, and the Indus Valley.

Questions for Analysis

- How do the different kinds of evidence—climatological, archaeological, and literary—for each river-basin society's collapse at the end of the third millennium BCE compare with one another, and how do they compare across the different regions?
- How might the changes suggested by these different types of evidence have laid the groundwork for the second-millennium BCE development of territorial states described in this chapter?
- What additional evidence would you want to see in order to be able to make arguments for a global climate crisis around 2000 BCE?

Explore Further

Behringer, Wolfgang, A Cultural History of Climate (2010).

Bell, Barbara, "The Dark Ages in Ancient History," American Journal of Archaeology 75 (January 1971): 1–26.

Butzer, Karl W., "Collapse, Environment, and Society," Proceedings of the National Academy of Science 109 (March 2012): 3632–39.

Cullen, H. M., et al., "Climate Change and the Collapse of the Akkadian Empire," Geology 28 (April 2000): 379–82.

Giosan, Liviu, et al., "Fluvial Landscapes of the Harappan Civilization," Proceedings of the National Academy of Science 109 (June 2012): E1688–94.

Weiss, Max, et al., "The Genesis and Collapse of Third Millennium North Mesopotamian Civilization," Science, New Series, 261 (August 20, 1993): 995–1004.

Luxury Imports This chest amulet from Tutankhamun's fourteenth-century BCE tomb highlights the use of luxury imports in Egyptian religious and visual culture. Lapis lazuli, turquoise, and carnelian from the east and gold from the south were combined to create uniquely Egyptian symbolism, including a falcon flanked with cobras and topped with an eye of Horus, with papyrus and lotus flowers dangling below. Scientists recently determined that the yellow glass that makes up the scarab forming the falcon's body contains reidite, a mineral that can be formed only when a meteorite strikes and melts the desert sand.

Merchants and Expanding Trade Networks Prosperity gave rise to an urban class of merchants and professionals who used their wealth and skills to carve out new opportunities for themselves. They indulged in leisure activities such as formal banquets with professional dancers and singers, and they honed their skills in hunting, fowling, and fishing. In a sign of their upward mobility and autonomy, some members of the middle class constructed tombs filled with representations of the material goods they would use in the afterlife as well as the occupations that would engage them for eternity. This new merchant class did not rely on the king's generosity and took burial privileges formerly reserved for the royal family and a few powerful nobles.

As they centralized power and consolidated their territorial state, Egyptians also expanded their trade networks. (See Map 3.2.) Because the floodplains had long since been deforested, the Egyptians needed to import massive quantities of wood by ship. Most prized were the cedars from Byblos (a city in the land soon known as Phoenicia, roughly present-day Lebanon), which were crafted into furniture and coffins. Commercial networks extended south through the Red Sea to present-day Ethiopia and were used to import precious metals, ivory, livestock, and exotic animals such as panthers and monkeys. They brought enslaved people as well. Expeditions to the Sinai Peninsula searched for copper and turquoise. Egyptians looked south for gold, which they prized for personal and architectural ornamentation. To acquire it, they crossed into Nubia, where they met stiff resistance. One Egyptian official from the reign of Amenemhet II (the third pharaoh of the long-lasting Twelfth Dynasty) bragged about his expeditions into the Sinai and south into Nubia: "I forced the (Nubian) chiefs to wash gold. . . . I went overthrowing by the fear of the Lord of the Two Lands [i.e., the pharaoh]." Eventually, the Egyptians colonized Nubia to broaden their trade routes and secure these coveted resources. As part of Egyptian colonization southward, a series of forts extended as far south as the second cataract of the Nile River (just south of the modern-day border between Egypt and Sudan).

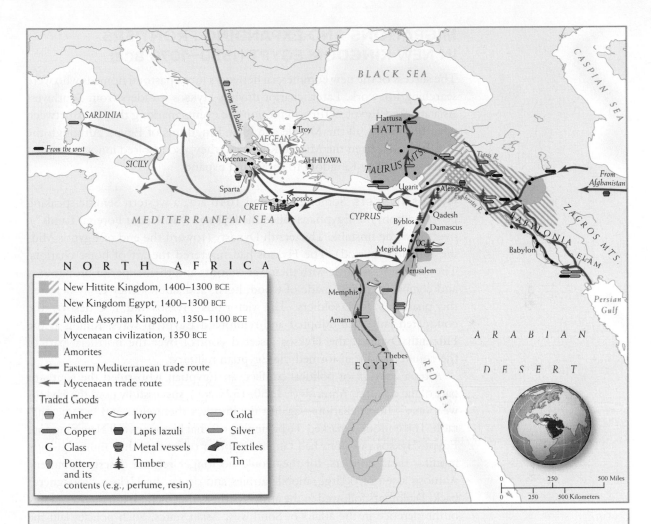

Legend

/// New Hittite Kingdom, 1400–1300 BCE

New Kingdom Egypt, 1400–1300 BCE

/// Middle Assyrian Kingdom, 1350–1100 BCE

Mycenaean civilization, 1350 BCE

Amorites

← Eastern Mediterranean trade route

← Mycenaean trade route

Traded Goods

- Amber
- Copper
- G Glass
- Pottery and its contents (e.g., perfume, resin)
- Ivory
- Lapis lazuli
- Metal vessels
- Timber
- Gold
- Silver
- Textiles
- Tin

Map 3.2 Territorial States and Trade Routes in Southwest Asia, North Africa, and the Eastern Mediterranean, 1500–1350 BCE

Trade in many commodities brought the societies of the Mediterranean Sea and Southwest Asia into increasingly closer contact.

- What were the major trade routes and the major trading states in Southwest Asia, North Africa, and the eastern Mediterranean during this time?
- What were the major trade goods? Which regions appear to have had more, and more unique, resources than the others?
- What did each region need from the others? What did each region have to offer in exchange for the goods it needed?

MIGRATIONS AND EXPANDING FRONTIERS IN NEW KINGDOM EGYPT (1550–1070 BCE)

The success of the new commercial networks lured pastoral nomads who were searching for work. Later, chariot-driving Hyksos invaders from Southwest Asia attacked Egypt, setting in motion the events marking the break between what historians call the Middle and New Kingdoms of Egypt. Although the invaders challenged the Middle Kingdom, they also inspired innovations that enabled the New Kingdom to thrive and expand.

Hyksos Invaders Sometime around 1640 BCE, a western Semitic-speaking people, whom the Egyptians called the **Hyksos** ("Rulers of Foreign Lands"), overthrew the unstable Thirteenth Dynasty (toward the end of Egypt's Middle Kingdom period). The Hyksos had mastered the art of horse chariots. Thundering into battle with their war chariots and their superior bronze axes and composite bows (made of wood, horn, and sinew), they easily defeated the pharaoh's foot soldiers. The victorious Hyksos did not destroy the conquered land, but adopted and reinforced Egyptian ways. Ruling as the Fifteenth Dynasty, the Hyksos asserted control over the northern part of the country and transformed the Egyptian military.

After a century of political conflict, an Egyptian who ruled the southern part of the country, Ahmosis (r. 1550–1525 BCE), successfully used the Hyksos weaponry—horse chariots—against the invaders themselves and became pharaoh. This conquest marked the beginning of what historians call New Kingdom Egypt. Hyksos invasions had taught Egyptian rulers that they must vigilantly monitor their frontiers, for they could no longer rely on deserts as buffers. Ahmosis assembled large, mobile armies and drove the Hyksos "foreigners" back. Diplomats followed in the army's path, as the pharaoh initiated a strategy of interference in the affairs of Southwest Asian states. Such policies laid the groundwork for statecraft and an international diplomatic system that future Egyptian kings used to dominate the eastern Mediterranean world.

Migrations and invasions introduced new techniques that the Egyptians adopted to consolidate their power. These included bronze working (which the Egyptians had not perfected), an improved potter's wheel, and a vertical loom. South Asian animals such as humped zebu cattle, as well as vegetable and fruit crops, now appeared on the banks of the Nile for the first time. Other significant innovations pertained to war, such as the horse and chariot, the composite bow, the scimitar (a sword with a curved blade), and other weapons from western Eurasia. These weapons transformed the Egyptian army from a standing infantry to a high-speed, mobile, and deadly fighting force. Egyptian troops extended the military frontier as far south as the fourth cataract of the Nile River (in northern modern-day Sudan), and the kingdom now stretched from the Mediterranean shores to Ethiopia.

Hyksos
Chariot-driving, axe- and composite-bow-wielding, Semitic-speaking people (their name means "rulers of foreign lands"), who invaded Egypt, overthrew the Thirteenth Dynasty, set up their own rule over Egypt, and were expelled by Ahmosis to begin the period known as New Kingdom Egypt.

Expanding Frontiers By the beginning of the New Kingdom, the territorial state of Egypt was projecting its interests outward: it defined itself as a superior, cosmopolitan society with an efficient bureaucracy run by competent and socially mobile individuals. Paintings on the walls of Vizier Rekhmire's tomb from the mid-fifteenth century BCE record the wide-ranging tribute from distant lands that he received on behalf of the pharaoh, including a veritable menagerie: cattle, a giraffe, an elephant, a panther, baboons, and monkeys. The collected taxes that are enumerated in the accompanying inscriptions included offerings of gold, silver, linen, bows, grain, and honey. Rekhmire's tomb, with its paintings, tax lists, and instructions for how to rule, offers a prime example of how the bureaucracy managed the expanding Egyptian frontiers. Pushing the transnational connectivity even further, it has been argued that inscriptions and paintings from Rekhmire's tomb, together with other tomb paintings, show that Keftiu (people from Minoan Crete), along with Hittites from Asia Minor, Syrians from the Levant, and Nubians from the south, may have gathered for some major multinational event in Egypt, like a Sed festival.

As mentioned above, Egypt expanded its control southward into Nubia, as a source of gold, exotic raw materials, and manpower. Historians identify this southward expansion most strongly with the reign of Egypt's most powerful woman ruler, Hatshepsut. She served as regent for her young stepson, Thutmosis III, who came to the throne in 1479 BCE when his father—Hatshepsut's half brother and husband—Thutmosis II died. When her stepson was seven years old, Hatshepsut proclaimed herself "king," ruling as co-regent until

Exotic Tribute From the sumptuously painted tomb of the vizier Rekhmire (Theban Tomb 110), this scene depicts a range of tribute goods brought to Thutmosis III. Tribute from Nubia included oxen, dogs, and a giraffe (with a monkey clinging to its neck) and, from Syria, a baby elephant, a brown bear, horses, and a chariot. Other gifts not pictured here were gold and silver vessels from the Keftiu (of Minoan Crete) as well as incense and exotic animals from Punt (a region to the south of Egypt that scholars have not yet positively identified, likely located on the African coast of the Red Sea in modern Ethiopia and Somalia).

Hatshepsut The only powerful queen of Egyptian pharaonic history was Hatshepsut, seen here in two portraits created during her reign (1479–1458 BCE). In the earlier statue (*left*), a young, feminine Hatshepsut wears a masculine headdress and kilt but is labeled in the accompanying inscription as a "perfect goddess" and "daughter of Re." Because a woman on the throne of Egypt would offend the basic principles of order (*ma'at*), Hatshepsut usually portrayed herself as a man, especially late in her reign, as in the later image here (*right*). This masculine portrayal was reinforced by the use of male determinatives in the hieroglyphic renditions of her name.

she died two decades later. During her reign there was little military activity, but trade contacts into the Levant and Mediterranean and southward into Nubia flourished. When he ultimately came to power, Thutmosis III (r. 1479–1425 BCE) launched another expansionist phase, northeastward into the Levant. The famed Battle of Megiddo, the first recorded chariot battle in history, took place twenty-three years into his reign. Thutmosis III's army at Megiddo, including nearly 1,000 war chariots, defeated his adversaries and established an Egyptian presence in Palestine. The growth phase launched by Thutmosis III would continue for 200 years. Having evolved into a strong, expanding territorial state, Egypt was now poised to engage in commercial, political, and cultural exchanges with the rest of the region.

Territorial States in Southwest Asia

Core Objectives

COMPARE the varied processes by which territorial states formed and interacted with each other in Egypt and Southeast Asia.

Climate change and invasions by migrants also transformed the societies of Southwest Asia, and new territorial kingdoms arose in Mesopotamia and Anatolia (modern-day Iraq and Turkey, respectively). Here, as in Egypt, the drought at the end of the third millennium BCE was devastating. Harvests shrank, the price of basic goods rose, and the social order broke down. In southern Mesopotamia, cities were invaded by transhumant herders (not chariot-driving nomads) who sought grazing lands to replace those swallowed up by expanding deserts. A millennium of intense cultivation, combined with severe drought, brought disastrous consequences: rich soil in the river basin was depleted of nutrients; salt water from the Persian Gulf seeped into the marshy deltas, contaminating the water table; and the main branch of the Euphrates River shifted to the west. Many cities lost access to their fertile agrarian hinterlands and withered away. Mesopotamia's center of political and economic gravity shifted northward, away from the silted, marshy deltas of the southern heartland.

As scarcities mounted, transhumant peoples began to press in upon settled communities more closely. Mesopotamian city dwellers were scornful of the rustic migrants, whom they called **Amorites** ("westerners"), invading their cities. While these transhumant herders may have been western "foreigners"

Amorites
Name, which means "westerners," used by Mesopotamian urbanites to describe the transhumant herders who began to migrate into their cities in the late third millennium BCE.

to those living in the urban centers of Mesopotamia, they were not strangers. These rural folk had wintered in villages close to the rivers to water their animals, which grazed on fallow fields. In the scorching summer, they retreated to the cooler highlands. Their flocks provided wools, leather, bones, and tendons to the artisan-based industries of the urban centers of Mesopotamia. In return, the herders purchased crafted products and agricultural goods. They also paid taxes, served as warriors, and labored on public works projects, but had few political rights within city-states.

Around 2000 BCE, Amorites from the western desert joined allies from the Iranian plateau to bring down the Third Dynasty of Ur, which had controlled all of Mesopotamia and southwestern Iran for more than a century. These Amorites and their allies founded the Old Babylonian kingdom, centered on the southern Mesopotamian city of Babylon, near modern-day Baghdad. Other territorial states arose in Mesopotamia in the millennium that followed, sometimes with one dominating the entire floodplain and sometimes with multiple powerful kingdoms vying for territory. As in Egypt, a century of political instability followed the demise of the old city-state models. Here, too, pastoralists played a role in the restoration of order, increasing the wealth of the regions they conquered and helping the cultural realm to flourish. The Old Babylonian kingdom expanded trade and founded territorial states with dynastic ruling families and well-defined frontiers. Pastoralists also played a key role in the development of territorial kingdoms in Anatolia.

MESOPOTAMIAN KINGSHIP

The new rulers of Mesopotamia changed the organization of the state and promoted a distinctive culture, as well as expanding trade. Herders-turned-urbanite-rulers mixed their own nomadic social organization with that of the once-dominant city-states to create the structures necessary to support much larger territorial states. The basic social organization of the Amorites, out of which the territorial states in Mesopotamia evolved, was tribal (dominated by a ruling chief) and clan based (claiming descent from a common ancestor). Over time, chieftains drew on personal charisma and battlefield prowess to become kings; kings allied with the merchant class and nobility for bureaucratic and financial support; and kingship became hereditary.

Over the centuries, powerful Mesopotamian kings expanded their territories and subdued weaker neighbors, inducing them to pay tribute in luxury goods, raw materials, and manpower as part of a broad confederation of city-states under the kings' protection. Control over military resources (metals for weaponry and, later, herds of horses for pulling chariots) was necessary for dominance. The ruler's charisma also mattered. Unlike the more institutionalized Egyptian leadership, Mesopotamian kingdoms could vacillate from strong to weak, depending on the leader's personality.

Hammurabi's Code The inscription on the shaft of Hammurabi's Code is carved on a diorite stele in the Akkadian language using a beautiful and orderly rendition of cuneiform script. At the top of the stele, which is more than 7 feet tall, the seated sun god, Shamash, bestows authority on Hammurabi, illustrating the point of the code's prologue and epilogue, which describe Hammurabi's god-given authority.

Hammurabi's Code
Legal code created by Hammurabi (r. 1792–1750 BCE). The code divided society into three classes—"free," "dependent," and "slave"—each with distinct rights and responsibilities.

The most famous Mesopotamian ruler of this period was Hammurabi (r. 1792–1750 BCE). Continuously struggling with powerful neighbors, he sought to centralize state authority and to create a new legal order. Using diplomatic and military skills to become the strongest king in Mesopotamia, he made Babylon his capital. He implemented a new system to consolidate power, appointing regional governors to manage outlying provinces and to deal with local elites. Like the Egyptian pharaohs of the Middle Kingdom, Hammurabi was shepherd and patriarch of his people, responsible for proper preparation of the fields and irrigation canals and for his followers' well-being. Balancing elite privileges with the needs of the lower classes, the king secured his power. **Hammurabi's Code**, with its "eye-for-an-eye," if/then, reciprocity of crime and punishment, is an example of this balancing act. Its compilation of 282 edicts outlines crimes and their punishments. The laws dealt with theft, murder, professional negligence, and many other matters of daily life. The laws make it clear that governing public matters was man's work and upholding a just order was the supreme charge of rulers. Whereas the gods' role in ordering the world was distant, the king was directly in command of ordering relations among people. Accordingly, the code elaborated in exhaustive detail the social rules that would ensure the kingdom's peace through its primary instrument—the family. The code outlined the rights and privileges of fathers, wives, and children. The father's duty was to treat his kin as the ruler would treat his subjects, with strict authority and care. Adultery was harshly punished, resulting in the drowning of the adulterous wife and her lover, unless the husband or king intervened.

The code also divided the people in the Babylonian kingdom into three classes: "free persons," "dependents," and "slaves." Each class had an assigned value and distinct rights and responsibilities. While its eye-for-an-eye, tooth-for-a-tooth reciprocity is remarkable, the code also made it clear that Babylonia was a stratified society, in which some persons (and eyes and teeth!) were more valued than others. Punishments for offenses were determined by the status of the committer and that of the one who suffered. The code itself was inscribed in the last years of Hammurabi's reign, after his conquests had created a larger state, and represented a way to celebrate the king's achievements.

Power and Culture Mesopotamian rulers commissioned public art and works projects and promoted institutions of learning. To dispel their image as rustic foreigners and to demonstrate their familiarity with the region's core values, new Mesopotamian rulers valued the oral tales and written records of the earlier Sumerians and Akkadians. Scribes copied the ancient texts and preserved their tradition. Royal hymns portrayed the king as a legendary hero of quasi-divine status.

Heroic narratives about legendary founders, based on traditional stories about the rulers of ancient Uruk, legitimized the new rulers. The most

Gilgamesh in Image and Text *Left*: This terra-cotta plaque is one of the few visual depictions of Gilgamesh (on the left wielding the knife) and his sidekick, Enkidu. It illustrates one of the episodes in their shared adventures, the killing of Humwawa, the monster of the Cedar Forest. The style of the plaque indicates that it was made during the Old Babylonian period, between 2000 and 1600 BCE. *Right*: The text of the Gilgamesh epic was preserved on tablets of baked clay, like the now-fragmentary tablets shown here, which were found in the seventh-century BCE library of the Neo-Assyrian king Ashurbanipal. The *Epic of Gilgamesh* had enduring appeal for those in Mesopotamia, who passed the story along for millennia, first orally, then in images like the one here, then in text.

famous tale was the *Epic of Gilgamesh*, one of the earliest surviving works of literature. Originally composed more than a millennium earlier, in the Sumerian language, this epic narrated the heroism of the legendary king of early Uruk, Gilgamesh. This epic is probably best known for the passage in which Gilgamesh seeks out advice from Utnapishtim, the survivor of a terrible flood, in a story that resonates with that of Noah from Genesis in the Hebrew scriptures. Utnapishtim's flood story, however, is just one part of Gilgamesh's epic, which describes the title character's rivalry and, later, friendship with Enkidu and his quest for immortality after his friend Enkidu's death. Preserved by scribes in royal courts through centuries, the epic offers an example of how the Mesopotamian kings invested in cultural production to explain important political relations, unify their people, and distinguish their subjects from those of other kingdoms.

Trade and the Rise of a Private Economy Another feature of the territorial state in Mesopotamia was its shift away from economic activity dominated by the city-state and toward independent private ventures. Mesopotamian rulers designated private entrepreneurs rather than state bureaucrats to collect taxes. People paid taxes in the form of commodities such as grain, vegetables, and wool, which the entrepreneurs exchanged for silver. They, in turn, passed on the silver to the state after pocketing a percentage for their profit. This process generated more private economic activity and wealth, and more revenues for the state.

Mesopotamia was a crossroads for caravans leading east and west. Peace and good governance allowed trade to flourish. The ability to move exotic foodstuffs, valuable minerals, textiles, and luxury goods across Southwest Asia won Mesopotamian merchants and entrepreneurs a privileged position as middlemen. Merchants also used sea routes for trade with the Indus Valley. Before 2000 BCE, mariners had charted the waters of the Red Sea, the Gulf of Aden, the Persian Gulf, and much of the Arabian Sea. And during the second millennium BCE, shipbuilders figured out how to construct larger vessels and rig them with towering masts and woven sails—creating seaworthy craft that could carry bulkier loads. Shipbuilding required wood (particularly cedar from Phoenicia) as well as wool and other fibers (from the pastoral hinterlands) for sails. Such reliance on imported materials reflected a growing regional economic specialization and an expanding sphere of interaction across western Afro-Eurasia. The benefits and risks of trade in Mesopotamia are evident from royal edicts of debt annulment (to help merchants who had overstretched) and formalized commercial rules governing taxes and duties. In trade and other exchanges, Mesopotamia became a crucial link between Egypt, Anatolia, and southwestern Iran. Centralized control of the region facilitated a thriving trade in such precious commodities as horses, chariots, and lapis lazuli, which was exchanged for gold, wood, and ivory.

THE OLD AND NEW HITTITE KINGDOMS (1800–1200 BCE)

Chariot warriors known as the Hittites established territorial kingdoms in Anatolia, to the northwest of Mesopotamia. Anatolia was an overland crossroads that linked the Black and Mediterranean Seas. Like other plateaus of Afro-Eurasia, it had high tablelands, was easy to traverse, and was hospitable to large herding communities. During the third millennium BCE, Anatolia had become home to numerous communities run by native elites. These societies combined pastoral ways of life, agriculture, and urban commercial centers. Before 2000 BCE, peoples speaking Indo-European languages began to enter the plateau, probably coming from the steppe lands north and west of the Black Sea. The newcomers lived in fortified settlements and often engaged in regional warfare, and their numbers grew. Splintered into competing clans, they fought for regional supremacy. They also borrowed extensively from the cultural developments of the Southwest Asian urban cultures, especially those of Mesopotamia.

In the early second millennium BCE, the chariot warrior groups of Anatolia grew powerful on the commercial activity that passed through their region. Chief among them were the **Hittites**. Hittite lancers and archers rode chariots across vast expanses to plunder their neighbors and demand taxes and tribute. In the seventeenth century BCE, the Hittite leader Hattusilis I unified these chariot aristocracies, secured his base in Anatolia, defeated the kingdom that controlled northern Syria, and then campaigned along the

Hittites

An Anatolian chariot warrior group that spread east to northern Syria, though they eventually faced weaknesses in their own homeland. Rooted in their capital at Hattusa, they interacted with contemporary states both violently (as at the Battle of Qadesh against Egypt) and peacefully (as in the correspondence of the Amarna letters).

Akhenaten and Aten Akhenaten, one of the correspondents in the Amarna letters that reveal so much about international diplomacy among the community of major powers, also forged a revolutionary, if short-lived, change in Egyptian religion. His elevation of the sun disk, Aten, to supreme authority displaced the long-standing power of the god Amun-Re and his priestly elite. On this relief carving, the sun disk, Aten, beams down on Akhenaten and his family with rays that end in hands holding ankhs, the Egyptian symbol for life. This intimate scene depicts Akhenaten lovingly cradling his young daughter across from his wife, Nefertiti, who holds their other two daughters.

Euphrates River. His grandson and successor, Mursilis I, sacked Babylon in 1595 BCE. The Hittites ultimately built their capital at Hattusa, in central Anatolia, complete with massive walls, a monumental gate with lions carved into it, multiple temples and granaries, and a palace. Near Hattusa, the rock-cut sanctuary of Yazilikaya contains reliefs of gods and goddesses marching in procession, as well as images of Hittite kings.

Two centuries after the successes of Hattusilis I, the Hittites enjoyed another period of political and military success. In 1274 BCE, they fought the Egyptians at the Battle of Qadesh (in modern Syria), the largest and best-documented chariot battle of antiquity. Both sides claimed victory. The treaty that records reciprocal promises of nonaggression by the Egyptians and Hittites nearly fifteen years after the battle is the oldest surviving peace treaty, and a replica of it is displayed at the United Nations. Soon after Qadesh, the Egyptian forces withdrew from the region. Hittite control—spanning from Anatolia across the region between the Nile and Mesopotamia—was central to balancing power among the territorial states that grew up in the river valleys.

A COMMUNITY OF MAJOR POWERS (1400–1200 BCE)

Between 1400 and 1200 BCE, the major territorial states of Southwest Asia and Egypt perfected instruments of international diplomacy. A cache of 350 letters, referred to by modern scholars as the Amarna letters after the present-day Egyptian village of Amarna, where they were discovered, offers intimate views of the interactions among the powers of Egypt and Southwest Asia. The letters include communications between Egyptian pharaohs and various leaders of Southwest Asia, including Babylonian and Hittite kings. Powerful rulers referred to one another as brothers, suggesting not only a high degree of equality but also a desire to foster friendship among large states. Trade linked the regimes and was so vital to the economic and political well-being of rulers that if a commercial mission was plundered, the ruler of the area in which the robbery occurred assumed responsibility and offered compensation to the injured parties.

Because trade was so important, the leaders of these powers settled their differences through treaties and diplomatic negotiations rather than on the battlefield. Each state knew its place in the political pecking order. It was an order that depended on constant diplomacy, based on communication, treaties, marriages, and the exchange of gifts. As nomadic peoples combined with settled urban polities to create new territorial states in Egypt, Mesopotamia, and Anatolia, and as those territorial states came into contact with one another through trade, this diplomacy was vital to maintaining the interactions in this community of major powers in Southwest Asia.

Nomads and the Indus River Valley

Core Objectives

DESCRIBE the impact of transhumant herders and pastoral nomads on settled communities in Egypt, Southwest Asia, and the Indus River valley.

Vedic peoples

Indo-European nomadic group who migrated from the steppes of Inner Asia around 1500 BCE into the Indus basin, on to the Ganges River valley, and then as far south as the Deccan plateau, bringing with them their distinctive religious ideas (Vedas), Sanskrit, and domesticated horses.

Compared with those in Egypt and Mesopotamia, territorial states emerged more slowly in the Indus River valley. Late in the third millennium BCE, drought ravaged the Indus River valley as it did other regions. By 1700 BCE, the population of the old Harappan heartland had plummeted. Here, too, around 1500 BCE, yet another group of nomadic peoples, calling themselves Aryans ("respected ones"), emerged from their homelands in the steppes of Inner Eurasia. In contrast with developments in Egypt, Anatolia, and Mesopotamia, these pastoral nomads did not immediately establish large territorial states. Crossing the northern highlands of central Asia through the Hindu Kush, they descended into the fertile Indus River basin (see Map 3.3) with large flocks of cattle and horses. They sang chants from the Rig-Veda as they sacrificed some of their livestock to their gods. Known collectively as the Vedas ("knowledge"), these hymns served as the most sacred texts for the newcomers, who have been known ever since as the **Vedic peoples**. Sanskrit, the spoken language of the Vedic peoples, is one of the earliest known Indo-European languages and a source for virtually all the European languages, including Greek, Latin, English, French, and German.

Like other nomads from the northern steppe, Vedic peoples brought domesticated animals—especially horses, which pulled their chariots and established their military superiority. Not only were they superb horse

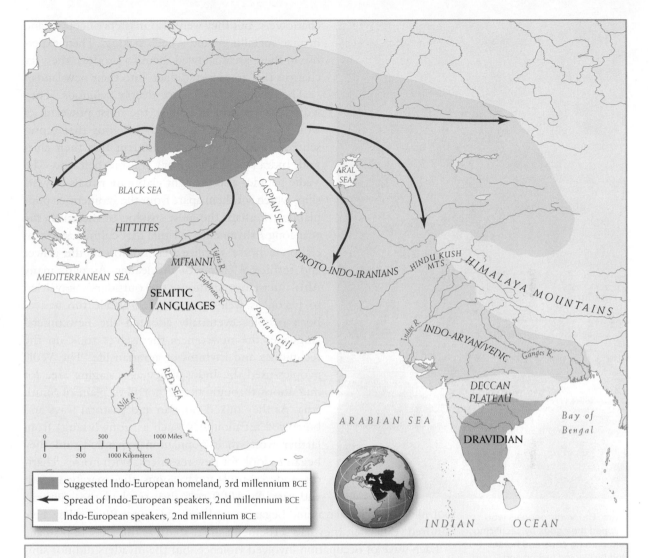

Map 3.3 Indo-European Migrations, Second Millennium BCE

Legend:
- Suggested Indo-European homeland, 3rd millennium BCE
- Spread of Indo-European speakers, 2nd millennium BCE
- Indo-European speakers, 2nd millennium BCE

Map 3.3 Indo-European Migrations, Second Millennium BCE

One of the most important developments of the second millennium BCE was the movement of Indo-European peoples.

- Where did the Indo-European migration originate?
- Where did Indo-European migrations spread to during this time?
- How do these migrations relate to the Afro-Eurasian developments that are traced in this chapter?

Indra The Vedic peoples worshipped their gods by sacrificing and burning cows and horses and by singing hymns and songs, but they never built temples or sculpted idols. Therefore, we do not know how they envisioned Indra and their other gods. However, when Buddhists started to make images of Buddha in the early centuries CE, they also sculpted Indra and other Vedic deities. This image of Indra riding his elephant, Airavata, dates to the second century BCE and was found in Bhaja Cave 19 on the northwest coast of India.

charioteers, but they were also masters of copper and bronze metallurgy and wheel making. Their expertise in these areas allowed them to produce the very chariots that transported them into their new lands.

The Vedic peoples were deeply religious. They worshipped a host of deities, the most powerful of which were the sky god and the gods that represented horses. They were confident that their chief god, Indra (the deity of war), was on their side. The Vedic peoples also brought elaborate rituals of worship, which set them apart from the indigenous populations. Perhaps the most striking of these was the year-long Ashvamedha, a ritual that culminated in an elaborate horse sacrifice that reinforced the power and territorial claims of the leader. As with many Afro-Eurasian migrations, the outsiders' arrival led to fusion as well as to conflict. While the native-born peoples eventually adopted the newcomers' language, the newcomers themselves took up the techniques and rhythms of agrarian life. The Vedic peoples used the Indus Valley as a staging area for migrations throughout the northern plain of South Asia. As they mixed agrarian and pastoral ways and borrowed technologies (such as ironworking) from farther west, their population expanded and they began to look for new resources. With horses, chariots, and iron tools and weapons, they marched south and east. By 1000 BCE, they reached the southern foothills of the Himalayas and began to settle in the Ganges River valley. Five hundred years later, they had settlements as far south as the Deccan plateau.

Each wave of occupation involved violence, but the invaders did not simply dominate the indigenous peoples. Instead, the confrontations led them to embrace many of the ways of the vanquished. In particular, the Vedic newcomers were impressed with inhabitants' farming skills and knowledge of seasonal weather. These they adapted even as they continued to expand their territory. They moved into huts constructed from mud, bamboo, and reeds. They refined the already sophisticated production of beautiful carnelian stone beads, and they further aided commerce by devising standardized weights. In addition to raising domesticated animals, they sowed wheat and rye on the Indus plain, and they learned to plant rice in the marshy lands of the Ganges River valley. Later they mastered the use of plows with iron blades, an innovation that transformed the agrarian base of South Asia. This turn to settled agriculture was a major shift for the nomadic pastoral Vedic peoples. After all, their staple foods had always been dairy products and meat, and they were used to measuring their wealth in livestock (horses were most valuable, and cows were more valuable than sheep). Moreover, because they could not breed their prized horses in South Asia's semitropical climate, they initiated a brisk import trade from central and Southwest Asia.

As the Vedic peoples filled the relative void left by the collapse of the Harappans and adapted to their new environment, their initial political organization took a somewhat different course from that of Southwest Asia. Whereas competitive kingdoms dominated the landscape in Southwest Asia, competitive and balanced regimes were slower to emerge in South Asia. The result was a slower process of political integration.

The Shang Territorial State in East Asia

China's first major territorial state combined features of earlier Longshan culture with new technologies and religious practices. Climate change affected East Asia much as it had central and Southwest Asia. Stories written on bamboo strips and later collected into what historians call the "Bamboo Annals" tell of a time at the end of the legendary Xia dynasty when the sun dimmed and frost and ice appeared in the summer, followed by heavy rainfall, flooding, and then a long drought. According to Chinese mythology, the first ruler of the Shang dynasty defeated a despotic Xia king and then offered to sacrifice himself so that the drought would end. This leader, Tang, survived to found the territorial state called Shang around 1600 BCE in northeastern China.

The Shang state was built on four elements that the Longshan peoples had already introduced: a metal industry based on copper; pottery making; walled towns; and divination using animal bones. To these Longshan foundations, the Shang dynasty added hereditary rulers whose power derived from their relation to ancestors and gods; written records; large-scale metallurgy (especially in bronze); tribute; and various rituals.

Core Objectives

COMPARE state formation in Shang China and in Mesopotamia and Egypt.

STATE FORMATION

A combination of these preexisting Longshan strengths and Shang innovations produced a strong Shang territorial state and a wealthy and powerful elite, noted for its intellectual achievements and aesthetic sensibilities.

Shang kings used a personalized style of rule, making regular trips around the country to meet, hunt, and conduct military campaigns. With no rival territorial states on its immediate periphery, the Shang state did not create a strongly defended, permanent capital, but rather moved its capital as the

Bronze At the height of the Shang state, circa 1200 BCE, its rulers erected massive palaces at the capital of Yin, which required bronze foundries for their wine and food vessels. In these foundries, skilled workers produced bronze weapons, ritual objects, and elaborate ceremonial drinking and eating vessels, like the one pictured.

frontier expanded and contracted. Bureaucrats used written records to oversee the large and expanding population of the Shang state.

Advanced Shang metalworking—the beginnings of which appeared in northwestern China at pre-Shang sites dating as early as 1800 BCE—was vital to the Shang territorial state. Shang bronze work included weapons, fittings for chariots, and ritual vessels. Because copper and tin were available from the North China plain, only short-distance trade was necessary to obtain the resources that a bronze culture needed. (See Map 3.4.) Shang bronze-working technique involved the use of hollow clay molds to hold the molten metal alloy, which, when removed after the liquid had cooled and solidified, produced firm bronze objects. The casting of modular components that artisans could assemble later promoted increased production and permitted the elite to make extravagant use of bronze vessels for burials. The bronze industry of this period shows the high level not only of material culture (in the practical function of the physical objects) but also of cultural development (in the aesthetic sense of beauty and taste conveyed by the choice of form). Since Shang metalworking required extensive mining, it necessitated a large labor force, efficient casting, and a reproducible artistic style. Although the Shang state highly valued its artisans, it treated its copper miners as lowly tribute laborers. By controlling access to tin and copper and to the production of bronze, Shang kings prevented their rivals from forging bronze weapons and thus increased their own power and legitimacy. With their superior weapons, Shang armies by 1300 BCE could easily destroy armies wielding wooden clubs and stone-tipped spears.

Chariots entered the Central Plains of China with nomads of the north around 1200 BCE, much later than their appearance in Egypt and Southwest Asia. They were quickly adopted by the upper classes. Chinese chariots were larger (fitting three men standing in a box mounted on eighteen- or twenty-six-spoke wheels) and much better built than those of their neighbors. As symbols of power and wealth, they were often buried with their owners. Yet, unlike elsewhere in Afro-Eurasia, they were at first little used in warfare during the Shang era, perhaps because of the effectiveness and shock value of large Shang infantry forces, composed mainly of foot soldiers armed with axes, spears, arrowheads, shields, and helmets, all made of bronze. In Shang China, the chariot was used primarily for hunting and as a mark of high status. Shang metalworking and the incorporation of the chariot gave the Shang state a huge advantage and unprecedented power over its neighbors.

AGRICULTURE AND TRIBUTE

The Shang dynastic rulers also understood the importance of agriculture for winning and maintaining power, so they did much to promote its development. The activities of local governors and the masses revolved around

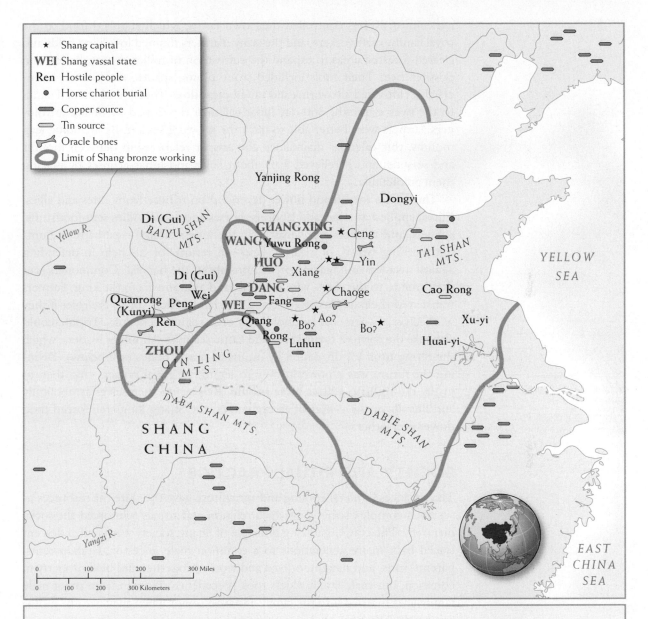

Map 3.4 Shang Dynasty in East Asia

The Shang state was one of the most important and powerful of early Chinese dynasties.

- Based on your analysis of this map, what raw materials were the most important to the Shang state?

- How were the deposits of these raw materials distributed across Shang territory and beyond? How might that distribution have shaped the area marked on the map as the limit of Shang bronze working?

- Locate the various Shang capitals. Why do you think they were located where they were?

agriculture. Rulers controlled their own farms, which supplied food to the royal family, craftworkers, and the army. Farmers drained low-lying fields and cleared forested areas to expand the cultivation of millet, wheat, barley, and possibly rice. Their tools included stone plows, spades, and sickles. Farmers also cultivated silkworms and raised pigs, dogs, sheep, and oxen. Thanks to the twelve-month, 360-day lunar calendar developed by Shang astrologers, farmers were better able to track the growing season. By including leap months, this calendar maintained the proper relationship between months and seasons, and it relieved fears about solar and lunar eclipses by making them predictable.

The ruler's wealth and power depended on tribute from elites and allies. Elites supplied warriors and laborers, horses and cattle. Allies sent foodstuffs, soldiers, and workers and "assisted in the king's affairs"—perhaps by hunting, burning brush, or clearing land—in return for his help in defending against invaders and making predictions about the harvest. Commoners sent their tribute to the elites, who held the land as grants from the king. Farmers transferred their surplus crops to the elite landholders (or to the ruler if they worked on his personal landholdings) on a regular schedule. Tribute could also take the form of turtle shells and cattle scapulas (shoulder blades), which the Shang used for divination by means of oracle bones (see below). Divining the future was a powerful way to legitimate royal power—and then to justify the right to collect more tribute. By placing themselves symbolically and literally at the center of all exchanges, the Shang kings reinforced their power over others.

SOCIETY AND RITUAL PRACTICE

The advances in metalworking and agriculture gave the state the resources to sustain a complex society, in which religion and rituals reinforced the social hierarchy. The core organizing principle of Shang society was familial descent traced back many generations to a common male ancestor. Grandparents, parents, sons, and daughters lived and worked together and held property in common, but male family elders took precedence. Women from other male family lines married into the family and won honor when they became mothers, particularly of sons.

The death ritual, which involved sacrificing humans to join the deceased in the next life, reflected the importance of family, male dominance, and social hierarchy. Members of the royal elite were often buried with their full entourage, including wives, consorts, servants, chariots, horses, and drivers. The inclusion of personal servants and people enslaved by the elite among those sacrificed indicates a belief that the familiar social hierarchy would continue in the afterlife. An impressive example of the burial practices of the Shang elite is the tomb of an exceptional prominent woman, Fu Hao (also known as Fu Zi), who was consort to the king, a military leader in her own right, and a ritual specialist. She was buried with a wide range of objects made from bronze and jade (including weapons), ivory, pottery, cowrie shells that were used as currency, and a large cache of oracle bones, as well as six dogs and sixteen humans who appear to have been sacrificed to accompany her at death.

The Shang state was a full-fledged theocracy: it claimed that the ruler at the top of the hierarchy derived his authority through guidance from ancestors and gods. Shang rulers practiced ancestral worship, which was the major form of religious belief in China during this period. Ancestor worship involved performing rituals in which the rulers offered drink and food to their recently dead ancestors with the hope that they would intervene with their more powerful long-dead ancestors on behalf of the living. Divination was the process by which Shang rulers communicated with ancestors and foretold the future by means of **oracle bones**. Diviners applied intense heat to the shoulder bones of cattle or to turtle shells and interpreted the cracks that appeared on these objects as auspicious or inauspicious signs from the ancestors regarding royal plans and actions. On these so-called oracle bones, scribes subsequently inscribed the queries asked of the ancestors to confirm the diviners' interpretations. Thus, Shang writing began as a dramatic ritual performance in which the living responded to their ancestors' oracular signs.

The oracle bones and tortoise shells offer a window into the concerns and beliefs of the elite groups of these very distant cultures. The questions put to diviners most frequently as they inspected bones and shells involved the weather—hardly surprising in communities so dependent on growing seasons and good harvests—and family health and well-being, especially the prospects of having male children, who would extend the family line.

In Shang theocracy, because the ruler was the head of a unified clergy and embodied both religious and political power, no independent priesthood emerged. Diviners and scribes were subordinate to the ruler and the royal pantheon of ancestors he represented. Ancestor worship sanctified Shang control and legitimized the rulers' lineage, ensuring that the ruling family kept all political and religious power. Because the Shang gods were ancestral deities, the rulers were deified when they died and ranked in descending chronological order. Becoming gods at death, Shang rulers united the world of the living with the world of the dead.

SHANG WRITING

As scribes and priests used their script on oracle bones for the Shang kings, the formal character-based writing of East Asia developed over time. So although Shang scholars did not invent writing in East Asia, they perfected it. Evidence for writing in this era comes entirely from oracle bones, which were central to political and religious authority under the Shang. Other written records

oracle bones
Animal bones inscribed, heated, and interpreted by Shang ritual specialists to determine the will of the ancestors.

may have been on materials that did not survive. This accident of preservation may explain the major differences between the ancient texts in China (primarily divinations on bones) and in the Southwest Asian societies that impressed cuneiform on clay tablets (primarily for economic transactions, literary and religious documents, and historical records). In comparison with the development of writing in Mesopotamia and Egypt, the transition of Shang writing from record keeping (for example, questions to ancestors, lineages of rulers, or economic transactions) to literature (for example, myths about the founding of states) was slower. Shang rulers initially monopolized writing through their scribes, who positioned the royal families at the top of the social and political hierarchy. And priests wrote on the oracle bones to address the otherworld and gain information about the future so that the ruling family would remain at the center of the political system.

As Shang China cultivated developments in agriculture, ornate bronze metalworking, and divinatory writing on oracle bones, the state did not face the repeated waves of pastoral nomadic invaders seen in other parts of Afro-Eurasia. It was nonetheless influenced by the chariot culture that eventually filtered into East Asia. Given that so many of the developments in Shang China bolstered the authority of the dynastic rulers and elite, it is perhaps not surprising that the chariot in China was initially more a marker of elite status than an effective tool for warfare.

Microsocieties in the South Pacific and in the Aegean

Core Objectives

EXAMINE the development of microsocieties in the South Pacific and the Aegean, and **EXPLAIN** the role geography played in their development.

microsocieties
Small-scale, fragmented communities that had little interaction with others. These communities were the norm for peoples living in the Americas and islanders in the Pacific and Aegean from 2000 to 1200 BCE.

As environmental circumstances drove pastoral nomads and transhumant herders toward settled agriculturalists, leading ultimately to the development of powerful and somewhat intertwined territorial states in Egypt, Southwest Asia, the Indus River valley, and Shang China, other pressures drove migrations across the South Pacific and Aegean. These maritime migrations led to the development after 2000 BCE, in such places as Austronesia and the Aegean, of **microsocieties**: small-scale, fragmented, and dispersed communities that had limited interaction with others.

THE SOUTH PACIFIC (2500 BCE–400 CE)

Austronesian-speaking peoples with origins in coastal South China migrated into the South Pacific and formed microsocieties there. While the precise date for the beginning of these migrations is debated among scholars, the proliferation of peoples across the South Pacific was well under way by the third millennium BCE. Using their double-outrigger canoes, which were 60 to 100 feet long and bore huge triangular sails, the early Austronesians

Austronesian Canoe Early Austronesians crossed the Taiwan Straits and colonized key islands in the Pacific using double-outrigger canoes from 60 to 100 feet long equipped with triangular sails. In good weather, such canoes could cover more than 120 miles in a day. This relief, from Borobudur, a later Buddhist temple in Java, shows an eighth-century CE depiction of a double-outrigger canoe.

crossed the Taiwan Straits and colonized key islands in the Pacific. Their vessels were much more advanced than the simple dugout canoes used in inland waterways. In good weather, double-outrigger canoes could cover more than 120 miles in a day. The invention of a stabilization device for deep-sea sailing sometime after 2500 BCE triggered further Austronesian expansion into the Pacific. By 400 CE, these nomads of the sea had reached most of the islands of the South Pacific. Their seafaring skills enabled the Austronesians to monopolize trade wherever they went.

By comparing the vocabularies and grammatical features of languages spoken today by the remaining tribal peoples in Taiwan, the Philippines, and Indonesia, scholars have traced the ancient Austronesian-speaking peoples back to coastal South China in the fourth millennium BCE. Pottery, stone tools, and domesticated crops and pigs also provide markers for tracking Austronesian settlements throughout the coastal islands and in the South Pacific. According to archaeologists, the same cultural features had spread from Taiwan to the Philippines (by 2500 BCE), to Java and Sumatra (by 2000 BCE), and to parts of Australia and New Guinea (by 1600 BCE). The Austronesians then ventured farther eastward into the South Pacific, apparently arriving in Samoa and Fiji in 1200 BCE and on mainland Southeast Asia in 1000 BCE. (See Map 3.5.) The Austronesians reached the Marquesas Islands, strategically located for northern and southern exploration, in the central Pacific around 200 CE. Over the next few centuries, some moved on to Easter Island to the south and Hawaii to the north. The immense 30-ton stone structures on Easter Island represent the monumental Polynesian architecture produced after their arrival.

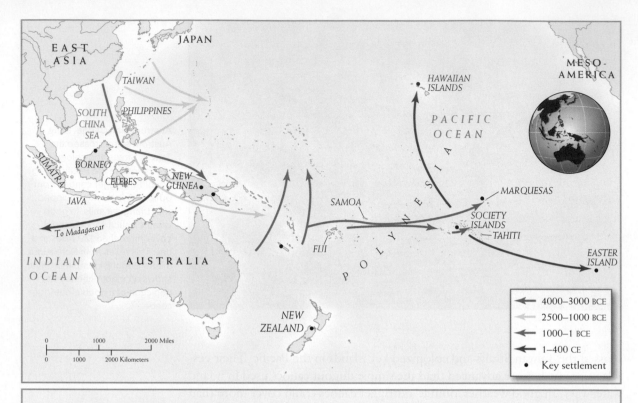

Map 3.5 Austronesian Migrations

The Pacific Ocean saw many migrations from East Asia.

- Where did the Austronesian migrants come from? What were the boundaries of their migration? Trace the stages of Austronesian migration over time. Why do you think these migrations took place over such a long time period?
- Why, unlike other migratory people during the second millennium BCE, did Austronesian settlers in Polynesia become a world apart?

Equatorial lands in the South Pacific have a tropical or subtropical climate and, in many places, fertile soils containing nutrient-rich volcanic ash. In this environment the Austronesians cultivated dry-land crops (yams and sweet potatoes), irrigated crops (more yams, which grew better in paddy fields or in rainy areas), and harvested tree crops (breadfruit, bananas, and coconuts). In addition, colonized areas beyond the landmass, such as the islands of Indonesia, had labyrinthine coastlines rich in maritime resources, including coral reefs and mangrove swamps teeming with wildlife. Island-hopping led the adventurers to encounter new food sources, but the shallow waters and reefs offered sufficient fish and shellfish for their needs.

In the South Pacific, the Polynesian descendants of the early Austronesians shared a common culture, language, technology, and stores of domesticated plants and animals. These later seafarers came from many different island communities (hence the name *Polynesian*, "belonging to many islands"), and after they settled down, their numbers grew. Their crop surpluses allowed more densely populated communities to support craft specialists and soldiers. Most settlements boasted ceremonial buildings to promote local solidarity and forts to provide defense. On larger islands, communities often cooperated and organized workforces to enclose ponds for fish production and to build and maintain large irrigation works for agriculture. In terms of political structure, Polynesian communities ranged from tribal or village units to multi-island alliances that sometimes invaded other areas.

The expansion of East Asian peoples throughout the South Pacific and their trade back and forth, however, did not integrate the islands into the mainland culture. Expansion could not overcome the tendency of these Austronesian microsocieties, dispersed across a huge ocean, toward fragmentation and isolation.

THE AEGEAN WORLD (2000–1200 BCE)

In the region around the Aegean Sea (the islands and the mainland of present-day Greece), no single power emerged before the second millennium BCE, but island microsocieties (the Minoans and the Mycenaeans) developed an expanding trade network and distinctive cultures. Settled agrarian communities were linked only by trade and culture. Fragmentation was the norm—in part because the landscape had no great river-basin systems or large common plain. In its fragmentation, the island world of the eastern Mediterranean initially resembled that of the South Pacific.

As an unintended benefit of the lack of centralization, there was no single regime to collapse when the droughts arrived. Thus, in the second millennium BCE, peoples of the eastern Mediterranean did not struggle to recover lost grandeur. Rather, they enjoyed a remarkable though gradual development, making advances based on influences they absorbed from Southwest Asia, Egypt, and Europe. Residents of Aegean islands like Crete and Thera enjoyed extensive trade with the Greek mainland, Egypt, Anatolia, Syria, and Palestine. It was also a time of population movements from the Danube region and central Europe into the Mediterranean. Groups of these migrants settled in mainland Greece in the centuries after 1900 BCE; modern archaeologists have named them Mycenaeans after their famous palace at Mycenae. Soon after settling in their new environment, the Mycenaeans turned to the sea to look for resources and interaction with their neighbors.

At the outset, the main influence on the Aegean world came from the east by sea. As the institutions and ideas that had developed in Southwest Asia moved westward, they found a ready reception along the coasts and on the islands of the Mediterranean. Trade was the main source of eastern influences, with vessels carrying cargoes from island to island and up and down

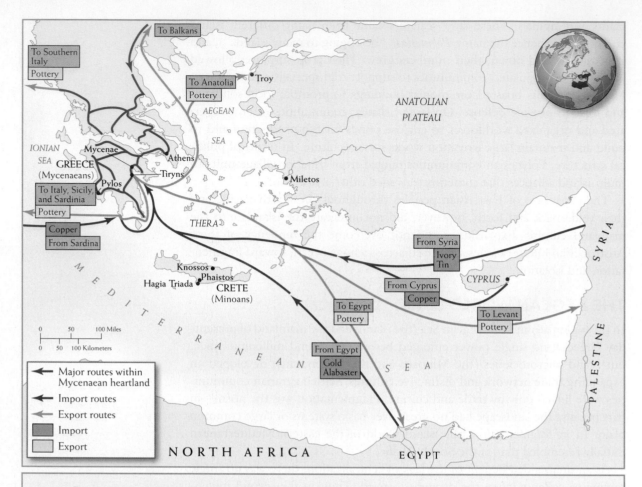

Map 3.6 Trade in the Eastern Mediterranean World

....

Greece, Egypt, and Cyprus were trade hubs in the eastern Mediterranean.

- What major commodities were traded in the eastern Mediterranean?
- Why did trade originally move from east to west?
- What role did geographic location play in the Mycenaeans' eventual conquest of the Minoans?

the commercial centers along the coast. (See Map 3.6.) Mediterranean trade centered on tin from the east and readily available copper, both essential for making bronze (the primary metal in tools and weapons). Islands such as Cyprus and Crete, located in the midst of the active sea-lanes, flourished. Cyprus had large reserves of copper ore, which started to generate intense activity around 2300 BCE. By 2000 BCE, harbors on the southern and eastern sides of the island were shipping and transshipping goods, along with copper ingots, as far west as Crete, east to the Euphrates River, and south to Egypt.

Minoan Culture Crete, too, was an active trading node in the Mediterranean, and its culture reflected outside influences as well as local traditions. Around 2000 BCE, a large number of independent palace centers began to emerge on Crete, at Knossos (ultimately the most impressive of them) and elsewhere. Scholars have named the people who built these elaborate centers the Minoans, after the legendary King Minos who may have ruled Crete at this time. The Minoans sailed back and forth across the Mediterranean, and by 1600 BCE they were colonizing other Aegean islands as trading and mining centers. The Minoans' wealth soon became a magnet for the Mycenaeans, their mainland competitors, who took over Crete around 1400 BCE.

Seaborne Trade Shipwrecks recovered by underwater archaeologists, who work methodically to document their cargo, demonstrate the scale of seaborne trade in the late second millennium BCE. The famous Uluburun shipwreck, which sunk off the southern coast of Turkey around 1325 BCE, was transporting 10 tons of copper and more than 100 amphorae (large two-handled jars) containing all kinds of high-value commodities.

As the island communities traded with the peoples of Southwest Asia, they borrowed some ideas but also kept their own cultural traditions. In terms of borrowing, the monumental architecture of Southwest Asia found small-scale echoes in the Aegean world—notably in the palace complexes built on Crete between 1900 and 1600 BCE.

In terms of a distinctive cultural element, worship on the islands focused on a female deity, the "Lady," but there are no traces of large temple complexes similar to those in Mesopotamia, Anatolia, and Egypt. Nor, apparently, was there any priestly class of the type that managed the temple complexes of Southwest Asian societies. Moreover, it is unclear whether these societies had full-time scribes. The so-called Phaistos disk, found in the palace of the city of Phaistos on Crete and measuring just over 6 inches across, is arguably an example of early Minoan writing. Its 242 symbols, spiraling inward from the rim of the disk, were impressed into the clay using 45 different stamps, including a rosette, an ear of grain, olives, fish, and birds. Some have suggested that the text might record a calendar or (most recently) a prayer to a mother goddess; still others insist the text is too limited to be convincingly deciphered.

Perhaps not surprisingly for a fragmented microsociety, there was significant regional diversity within this small Aegean world. On Crete, the large, palace-centered communities controlled centrally organized societies with a high order of refinement. Confident in their wealth and power, the sprawling, airy palaces had no fortifications and no natural defenses. On Thera (modern Santorini), a small island to the north of Crete, a trading city was not centered on a major palace complex but rather featured private houses, with bathrooms including toilets and running water and other rooms decorated with exotic wall paintings. It was this same island of Thera that was the center of a catastrophic volcanic eruption in the mid-second millennium BCE that likely contributed to the decline of the Minoans.

Mycenaean Culture The Mycenaean culture was more war oriented than that of the peaceful, seafaring Minoans. When the Mycenaeans migrated to Greece from central Europe, they brought their Indo-European language, their horse chariots, and their metalworking skills. Their move was gradual, lasting from about 1850 to 1600 BCE, but ultimately they dominated the indigenous population. They maintained their dominance with their powerful weapon, the chariot, until 1200 BCE. The battle chariots and festivities of chariot racing described in the centuries-later epic poetry of Homer's *Iliad* (recounting the legendary Trojan War in which Mycenaean Greeks attacked the city of Troy, in Anatolia) express memories of glorious chariot feats that echo Vedic legends from South Asia. Homer's "Catalog of Greek Ships" (*Iliad* 2.494–759), detailing the many different Greek communities that sent ships of warriors to fight at Troy, also illustrates the diffuse and fragmented

Aegean Fresco This is one of the more striking wall paintings, or frescoes, discovered by archaeologists in the 1970s and 1980s at Akrotiri on the island of Thera (modern Santorini) in the Aegean Sea. Its brilliant colors, especially the blue of the sea, evoke the lively essence of Minoan life on the island. Note the houses of the wealthy along the port and the flotilla of ships that reflects the seaborne commerce that was beginning to flourish in the Mediterranean in this period.

political situation, yet common culture and ideals, that bound together the Greek microsociety.

The Mycenaean material culture emphasized displays of weaponry, portraits of armed soldiers, and illustrations of violent conflicts. The main palace centers at Tiryns and Mycenae were the hulking fortresses of warlords surrounded by rough-hewn stone walls and strategically located atop large rock outcroppings. In these fortified urban hubs, a preeminent ruler (*wanax*) stood atop a complex bureaucratic hierarchy. At the heart of the palace society were scribes, who recorded in their Linear B script the goods and services allotted to local farmers, shepherds, and metalworkers, among others. Tombs of the Mycenaean elite contain many gold vessels and ostentatious gold masks. Amber beads in the tombs indicate that the warriors had contacts with inhabitants of northern European coniferous forest regions, whose trees secreted that highly valued resin.

Mycenaean expansion eventually overwhelmed the Minoans on Crete. The Mycenaeans created colonies and trading settlements, reaching as far as Sicily and southern Italy. The trade and language of these early Greek-speaking peoples created a veneer of unity linking the dispersed worlds of the Aegean

Sea. Yet, at the close of the second millennium BCE, the eastern Mediterranean faced internal and external convulsions that ended the heyday of these microsocieties. Most notable was a series of migrations of peoples from central Europe who moved through southeastern Europe, Anatolia, and the eastern Mediterranean (see Chapter 4 for more on these Sea Peoples). The invasions, although often destructive, did not extinguish but rather reinforced the creative potential of this frontier area. Because theirs was a closed maritime world—in comparison with the wide-open Pacific—the Greek-speaking peoples around the Aegean quickly reasserted dominance in the eastern Mediterranean that the Austronesians did not match in Southeast Asia or Polynesia.

Conclusion

The second millennium BCE was an era of migrations, warfare, and territorial state building in Afro-Eurasia. Whereas river-basin societies had flourished in the fourth and third millennia BCE in Mesopotamia, Egypt, the Indus Valley, and East Asia, now droughts shook the agrarian foundations of their economies. Old states crumbled; from the steppes and plateaus pastoral nomads and transhumant herders descended in search of food, grazing lands, and other opportunities. As transhumant herders pressed into the river-basin societies, the social and political fabric of these communities changed. Likewise, horse-riding nomads from steppe communities in Inner Eurasia conquered and settled in the agrarian states, bringing key innovations. Foremost were the horse chariots, which became a military catalyst sparking the evolution from smaller states to larger territorial states encompassing crowded cities, vast hinterlands, and broadened trade networks. The nomads and herders also adopted many of the settled peoples' beliefs and customs. On land and sea, migrating peoples created zones of long-distance trade that linked agrarian societies.

Through a range of trade, migrations, and conquest throughout the second millennium BCE, the Nile Delta, the basin of the Tigris and Euphrates Rivers, the Indus Valley, and the Yellow River basin were brought into even closer contact than before. In Southwest Asia and the Nile River basin, the interaction led to an elaborate system of diplomatic relations. The first territorial states appeared in this millennium, composed of multiple communities living under common laws and customs. An alliance of farmers and warriors united agrarian production with political power to create and defend territorial boundaries. The new arrangements overshadowed the nomads' historic role as predators and enabled them to become military elites within these new states. Through taxes and drafted labor, villagers repaid their rulers for local security and state-run diplomacy.

The rhythms of state formation differed where regimes were not closely packed together. In East Asia, for example, the absence of strong rivals allowed the emerging Shang dynasty to develop more gradually. Where landscapes had sharper divisions—as in the island archipelagos of the South Pacific and in the Mediterranean—small-scale, decentralized, and fragmented microsocieties emerged. But fragmentation is not the same as isolation. Even peoples in the worlds apart from the developments across Afro-Eurasia were not entirely secluded from the increasing flows of technologies, languages, goods, and migrants.

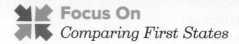

Focus On
Comparing First States

Egypt and Southwest Asia

- Invasions by nomads and transhumant herders lead to the creation of larger territorial states: New Kingdom Egypt, the Hittites, and Mesopotamian states.

- Creating a centuries-long peaceful era, a community of major powers emerges among the major states as the result of shrewd statecraft and diplomacy.

Indus River Valley

- Migratory Vedic peoples from the steppes of Inner Eurasia use chariots and rely on domesticated animals to spread out and begin integrating the northern half of South Asia.

Shang State (China)

- Shang dynastic rulers promote improvements in metalworking, agriculture, and the development of writing, leading to the growth of China's first major state.

Microsocieties

- Substantial increases in population, migrations, and trade lead to the emergence of microsocieties among peoples in the South Pacific (Austronesians) and the Aegean world (Minoans and Mycenaeans).

Key Terms

Amorites p. 124	Hittites p. 128	microsocieties p. 138	territorial state p. 116
chariot p. 114	Hyksos p. 122	oracle bones p. 137	transhumant herders p. 111
Hammurabi's Code p. 126	Indo-European migrations p. 111	pastoral nomads p. 111	Vedic peoples p. 130

CHRONOLOGY

	2500 BCE	2000 BCE
Egypt and Southwest Asia		Middle Kingdom in Egypt 2055–1650 BCE
		Hammurabi's Babylonia 1792–1750 BCE
South Asia		
East Asia		
The Mediterranean		
South Pacific	Austronesian migrations 2500 BCE–400 CE	

THINKING ABOUT GLOBAL CONNECTIONS

- **Thinking about Environmental Impacts and Territorial States** Around 2000 BCE, a series of environmental disasters helped destroy the societies that had thrived in parts of Afro-Eurasia in the third millennium BCE. What were the short-term and long-term impacts of these environmental troubles? How did they influence the movement of peoples and the formation of territorial states in the second millennium BCE?

- **Thinking about Transformation & Conflict and Territorial States** The second millennium BCE witnessed large-scale migrations of nomadic peoples who brought with them their domesticated horses and their chariot technology. These people are referred to by scholars as Indo-Europeans, largely on the basis of their languages. Contrast the impact of migrations into Southwest Asia (Anatolia and Mesopotamia), Egypt, South Asia, and East Asia. To what extent did conflict play a role in the impact of Indo-European-language speakers on the formation of territorial states?

- **Thinking about Interconnection & Divergence and Territorial States** While territorial states formed in Egypt, Mesopotamia, South Asia, and East Asia, microsocieties formed in the South Pacific and in the Aegean Sea. What factors influenced whether a region might host a territorial state as opposed to a microsociety? What areas of the planet were still worlds apart? What ways of life continued to predominate in those worlds apart from the territorial states and microsocieties discussed in this chapter?

 Go to INQUIZITIVE to see what you've learned—and learn what you've missed—with personalized feedback along the way.

1500 BCE	1000 BCE	500 BCE

New Kingdom in Egypt 1550–1070 BCE

Community of major powers 1400–1200 BCE

Vedic migration into Indus River valley begins 1500 BCE

Vedic migration into Ganges River valley begins 1000 BCE

Shang state 1600–1046 BCE

Minoan culture in Aegean 2000–1600 BCE

Mycenaean culture in Greece and Aegean 1850–1200 BCE

Global Themes and Sources

Law Codes in the Context of Territorial States and Pastoral Nomads

In addition to charismatic monarchs and complex bureaucracies, one of the ways territorial states brought order to the large regions under their control was through clear codes of law. These could range from elaborate legal codes, such as that of Hammurabi, to more general instructions to leaders on how to administer justice. Pastoral nomadic groups, like the Hebrews and Vedic peoples, also developed law codes, especially as they began to settle down.

The logic of the law codes is as varied as their historical context. Some law codes operated on an "if/then" formula (*if* a certain crime is committed, *then* a certain punishment is to be meted out), others laid out clear and forceful rules for proper behavior, and others deliberated on procedure and punishment. Some law codes mention gods specifically, while others appear to focus primarily on human interactions and appeal to earthly authority. Many of the law codes reveal distinctions based on class, occupation, and gender.

What is unclear from the laws themselves is the extent to which they describe ideal behavior or the realities of everyday life in the communities to which they applied. For instance, scholars do not know how often either the penalties of Hammurabi's Code in Mesopotamian Babylon or the *Punishments of Tang* in Shang China were applied. Nor do scholars know for sure how frequently the scene of supplicants assembling before the vizier in New Kingdom Egypt played out or how true to life the husband-wife relations and attitudes toward women in the Code of Manu were. These law codes do, however, allow us to compare the varied historical contexts from which they come and to consider what the laws suggest about power and community in the second millennium BCE.

Analyzing the Context of Early Law Codes

- What issues do territorial states, such as those of Babylon, New Kingdom Egypt, and Shang China, attempt to legislate? What sorts of issues appear to matter to the nomadic Hebrews and Vedic peoples?

- What sorts of social distinctions (class, gender, occupation) are evident in the codes?

- What do the variations in the laws—with respect to issues such as source of authority, punishment, and enforcement—suggest about the source of power at the heart of these societies?

- What can you generalize about the concerns of a settled territorial state as compared with those of a more nomadic group?

PRIMARY SOURCE 3.1

Hammurabi's Code (c. eighteenth century BCE)

From a Babylonian territorial state in Mesopotamia, Hammurabi's Code, with its 282 laws covering everything from property ownership to marriage, is one of the earliest recorded law codes. Dating to the eighteenth century BCE, the code was produced in the context of the blending of Amorite herders and Mesopotamian urbanites. While the prologue to the law code describes how the gods have invested Hammurabi with the power to establish this code of laws and "to bring about the rule of righteousness in the land, to destroy the wicked and evil-doers, so that the strong should not harm the weak," the laws themselves are focused primarily on humans' relationships with one another.

- What are some of the crimes outlined in these laws? What are the punishments for those crimes?

- What evidence do you see in Hammurabi's laws for the relationship between men and women? Between parents and children? Between different levels of society?

- What do these laws suggest about the eighteenth-century BCE Mesopotamian context from which they come? What sorts of issues seem to matter to this community (or its ruler)?

§1. If a man bring an accusation against a man, and charge him with a (capital) crime, but cannot prove it, he, the accuser, shall be put to death.

§2. If a man charge a man with sorcery, and cannot prove it, he who is charged with sorcery shall go to the river, into the river he shall throw himself and if the river overcome him, his accuser shall take to himself his house (estate). If the river show that man to be innocent and he come forth unharmed, he who charged him with sorcery shall be put to death. He who threw himself into the river shall take to himself the house of his accuser.

§3. If a man, in a case (pending judgment), bear false (threatening) witness, or do not establish the testimony that he has given, if that case be a case involving life, that man shall be put to death.

§4. If a man (in a case) bear witness for grain or money (as a bribe), he shall himself bear the penalty imposed in that case.

§5. If a judge pronounce a judgment, render a decision, deliver a verdict duly signed and sealed and afterward alter his judgment, they shall call that judge to account for the alteration of the judgment which he had pronounced, and he shall pay twelve-fold the penalty which was in said judgment; and, in the assembly, they shall expel him from his seat of judgment, and he shall not return, and with the judges in a case he shall not take his seat.

§6. If a man steal the property of a god (temple) or palace, that man shall be put to death; and he who receives from his hand the stolen (property) shall also be put to death.

§7. If a man purchase silver or gold, manservant or maid servant, ox, sheep or ass, or anything else from a man's son, or from a man's servant without witnesses or contracts, or if he receive (the same) in trust, that man shall be put to death as a thief.

§8. If a man steal ox or sheep, ass or pig, or boat—if it be from a god (temple) or a palace, he shall restore thirtyfold; if it be from a freeman, he shall render tenfold. If the thief have nothing wherewith to pay he shall be put to death.

***

§14. If a man steal a man's son, who is a minor, he shall be put to death.

§15. If a man aid a male or female slave of the palace, or a male or female slave of a freeman to escape from the city gate, he shall be put to death.

§16. If a man harbor in his house a male or female slave who has fled from the palace or from a freeman, and do not bring him (the enslaved man) forth at the call of the commandant, the owner of that house shall be put to death.

§17. If a man seize a male or female slave, a fugitive, in the field and bring that (person) back to his owner, the owner of the slave shall pay him two shekels of silver.

***

§38. An officer, constable or tax-gatherer shall not deed to his wife or daughter the field, garden or house, which is his business (*i.e.*, which is his by virtue of his office), nor shall he assign them for debt.

§39. He may deed to his wife or daughter the field, garden or house which he has purchased and (hence) possesses, or he may assign them for debt.

§40. A woman, merchant or other property-holder may sell field, garden or house. The purchaser shall conduct the business of the field, garden or house which he has purchased.

§41. If a man have bargained for the field, garden or house of an officer, constable or tax-gatherer and given sureties, the officer, constable or tax-gatherer shall return to his field, garden, or house and he shall take to himself the sureties which were given to him.

§42. If a man rent a field for cultivation and do not produce any grain in the field, they shall call him to account, because he has not performed the work required on the field, and he shall give to the owner of the field grain on the basis of the adjacent (fields).

§43. If he do not cultivate the field and neglect it, he shall give to the owner of the field grain on the basis of the adjacent (fields); and the field which he has neglected, he shall break up with hoes, he shall harrow and he shall return to the owner of the field.

***

§45. If a man rent his field to a tenant for crop-rent and receive the crop-rent of his field and later Adad (*i.e.*, the Storm God) inundate the field and carry away the produce, the loss (falls on) the tenant.

§46. If he have not received the rent of his field and he have rented the field for either one-half or one-third (of the crop), the tenant and the owner of the field shall divide the grain which is in the field according to agreement.

***

§128. If a man take a wife and do not arrange with her the (proper) contracts, that woman is not a (legal) wife.

§129. If the wife of a man be taken in lying with another man, they shall bind them and throw them into the water. If the husband of the woman would save his wife, or if the king would save his male servant (he may).

§130. If a man force the (betrothed) wife of another who has not known a male and is living in her father's house, and he lie in her bosom and they take him, that man shall be put to death and that woman shall go free.

§131. If a man accuse his wife and she has not been taken in lying with another man, she shall take an oath in the name of god and she shall return to her house.

§132. If the finger have been pointed at the wife of a man because of another man, and she have not been taken in lying with another man, for her husband's sake she shall throw herself into the river.

§133. If a man be captured and there be maintenance in his house and his wife go out of her house, she shall protect her body and she shall not enter into another house.

§133A. [If] that woman do not protect her body and enter into another house, they shall call that woman to account and they shall throw her into the water.

§134. If a man be captured and there be no maintenance in his house and his wife enter into another house, that woman has no blame.

§135. If a man be captured and there be no maintenance in his house, and his wife openly enter into another house and bear children; if later her husband return and arrive in his city, that woman shall return to her husband (and) the children shall go to their father.

§136. If a man desert his city and flee and afterwards his wife enter into another house; if that man return and would take his wife, the wife of the fugitive shall not return to her husband because he hated his city and fled.

§137. If a man set his face to put away a concubine who has borne him children or a wife who has presented him with children, he shall return to that woman her dowry and shall give to her the income of field, garden and goods and she shall bring up her children; from the time that her children are grown up, from whatever is given to her children they shall give to her a portion corresponding to that of a son and the man of her choice may marry her.

§138. If a man would put away his wife who has not borne him children, he shall give her money to the amount of her marriage settlement and he shall make good to her the dowry which she brought from her father's house and then he may put her away.

§139. If there were no marriage settlement, he shall give to her one mana of silver for a divorce.

§140. If he be a freeman, he shall give her one-third mana of silver.

§141. If the wife of a man who is living in his house, set her face to go out and play the part of a fool, neglect her house, belittle her husband, they shall call her to account; if her husband say "I have put her away," he shall let her go. On her departure nothing shall be given to her for her divorce. If her husband say: "I have not put her away," her husband may take another woman. The first woman shall dwell in the house of her husband as a maid servant.

§142. If a woman hate her husband, and say: "Thou shalt not have me," they shall inquire into her antecedents for her defects; and if she have been a careful mistress and be without reproach and her husband have been going about and greatly belittling her, that woman has no blame. She shall receive her dowry and shall go to her father's house.

§143. If she have not been a careful mistress, have gadded about, have neglected her house and have belittled her husband, they shall throw that woman into the water.

***

§148. If a man take a wife and she become afflicted with disease, and if he set his face to take another, he may. His wife, who is afflicted with disease, he shall not put away. She shall remain in the house which he has built and he shall maintain her as long as she lives.

§149. If that woman do not elect to remain in her husband's house, he shall make good to her the dowry which she brought from her father's house and she may go.

§150. If a man give to his wife field, garden, house or goods and he deliver to her a sealed deed, after (the death of) her husband, her children cannot make claim against her. The mother after her (death) may will to her child whom she loves, but to a brother she may not.

***

§162. If a man take a wife and she bear him children and that woman die, her father may not lay claim to her dowry. Her dowry belongs to her children.

§163. If a man take a wife and she do not present him with children and that woman die; if his father-in-law return to him the marriage settlement which that man brought to the house of his father-in-law, her husband may not lay claim to the dowry of that woman. Her dowry belongs to the house of her father.

§164. If his father-in-law do not return to him the marriage settlement, he may deduct from her dowry the amount of the marriage settlement and return (the rest) of her dowry to the house of her father.

***

§194. If a man give his son to a nurse and that son die in the hands of the nurse, and the nurse substitute another son without the consent of his father or mother, they shall call her to account, and because she has substituted another son without the consent of his father or mother, they shall cut off her breast.

§195. If a son strike his father, they shall cut off his fingers.

§196. If a man destroy the eye of another man, they shall destroy his eye.

§197. If one break a man's bone, they shall break his bone.

§198. If one destroy the eye of a freeman or break the bone of a freeman, he shall pay one mana of silver.

§199. If one destroy the eye of a man's slave or break a bone of a man's slave he shall pay one-half his price.

§200. If a man knock out a tooth of a man of his own rank, they shall knock out his tooth.

§201. If one knock out a tooth of a freeman, he shall pay one-third mana of silver.

§202. If a man strike the person of a man (*i.e.*, commit an assault) who is his superior, he shall receive sixty strokes with an ox-tail whip in public.

§203. If a man strike another man of his own rank, he shall pay one mana of silver.

§204. If a freeman strike a freeman, he shall pay ten shekels of silver.

§205. If a man's slave strike a man's son, they shall cut off his ear.

Source: *The Code of Hammurabi, King of Babylon, about 2250 B.C.*, 2nd ed., translated by Robert Francis Harper (Union, NJ: University of Chicago Lawbook Exchange, 1999), pp. 11, 13, 17, 25, 27, 45, 47, 49, 51, 53, 57, 59, 73, 75.

PRIMARY SOURCE 3.2

Instruction to Vizier Rekhmire (c. fifteenth century BCE)

No comprehensive law codes survive from Middle or New Kingdom Egypt, but a set of instructions from Thutmosis III (stepson of, and co-ruler with, Hatshepsut, before his solo reign) to Rekhmire, a pharaoh's vizier (chief minister), from around 1450 BCE gives a keen sense of how judgments were made at the Egyptian court. These instructions, along with a biography of Rekhmire, were preserved in hieroglyphs on the wall of the mortuary chapel of Rekhmire in Thebes, along with beautifully painted scenes of the collection of taxes and tribute, the labors of workers and other craftspeople, and funerary practices.

- What scene does the opening of these instructions conjure? How does this scene help you imagine the social and political context in which the instructions were meant to be followed?

- Over what issues does the vizier have authority?

- How does this administration of authority and justice by the vizier align with your understanding of the post-Hyksos territorial state context of New Kingdom Egypt?

667. Mayest thou see to it for thyself, to do everything after that which is in accordance with law; to do everything according to the right thereof.

* * *

669. Be not enraged toward a man unjustly, but be thou enraged concerning that about which one should be enraged; show forth the fear of thee; let one be afraid of thee, (for) a prince is a prince of whom one is afraid. Lo, the true dread of a prince is to do justice. Behold, if a man show forth the fear of him a myriad of times, there is something of violence in him. Be not known to the people; and they shall not say: "He is (only) a man."

670. Lo, one shall say of the chief scribe of the vizier: "A scribe of justice," shall one say of him. Now, as for the hall, wherein thou holdest hearings there shall be a broad-hall therein. ⌜He who dispenses⌝ justice before all the people, he is the vizier. Behold, a man shall be in his office, (as long as) he shall do things according to that which is given to him.

* * *

675. Arrangement of the sitting of the governor of the (residence) city, and vizier of the Southern City, (and) of the court, in the hall of the vizier. As for every act of this official, the vizier while hearing in the hall of the vizier, he shall sit upon a chair, with a rug upon the floor, and a dais upon it, a cushion under his back, a cushion under his feet, a—upon it, and a baton at his hand; the 40 skins shall be open before him. Then the magnates of the South (shall stand) in the two aisles before him, while the master of the privy chamber is on his right, the ⌜receiver of income⌝ on his left, the scribes of the vizier at his (either) hand; one ⌜corresponding⌝ to another, with each man at his proper place. One shall be heard after another, without allowing one who is behind to be heard before one who is in front. If one in front says: "There is none being heard at my hand," then he shall be taken by the messenger of the vizier.

* * *

681. Let not any official be empowered to judge ⌜against a superior⌝ in his hall. If there be any assailant against any of these officials in his hall, then he shall cause that he be brought to the judgment-hall. It is the vizier who shall punish him, in order to expiate his fault. . . .

682. As for every messenger whom the vizier sends with a message for an official, from the first official to the last, let him not be ⌜swerved⌝, and let him not be conducted; the official shall repeat his vizierial message while he stands before the official, repeating his message and going forth to wait for him. His messenger shall seize the mayors and village sheiks for the judgment-hall; . . . saying: "I have been sent with a message for the official so and so; he caused that I be conducted, and he caused that something be entrusted to me.

683. He who has not disproved the charge at his hearing, which takes place ⌜—⌝, then it shall be entered in the criminal docket. He who is in the great prison, not able to disprove the charge of his messenger, likewise; when their case comes on another time, then one shall report and determine whether it is in the criminal docket, and there shall be ⌜executed⌝ the things concerning which entry was made, in order to expiate their offense.

* * *

698. It is he who dispatches the official staff, to attend to the water-supply in the whole land.

699. It is he who dispatches the mayors and village sheiks to plow for harvest time.

700. It is he who ⌜appoints⌝ the overseers of hundreds in the hall of the king's-house.

701. It is he who ⌜arranges⌝ the hearing of the mayors and village sheiks who go forth in his name, of South and North.

702. Every matter is reported to him; there are reported to him the affairs of the southern fortress; and every arrest which is for seizing — — —.

703. It is he who makes the ⌜—⌝ of every nome; it is he who "hears" it. It is he who dispatches the ⌜district⌝

soldiers and scribes to carry out the ⌈administration⌉ of the king. The records of the nome are in his hall. It is he who hears concerning all lands. It is he who makes the boundary of every nome, the field ⌈—⌉, all divine offerings and every contract.

704. It is he who takes every deposition; it is he who hears the rejoinder when a man comes for argument with his opponent.

705. It is he who appoints every appointee to the hall of judgment, when any litigant comes to him from the king's-house. It is he who hears every edict.

Source: *Ancient Records of Egypt: Historical Documents from the Earliest Times to the Persian Conquest*, vol. 2, translated by James Henry Breasted (Chicago: University of Chicago Press, 1906), pp. 269–70, 273, 275–76, 279.

PRIMARY SOURCE 3.3

The Ten Commandments, Exodus 20:1–17 and Leviticus from the Bible

The Ten Commandments are perhaps the clearest, most direct statement of the laws binding the nomadic Hebrew peoples with their god and with one another. Hebrew scriptures describe the scene in which God delivers the Ten Commandments to Moses in the wilderness of Sinai during the Hebrews' sojourn from Egypt. A more elaborate set of laws touching on a wider range of issues, including dietary concerns, sexuality, blasphemy, and religious observances, is contained in the priestly Levitical Code of Hebrew scripture, especially in Leviticus 17–26. Examined together, the Ten Commandments and the Levitical Code give a better context for the laws and penalties by which the Hebrew peoples lived and governed their community.

- What are the range of behaviors addressed by the Ten Commandments? What, if any, rationale is offered in Exodus for why these rules should be followed and the penalty for not doing so?

- How do the Ten Commandments (Exodus 20:1–17) compare with the punishments for disobedience in Leviticus 26?

- What do the concerns addressed in the Ten Commandments and the punishments described in Leviticus suggest about the context of the community living by these rules?

Exodus 20: [1]And God spoke all these words, saying,

[2]"I am the Lord your God, who brought you out of the land of Egypt, out of the house of bondage.

[3]"You shall have no other gods before me.

[4]"You shall not make for yourself a graven image, or any likeness of anything that is in heaven above, or that is in the earth beneath, or that is in the water under the earth; [5]you shall not bow down to them or serve them; for I the Lord your God am a jealous God, visiting the iniquity of the fathers upon the children to the third and the fourth generation of those who hate me, [6]but showing steadfast love to thousands of those who love me and keep my commandments.

[7]"You shall not take the name of the Lord your God in vain; for the Lord will not hold him guiltless who takes his name in vain.

[8]"Remember the sabbath day, to keep it holy. [9]Six days you shall labor, and do all your work; [10]but the seventh day is a sabbath to the Lord your God; in it you shall not do any work, you, or your son, or your daughter, your manservant, or your maidservant, or your cattle, or the sojourner who is within your gates; [11]for in six days the Lord made heaven and earth, the sea, and all that is in them, and rested the seventh day; therefore the Lord blessed the sabbath day and hallowed it.

[12]"Honor your father and your mother, that your days may be long in the land which the Lord your God gives you.

[13]"You shall not kill.

[14]"You shall not commit adultery.

[15]"You shall not steal.

[16]"You shall not bear false witness against your neighbor.

[17]"You shall not covet your neighbor's house; you shall not covet your neighbor's wife, or his manservant, or his maidservant, or his ox, or his ass, or anything that is your neighbor's."

***

Leviticus 26: [14]"But if you will not hearken to me, and will not do all these commandments, [15]if you spurn my statutes, and if your soul abhors my ordinances, so that you will not do all my commandments, but break my covenant, [16]I will do this to you: I will appoint over you sudden terror, consumption, and fever that waste the eyes and cause life to pine away. And you shall sow your seed in vain, for your enemies shall eat it; [17]I will set my face against you, and you shall be smitten before your enemies; those who hate you shall rule over you, and you shall flee when none pursues you. [18]And if in spite of this you will not hearken to me, then I will chastise you again sevenfold for your sins, [19]and I will break the pride of your power, and I will make your heavens like iron and your earth like brass; [20]and your strength shall be spent in vain, for your land shall not yield its increase, and the trees of the land shall not yield their fruit.

[21]"Then if you walk contrary to me, and will not hearken to me, I will bring more plagues upon you, sevenfold as many as your sins. [22]And I will let loose the wild beasts among you, which shall rob you of your children, and destroy your cattle, and make you few in number, so that your ways shall become desolate.

[23]"And if by this discipline you are not turned to me, but walk contrary to me, [24]then I also will walk contrary to you, and I myself will smite you sevenfold for your sins. [25]And I will bring a sword upon you, that shall execute vengeance for the covenant; and if you gather within your cities I will send pestilence among you, and you shall be delivered into the hand of the enemy. [26]When I break your staff of bread, ten women shall bake your bread in one oven, and shall deliver your bread again by weight; and you shall eat, and not be satisfied."

Source: *The New Oxford Annotated Bible: New Revised Standard Version with the Apocrypha*, 4th ed. (New York: Oxford University Press, 2010), pp. 92–93, 156–57.

PRIMARY SOURCE 3.4

The Code of Manu (c. 200 BCE)

The Code of Manu is thought to represent some of the earliest legal ideas of the nomadic Vedic peoples of South Asia. The code's nearly 2,700 verses were written down in Sanskrit sometime after 200 BCE, but the laws about social interactions in the excerpt here may well date to a much earlier time. They are presented in the form of a dialogue between the legendary first man, Manu, and wise men who come before him to hear his ideas about social order.

- How does the opening of this code engage the class distinctions you might expect in a Vedic South Asian context?
- What expectations for behavior are outlined in this code?
- What do these "eternal laws for a husband and his wife" suggest about the relationship between men and women in a Vedic context?

Chapter I. 1. The great sages approached Manu, who was seated with a collected mind, and, having duly worshipped him, spoke as follows:

2. 'Deign, divine one, to declare to us precisely and in due order the sacred laws of each of the (four chief) castes (varna) and of the intermediate ones.

3. 'For thou, O Lord, alone knowest the purport, (i.e.) the rites, and the knowledge of the soul, (taught) in this whole ordinance, which is unknowable and unfathomable.

4. He [Manu] whose power is measureless, being thus asked by the high-minded great sages, duly honoured them, and answered, 'Listen!'

***

Chapter IX. 1. [Manu] will now propound the eternal laws for a husband and his wife who keep to the oath of duty, whether they be united or separated.

2. Day and night women must be kept in dependence by the males (of) their (families), and, if they attach themselves to sensual enjoyments, they must be kept under one's control.

3. Her father protects (her) in childhood, her husband protects (her) in youth, and her sons protect (her) in old age; a woman is never fit for independence.

4. Reprehensible is the father who gives not (his daughter in marriage) at the proper time; reprehensible is the husband who approaches not (his wife in due season), and reprehensible is the son who does not protect his mother after her husband has died.

5. Women must particularly be guarded against evil inclinations, however trifling (they may appear); for, if they are not guarded, they will bring sorrow on two families.

6. Considering that the highest duty of all castes, even weak husbands (must) strive to guard their wives.

7. He who carefully guards his wife, preserves (the purity of) his offspring, virtuous conduct, his family, himself, and his (means of acquiring) merit.

***

9. As the male is to whom a wife cleaves, even so is the son whom she brings forth; let him therefore carefully guard his wife, in order to keep his offspring pure.

10. No man can completely guard women by force; but they can be guarded by the employment of the (following) expedients:

11. Let the (husband) employ his (wife) in the collection and expenditure of his wealth, in keeping (everything) clean, in (the fulfilment of) religious duties, in the preparation of his food, and in looking after the household utensils.

12. Women, confined in the house under trustworthy and obedient servants, are not (well) guarded; but those who of their own accord keep guard over themselves, are well guarded.

13. Drinking (spirituous liquor), associating with wicked people, separation from the husband, rambling abroad, sleeping (at unseasonable hours), and dwelling in other men's houses, are the six causes of the ruin of women.

***

46. Neither by sale nor by repudiation is a wife released from her husband; such we know the law to be, which the Lord of creatures (Pragâpati) made of old.

***

76. If the husband went abroad for some sacred duty, (she) must wait for him eight years, if (he went) to (acquire) learning or fame six (years), if (he went) for pleasure three years.

77. For one year let a husband bear with a wife who hates him; but after (the lapse of) a year let him deprive her of her property and cease to cohabit with her.

***

81. A barren wife may be superseded in the eighth year, she whose children (all) die in the tenth, she who bears only daughters in the eleventh, but she who is quarrelsome without delay.

82. But a sick wife who is kind (to her husband) and virtuous in her conduct, may be superseded (only) with her own consent and must never be disgraced.

***

95. The husband receives his wife from the gods, (he does not wed her) according to his own will; doing what is agreeable to the gods, he must always support her (while she is) faithful.

96. To be mothers were women created, and to be fathers men; religious rites, therefore, are ordained in the Veda to be performed (by the husband) together with the wife.

***

101. 'Let mutual fidelity continue until death,' this may be considered as the summary of the highest law for husband and wife.

Source: *The Laws of Manu, Translated with Extracts from Seven Commentaries,* translated by Georg Bühler (Oxford: Clarendon Press, 1886), pp. 1–2, 327–29, 335, 341–42, 344–45.

PRIMARY SOURCE 3.5

Adviser Zichan of Zheng's Compilation of Laws (c. sixth century BCE)

The Chinese text included here describes the first set of formal laws in China, dating to the sixth century BCE. The text comes from the Spring and Autumn period (722–481 BCE), whose latter years also produced the thoughtful musings of Confucius. This passage, however, describes a series of earlier contexts for how law worked in early China and offers reflections on rule by king versus rule of law. It suggests that Shang kings did not publicize a penal code, but rather created a clear system of punishments for disorderly conduct brought before the king.

- **What are the problems with law codes, according to this text?**

- **How does this text suggest that Chinese kings established order before there were laws?**

- **Based on this text, what do you imagine was the second-millennium BCE legal context of the Shang territorial state? Would people living under Shang authority have known the laws that governed them? Explain.**

In the third month, the people of Zheng cast a penal text. Shu Xiang dispatched to Zichan a text. It stated, "Formerly, I had hope for you, but have now given it up. In the past, former kings consulted on affairs to decide them but did not make penal compilations, for they feared that the people would grow litigious. Still unable to control them, they restrained them with rightness, bound them with [good] governance, and raised them with humanness. They institutionalized emoluments and ranks to encourage their obedience and determined strict punishments so as to overawe their perversity. Fearing that that was not enough, they taught them of loyalty, rewarded good conduct, instructed them in their duties, deployed them with harmony, supervised them respectfully, supervised them with might, and adjudged them with firmness. Still they sought sagacious and erudite superiors, intelligent and astute officials, loyal and trustworthy elders, and kind and beneficent masters. It was only under such conditions that the people could be employed without disaster or disorder resulting. When the people are aware of a legal compilation, they will have no wariness of their superiors. All become contentious, appealing to the texts, and achieve their goals through lucky conniving. They cannot be governed. When the Xia had a disorderly government, they composed the *Punishments of Yu*. When the Shang had disorderly administration, they composed the *Punishments of Tang*. When the Zhou had disorderly administration, they composed the *Nine Punishments*. All three of these penal compilations arose in terminal ages. Now as advisor to the kingdom of Zheng you have rectified fields and ditches, established a reviled administration, instituted the tripartite compilation, and cast the penal text [in bronze], in order to calm the populace. Is this not difficult?

Source: *Zuozhuan*, translated by Earnest Caldwell, in "Social Change and Written Law in Early Chinese Legal Thought," *Law and History Review* 32 (February 2014): 15.

Interpreting Visual Evidence

Bronze Working

An important development in many of the territorial states of the second millennium BCE was bronze working, which involved the smelting of copper and tin to make durable objects. Bronze was used for weapons, chariot parts (wheel rims and lynchpins), tools, decorative objects, and ritual vessels.

The methods for casting bronze varied in different parts of Afro-Eurasia. In the east, in Shang China, artisans used an approach called the piece-mold method. In this method, artists would make a model of the item to be cast, cover it in clay to make a mold, cut the clay mold away in pieces (even etching the clay mold to add further detail), cast the bronze into the cut pieces of the clay mold, and then reassemble the bronze pieces to make the finished product. This process allowed the artists to achieve a much greater level of detail than the lost-wax method used in the Mediterranean, in which a model is made in wax, clay is formed around it, the clay form is heated to melt and remove the wax, and then bronze is poured into the cavity where the wax had been.

While bronze working thrived across Afro-Eurasia in the second millennium BCE, scholars agree that Shang bronze metallurgy was far and away the most advanced. Stunning examples of intricate Shang bronze work have been unearthed in tombs in the Yellow River valley. The Shang Chinese developed a range of vessel types, one of which was the jia-type vessel (an example from the fifteenth to fourteenth century BCE is pictured here), used for heating wine libations for ceremonies venerating ancestors. To the far west, bronze casters in Middle and New Kingdom Egypt crafted a range of items that have been found in burials. One example, dating to the sixteenth to thirteenth century BCE, is this razor handle depicting an African man playing an instrument. From Mycenae in Greece, a gold-inlay dagger from the sixteenth century BCE shows a lion hunt, with five hunters (one of whom has been killed) and three lions.

Shang "jia" vessel.

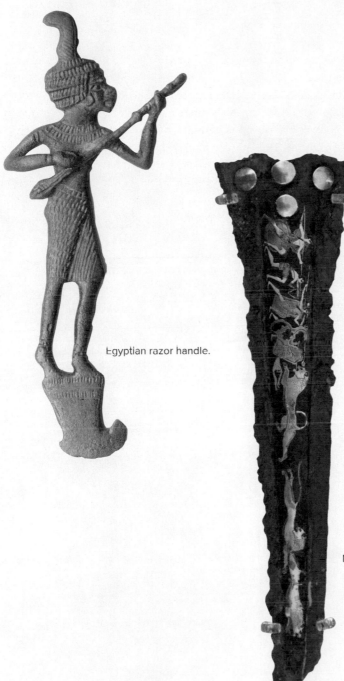

Egyptian razor handle.

Mycenaean bronze dagger.

1. Compare the bronze work from China, Egypt, and Greece. What does the varied craftsmanship suggest about the spread of this vital skill among territorial states in the second millennium BCE?

2. Compare what each of these items was used for and where they were found. What can you surmise about territorial states—about their hierarchies, their similarity to river-basin societies—based on the findspots for these items (elite graves) and their purpose (ritual, decorative, and so on)?

3. What does the decorative imagery on these bronze items suggest about trade and exchange among territorial states?

4

First Empires and Common Cultures in Afro-Eurasia

1250-325 BCE

Sennacherib—ruler of the Neo-Assyrian Empire early in the seventh century BCE—writes that at the end of one successful campaign he took "200,150 people, great and small, male and female, horses, mules, asses, camels, and sheep without number, I brought away from them and counted them my spoil." The booty about which Sennacherib boasts was unheard of in earlier ages. The immensity of such conquest highlights the arrival of a new era that involved empires with even larger geographical, political, economic, and cultural ambitions and achievements than the territorial states that preceded them (see Chapter 3). Given the nature and process of their formation, these early empires arguably replaced, rather than descended from, the earlier territorial states.

One key factor shaping these developments was warfare spurred by military innovation. Additionally, radical climate change drove many of the warrior/political leaders from the fringes of formerly powerful territorial states to the centers of power. There they established hybrid societies uniting cities and their hinterlands among the Neo-Assyrians and Persians of Southwest Asia, in the Vedic parts of South Asia, and in Zhou China. Imperial ideologies and religious beliefs supported the new empires. Farming yields

Chapter Outline

- Forces of Upheaval and the Rise of Early Empires
- Empire in Southwest Asia. The Neo-Assyrian and Persian Empires
- Imperial Fringes in Western Afro-Eurasia
- Foundations of Vedic Culture in South Asia
- The Early Zhou Empire in East Asia
- Conclusion

Core Objectives

- **DESCRIBE** the factors that contributed to the rise of early empires in the centuries after 1200 BCE and the characteristics of these empires.
- **COMPARE** empire formation, or the lack thereof, in Southwest Asia, South Asia, and East Asia in this period.
- **EVALUATE** the connection between empires and war, religion, and trade.
- **ANALYZE** the relationships between empires and the peoples on their peripheries.

increased and populations grew. On the fringes of empires, microsocieties arose and made significant contributions to human development: the seafaring Phoenicians developed a simplified alphabet, the Israelites espoused a strict monotheism, and Greek city-states came to the fore and even began to challenge the power of the Persian Empire.

Global Storyline

Comparing First Empires and the Beginnings of Judaism

- Climate change, migrations, technological advances, and administrative innovations contribute to the development of the world's first great empires.

- The Neo-Assyrians and then the Persians employ two different approaches to consolidate and maintain empires in Southwest Asia.

- South Asia becomes more culturally integrated despite the absence of a strong, centralized political authority.

- The Zhou dynasty establishes loose political integration in East Asia.

Forces of Upheaval and the Rise of Early Empires

Four related forces shaped the development of early empires in the first millennium BCE: climate change, migrations, new technologies, and administrative innovations. Migrants driven by climate change mingled with settled peoples. Ambitious leaders used innovations in technology and administration to create new states that went on to conquer other kingdoms. Gradually, a new political organization came into being: the **empire**. An empire is a group of states or different ethnic groups brought together under a single sovereign power. With varying degrees and types of centralization (as we will see in Southwest Asia, South Asia, and East Asia), empires connected distant regions through common languages, unifying political systems, trade, and shared religious beliefs. While most regions of Afro-Eurasia did not experience the rise of empire, those that did, and their neighbors, were profoundly affected by the development.

CLIMATE CHANGE

Beginning around 1200 BCE, another prolonged period of drought gripped Afro-Eurasia, causing social upheavals and migrations and utterly destroying settled societies and long-established governments. Many regions that had enjoyed rapid population growth in the second millennium BCE now found themselves unable to support such large numbers, forcing peoples to leave their homes in search of food and fertile land. (See Map 4.1.)

From the Mediterranean to East Asia, this wave of drought led to dramatic political shifts. In Egypt, low Nile floods forced pharaohs to spend their time securing food supplies and repelling Libyans from the desert and "Sea People" marauders from the coast. In Anatolia, Hittite kings dispatched envoys to the rulers of all the major agricultural areas, pleading for grain shipments to save their starving people. Even the drastic step of moving their capital to northern Syria, where food was more plentiful, did not prevent Hittite collapse. In mainland Greece, Mycenaean culture disintegrated when diminished rains made it impossible for farmers there to export wine, olives, and timber. Likewise in East Asia, radical climate change was a major factor in political developments. Arid conditions on the plains of central Asia resulted in powerful hot and dry winds that carried immense quantities of dust onto the North China plain. The dust storms reduced the soil's ability to retain moisture and led to a sharp decline in soil fertility. Some groups, like the Zhou peoples, went on the move in search of arable land.

THE BIG PICTURE

What were the factors that contributed to the rise of early empires in the centuries after 1200 BCE, and what were the characteristics of these empires?

empire
Group of states or ethnic groups governed by a single sovereign power with varying degrees of centralization using a range of methods, including common language, shared religious beliefs, trade, political systems, and military might.

The Global View

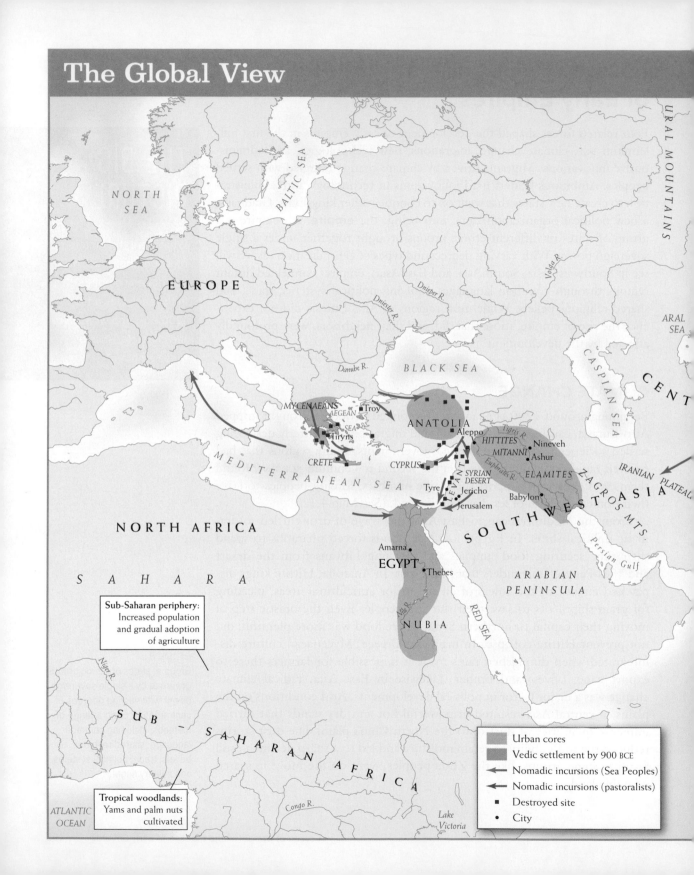

NORTH SEA

BALTIC SEA

EUROPE

Dnieper R.

Dniester R.

URAL MOUNTAINS

Volga R.

ARAL SEA

BLACK SEA

CASPIAN SEA

CENT

Danube R.

MYCENAEANS   Troy
AEGEAN   ANATOLIA
SEA   Aleppo
Tiryns   *HITTITES*   Nineveh
CRETE   CYPRUS   *MITANNI*   Ashur
SYRIAN
DESERT
Tyre   Jericho   *ELAMITES*
Jerusalem   Babylon

Tigris R.
Euphrates R.

IRANIAN
PLATEAU

ZAGROS MTS.

SOUTHWEST ASIA

Persian Gulf

MEDITERRANEAN SEA

NORTH AFRICA

Amarna
EGYPT   Thebes

ARABIAN
PENINSULA

S A H A R A

RED SEA

Sub-Saharan periphery:
Increased population
and gradual adoption
of agriculture

NUBIA

Nile R.

Niger R.

S U B - S A H A R A N   A F R I C A

ATLANTIC
OCEAN

Congo R.

Lake
Victoria

Tropical woodlands:
Yams and palm nuts
cultivated

	Urban cores
	Vedic settlement by 900 BCE
←	Nomadic incursions (Sea Peoples)
←	Nomadic incursions (pastoralists)
■	Destroyed site
•	City

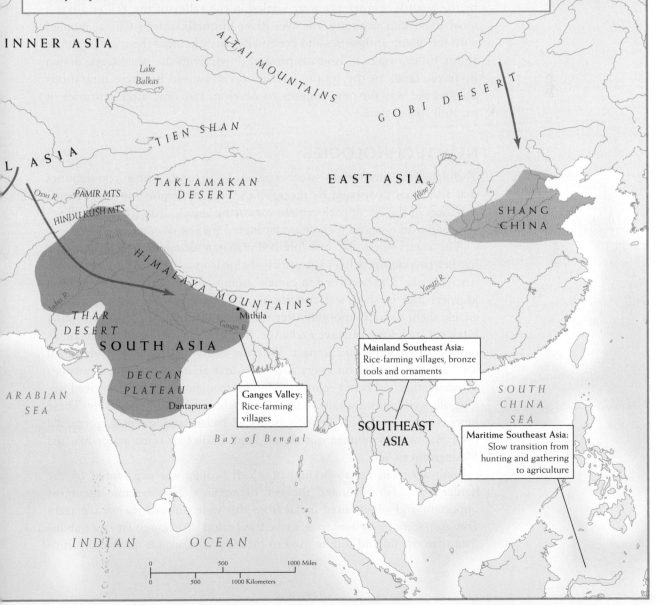

Map 4.1 Afro-Eurasia, 1200 BCE—Urban Cores and Migrations

Nomadic incursions shattered the social and political status quo in Afro-Eurasia at this time. While destroying old polities, these migrations fostered a new social and political order in a variety of regions.

- Where did nomadic groups originate, and where did they migrate to?
- What is a major difference between the invasions of the Sea Peoples and the movements of pastoralists in this period?
- Why do you think that so many of the nomadic movements were toward populated areas?

INNER ASIA

ALTAI MOUNTAINS

Lake Balkas

GOBI DESERT

TIEN SHAN

L ASIA

Oxus R. PAMIR MTS.

HINDU KUSH MTS.

TAKLAMAKAN DESERT

EAST ASIA

Yellow R.

SHANG CHINA

HIMALAYA MOUNTAINS

Indus R.

THAR DESERT

Mithila

Ganges R.

SOUTH ASIA

Yangzi R.

DECCAN PLATEAU

Dantapura

ARABIAN SEA

Ganges Valley:
Rice-farming villages

Bay of Bengal

Mainland Southeast Asia:
Rice-farming villages, bronze tools and ornaments

SOUTHEAST ASIA

SOUTH CHINA SEA

Maritime Southeast Asia:
Slow transition from hunting and gathering to agriculture

INDIAN   OCEAN

| 0 | 500 | 1000 Miles |
| 0 | 500 | 1000 Kilometers |

MIGRATIONS

The violent movement of peoples, driven in part by climate change, disrupted urban societies and destroyed the administrative centers of kings, priests, and dynasties. Invaders, moving out of loosely organized peripheral societies, assaulted the urban centers and territorial kingdoms of mainland Greece, Crete, Anatolia, Mesopotamia, Egypt, and East Asia, causing the collapse of many of these once powerful states. Marauders from the Mediterranean basin and the Syrian desert upset the diplomatic relations and the elaborate system of international trade that had linked Southwest Asia and North Africa. In East Asia, the Zhou peoples, who by the twelfth century BCE were settled in the valley of the Yellow River's most important tributary, the Wei River in northwestern China, tangled with the Shang authorities and eventually overwhelmed the regime. In the Indus Valley, waves of nomads pressed down from the northwest, drawn by fertile lands to the south. The upheavals caused by these migrations opened the way for new empires to develop, but only after centuries of turmoil and decline.

NEW TECHNOLOGIES

Technological innovations were crucial in reconstructing communities that had been devastated by drought and violent population movements. Advances in the use of pack camels, seaworthy vessels, iron tools for cultivation, and iron weapons for warfare facilitated the rise of empires.

The camel—first the one-humped Saharan dromedary and later the hardier two-humped Bactrian camel—helped open up trade routes across Afro-Eurasia. The fat stored in camels' humps allows them to survive long journeys and harsh desert conditions, and thick pads under their hoofs enable them to walk smoothly over the difficult terrain that had previously hindered such long-distance exchange. Similarly, new shipbuilding technologies made a significant impact. Whereas boats had once been designed for limited transport on rivers and lakes and along shorelines, new ships boasted larger and better-reinforced hulls. Stronger masts and improved rigging allowed billowing sails to harness wind power more effectively. These innovations, along with improvements in ballast and steering, propelled bold mariners to venture out across large bodies of open water like the Mediterranean Sea.

Innovations in metalworking, in which bronze was supplanted by the harder iron, also facilitated the rise of empires. Iron became the most important and widely used metal from this time onward (hence the term *Iron Age*, sometimes used to describe this period). Although far more abundant than the tin and copper used to make bronze, iron is more difficult to

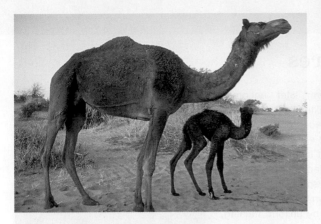 

Camels Dromedary camels (*left*) are good draft animals for travel and domestic work in the deserts of Arabia, Afghanistan, and India. Two-hump camels (*right*) are much bigger than dromedary camels. They are more suited to the extreme dry and cold weather in Iran and central Asia. Over time, both types of camel become important for Afro-Eurasian trade.

extract from ore and to fabricate into useful shapes. When the technology to smelt and harden iron advanced, iron tools and weapons replaced those made of bronze. This revolution in metallurgy brought shifts in agrarian techniques, such as forged-iron-edged plows that allowed farmers to cultivate crops far beyond the traditional floodplains of riverbanks. Farmers could now till more difficult terrain to remove weeds, break up sod, and unearth fertile subsoil. These technological innovations supported larger, more integrated societies.

ADMINISTRATIVE INNOVATIONS

The expansion of the first empires depended on military might, and control of expanded territories required new administrative techniques. Beginning in the ninth century BCE, fierce Neo-Assyrian soldiers, equipped with iron weaponry and armor, established their king's rule over the countryside. The Neo-Assyrians used mass deportations to break resisters' unity, to provide enslaved laborers in parts of the empire that needed manpower, and to integrate the realm. Over 300 years, they constructed an infrastructure of roads, garrisons, and relay stations throughout the entire territory, making it easier to communicate and to move troops. Moreover, they forced subject peoples to send tribute in the form of grains, animals, raw materials, and people, in addition to precious goods such as gold and lapis lazuli, which they used to build imperial cities and to enrich the royal coffers. In later centuries, such innovations—well-equipped armies, deportation, road systems for transit and communication, and tribute—became common among empires. (See Current Trends in World History: Big Forces in Early Empires.)

Big Forces in Early Empires

Conflict has always been a part of the human condition. But organized warfare and the use of "big force"—that is, large, well-disciplined armies—appears only with the formation of complex societies. The military units created in these complex societies became crucial vehicles for expanding the lands and peoples under the control of single states and broadcasting the influence of these states well beyond the territories that they controlled militarily.

Evidence for intermittent conflict among the city-states of Sumer in the fourth millennium BCE and in Old Kingdom Egypt (2686–2181 BCE), discussed in Chapter 2, shows that local populations were drafted into a common army when needed. Permanent forces, first recorded in the Old Akkadian period in the third millennium BCE, were used to forge unity, dominate trade routes, and repel threatening "barbarians." Over the next two millennia, across the full extent of Afro-Eurasia, the technologies and structure of war machines developed along similar paths, leading to large standing armies equipped with new and improved weapons, marked by continual innovation and addition of new capabilities.

The earliest armies of Sumer were soldiers on foot arranged in a boxlike formation (generally called a *phalanx*, although that term later becomes associated with military innovations by Alexander of Macedon and his father, Philip II). The men were protected by the same types of leather capes and helmets and carried the same large shields to deflect spears and arrows. This mass-formation fighting of infantry that was enabled by uniform training, uniform armaments, and state provisioning became the norm for land forces in Egypt, Neo-Assyria, and, later, the Greek city-states. By the early second millennium, horse-drawn chariots were added to the force, adding mobility and the potential of surprise to an ever-larger infantry force (see Chapter 3). Mounted cavalry was introduced later, toward the middle of the first millennium BCE, by the Neo-Assyrians when fighting in mountainous terrain rendered the chariot impractical. Camels, long used as pack animals, were also used in warfare, primarily by Arab tribesmen conscripted into the Neo-Assyrian army. And elephants were one of the four components of the South Asian Vedic armies, who combined them with cavalry, infantry, and chariots to create a highly effective fighting force.

Even before the rise of complex societies and large military forces, the weapons of warfare had been those of the hunter: bows and arrows,

Assault on -alammu On the reliefs of the palace of Sennacherib (r. c. 700–692 BCE) at Nineveh, slingers launch projectiles while shield-bearing spearmen form up behind them in an assault on a city known from a fragmentary inscription as -alammu.

spears, and slings. Like these weapons, knives, daggers, axes, and maces were also incorporated into armies and were wielded by infantries in hand-to-hand combat. The compound bow, first used in warfare by the Sumerians, was refined by the Neo-Assyrians into a powerful projectile that could achieve an arc of more than 200 yards, raining destruction down on the opposing infantry. Although bronze was the most important metal for weapons, the introduction of iron toward the end of the second millennium BCE expanded the availability of metal for these state war machines. Since war was often conducted to acquire land, cities had to be conquered by force. Battering rams, first documented in Egypt, were added to mobile siege machines; towers supporting archers are pictured on the Neo-Assyrian stone sculptures. Levers and breaking bars as well as tunneling were used to undermine the integrity of the walls. And scaling ladders were thrown against the fortification for the final assault.

In China, the same elements of infantry, chariots, and archers were at the core of the army from as early as the Shang dynasty. While the original goal of the Shang was to capture prisoners needed for sacrifice to the ancestors, soon defensive forces were needed to protect them against their neighbors. The Zhou gradually defeated the Shang through their superior forces and more ingenious and agile tactics. A fundamental advance was made with the invention around 475 BCE of the crossbow, a far more powerful personal killing machine, and the torsion catapult, which threw both heavy projectiles and fiery masses onto the enemy. From the beginning, the techniques and technologies of war were rapidly shared across cultural boundaries as a natural result of adapting

and improving on the achievements of the enemy. What mattered most for success was the ability to integrate and coordinate the increasing number of elements that went into a fighting force. The Persians learned at the hands of the Greeks that numbers and sheer firepower could not overcome agility, communication, and integration.

Toward the end of the second millennium BCE, new forms of force were appearing not just on land but also on the sea. The construction of purpose-built ships for the conduct of war on water—the world's first "battleships"—occurred over the course of the eighth century BCE in the eastern Mediterranean. These special ships were built mainly by the Phoenician and the Greek city-states, whose livelihood depended on commerce on the high seas. They were not designed like the slow-sailing bulky ships used for the transport of large cargoes; instead, they were sleek and slim—about 120 feet long and only 15 feet wide—with little room for anything other than the men rowing them. With up to 170 rowers, they were designed and constructed for speed and power. They had no purpose other than the deliberate sinking of other ships. At first, the rowers in ships were arranged with two banks (called *biremes* by the Greeks) and later with three (called *triremes*). The ships were

armed with bronze "beaks," or rams, that were used to cave in the sides of enemy ships. These ships were costly to construct, to man, to provision, and to command. As with the maintenance, training, and arming of large land forces, only relatively wealthy states and governments could afford to mount this kind of power on the high seas.

Questions for Analysis

- What were some of the military innovations that were characteristic of "big forces"? In infantry? Cavalry? Naval forces?
- In what specific ways did these military innovations shape the development of empires?
- From your reading of this chapter, in what other ways could you compare empires, in addition to comparing their use of "big forces"?

Explore Further

Briant, Pierre, *From Cyrus to Alexander: A History of the Persian Empire* (2002).

Tanner, Harold M., *China: A History: From Neolithic Cultures through the Great Qing Empire (10,000 BCE–1799 CE)* (2009).

Empire in Southwest Asia: The Neo-Assyrian and Persian Empires

Core Objectives

COMPARE empire formation, or the lack thereof, in Southwest Asia, South Asia, and East Asia between 1250 and 325 BCE.

In Southwest Asia, the Neo-Assyrians and then the Persians offered some of the world's first experiments with true imperial control. The Neo-Assyrians (911–612 BCE) perfected early techniques of imperial rule, many of which became standard in later empires. The Neo-Assyrians also revealed the raw military side of imperial rule: constant, harsh warfare and the brutal exploitation of subjects. On the other hand, the Persians (560–331 BCE), who took control of Southwest Asia after the Neo-Assyrians, balanced their vast multicultural empire through a gentler combination of centralized administration and imperial ideology.

THE NEO-ASSYRIAN EMPIRE (911–612 BCE)

Defining features of the Neo-Assyrian Empire included deportations, forced labor, and a rigid social hierarchy. Neo-Assyrian rulers divided their empire into two parts and ruled them in different ways. The core of the empire, which the Neo-Assyrians called the "Land of Ashur," included such ancient cities as Ashur and Nineveh on the upper reaches of the Tigris River, and the lands between the Zagros Mountains and the Euphrates River. (See Map 4.2.) The king's appointees governed these interior lands, whose inhabitants had to supply food for the temple of the national god Ashur, manpower for the god's residence in the city of Ashur, and officials to carry out the state's business. Outside the "Land of Ashur" proper lay "the Land under the Yoke of Ashur," whose inhabitants were not considered Neo-Assyrians. In these peripheral territories, local rulers held power as subjects of the Neo-Assyrian Empire. These subordinated states were expected to deliver massive amounts of tribute in the form of gold and silver, as opposed to the manpower or agricultural goods supplied by those in the "Land of Ashur." Tribute went directly to the king, who used it to pay for his extravagant court and ever-increasing military costs.

Forced labor—including serving in the military—and deportations helped integrate the empire and undermine local resistance. The Neo-Assyrian armies were hardened and disciplined professional troops led by officers promoted on the basis of merit, not birth. Their military combined infantry, cavalry, iron weapons, horse-drawn chariots armored with iron plates and carrying expert archers, and siege warfare (complete with massive wheeled siege towers and iron-capped battering rams). The Neo-Assyrian army evolved over time from an all-Neo-Assyrian force that conducted annual summer campaigns to a several-hundred-thousand-strong, year-round force composed of Neo-Assyrians and conquered peoples. By the seventh century BCE, different ethnic groups in the Neo-Assyrian army performed specialized military functions:

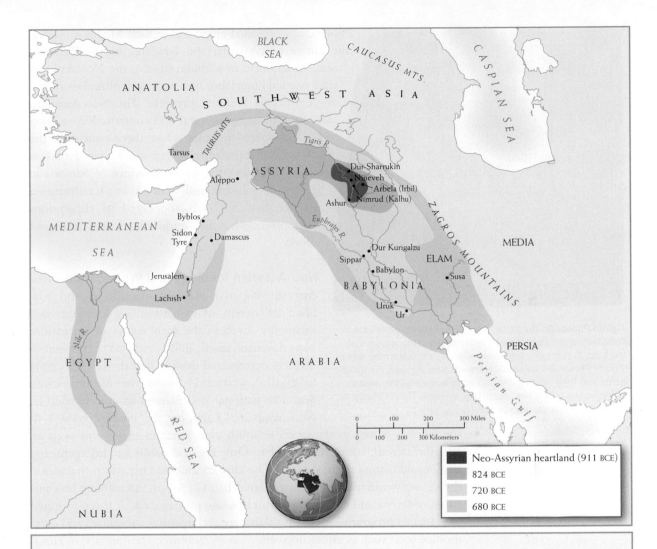

Map 4.2 The Neo-Assyrian Empire

The Neo-Assyrians built the first strong regional empire in Afro-Eurasia. In the process, they faced the challenge of promoting order and stability throughout their diverse realm.

- Where did the Neo-Assyrian Empire expand? How would you compare the various stages of expansion, in terms of timing and geographic reach?
- Which parts of the empire were "the Land of Ashur" and which were "the Land under the Yoke of Ashur"?
- Why do you think expansion after 720 BCE led to the empire's destruction?

Tiglath Pileser III The walls of the Neo-Assyrian palaces were lined with stone slabs carved with images of the victories of the king. This fragmentary slab originally decorated the wall of Tiglath Pileser III's palace at Nimrud/Kalhu. It shows the inhabitants and their herds being forced to leave after the defeat of their town by the Neo-Assyrians. Below is Tiglath Pileser III, shaded by his royal umbrella, in his war chariot.

Phoenicians provided ships and sailors; Medes served as the king's bodyguards; and Israelites supplied charioteers. In addition to a military force, the Neo-Assyrian state needed huge labor forces for agricultural work and for enormous building projects. The Neo-Assyrians recruited most agricultural and construction workers from conquered peoples. Over three centuries, the Neo-Assyrian Empire relocated more than 4 million people, including the whole province of Samaria in present-day Israel and Palestinian territories—a practice that not only supported its stupendous work projects but also undermined local resistance efforts.

Neo-Assyrian Ideology and Propaganda Neo-Assyrian imperial ideology supported and justified its system of expansion, exploitation, and inequality. Even in the early stages of expansion, Neo-Assyrian inscriptions and art expressed a divinely determined destiny that drove the regime to expand westward toward the Mediterranean Sea. The national god Ashur had commanded all Neo-Assyrians to support the forcible growth of the empire, whose goal was to establish and maintain order and keep an ever-threatening cosmic chaos at bay. Only the god Ashur and his agent, the king, could bring universal order. The king conducted holy war to transform the known world into the well-regulated Land of Ashur, intensifying his campaign of terror and expansion with elaborate propaganda. A three-pronged propaganda program—including elaborate architectural complexes and ceremonies, texts such as inscriptions and year-by-year accounts (annals) of kings' achievements, and vivid images of the army's brutal campaigns—proclaimed that Neo-Assyria's triumph was inevitable.

Neo-Assyrian Social Structure The Neo-Assyrians also exploited a rigid social hierarchy. At the top was the king, who as the sole agent of the god Ashur conducted war to expand the Land of Ashur. Below the king were military elites, rewarded through gifts of land, silver, and exemptions from royal taxes. Over time, these military elites became the noble class and controlled vast estates that included both the land and the local people who worked it. The king and the elites also controlled the most populous part of the society, the peasantry, in which various categories of workers had differing privileges. Many workers were enslaved because they could not pay their debts, but they were allowed to marry partners who were free, conduct financial transactions, and even own property with other enslaved people attached to it. Foreigners enslaved through conquest, however, had no rights and were forced to do hard manual labor on the state's monumental building projects. Those peoples forcibly relocated were not enslaved but they did become attached to the lands that they had to work. Families were small and lived on modest plots of land, where they raised vegetables and planted vineyards.

Neo-Assyrian women were far more restricted than their counterparts in the earlier periods of Sumerian and Old Babylonian Mesopotamia. Under the Neo-Assyrians' patriarchal social system, women had almost no control over their lives. Because all inheritance passed through the male line, it was crucial that a man be certain of the paternity of the children borne by his wives. As a result, all interactions between men and women outside the family were highly restricted. The so-called Middle Assyrians of the thirteenth century BCE had introduced the practice of veiling, requiring it of all respectable women. Prostitutes who serviced the men of the army and worked in the taverns were forbidden to wear the veil, so that their revealed faces and hair would signal their disreputable status. Any prostitute found wearing the veil would be dragged to the top of the city wall, stripped of her clothing, flogged, and sometimes even killed.

The queens of Neo-Assyria obeyed the same social norms, but their lives were more comfortable and varied than the commoners'. They lived in a separate part of the palace with servants who were either enslaved women or eunuchs (castrated males). Though Neo-Assyrian queens rarely wielded genuine power, they enjoyed respect and recognition, especially in the role of mother of the king. In fact, a queen could serve as regent for her son if the king died while his heir was still a child.

Such was the case with Sammuramat, associated with the quasi-mythical queen Semiramis in Greek sources. Sammuramat served as regent from 810 to 806 BCE, successfully ruling the empire until her son came of age. An early "world historian," the Greek Diodorus Siculus, described the legendary Semiramis as a brilliant military strategist who wore clothes that disguised her gender, beguiled a king through her beauty and intellect into marrying her, built a massive city at Babylon, and undertook daring and far-reaching military campaigns from Egypt to India after her husband's death. The memorial in Ashur to the real Sammuramat, however, in true patriarchal Neo-Assyrian fashion, commemorates her merely by noting her relationship with various male figures: "queen [wife] of Shamshi-Adad, king of the universe, king of Assyria, mother of Adad-nirari, king of the universe, king of Assyria, daughter-in-law of Shalmaneser, king of the four regions."

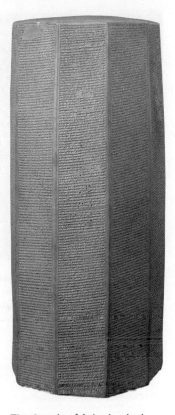

The Annals of Ashurbanipal
This ten-sided baked clay cylinder carries a portion of the annals of the Neo-Assyrian king Ashurbanipal (r. 668–627 BCE). It was found at Nineveh along with thousands of other tablets preserved in his famous library, including many of the earliest fragments of the *Epic of Gilgamesh*. The annals of Ashurbanipal were detailed, almost novelistic accounts of his military and civic achievements. Unlike earlier annals, they include first-person discourse, indirect discourse, flashbacks, and lively descriptions of events and places.

The Instability of the Neo-Assyrian Empire At their peak, the Neo-Assyrians controlled most of the lands stretching from Persia to Egypt. Yet their empire was unstable, as it required occupying armies to be spread across

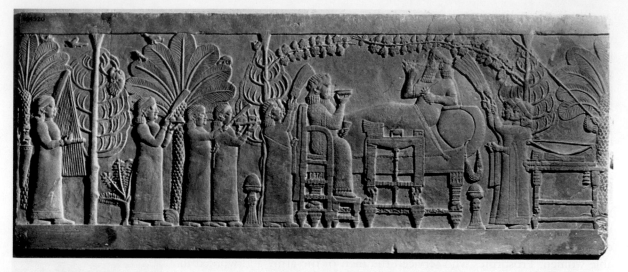

Ashursharrat, Neo-Assyrian Queen While no contemporary images of the exceptional Queen Sammuramat/Semiramis exist, we do get a rare glimpse of a later Neo-Assyrian queen in this relief from Ashurbanipal's palace at Nimrud/Kalhu. Ashursharrat, bedecked in an ornate robe, sits on an elaborately carved chair at the feet of her reclining husband as they celebrate victory in 653 BCE over the Elamite king Te-umman, whose head—in brutal Neo-Assyrian fashion—hangs from the tree on the left.

vast territories and a relentless propaganda machine. Discontent among nobles ultimately led to civil war, which made the Neo-Assyrian Empire vulnerable to external threats as well. The conquest of Nineveh by a combined force of Medes, Neo-Babylonians, and other groups contributed to the collapse of the Neo-Assyrian Empire in 612 BCE.

THE PERSIAN EMPIRE (560–331 BCE)

After a brief interlude of Neo-Babylonian rule—including the reign of Nebuchadnezzar II (r. c. 605–562 BCE) and the creation of his legendary Hanging Gardens of Babylon—the Persians asserted power and created a gentler form of imperial rule in Southwest Asia, based more on persuasion and mutual benefit than on raw power. A nomadic group speaking an Indo-Iranian language, the Persians had arrived on the Iranian plateau from central Asia during the second millennium and gradually spread to the plateau's southwestern part. These expert horsemen shot arrows from horseback with deadly accuracy in the midst of battle. After Cyrus the Great (r. 559–529 BCE) united the Persian tribes, his armies defeated the Lydians in southwestern Anatolia and took over their gold mines, land, and trading routes. He next overpowered the Greek city-states on the Aegean coast of Anatolia. In building their immense empire, the Persians, whose ancestors were pastoralists and had no urban traditions to draw on, adapted the ideologies and institutions of the Neo-Babylonians, the Neo-Assyrians, and indigenous peoples, modifying them to fit their own customs and political aims.

The Integration of a Multicultural Persian Empire From their base on the Iranian plateau, the Persian rulers developed a centralized yet multicultural empire that reached from the Indus Valley to northern Greece and from central Asia to the south of Egypt. (See Map 4.3.) Cyrus, the founder of the Persian Empire, presented himself as a benevolent ruler who had liberated his subjects from the oppression of their own kings. He pointed to his victory in Babylon as a sign that the city's gods had turned against its king as a heretic. Cyrus released the Jews from their captivity in Babylon, to which they had

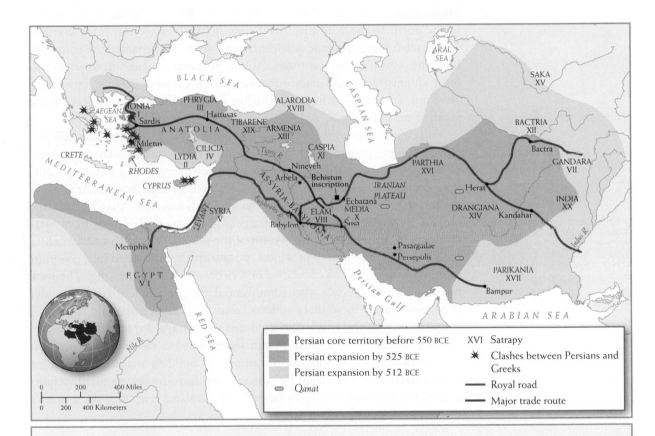

Map 4.3 The Persian Empire, 550–479 BCE

Starting in the sixth century BCE, the Persians succeeded the Neo-Assyrians as rulers of the large regional empire of Southwest Asia and parts of North Africa. Compare the Persian Empire's territorial domains with those of the Neo-Assyrian Empire in Map 4.2.

- Geographically, how did the Persian Empire differ from the Neo-Assyrian state?
- Analyzing the map, how many Persian satrapies existed? What role do you think they played in the success of the Persian Empire?
- How did *qanats* and road systems help the Persians consolidate their imperial power?

been exiled by the Neo-Babylonian king Nebuchadnezzar II around 587 BCE; they then returned to Jerusalem in 538 BCE to begin rebuilding their temple. Even the Greeks, who later defeated the Persians, saw Cyrus as a model ruler.

In the aftermath of Cyrus's death on the battlefield, Darius I (r. 522–486 BCE) overcame his main rival for power and put the new empire on a solid footing. First, he suppressed revolts across the lands, recording this feat on the Behistun inscription, a monumental rock relief overhanging the road to his capital, Persepolis. Then he conquered territories held by dozens of different ethnic groups, stretching from the Indus River in the east to the Aegean and Mediterranean Seas in the west, and from the Black, Caspian, and Aral Seas in the north to the Nile River in the south. To manage this huge domain, Darius introduced dynamic administrative systems that enabled the empire to flourish for another two centuries. Its new bureaucracy combined central and local administration and made effective use of the strengths of local tradition, economy, and rule—rather than forcing Persian customs on subject people via rigid central control.

This empire was both centralized and multicultural. The Persians believed that all subject peoples were equal; the only requirements were to be loyal to the king and to pay tribute—which was considered an honor, not a burden. Although local Persian administrators used local languages, Aramaic (a dialect of a Semitic language long spoken in Southwest Asia) became the empire's official language because many of its literate scribes came from Mesopotamia. Darius brought the wealth of the periphery to the imperial center by establishing a system of provinces, or **satrapies**, each ruled by a governor (called a satrap) who was a relative or a close associate of the king. The local bureaucrats and officials who administered the government worked under close monitoring by military officers, central tax collectors, and spies (the so-called eyes of the king) who enforced the satraps' loyalty. Darius established a system of fixed taxation and formal tribute allocations. Moreover, he promoted trade throughout the empire by building roads, establishing a standardized currency including coinage, and introducing standard weights and measures. These strategies helped integrate and centralize the empire's vast territories.

Zoroastrianism, Ideology, and Social Structure The Persians built their ideology of kingship and their social structure on religious foundations. They drew their religious ideas from their pastoral and tribal roots, and thus their ideology reflected traditions of warrior and priestly classes similar to those preserved in the Vedic texts of the Indus Valley. Zoroaster (also known as Zarathustra), who most likely lived sometime after 1000 BCE in eastern Iran, crystallized the region's traditional beliefs into a formal religious system. The main source for the teachings of Zoroaster is the Avesta, a collection of holy works initially transmitted orally by priests and then, according to legend,

satrapy
Province in the Persian empire, ruled over by a governor, called a satrap, who was usually a relative or associate of the king.

written down in the third century BCE. **Zoroastrianism** ultimately became the religion of the empire.

Zoroaster promoted belief in the god Ahura Mazda, who had created the world and all that was good. In dualistic contrast, Ahura Mazda's adversary, Ahriman, was deceitful and wicked. The Persians saw these two forces—light and truth versus darkness and lies—as engaged in a cosmic struggle for control of the universe. Zoroastrianism treated humans as capable of choosing between good and evil. Human choices had consequences: rewards or punishments in the afterlife. Strict rules of behavior determined the fate of each individual. For example, because animals were good, they deserved to be treated well. Intoxicants, widely used in tribal religions, were forbidden. Also, there were strict rules for treatment of the dead. For example, to prevent death from contaminating the sacred elements of earth, fire, and water, it was forbidden to bury, burn, or drown the deceased. Instead, people left corpses out for beasts and birds of prey to devour. The Greek historian Herodotus, who investigated the customs of the Persians in his attempt to explore the background of the Greco-Persian wars in the early fifth century BCE, was perplexed by this practice and reported that Persian corpses were mangled by birds or dogs and then encased in wax before burial.

Persians believed that their kings were appointed by Ahura Mazda as ruler over all peoples and all lands of the earth and charged by him with maintaining perfect order from which all creation would benefit. As such, kings enjoyed absolute authority. In return, they were expected to follow moral and political guidelines that reflected Zoroastrian notions of ethical behavior. Kings also had to show physical superiority that matched their moral standing. They had to be expert horsemen and peerless in wielding bows and spears. These were qualities valued by all Persian nobles, who revered the virtues of their nomadic ancestors. According to the ancient Greek historian Herodotus, Persian boys were taught three things only: "to ride, to shoot with the bow, and to tell the truth."

The Persian social order included four diverse groups with well-defined roles. A ruling class consisted of priests maintaining the ritual fire in temples, nobles administering the state, and warriors protecting and expanding the empire. An administrative and commercial class included scribes and bureaucrats who kept imperial records and merchants who secured goods from distant lands. The other two groups were made up of artisans and, finally, peasants who grew the crops and tended the flocks that fed the imperial machine.

The powerful Persian hereditary nobility surrounded and supported the king. These nobles had vast landholdings and often served the king as satraps or advisers. Also close to the king were wealthy merchants who directed trade across the vast empire. Royal gifts solidified the relations between king and nobles, reinforcing the king's place at the top of the political and social pyramid. In public ceremonies the king presented gold vessels, elaborate textiles,

Zoroastrianism
Dualistic Persian religion, based on the teaching of Zoroaster, in which forces of light and truth battle with those of darkness and falsehood.

and jewelry to reward each recipient's loyalty and demonstrate dependence on the crown. Any kind of failure would result in the withdrawal of royal favor. Should such failures be serious or treasonous, the offenders faced torture and death. In Persian society, class and royal favor counted for everything.

Public Works and Imperial Identity The Persians undertook significant building projects that helped unify their empire and consolidate imperial identity. For one, the Persians engaged in large-scale road building and constructed a system of rapid and dependable communication. The key element in the system was the Royal Road, which followed age-old trade routes some 1,600 miles from western Anatolia to the heart of the empire in southwestern Iran; trade routes continued eastward across the northern Iranian plateau and into central Asia. Traders used the Royal Road, as did the Persian army; subjects took tribute to the king, and royal couriers carried messages to the satraps and imperial armies over this road. As the Neo-Assyrians had done, the Persians placed way stations with fresh mounts and provisions along the route. Known routes and connections like these helped merchants conduct long-distance trade. Many examples of this trade can be found in the Egibi family's archive of more than 1,700 texts that span more than 120 years, from 606 to 484 BCE. These texts document the Egibis' trade in agricultural goods like barley, dates, onions, and wool across the region controlled by the Neo-Babylonians and then the Persians.

In addition to the Royal Road, the Persians devised other ways to connect the far reaches of the empire with its center. Darius oversaw the construction

Persian Water-Moving Technique The Persians perfected the channeling of water over long distances through underground channels called *qanats*. This technique, an efficient way to move water without evaporation, is still used today in hot, arid regions. In this example near Yazd, in central Iran, the domed structure leading to the underground tunnel is flanked by two brick towers called *badgir* (wind towers), an ancient form of air conditioning that cools the water using *bad* (the Persian word for wind).

Persepolis In the highland valley of Fars, the homeland of the Persians, Darius and his successors built a capital city and ceremonial center at the site of Persepolis. On top of a huge platform, there were audience halls, a massive treasury, the harem, and residential spaces. The largest palace, called the Apadana, was constructed of mud brick. The roof was supported by enormous columns projecting the images of bulls.

of a canal more than 50 miles long linking the Red Sea to the Nile River. Additionally, Persians developed a system of *qanats,* underground tunnels through which water flowed over long distances without evaporating or being contaminated. Laborers from local populations toiled on these feats of engineering as part of their obligations as subjects of the empire.

Until Cyrus's time, the Persians had been pastoral nomads who lacked traditions of monumental architecture, visual arts, or written literature or history. Multiple capitals—at Persepolis, Pasargadae, and Susa—expressed a Persian imperial identity. Skilled craftworkers from all over the empire blended their distinct cultural influences into a new Persian architectural style. The Persians used monumental architecture with grand columned halls and huge open spaces to provide reception rooms for thousands of representatives bringing tribute from all over the empire and to help integrate subject peoples by connecting them to one central, imperial authority. In the royal palace, three of the columned halls stood on raised platforms accessed via processional stairways that were lined with elaborate images of subjects bringing gifts and tribute to the king. This highly refined program of visual propaganda showed the Persian Empire as a society of diverse but obedient peoples. The carvings on the great stairway of Persepolis demonstrate the range of peoples who visited the palace, each bringing distinctive tribute: the Armenians presenting precious metal vessels, the Lydians carrying gold armlets and bowls, the Egyptians offering exotic animals, and the Sogdians leading proud horses.

While the stream of tribute ebbed and flowed over time, the multicultural Persian Empire was able to hold power in Southwest Asia for more than 200 years. Although the empire was weakened by challenges posed by Greek city-states to its west in the fifth century BCE, it persisted until it fell to the invading army of Alexander the Great in 331 BCE. First the Neo-Assyrians, and then later the Persians, had fashioned their own brands of empire that used a combination of military force, rigid political and social organization, and religious ideology to maintain successive control over Southwest Asia.

Imperial Fringes in Western Afro-Eurasia

A very different world emerged on Afro-Eurasia's western edges. Although their powerful neighbors affected them, western peoples—such as the Sea Peoples, the Greeks, the Phoenicians, and the Israelites—retained their own languages, beliefs, and systems of rule. While their communities were smaller than those in Southwest Asia, each asserted power and had long-lasting influence disproportionate to their size.

Core Objectives

ANALYZE the relationships between empires and the peoples on their peripheries in Southwest Asia, South Asia, and East Asia.

SEA PEOPLES

New migrations brought violent change to long-established kingdoms and states in the Mediterranean and Southwest Asia. Beginning around 1200 BCE, as the full effects of drought struck, new waves of Indo-European-speaking peoples left the Danube River basin in central Europe. A rapid rise in population and the development of local natural resources, particularly iron, spurred this group, who came to be known as the **Sea Peoples**, to move down the Danube toward the Black Sea. The invaders, armed with iron weaponry, brought turmoil to the peoples living in southeastern Europe, the Aegean, and the eastern Mediterranean.

The Hittites of Anatolia were the first to fall to the migrants' invasion. Once the invaders reached the Mediterranean, they mainly used boats for transportation, hence the label Sea Peoples (not a name they called themselves but rather one from the perspective of those whom they attacked). The Egyptians knew them as the Peleset, and only with great difficulty did the pharaohs repel them. Ramses III's mortuary temple in Thebes displays a massive relief depicting the so-called Battle of the Delta (c. 1175 BCE), in which he and his Egyptian forces fought off their invasions. Outside Egypt,

Sea Peoples
Migrants from north of the Mediterranean who invaded cities of Egypt, Asia Minor, and the Levant in the second millennium BCE.

other states and kingdoms suffered heavily from their ravages. The great trading cities of the Levant, especially Ugarit, an important port city in what is today northern Syria, were destroyed in the tumultuous movement of peoples in the twelfth century BCE. In the remains of the destroyed palace, cuneiform tablets were found that report on the impending disaster in vivid detail. One of the tablets sent to the king warns of the arrival of the *hapiru*, one of the threatening nomad peoples, and asks the ruler to prepare 150 ships for defense. Another, earlier tablet sent by the king of Ugarit to the king of Alashia (Cyprus) describes the threat, saying, "Behold, the enemy's ships came [here]; my cities were burned, and they did evil things to my country. . . . May my father know it: the seven ships of the enemy that came here inflicted much damage to us." All the major centers of the coast and inland were burned to the ground, including Alalakh, Hamath, Qatna, and Kadesh. Many were never reoccupied. The Sea Peoples ultimately settled along the southern coast of Southwest Asia, where they became known as the Philistines.

In the Mediterranean, the Sea Peoples' intrusion shook the social order of the Minoans on the island of Crete (see Chapter 3). Agricultural production in the region declined, and as the palace-centered bureaucracies and priesthoods of the second millennium BCE vanished, more violent societies emerged that relied on the newcomers' iron weapons. These more warlike Mycenaeans, who lived in one of the marginal areas of the Greek mainland and were dependent for their livelihood on exporting olives, wine, and timber, were hard hit by the political, economic, and climate-related problems wracking the eastern Mediterranean at the end of the second millennium BCE. Diminished rains made it impossible for farmers there to export these products and led to the disintegration of their culture. As a result, the Greek mainland experienced a 400-year period of economic decline, vividly captured by the Athenian historian Thucydides, writing in the fifth century BCE. Looking back on a dismal past, he remembered a dark age, "when there was no commerce, when people did not have dealings with each other without fear either on land or sea, when they only cultivated enough of their own land to provide a living for themselves." This was the culture of warrior-heroes described in the *Iliad*, an epic poem about the Trojan War, based on oral tales passed down for centuries before their compilation by Homer in the eighth century BCE. The Greek descendants of these warrior-heroes of the Mycenaean past developed dynamic communities and, as we will see in the next section, offered one of the most significant challenges to the Persians.

Mycenaean Arms and Armor
This Mycenaean vase illustrates the central role of arms and war to the societies on mainland Greece through 1200 BCE. The men bear common suits of armor and weapons—helmets, corsets, spears, and shields—most likely supplied to them by the palace-centered organizations to which they belonged. Despite these advantages, they were not able to mount a successful defense against the land incursions that destroyed the Mycenaean palaces toward the end of the thirteenth century BCE.

THE GREEKS

While the Neo-Assyrians and then the Persians thrived in Southwest Asia, the Greek city-states of the Peloponnese, of the Aegean islands, and along the west coast of Anatolia were experimenting with a range of political systems, from the dual kingship of warlike Sparta to the aristocracy, brief tyranny, and then democracy of Athens. Even with their political differences, the Greeks of the so-called Archaic period (from the eighth through the sixth century BCE) shared a language, religion, and culture that united them. The Olympic Games, celebrated to honor Zeus beginning in 776 BCE, were an example of that shared Panhellenic ideal. The Greek city-states, for all their differences, offer a good example of the energy and dynamism of a comparably small-scale society emerging in the shadow of the Persians. In areas of contact with the Persian Empire, Greek-speaking people in different cities sometimes cooperated with the Persians, even borrowing their ideas, but sometimes strongly resisted them.

In 499 BCE, some Greek city-states and others in the eastern Mediterranean revolted against the Persians, who claimed control over the Greek islands and mainland. During the six-year struggle, some Greek communities sided with the Persians and suffered condemnation by other Greeks for doing so. On the mainland, most Greek cities resisted the Persian king's authority. In 490 BCE, Darius and his vast army invaded mainland Greece but suffered a humiliating defeat at the hands of the much smaller force of Athenians at Marathon, near Athens. The Persians retreated and waited another decade before challenging their western foe again. Meanwhile, however, Athens was becoming a major sea power.

Under the leadership of Themistocles in the 480s BCE, Athens became a naval power whose strength was its fleet of triremes (battleships). When Greek and Persian forces clashed again in 480 BCE, Persian land forces led by Darius's successor Xerxes fought through Leonidas's 300 Spartans (and other Greeks) at Thermopylae only to have their navy lose the pivotal sea battle at Salamis. A year later, the Persians suffered a decisive defeat on land and eventually lost the war. Persian military defeats changed the balance of power. For the next 150 years, Persia lost ground to the Greeks, who gradually regained territory in southeastern Europe and western Anatolia. That expanded territory, and its governance, would become in the fifth century BCE the root of Greek civil discord (see Chapter 5).

THE PHOENICIANS

Another important group on the fringes extended its influence across the Mediterranean through its seafaring and trade: this group was the Chanani (called "Canaanites" in Hebrew scriptures), living in the region of

Greeks at War This fifth-century BCE krater (a 2-foot-tall wine-mixing vessel) illustrates an Amazonomachy. This scene—oft repeated in a variety of media—shows helmeted, shield-carrying, spear-wielding Greek warriors fighting against Amazons who serve as a stand-in for the recently defeated Persian foe. Fifth-century BCE art, including murals and large-scale friezes over the entryways of temples as well as smaller-scale imagery on pottery, focused more on such mythical/legendary events than on recent historical battles.

modern-day Lebanon. We know these entrepreneurial people by the name that the Greeks gave them—**Phoenicians** ("purple people")—because of an expensive purple dye that they manufactured and traded. A mixture of the local population and the more recently arrived Sea Peoples, these traders preferred opening up new markets and new ports to subduing frontiers. The Phoenicians maintained their autonomy from Neo-Assyrian kings by supplying them with exotic luxuries. Phoenician coastal cities were ideally situated to develop trade throughout the entire Mediterranean basin. Inland stood an extraordinary forest of massive cedars—perfect timber for making large, seaworthy craft, and a highly desirable export to the treeless heartlands of Egypt and Mesopotamia. (See Map 4.4.)

Innovations in shipbuilding and seafaring enabled Phoenicians to sail as far west as present-day Morocco and Spain, carrying huge cargoes of such goods as timber, dyed cloth, glassware, wines, textiles, copper ingots, and carved ivory. Their trading colonies all around the southern and western rims of the Mediterranean (including Carthage in modern-day Tunisia) became major ports that shipped goods from interior regions throughout the Mediterranean. There they competed with Greek colonies that were similarly settling in the western Mediterranean to pursue commerce and relieve population pressures. While the Phoenicians are noteworthy for their seafaring and trade, they are perhaps best known for their revolutionizing of commerce and communication through their development of the **alphabet** in the mid-second millennium BCE. This new method of writing arrived in the west in 800 BCE, probably through Greek traders working in Phoenician centers. The alphabet allowed educated people to communicate directly with one another, dramatically reducing the need for professional scribes. The Phoenicians' trade and their alphabet allowed this "fringe" group to exert influence far beyond the confines of their political borders.

THE ISRAELITES

To the south of the mountains of Lebanon, the homeland of the Phoenicians, another minor region extended to the borderlands of Egypt. In this narrow strip of land between the Mediterranean Sea to the west and the desert to the east, an important microsociety emerged, that of the Israelites. The Israelites' own later stories emphasized their beginnings in Mesopotamia to the east and their patriarch Abraham's origin in the city of Ur on the Euphrates. Later stories stressed their connections with pharaonic Egypt to the west and the mass movement of a captive Israelite population out of Egypt under Moses in the late second millennium BCE. Archaeological evidence suggests that a local culture emerged in the area of present-day Israel between 1200 and 1000 BCE. These developments culminated in a kingdom centered at Jerusalem under King David (r. c. 1000–960 BCE). The kingdom that David

Phoenicians
An ethnic group in the Levant known for their ships, trading, and alphabet, and referred to in Hebrew scripture as the Canaanites. The term *Phoenician* (Greek for "purple people") derives from the major trade good they manufactured, a rare and expensive purple dye.

alphabet
A mid-second-millennium BCE Phoenician system of writing based on relatively few letters (twenty-two) that combined to make sounds and words. Adaptable to many languages, the alphabet was simpler and more flexible than writing based on symbols for syllables and ideas.

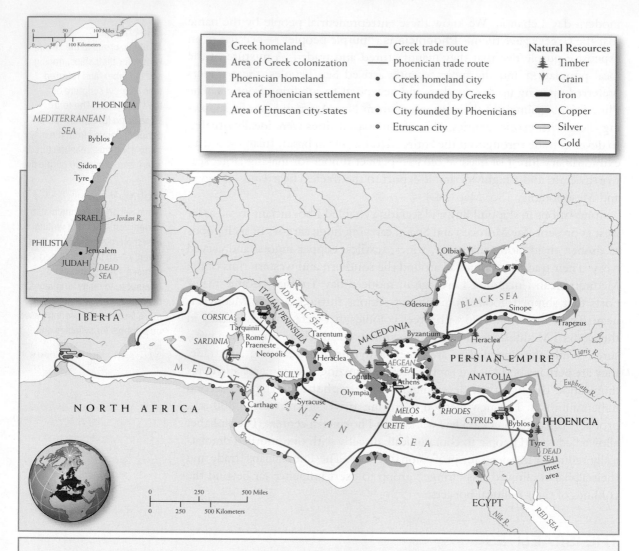

Map 4.4 The Mediterranean World, 1000–400 BCE

Peoples on the fringes of the great regional empires of Southwest Asia and North Africa had strong influences beyond their borders, despite their political marginalization. Though politically dwarfed by the Neo-Assyrian and Persian Empires, various groups in the Mediterranean basin displayed strong cultural and economic power.

- What were the borderland communities, and what did they trade?
- How far did their trading networks and settlement patterns extend?
- Why were such small communities able to flourish in terms of trade and settlement?

PHŒNICIAN	ANCIENT GREEK	LATER GREEK	ROMAN

The Phoenician Alphabet *Left:* The first alphabet was written on clay tablets using cuneiform script. It was developed by Phoenician traders who needed a script that was easy to learn so that they could record transactions without specially trained scribes. This tablet was found at the port town of Ugarit (Ras Shamra), in Syria, and is dated to the fourteenth century BCE. *Right:* The forms of the letters in the Phoenician alphabet of the first millennium BCE are based on signs used to represent the Aramaic language. These Phoenician letters were then borrowed by the ancient Greeks. Our alphabet is based on that used by the Romans, who borrowed their letter forms from the later Greek inscriptions.

and his successor Solomon (r. c. 960–930 BCE) established around Jerusalem, centered on the great temple that Solomon built in the city, did not last long. It fragmented immediately after Solomon's reign, forming the small kingdom of Israel in the north and the smaller Judah in the south.

Within the small kingdom founded by David and Solomon, profound religious and cultural changes took place. Solomon's great temple in Jerusalem outranked all other shrines in the land. The educated upper classes especially, who were linked to the temple, focused on one god, YHWH, over other regional deities in a form of reverence modern scholars call *henotheism* (the recognition of the power of one god over other spirits and deities that still exist). Gradually, however, there was a move to **monotheism** (the acceptance of only one god to the exclusion of all others).

The long transition to monotheism, completed by the seventh century BCE, did not take place without resistance. Challenging the power of kings

monotheism
The belief in only one god; to be distinguished from polytheism (the belief in many gods) and henotheism (the belief that there may be many gods but one is superior to the others).

and priests, prophets like Isaiah (c. 720s BCE), Ezra (c. 600s BCE), and Jeremiah (c. 590s BCE) helped articulate the Israelites' monotheistic religion. Prophets threatened divine annihilation for groups that opposed the new idea of one temple, one god, and one moral system to the exclusion of all others. The Neo-Assyrians to the east figured large in many of the prophets' warnings. Ultimately, the Torah—a series of five books that encapsulated the laws governing all aspects of life, including family and marriage, food, clothing, sex, and worship—became an exclusive "contract" between all these people and their one and only god. As Jewish people scattered over time across Afro-Eurasia, their monotheism would come to have a far-reaching impact.

Foundations of Vedic Culture in South Asia

In South Asia, language and belief systems—rather than a unified political system enforced and enlarged by military conquests—brought people together. Indo-European-speaking peoples, also known as Vedic peoples for the religious traditions they brought with them, entered South Asia through the passes in the Hindu Kush Mountains in the middle of the second millennium BCE and eventually occupied the whole of what are today Pakistan, Bangladesh, and northern India (see Chapter 3). Here the migrant population, together with the indigenous inhabitants, fostered a flourishing culture. Unlike in societies in Southwest Asia, the new rulers in this region did not have previous states on which to found their power. Floods and earthquakes had weakened the earlier Harappan urban centers in the Indus River valley (see Chapter 2), and their urban culture had died out several centuries earlier. Vedic newcomers integrated this territory through a shared culture. Even though the Vedic migrants changed the social and cultural landscape of the region, they did not give it greater political coherence by creating a single, unified regional kingdom.

VEDIC PEOPLES SETTLE DOWN

The men and women who migrated into the northern lands of South Asia were illiterate, chariot-riding, and cattle-keeping pastoral peoples, who lacked experience of cities and urban life. They brought with them much beloved and elaborate rituals, mainly articulated in hymns, called **Vedas** (Sanskrit for "wisdom" or "knowledge"), which they retained as they entered a radically different environment and which they relied on to provide a foundation for assimilating new ways. Transmitted orally, but eventually written down in Sanskrit, Vedic hymns reflected their earlier lives on the plains of central Asia and were infused with images of animals and gods. For example, in some of

Vedas
Rituals, hymns, and other explanatory texts composed and orally transmitted in Sanskrit by Brahman priests. They shaped the society and religious rituals of Vedic peoples and became central texts in Hinduism.

these Vedic poems storms "gallop" across the heavens, and thunder sounds like the "neigh of horses."

These Indo-European-speaking migrants, equipped with their Vedic traditions, encountered indigenous people who either lived in agricultural settlements or were herders like themselves. They allied themselves with some peoples and made enemies of others. In their interactions with local peoples, the Vedic migrants kept their own language and religious rituals but also absorbed local words and deities. Allies and defeated enemies who became part of their society had to accept Vedic culture. By the middle of the first millennium BCE, the Vedic peoples covered all of what is now northern India, and their language and rituals had become dominant in their new land. (See Map 4.5.)

Vedic elites, with their pastoral nomadic roots, never lost their passion for fine horses, and they created trading routes to the northwest, beyond the Hindu Kush, to maintain a supply of these horses. But as the Vedic peoples entered the fertile river basins, they gradually settled down and turned to agriculture and herding. Indigenous farmers taught the Vedic newcomers farming techniques. For example, the iron plow was crucial for tilling the Ganges plain and transforming the Deccan plateau into croplands. In the drier north, the Vedic peoples grew wheat, barley, millet, and cotton; in the wet lowlands, they cultivated rice paddies. Farmers also produced tropical crops such as sugarcane and spices like pepper, ginger, and cinnamon. With farming success came increased populations and urban settlements across the region, fueled by agricultural surplus and trade in goods, both raw (grain) and manufactured (sugarcane into sugar).

SOCIAL DISTINCTIONS: CLANS AND *VARNA*

Over time, Vedic societies became more complex and less egalitarian than those of their pastoral ancestors. In the process of fanning out across the five tributaries of the Indus River and settling in the plain between the Ganges and Yamuna Rivers, the Vedic peoples created small regional governments and chieftainships. Jockeying for land and resources, they fought fiercely with the indigenous peoples and even more fiercely among themselves.

Vedic chieftainships eventually became small kingdoms with inhabitants bound to each other through lines of descent from a common ancestor. They traced their lineage—identified as either solar or lunar—through blood ties, marriage alliances, and invented family relations. The two lineages, solar and lunar, included many *clans* (groups of households claiming descent from a common ancestor) in which seniority determined one's power and importance. The Vedic peoples absorbed many local clans into their own lineages. Clans that adopted the Vedic culture became part of the lineage (through marriage or made-up ties) and were considered insiders.

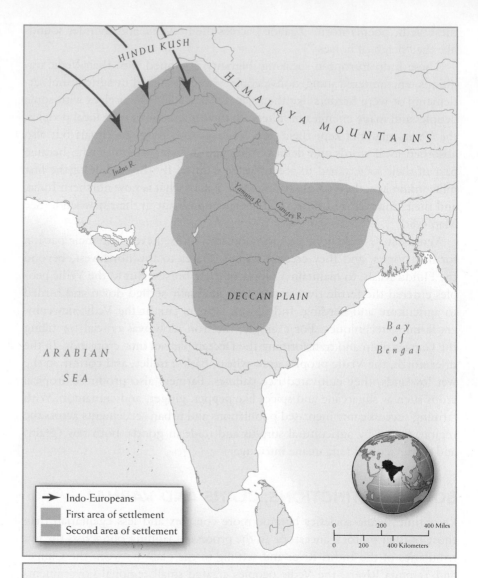

Map 4.5 South Asia, 1500–400 BCE

Indo-European peoples crossed over mountainous areas and entered northern South Asia, bringing with them their nomadic ways. They were, however, quick to learn settled agriculture from the local inhabitants.

- Where did the Indo-Europeans originally come from?
- Where did they settle? What geographical features may have influenced the stages of expansion southward?
- Based on your reading, why did Vedic culture prosper and provide a basis of unity for such large populations?

In contrast, clans that had other languages and rituals were considered to be uncivilized outsiders. These two lineages became less important over time, but were memorialized in the later *Mahabharata*, one of the two major Sanskrit epics of ancient India, which relates the last phase of the lunar lineage, and the *Ramayana*, the second Sanskrit epic, which celebrates a hero of the solar lineage.

As Vedic peoples settled into agrarian communities after 1000 BCE, their social structure became even more complex and hierarchical. Among other distinctions, divisions developed between those who controlled the land and those who worked it. Vedic peoples used the term **varna** to refer to their rigid status distinction and recognized four ranked social groups into which one was born—Brahmans, Kshatriyas, Vaishyas, and Shudras. Since the Sanskrit word *varna* means "color," its use suggests that the four-class system originated in the encounter between clans and communities of different complexions and cultures. Vedic hymns described the origins of the *varnas* in their creation narrative. When the gods sacrificed Purusha to create the universe, the Brahmans (priests) came from his mouth, his arms produced the Kshatriyas (warriors), the thighs gave birth to the Vaishyas (commoners), and from the feet emerged the Shudras (laborers and servants).

Clan members who had been politically the most powerful and had led their communities into northern India claimed the status of Kshatriyas. It was they who controlled the land. Less powerful clan members, who worked the land and tended livestock, became Vaishyas. Paid and enslaved laborers who served in the households and fields of the Vaishyas came from outside the Vedic lineages and became known as Shudras. Brahmans claimed the

varna

Sanskrit for "color"; refers to the four ranked social groups within early Vedic society (priests, warriors, commoners, and laborers). The term *caste*, which derives from the term *casta* ("race/breed" in Spanish and Portuguese), is a later, anachronistic term often used for these divisions.

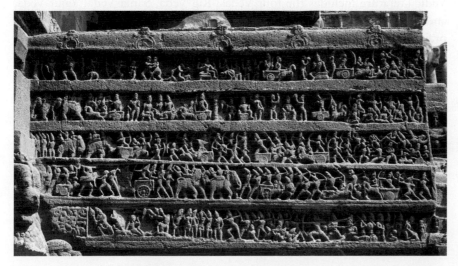

Scenes from the Mahabharata Reliefs on the walls of the Kailasa Temple in the Ellora Cave complex in northwest India depict scenes from the *Mahabharata* and the *Ramayana*. While these images were carved in the eighth century CE, they illustrate scenes from these epics that recount the distant Vedic past thousands of years earlier, when the lunar and solar lineages struggled against one another and among themselves. Archers, war elephants, chariots, hand-to-hand combat, and diplomatic scenes combine on this relief to narrate the main battle from the *Mahabharata* between two rival factions of the lunar lineage.

Gold Coin of Kumaragupta I
Kumaragupta I's coin, dating from the fifth century CE, intentionally drew on much older Vedic concepts (including the Ashvamedha, or horse sacrifice from the Yajur-Veda) and imagery (here, a Hindu goddess).

Upanishads
First-millennium BCE Vedic wisdom literature, in the form of a dialogue between students and teacher; together with the Vedas, they brought a cultural and spiritual unity to much of South Asia.

highest status, for they performed the rituals and understood the religious principles without which life was believed to be unsustainable. Brahmans and Kshatriyas reinforced each other's high status. Brahmans performed the sacrifices that converted warriors into kings, and kings reciprocated by paying fees and gifts to the Brahmans. Vaishyas and Shudras were left with the tasks of ensuring the sustenance of the elite. The Brahmans guided a society in which the proper relationship with the forces of nature as represented by the deities constituted the basis of prosperity. As agriculture became ever more important, Brahmans acted as agents of Agni, the god of fire, to purify the new land for cultivation. This complex hierarchy, so inextricably connected with Vedic religion, provided the primary unifying structure for society in South Asia.

UNITY THROUGH THE VEDAS AND UPANISHADS

A Vedic culture, transmitted from generation to generation by the Brahmans, unified what political rivalries had divided. A common language (Sanskrit); belief in Agni, Indra, and other gods; and shared cultural symbols linked the dispersed communities and gave Vedic peoples a collective identity. Though Sanskrit was a language imported from central Asia, the people used it to transmit the Vedas orally. By expressing sacred knowledge in the rhythms and rhymes of Sanskrit, the Vedic peoples effectively passed on their culture from one generation to the next.

The Vedas promoted cultural unity and pride through common ritual practices and support for hereditary leaders. As the priests of Vedic society, the Brahmans were responsible for memorizing the Vedic works. These included commentaries on sacred works from early nomadic times as well as new rules and rituals explaining the settled, farming way of life. The main body of Vedic literature includes the four Vedas: Rig-Veda, Sama-Veda, Yajur-Veda, and Atharva-Veda. The Rig-Veda, the earliest text, is a collection of hymns praising the gods, including Indra (god of war), Agni (god of fire), and Varuna (god of water). The Sama-Veda is a textbook of songs for priests to perform when making ritual sacrifices; most of its stanzas also appear in the Rig-Veda. The Yajur-Veda is a prayer book for the priest who conducted rituals for chariot races, horse sacrifices, or the king's coronation. The Atharva-Veda includes charms and remedies; many address problems related to agriculture, a central aspect of life. Although the Vedic period left no impressive buildings and artifacts, the Vedas laid the socioreligious foundations for South Asia.

During the middle of the first millennium BCE, some thinkers (mostly Brahman ascetics dwelling in forests) felt that the Vedic rituals no longer provided satisfactory answers to the many questions of a rapidly changing society. The result was a collection of works known as the **Upanishads**, or "the supreme knowledge," which expanded the Vedic cultural system. Taking the form of dialogues between disciples and a sage, the Upanishads offered insights into the ideal social order. The Upanishads teach that people are not separate from each other but belong to a cosmic universe called Brahma. While the physical world is always changing and is filled with chaos and illusion, *atman*, the eternal being, exists in all people and all creatures. Atman's presence in each living being makes all creatures part of a universal soul. Although all living beings must die, atman guarantees eternal life, ensuring that souls are reborn and transmigrate into new lives. This cycle continues with humans as they are reborn either as humans or as other living creatures, like cows, insects, or plants.

These unique views of life and the universe, as outlined in the Vedas and Upanishads, were passed along as principles of faith, bringing spiritual unity to the northern half of South Asia because local gods could easily be absorbed into the system. Unlike in Southwest Asia, here in the kingdoms of the Indus Valley and the Ganges plain the common Vedic culture—rather than larger political units—was the unifying bond.

The Early Zhou Empire in East Asia

In China, the Zhou succeeded the Shang state, and Zhou rulers built a powerful tributary empire, claiming the "mandate of heaven." The Zhou had been only a minor state during the Shang's political preeminence; during that period, the Zhou and the Shang had lived side by side, trading and often allying with each other to fend off raiders from the northwest. The appearance of a dynamic leader among the Zhou peoples, King Wu, and the need to find more resources after drought-related dust storms swept across the North China plain, emboldened the Zhou to challenge the Shang. At a battle in 1045 BCE, the Zhou prevailed. King Wu of the Zhou owed his success to his army of 45,000 troops and their superior weaponry, which included dagger axes, bronze armor, and 300 war chariots (small numbers by Southwest Asian standards, but overwhelming in East Asia). (See Map 4.6.) In the centuries that followed, innovations in politics, agriculture, and social structures helped the Zhou integrate their empire.

Core Objectives

EVALUATE the connection between empires and war, religion, and trade in Southwest Asia and East Asia.

DYNASTIC INSTITUTIONS AND CONTROL OF THE LAND

When the Zhou took over from the Shang, their new state consisted of more than seventy small states, whose rulers accepted the overarching authority of the Zhou kings. To solidify their power, the Zhou copied the Shang's patrimonial state structure, centered on ancestor worship in which the rulers' power passed down through a lineage of male ancestors reaching back to the

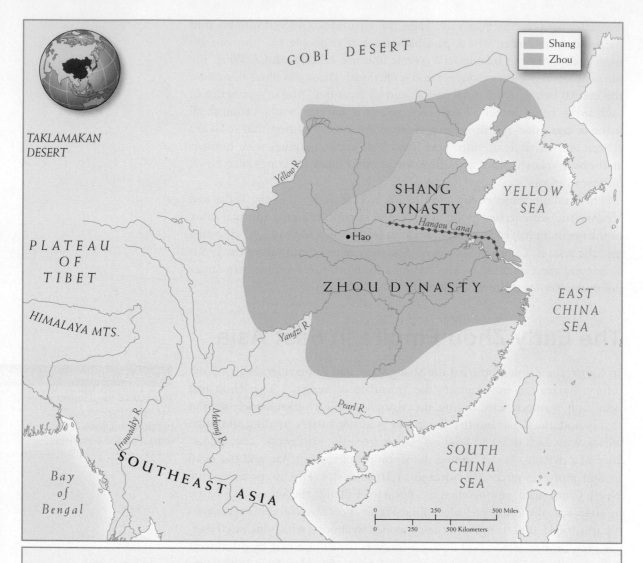

Map 4.6 The Shang and Zhou Dynasties, 2200–256 BCE

Toward the end of the second millennium BCE, the Zhou state supplanted the Shang state as the most powerful political force in East Asia. Using the map, compare and contrast the territorial reach of the Zhou state with that of the Shang.

- In what direction did the Zhou state expand most dramatically?
- As you view the map, why do you think that the Zhou did not expand farther northward and westward?
- Based on your reading, how did the Zhou integrate their geographically large and diverse state?

gods. Thirty-nine Zhou kings followed one after the other, mostly in an orderly father-to-son succession, over a span of eight centuries.

Even though the Zhou drew heavily on Shang precedents, their own innovations produced some of the most significant contributions to China's distinctive cultural and political development. Regarding all those whom they governed as a single people, the Zhou referred to their subjects using the term *Huaxia*, or "Chinese." Although the various Zhou states were not fully unified, Zhou leaders called their lands *Zhongguo*, a term that came to mean "the middle kingdom" (and is still used for the modern state of China). Moreover, the Zhou kings of this middle kingdom, in addition to being required to rule justly, believed that they had a duty to extend their culture to "less civilized" peoples living in outlying regions.

Having defeated the Shang and established Zhou control in northwestern China, King Wu (r. 1049–1043 BCE) and his successors expanded north toward what is now Beijing and south toward the Yangzi River valley. Seeking to retain the allegiance of the lords of older states and to gain the support of new lords, whom they appointed in annexed areas, Zhou kings rewarded their political supporters with lands that they could pass on to their descendants. As the Zhou expanded their territory, their new colonies often consisted of garrison towns where the Zhou colonizers lived, surrounded by fields (inhabited by local farmers). As under the Shang, Zhou regional lords supplied military forces as needed, paid tribute, and appeared at the imperial court to pledge their continuing allegiance.

The Zhou leaders promoted the integration of China not only through dynastic institutions but also through agricultural advances (including the iron plow, irrigation, and canals). Wooden and, much later, iron plows enabled farmers to break the hard sod of lands beyond the river basins, and over time cultivators learned the practice of field rotation to prevent soil nutrients from being exhausted. In the middle of the first millennium BCE, regional states organized local efforts to regulate the flow of the main rivers. They built long canals to promote communication and trade, and they dug impressive irrigation networks to convert arid lands into fertile belts. This slow agrarian revolution enabled the Chinese population to soar, reaching perhaps 20 million by the late Zhou era.

Under the Zhou, landowners and rulers organized the construction of dikes and irrigation systems to control the floodplain of the Yellow River and Wei River valley surrounding the capital at Hao (present-day Xi'an). For

Zhou Chariots This seventeenth-century CE painting (on silk) recalls the memory of a pivotal Zhou king, Emperor Mu Wang (of the tenth century BCE), riding in a chariot driven by a legendary charioteer. The Zhou adapted the use of chariots and archers from their predecessors to defeat the Shang around 1045 BCE. Regional lords who owed allegiance to the Zhou king distinguished themselves in the aristocratic hierarchy by using chariots for battle and travel.

centuries, peasants labored over this floodplain and its tributaries—building dikes, digging canals, and raising levees as the waters flowed to the sea. When their work was done, the bottom of the floodplain was a latticework of rich, well-watered fields, with carefully manicured terraces rising in gradual steps to higher ground. Eventually, irrigation works grew to such a scale that they required management by the Zhou rulers, centered in the Wei River valley, and their skilled engineers. The engineers also designed canals that connected rivers and supported commerce and other internal exchanges. Tens of thousands of workers spent countless days digging these canals, paying tribute in the form of labor.

The canals linked China's two breadbaskets: wheat and millet fields in the north and rice fields in the south. And as with the Yellow River in the north, engineers controlled the Yangzi River in the south. Nomads in mountainous areas or on the Zhou frontiers, who often fought with the Zhou ruler and his regional lords, began to depend on trade with the fertile heartlands. In these ways, the Zhou promoted greater unity within their territory and among the peoples living in and around it.

"MANDATE OF HEAVEN"

In addition to promoting a Chinese ethnic and political identity and cultivating advances in agriculture, Zhou rulers introduced the long-enduring concept of the **mandate of heaven**, which provided a justification for their rule. Attributed by later Chinese intellectuals to King Wu's younger brother Zhou Gong (often referred to as the Duke of Zhou), the mandate asserted that Zhou moral superiority justified taking over Shang wealth and territories and that heaven had imposed a moral mandate on them to replace the Shang, whom they characterized as evil men whose policies brought pain to the people through waste and corruption, and return good governance to the people.

At first Zhou leaders presented the mandate of heaven as a religious compact between the Zhou people and their supreme "sky god" in heaven, but over time Zhou kings and the court detached the concept from the sky god and made the mandate into a freestanding Chinese political doctrine. The Zhou argued that since worldly affairs were supposed to align with those of the heavens, heavenly powers conferred legitimate rights to rule only on their chosen representative. In return, the ruler was duty-bound to uphold heaven's principles of harmony and honor. Any ruler who failed in this duty, who let instability creep into earthly affairs, or who let his people suffer, would lose the mandate. Under this system, spiritual authority withdrew support from any wayward dynasts and found other, more worthy, agents. The Zhou rulers had to acknowledge that any group of rulers, even they themselves, could be ousted if they lost the mandate of heaven because of improper practices.

mandate of heaven
Religious ideology established by Zhou leaders to communicate legitimate transfer and retention of royal power as the will of their supreme god. The mandate later became Chinese political doctrine.

As part of maintaining their mandate and their legitimacy as rulers, Zhou kings created royal calendars, official documents that defined times for undertaking agricultural activities and celebrating rituals. Unexpected events such as solar eclipses or natural calamities could throw into question the ruling house's mandate. Since rulers claimed that their authority came from heaven, the Zhou perfected the astronomical system on which they based their calendar. Zhou astronomers precisely calculated the length of a lunar month (29.53 days) and the solar year. To resolve the discrepancy between a solar year (365.25 days) and a lunar year (354.36 days), the Zhou occasionally inserted a leap month. Scribes dated the reigns of kings by days and years within a repeating sixty-year cycle.

The Zhou's legitimacy was also grounded in their use of bronze ritual vessels, statues, ornaments, and weapons, the large-scale production of which they borrowed from their Shang predecessors. Like the Shang, the Zhou developed an extensive system of bronze metalworking that required a large force of tribute labor. Many of its members were Shang, who were sometimes forcibly transported to new Zhou towns to produce the bronze ritual objects. These objects, sold and distributed across the lands and used in ceremonial rituals, symbolized Zhou legitimacy.

Zhou Wine Vessel Under the Zhou, bronze metallurgy depended on a large labor force. Many workers initially came from Shang labor groups, who were superior to the Zhou in technology. The use of bronze, such as for this wine vessel, exemplified dynastic continuity between the Shang and Zhou.

SOCIAL AND ECONOMIC CONTROLS

As the Chinese social order became more integrated, it also became more class based. Directly under the Zhou ruler and his royal ministers were the hereditary nobles, divided into ranks. These regional lords had landholdings of different sizes. They all owed allegiance to the Zhou king, and they supplied warriors to fight in the king's army and laborers to clear land, drain fields, and do other work. The regional lords periodically appeared at court and took part in complex rituals to reaffirm their allegiance to the king. Below the regional lords were high officers at the Zhou court, as well as ministers and administrators who supervised the people's work. Aristocratic warriors stood at the bottom of the noble hierarchy.

Among commoners, an elaborate occupation-based hierarchy developed over time. Early on, most of the population worked as farmers on fields owned by great landholding families, while some commoners were artisans, such as bronze workers or silk weavers. The later occupation-based system, however, divided people more precisely by function—landholders who produced grain, growers of plants and fruit trees, woodsmen, breeders of cattle and chickens, artisans, merchants, weavers, servants, and those with no fixed occupation—and the central government exerted considerable control over how each group did its job. While reports of this control may be overstated, the system does show a unique attempt by the Zhou government to assert power over the empire's diverse peoples.

The Zhou also made political and legal use of family structures. In their patrilineal society, the Zhou established strict hierarchies for both men and women. Both art and literature celebrated the son who honored his parents. Men and women had different roles in family and ceremonial life. On landholdings, men farmed and hunted, while women produced silk and other textiles and fashioned them into clothing. Wealth increasingly trumped other distinctions, however. In particular, rich women high in the Zhou aristocracy enjoyed a greater range of actions than other women did. And wealthy merchants in emerging cities challenged the authority of local lords.

LIMITS AND DECLINE OF ZHOU POWER

The Zhou state relied on culture (its bronzes) and statecraft (the mandate of heaven) to maintain its leadership among competing powers and lesser principalities in its territories. Rather than having absolute control of an empire (like the Neo-Assyrians and Persians had) or a primarily socioreligious unity (like the Vedic peoples of South Asia had), the Zhou state was first among many regional economic and political allies.

The Zhou dynasty was not highly centralized; instead, it expected regional lords to control the provinces. Military campaigns continued to press into new lands or to defend Zhou holdings from enemies. Rulers interacted with neighbors and allies by giving them power, protecting them from aggression, and intermarrying between dynastic family members and local nobles. Consequently, Zhou subordinates had more than autonomy; they had genuine resources that they could turn against the dynasts at opportune moments.

The power of the Zhou royal house over its regional lords declined in the ninth and eighth centuries BCE. In response, the Zhou court at Hao introduced ritual reforms with grandiose ceremonies featuring larger, standardized bronze vessels. Even this move could not reverse the regime's growing political weakness in dealing with its steppe neighbors and internal regional lords. In 771 BCE, northern steppe invaders forced the Zhou to flee their western capital, ushering in the beginning of what would come to be known as the Spring and Autumn period of the Eastern Zhou dynasty centered at Luoyi (modern Luoyang).

The Zhou dynastic period, like the Shang, was later idealized by Chinese historians as a golden age of wise kings and officials. In fact, the Zhou model of government, culture, and society became the standard for later generations. Though the Neo-Assyrian and Persian superpowers were capable of greater expansion during this period, China was sowing the seeds of a more durable state.

Conclusion

Around 1000 BCE, dramatic changes in political and social structures took place across Afro-Eurasia. Consolidations of power, with varying degrees and types of centralization, formed in Southwest Asia (Neo-Assyrians and Persians), Vedic South Asia, and East Asia (among the Zhou). Driving these sociopolitical developments were changes in climate, invasions by nomadic peoples, technological innovations, and new administrative strategies.

A spectrum of power consolidation—from the highly centralized to the more culturally unified—occurred across Afro-Eurasia. The tightly consolidated Neo-Assyrian and Persian Empires differed in fundamental ways from the earlier city-states and territorial states of this area. They created ideologies, political institutions, and economic ties that extended their power across vast regions. Their strong imperial institutions enabled them to exploit human and material resources at great distances from the imperial centers. At the other end of Afro-Eurasia, the Zhou in East Asia established loose integration of diverse peoples and territories through a powerful dynastic arrangement buttressed by a mandate from heaven, but they could not overcome the power of local nobles or fully protect the western frontier from nomadic attacks. In the Vedic world of the Indus Valley and Ganges plain, shared values and revered texts did not lead to a single major state. An unparalleled degree of cultural, as opposed to political or economic, integration bound together northern South Asia. Many centuries would pass before a regime would layer a state over this shared cultural world.

Empire building did not occur everywhere. The majority of the world's people still lived in smaller political groupings. Even within Afro-Eurasia, some areas were completely untouched. And even where the Neo-Assyrian and Persian rulers, soldiers, and traders came into contact with certain groups, they did not necessarily crush them. For example, the nomadic peoples of the northern steppes and the southern desert locations throughout Eurasia continued to be autonomous. But fewer and fewer were untouched by the technological, cultural, and political pulses of empires.

The peoples living in Southwest Asia (under the Neo-Assyrians and then Persians), in the Vedic society of South Asia, and in the Zhou kingdom of East Asia made lasting contributions to the cultural and religious history of humanity. Late Vedic South Asia spun out the concept of cyclic universal time in the form of reincarnation. And in late Zhou China, an ideal of statecraft and social order took shape. On the fringes of these empires, other groups made lasting contributions. The Phoenicians traversed the whole of the Mediterranean basin and spread their simplified alphabet. From the land of Israel, a budding monotheism sprouted. All evolved into powerful cultural forms that in time spread their influences far beyond their sites of origin.

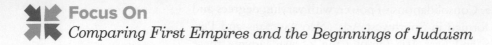

Focus On
Comparing First Empires and the Beginnings of Judaism

Ancient Near East

- Neo-Assyrians use raw military power and massive population relocations to build and maintain the world's first empire.

- Persians rely on tolerance, their system of satrapies, and Zoroastrianism to build a cosmopolitan empire.

Mediterranean World

- Greeks, Phoenicians, and Israelites show the advantages of small-scale states with innovations in writing, trading, and religious thought.

- Sea Peoples migrate into the region, attacking empires in the eastern Mediterranean, including the Hittites and Egyptians, before settling down in the Levant.

South Asia

- Vedic migrants combine with local populations to build a unified but *varna*-stratified common culture through religious and economic ties.

- Religious texts, like the Vedas and the Upanishads, bring a cultural unity through their rules, rituals, and traditions.

China

- The Zhou dynasty constructs a powerful tributary state through dynastic institutions and agricultural advances.

- Zhou dynasts legitimate their rule through claiming the mandate of heaven (good governance together with upright behavior equates to legitimate rule), a concept that will become a long-lasting political doctrine in China.

CHRONOLOGY	1500 BCE	1200 BCE
Southwest Asia and North Africa		
The Mediterranean		
South Asia		
East Asia		

THINKING ABOUT GLOBAL CONNECTIONS

- **Thinking about Power Relationships and the Formation of Empires** From 1250 to 325 BCE, several regional empires with centralized rule developed: in Southwest Asia, the Neo-Assyrians and then the Persians established tightly controlled empires; in East Asia, the Zhou achieved loose political unification; and a culturally integrated people thrived in South Asia. Compare the use of military force and its relationship to political centralization in each of these cases. How does religion help bring unification?

- **Thinking about the Environment and the Formation of Empires** Just as climate change around 2000 BCE contributed to the demise of earlier societies, prolonged drought around 1200 BCE again brought dramatic changes to many areas. Compare the environmental crises in Egypt, Southwest Asia, and East Asia in the late second millennium BCE and their results, especially with respect to empire formation.

- **Thinking about Exchange Networks and the Formation of Empires** While this chapter focuses on the formation of empires, the majority of the world's people lived outside or on the fringes of these empires. The Sea Peoples, after disrupting the Hittites, Greeks, and Egyptians, settled down on the coast of Southwest Asia and became the Philistines; the Phoenicians expanded their trade across the Mediterranean; the Greeks effectively resisted Persian authority; and Jewish Israelites founded a kingdom centered on monotheism. Which had the most significant impact on human history: the centralized empires or the peoples on the fringes and beyond? Why?

Key Terms

alphabet p. 185	monotheism p. 187	Sea Peoples p. 182	Vedas p. 188
empire p. 165	Phoenicians p. 185	Upanishads p. 192	Zoroastrianism p. 179
mandate of heaven p. 196	satrapy p. 178	*varna* p. 191	

 Go to INQUIZITIVE to see what you've learned—and learn what you've missed—with personalized feedback along the way.

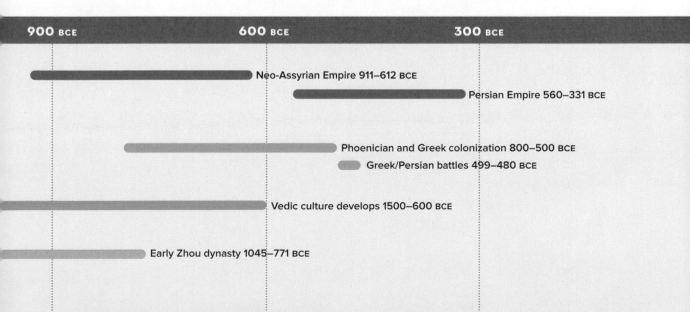

900 BCE — 600 BCE — 300 BCE

Neo-Assyrian Empire 911–612 BCE

Persian Empire 560–331 BCE

Phoenician and Greek colonization 800–500 BCE

Greek/Persian battles 499–480 BCE

Vedic culture develops 1500–600 BCE

Early Zhou dynasty 1045–771 BCE

Global Themes and Sources

Comparing First Empires

....

The early empires described in this chapter used a combination of military might, political organization, and religious ideology to control the peoples who lived within their territory. The Neo-Assyrians, for instance, combined brute force and tight political administration to consolidate a highly centralized empire. The Persians used some of the same strategies but allowed greater multicultural variation and self-rule within their domain. Zhou leaders in East Asia justified their rule via the mandate of heaven, but this justification required ongoing demonstration of a mandate in a world of unpredictable events such as sickness and crop devastation. In South Asia, Indo-European Vedic immigrants brought a degree of social, but not political, unification through their religious ideas, most notably the hierarchically arranged *varna* and understandings of reincarnation.

The texts presented here facilitate a comparison of the varied methods of control utilized in each of these regions, on a spectrum from the harsh centralized control of the Neo-Assyrians to the looser political, yet strong ideological, ties of South Asia. The Dur-Sharrukin building inscription describes the construction by Sargon II (r. 721–705 BCE) of a new capital for the Neo-Assyrian Empire in Southwest Asia. Over the course of the two decades during which the lavish capital was under construction, Sargon II expanded his empire by force and tribute exaction. Two centuries later, Darius I (r. 522–486 BCE) commissioned the Behistun inscription to commemorate his consolidation of power over the Persian state in roughly the same region of Southwest Asia that the Neo-Assyrians had controlled. This blend of Zoroastrian ideals and military force demonstrates some of the key elements of Persian imperial control. The *Shangshu* (Book of Documents) preserves a narrative of the transition of power around 1043 BCE in East Asia from King Wu to his brother the Duke of Zhou, who was acting as regent for Wu's son, King Ch'eng.

In this account, ancestors were consulted via oracle bones and the mandate of heaven was in doubt. The last excerpt comes from the Upanishads, a collection of works sacred to the Vedic peoples of South Asia, dating to the seventh century BCE or earlier. The reassuring message from this text underscores the potentially unifying power of the belief in reincarnation. Each text gives a glimpse of the practical and ideological forces that bound peoples and empires together in the first millennium BCE.

Analyzing Early Empires

- What similarities and differences do you see in the central focus of each text? What does the central focus of each text reveal about political and social control? How is the nature of empire, or social control, within each text a reflection of what you know (from this chapter) about the degree of imperial centralization in each region?

- What is the role of religion in each text? How is the role of religion similar across these texts and the empires they reflect? How is it different?

- Compare the genre and perspective of each text. How do the type of source and the point of view from which it is written add something to your consideration of the nature of empire, or the lack of a consolidated empire, in each region?

PRIMARY SOURCE 4.1

Sargon II's Lamassu Inscription at Dur-Sharrukin (c. 720 BCE)

Sargon II (r. 721–705 BCE) ruled during a time of militaristic expansion for the Neo-Assyrians, undertaking brutal campaigns both within and beyond the borders of his empire. Toward the beginning of his reign, he began the construction of the new capital city of Dur-Sharrukin (modern Khorsabad, near Mosul in Iraq). At the entrance to Sargon II's throne room in the palace at Dur-Sharrukin sat a 40-ton, 16-foot-tall lamassu (human-headed winged bull). The inscriptions included here were carved onto the front and back of this massive creature. Beneath the descriptions of beauty and splendor is a reality of conquest, tribute extraction, and tight-fisted rule.

....

- What actions and traits does Sargon II highlight throughout the inscription that could justify his imperial power and authority?

- What details does the inscription offer about the construction of Dur-Sharrukin, including its park, the buildings, the city walls, the gates, and other features? Why do you think the text offers such details?

- What does the tone and content of this inscription suggest about the nature of Neo-Assyrian rule?

....

[Inscription on the back of the lamassu]: Palace of Sargon, ruler appointed by Enlil, priest of Ashur, mighty king, king of the world, king of Assyria, king of the four quarters of the world, favorite of the great gods; who established the exempt status of Sippar, Nippur, and Babylon, and protects them in their weakness; who provides food for the destitute, who makes restitution for their wrongful losses; who reestablished for the city Assur its privileged status which had lapsed; who abolished forced labor for Der and brought rest to its weary people; most powerful of all princes, who stretched his protection over Harran and recorded that city's freedom from taxation in accordance with the will of Anu and Dagan; the king, who since the day he became ruler, has had no equal and has encountered no one superior to him in war or battle; who has smashed all lands like clay pots and has imposed reins on the four quarters of the world, who has set his officials over them as governors, and has imposed tax and tribute upon them comparable to those paid by Assyria.

[Inscription on the front of the lamassu]: [At that time I constructed a city above the water holes at the foot of Mt. Musri north of Nineveh, and I named it Dur-Sharrukin. Around it I laid out a great park

resembling Mt. Amanus, planted with every Syrian aromatic tree and mountain fruit tree. Not one of the 350 ancient princes who reigned over Assyria before me and ruled the subjects of Enlil had thought of this location; not one had known how to settle it or dig its canal or to set out its orchards.] I planned day and night how to settle that city and how to raise its great shrines, the dwellings of the great gods, and my royal residential palaces. I spoke and commanded it to be built. In an auspicious month, on a favorable day, the month Simanu (May/June), on a festival day, I made my workers take up the hoe and mold bricks.

In the month Abu (July/August) . . . , I set out its limestone (masonry) upon (foundation deposits of) gold, silver, precious stones, and aromatic plants of Mt. Amanus; I laid its foundations and firmly set its bricks. There I built awesome shrines, firm as the mass of a mountain, for Ea, Sin, Ningal, Shamash, Nabu, Adad, and Ninurta. At the exalted command of these gods, I constructed palaces of ivory, ebony, boxwood, musukkannu-wood, cedar, cypress, juniper, burashu-juniper, and pistachio-wood for my royal dwelling. I roofed them with large cedar beams. I bound doors made of cypress and musukkannu-wood with bands of shining copper and made them fast in their entrances. In front of the palace gates, I built a portico resembling that of a Hittite palace. . . . Eight lions, in pairs, each weighing 4,610 talents (ca. 14 tons) full measure of shining copper, cast according to the workmanship of Ninagal and of dazzling brightness—on top of these lion figures I placed four equally tall cedar columns, each one ninda (ca. 20 ft.) in diameter, products of Mt. Amanus, and there supported the boards forming the cornice of the palace gates. I skillfully made mountain sheep and great protective deities out of massive mountain stone and set them facing the four directions. I depicted on large limestone slabs the regions which I had personally captured and set these slabs around the walls for display.

I made the length of the wall 16,261½ ninda and 2 cubits (ca. 60 miles) and laid its foundation platform upon a high mountain. In front and in back, on both sides, and facing the four winds I opened eight gates. I called the gates of Shamash and Adad on the east side of the city: "Shamash Gains Victories for Me" and "Adad Establishes My Abundance." I named the gates of Enlil and Ninlil on the north side: "Enlil Makes the Foundation of My City Firm" and "Ninlil Creates Abundance." I named the gates of Anu and Ishtar on the west side: "Anu Makes the Work of My Hands Flourish" and "Ishtar Enriches Its People." I named the gates of Ea and Belet-ili on the south side: "Ea Makes Its Springs Flow Prosperously" and "Belet-ili Increases His Offspring." Its inner wall was called "Ashur Allows the Reign of the King, Its Builder, to Last for Many Years and Guards His Troops"; its outer wall was called "Ninurta Establishes the Foundation Platform of His City So That It Will Last until the Distant Future."

There under a single administration I settled peoples from the four quarters of the world, of alien tongues and different speech, mountain dwellers and lowlanders, as many as the Light of the Gods (Shamash), Lord of All, has shepherded; these peoples I had captured at the command of the god Ashur by the power of my scepter. I commissioned native Assyrians, masters of every craft, as overseers and officials to instruct them (the settlers) in their duties as tenants and in their obligations toward god and king.

When I had finished building the city and my palaces, in the month Tashritu (September/October) I invited the great gods who dwell in Assyria to come here. I held a feast to dedicate the city and palaces. I received rich gifts from the princes of the East and West: gold, silver, and all kinds of costly objects fitting for these palaces. May the gods who dwell in this city deem all my works acceptable. May they decree that they will dwell in their temples here and that my reign may remain firm for ever and ever. Whoever destroys the work of my hands, alters the features of my statue, obliterates the representations which I have had depicted, or erases my insignia—may Sin, Shamash, Adad, and all the great gods who live here pluck out his name and his seed from the land; and may they make him live as a captive under his enemies.

Source: "Featured Object Number 8, May 1990, Human-Headed Winged Bull from Khorsabad (OIM A7369)," translated by John A. Brinkman, Oriental Institute Museum, 1990, pp. 3–4, https://oi.uchicago.edu/sites/oi.uchicago.edu/files/uploads/Lamassu_A7369_1990_factsheet.pdf.

The Behistun Inscription (c. 520 BCE), Darius I

The Behistun inscription was commissioned by Darius I, king of Persia, sometime after 520 BCE. It commemorates a series of nineteen battles over the course of which he defeated nine rebellious kings. The trilingual cuneiform inscription—in Old Persian, Elamite, and Babylonian—was posted high up on a cliff face on a major road connecting Mesopotamia with western Iran. The text was accompanied by a relief that shows the nine kings, ropes around their necks and hands bound, led before the victorious Darius. Zoroastrian themes of truth and righteousness vanquishing lies and wrongdoing are central to the text.

- What role does Ahura Mazda, and Zoroastrianism more generally, play in Darius's claims to have defeated his enemies?

- Apart from religious justification, what other evidence do you see for the way that Darius I asserted power and consolidated his empire?

- Given that this copy at Behistun was high up on the side of a cliff and not likely to have been legible to passersby, why might Darius have posted an inscription like this on a major route through his empire?

4.1–2. Saith Darius the King: This is what was done by me in Babylon.

4.2–31. Saith Darius the King: This is what I did by the favor of Ahuramazda in one and the same year after that I became king. XIX battles I fought; by the favor of Ahuramazda I smote them and took prisoner IX kings. One was Gaumata by name, a Magian; he lied . . . he made Persia rebellious. One, Açina by name, an Elamite; he lied . . . he made Elam rebellious to me. One, Nidintu-Bel by name, a Babylonian; he lied; thus he said: "I am Nebuchadnezzar, the son of Nabonidus; he made Babylon rebellious. One, Martiya by name, a Persian; he lied . . . he made Elam rebellious. One, Phraortes by name, a Mede; he lied . . . he made Media rebellious. One Ciçantakhma by name, a Sagartian; he lied . . . he made Sagartia rebellious. One, Frada by name, a Margian; he lied . . . he made Margiana rebellious. One, Vahyazdata by name, a Persian; he lied . . . he made Persia rebellious. One, Arkha by name, an Armenian; he lied . . . he made Babylon rebellious.

4.31–32. Saith Darius the King: These IX kings I took prisoner within these battles.

4.33–36. Saith Darius the King: These are the provinces which became rebellious. The Lie made them rebellious, so that these [men] deceived the people. Afterwards Ahuramazda put them into my hand; as was my desire, so I did unto them.

4.36–40. Saith Darius the King: Thou who shalt be king hereafter, protect thyself vigorously from the Lie; the man who shall be a Lie-follower, him do thou punish well, if thus thou shalt think, "May my country be secure!"

4.40–43. Saith Darius the King: This is what I did; by the favor of Ahuramazda, in one and the same year I did [it]. Thou who shalt hereafter read this inscription, let that which has been done by me convince thee; do not thou think it a lie.

4.43–45. Saith Darius the King: I turn myself quickly to Ahuramazda, that this [is] true, not false, [which] I did in one and the same year. . . .

4.52–56. Saith Darius the King: Now let that which has been done by me convince thee; thus to the people impart, do not conceal it: if this record thou shalt not conceal, [but] tell it to the people, may Ahuramazda be a friend unto thee, and may family be unto thee in abundance, and may thou live long!

4.57–59. Saith Darius the King: If this record thou shalt conceal, [and] not tell it to the people, may Ahuramazda be a smiter unto thee, and may family not be to thee!

4.59–61. Saith Darius the King: This which I did, in one and the same year by the favor of Ahuramazda I did; Ahuramazda bore me aid, and the other gods who are.

4.61–67. Saith Darius the King: For this reason Ahuramazda bore aid, and the other gods who are, because I was not hostile, I was not a Lie-follower, I was not a doer of wrong—neither I nor my family. According to righteousness I conducted myself. Neither to the weak nor to the powerful did I do wrong. The man who cooperated with my house, him I rewarded well; whoso did injury, him I punished well.

4.67–69. Saith Darius the King: Thou who shalt be king hereafter, the man who shall be a Lie-follower or who shall be a doer of wrong—unto them do thou not be a friend, [but] punish them well.

4.69–72. Saith Darius the King: Thou who shalt hereafter behold this inscription which I have inscribed, or these sculptures, do thou not destroy them, [but] thence onward protect them; as long as thou shalt be in good strength! . . .

4.76–80. Saith Darius the King: If thou shalt behold this inscription or these sculptures, (and) shalt destroy them and shalt not protect them as long as unto thee there is strength, may Ahuramazda be a smiter unto thee, and may family not be unto thee, and what thou shalt do, that for thee may Ahuramazda utterly destroy!

4.80–86. Saith Darius the King: These are the men who were there at the time when I slew Gaumata the Magian who called himself Smerdis; at that time these men cooperated as my followers. . . .

4.86–88. Saith Darius the King: Thou who shalt be king hereafter, protect well the family of these men.

4.88–92. Saith Darius the King: By the favor of Ahuramazda this is the inscription which I made. . . . [O]n clay tablets and on parchment it was composed. Besides, a sculptured figure of myself I made. Besides, I made my lineage. And it was inscribed and was read off before me. Afterwards this inscription I sent off everywhere among the provinces. The people unitedly worked upon it.

Source: Roland G. Kent, *Old Persian: Grammar, Texts, Lexicon*, 2nd rev. ed. (New Haven, CT: American Oriental Society, 1953), pp. 131–32.

Zhou Succession Crisis (c. 1043 BCE)

This account of the Zhou succession crisis derives from a much larger set of texts known as the *Shangshu*, or Book of Documents. While portions of the collection report on earlier periods of Chinese history (the legendary Xia dynasty, as well as the historical second-millennium BCE Shang dynasty), the majority of the *Shangshu* reports on the history of the Zhou. Despite the complex transmission history of the *Shangshu*, its combination of speeches and narrative provides some of the best evidence for developments in the Zhou dynasty. This particular excerpt describes the tricky situation that occurred when the first king of the Zhou dynasty, King Wu, died and his brother the Duke of Zhou (spelled "Chou" in the document) assumed the position of regent for the dead king's young son King Ch'eng (the second king of the Zhou dynasty).

- In what ways does divination by oracle bone and other means factor into this account?
- What role does the mandate of heaven play in establishing Zhou authority?
- What does this account suggest about the nature of imperial rule in Zhou China?

After he had completed the conquest of the Shang people, in the second year, King Wu fell ill and was despondent. The two lords, the duke of Shao and Tai-kung Wang, said, "For the king's sake let us solemnly consult the tortoise oracle." But the duke of Chou [King Wu's younger brother, named Tan] said, "We must not distress the ancestors, the former kings."

The duke of Chou then offered himself to the ancestors, constructing three altars within a single compound. . . . Then he made this announcement to the Great King, to King Chi, and to King Wen, his great grandfather, grandfather, and father, and the scribe copied down the words of his prayer on tablets:

"Your chief descendant So-and-so [King Wu's personal name is tabooed] has met with a fearful disease and is violently ill. If you three kings are obliged to render to Heaven the life of an illustrious son, then substitute me, Tan, for So-and-so's person. I am good and compliant, clever and capable. I have much talent and much skill and can serve the spirits. . . ."

Then he divined with three tortoises, and all were auspicious. He opened the bamboo receptacles and consulted the documents, and they too indicated an auspicious answer. The duke of Chou said to the king, "According to the indications of the oracle, you will suffer no harm."

[The king said,] "I, the little child, have obtained a new life from the three kings. I shall plan for a distant end. I hope that they will think of me, the solitary man."

After the duke of Chou returned, he placed the tablets containing the prayer in a metal-bound casket. The next day the king began to recover.

[Later, King Wu died and was succeeded by his infant son, King Ch'eng. The duke of Chou acted as regent and was slandered by King Wu's younger brothers, whom he was eventually forced to punish.]

In the autumn, when a plentiful crop had ripened but had not yet been harvested, Heaven sent great thunder and lightning accompanied by wind. The grain was completely flattened and even large trees were uprooted. The people of the land were in great fear. The king and his high ministers donned their ceremonial caps and opened the documents of the metal-bound casket and thus discovered the record of how the duke of Chou had offered himself as a substitute for King Wu. The two lords and the king then questioned the scribe and the various other functionaries, and they replied. "Yes it is true. But his lordship forbade us to speak about it."

The king grasped the document and wept. "There is no need for us to make solemn divination about what has happened," he said. "In former times the duke of Chou toiled diligently for the royal house, but I, the youthful one, had no way of knowing it. Now Heaven has displayed its terror in order to make clear the virtue of the duke of Chou. I, the little child, will go in person to greet him, for the rites of our royal house approve such action."

When the king came out to the suburbs to meet the duke of Chou, Heaven sent down rain and reversed the wind, so that the grain all stood up once more. The two lords ordered the people of the land to right all the large trees that had been blown over and to earth them up. Then the year was plentiful. (*Chin t'eng.*)

Source: Burton Watson, *Early Chinese Literature* (New York: Columbia University Press, 1962), pp. 35–36.

PRIMARY SOURCE 4.4

On Karma and Reincarnation (before seventh century BCE), from the Upanishads

The Upanishads began to take their current form in the first millennium BCE. They reflect on the social and cosmic order of which humans and other creatures are a part. While they do not seek to replace Vedic rituals or undermine *varna* structures, they did offer a unifying spiritual message that all living creatures possessed a spark of universal soul (*atman*). The excerpt included here comes from the fourth chapter of the Brihadaranyaka Upanishad and is focused on a somewhat philosophical discussion of the freedom of the soul and its escape from earthly attachments. While Brahmans (the highest of the *varna* levels of Vedic society) are mentioned in this text and the text is divided into Brāhmaṇas (commentaries), neither are to be confused with the larger theme of Brahma (the cosmic universe of everything).

....

- According to this text, what happens to the self at death?

- What evidence in the text offers a view into the realities and political structures of the world that produced it?

- How might the ideas expressed in this text offer a sense of unity and belonging to the people who believed its message?

....

[Third Brāhmaṇa] 35. As a heavily loaded cart goes creaking, just so this bodily self, mounted by the intelligent Self, goes groaning when one is breathing one's last. 36. When he comes to weakness—whether he come to weakness through old age or through disease—this person frees himself from these limbs just as a mango, or a fig, or a berry releases itself from its bond; and he hastens again, according to the entrance and place of origin, back to life. 37. As noblemen, policemen, chariot-drivers, village-heads wait with food, drink, and lodgings for a king who is coming, and cry: "Here he comes! Here he comes!" so indeed do all things wait for him who has this knowledge and cry: "Here is Brahma coming! Here is Brahma coming!" 38. As noblemen, policemen, chariot-drivers, village-heads gather around a king who is about to depart, just so do all the breaths gather around the soul and the end, when one is breathing one's last.

[Fourth Brāhmaṇa] 1. When this self comes to weakness and to confusedness of mind, as it were, then the breaths gather around him. He takes to himself those

particles of energy and descends into the heart. When the person in the eye turns away, back [to the sun], then one becomes non-knowing of forms. 2. "He is becoming one," they say; "he does not see." "He is becoming one," they say; "he does not smell." "He is becoming one," they say; "he does not taste." "He is becoming one," they say; "he does not speak." "He is becoming one," they say; "he does not hear." "He is becoming one," they say; "he does not think." "He is becoming one," they say; "he does not touch." "He is becoming one," they say; "he does not know." The point of his heart becomes lighted up. By that light the self departs, either by the eye, or by the head, or by other bodily parts. After him, as he goes out, the life goes out. After the life, as it goes out, all the breaths go out. He becomes one with intelligence. What has intelligence departs with him. His knowledge and his works and his former intelligence [i.e., instinct] lay hold of him. 3. Now as a caterpillar, when it has come to the end of a blade of grass, in taking the next step draws itself together towards it, just so this soul in taking the next step strikes down this body, dispels its ignorance, and draws itself together [for making the transition]. 4. As a goldsmith, taking a piece of gold, reduces it to another newer and more beautiful form, just so this soul, striking down this body and dispelling its ignorance, makes for itself another newer and more beautiful form like that either of the fathers or of the Gandharvas, or of the gods, or of Prajāpati, or of Brahma, or of other beings. 5. Verily, this soul is Brahma, made of knowledge, of mind, of breath, of seeing, of hearing, of earth, of water, of wind, of space, of energy and non-energy, of desire and non-desire, of anger and of non-anger, of virtuousness and of non-virtuousness. It is made of everything. . . . According as one acts, according as one conducts himself, so does he become. The doer of good becomes good. The doer of evil becomes evil. One becomes virtuous by virtuous action, bad by bad action. . . . As is his desire, such is his resolve; as is his resolve, such the action he performs; what action (*karma*) he performs, that he procures for himself. . . . [6.] Now the man who does not desire.—He who is without desire, who is freed from desire, whose desire is satisfied, whose desire is the Soul—his breaths do not depart. Being very Brahma, he goes to Brahma. 7. On this point there is this verse:—

When are liberated all

The desires that lodge in one's heart,

Then a mortal becomes immortal!

Therein he reaches Brahma!

As the slough of a snake lies on an ant-hill, dead, cast off, even so lies this body. But this incorporeal, immortal Life is Brahma indeed, is light indeed. . . . 22. Verily, he is the great, unborn Soul, who is this [person] consisting of knowledge among the senses. In the space within the heart lies the ruler of all, the lord of all, the king of all. He does not become greater by good action nor inferior by bad action. He is the lord of all, the overlord of beings, the protector of beings. He is the separating dam for keeping these worlds apart.

Such a one the Brahmans desire to know by repetition of the Vedas, by sacrifices, by offering, by penance, by fasting. On knowing him, in truth, one becomes an ascetic. Desiring him only as their home, mendicants wander forth. . . . [23.] Therefore, having this knowledge, having become calm, subdued, quiet, patiently enduring, and collected, one sees the Soul just in the soul. One sees everything as the Soul. Evil does not overcome him; he overcomes all evil. Evil does not burn him; he burns all evil. Free from evil, free from impurity, free from doubt, he becomes a Brahman. . . . 25. Verily, that great, unborn Soul, undecaying, undying, immortal, fearless, is Brahma. Verily, Brahma is fearless. He who knows this becomes the fearless Brahma.

Source: *The Thirteen Principal Upanishads*, translated by Robert Ernest Hume (New York: Oxford University Press, 1934), pp. 139–41, 143–44.

Interpreting Visual Evidence

Tribute in First Empires

Black obelisk of Shalmaneser III.

One method early empires of the first millennium BCE used to consolidate their power was the collection of tribute from the areas under their control. The examples gathered here depict the payment of various forms of tribute in different empires.

In his palace complex at Nimrud/Kalhu, the Neo-Assyrian king Shalmaneser III (r. 858–824 BCE) erected a black limestone obelisk decorated on four sides with reliefs and inscriptions commemorating his conquests and the peoples who paid tribute to him. This obelisk includes a famous scene thought to show the tribute offered by King Jehu of Israel. Another series of images on the obelisk, shown here, records

Tribute scene from palace at Persepolis.

the exotic gifts from Musri (literally, "Borderlands"), including two-humped Bactrian camels, an elephant, and three monkeys. At the Persian capital of Persepolis, grand staircases leading to the main audience hall of the palace were decorated with scenes of the king and his courtiers as well as the delegations bringing tribute to the center of the empire. The second image depicts tribute bearers bringing animals and other items (in bowls) as gifts to the Persian king. Those delivering their tribute would have walked past these scenes on their way to pay obeisance to the Persian king. In Zhou China, tribute was often rendered in human labor, which was needed to build the irrigation system of canals and dikes. But another form of tribute

to Zhou dynasts may have been textiles, such as the woven silk with a geometric and dragon motif shown in the final image. The silk was dyed red with cinnabar, a rare and expensive ingredient whose use would have been limited to luxury textiles of the elite. The differing types of tribute and their display indicate the varying levels of centralized control these first-millennium BCE empires exerted over their subject peoples.

Woven textile from Eastern Zhou.

Questions for Analysis

1. Compare the grand display of tribute in the Neo-Assyrian and Persian Empires with the tribute suggested by the Zhou textile. What do these varied tributes (their type and display) suggest about the nature of early empire in each of these regions?

2. Compare the symbolic political value with the actual economic impact of the specific tributes visible here.

3. Imagine yourself as a tribute bearer ascending the steps to the reception hall of the Persian king or visiting the Neo-Assyrian capital of Shalmaneser III. Now imagine yourself as a member of the Persian or Neo-Assyrian elite. How would your experience of viewing these scenes differ depending on your identity?

先師孔子行教像

德侔天地道冠古今

刪述六經垂憲萬世

唐吳道子筆

5

Worlds Turned Inside Out

1000–350 BCE

In the midst of violent struggles for power and territory in China in the sixth century BCE, Master Kong Fuzi instructed his disciples on how to govern, saying: "Guide them by edicts, keep them in line with punishments, and the people will stay out of trouble but will have no sense of shame. Guide them by virtue, keep them in line with the rites, and they will, besides having a sense of shame, reform themselves."

Master Kong, also known as Confucius, represented a new breed of influential leaders who were teachers and thinkers, not kings, priests, or warriors. Nonetheless, it was the convulsions around them—incessant warfare, population growth, migrations, and the emergence of new cities—that motivated their search for insights. By viewing the world in innovative ways, these teachers instructed rulers on how to govern justly and showed ordinary individuals how to live ethically.

The teachers and founders of new ways of thinking from the first millennium BCE, who figure prominently in this chapter, were some of the most influential in history. And their students preserved and passed along their radical new thought. In China, Confucius elaborated a set of principles for ethical living that has guided the Chinese population up to modern times. In South Asia, Siddhartha Gautama (the Buddha) laid out social and spiritual tenets that challenged the traditional social hierarchy based on birth and, with it, the power of the ruling priests and warriors. In Greece, Socrates,

Core Objectives

- **DESCRIBE** the challenges that Afro-Eurasian empires and states faced in the first millennium BCE, and **COMPARE** the range of solutions they devised.

- **IDENTIFY** Axial Age thinkers and **ANALYZE** their distinctive ideas.

- **EXPLAIN** the relationship between Axial Age thinkers across Afro-Eurasia (East Asia, South Asia, and the Mediterranean) and the political and social situations to which they were responding.

- **COMPARE** the political, cultural, and social developments across Afro-Eurasia with those occurring in the Americas and sub-Saharan Africa.

Plato, and Aristotle offered ideas that ranged from shaking Greek citizens from their complacency and questioning what they thought they knew about reality to offering a system of logic that conformed to natural and intelligible laws.

The philosophers, theologians, poets, political leaders, and merchants of this era founded literary traditions, articulated new belief systems, and established new political and economic institutions that spread well beyond the places where they began. While wars and havoc raged within their societies and long-distance trade and travel linked societies, these thinkers influenced a world shaped by a search for order and an appetite for new thinking.

Global Storyline

The Axial Age

- A range of challenges—warfare, political upheaval, economic pressures, and social developments—transform the empires and states of Afro-Eurasia.

- "Second-generation" societies arise across Afro-Eurasia in a pivotal period sometimes called the "Axial Age."

- Axial Age thinkers in Afro-Eurasia reshape peoples' views of the world and their place in it.

- Complex new societies develop in the Americas and sub-Saharan Africa.

An "Axial Age"

Some modern thinkers call the mid-first millennium BCE the **Axial Age** to emphasize its pivotal and transitional role between the declining old empires of ancient Egypt, Southwest Asia, northern India, and Zhou China and the later empires of Alexander the Great, Chandragupta's Mauryan Empire in India, Augustus's Rome, and Han Wudi's China (see Chapters 6 and 7). Instrumental to this dynamic period were the ethical, philosophical, and religious innovations taking place in India, China, and Europe.

In this Axial Age, societies on the edges of regional empires or within declining empires of Afro-Eurasia started to follow innovative paths. (See Map 5.1.) These new communities were not just extensions of old ways of life. In each, dramatic innovations in cultural and religious beliefs were expanding people's social, political, and cultural options. Although each of the resulting cultures—in East Asia, South Asia, and the Mediterranean—was distinct from the others, we might call them all **second-generation societies**, given that they built on their predecessors yet represented a departure from ancient legacies. (See Current Trends in World History: What Makes an "Axial Age"?)

While Afro-Eurasia experienced an Axial Age and the emergence of second-generation societies, other parts of the world saw complex, urban-based societies emerge for the first time. The first of these in the Americas was established by the Olmecs in Mesoamerica, with artistic and religious reverberations well beyond their homelands. In Africa, distinct regional identities spread in the Upper Nile (in Nubia) and West Africa (among the Nok). One of the most striking features of the first millennium BCE is the long-lasting impact of both the Axial Age second-generation societies that stretched across Afro-Eurasia and the first complex societies isolated from them by oceans and desert.

Eastern Zhou China

Destruction of the old political order paved the way for radical thinkers and cultural flourishing in Eastern Zhou China. Centered at Luoyang, the turbulent Eastern Zhou dynasty was divided by ancient Chinese chroniclers into the Spring and Autumn period (722–481 BCE) and the Warring States period (403–221 BCE). One writer from the Spring and Autumn period described over 500 battles among states and more than 100 civil wars within states, all taking place within 260 years. Fueling this warfare was the spread of cheaper and more lethal weaponry, made possible by new iron-smelting techniques, which in turn shifted influence from the central government to local authorities and allowed warfare to continue unabated into the Warring States period. Regional states became so powerful that they undertook large-scale projects, including dikes and irrigation systems, which had to this point been feasible

THE BIG PICTURE

Explain why historians refer to the mid-first millennium bce as the "Axial Age." Was this period an Axial Age in your opinion?

Axial Age
Pivotal period in the mid-first millennium BCE when radical thinkers, such as Zoroaster in Persia, Confucius and Master Lao in East Asia, Siddhartha Gautama (the Buddha) in South Asia, and Socrates in the Mediterranean, offered dramatically new ideas that challenged their times.

second-generation societies
First-millennium BCE societies that innovated on their older political, religious, and cultural ideas by incorporating new aspects of cultures they encountered to reshape their way of life.

Core Objectives

DESCRIBE the challenges that Afro-Eurasian empires and states faced in the first millennium BCE, and **COMPARE** the range of solutions they devised.

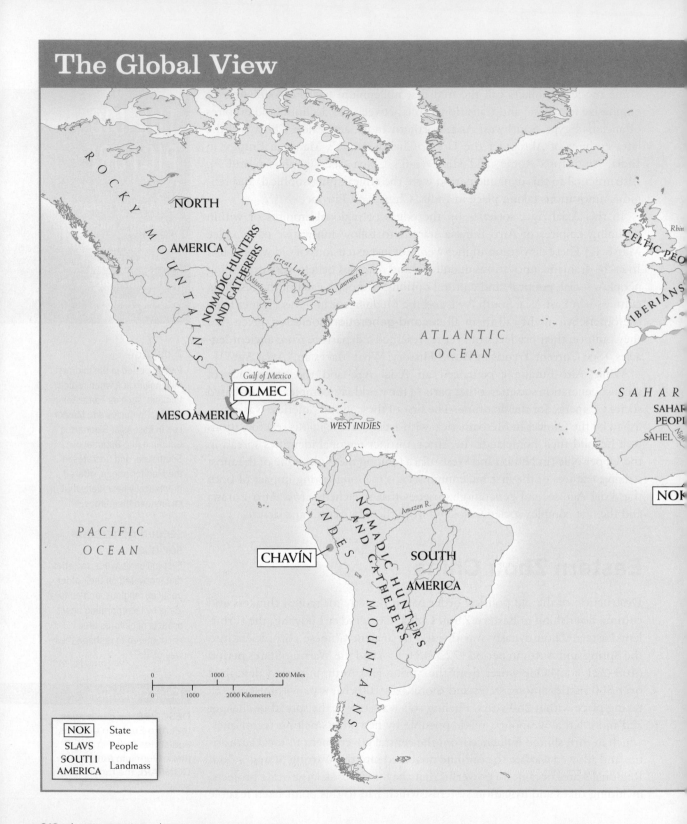

ROCKY MOUNTAINS

NORTH

AMERICA

NOMADIC HUNTERS AND GATHERERS

Great Lakes

St. Lawrence R.

Mississippi R.

Gulf of Mexico

OLMEC

MESOAMERICA

WEST INDIES

ATLANTIC OCEAN

CELTIC PEO

Rhin

IBERIANS

SAHAR

SAHAR
PEOPL

SAHEL

NOK

PACIFIC OCEAN

Amazon R.

ANDES

NOMADIC HUNTERS AND GATHERERS

CHAVÍN

SOUTH

AMERICA

MOUNTAINS

| 0 | 1000 | 2000 Miles |
| 0 | 1000 | 2000 Kilometers |

NOK	State
SLAVS	People
SOUTH AMERICA	Landmass

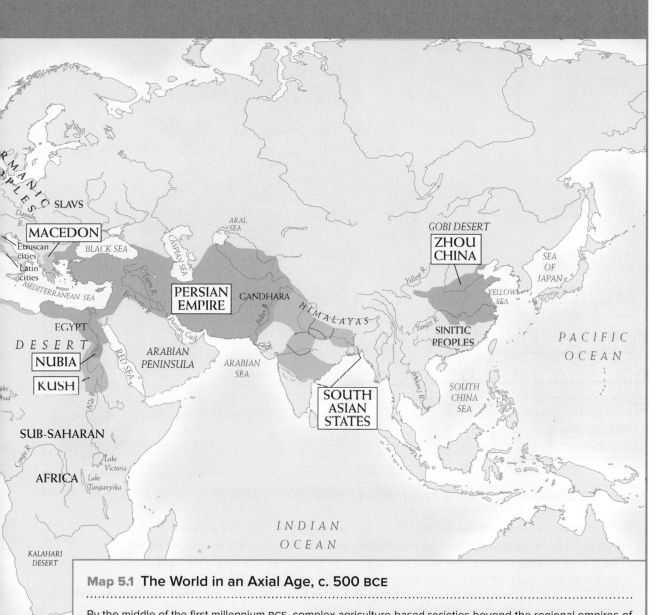

Map 5.1 The World in an Axial Age, c. 500 BCE

By the middle of the first millennium BCE, complex agriculture-based societies beyond the regional empires of Southwest Asia, North Africa, and East Asia contributed to the flowering of new cultural pathways and ideas that reshaped the old empires and territorial states into what we might call second-generation societies.

- According to your reading, where did these second-generation societies appear? What had been located there before?

- Examining the map, how are these second-generation societies influenced by peoples on their margins?

- Which states are in regions closely connected to others? Which appear to be geographically isolated? How might proximity to others or relative isolation have shaped these societies' development?

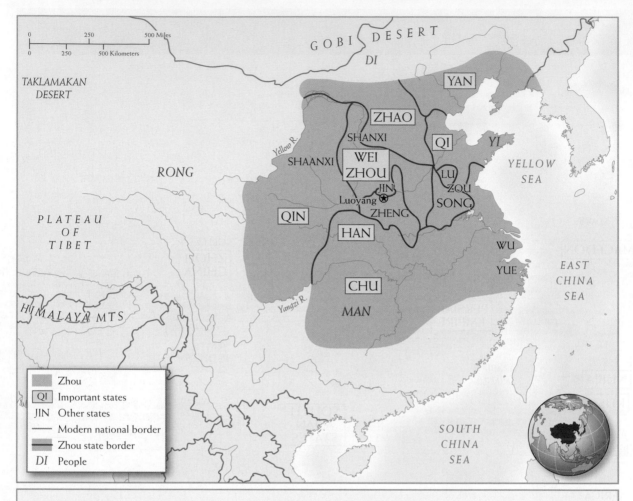

Map 5.2 Zhou China in the Warring States Period, 403–221 BCE

The Warring States period witnessed a fracturing of the Zhou dynasty into a myriad of states.

- Find the Zhou capital of Luoyang on the map. Where was it located relative to the other key states?
- Trace the Zhou state borders. How would you compare the boundaries and sizes of the various Zhou states? What does this suggest about the importance of diplomacy during this period?
- How do you think so many smaller polities could survive when they were surrounded first by seven and then by three even larger and more powerful states (Qin, Qi, and Chu)?

only for empires. By the beginning of the Warring States period, seven large territorial states dominated the Zhou world. (See Map 5.2.) Their wars and shifting political alliances involved the mobilization of armies and resources on an unprecedented scale. Qin, the most powerful state, which ultimately replaced the Eastern Zhou dynasty in 221 BCE, fielded armies that combined huge infantries in the tens of thousands with lethal cavalries and skilled archers using state-of-the-art crossbows.

The conception of central power changed dramatically during this era. Royal appointees replaced hereditary officeholders. By the middle of the fourth century BCE, power was so concentrated in the major states' rulers that each began to call himself "king" (*wang*). Despite—or perhaps even as a result of—the constant warfare, scholars, soldiers, merchants, peasants, and artisans thrived in the midst of an expanding agrarian economy and interregional trade.

INNOVATIONS IN THOUGHT

Out of this turmoil came new visions that would shape Chinese thinking about the individual's place in society and provide the philosophical underpinnings for the world's most enduring imperial system (lasting from the establishment of the Qin dynasty in 221 BCE until the abdication of China's last monarch in 1912). Often it was the losers among the political elites, seeking to replace their former advantages with new status gained through service, who sparked this intellectual creativity. Many important teachers emerged in China's Axial Age, each with disciples. The philosophies of these "hundred masters," a term mostly used at the time by itinerant scholars, constituted what came to be known as the Hundred Schools of Thought. Among the most influential were Confucianism and Daoism.

Confucius (551–479 BCE) was very much the product of the violent Spring and Autumn period. Serving in minor governmental positions, he believed the founders of the Zhou dynasty had established ideals of good government and principled action. Frustrated, however, by the realities of division and war among rival states all around him, Confucius set out in search of an enlightened ruler. Confucius's teachings stemmed from his belief that human beings behaved ethically not because they wanted to achieve salvation or a heavenly reward but because it was in their human makeup to do so. Humanity's natural tendencies, if left alone, produced harmonious existence. Confucius saw family and filial submission (the duty of children to parents) as the foundation of proper ethical action, including loyalty to the state and rulers. His idea of modeling the state on the patriarchal family—with the ruler respecting heaven as if it were his father and protecting his subjects as if they were his children—became a bedrock principle of Confucian thought. Although he regarded

Intricate Jade Carving This small jade plaque, measuring just under 2 inches across, demonstrates the aesthetic sensibility and artistic accomplishment of jade carvers in the Warring States period (403–221 BCE). The intricate design of two facing dragons complete with tiny scales and enclosed within a circular frame carefully etched with a swirling pattern—all on so small an object—required the skilled use of fine rotary tools for carving and polishing jade.

Core Objectives

IDENTIFY Axial Age thinkers and **ANALYZE** their distinctive ideas.

Confucius
(551–479 BCE) Radical thinker whose ideas—especially about how ethical living that was centered on *ren* (benevolence), *li* (proper ritual), and *xiao* (filial piety toward ancestors living and dead) shaped the politically engaged superior gentleman—transformed society and government in East Asia.

himself as a transmitter of ancient wisdom, Confucius established many of the major guidelines for Chinese thought and action: respect for the pronouncements of scholars, commitment to a broad education, and training for all who were highly intelligent and willing to work, whether noble or humble in birth. This equal access to training for those willing and able offered a dramatic departure from past centuries, when only nobles were believed capable of ruling. Nonetheless, Confucius's distinctions between gentlemen-rulers and commoners continued to support a social hierarchy—although an individual's position in that hierarchy now rested on education rather than on birth.

Confucius's ethical teachings were preserved by his followers in a collection known as *The Analects*. These texts record Confucius's conversations with his students. In his effort to persuade his contemporaries to reclaim what he regarded as the lost ideals of the early Zhou, Confucius proposed a moral framework stressing benevolence (*ren*), correct performance of ritual (*li*), loyalty to the family (*xiao*), and perfection of moral character to become a "superior man" (*junzi*)—that is, a man defined by benevolence and goodness rather than by the pursuit of profit. Confucius believed that a society of such superior men would not need coercive laws and punishment to achieve order. Confucius ultimately left court in 484 BCE, discouraged by the continuing state of warfare. His transformational ideology remained, however, and has shaped Chinese society for millennia, both through its followers and through those who adopted traditions that developed as a distinct counterpoint to Confucian engagement.

Another key philosophy was **Daoism**, which diverged sharply from Confucian thought by scorning rigid rituals and social hierarchies. Its ideas originated with a Master Lao (Laozi, "Old Master"), who—if he actually existed—may have been a contemporary of Confucius. His sayings were collected in *The Daodejing*, or *The Book of the Way and Its Power* (c. third century BCE). Master Lao's book was then elaborated by Master Zhuang (Zhuangzi, c. 369–286 BCE). Master Lao is credited with saying, "The Sage, when he governs, empties [people's] minds and fills their bellies. . . . His constant object is to keep the people without knowledge and without desire, or to prevent those who have knowledge from daring to act." Daoism stressed that the best path (*dao*) for living was to follow the natural order of things. Its main principle was *wuwei*, "doing nothing." Spontaneity, noninterference, and acceptance of the world as it is, rather than attempting to change it through politics and government, were what mattered. In Laozi's vision, the ruler who interfered least in the natural processes of change was the most successful. Zhuangzi focused on the enlightened individual living spontaneously and in harmony with nature, free of society's ethical rules and laws and viewing life and death simply as different stages of existence.

Xunzi and Han Fei Legalism, or Statism, another view of how best to create an orderly life, grew out of the writings of Master Xun (Xunzi, 310–237 BCE)

Daoism
East Asian philosophy of the Axial Age introduced by Master Lao and expanded by his student Zhuangzi. It was remarkable for its emphasis on following the *dao* (the natural way of the cosmos) and held that the best way to do that was through *wuwei* (doing nothing).

toward the end of the Warring States period. He believed that men and women are innately bad and therefore require moral education and authoritarian control. In the decades before the Qin victory over the Zhou, the Legalist thinker Han Fei (280–233 BCE) agreed that human nature is primarily evil. He imagined a state with a ruler who followed the Daoist principle of *wuwei,* detaching himself from everyday governance—but only after setting an unbending standard (strict laws, accompanied by harsh punishments) for judging his officials and people. For Han Fei, the establishment and uniform application of these laws would keep people's evil nature in check. As we will see in Chapter 7, the Qin state, before it became the dominant state in China, systematically followed the Legalist philosophy.

Apart from the philosophical discourse of the "hundred masters," with its far-reaching impact across Chinese society, elites and commoners alike tried to maintain stability in their lives through religion, medicine, and statecraft. The elites' rites of divination to predict the future and medical recipes to heal the body found parallels in the commoners' use of ghost stories and astrological almanacs to understand the meaning of their lives and the significance of their deaths. Elites recorded their political discourses on wood and bamboo slips, tied together to form scrolls. They likewise prepared military treatises, ritual texts, geographic works, and poetry. The growing importance of statecraft and philosophical discourse promoted the use of writing, with 9,000 to 10,000 graphs or signs required to convey these elaborate ideas.

Qu Yuan In addition to the innovations of Confucian and Daoist thought, the first millennium BCE also saw an outpouring of poetic work. Qu Yuan (339–278 BCE), shown here in a seventeenth-century painting, is known both from his own writing and from the works of later writers who mention him, such as the famous Chinese historian Sima Qian (145–86 BCE). A disgraced politician, diplomat, and poet, Qu Yuan wrote his famous poem *Li Sao* in the context of the decline of his home state, Chu, over the course of the Warring States period.

What emerged from all this activity was a foundational alliance between scholars and the state. Scholars became state functionaries who were dependent on rulers' patronage. In return, rulers recognized scholars' expertise in matters of punishment, ritual, astronomy, medicine, and divination. Philosophical deliberations focused on the need to maintain order and stability by preserving the state. These bonds that rulers forged with their scholarly elites were a distinguishing feature of governments in Warring States China, as compared with other Afro-Eurasian societies at this time.

INNOVATIONS IN STATE ADMINISTRATION

Regional rulers of the Spring and Autumn period enhanced their ability to obtain natural resources, to recruit men for their armies, and to oversee conquered areas. This trend continued in the Warring States period, as the elites in the major states created administrative districts with stewards, sheriffs, and judges and a system of registering peasant households to facilitate tax collection and army conscription. These officials, who had been knights under the Western Zhou, were now bureaucrats in direct service to the ruler. These administrators were the "superior men" (*junzi*) of Confucian thought. They were paid in grain and sometimes received gifts of gold and silver, as well as titles and seals of office, from the ruler. The most successful of these ministers was the Qin statesman Shang Yang (fourth century BCE). Lord Shang's reforms—including a head tax, administrative districts for closer bureaucratic control of hinterlands, land distribution for individual households to farm, and reward or punishment for military achievement—positioned the Qin to become the dominant state of its time.

INNOVATIONS IN WARFARE

With administrative reforms came reforms in military recruitment and warfare. In earlier periods, nobles had let fly their arrows from chariots while conscripted peasants fought beside them on the bloodstained ground. The Warring States, however, relied on massed infantries of peasants, whose conscription was made easier by the registration of peasant households. Bearing iron lances and unconstrained by their relationships with nobles, these peasants fought fiercely. In addition to this conscripted peasant infantry, armies boasted elite professional troops equipped with iron armor and weapons, and wielding the recently invented crossbow. The crossbow's tremendous power, range, and accuracy enabled archers to kill lightly armored cavalrymen or charioteers at a distance. With improved siege technology, enemy armies assaulted the new defensive walls of towns and frontiers, either digging under them or using counterweighted siege ladders to scale them. Campaigns were no longer limited to an agricultural season and instead might stretch over a year or longer. The huge state armies contained as many as 1 million commoners in the infantry, supported by 1,000 chariots and 10,000 bow-wielding cavalrymen. During the Spring and Autumn period one state's entire army would face another state's, but by the Warring States period armies could divide into separate forces and wage several battles simultaneously.

ECONOMIC, SOCIAL, AND CULTURAL CHANGES

While a growing population presented new challenges, the continuous warfare in these periods spurred economic growth in China. An agricultural revolution on the North China plain along the Yellow River led to rapid population growth, and the inhabitants of the Eastern Zhou reached approximately 20 million. Several factors contributed to increased agricultural productivity beginning in the Spring and Autumn period. Some rulers gave peasants the right to own their land in exchange for taxes and military service, which in turn increased productivity because the farmers were working to benefit themselves. Agricultural productivity was also enhanced by innovations such as crop rotation (millet and wheat in the north, rice and millet in the south) and oxen-pulled iron plowshares to prepare fields.

With this increased agricultural yield came the pressures of accompanying population growth. Ever-attentive peasant farmers tilling the fields of North and South China produced more rice and wheat than anyone else on earth, but that agricultural success was often outpaced by their growing families. As more people required more fuel, deforestation led to erosion of the fields. Many animals were hunted to extinction. Many inhabitants migrated south to domesticate the marshes, lakes, and rivers of the Yangzi River delta, here they created new arable frontiers out of former wetlands. When the expansion into arable land invariably hit its limits, Chinese families faced terrible food shortages and famines. The long-term economic result was a declining standard of living for massive numbers of Chinese peasants.

Despite these long-term cycles of population pressures and famine, larger harvests and advances in bronze and iron casting enabled the beginning of a market economy: trade in surplus grain, pottery, and ritual objects. Peasants continued to barter, but elites and rulers used minted coins. Grain and goods traveled along roads, rivers, and canals. Rulers and officials applied their military and organizational skills for public projects enhancing waterworks.

Economic growth had repercussions at all levels of society. Rulers attained a high level of cultural sophistication, as reflected in their magnificent palaces and burial sites. Archaeological evidence also suggests that commoners could purchase bronze metalwork, whereas previously only Zhou rulers and aristocrats could afford to do so. Social relations became more fluid as commoners gained power and aristocrats lost it. In Qin, for example, peasants who served in the ruler's army could be rewarded with land, houses, enslaved servants, and even status change for killing enemy soldiers. While class relations had a

Bamboo-Strip Texts Over the past fifty years, Chinese texts dating to the Warring States (403–221 BCE) and Western Han (206 BCE–9 CE) periods have been unearthed from tombs at various sites, including Jingmen (Guodian tombs) and Changsha (Mawangdui tombs). Written on bamboo strips (as pictured here) and on silk, these texts include philosophical and medical treatises, as well as mathematical and calendrical calculations.

revolutionary fluidity, gender relations became more rigid for elites and non-elites alike as male-centered kinship groups grew. The resulting separation of the sexes and male domination within the family affected women's position. An emphasis on monogamy, or at least the primacy of the first wife over additional wives and concubines, emerged. Relations between the sexes became increasingly ritualized and constrained by moral and legal sanctions against any behavior that appeared to threaten the purity of authoritarian male lineages.

Even with the endless cycles of warfare and chaos—or perhaps because of them—many foundational beliefs, values, and philosophies for later dynasties sprang forth during the Spring and Autumn and Warring States periods. By the middle of the first millennium BCE, China's political activities and institutional and intellectual innovations affected larger numbers of people, over a much broader area, than did comparable developments in South Asia and the Mediterranean.

South Asia

While Chinese scholar-officials were theorizing about how to govern and organize their society, the Vedic peoples who settled in the Ganges Valley were assimilating earlier residents and forging their own new political institutions, economic activities, and belief systems. The heartland of South Asian developments in this period was the mid-Ganges plain, a roughly 70,000-square-mile area in the northeast of present-day India and the southern tip of Nepal. (See Map 5.3.) Waves of Vedic peoples migrated into this region around 600 BCE, clearing land, establishing new cities and trade routes, expanding rice cultivation, and experimenting with new political forms. Abundant monsoon rains made the land suitable for rice farming, as opposed to the wheat and barley farming of the Indus Valley. Vedic migrants cleared land by setting fire to the forests and using iron tools—fashioned from ore mined locally—to remove what was left of the jungle. Two major kinds of states appeared in the mid- and lower Ganges plain: those ruled by hereditary monarchs and those ruled by a small elite (oligarchy). South Asian oligarchies were led by the Kshatriya class of warriors and officials. Kshatriya oligarchs controlled the land and other resources, overseeing the enslaved and foreign workers

Eastern Zhou Coinage Coins in the Eastern Zhou state were made of bronze and were cast in a variety of shapes, some resembling farming tools such as spades and others resembling knives. The variety of shapes might reflect a time when tools were exchanged as a form of currency. In the Warring States period, each region had its own currency.

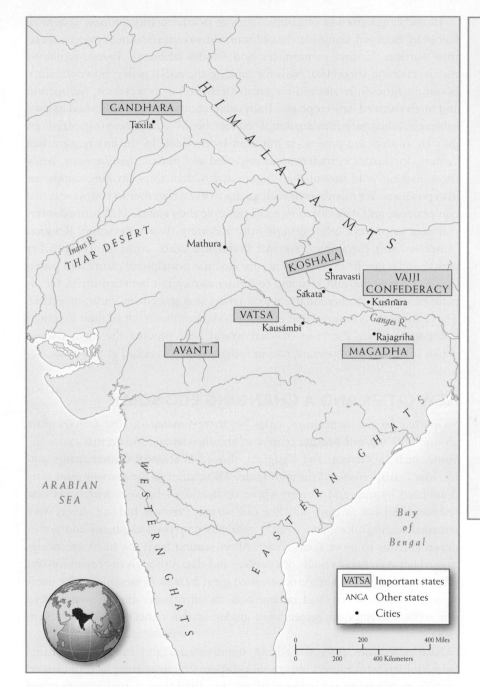

Map 5.3 Major States in the First Millennium BCE in South Asia

South Asia underwent profound transformations in the first millennium BCE that reflected growing urbanization, increased commerce, and the emergence of two types of states: monarchies and oligarchies.

- Where did the new states and cities appear? How do these compare with the location of the earlier cities of the Harappans (Map 2.5)?

- What geographic and environmental features encouraged or hindered social and cultural integration?

- What other regions had influence on South Asia, and where might South Asian culture spread?

GANDHARA

Taxila

HIMALAYA MTS

Indus R.

THAR DESERT

Mathura

KOSHALA

Shravasti

Sakata

VAJJI CONFEDERACY

Kusinara

VATSA

Kausámbi

Ganges R.

Rajagriha

AVANTI

MAGADHA

ARABIAN SEA

WESTERN GHATS

EASTERN GHATS

Bay of Bengal

VATSA	Important states
ANGA	Other states
•	Cities

0   200   400 Miles
0   200   400 Kilometers

In the kingdoms and oligarchic cities of northern India, a new system of hierarchy emerged alongside the old fourfold *varnas* (Brahman priests, Kshatriya warriors, Vaishya commoners, and Shudra laborers). *Varnas* remained the overarching theoretical basis for ranking the social order; however, since booming agriculture allowed for greater variation in professions, occupation and birth received new emphasis. Each occupational group established its own sublevels, called *jatis* (the Sanskrit word for "birth"). *Jatis* were organized not only by kinship and profession but even by product. In the emerging urban centers, for instance, traders were regarded as "purer" than artisans, while those making gold utensils had higher status than those making copper or iron products. Yet members of each group worked together to restrict internal competition, and they closed ranks to preserve their status. *Jatis* banned intermarriage to prevent other groups from accessing their knowledge. Religion buttressed this hierarchical system. Brahmanic texts, some from an earlier period and some from the present, invoked the principle of purity and pollution to rank *varnas* and *jatis* and to hinder movement between them. Occupations were made hereditary, and a taboo was placed on eating together. These injunctions ensured that individuals did not move out of their inherited occupation. Thus, the basis of what would later become the caste system, which still plays an important role in Indian society, was laid at this time.

NEW CITIES AND A CHANGING ECONOMY

Supported by rice agriculture, cities began to emerge on the Ganges plain around 500 BCE and became centers of commercial and intellectual exchange. Some, such as Shravasti and Rajagriha, thrived as artisanal centers, while others, like Taxila, prospered through trade. These cities of the Ganges plain were dominated by men and women whose occupations—bankers, merchants, and teachers—did not fit easily into the old *varnas*. Precisely laid-out streets were crowded with vendors, and wealthy residents employed elephants and horse-drawn chariots to move them about. Alleys leading from the main streets zigzagged between houses built with pebbles and clay. Although city expansion was often haphazard, civic authorities showed great interest in sanitation. The many squares dotting each city had garbage bins, and dirty water drained away in deep sink wells underground. Streets were graded so that rainfall would wash them clean.

The new cities offered exciting opportunities and innovations. Rural householders who moved into them prospered by importing rice and sugar-cane from villages to sell in the markets; they then transported manufactured goods such as sugar, salt, and utensils back to their villages. The less affluent turned to craftwork, fashioning textiles, needles, fine pottery, copper plates, ivory decorations, and gold and silver utensils. Other professions included physicians, launderers, barbers, cooks, tailors, and entertainers. The elaborate

Taxila *Left:* Taxila became the capital of Gandhara, a kingdom located in what is today northern Pakistan and eastern Afghanistan, when it was occupied by the Persian Empire in the fifth century BCE. Dharmarajika was one of the most important monasteries. The walkway around the stupa, a moundlike structure containing Buddhist relics, was covered with glass tiles, and the stupa itself was decorated with jewels. *Right:* This corner of a stupa exhibits a variety of the architectural styles that prevailed in Gandharan art. Both square and round columns are covered by Greek-influenced Corinthian capitals. The arch on the right shows the stacked-beam style of Sanchi, the famous stupa in central India.

division of labor suggests high degrees of specialization and commercialization. Those with money became bankers who financed trade and industry. As in Greece and China, coins came into use in these cities at about this time. Traders and bankers established municipal bodies that issued the coins and vouched for their worth. Made of silver, the coins had irregular shapes but specific weights, which determined their value; they also were punch-marked, or stamped with symbols of authority on one side.

Yet the opportunities and innovations of the new cities did not ensure success for everyone. Many came to cities in search of work, and some fared better than others. As a whole, city dwellers had more material wealth, but their lives were far more uncertain. In addition, urban life created a new social class: those who did the dirtiest jobs, such as removing garbage and sewage, and were therefore viewed as physically and ritually impure "untouchables." Even though their work kept the cities clean, they were forced to live in shantytowns outside the city limits. These outcasts became receptive audiences for those who would challenge Vedic rituals and Brahman priests.

BRAHMANS, THEIR CHALLENGERS, AND NEW BELIEFS

To the Brahmans, nothing about the cities seemed good, and their efforts to retain their superior status prompted new challenges to traditional beliefs. The Brahmans thought that *varnas* and *jatis* mixing indiscriminately polluted society. Moreover, lowborn persons grasping at higher status by acquiring wealth or skill skewed established hierarchies. When an alphabetic script appeared around 600 BCE, sacred knowledge became more accessible, and thus the Brahmans' ability to control the definition of right and wrong was undermined. Formerly, all of Vedic literature had been memorized, and only the brightest Brahmans could master the tradition (see Chapter 4).

Frightened by these urban threats, Brahmans sought to strengthen their relationships with the kings by establishing the idea of a monarch endowed with divine power. Kingship had been unnecessary in a long-ago golden age, according to Brahmanic scripts; a moral code and priests to uphold it had been enough to keep things in order. Over time, though, the world deteriorated due to rivalry for wealth. According to Brahmanic writings, the gods then decided that people on earth needed a king to maintain order. The gods enticed a reluctant Manu ("Man") with a range of promises, including one-tenth of the grain harvest, one-fiftieth of the cattle, merits for subjects' good behavior, and the most beautiful woman in his domain. The Laws of Manu are associated with this tradition. In the Brahmanic accounts, royal power had a divine origin: the gods chose the king and protected him. Priests and Vedic rituals were essential to royal power, since kingly authority was validated through religious ceremonies carried out by Brahman priests. This emphasis on divine kingship solved some problems but created new ones. The Brahmans' claim to moral authority caused resentment among the Kshatriyas—especially those in the oligarchic republics, whose leaders did not assert divine power. Merchants and artisans also chafed at the Brahmans' claims to superiority. Such resentments provoked challenges to the Brahmans' domination. Some thinkers in South Asia believed that they were in an age of acute crisis because their culture's ancient harmony had been lost. And like many scholars and philosophers elsewhere in this Axial Age, a new group of South Asian scholars and religious leaders developed their own answers to questions about human existence.

Revolutionary South Asian thinkers challenged the Brahmans' worldview by refusing to recognize the gods that populated the Vedic world. Some of these rebels sprang from inside the Vedic tradition; though Brahmans, they rejected the idea that sacrificial rituals pleased the gods. To them, God was a universal concept, not a superhuman creature. Also, they felt that the many cows that priests slaughtered for ritual sacrifices could serve more practical uses, such as plowing the land and producing milk. Their discussions and teachings about the universe and life were later collected in the Upanishads. Other dissidents, such as Mahavira and the Buddha, came from outside the Vedic tradition.

Mahavira and Jainism Vardhamana Mahavira (c. 540–468 BCE) popularized the doctrines of **Jainism**, which had emerged in the seventh century BCE. Born a Kshatriya in an oligarchic republic, Mahavira left home at age thirty to seek the truth about life; he spent twelve years as an ascetic (one who rejects material possessions and physical pleasures) wandering throughout the Ganges Valley before reaching enlightenment. He taught that the

Jainism
System of thought, originating in the seventh century BCE, that challenged Brahmanism. Spread by Vardhamana Mahavira, Jainism encouraged purifying the soul through self-denial and nonviolence.

universe obeys its own everlasting rules and cannot be affected by any god or other supernatural being. He also believed that the purpose of life is to purify one's soul through asceticism and to attain a state of permanent bliss. The Jains' religious doctrines emphasized the idea that asceticism, rather than knowledge, would enable one to avoid harming other creatures and thereby purify the soul. Since the doctrine of *ahimsa* ("no hurt") held that every living creature has a soul—killing even an ant would result in an unfavorable rebirth—believers had to watch every step to avoid inadvertently becoming murderers. The extreme nonviolence of Jainism was impossible for peasants, who could not work the land without killing insects. Instead, Jainism became a religion of city dwellers and traders. Mahavira's teachings were transmitted orally for nearly a millennium before being compiled into writing by followers in the fifth century CE.

The Buddha and Buddhism The most direct challenge to traditional Brahmanic thinking came from Siddhartha Gautama (c. 563–483 BCE), a contemporary of Mahavira and Confucius. Later known as the **Buddha** (Enlightened One), Gautama objected to Brahmanic beliefs, their rituals and sacrifices, and their preference for kingship that kept the priestly class in power. His Axial Age teachings provided the peoples of South Asia and elsewhere with alternatives to established traditions.

The son of a highly respected Kshatriya warrior, Gautama was born into a comfortable life in a small oligarchic community nestled in the foothills of the Himalayas. Yet, at the age of twenty-nine, he walked away from everything, leaving behind his father, wife, and newborn son. Family and friends wept as he donned a robe and shaved his head and beard, symbols of the ascetic life that he intended to pursue. Gautama struggled with the belief that the life that he and most others were destined to live would consist of little more than endless episodes of suffering, which began with the pain of childbirth, followed by aging, illness, disease, and death, after which reincarnated beings would experience more of the same.

For six years, Gautama lived as an ascetic wanderer before a forty-nine-day meditation led him to the enlightened moment in which he realized that nirvana (spiritual contentment) could be achieved by finding a middle ground between self-indulgence and self-denial. He expressed this new credo as the Four Noble Truths: (1) life, from birth to death, is full of suffering; (2) all suffering is caused by desires; (3) the only way to avoid suffering is to renounce

Brahman Recluse When Buddhists started to tell stories in sculptures and paintings, Brahmans were included when appropriate. This character in Gandharan Buddhist art probably represents a Brahman who lived as a recluse, instead of as a priest. He is not shaved or dressed, but his expression is passionate.

Buddha
"Enlightened One." The term was applied to Kshatriya-born Siddhartha Gautama (c. 563–483 BCE), whose ideas—about the relationship between desire and suffering and how to eliminate both through wisdom, ethical behavior, and mental discipline in order to achieve contentment (nirvana)—offered a radical challenge to Brahmanism.

desire; and (4) the only way to rid oneself of desire is through adherence to the Eightfold Path, which includes wisdom (right views and right intentions), ethical behavior (right conduct, right speech, and right livelihood), and mental discipline (right effort, right thought, and right meditation). This teaching represented a dramatic shift in thinking about humanity and correct behavior. Like the Jain teachings of Mahavira, the Buddha's doctrines left no space for Brahmanic deities to dictate human lives. The Buddha's logical explanation of human suffering and his guidelines for renouncing desire appealed to many people for their simplicity, accessibility, and challenge to the Vedic hierarchies.

Like other dissident thinkers of this period, the Buddha delivered his message in a vernacular dialect of Sanskrit that all could understand. His many followers soon formed a community of monks called a *sangha* ("gathering"). The Buddha and his followers wandered from one city to another on the Ganges plain, where they found large audiences as well as the alms needed to sustain the expanding *sangha*. It was these followers who would pass on and eventually compile the Buddha's sayings into the Dhammapada. The Buddha's most influential patrons were urban merchants. In struggles between oligarchs and kings, the Buddha sided with the oligarchs, reflecting his upbringing in an oligarchic republic. He inevitably aroused opposition from the Brahmans, who favored monarchical government. While the Buddha himself did not seek to erase the Vedic hierarchies, Buddhism provided an escape from its oppressive aspects and the prestige that it afforded the Brahmans. Together with Jainism, Buddhism's challenge to Brahmanic thinking appealed particularly in the new urban contexts of South Asia and to those who felt disadvantaged by prevailing Vedic hierarchies in the first millennium BCE.

The Mediterranean World

Political, economic, and social changes also stimulated new thinking in the Mediterranean world. The violent upheavals that tore through the borderland areas of the northern Levant, the coastal lands of Anatolia, the islands of the Aegean and Mediterranean Seas, and mainland Greece in the few centuries after 1000 BCE freed the people in these regions from the domination of the Neo-Assyrians and Persians (see Chapter 4). These borderland communities encircling the Mediterranean basin also created second-generation societies that developed new social and political methods of organization and explored new Axial Age ideas. Phoenicians, Greeks, Cretans, Cypriots, Lydians, Etruscans, and many others exchanged not only trade goods but also ideas about the virtues of self-sufficient cities whose inhabitants shared power more widely than before. (See Map 5.4.)

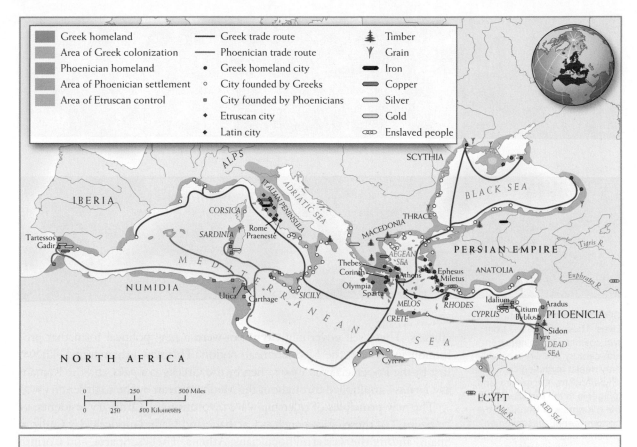

Map 5.4 The Mediterranean World, 1000–350 BCE

Phoenician and Greek city-states, as well as the colonies they founded, dotted the coastline of both the Mediterranean and Black Seas.

- What were the main goods traded in the Mediterranean world in this period? Where were they located?
- To what extent might the concentration of goods in certain regions have driven colonization and fostered trade?
- What areas did the Greeks and Phoenicians control with their homeland cities and their colonies? What was their main settlement pattern?

FORMATION OF NEW CITY-STATES

In the ninth and eighth centuries BCE, as order returned to the eastern Mediterranean and the population rebounded, peoples who were clustered in more concentrated settlements formed city-states. Unlike the city-states of earlier Mesopotamia, which were governed by semidivine monarchs, or the great urban centers of Southwest Asian empires, which were run by elite scribes, high priests, and monarchs, the Mediterranean city-states were governed by their

Core Objectives

EXPLAIN the relationship between Axial Age thinkers across Afro-Eurasia and the political and social situations to which they were responding.

Glimpsing Women's Lives These panels are from two cosmetic containers from fifth-century BCE Greece. While they depict mythological women (Clytemnestra, Cassandra, and Iphigenia in the top scene and the daughters of Nereus in the bottom scene), these women are engaged in activities—such as spinning (*top left*) and marriage preparation (*bottom*)—that would have been meaningful to the women who used these containers to hold their cosmetics and jewelry. The woman on the far right of the marriage scene (*bottom*) uses a device called an *iunx* to cast a love spell.

citizens. These self-governing city-states were a new political form that profoundly influenced the Mediterranean region. This new urban entity—known first by the Phoenicians as a *qart*, then by the Greeks as a *polis*, and the Romans as a *civitas*—multiplied throughout the Mediterranean by the sixth century BCE.

The new principles of rulership were revolutionary. Ordinary residents, or "citizens," of these cities—such as Carthage and Gadir (modern-day Cádiz in Spain) among the western Phoenicians; Athens, Thebes, Sparta, and Corinth among the Greeks; and Rome and Praeneste among the early Latins—governed themselves and selected their leaders. Their self-government took various forms, including tyranny (rule by a popularly approved individual), oligarchy (rule by the few), and democracy (rule by all free adult males).

The new cities of the Mediterranean basin included adult male citizens, other free persons (including women, who could not vote or hold office), foreign immigrants, and large numbers of unfree persons (including enslaved people and people tied to the land who could not vote or fight for the polis). The small family unit, or household, was the most important social unit of the city-state, and the city-state was seen as a natural outgrowth of the household. Thus, the free adult male was fully entitled to engage in the city's public affairs. Those enjoying full citizenship rights—the adult freeborn males—in each community decided what tasks, from warfare to public works, the city-state would undertake and what kind of government and laws it would adopt. In contrast, adult women of free birth remained enclosed within the private world of the family and had no standing to debate policy in public, vote, or hold office, although they did go out in public for religious festivals of which there were many. Upperclass women who did carry on intelligent conversations with men in public about public matters were criticized. Families of the lower classes could not afford the luxury of secluding women in such a way, however, when they might be needed to work as agricultural laborers or market vendors or just to do the chores outside the house that wealthy families could employ someone else to do. Spartan women were a partial exception, and their unusual behavior—such as exercising in the nude in public (as did men) or holding property in their own right—evoked humor and hostility from men in the other Greek city-states.

Athens developed into one of the most dynamic of these city-states. The Athenian city-state was tiny by the standards of the ancient empires. It covered less than 2,000 square miles, barely big enough to be a Persian satrapy, and its population of roughly 300,000, not counting 60,000 "chattel slaves," was significantly smaller than the population of 35 million who lived under Persian rule. Nonetheless, city-states were competitive places. Their histories relate rivalries between individuals, social classes, and other groups. Competition for honor and prestige was a value that shaped behavior in the city-states. This extreme competitive ethic found an outlet in organized sporting events. Almost from the moment that Greek city-states emerged, athletic contests sprang up. The greatest of these competitions were the Olympic Games, which began in 776 BCE at Olympia in southern Greece.

The competitive spirit among communities also took the destructive form of armed conflicts over borderlands, trade, valuable resources, religious shrines, and prestige. The incessant battles among city-states fueled new developments in military equipment, such as the heavy armor that gave its name to the hoplites, or infantrymen, and in tactics, such as the standard blocklike configuration (which the Greeks called a *phalanx*) in which the regular rank

Hoplite Warfare Two lines of helmeted hoplites advance on each other in lockstep, marching shield to shield with spears raised. A pipe player's tune sounds out the pace and maneuvers. The troops in the center offer a view of the inside of the *hoplon* (shield) and how it was grasped by the hoplite, while on the right we see the range of menacing heraldry emblazoned on the shield faces. The scene comes from the Chigi vase, which dates to the seventh century BCE and was found in a tomb in Greek-influenced Etruscan territories on the Italian Peninsula.

and file fought. These wars were so destructive that they threatened to desta-bilize the city-states' world. The most famous conflicts were the Pelopon-nesian War (431–404 BCE) between Athens and Sparta and their respective allies, and the ongoing rivalry between the city-states of Rome and Phoeni-cian Carthage (from c. 500 BCE onward) that led to the Punic Wars. Despite the destabilizing effects of warfare, city-states prospered, and economic inno-vations facilitated trade and exchange throughout the Mediterranean.

ECONOMIC INNOVATIONS

Without an elaborate top-down bureaucratic and administrative structure, res-idents of the new cities devised other ways to run their commercial affairs. They developed open trading markets and a system of money that enabled buyers and sellers to know the precise value of commodities so that exchanges were efficient. At their center, the new city-states had a marketplace (*agora* or *forum*), a large open area where individuals bought and sold commodities. These increasingly complex transactions required money, rather than barter or gift exchange. Like the states in Eastern Zhou China and Vedic South Asia, the Greek city-states were issuing a striking variety of coins by the end of the fifth century BCE, and other peoples such as the Phoenicians, Etruscans, and Persians were using them. Each Greek city-state minted coins with distinct features, making them recognizable at a glance. For example, Athens stamped its coins with the image of an owl, Corinth with a Pegasus, Aegina with a turtle, Knossos with a maze, and Akragas with a crab. Coins bought services as well, perhaps at first the services of mercenary soldiers. In the absence of large bureaucracies, Mediterranean cities relied on money to connect the producers and buyers of goods and services, especially as city-states became more far-flung.

Indeed, the search for silver, iron, copper, and tin drove traders westward across the Mediterranean. By about 500 BCE, the Phoenicians, Greeks, and others from the eastern Mediterranean had planted new city-states around

The Agora The agora, or cen-tral open marketplace, was one of the core defining features of Mediterranean city-states. At its center, each city had one of these open-air plazas, the heart of its commercial, religious, social, and political life. When a new city was founded, the agora was one of the first places that the colonists measured out. The large, rectangular, open area in this picture is the agora of the Greek colonial city of Cyrene (in modern-day Libya).

the shores of the western Mediterranean and the Black Sea. Once established, these colonial communities became completely independent and might even found other colonies. For instance, Corinth founded Syracuse (in Sicily) and then Syracuse went on to settle several Sicilian colonies of its own. Sparta founded Thera (a city-state on the modern island of Santorini in the Aegean), which then went on to found Cyrene (in North Africa). At Cyrene, a foundation inscription hints at the tricky citizenship and property issues involved in creating a new colony, as well as the potential dangers of colonization. One man from each Theran family was required to join the expedition and the expedition had to make a go of it for five years before being allowed to return home. The oath the colonists swore as they set out included burning wax images fashioned in the shape of the would-be colonists and proclaiming that just as these wax images melted away so would the fortunes and lives of the settlers and their descendants should they break their oath to found the Theran colony at Cyrene.

Coinage and Commodities
From the sixth century BCE onward, the use of metal coins minted by individual city-states began spreading throughout the Mediterranean. This coin from Barce, a Greek town in North Africa, depicts a precious regional commodity, silphium, on one side and the image of Zeus Ammon on the other. Silphium was a plant that when ingested orally (eaten or brewed as a tea) served as an effective contraceptive.

Whether driven by internal competition, population pressures, or economic possibilities, the far-flung colonies of the Greeks and Phoenicians transformed the coastal world. City-based life was common from southern Spain and western Italy to the Crimea on the Black Sea. With amazing speed, seaborne communications spread a Mediterranean-wide urban culture that bolstered the region's wealthy and powerful elites. Among the local elites of Tartessos in southern Spain, the Gallic chiefs in southern France, and the Etruscan and Roman nobles of central Italy, a new aristocratic culture featured similar public displays of wealth: richly decorated chariots, elaborate armor and weapons, fine dining ware, elaborate houses, and public burials. From the western end of the Mediterranean to the Black Sea, the city-state communities developed a culture founded on market-based economies and private property.

In contrast to the privilege enjoyed by these elites was the traffic in human flesh: slavery. Treating men, women, and children as objects of commerce, to be bought and sold in markets, created a new form of commercial slavery called chattel slavery. Slavery—the forced, unfree labor of war captives or of those who sold themselves to pay debt—had existed since the third millennium BCE, but what was new in this Mediterranean context was the commodification of bodies and the scale of the exchange. When dangerous and exhausting tasks such as mining and farming required extra labor, freeborn citizens purchased enslaved laborers. The primary source of enslaved laborers was still mainly war captives. In some city-states, enslaved people may have constituted up to a quarter of the population. In every one of the new city-states, the enslaved provided manual and technical labor of all kinds and produced the agricultural surpluses that supported the urban population.

Encounters with Frontier Communities The forces that transformed the Mediterranean region's mosaic of urban communities and surrounding rural areas also affected those in northern and central Europe. Whether they wished it or not, diverse tribes and ethnic groups—such as the Celts and Germans in western Europe and the Scythians to the north of the Black Sea—who were living in nomadic bands, isolated settlements, and small villages became integrated into the expanding cities' networks of violence, conquest, and trade.

Increasingly drawn to the city-states' manufactured goods—money, wine, ornate clothing, weapons—these tribal peoples became an armed threat to the region's core societies. Seeking to acquire the desired commodities through force rather than trade, frontier peoples convulsed the settled urban societies in wavelike incursions between 2200 and 2000 BCE, 1200 and 1000 BCE, and 400 and 200 BCE. Called "barbarians" (the Greeks' mocking name for foreigners unable to speak their language), the invaders actually were not much different from the Phoenicians or Greeks—who themselves had sought new homes and a better future by migrating. In colonizing the Mediterranean, they, too, had dispossessed the original inhabitants. The Celts, Gauls, Germans, Scythians, and other northerners came to the Mediterranean first as conquerors. Later, when Mediterranean empires grew more powerful and could keep them at bay, they were imported as enslaved laborers. Regarding these outsiders as uncivilized, the Greeks and western Phoenicians seized and colonized their lands—and sold the captives as commodities in their marketplaces.

NEW IDEAS

New ways of thinking about the world emerged from the competitive atmosphere that the Greek city-states fostered. In the absence of monarchical or priestly rule, ideas were free to arise, circulate, and clash. Individuals argued publicly about the nature of the gods, the best state, what is good, and whether to wage war. There was no final authority to give any particular idea a final stamp of approval and force its acceptance. New ideas emerged in science and the arts, and Greek philosophers proposed theories on human society and many other topics.

Naturalistic Science and Realistic Art In this competitive marketplace of ideas, some daring thinkers developed novel ways of perceiving the cosmos and representing the environment. Rather than seeing everything as the handiwork of all-powerful deities, they took a naturalistic view of humans and their place in the universe. This new thinking was evident in their art, which idealized the natural world. Artists increasingly represented humans, objects, and landscapes not in abstract, idealized, or formal ways but in "natural" ways, as they appeared to the human eye. Even their portrayals of gods became more human-like. Later, these objective and natural views of humans and nature became the new ideals, the highest of which was the unadorned human figure: the nude became the centerpiece of Greek art. Individual artists and writers—such as the vase painter Exekias, the sculptor Praxiteles, and the poet Sappho—began to sign their works in a clear manifestation of the new sense of the individual being freed from the restraints of an autocratic state or a controlling religious system.

New Thinking and Greek Philosophers Axial Age thinkers in city-states such as Miletus and Ephesus in western Anatolia did not accept traditional explanations of how and why the universe worked. Each thinker competed to outdo his peers in offering persuasive and comprehensive explanations of the cosmos, and their theories became ever more radical. For instance, Thales (c. 636–546 BCE) believed that water was the primal substance from which all other things were created. Xenophanes (c. 570–480 BCE) doubted the very existence of gods as they had been portrayed, asserting instead that only one general divine aura suffused all creation but that ethnic groups produced images of gods in their own likeness. Pythagoras (c. 570–495 BCE), who devoted himself to the study of numbers, held that a wide range of physical phenomena, like musical sounds, were in fact based in numbers. Democritus (c. 460–370 BCE) claimed that everything was composed of small and ultimately indivisible particles, which he called *atoma* ("uncuttables"). This rich competition among ideas led to a more aggressive mode of public thinking, which the Greeks called *philosophia* ("love of wisdom").

In the fifth century BCE, **Greek philosophers** ("wisdom lovers") were focusing on humans and their place in society. Some of these professional thinkers tried to describe an ideal state, characterized by harmonious relationships and free from corruption and political decline. One such thinker was Socrates (469–399 BCE), a philosopher who frequented the agora at Athens and encouraged people to reflect on ethics and morality, even as the Peloponnesian War raged on. He stressed the importance of honor and integrity as opposed to wealth and power (just as Confucius had done in Eastern Zhou China and the Buddha had done in Vedic South Asia). Plato (427–347 BCE), a student of Socrates, presented Socrates's philosophy in a series of dialogues (much as Confucius's students had written down his thoughts). In *The Republic*, Plato envisioned a perfect city that philosopher-kings would rule.

The Human Form The human body as it appeared naturally, without any adornment, became the ideal set by Greek art. Even gods were portrayed in this nude human form. This statue by Praxiteles is of the god Hermes with the infant Dionysus. Such bold nude portraits of humans and gods were sometimes shocking to other peoples.

Greek philosophers

"Wisdom lovers" of the ancient Greek city-states, including Socrates, Plato, Aristotle, and others, who pondered such issues as self-knowledge, political engagement and withdrawal, and evidence-based inquiry to understand the order of the cosmos.

Chavín

Agrarian people living from 1400 to 200 BCE in complex societies in what is now Peru. They manufactured goods (ceramics, textiles, and precious metals), conducted limited long-distance trade, and shared an artistic and religious tradition, most notably at Chavín de Huántar.

Core Objectives

COMPARE the political, cultural, and social developments across Afro-Eurasia with those occurring in the Americas and sub-Saharan Africa.

He thought that if fallible humans could imitate this model city more closely, their states would be less susceptible to the decline that was affecting the Greek city-states of his own day.

Plato's most famous pupil answered the same questions about nature and the acquisition of knowledge differently. Deeply interested in the natural world, Aristotle (384–322 BCE) believed that by collecting and studying all the facts one could about a given thing, one could achieve a better understanding. His main idea was that the interested inquirer can find out more about the world by collecting as much evidence as possible about a given thing and then making deductions from these data about general patterns. This evidence-based inquiry stood in stark contrast to Plato's claim that everything a person observes is in fact only a flawed copy of the "real" thing that exists in a thought-world of abstract patterns accessible only by pure mental meditation—completely the opposite of Aristotle's method.

This competition of ideas raged on for centuries, with the new thinking of these Mediterranean Axial Age philosophers at times fueling the aspirations of the city-states and at other times challenging them.

Common Cultures in the Americas and Sub-Saharan Africa

During what we have termed the Axial Age in Eurasia and North Africa, peoples living in the Americas and most of sub-Saharan Africa built complex, urban-based societies for the first time. These regions did not have the large number of immense cities, the presence of increasingly complex empires, the proliferation of elaborate written texts, the wide variety of load-bearing domesticated animals, and the other ingredients that underlay the radical new ideas of this era in the narrow band above the equator in the Eastern Hemisphere. Nonetheless, among the Chavín of the Andes, the Olmecs of Mesoamerica, the peoples of Nubia, and the West African Nok, exciting new developments were taking place in the first millennium BCE. Since the written record from these communities is limited, however, knowledge of their societies and beliefs is based largely on archaeological remains.

THE CHAVÍN IN THE ANDES

Around 1400 BCE, as the **Chavín** peoples began to share a common belief system, they also began to organize their societies vertically along the steep mountainsides and deep fertile valleys of the Andes. (See Map 5.1.) Valley floors yielded tropical and subtropical produce; the mountains supported maize and other crops; and in the highlands, potatoes became a staple and llamas produced wool and dung (used as fertilizer and fuel) and, eventually, served as beasts of burden. Llamas could not transport humans, however, so the Chavín migratory and political reach remained limited. While most necessities were available nearby thanks to the ecological diversity of the region, the Chavín did undertake some long-distance trade—mainly in dyes and precious stones, such as obsidian. By 900 BCE, the Chavín were erecting elaborate stone carvings, using advanced techniques to weave fine cotton textiles, and making gold, silver, and copper metal goods. Scholars have found evidence that by 400 BCE trade in painted textiles, ceramics, and gold objects spanned the Pacific coast, the Andean highlands, and the watershed eastward to the tropical rain forests of the Amazon basin.

What unified the fragmented Chavín communities was a shared artistic tradition manifested in their devotion to powerful deities. Their spiritual capital was the central temple complex of Chavín de Huántar, in modern Peru's northeastern highlands. The temple boasted a U-shaped platform whose opening to the east surrounded a sunken, circular plaza. From its passageways and underground galleries, priests—whom the Chavín believed were transformed into jaguars through their consumption of hallucinogenic drugs—could make dramatic entrances during ceremonies. Pilgrims brought tribute to Chavín de Huántar, where they worshipped and feasted together. The Chavín drew on influences from as far away as the Amazon and the Pacific coast as they created devotional cults that revered wild animals as representatives of spiritual forces. Carved stone jaguars, serpents, and hawks, baring their large fangs and claws to remind believers of nature's powers, dominated the spiritual landscape. The

Chavín de Huántar and El Lanzón Chavín de Huántar is nestled in the Peruvian Andes. The temple complex contains several structures; the so-called Northern Platform is pictured here (*above*). Deep within one of the labyrinthine structures stands El Lanzón (*right*), etched with snakes, felines, and humans combined into one hybrid supernatural form.

Olmecs

Mesoamerican people, emerging around 1500 BCE, whose name means "inhabitants in the land of rubber," one of their major trade goods. Living in decentralized agrarian villages, this complex, stratified society shared language and religious ideas that were practiced at sacred ritual centers.

Chavín cult gave way around 400 BCE to local cultural heirs, but some elements of it survived in successor religions adopted by stronger states to the south.

THE OLMECS IN MESOAMERICA

Farther to the north, the first complex society in Mesoamerica emerged about 1500 BCE between the highland plateaus of central Mexico and the Gulf Coast around modern-day Veracruz. (See Map 5.5.) The **Olmecs** are an example of a first-generation community that created new political and economic institutions while contemplating profound questions about the nature of humanity and the world beyond. The culture of the Olmecs—a name meaning "inhabitants in the land of rubber," one of their staples—sprang up from local village roots. The region's peoples formed a loose confederation of villages scattered from the coast to the highlands, mainly nestling in river valleys and along the shores of swampy lakes. Their residents traded with one another, shared a common language, and worshipped the same gods. Around 1500 BCE, the residents of hundreds of hamlets began to develop a single culture and to spread their beliefs, artistic achievements, and social structure far beyond their heartland.

At the core of Olmec culture were its decentralized villages, which housed hundreds—possibly thousands—of households apiece. In these settlements productive subsistence farmers cultivated most of the foodstuffs their communities needed (especially maize, beans, squash, and cacao), while shipping lightweight products including ceramics and precious goods (such as jade, obsidian, or quetzal feathers, used to create masks and ritual figurines) to other villages. Most of the precious objects were for religious purposes rather than everyday consumption. Despite their dispersed social landscape, the Olmec peoples created shared belief systems, a single language, and a priestly class who ensured that villagers and residents of the new urban centers followed highly ritualized practices.

Cities as Sacred Centers The primary Olmec cities, including San Lorenzo, La Venta, and Tres Zapotes, were small compared with the urban centers of Afro-Eurasia, but they served as devotional and secular hubs. The cities featured specialized structures that included massive earthen mounds, platforms, palaces, capacious plazas, and large stone monuments (colossal heads, jaguar sculptures, and basalt thrones). Beneath the mounds of the devotional centers, archaeologists have found axes, knives of sharpened obsidian, other tools, and jade figurines, buried as tokens for those who dwelled in the supernatural world. Olmec devotional art depicted natural and supernatural entities—not just snakes, jaguars, and crocodiles, but also certain humans called shamans, whom the Olmecs believed could commune with the supernatural and transform themselves wholly or partly into beasts. A common figurine is the "were-jaguar," a being that was part man, part animal. Shamans representing jaguars invoked the Olmec rain god, a jaguar-like being, to bring rainfall and secure the land's fertility.

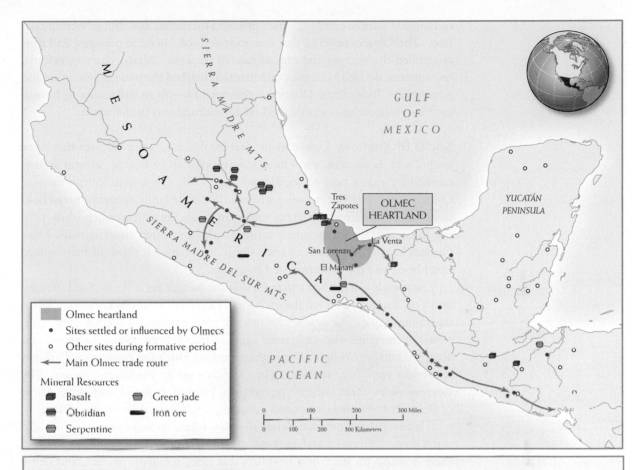

Map 5.5 The Olmec World, 1500–350 BCE

The Olmecs had a strong impact on Mesoamerica's early cultural integration.

- According to this map, how did the Olmecs influence people living beyond the Olmec heartland?
- What geographical factors limited the extent of Olmec influence?
- What is the relationship between resources, trade routes, and Olmec settlements?

A range of agriculture-linked devotional activity thrived in the Olmecs' major cities. Noble players competed in a complex ball game to honor the rain god, as fans cheered them on. Olmec archaeological sites are filled with the remains of game equipment and trophies, some of which were entombed with dead rulers so they could play ball with the gods in the otherworld. It is likely that athletics and human sacrifice were blended in the same rituals. Many monuments depict a victorious and costumed ballplayer (sporting a jaguar headdress or a feathered serpent helmet) atop a defeated, bound human, though scholars are not sure whether the losers were literally executed. Nevertheless, rainmaking rites did include human sacrifice, which involved executing and dismembering captives. The Olmecs believed that the gods defined calendric passages, and thus controlled the seasons and crucial rainfall patterns. Priests, charting celestial movements, devised a complex calendar that marked the passage of seasons and generations. Indeed, the Olmecs' ceremonial life—from ball games to human sacrifice to calendars—was focused on agricultural and rainfall cycles.

Social Distinctions Unlike many decentralized agrarian cultures that were simple and egalitarian, the Olmecs developed an elaborate cultural system marked by many tiers of social rankings. Daily labor kept village-focused Olmecs busy. The vast majority worked the fertile lands as part of household units, with children and parents toiling in the fields with wooden tools, fishing in streams with nets, and hunting turtles and other small animals. Most Olmecs juggled the needs of their immediate families, those of their village neighbors, and the taxes imposed by rulers.

The priestly class, raised and trained in the palaces at La Venta, San Lorenzo, and Tres Zapotes, directed the exchanges of sacred ritual objects among farming communities. Alongside the priestly elite emerged a secular elite composed of chieftains who supervised agrarian transactions, oversaw artisans, and accepted villagers' tribute. The highest-ranking chieftains commanded villages scattered over a large territory. The chieftains set up workshops, managed by foremen, where craftworkers created pots, painted, sculpted, and wove. Some of their work featured stones and gems imported from surrounding villages.

It is likely that a merchant class also developed to facilitate trade throughout Olmec territories and beyond. As the Olmecs' arts expanded, so did their demand for imported obsidian and jade, seashells, plumes, and other precious goods. The Olmecs exported rubber, cacao, pottery, ceramics, figurines, jaguar pelts, and crocodile skins throughout Mesoamerica. They also conveyed their belief system to neighbors—if not to convert them, at least to influence them and reinforce a sense of superiority.

The Loss of Centers The breakdown of the Olmec culture around the middle of the first millennium is shrouded in mystery. The decline was abrupt in some centers and drawn out in others. At La Venta, the altars and massive basalt heads were defaced and buried, indicating a dramatic shift. Yet there is little evidence of a spasm of war, a peasant uprising, a population shift, or conflict within the ruling classes. Indeed, in many parts of the heartland, the religious centers that had been the hubs of the Olmec world were abandoned but not destroyed. As the bonds between rulers and subjects weakened, so did the exchange of ritual objects that had enlivened the Olmec centers and made them magnets for obedience and piety. Although Olmec hierarchies collapsed, much of the Olmec hinterland remained heavily populated and highly productive. While it lasted, the Olmec combination of an integrated culture, a complex hierarchical social structure, and urban-centered devotional practice offered a degree of cohesion unprecedented in the Americas.

COMMON CULTURES IN SUB-SAHARAN AFRICA

In Africa, too, widespread common cultures emerged in a number of favorable locations. Africa's most significant climate-related historical development in the first millennium BCE was the continued drying up of the northern and central landmass and the sprawl of the great Sahara Desert. (See Map 5.6.) Large areas that had once supported abundant plant and animal life, including human settlements, now became sparsely populated. As a result, the African peoples began to coalesce in a few locations. Most important was the Nile Valley, which may have held more than half of the entire population of Africa at this time.

Climatic change divided Africa from the equator northward to the Sahara Desert into four zones. The first zone was the Sahara itself, which never completely emptied out despite its extreme heat and aridity. Its oases supported pastoral peoples, who raised livestock and promoted contacts between the northern and western parts of the landmass. South of the Sahara was the Sahel, literally the "coast" (Arabic *sahil*) of the great ocean of sand, which saw no city of great size in this period. The next zone was the Sudanic savanna, an area of high grasslands stretching from present-day Senegal along the Atlantic Ocean in the west to the Nile River and the Red Sea in the east. Many of West Africa's kingdoms later emerged there because the area was free of the tsetse fly, which was as lethal to animals as to humans, killing off cattle, horses, and goats. The fourth zone comprised the western and central African rain forests, a sparsely populated region characterized by small-scale societies.

Although there was contact across the Sahara by means of trans-Saharan trade routes traversed by camel and via the Nile Valley, Africa below the Sahara differed markedly from North Africa and Eurasia. It did not develop plow agriculture; instead, its farmers depended on hoes. Also, except in densely populated regions, land was held communally and never carried as much value as labor, which was in short supply. African peoples could always move into new locations. They had more difficulty finding workers to turn the soil. In the savanna, millet and sorghum were the primary food crops; in the rain forests, yams and other root crops predominated. Relatively large populations inhabited the Sudanic savanna, the sole area for which substantial historical records exist. Here, in fact, a way of life that historians call Sudanic began to crystallize.

These Sudanic peoples were not completely dependent on their feet to get around (in contrast to their llama-reliant counterparts in the Americas). They had domesticated several animals, including cattle and goats, and even possessed small horses. Although their communities were scattered widely across this region of Africa, they had much in common. For example, they all possessed religious beliefs dominated by a high god, polities led by sacred kings, and burial

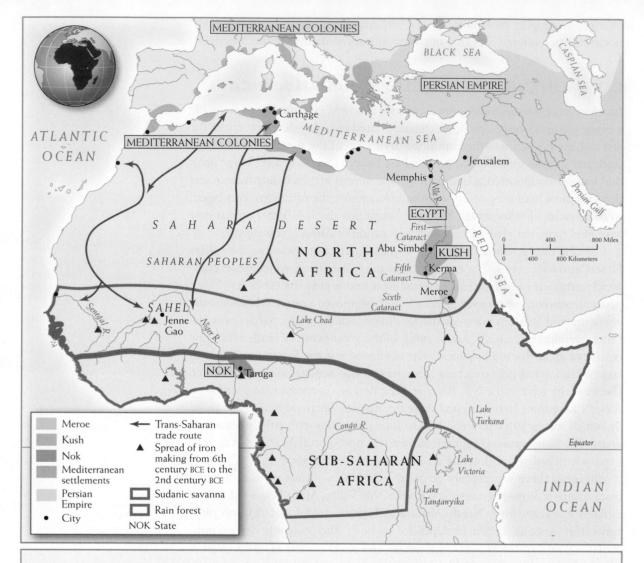

Map 5.6 Africa, 500 BCE

The first millennium BCE was a period of cultural, economic, and political integration for North and sub-Saharan Africa.

- According to this map, what effect did the Mediterranean colonies have on Africa?
- What main geographic feature integrated Kush and Egypt? What impact might cataracts have had on integration?
- Where does the map indicate there was a spread of ironworking? What features on the map may have influenced where ironworking spread?

customs of interring servants alongside dead rulers to serve them in the afterlife. Sudanic peoples were skilled cultivators and weavers of cotton, which they had domesticated. Archaeologists and historians used to believe that the Sudanic peoples borrowed their institutions, notably their sacred kingships, from their Egyptian neighbors, but linguistic evidence and their burial customs indicate that the Sudanic communities developed these practices independently.

Nubia: Kush and Meroe One of the most highly developed locations of common culture in sub-Saharan Africa was Nubia, a region lying between the first Nile cataract (a large waterfall) and the sixth, just north of where the Blue and White Niles come together. From at least the fourth millennium BCE onward, peoples in this region had contact with both the northern and southern parts of the African landmass. It was one of the few parts of sub-Saharan Africa known to the Eurasian world during this period.

In the second and first millennia BCE, complex societies formed and developed into states in Nubia. The first of the important Nubian states was Kush. A thriving contemporary of Middle Kingdom Egypt, it flourished between 1700 and 1500 BCE between the first and third cataracts and had its capital at Kerma. Because of its proximity to Egypt, it adopted many Egyptian cultural and political practices, even as it was under constant pressure from the northern powerhouse. Its successor states had to move farther south, up the Nile, to keep free from the powerful Egyptians; the kingdom's capitals were repeatedly uprooted and relocated upriver.

Nubia was Egypt's corridor to sub-Saharan Africa; a source of ivory, gold, and enslaved men and women; and an area that Egyptian monarchs wanted to dominate.

Temple of the Lion God at Naqa The small, steep Nubian pyramids of the Meroitic kingdom, reflecting its Egyptian connections up the Nile, are familiar to many. But the kings and queens of Meroe also built other structures that echoed Egyptian themes and architecture. Pictured here is the façade of the temple of the Lion God, Apedemak, at Naqa in the ancient Meroitic kingdom. To the right of the entrance, Queen Amanitore (c. 50 CE) strikes down her enemies in a scene reminiscent of images of Thutmosis III (fifteenth century BCE) or Ramses III (twelfth century BCE) at Luxor.

What Makes an "Axial Age"?

In the mid-twentieth century, the German philosopher Karl Jaspers invented the term "Axial Age" to describe the importance of ideas that originated in the first millennium BCE. These thinkers and their ideas are characterized as "axial" because (1) they were a pivot point, or axis, that seemed to turn the world in a new direction, (2) they occurred along an east-west axis stretching from the Mediterranean to East Asia, and (3) they are central to ethical thought even down to the present day. These Axial Age philosophers were both the product of, and a challenge to, the societies from which they came. Each was responding to a context of economic growth and political infighting. Although the specific socioeconomic and political contexts that spurred them to develop their new ideas were unique—the stratifications of *varna* in South Asia for the Buddha, the warfare of the late Spring and Autumn period in China for Confucius, and the civil war among Greek city-states for Socrates—across the board these new thinkers critiqued and offered alternatives to the status quo.

Ideas about the Axial Age have come a long way since Jaspers. World historians today have a better understanding of how connectedness may have affected the development of these ideas. Where Jaspers saw a relatively disconnected world and marveled at the similarities among the independently proposed ideas, scholars today recognize that exchange between the Mediterranean, Southwest Asia, and South Asia predated these thinkers by almost 2,000 years and may have even had an impact on these developments. Scholars have refined the definition of what makes a tradition axial. For instance, Shmuel Eisenstadt has remarked that the axial philosophers were a sort of intellectual elite who, in a self-examining way, helped negotiate between what he refers to as an "otherworldly" and "worldly" order. David Christian, the historian known for his work with "Big History," has noted the relationship between large, connected empires and these universal

philosophical ideas, with their "universal truths and . . . all-powerful gods"; he has even interpreted the spread of these similar ideas as evidence of the connections across Afro-Eurasia. Others have also begun to reflect more critically on the limitations of Axial Age thought as an organizing concept. For instance, although the tenets of Axial Age philosophers were accessible and applicable to urban-living elite men, historians such as Karen Armstrong raise the question of whether they also applied to women, nonelites, and those living in rural contexts. Other scholars, of whom Iain Provan

First-Millennium Thinkers Confucius, the Buddha, and Socrates, in representations from Eastern Zhou China, Brahmanic South Asia, and the Mediterranean, respectively. These thinkers are still influential today.

Meroitic kingdom

Thriving kingdom from the fourth century BCE to 300 CE. A successor to Kush, it was influenced by both Egyptian and Sudanic cultures.

To the Egyptians, the land of Kush and its people were there to be exploited, not conquered, as Egyptians had no desire to live there. Ramses II left his mark with his magnificent monuments at the Nubian site Abu Simbel around 1250 BCE.

Building on the foundations of earlier kings who had ruled the region of Nubia, the **Meroitic kingdom** arose in the fourth century BCE and flourished until 300 CE. This kingdom was centered in the city of Meroe farther is the most recent and vocal, raise concerns about generalizing across very different cultures and not giving enough attention to the unique political situation of each region. Some have challenged outright the concept of the Axial Age, arguing that it is merely a modern, oversimplifying construct that is in no way useful for interpreting the complex philosophical developments of the first millennium BCE.

Even with the modern tweaks and strong critiques of his theory, it is hard to disagree with Jaspers that these mid-first-millennium BCE thinkers, such as Confucius, the Buddha, and Socrates, offered transformational ideas that are still with us today. The axial traditions offer surprisingly similar moral codes that address issues such as the nature of wisdom and divine justice, the need for kindness, and the value of following the "Golden Rule."

Questions for Analysis

- Based on your reading of this chapter, what connections, if any, can be made between the geopolitical situation of a society and the Axial Age philosophy that sprang from that region? In what ways did each philosopher support or challenge the status quo?
- Karl Jaspers was particularly impressed that societies he understood as being disconnected from one another could develop philosophical ideas that were so similar. How might connections with other regions, or the lack thereof, have affected the development of these ideas? What might account for similarities and differences in these Axial Age philosophies?
- How useful, or not, do you find the concept of the Axial Age for thinking about global developments in the first millennium BCE? What are some arguments for and against using such a term/concept?

Explore Further

Armstrong, Karen, *The Great Transformation: The Beginning of Our Religious Traditions* (2006).

Bellah, Robert N., "What Is Axial about the Axial Age?" *European Journal of Sociology* 46, no. 1 (2005): 69–89.

Eisenstadt, S. N., (ed.), *The Origins and Diversity of the Axial Age* (1986).

Jaspers, Karl, *The Origin and Goal of History,* translated by Michael Bullock (1953).

Provan, Iain, *Convenient Myths: The Axial Age, Dark Green Religion, and the World That Never Was* (2013).

Sources: Karen Armstrong, *The Great Transformation: The Beginning of Our Religious Traditions* (New York: Knopf, 2006), pp. xxi–xxii; Robert N. Bellah, "What Is Axial about the Axial Age?" *European Journal of Sociology* 46, no. 1 (2005): 69–89; David Christian, *Maps of Time: An Introduction to Big History* (Berkeley: University of California Press, 2004), p. 319; S. N. Eisenstadt (ed.), *The Origins and Diversity of the Axial Age* (Albany: State University of New York Press, 1986); Karl Jaspers, *The Origin and Goal of History,* translated by Michael Bullock (New Haven, CT: Yale University Press, 1953); Iain Provan, *Convenient Myths: The Axial Age, Dark Green Religion, and the World That Never Was* (Waco, TX: Baylor University Press, 2013).

south along the Nile, close to its sixth cataract, in the region today known as Sudan. The Meroitic kingdom's rulers were influenced by pharaonic culture, adapting hieroglyphs, erecting pyramids in which to bury their rulers, viewing their kings as divine, and worshipping the Egyptian god Amun. Meroe became a thriving center of production and commerce. Its residents were especially skilled in iron smelting and the manufacture of textiles, and their products circulated widely throughout Africa. However, Meroe was equally a part of the Sudanic savanna way of life—as evidenced by the distinctiveness of its language and the determination of its inhabitants to retain political autonomy, including, if necessary, moving farther south, out of the orbit of Egypt and more into the orbit of Sudanic polities. Although they called their kings pharaohs, the influential leaders of Meroe selected them from among the many members of the royal family, attempting to ensure that their rulers were men of proven talents. In addition, the Nubian states had close commercial contacts with other merchants and commercial hubs in Sudanic Africa.

West African Kingdoms Complex societies also thrived in West Africa. The most spectacular West African culture of the first millennium BCE was the Nok culture, which arose in the sixth century BCE in an area that is today the geographical center of Nigeria. Though slightly south of the savanna lands of West Africa, the area was (and still is) in regular contact with that region. At Taruga, near the present-day village of Nok, early iron smelting occurred in 600 BCE. Taruga may well have been the first place in western Africa where iron ores were smelted. Ironworking was significant for the Nok peoples, who moved from using stone materials directly to iron, bypassing the bronze working that had been a transitional stage in the technology characteristic of other advanced metallurgists in Afro-Eurasia (as in second-millennium BCE Shang China and the Mediterranean). The Nok made iron axes and hoes, iron knives and spears, and luxury items for trade. However, they achieved historical fame not for their iron-smelting prowess but for their magnificent terra-cotta figurines, discovered in the 1940s in the tin-mining region of central Nigeria. These naturalistic figures date to at least 500 BCE. They were likely altarpieces for a cult associated with the land's fertility. Placed next to new lands that were coming into cultivation, they were believed to bless the soil and enhance its productivity.

The Nok were not the only culture developing in this region. Peoples living in the Senegal River basin and Mande peoples around the western branch of the Niger River also began to establish large settlements, in which artisans smelted iron ore and wove textiles and merchants engaged in long-distance trade. West Africa was also home to the Bantu-speaking peoples destined to play a major role in the history of the landmass. Around 300 BCE, small Bantu groups began to migrate southward into the equatorial rain forests, where they cleared land for farming; from there, some moved on to southern Africa. (See Chapter 8 for a discussion of the Bantu peoples.) As impressive as the ironworking, figurines, and trade of West Africa were, these cultures were not yet producing—or at least there is no record of—the type of Axial Age developments that were happening in much of Eurasia.

Conclusion

Afro-Eurasia's great river-basin areas—the Nile, the Tigris-Euphrates, the Indus—were still important in the first millennium BCE, but their time as centers of world cultures was passing. With the development of second-generation societies, these river-basin areas yielded some of their prominence to regions that had been on their fringes, whether the Mediterranean in the west or the Ganges in the east. Within the territorial states in China, the kingdoms and oligarchies in urbanizing South Asia, and the city-states in the Mediterranean world, great social and intellectual dynamism occurred.

During this Axial Age across much of Eurasia, influential thinkers came to the fore with perspectives quite different from those of the earlier river-basin societies and other contemporary developments elsewhere in worlds apart. In China, the political instability of the Warring States period propelled scholars such as Confucius to engage in political debate, in which they stressed respect for social hierarchy. In South Asia, dissident thinkers challenged the Brahmanic spiritual and political order, and the Buddha articulated a religious belief system that was much less hierarchical than its Vedic predecessor. Mediterranean Greek philosophers offered new views about nature, their political world, and human relations and values—based primarily on secular rather than religious ideas.

Even where contacts with other societies were less intense, innovations occurred as the first complex societies began to arise in the Americas and in sub-Saharan Africa. In the Americas, the Olmecs developed a worldview in which mortals had to appease angry gods through human sacrifice, and built elaborate temples where many peoples could pay homage to the same deities. In West Africa, the Nok peoples promoted interregional trade and cultural contact as they expanded their horizons. In sub-Saharan Africa, settled pockets devised complex cultural foundations for community life. One spectacular example of sub-Saharan and Egyptian synthesis was the Nubian culture of the Meroitic kingdom. As the world was coalescing into culturally distinct regions, many of the ideas newly forged in Eurasia, the Americas, and sub-Saharan Africa had a continuing impact on societies that followed.

Focus On
The Axial Age

China

- A multistate system emerges from warfare, revolutionizing society and thought.
- Confucius and Master Lao outline new ideals of governing and living.

South Asia

- Small monarchies and urban oligarchies emerge after the Vedic peoples' migrations and rule over societies organized around the *varna* and *jati* system.
- Dissident thinkers like Mahavira and the Buddha challenge Brahman priests and the *varna* and *jati* system.

The Mediterranean World

- Independent city-states emerge from social destruction and facilitate revolutionary principles in rulership, commerce, and thought.

- Thinkers like Socrates, Plato, and Aristotle challenge conventions and encourage public discourse about the role of the individual in society and the way the universe works.

The Americas

- Chavín peoples and the Olmecs produce increasingly hierarchical, agriculture-based societies and connect villages via trade.
- Large-scale common cultures emerge.

Sub-Saharan Africa

- Expansion of the Sahara Desert and population migrations cause people to coalesce in a few locations.
- Early signs of a common culture appear across the Sudanic savanna.

 Go to INQUIZITIVE to see what you've learned—and learn what you've missed—with personalized feedback along the way.

CHRONOLOGY

	1600 BCE	1400 BCE	1200 BCE
East Asia			
South Asia			
The Mediterranean			
The Americas			
Sub-Saharan Africa			

Olmec culture emerges and diffuses through Mesoamerica 1500–400 BCE

Chavín culture flourishes in Central Andes of South America 1400–400 BCE

THINKING ABOUT GLOBAL CONNECTIONS

- **Thinking about Transformation & Conflict and the Axial Age** In the first millennium BCE across Afro-Eurasia, Axial Age thinkers developed radical new ideas in response to their respective political and cultural situations. In what ways did Axial Age thinkers in East Asia (Confucius and Master Lao), South Asia (Mahavira and the Buddha), and the Mediterranean (naturalist philosophers and Socrates) address the unique transformations and conflicts that were taking place where they lived? How do Zoroaster of Persia and the Jewish prophets of Israel, discussed in Chapter 4, fit this model?

- **Thinking about Worlds Together, Worlds Apart and the Axial Age** From the mid-second through the mid-first millennium BCE, "second-generation" societies developed in Eastern Zhou China, the Ganges plain of South Asia, and the Mediterranean, while parts of South America, Mesoamerica, and sub-Saharan Africa birthed their first complex societies. What are the differences between the second-generation societies of Afro-Eurasia and the first complex societies elsewhere, and what might account for these very different, yet contemporary, developments across the globe?

- **Thinking about Changing Power Relationships and the Axial Age** Axial Age thinkers in East Asia, South Asia, and the Mediterranean offered challenges to both political and social traditions. How did the innovative ideas of thinkers such as Confucius, the Buddha, and Socrates contest and help reshape power relationships ranging from the political to the familial?

Key Terms

Axial Age p. 215

Buddha p. 229

Chavín p. 238

Confucius p. 219

Daoism p. 220

Greek philosophers p. 237

Jainism p. 228

Meroitic kingdom p. 246

Olmecs p. 240

second-generation societies p. 215

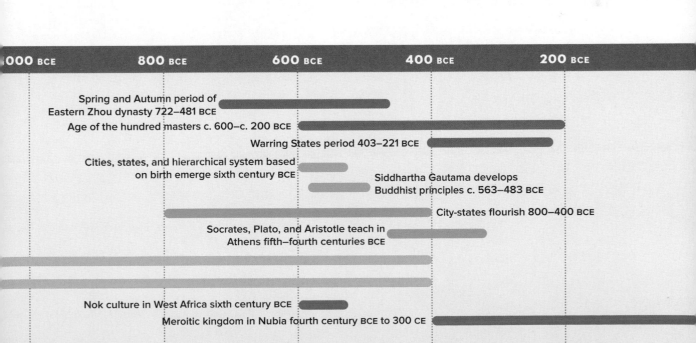

1000 BCE	800 BCE	600 BCE	400 BCE	200 BCE

Spring and Autumn period of Eastern Zhou dynasty 722–481 BCE

Age of the hundred masters c. 600–c. 200 BCE

Warring States period 403–221 BCE

Cities, states, and hierarchical system based on birth emerge sixth century BCE

Siddhartha Gautama develops Buddhist principles c. 563–483 BCE

City-states flourish 800–400 BCE

Socrates, Plato, and Aristotle teach in Athens fifth–fourth centuries BCE

Nok culture in West Africa sixth century BCE

Meroitic kingdom in Nubia fourth century BCE to 300 CE

Global Themes and Sources

Comparing Axial Age Thinkers and Their Ideas

Zoroastrianism. Confucianism. Buddhism. Socratic philosophy and questioning. Each of these major developments in the world of ideas is named for a thinker who lived in the first millennium BCE: Zoroaster (after 1000 BCE); Confucius (551–479 BCE); Siddhartha Gautama, later called the Buddha (c. 563–483 BCE); and Socrates (469–399 BCE). But what can we know of these individuals whose ideas were so transformational in their own time and continue to be influential even today? How were their ideas preserved? How can we explore the texts that preserve the ideas attributed to these thinkers in order to get a better sense of the philosophers and the world to which each was responding? Although the "Axial Age" is a contested concept—with scholars ranging from those who find it a useful concept but argue about how best to define it, why it happened, and what impact it may have had, to those who question whether it is a meaningful category for understanding disparate philosophical developments—this chapter has emphasized the challenge that these exceptional thinkers posed to their second-generation societies.

Axial Age thinkers and the ideas they proposed offer an opportunity to compare the radical teachings that surfaced in the first millennium BCE and the distinct contexts within which they were initially put forward. The following excerpts are drawn from Zoroaster's teachings preserved in the Gathas, from Confucius's dialogues with his students in *The Analects*, from the Buddha's reflections in the Dhammapada, and from Socrates's defense of himself in the *Apology*. These texts demonstrate the similarities and differences in how each thinker expressed his ideas—in bold statements and interactive dialogue with others, or rather in poetic phrases and cryptic comments. These selections offer differing ideas about the divine, ranging from the all-powerful Ahura Mazda of the Zoroastrian tradition to the oracular Apollo with whom Socrates had a more transactional relationship, as well

as differing ideas about the role of the individual, ranging from participating in a cosmic battle between good and evil (as in the Gathas of Zoroastrianism) to engaging in a personal struggle to attain inner peace (as in the Dhammapada of Buddhism). These texts show the vibrant nature of political debate involved in axial thought, as students converse with Confucius about the traits of a superior gentleman and as Socrates recounts the charges against him to the men of Athens assembled to hear his defense. We see each of the thinkers reflect on what it means to be wise and what the meaning of truth is. These texts give us a chance to combine what we know from this chapter about each region with what we see of these philosophical developments in order to investigate why these differences and similarities in thought may have developed in these places at this particular moment in time.

Analyzing Axial Age Thinkers and Their Ideas

- What elements of each Axial Age thinker's ideas, as outlined in this chapter, do you find in these excerpts? What are the similarities and differences among these Axial Age ideas? What do you think accounts for the similarities and differences?

- How do the similarities and differences among these thinkers' ideas help you understand how the so-called Axial Age may have played out in the various regions? Given what you know from this chapter about the political context for each thinker, what is so radical about the ideas in each excerpt?

- The teachings of each of these thinkers were recorded not by the thinker himself but by his students. What evidence in the excerpts suggests transmission of these ideas by disciples? Why do you think these Axial Age thinkers did not write down their own ideas?

- To what extent do these Axial Age ideas apply to nonelite men? To women? Which regions of the world are represented by these Axial Age texts? Which regions are not? Why is this the case, and how might this affect the usefulness of the term "Axial Age" as a global concept for making sense of the first millennium BCE?

PRIMARY SOURCE 5.1

The Gathas from the Hymns of Zoroaster (1000–600 BCE)

In the Gathas, Zoroaster (also called Zarathustra) outlines a philosophy in which opposing forces of light and truth battle those of darkness and lies. These hymns, which are addressed by Zoroaster to the god of light, Ahura Mazda, praise the god and seek his guidance. Initially a challenge to the spirit-focused tradition of the pastoral nomadic culture from which the Persians came, Zoroaster's ideas were eventually adopted by kings to undergird the Persian state and justify their rule.

- How are the ideas in this text about truth and falsehood supposed to influence the actions of the believer?

- What are the rewards for following the ideas and ideals of Ahura Mazda?

- How could a ruler, like Darius in Persia, use these ideas to support his imperial power?

33.1 In accordance with the Primeval Laws of this existence,

The Ratu (Judge) shall deal perfect justice to all;
To the good who chose the Truth,
To the evil who chose Falsehood,
And to those in whom good and evil are mixed.

33.2 He who opposes Evil by his thought or word
Or by the work of his own two hands,
He who instructs people to their good,
Makes a worthy offering of faith to Thy Purpose,
O Ahura Mazda!

33.3 He who is most good to the righteous,
Be he a noble, or a peasant, or a dependent,

He who zealously makes the good living creation flourish,
He shall come to dwell with Truth in the realm of the Good Mind.

33.4 I [Zarathustra] am he who by devotion and prayer shall
Keep disobedience and the Evil Mind far from Thee, O Mazda,
Keep insolent heresy away from the nobles,
The distrust spread by slanderers, from the community,
And the evil of destruction from the pastures of cattle.

33.5 I invoke Thy Sraosha (Inspiration) as the greatest of all aids at the Consummation,
To attain Life Eternal in Thy Kingdom of the Good Mind,
To attain the straight path of Truth wherein Thou dwelleth, O Mazda Ahura!

33.6 I, who as Thy steadfast priest, have learned the straight path of Asha (Truth and Righteousness),
And would learn from the Best Mind how best to do what should be done,
Therefore I ask of Thee, My Lord,
Bless me with Thy Vision and grant me a consultation with Thee!

33.7 Come hither to me, in Thine own self, O Mazda!
Come unmistakably, O Thou Best One, with
The Spirit of Truth and The Good Mind!
Let my message be heard beyond the limits of the community of adherents.
Let the brilliant offerings of reverential prayers be manifest to all.

33.8 Do Thou make known to me, the Ultimate Good, the final end,
That I may bring it about with the help of the Good Mind.
Accept, O Mazda, the homage of Thy faithful worshipper.

Accept, O truth, my hymn of praise for Thee,
Grant to us, O Spirits of Deathless Weal and
Immortality, your own two blessings.

33.9 And with the blessings of these comrade
Spirits of
Perfection and Immortality,
Let all advance to Thee, O Mazda!
Let all promote the cause of Truth!

33.10 All the felicities of life, which have been, which
are, which shall be,
Come to us through Thy Divine Grace, O Mazda:
Through thy Holy Power, let our persons advance to
the wished-for beatitude,
With the help of the Good Mind, with the help of
Truth!

33.11 Hearken unto me, O Most Benevolent Ahura
Mazda!
O ye Spirits of Piety and Truth that bless our
existence!
O ye Good Mind, and the Dominion of Heaven!
Be gracious unto us as we receive our recompense!

33.12 Arise for me, O Ahura!
Through my devotion give me steadfastness of purpose,
Through Thy Most Bounteous Spirit make me pure
in goodness,
Through the Spirit of Righteousness grant me the
courage of spiritual might,
And through the Good Mind give me the trust of
the people.

3.13 With thy divine grace, O Lord.
Make wide the vision of my mind;
Make manifest Thy everlasting attributes;
Make known the blessings of Thy Kingdom of Heaven,
and the joyous recompense of the Good Mind,
. . . inspire our consciousness with the Ultimate Truth.

33.14 To the Lord Mazda, as an offering,
Zarathustra dedicates the works of his life, even his
very self.

The noblest essence of his Good Thought.
To Truth, he consecrates obedience to its
principles
In word and deed, and all the might of his spiritual
authority.

Source: Yasna 33, *The Gathas: The Hymns of Zarathushtra*, translated by
D. J. Irani, edited by K. D. Irani (Newton, MA: Center for Ancient Iranian
Studies, 1998), pp. 47–50.

PRIMARY SOURCE 5.2

The Analects (c. 480 BCE), Confucius

Confucius engaged in philosophical dialogues with his
students in the 480s BCE, during the transition from
the Spring and Autumn period to the Warring States
period. Confucius's teachings about what it meant to
be a superior gentleman (*junzi*) became the foundation
for Chinese government and society for thousands of
years. The passage here shows the lively conversation
between Confucius, "the Master" in the text, and his
students, including Master You, Master Zeng, Zixia,
Ziqin, and Zigong.

• **What evidence in the text do you see for the
  Confucian principles of *ren* (benevolence),
  li (proper ritual), and *xiao* (filial piety)?**

• **Based on the exchanges here between Confucius
  and his pupils, and among his students, what would
  it have been like to study with Confucius?**

• **What would be the implications for governing if
  elite men lived according to the principles laid out
  in this text?**

1.1. The Master said: "To learn something and then to
put it into practice at the right time, is this not a joy?
To have friends coming from afar: is this not a delight?
Not to be upset when one's merits are ignored: is this
not the mark of a gentleman?"

1.2. Master You said: "A man who respects his parents and his elders would hardly be inclined to defy
his superiors. A man who is not inclined to defy his
superiors will never foment a rebellion. A gentleman
works at the root. Once the root is secured, the Way
unfolds. To respect parents and elders is the root of
humanity."

1.3. The Master said: "Clever talk and affected manners are seldom signs of goodness."

1.4. Master Zeng said: "I examine myself three times a day. When dealing on behalf of others, have I been trustworthy? In intercourse with my friends, have I been faithful? Have I practiced what I was taught?"

1.5. The Master said: "To govern a state of middle size, one must dispatch business with dignity and good faith; be thrifty and love all men; mobilize the people only at the right times."

1.6. The Master said: "At home, a young man must respect his parents; abroad, he must respect his elders. He should talk little, but with good faith; love all people, but associate with the virtuous. Having done this, if he still has energy to spare, let him study literature."

1.7. Zixia said: "A man who values virtue more than good looks, who devotes all his energy to serving his father and mother, who is willing to give his life for his sovereign, who in intercourse with friends is true to his word—even though some may call him uneducated, I still maintain he is an educated man."

1.8. The Master said: "A gentleman who lacks gravity has no authority and his learning will remain shallow. A gentleman puts loyalty and faithfulness foremost; he does not befriend his moral inferiors. When he commits a fault, he is not afraid to amend his ways."

1.9. Master Zeng said: "When the dead are honored and the memory of remote ancestors is kept alive, a people's virtue is at its fullest."

1.10. Ziqin asked Zigong: "When the Master arrives in another country, he always becomes informed about its politics. Does he ask for such information, or is it given him?" Zigong replied: "The Master obtains it by being cordial, kind, courteous, temperate, and deferential. The Master has a way of enquiring which is quite different from other people's, is it not?"

1.11. The Master said: "When the father is alive, watch the son's aspirations. When the father is dead, watch the son's actions. If three years later, the son has not veered from the father's way, he may be called a dutiful son indeed."

1.12. Master You said: "When practicing the ritual, what matters most is harmony. That is what made the beauty of the way of the ancient kings; it inspired every move, great or small. Yet they knew where to stop: harmony cannot be sought for its own sake, it must always be subordinated to the ritual; otherwise it would not do."

1.13. Master You said: "If your promises conform to what is right, you will be able to keep your word. If your manners conform to the ritual, you will be able to keep shame and disgrace at bay. The best support is provided by one's own kinsmen."

1.14. The Master said: "A gentleman eats without stuffing his belly; chooses a dwelling without demanding comfort; is diligent in his office and prudent in his speech; seeks the company of the virtuous in order to straighten his own ways. Of such a man, one may truly say that he is fond of learning."

1.15. Zigong said: "'Poor without servility; rich without arrogance.' How is that?" The Master said: "Not bad, but better still: 'Poor, yet cheerful; rich, yet considerate.'" Zigong said: "In the *Poems*, it is said: 'Like carving horn, like sculpting ivory, like cutting jade, like polishing stone.' Is this not the same idea?" The Master said: "Ah, one can really begin to discuss the *Poems* with you! I tell you one thing, and you can figure out the rest."

1.16. The Master said: "Don't worry if people don't recognize your merits; worry that you may not recognize theirs."

Source: Confucius, *The Analects*, translated by Simon Leys, edited by Michael Nylan, A Norton Critical Edition (New York: Norton, 2014), pp. 3–4.

PRIMARY SOURCE 5.3

The Dhammapada (third century BCE), Buddha

The wisdom of Siddhartha Gautama, later called the Buddha, was passed along in a text called the Dhammapada, which was recorded by his followers in the third century BCE. The Buddha's ideas about suffering, desire, and how to escape both, offered a distinct challenge to the prevailing hierarchies of the *varna* system that had thrived in South Asia since the influx of pastoral nomads into the region in the mid-second millennium BCE.

....

- According to this text, what distinguishes the behavior of a fool from that of a wise person? How does one know if one is wise?

- What ways of thinking and acting are encouraged by this text? How do those fit with what you know of Buddhism?

- In what specific ways do the principles laid out in this text challenge the *varna*-stratified community and the religious ideas of South Asia at the time of the Buddha?

....

Long is the night for the sleepless. Long is the road for the weary. Long is samsara (the cycle of continued rebirth) for the foolish, who have not recognized the true teaching.   60

If on one's way one does not come across one's better or an equal, then one should press on resolutely alone. There is no companionship with a fool.   61

"I've got children," "I've got wealth." This is the way a fool brings suffering on himself. He does not even own himself, so how can he have children or wealth?   62

A fool who recognises his own ignorance is thereby in fact a wise man, but a fool who considers himself wise—that is what one really calls a fool.   63

Even if a fool lived with a wise man all his life, he would still not recognise the truth, like a wooden spoon cannot recognise the flavour of the soup.   64

Even if a man of intelligence lives with a wise man only for a moment, he will immediately recognise the truth, like one's tongue recognises the flavour of the soup.   65

Stupid fools go through life as their own enemies, doing evil deeds which have bitter consequences.   66

A deed is not well done if one suffers after doing it, if one bears the consequences sobbing and with tears streaming down one's face.   67

But a deed is well done if one does not suffer after doing it, if one experiences the consequences smiling and contented.   68

A fool thinks it like honey so long as the bad deed does not bear fruit, but when it does bear fruit he experiences suffering.   69 . . .

Like fresh milk a bad deed does not turn at once. It follows a fool scorching him like a smouldering fire.   71

A fool acquires knowledge only to his own disadvantage. It destroys what good he has, and turns his brains.   72 . . .

One way leads to acquisition, the other leads to nirvana. Realising this a monk, as a disciple of the Buddha, should take no pleasure in the respect of others, but should devote himself to solitude.   75

***

Better than a thousand pointless words is one saying to the point on hearing which one finds peace.   100

Better than a thousand pointless verses is one stanza on hearing which one finds peace.   101

Better than reciting a hundred pointless verses is one verse of the teaching (one dhammapada) on hearing which one finds peace.   102

Though one were to defeat thousands upon thousands of men in battle, if another were to overcome just one—himself, he is the supreme victor.   103

Victory over oneself is better than that over others. When a man has conquered himself and always acts with self-control, neither devas, spirits, Mara or Brahma can reverse the victory of a man like that.   104, 105

Though one were to perform sacrifices by the thousand month after month for a hundred years, if another were to pay homage to a single inwardly perfected man for just a moment, that homage is better than the hundred years of sacrifices.   106

Though one were to tend the sacrificial fire for a hundred years in the forest, if another were to pay homage to a single inwardly perfected man for just a moment, that homage is better than the hundred years of sacrifice.   107 . . .

Four principal things increase in the man who is respectful and always honours his elders—length of life, good looks, happiness and health.   109

Though one were to live a hundred years immoral and with a mind unstilled by meditation, the life of a single day is better if one is moral and practises meditation.   110

Though one were to live a hundred years without wisdom and with a mind unstilled by meditation, the life of a single day is better if one is wise and practises meditation.   111 . . .

Though one were to live a hundred years without seeing the rise and passing of things, the life of a single day is better if one sees the rise and passing of things.   113 . . .

Though one were to live a hundred years without seeing the supreme truth, the life of a single day is better if one sees the supreme truth.   115

Source: "The Fool" and "The Thousands," in *The Dhammapada*, translated by John Richards, Electronic Buddhist Archives, 1993, http://www.cheraglibrary.org/buddhist/dhammapada/.

<hr>

PRIMARY SOURCE 5.4

The Apology of Socrates (c. 400 BCE), Plato

The ideas of the Greek philosopher Socrates, recorded in dialogues and the speech called the *Apology* (in defense of his influence on youth), called on Athenians to look within, to question, and to reason for themselves. As a citizen of democratic Athens, Socrates was a full participant in the political system and in the Peloponnesian War (431–404 BCE), as well as an influential teacher. The defense speech included here, as reported by his student Plato, preserves Socrates's reflections on wisdom and how his pursuit of understanding led to the charges against him.

- What are the charges against Socrates? From what you can tell of him from this passage, do you think they are justified?

- What does Socrates think of teachers? Of wisdom?

- How could the behaviors and ideas promoted by Socrates in this passage have been interpreted

by his contemporaries as radical and youth-corrupting?

<hr>

19b–e: Let us consider, then, from the beginning, what the accusation is, from which the prejudice against me arose that Meletos believed when he brought this charge against me. Well then. What precisely did the accusers say when they accused me? Just as if they were charging me, it is necessary to read out the indictment: "Socrates is guilty of meddling, of inquiring into things under the earth and in the heavens, of making the weaker speech the stronger and of teaching these very things"—something like this. . . . I call on the majority of you as witnesses, and I expect you to teach and inform one another, those of you who have ever heard me in discussion—and this includes many of you. Inform one another if any of you heard me ever discussing such things, either a lot or a little. And from this you will realize that the same is true of the other things that the many say about me, when really none of this is the case. And if you have heard from anyone that I endeavor to teach people and make money, this is certainly not true. Though again, I think that it is a fine thing if an individual is able to teach people. . . .

20d: Perhaps some of you might respond, "But Socrates, what is your profession? Where have these slanders against you come from? For surely it's not by busying yourself with the usual things that so much hearsay and talk has arisen, but by doing something different from most people. Then tell us what it is, so that we don't judge your case rashly." [Socrates replies:] Listen then. And while I will perhaps appear to some of you to be joking, rest assured that I will tell you the whole truth. For I, men of Athens, have acquired this reputation due to nothing other than a certain wisdom. What sort of wisdom is this? Quite likely a human wisdom. . . .

21a–e: You know Chairephon, I presume. He was a companion of mine from youth and a comrade of yours in the democracy. . . . [W]hen he went to Delphi he was so bold as to ask this—and, as I say, don't interrupt, gentlemen—he asked if there was anyone wiser than me. The Pythia [a priestess of Apollo who was renowned for her advice, which was thought to come from Apollo] then replied that there was no one wiser. And his brother here will bear witness to you about these things, since he [Chairephon] himself has died.

Think about why I am bringing this up: it's because I am going to teach you where the prejudice against me came from. Because when I heard this I pondered in the following way: "Whatever does the god mean? And what riddle is he posing? For I am not aware of being wise in anything great or small. What in the world does he mean, then, when he says that I am wisest? For certainly he does not lie; he is not permitted to." And I for a long time puzzled over his meaning.

Then, very reluctantly, I embarked on a sort of trial of him [Apollo]. I went to one of the people who are thought to be wise, hoping to refute the oracle there if anywhere, and reply to its pronouncement: "This man here is wiser than me, though you said I was." So, scrutinizing this fellow—there's no need to refer to him by name, he was one of the politicians with whom I experienced something of the following sort when examining him, men of Athens—in talking with him it seemed to me that while this man was considered to be wise both by many other people and especially by himself, he was not. And so I tried to show him that he took himself to be wise, but was not. As a result I became hated by this man and by many of those present.

And so, as I was going away, I was thinking to myself, "I am at least wiser than this man. It's likely that neither of us knows anything worthwhile, but whereas he thinks he knows something when he doesn't know it, I, when I don't know something, don't think I know it either. It's likely, then, that by this I am indeed wiser than him in some small way that I don't think myself to know what I don't know." Next, I went to another one of the people thought to be wiser than him and things seemed the same to me, and so I made an enemy of him as well as of many others.

Source: Plato, *Socrates' Defense (The Apology of Socrates)*, translated by Cathal Woods and Ryan Pack, 2016, pp. 2–4, doi:10.2139/ssrn.1023144.

Interpreting Visual Evidence

Elsewhere in the Axial Age

During the time that the Axial Age thinkers such as Confucius, the Buddha, and Socrates were sharing their radical ideas with disciples who recorded them in written texts, other major developments were taking place in preliterate societies. Some of the complex civilizations that formed in this period, like the Nok (in sub-Saharan Africa) and the Olmecs (in Mesoamerica), apparently did not leave written records, so historians rely on artwork—as well as many other sources, such as oral traditions and linguistic analysis—to learn about these peoples.

For example, although the Nok left no written texts that would tell us of their thinking, they did leave behind intriguing figurines. The Nok figurines were shaped from terra-cotta. Their impressive craftsmanship, with finely sculpted poses and carefully shaped hair, clothing, jewelry, and facial features, conveys the artistic tastes of these African peoples dating back to the mid-first millennium BCE. Who these figurines represent, however, is not clear, nor is their purpose.

The second Nok terra-cotta pictured here offers a glimpse of everyday life with its scenes of the harvest and mothers caring for their children.

The Olmecs, who thrived on the other side of the world in first-millennium BCE Mesoamerica, constructed ceremonial centers and also produced a wide range of artifacts, many of which provide evidence of their religious beliefs. So-called Offering 4 from the ritual center at La Venta dates to the mid-first millennium BCE. These seventeen figurines (between 6 and 8 inches tall), including at least one female, were buried together apparently to reenact some political or religious event, perhaps a high-status marriage or an important sacrifice. Wearing a mask that resembles classic Olmec shamanic images—like a jaguar's snarling mouth (see fourth image) and an eagle's beak—these figurines suggests the shape-shifting powers of a shaman. Even without written texts from these first-millennium BCE peoples, artifacts like these help us reconstruct their ideas.

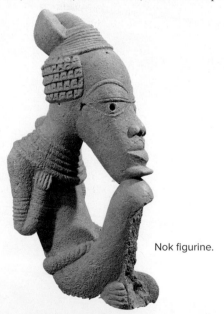

Nok figurine.

Nok terra-cotta.

Offering 4 at La Venta.

Olmec jaguar.

Questions for Analysis

1. Compare the Nok and Olmec figurines with the depictions of the Axial Age thinkers on the first page of this chapter. What do these depictions suggest about what matters to the people who produced them?

2. Looking at Map 5.6, what connection might the Nok have had with the Mediterranean in the first millennium BCE? How might transregional exchange, not just of goods but also of ideas, have affected both the Mediterranean and the sub-Sahara?

3. Looking at Map 5.5, how might trade in Mesoamerica in raw materials such as jade and obsidian have influenced the creation of objects such as Offering 4 from La Venta and the jaguar figurines?

4. Given that the Nok and Olmec cultures were sophisticated and expressed their beliefs through artworks like these, why do you think there is no evidence of singular Axial Age thinkers (like Confucius, the Buddha, or Socrates) among the Nok and the Olmecs?

6

Shrinking the Afro-Eurasian World

350–100 BCE

In the blistering August heat of 324 BCE, at a town on the Euphrates River that the Greeks called Opis (not far from modern Baghdad), Alexander the Great's experienced Macedonian troops declared that they had had enough. They had been fighting far from their homeland for more than a decade. They had marched eastward from the Mediterranean, forded wide rivers, traversed great deserts, trudged over high mountain passes, and slogged through rain-drenched forests. Along the way they had defeated massive armies that not only outnumbered Alexander's own forces but also were armed with fearsome war elephants. Some of his troops had taken wives from the cities and tribes they vanquished, so the army had become a giant swarm of ethnically mixed families. This was an army like no other. It did more than just defeat neighbors and rivals—it forcefully connected entire worlds, bringing together diverse peoples and lands.

Conquering in the name of building a new world, however, was not what the soldiers had bargained for. They loved their leader, but many thought he had gone too far. They had lost companions and grown weary of war. Some had mutinied at a tributary of the Indus River, halting Alexander's advance into South Asia. Now, at Opis, they threatened to desert him altogether. Summoning up their courage, they voiced these resentments to their supreme commander. Alexander's response was immediate and inspired. In order to persuade his troops not to desert him, he evoked

Chapter Outline

- Alexander and the Emergence of a Hellenistic World
- Converging Influences in Central and South Asia
- The Transformation of Buddhism
- The Formation of the Silk Roads
- Conclusion

Core Objectives

- **DESCRIBE** what enabled and motivated Alexander's military pursuits, and **EXPLAIN** why his conquests matter for understanding a connected Afro-Eurasia.
- **DESCRIBE** Hellenism and **EXPLAIN** its impact across Afro-Eurasia.
- **ANALYZE** the political changes that shaped central and South Asia in the aftermath of Alexander's incursion into the region.
- **TRACE** the spread of Buddhism in this period and **EVALUATE** the forces that influenced its spread.
- **TRACE** the early routes of the "Silk Roads" and **ASSESS** their importance in connecting Afro-Eurasia by land and sea.

the astounding military triumphs and historic achievement they had accomplished: establishing his rule from Macedonia to the Indus Valley. This far-reaching political vision came to a sudden end with Alexander's death a year later, when he was just thirty-two years old. Even in his short lifetime, though, he had set in motion cultural and economic forces that would transform Afro-Eurasia. As Alexander was expanding eastward, another development was taking form: the Silk Roads. This system of routes constituted the primary commercial network linking East Asia and the Mediterranean world for nearly a thousand years. Many different types of precious commodities were exchanged along its more than 5,000 miles, but the network ultimately took its name from the huge quantities of precious silk that passed along it. At the same time, exchange routes by sea were also taking shape.

As a result of Alexander's conquests and the political developments that followed, as well as the intensifying of trade along land and sea routes, two broad cultural movements came to link diverse populations across wide expanses of the Afro-Eurasian landmass: Hellenism and Buddhism. Hellenism, briefly defined, was a shared Greek identity that spread throughout the lands in which Greeks settled and was expressed in their language, art, architecture, politics, and more. Buddhism, as an Axial Age philosophy, was introduced in the previous chapter. A new form of Buddhism, called Mahayana Buddhism, took shape in the period described in this chapter. New empires—namely Alexander's successor states of the Mediterranean and the Mauryan Empire in South Asia—and newly deepening trade routes created the circuits through which Hellenism and Buddhism flowed.

Imperial conquests and long-distance trade laid the foundations for widespread cultural systems that were far more enduring than the empires themselves. Merchants, monks, and administrators helped connect widespread parts of Afro-Eurasia, as the busy sea-lanes and Silk Roads flourished. Merely a few centuries after the conquests of Alexander and Mauryan kings, the world looked very different from the realms their armies had traversed.

Global Storyline

The Creation of the Silk Roads and the Beginnings of Buddhism

- Conquests by Alexander the Great and the influence of his successor states spread Hellenism across Southwest Asia and into South Asia.

- The Mauryan Empire accelerates the integration of South Asia and helps Buddhism spread throughout that region and beyond.

- "Silk Roads," both overland and by sea, facilitate the movement of commodities (spices, metals, and silks) and ideas (especially Buddhism and Hellenism) across Afro-Eurasia.

Alexander and the Emergence of a Hellenistic World

The armed campaigns of the Macedonians led by Alexander the Great (356–323 BCE) began a drive for empire from the west that connected distant regions and spread a Hellenistic culture throughout the conquered lands. (See Map 6.1.) Alexander came from the frontier state of Macedonia to the north of Greece and commanded a highly mobile force armed with advanced military technologies that had developed during the incessant warfare among Greek city-states in the fifth and fourth centuries BCE. Alexander's novel use of new kinds of armed forces in a series of lightning attacks on the Persian Empire, the nemesis of the Greeks over the previous 200 years, further undermined barriers that separated the Mediterranean world from the rest of Southwest Asia.

Under Alexander's predecessors—especially his father, Philip II—Macedonia had become a large ethnic and territorial state. Philip had unified Macedonia and then gone on to conquer neighboring states. Macedonia boasted gold mines that could finance Philip's new military technology and his disciplined army. Philip's troops included heavily armored infantry that maneuvered in closely arrayed units called phalanxes as well as in large-scale cavalry formations for shock tactics. These infantry and cavalry forces were supported by income not only from Macedonian gold mines but also from the slave trade that passed through Macedonia. By the early 330s BCE, Philip had crushed the Greek city-states to the south, including Athens. After Philip's assassination, his son Alexander steered this new military machine toward the Persian Empire and its king, Darius III.

Historians and biographers have filled libraries with books about Alexander the Great, yet he remains one of the more perplexing figures in world history. Many have explored what motivated Alexander to embark on such an audacious campaign of conquest. To begin with, Alexander was deeply steeped in Greek culture, had absorbed Homer, and hoped to emulate the military exploits of heroic figures like Achilles, Hercules, and Dionysus. Moreover, he had a deep hatred of the Persian Empire; he sought to avenge the Persian invasion of Thrace and the murder of his father, Philip II, which some Macedonian sources attributed to Persian intrigue at Philip's court. Also, the influence of his mother, Olympias, a complex figure much maligned in the historical record, should not be underestimated. Olympias was one of several wives of Philip II (she was also implicated, by some sources, in his assassination), and after Philip's death she may have helped secure Alexander's succession by ordering his rivals killed. For several years after Alexander's death in 323 BCE, she continued to advocate for her son's legacy by advancing the claim of Alexander's son (her grandson) to the throne of Macedonia.

THE BIG PICTURE

How did Hellenism, Buddhism, and the Silk Roads shape Afro-Eurasia?

Core Objectives

DESCRIBE what enabled and motivated Alexander's military pursuits, and **EXPLAIN** why his conquests matter for understanding a connected Afro-Eurasia.

The Global View

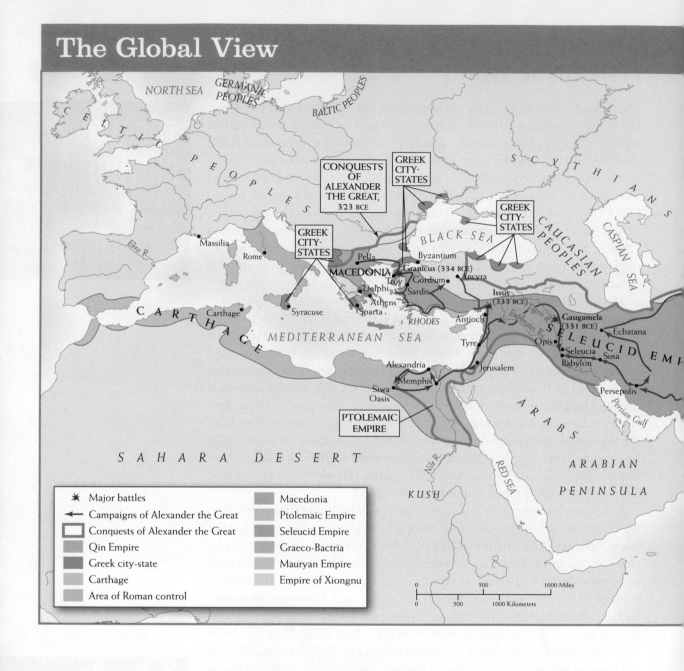

NORTH SEA

GERMANIC PEOPLES

BALTIC PEOPLES

CELTIC PEOPLES

CONQUESTS OF ALEXANDER THE GREAT, 323 BCE

GREEK CITY-STATES

GREEK CITY-STATES

GREEK CITY-STATES

BLACK SEA

SCYTHIANS

CAUCASIAN PEOPLES

CASPIAN SEA

Massilia

Rome

Ebro R.

Pella

MACEDONIA

Byzantium

Granicus (334 BCE)

Gordium

Ancyra

Troy

Delphi

Sardis

Issus (333 BCE)

Euphrates R.

Tigris R.

Gaugamela (331 BCE)

Ecbatana

Athens

Sparta

RHODES

Antioch

Opis

SELEUCID EMP

Seleucia

Susa

Carthage

CARTHAGE

Syracuse

MEDITERRANEAN SEA

Tyre

Babylon

Jerusalem

Alexandria

Memphis

Persepolis

Persian Gulf

Siwa Oasis

ARABS

PTOLEMAIC EMPIRE

SAHARA DESERT

Nile R.

RED SEA

ARABIAN PENINSULA

KUSH

* Major battles
← Campaigns of Alexander the Great
☐ Conquests of Alexander the Great
Qin Empire
Greek city-state
Carthage
Area of Roman control

Macedonia
Ptolemaic Empire
Seleucid Empire
Graeco-Bactria
Mauryan Empire
Empire of Xiongnu

0   500   1000 Miles
0   500   1000 Kilometers

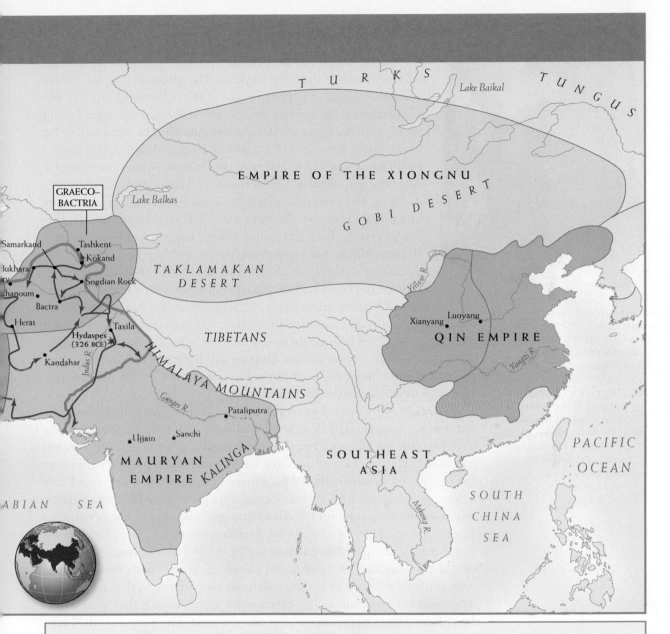

Map 6.1 Afro-Eurasia in 250 BCE, after Alexander's Conquests

Alexander of Macedon did not live long enough or establish the institutions necessary to create one large politically unified empire, but his conquests integrated various Afro-Eurasian worlds culturally and economically. Trace the pathways that Alexander followed on his conquests.

- Locate on the map the Hellenistic successor states. What did these states have in common? How were they different from one another?
- Which areas on the map did Greeks *not* rule? How did the spread of Hellenism affect these areas?
- What features illustrated on the map may have encouraged the spread of Hellenism? What features may have limited the spread of Hellenism?

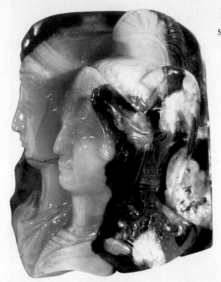

Alexander and Olympias Cameo carved in sardonyx and thought to depict Alexander and his mother, Olympias, in a style used to depict later Hellenistic kings and their queens. A fascinating character in her own right, Olympias exerted a powerful influence on Alexander, helping to strategize his rise to power and working to secure his legacy after his death.

Like many other successful conquerors, Alexander owed much of his success to a readiness to take risks. In his initial forays into Southwest Asia he outpaced, outflanked, and outthought his adversaries, repeatedly taking them by surprise. The Persians had substantial armed forces and an impressive navy. On the battlefield in 331 BCE at Gaugamela (in modern-day northern Iraq), even after having already suffered losses to Alexander in Anatolia (modern Turkey) at the Granicus River in 334 BCE and at Issus in 333 BCE, the Persian king Darius was able to assemble troops from Bactria (modern-day Afghanistan), Scythia (modern-day Ukraine and Kazakhstan), Armenia, and parts of modern-day Turkey that numbered as many as 1,000,000 infantry, 40,000 cavalry, 200 scythed chariots, and 15 war elephants. Even accounting for the tendency of Greek sources to overestimate troop numbers, this assemblage far outnumbered Alexander's infantry of 25,000 and cavalry of 2,000 Macedonians, supported by Greek and mercenary contingents of 10,000. Moreover, the Persians had virtually unlimited financial resources. Yet Alexander's forces were superior in technique, maneuverability, and resourcefulness. Through his military successes he brought under the rule of his Greek-speaking elites all the lands of the former Persian Empire, which extended from Egypt and the shores of the Mediterranean to the interior of what is now Afghanistan, and as far to the east as the Indus River valley.

The result of this expansion was hardly an empire, given that Alexander did not live long enough to establish institutions to hold the distant lands together. But his military campaigns continued a process that the Persians had already set in motion of smashing barriers that had separated peoples on the eastern and western ends of Afro-Eurasia. The conqueror saw himself as a new universal figure, a bridge connecting distant cultures. He demonstrated this vision in his adoption of Persian dress and customs; in his marriage to Roxana, the daughter of a chief from Bactria (present-day Afghanistan); and then later in a group wedding at Susa in 324 BCE in which he married Stateira, one of the daughters of the defeated Darius. Eager to create bonds linking west and east at every level, Alexander not only married off many Persian women to his Companions (his elite cavalry force), even if they already had Macedonian wives back at home, but also recognized as many as 10,000 pre-existing marriages between rank-and-file Macedonians and Persian women.

Alexander's conquests increased exposure of formerly Persian lands to the commodities of the Mediterranean and to cultural ideas associated with the Greek city-states. Alexander founded dozens of new cities named after himself, not only the famed Alexandria in Egypt but also Iskandariya and Kandahar in modern-day Iraq and Afghanistan. Alexander seized the accumulated wealth that the Persian kings stored in their immense palaces, especially at Persepolis, and dispersed it into the money economies of the Mediterranean

Battle of Issus Mosaic of the Battle of Issus (333 BCE) between Alexander the Great of Macedon and Darius, the king of Persia (found in a house at Pompeii in southern Italy). Alexander is the bareheaded figure to the far left; Darius is the figure to the right, gesturing with his right hand. The men represent two different types of warfare. On horseback, Alexander leads the cavalry-based shock forces of the Macedonian Greeks, while Darius directs his army from a chariot in the style of the great kings of Southwest Asia.

city-states. This massive redistribution of wealth fueled a widespread economic expansion in the Mediterranean and beyond.

ALEXANDER'S SUCCESSORS AND THE TERRITORIAL KINGDOMS

Alexander died in Babylon in 323 BCE at age thirty-two. Whether he was struck down by some infectious disease like malaria or by cirrhosis of the liver from his overconsumption of alcohol (which was legendary), Alexander's death brought on the collapse of the regime he had personally held together. The conquered lands fragmented into large territories over which his generals squabbled for control.

Alexander's successors—his generals Seleucus, Antigonus, Ptolemy, Lysimachus, and others—thought of themselves not as citizens of a Greek city-state but rather as absolute rulers over large blocks of territory, modeling themselves on the regional rulers they had defeated. One effect of powerful families' control of whole kingdoms was that some women could now hold great power. Queens in Egypt, Syria, and Macedonia—whether independent or as co-regents with their husbands—established new public roles for women. For example, Berenice I of Egypt (r. c. 320–280 BCE) was the first in a series of powerful women who helped rule the kingdom of the Nile, a line that ended with the famous Cleopatra VII in the 30s BCE. In Macedonia, a series of royal women whose husbands were either dead or incapacitated—Cynane (the widowed half sister of Alexander), Adea Eurydice (the wife of Alexander's half brother Philip III Arrhidaeus, whom sources report to have

Berenice and Ornamental Gorytos *Left:* Portrait head of Berenice, wife and consort of Ptolemy I, the first Macedonian king of Egypt after its conquest by Alexander the Great. Berenice was one of the women who, as queens of huge empires, wielded power and commanded wealth in their own right. *Right:* This ceremonial *gorytos* (bow and arrow case), fashioned from gold and depicting the brutal sacking of a city, was excavated from one of a series of Macedonian royal tombs in Vergina (outside Thessaloniki, in northern Greece). While debates rage over who exactly was buried in these tombs, some argue that this *gorytos* (which is similar to others found in Scythian graves), along with other materials in Tomb II, points to one of the Hellenistic warrior queens, perhaps even Adea Eurydice (the wife of Alexander's half brother Philip III Arrhidaeus).

had some intellectual disability), and Cratesipolis (the widow of one of the generals battling for power in the aftermath of Alexander's death)—not only ruled but also effectively led troops into battle.

Three large territorial states stood out in the new Hellenistic world: the Seleucid Empire (established by Seleucus), stretching from Syria to present-day Afghanistan; Macedonia, ruled by the Antigonids (established by Antigonus); and Egypt, ruled by the Ptolemies (established by Ptolemy). The Seleucid Empire was the largest, comprising much of the territory that had been the Persian Empire, before Alexander's conquest. Macedonia was the smallest but had the distinction of being the homeland of Alexander. The Ptolemaic state, smaller in territory and population than the Seleucid Empire, lasted the longest of Alexander's successor kingdoms, a full 275 years.

The Ptolemies are remarkable for how they effectively merged pharaonic institutions of kingship and priestly power with Hellenistic culture and practices. The Rosetta Stone offers evidence for this cultural hybridity in Hellenistic Egypt. Known for its role in deciphering hieroglyphs, its three scripts record a decree dating to 196 BCE that outlines Ptolemy V's relationship with the Egyptian temples and priesthood. The Ptolemies also united Upper and Lower Egypt, which had been fragmented into as many as eleven political units once the New Kingdom fell, into a centralized state, ruled from Alexandria. The Ptolemies, however, were unwilling to share power with Egyptian nobles. They married within their own royal family; often brothers married sisters or cousins. And despite the trilingualism of the Rosetta Stone, the Ptolemies remained committed to the Greek language and culture. Cleopatra VII, the last of the Ptolemaic line to rule in Egypt, was exceptional in her ability to speak Egyptian, but then again, she was a talented linguist, who also spoke the languages of the Ethiopians, Hebrews, Arabians, Syrians, Medes, and Parthians, according to the later biographer Plutarch.

In areas between these larger Hellenistic kingdoms, middle-sized kingdoms emerged. The old city-states of the Mediterranean, such as Athens and Corinth, still thrived, but now they interacted with a world dominated by these much larger power blocs. On mainland Greece, larger confederations of previously independent city-states formed.

Competition in war remained an unceasing fact of life, but the wars among the kingdoms of Alexander's successors were broader in scope and more complex in organization than ever before. Since the successor kingdoms were nearly equal in strength and employed the same advanced military technology, however, the near-constant state of war between the new kings never achieved much. After battles that killed tens of thousands, and severely injured and wounded hundreds of thousands more, the three major kingdoms—and even the minor ones—remained largely unchanged.

The great powers therefore settled into a centuries-long game of watching one another and balancing threats with alliances. What emerged was a fierce competition that dominated international relations, in which diplomacy and treaty-making sometimes replaced actual fighting. This equilibrium was reminiscent of the first age of international relations in the second millennium BCE (see Chapter 3). Long periods of peace began to grace the intervals between the new kingdoms' violent and destructive wars.

HELLENISTIC CULTURE

The unification of large blocks of territory under Alexander's successors helped spread a common Hellenistic culture. Following existing commercial networks, **Hellenism** was a shared Greek culture that extended across the entire Mediterranean basin and into Southwest Asia. Hellenistic culture included philosophical and political thinking, secular disciplines ranging from history to biology, popular entertainment in theaters, exercising and socializing in gymnasia, competitive public games, and art in many

Hellenism
A uniform culture that stressed the common identity of all who embraced Greek ways. This culture emphasized the common denominators of language, style, and politics to which anyone, anywhere in the Afro-Eurasian world, could have access.

forms. By diffusing well beyond its homeland, it brought worlds together: its influence spread from Greece to all shores of the Mediterranean, into parts of sub-Saharan Africa, across Southwest Asia, and through the Iranian plateau into central and South Asia. It even had echoes in China. Like "Americanization" in the modern world, Hellenism took the attractive elements of one culture—its language, its music, its modes of dress and entertainment—and made these parts of a new global culture. And like "Americanization," in some regions Hellenism was welcomed and in others it was resisted.

Despite pockets of resistance, Hellenism was remarkably successful at taking root across a large swath of Afro-Eurasia and spreading its influence even farther. Archaeologists have found a Greek-style gymnasium and theater in the town of Aï Khanoum in modern Afghanistan and adaptations of Greek sculptures made at the order of the Indian king Chandragupta, of the Mauryan Empire (discussed shortly). We also know of Carthaginians in North Africa who became "Greek" philosophers, and Gallic and Berber chieftains from the far west of France and North Africa had fine Greek-style drinking vessels buried with them.

Common Language The core element of Hellenism was a common language known as *Koine*, or "common," Greek. It replaced the city-states' numerous dialects with an everyday form that people anywhere could understand. **Koine Greek** quickly became the international language of its day. Peoples in Egypt, Judea, Syria, and Sicily, who all had distinct languages and cultures, could now communicate more easily with one another and enjoy the same dramatic comedies and new forms of art and sculpture.

Koine Greek

Simpler than regional versions of Greek such as Attic or Ionic, this "common Greek" dialect became an international language across the regions influenced by Hellenism and facilitated trade of goods and ideas.

cosmopolitans

Meaning "citizens of the world," as opposed to a city-state, this term refers particularly to inhabitants of the large, multiethnic cities that were nodes of exchange in the Hellenistic world.

Cosmopolitan Cities Individuals were no longer citizens of a particular city (*polis*); instead they were the first **cosmopolitans**, that is, citizens (*polites*) belonging to the whole world or universe (*kosmos*). Much as Athens had been the model city of the age of the Greek city-state, Alexandria in Egypt became exemplary in the Hellenistic age. Whereas citizens of fifth-century BCE city-states had zealously maintained their exclusive civic identities (as Athenians, Spartans, or Corinthians, for example), Alexandria was a multiethnic city built by immigrants, who rapidly totaled half a million as they streamed in from all over the Mediterranean and Southwest Asia seeking new opportunities. Members of Alexandria's dynamic population, representing dozens of Greek and non-Greek peoples, communicated in the common language that supplanted their original dialects. Soon a new urban culture emerged to meet the needs of so diverse a population.

Hellenistic entertainment in this more connected world had to appeal to broad audiences. Plays were now staged in any city touched by Greek influence and had to translate to any environment. Consequently, the distinctive

The Theater at Syracuse The great theater in the city-state of Syracuse, in Sicily, was considerably refurbished and enlarged under the Hellenistic kings. It could seat 15,000 to 20,000 persons. Here the people of Syracuse attended plays written by playwrights who lived on the far side of their world, but whose works they could understand as if the characters were from their own neighborhood. In the common culture of the Hellenistic period, plays deliberately featured typecast characters and situations, thereby broadening their audience.

regional humor and local characters of fifth-century BCE Greek city-state drama gave way to performances populated by the stock characters of standard sitcoms with whom any audience could identify: the greedy miser, the old crone, the jilted lover, the golden-hearted whore, the boastful soldier, the befuddled father, the cheated husband, the rebellious son. Plays were performed in theaters with nearly identical architecture throughout the Mediterranean basin, and laughter would be just as loud in Syracuse on the island of Sicily as in Scythopolis in the Jordan Valley of Judea.

A new political style of distant, almost godlike kings developed, in part due to the size of the territories over which they ruled. Instead of being accessible, which was not possible when Hellenistic kingdoms and states were so enormous, Hellenistic leaders became larger-than-life figures. Individuals related to political leaders primarily through the personality of the kings and their families. Rulership was personality, and personality could unite large numbers of subjects. For example, Demetrius Poliorcetes, the ruler of Macedonia, stood out in his platform shoes and heavy makeup, and he decorated his elaborate, flowing cape with images of the sun, the stars, and the planets. In the presence of a powerful sun-king like Demetrius, ordinary individuals felt small and inconsequential.

Philosophy and Religion Hellenistic religion and philosophy increasingly focused on the individual and his or her place in the larger world. This growing concern with the individual found expression in many new philosophical schools that proposed a range of ideas, including self-sufficiency (Cynicism), detachment (Epicureanism), and civic involvement (Stoicism). As mentioned in the previous chapter, given the connectedness of Eurasia that was heightened in the late first millennium BCE, echoes with East and South Asian philosophy are not surprising.

For instance, the Athenian Diogenes (c. 412–323 BCE), an early proponent of the Cynic school of philosophy, vividly demonstrates the Hellenistic manifestation of philosophy focused on the self. Diogenes sought freedom from society's laws and customs, rejecting cultural norms as human-made inventions not in tune with nature and therefore false. Similarly turning thoughts to the self, Epicurus (341–270 BCE), the founder of a school in Athens that he called The Garden, envisioned an ideal community of adherents regardless of their gender and social status, centered on his school. Seeking out pleasure and avoiding pain, these Epicureans contemplated the answer to the question "What is the good life?" and struggled to develop a sense of "not caring" (*ataraxia*) about their worries. More widespread than Diogenes's Cynicism and Epicurus's philosophy was Zeno's Stoicism. Zeno (c. 334–262 BCE), from the island of Cyprus, initiated it, and other cosmopolitan figures across the Hellenistic world—from Babylon in Mesopotamia to Sinope on the Black Sea—developed its beliefs. Named after the Stoa Poikilē, the roofed colonnade in the Athenian agora in which Zeno first presented his ideas, Stoicism argued that everything was grounded in nature. Stoicism regarded cities and kingdoms as human-made things, important but transient. Being in tune with nature and living a good life required understanding the rules of the natural order and being in control of one's passions, and thus required indifference to pleasure and pain. Stoicism, Epicureanism, and Cynicism offered the individual a range of philosophical responses to the Hellenistic world developing all around.

Long-established religions were also shaped by Hellenism and then re-exported throughout the Mediterranean. For example, Greeks in Egypt drew on the indigenous cult of Osiris and his consort, Isis, to fashion a new narrative about Osiris's death and rebirth that represented personal salvation from death. Isis became a supreme goddess whose "supreme virtues" encompassed the powers of dozens of other Mediterranean gods and goddesses. Believers experienced personal revelations and out-of-body experiences (*exstasis*, "ecstasy"). A ritual of dipping in water (*baptizein*, "to baptize") marked the transition of believers, "born again" into lives devoted to a "personal savior" who delivered an understanding of a new life by direct revelation. These new beliefs, like the worship of Isis, emphasized the spiritual concerns of humans as individuals, rather than the collective worries of kingdoms or city-states. Other Hellenistic adaptations from earlier Greek religion, including cults centered on the Eleusinian Mysteries of Demeter and Bacchic worship of Dionysus, similarly focused on the salvation of the individual as they spread throughout the Hellenistic world.

Dionysus in India While dating to a later period (third century CE), this sarcophagus illustrates the connection of Dionysus with India in stories that reached back to Hellenistic times. In this scene, Dionysus rides in a chariot pulled by two Indian elephants, and even a giraffe and lion join the parade. The presence of this Dionysian scene on a burial container shows the personal value that these Greek cults had for addressing the spiritual concerns of their adherents.

PLANTATION SLAVERY AND MONEY-BASED ECONOMIES

Ironically, philosophical and religious innovations focused on the self were accompanied by the rise of plantation slavery—the ultimate devaluing of an individual—as an engine of the Hellenistic economy. Large numbers of enslaved people were used in agricultural production, especially in Italy, Sicily, and North African regions close to Carthage. Alexander's conquests and Rome's political rise had produced unprecedented wealth for a small elite. These men and women used their riches to acquire huge tracts of land and to purchase enslaved people (either kidnapped individuals or conquered peoples) on a scale and with a degree of managerial organization never seen before. The slave plantations, wholly devoted to producing surplus crops for profit, helped drive a new Mediterranean economy. The estates created vast wealth for their owners—though at a heavy price to others, as reliance on enslaved laborers now left the free peasants who used to work the fields with no option but to move into overcrowded cities, where employment was hard to find.

The sudden importation of so many enslaved people to work in harsh conditions also had unanticipated outcomes. In 135 BCE, authorities on Sicily faced a massive uprising, led by a Syrian named Eunus, whose followers were amazed at his wonder-working and fortune-telling. A few mistreated enslaved people who resisted their cruel enslavers became a band of 400, whose ranks swelled to tens of thousands of enslaved men, women, and children.

Roman Slavery One of the most profitable occupations for peoples living beyond the northwestern frontiers of the Roman Empire, in what was called Germania, was providing bodies for sale to Roman merchants. In this relief, we see chained German prisoners whose fate was to become enslaved in the empire. This stone picture supported columns in front of the headquarters of the Roman fortress at Mainz-Kästrich.

The mighty Roman army only with difficulty subdued their revolt. Perhaps more well known is the uprising led by the enslaved gladiator Spartacus on the Italian Peninsula in the late 70s BCE. Again, the superior military force of the Roman state prevailed, but the political repercussions of the slave wars had a fundamental impact in the subsequent political crises that transformed the Roman state.

The circulation of money reinforced the effects of forced labor. With more cash in the economy, wealthy landowners, urban elites, and merchants could more easily do business. The increasing use of Greek-style coins to pay for goods and services (in place of barter) promoted the importation of commodities such as wine from elsewhere in the Mediterranean. As coined money became even more available, even more commercial exchanges occurred. The forced transfer of precious metals to the Mediterranean from Southwest Asia by Alexander's conquests was so large that it actually caused the price of gold to fall.

In the west, Carthage began to mint its own coins—at first mainly in gold, but later in other metals. Rome moved to a money economy at the same time. By the 270s and 260s BCE, the Romans were issuing coins on a large scale under the pressures of their first war with Carthage (264–241 BCE). By the end of the third century BCE, borderland peoples such as the Gauls had begun to mint coins, imitating the galloping-horse images found on Macedonia's gold coins. So, too, did kingdoms in North Africa, where the coins of Numidian kings bore the same Macedonian royal imagery. By around 100 BCE, inhabitants of the entire Mediterranean basin and surrounding lands were using coins minted by this range of political entities to buy and sell all manner of commodities.

Adaptation and Resistance to Hellenism The new high Greek culture spread far and wide, though it was not fully accepted everywhere in the Mediterranean. It appealed particularly to elites who sought to enhance their position by embracing Hellenistic culture over local values. Syrian,

Jewish, and Egyptian elites in the eastern Mediterranean adopted this attitude, as well as Roman, Carthaginian, and African elites in the western Mediterranean.

The Hellenistic influences reached sub-Saharan Africa, where the Meroitic kingdom (see Chapter 5), already influenced by pharaonic forms, now absorbed characteristics of Greek culture as well. It is not surprising that Greek influences were extensive in Meroe, because continuous interaction with the Egyptians also exposed its people to the world of the Mediterranean. Both Meroe and its rival, Axum, located in the Ethiopian highlands, used Greek-style steles (inscribed stone pillars) to boast of their military exploits. Citizens of Meroe worshipped Zeus and Dionysus. The rulers of Meroe, understanding the advantages of the Greek language, employed Greek scribes to record their accomplishments on the walls of Greek-Egyptian temples. In this way, Meroe developed a mix of Greek, Egyptian, and African cultural and political elements.

Not every community succumbed to the allure of Hellenism. The Jews in Judea offer a striking case of resistance and accommodation to its universalizing forces. Having been released from their Babylonian exile by the Persian monarch Cyrus in 538 BCE, the Jews returned to Judea—now a Persian province—and began rebuilding Jerusalem, including a magnificent "second" temple to replace the Temple of Solomon that had been destroyed by the Neo-Babylonians fifty years earlier. While the Persians tolerated local customs and beliefs (see Chapter 4), the Hellenism brought by the Seleucid successor state that took Persia's place after Alexander's conquest brought a shock to Judaism. While some among the Jewish ruling elite began to adopt Greek ways—to wear Greek clothing, to participate in the gymnasium with its cult of male nudity, to produce images of gods as art—others rejected the push. Those who spurned assimilation rebelled against the common elements of Hellenism—its language, music, gymnasia, nudity, public art, and secularism—as being deeply immoral and threatening to their beliefs.

Ultimately, this resistance to Hellenism led to full-scale armed revolt, headed up by the family of the Maccabees. In 167 BCE, the Seleucids provoked the Maccabees by forbidding the practice of Judaism (by outlawing worship and circumcision) and profaning the Jews' temple (by erecting an altar to Zeus in the sanctuary of the temple and sacrificing pigs on it). Though the Maccabees succeeded in establishing an independent Jewish state centered on the temple in Jerusalem, they did not entirely overcome the impact of the new universal culture on Judaism. A huge Jewish community in the Hellenistic city of Alexandria in Egypt embraced the new culture. Scholars there produced a version of the Hebrew scriptures in *Koine* Greek, and historians (such as Jason of Cyrene) and philosophers (such as Philo of Alexandria) wrote in Greek, imitating Greek models.

Menorah as Resistance Symbol The menorah—and its miraculous burning for eight days during the rededication of the Jewish temple after it had been profaned by the Hellenistic king Antiochus IV in 167 BCE—became a symbol of Jewish resistance against Hellenistic influence. This image comes from the Roman emperor Titus's triumphal arch (dated to around 81 CE), on which the Romans celebrated their conquest of Judea in the late first century CE.

Similar resistance and accommodation were taking place elsewhere. In the 330s and 320s BCE, when Alexander was uniting the eastern Mediterranean, the city-state of Rome took the first critical military actions to unify Italy. Rather than beginning as a kingdom like Macedonia, Rome went from being a city-state to flourishing as a large territorial state. During this transformation it adopted significant elements of Hellenistic culture: Greek-style temples, elaborately decorated Greek-style pottery and paintings, and an alphabet based on that of the Greeks. Many Roman elites saw immersion in Hellenistic ideals as a way to appear to the rest of the world as "civilized," while others resisted Greek ways as being overly luxurious and contrary to Roman ideals of manliness. The conservative Roman senator Cato the Elder (234–149 BCE) struggled with the tensions that Hellenism introduced to traditional Roman ways. Although he was devoted to the Roman past, the Latin language, and the ideal of small-scale Roman peasant farmers and their families, Cato embraced many Hellenistic influences. He wrote a standard manual for the new economy of slave plantation agriculture, invested in shipping and trading, learned Greek rhetoric (both speaking and writing the language), and added the genre of history to Latin literature. Cato blended an extreme devotion to Roman tradition with bold Hellenistic innovations in most aspects of daily life.

Rome's long-time rival, the Phoenician colony of Carthage, also adopted Hellenism but with less internal conflict than in Rome. Carthaginian culture took on important elements of Hellenistic culture. For example, some Carthaginians went to Athens to become philosophers, and innovative ideas on political theory and warfare came from the Greek city-states. The design of sanctuaries, temples, and other public buildings in Carthage reveals a mix of Greek-style pediments and columns, Carthaginian designs and measurements, and local North African motifs and structures. Carthaginian women adorned themselves with jewelry that reflected styles from Egypt, such as ornate necklaces of gold and earrings of lapis lazuli.

Already well integrated into the Mediterranean economy, Carthage welcomed the increased communication and exchange that Hellenism facilitated.

Carthaginian merchants traded with other Phoenician colonies in the western Mediterranean, with the towns of the Etruscans and the Romans in Italy, with the Greek trading city of Massilia (modern Marseilles) in southern France, and with Athens in the eastern Mediterranean. In addition, the Carthaginians expanded their commercial interests into the Atlantic, moving north along the coast of Iberia and south along the coast of West Africa, even establishing a trading post at the island of Mogador more than 600 miles down the Atlantic coast of Africa. Profoundly shaped by Alexander's conquests, Hellenism spread even farther across Afro-Eurasia with Alexander's successors.

Converging Influences in Central and South Asia

During this period, tighter political organization in South Asia helped spread new influences, like Hellenism and Buddhism, across the region. The high mountains of modern-day Afghanistan were a major geographical barrier to east-west exchange, but they were not impassable. Mountain passes—pinched like the narrow neck of an hourglass between the high plateau of Iran to the west and the towering ranges of Tibet to the east—offered the shortest route through the formidable Hindu Kush range. By crossing these passes, Alexander's armies expanded the routes between the eastern and western portions of Afro-Eurasia and brought about massive political and cultural changes in central and South Asia. Conquerors moved from west to east (like Alexander), from east to west (like the later nomads from central Asia), and from north to south, through the mountains and into the rich plains of the Indus and Ganges River valleys. At the same time, South Asian trade and religious influences, especially Buddhism, moved northward toward routes running west to east along what became known as the Silk Roads.

Core Objectives

ANALYZE the political changes that shaped central and South Asia in the aftermath of Alexander's incursion into the region.

CHANDRAGUPTA AND THE MAURYAN EMPIRE

Alexander's brief occupation of the Indus Valley (327–325 BCE) helped pave the way for one of the largest empires in South Asian history, the Mauryan Empire. Before the arrival of Alexander's forces, South Asia had been a conglomerate of small warring states. This political instability came to an abrupt halt when, in 321 BCE, an ambitious young man named Chandragupta Mori (or Maurya), inspired by Alexander, seized the throne of the Magadha kingdom and launched a series of successful military expeditions in what is now northern India. These campaigns would lead to the founding of his new Mauryan Empire.

The Magadha kingdom that Chandragupta overthrew had thrived on the lower Ganges plain since the sixth century BCE and had held great strategic advantages over other states. For one thing, it contained rich iron ores and fertile rice paddies. Moreover, on the northeast Deccan plateau ample woods supported herds of elephants, a mainstay of the powerful Magadha mobile military forces, which used elephants to charge down and terrify the enemy. According to Alexander's contemporary Megasthenes (more on him, shortly), fear of facing those elephants and the large army of Magadha was one of the reasons Alexander's troops refused to cross the Ganges. However, by the time Chandragupta Maurya took over the Magadha kingdom, it was suffering under the heavy taxation and greed of its king.

The Mori family, or Mauryans, did not start out as a distinguished ruling family, but economic strength and military skill elevated them over their rivals. Chandragupta (r. 321–297 BCE), though of lowly origins, probably from the Vaishya *varna*, grew up in the Punjab region of the Indus Valley observing Alexander's onslaught and aspiring to be an equally powerful military and political leader. When Alexander withdrew his forces from northern India, Chandragupta inserted himself into the political vacuum created by the Greek withdrawal.

The **Mauryan Empire** (321–184 BCE), founded by Chandragupta, constituted South Asia's first empire and served as a model for later Indian empire builders. The contemporary Greek world knew this empire as "India," stretching from the Indus River eastward. After supplanting Magadha's Nanda monarchic dynasty, which had been in place for just over a century, Chandragupta used his military resources to reach westward beyond the Ganges plain into the area where four tributaries join the Indus. Here he pushed up to the border with the Seleucid kingdom, the largest successor kingdom of Alexander's empire, based in Mesopotamia.

Alexander's eastern successor, the Seleucid king Seleucus Nicator (358–281 BCE), responded by invading Mauryan territory—only to face Chandragupta's impregnable defenses. Soon thereafter, a treaty between the two powers gave a large portion of Afghanistan to the Mauryan Empire. One of the daughters of Seleucus went to the Mauryan court, accompanied by a group of Greek women. Seleucus also sent to Chandragupta's court an ambassador named Megasthenes—the same Megasthenes who reported on the elephants of Magadha's army. In return for these gifts and diplomacy, the Mauryans sent Seleucus many South Asian valuables, including hundreds of elephants, which the Greeks soon learned to use in battles.

The Seleucid ambassador Megasthenes lived in South Asia for years and gathered his observations while at the Mauryan court into a book titled *Indica*, after the Greek term for this region. Megasthenes's *Indica* depicted a well-ordered and highly stratified society divided into seven groups: philosophers, farmers, soldiers, herdsmen, artisans, magistrates, and councilors.

Mauryan Empire
(321–184 BCE) The first large-scale empire in South Asia, stretching from the Indus in the west to the mouth of the Ganges in the east and nearly to the southern tip of the Indian subcontinent; begun by Chandragupta Maurya, in the aftermath of Alexander's time in India, and expanded to its greatest extent by his grandson Aśoka.

People respected the boundaries between groups and honored rituals that reinforced their identities: members of different groups did not intermarry or even eat together. Megasthenes also noted the ways in which rulers integrated the region—for example, connecting major cities with extensive tree-lined roads, complete with mile markers. These roads facilitated both trade and the movement of troops. (See Current Trends in World History: Modern Destruction and Repatriation of Our World Cultural Heritage.) Contrary to Greek expectations of a military closely integrated into civil society, Megasthenes reported that soldiers in India were a profession separate from the rest of the population. Mauryan troops did not pursue any other occupation and stood ready to obey their commander. This military force was huge, boasting cavalry divisions of mounted horses, war elephants, and scores of infantry.

The Regime of Aśoka The Mauryan Empire reached its height during the reign of its third king, Aśoka (r. 268–231 BCE), Chandragupta's grandson. Aśoka's lands included almost all of South Asia; only the southern tip of the subcontinent remained outside his control. In 261 BCE, Aśoka launched the conquest of Kalinga, a kingdom on the east coast of the South Asian subcontinent. The Mauryan army triumphed, but at a high price: about 100,000 soldiers died in battle, many more perished in its aftermath, and some 150,000 people endured forcible relocation. Aśoka was appalled and shamed by the brutal devastation his army had wrought. He vowed to cease inflicting pain on his people and pledged to follow the peaceful doctrines of Buddhism, issuing a famous edict that renounced brutal ways.

In his Kalinga Edict, Aśoka proclaimed his intention to rule according to the Indian concept of *dhamma*, a vernacular form of the Sanskrit word *dharma*, understood widely in Mauryan lands to mean tolerance of others, obedience to the natural order of things, and respect for all of earth's life forms. *Dhamma* was to apply to everyone, including the priestly Brahmans, Buddhists, members of other religious sects, and even Greeks. *Dhamma* became an all-encompassing moral code that all religious sects in South Asia accepted. With *dhamma* as a unifying symbol, Aśoka required all people, whatever their religious practices and cultural customs, to consider themselves his subjects, to respect him as their father, and to conform to his moral code—starting with the precept that people of different religions or sects should get along with one another. He also praised the benefits of agrarian progress and banned large-scale cattle sacrifice as detrimental to agriculture. Meanwhile, he warned the "forest people," the hunters and gatherers living beyond the reach of government, to avoid making trouble.

To disseminate the ideals of *dhamma*, Aśoka regularly issued decrees, which he had chiseled on stone pillars and boulders in every corner of his

Stupa and Pillar at Sarnath King Aśoka had stupas built across his domain, each holding relics of the Buddha. The stupa at Sarnath at the Deer Garden (*left*), is one of the few that has remained standing since Aśoka's time and marks the place where the Buddha delivered his first sermon. Also in the Deer Garden stands this edict pillar (*right*). Aśoka had his policies carved on grand pillars like this one, capped by majestic sculptures of animals. This pillar capital has been established as the national emblem of the Republic of India since its independence.

domain, selecting locations where people were likely to congregate and where they could hear the words as read to them by the few who were literate. Occasionally he also issued edicts to explain his Buddhist faith. All were inscribed in local languages, including Sanskrit, as well as Greek and Aramaic in the Hellenistic- and Persian-influenced northwest.

The Mauryan Empire at its height encompassed 3 million square miles, including all of what is today Pakistan, much of what is Afghanistan, the southeastern part of Iran, and the whole of the Indian subcontinent except for the lands at the southern tip. Its extraordinarily diverse geography consisted of jungles, mountains, deserts, and floodplains, and its equally disparate population of 50 to 60 million inhabitants was made up of pastoralists, farmers, forest dwellers, merchants, artisans, and religious leaders. Yet Aśoka's promotion of the Buddhist tenet of *dhamma* and his elaborate administrative structure were not enough to hold together his empire, which did not last long after his death in 231 BCE. The proliferation of Buddhism made possible by Aśoka's adoption and wholehearted sponsorship of the faith, however, was a lasting impact of his reign.

GREEK INFLUENCES IN CENTRAL ASIA

Hellenistic influences shaped politics and culture in the regimes that succeeded direct Greek control in central Asia. Alexander's military had thrust into Asia and reached as far as the Punjab. There he defeated several rulers of Gandhara in 326 BCE. In the course of this campaign he planted many garrison towns—especially in eastern Iran, in northern Afghanistan, and in the

Punjab, where he needed to protect his easternmost territorial acquisition. These towns were originally stations for soldiers, but they soon became centers of Hellenistic culture. Many of these outposts displayed the characteristic features of a Greek city-state: a colonnaded main street lined by temples to patron gods or goddesses, a theater, a gymnasium for education, an administrative center, and a marketplace. Following Alexander's death, Seleucus Nicator built more of these Greek garrison towns before he concluded peace with Chandragupta Maurya and withdrew from the region.

The garrison towns founded by Alexander and Seleucus remained and grew into Hellenistic centers. Once the Greek soldiers who had been stationed in them realized they would be spending their lives far from their homeland, they married local women and started families. Bringing their Hellenistic customs to the local populations, the soldiers established institutions familiar to them from the Greek city-states. *Koine* Greek was the official language, but because locals used their own languages in daily life, subsequent generations were bilingual. For centuries, traditional Greek institutions—especially Greek language and writing—survived many political changes and much cultural assimilation, providing a common basis of engagement in a long zone stretching from the Mediterranean to South Asia.

Hellenistic influences were even more pronounced in the regimes that succeeded Seleucid control in central Asia in the late third century BCE. The Seleucid state had taken over the entirety of the former Persian Empire, including its central Asian and South Asian territory. The Hellenistic kingdom of **Bactria** broke away from the Seleucids around 200 BCE to establish a strong state that included the Gandhara region in modern Pakistan. As Mauryan power receded from the northwestern part of India, the Bactrian rulers extended their conquests into this area. Because the cities that the Bactrian Greeks founded included many Indian residents, they have been called "Indo-Greek." Those in Gandhara incorporated familiar features of the Greek polis, but inhabitants still revered Indian gods and goddesses.

Hellenistic Bactria served as a bridge between South Asia and the Greek world of the Mediterranean. Among the goods that the Bactrians sent west were elephants, which were vital to the Greek armies there. Not only did the Bactrian Greeks revive the cities in India left by Alexander, but they also founded new Hellenistic cities in the Gandhara region. The Greek king Demetrius, who invaded India around 200 BCE, entrusted the extension of his empire in the northern region of India to his generals, many of whom became independent rulers after his death. Sanskrit literature refers to these Greek rulers as the Yavana kings—a word derived from "Ionia," a region whose name applied to all those who spoke Greek or came from the Mediterranean.

Aï Khanoum, on the Oxus River (now the Amu) in present-day Afghanistan, was the site of an administrative center, possibly the capital of the Bactrian

Bactria
(c. 250–50 BCE) Hellenistic kingdom in Gandhara region (modern Pakistan) that became an independent state around 200 BCE, with a major city at Aï Khanoum. Its people and culture are sometimes called "Indo-Greek" because of the blending of Indian and Greek populations and ideas.

state. Unearthed by archaeologists in the 1960s, Aï Khanoum had avoided the devastations that befell so many other Hellenistic cities in this region. Greek-style architecture and inscriptions indicate that the original residents of Aï Khanoum were soldiers from Greece. Following the typical pattern, they married local women and established the basic institutions of a Greek polis. Aï Khanoum's characteristic Greek structures included a palace complex, a gymnasium, a theater, an arsenal, several temples, and elite residences. Featuring marble columns with Corinthian capitals, the palace contained an administrative section, storage rooms, and a library. A main road divided the city into lower and higher parts, with the main religious buildings located in the lower city. Though far from Greece, the elite Greek residents read poetry and philosophy and staged Greek dramas in the theater. Grape cultivation supported a wine festival associated with the god Dionysus. The remains of various statues indicate that the residents not only revered the Greek deity Athena and the demigod Heracles but also paid homage to the Persian Zoroastrian religion.

Three Coins *Top:* Wearing an elephant cap, Demetrius of Bactria titled himself the king of Indians as well as Greeks. On the other side of the coin is Hercules. *Middle:* The king Menander is remembered by Buddhists for his curiosity about their theology. His image appears on one side of the coin with a Greek legend of his name and title. On the other side, Athena is surrounded by Kharosthi script, an Indian type of writing. *Bottom:* The Scythian king Maues used Greek to assert his position as "King of Kings" on one side of his coin. On the other side, the goddess Nike is surrounded by Kharosthi letters.

Perhaps the ruler most adept at mingling Greek and Indian influences was Menander (also known as Milinda), the best-known Yavana/Hellenistic city-state king of the mid-second century BCE. Using images and legends on coins to promote both traditions among his subjects, Menander claimed legitimacy as an Indian ruler who also cultivated Greek cultural forms. The face of his coins bore his regal image surrounded by the words "King, Savior, Menander," in Greek. The reverse side featured the Greek goddess Athena and the king's title in the local Prakrit language, using Kharosthi script. This mixed Indo-Greek identity was not confined to coins. In his discussions with a Buddhist sage, King Menander debated the nature of the Buddha (was he human or divine?) and showed a keen interest in South Asian religious influences even as he embraced Hellenism. These Indo-Greek legacies persisted long after the Hellenistic regimes collapsed, because they remained essential to communication and trade around the rim of the Indian Ocean.

The Transformation of Buddhism

During this time of political and social change, South Asia also experienced upheavals in the religious sphere, as Hellenism and other east-west connections transformed Buddhism. Impressed by Hellenistic thought, South Asian peoples blended it with their own ethical and religious traditions. Beginning among the Yavana city-states in the northwest, where Buddhism's sway was most pronounced, this blended Buddhism rapidly spread to other regions that were experiencing the same changes. In addition to Hellenism, other layers of influence came together in South Asia through increased seafaring and interactions with nomadic peoples. This cultural fusion profoundly transformed and enriched Buddhism.

Core Objectives

TRACE the spread of Buddhism in this period and **EVALUATE** the forces that influenced its spread.

INDIA AS A SPIRITUAL CROSSROADS

Many land and sea routes now converged in India, rendering the region a melting pot of ideas and institutions. Improved mastery of the monsoon trade winds in this period opened the Indian Ocean to commerce and made India the hub for long-distance ocean traders and travelers. Another major influence on Buddhism was the Kushans, a horse-riding nomadic group who stabilized east-west connectivity through central Eurasia in the first century CE. With Kushan patronage and the thriving commerce their stability brought to the region, Buddhist communities grew so rich that monks began to live in elegant monastic complexes. (We will discuss the Kushans and their role in Silk Road trade later in this chapter.) The center of each monastic community was a stupa, with its Buddhist relics and sculptures depicting the Buddha's life and teachings. Such monasteries provided generously for the monks, furnishing them with halls where they gathered and worshipped and rooms where they meditated and slept. Buddhist monasteries were also open to the public as places for worship.

THE NEW BUDDHISM: THE MAHAYANA SCHOOL

This mixing of new ways—nomadic, Hellenistic, Mesopotamian, and Persian—with traditional Buddhism produced a spiritual and religious synthesis: **Mahayana** ("Great Vehicle") **Buddhism**. In the first two centuries of the

Mahayana Buddhism
"Great Vehicle" Buddhism; an accessible form of Buddhism that spread along the Silk Roads and included in its theology a divine Buddha as well as bodhisattvas.

Buddhist Cave Temple at Ajanta Buddhists excavated cave temples along the trade routes between ports on the west coast of India and places inland. Paintings and sculptures from Ajanta became the models of Buddhist art in central Asia and China.

Common Era, Mahayana Buddhists resolved a centuries-long dispute over whether the Buddha was a god or a wise human. They affirmed that the Buddha was indeed a deity. However, Mahayana Buddhism was accommodating; it offered a spiritual pluralism that incorporated outside influences and positioned Indian believers as a cosmopolitan people.

Mahayana Buddhism appealed especially to foreigners and immigrants who traded or settled in India because it made the Buddha easier to understand. The Buddha's preaching had stressed life's suffering and the renunciation of desire to end suffering and achieve nirvana. Newcomers to the region and to Buddhism—such as migrants or traders—saw no attraction in a belief that life consisted of painful cycles of birth, growth, death, and rebirth. This sharp dichotomy between a real world of hardship and the Buddha's abstract world of nirvana gave way to the Mahayana Buddhists' vision that **bodhisattvas**—enlightened demigods, ready to reach nirvana—delayed doing so in order to help others attain it. Early Mahayana texts, like "The Practice of Perfect Wisdom," describe in detail the characteristics of bodhisattvas. These bodhisattvas prepared spiritual halfway points to welcome deceased devotees not yet ready to release their desires and enter nirvana. The universe of the afterlife in **Mahayana Buddhism** presented an array of alternatives to the harsh real existence of worldly living. With its bodhisattvas, Mahayana Buddhism enabled all individuals—the poor and powerless as well as the rich and powerful—to move from a life of suffering into a happy existence.

bodhisattvas
In Mahayana Buddhism, enlightened beings who have earned nirvana but remain in this world to help others reach it.

NEW IMAGES OF THE BUDDHA IN LITERATURE AND ART

Just as Buddhism absorbed outside influences and became more appealing, it also inspired literature and art that appealed to diverse peoples. A new genre of literature dealing with the Buddha and the bodhisattvas emerged. Buddhist texts written in Sanskrit disseminated the life of the Buddha and his message far and wide, reaching far corners of Asia. Aśvaghosa (c. 80–c. 150 CE), a great Buddhist thinker, wrote a biography of the Buddha, which set the Buddha's life story within the commercial urban environment of the Kushan Empire (instead of in the rural Shakya republic in the Himalaya foothills, where he had actually lived). Aśvaghosa's largely fictive version of the Buddha's life story spread rapidly throughout India and beyond, introducing the Buddha and his teachings to many potential converts.

The colorful images of Sanskrit Buddhist texts of the first centuries CE gave rise to a large repertoire of Buddhist sculptural art and drama. On Buddhist stupas and shrines, artisans carved scenes of the Buddha's life, figures of bodhisattvas, and statues of patrons and donors. Fashioned from gray schist rock, these Buddhist sculptures from the Kushan territory (modern Pakistan and northwest region of India), follow what is called the **Gandharan style**. Those from the central region of India, created mainly from local red sandstone, follow what is called Mathuran style. Gandharan Buddhist art shows strong Greek and Roman influences, whereas the Mathuran style evolved from the carved idols of South Asian folk gods and goddesses.

Despite their stylistic differences, the schools shared themes and cultural elements. Inspired by Hellenistic art and religious tradition, both took the bold step of sculpting the Buddha and bodhisattvas in realistic human form, rather than symbolic form (such as a bodhi tree, which symbolizes the Buddha's enlightenment). Though the Buddha wore no decorations because he had cut off all links to the world, bodhisattvas were dressed as princes because they were still in this world, generously helping others. What was important was bringing the symbolic world of Buddhism closer to the people.

Stupa Staircase The risers from the staircase of a large stupa in the Gandhara region display scenes from Buddhist stories. The upper one shows men in nomads' clothing playing music, including the Greek-style lyre. On the middle and lower ones, men and women in Greek clothing drink and make merry. The pictures are Buddhist versions of performances in a Greek theater.

Gandharan style

Style of artwork, especially statuary, originating in the Gandharan region of modern Pakistan, that blends Hellenistic artistic influences with Buddhist stylistic features and subjects.

Buddhas Greco-Roman influence on the iconography of the Buddha was probably responsible for the Gandharan-style attire and facial expression of Buddhas and bodhisattvas. The seated Buddha (*left*) was crafted from bronze and, with its sun-like crown, looks a lot like Hellenistic images of Helios or Apollo. The Mathuran Buddha of the later Gupta period (*right*), carved from red sandstone, wears a robe so transparent that the artist must have had very fine silk in mind when sculpting it.

Buddhist art reflected a spiritual system that appealed to people of diverse cultural backgrounds. Consider the clothes of the patron figures. For male and female figures alike, the garments were simple and well adapted to tropical climates. Those indigenous to the semitropical land had nude upper bodies and a wrapping like the modern *dhoti*, or loincloth, on their lower bodies. Jewelry adorned their headdresses and bodies. By contrast, the nomadic patron figures wore traditional cone-shaped leather hats, knee-length robes, trousers, and boots. Figures with Greek clothing demonstrate continuing Hellenistic influence. The jumble of clothing styles illustrates that Buddhist devotees could share a faith while retaining their ethnic or regional differences.

The Formation of the Silk Roads

Core Objectives

TRACE the early routes of the "Silk Roads" and **ASSESS** their importance in connecting Afro-Eurasia by land and sea.

Although the Silk Roads were not among human history's more trafficked routes, they thoroughly altered history's course because the travelers along them spread their cultures everywhere they stepped. (See Map 6.2.) The Silk Roads were not straight and paved like the Appian Way in the Roman Empire. They were not human made but entirely natural, traversing mountain passes, valleys, and desert oases—and mapped for the first time only in the twentieth century. Often, they were no more than footpaths. Travelers wishing to journey through remote regions were compelled to hire guides.

In the first century BCE, trade routes along these footpaths and passes stretching from China to central Asia and westward had merged into one big intertwined series of routes famously referred to as the **Silk Roads**, even though caravans transported many other precious commodities, such as incense, gemstones, and metals. The first use of the term by modern Europeans occurred when a German traveler and geographer, Baron Ferdinand von Richthofen, entered the term on a map in 1877. But long before that, Roman writers knew the importance of these routes for bringing silk from the east. Most of the trade along the routes took place over short distances and involved barter. Traders traveled only segments of the routes, passing their goods on to others who took them farther along the road and, in turn, passed them on again. The Silk Roads owed much to earlier overland routes through which merchants exchanged frankincense and myrrh from the Arabian Peninsula for copper, tin, iron, gemstones, and textiles. Even so, silk was the routes' most expensive and prized commodity, and hence they are deserving of their present name. The Silk Roads, in addition, were routes through which Buddhists, Zoroastrians, Syrian Christians, and later on Muslims spread their religions eastward, translating their scriptures and modifying their beliefs as believers moved from one culture to another.

The effects of these long-distance exchanges altered the political geography of Afro-Eurasia. Egypt and Mesopotamia faded as sources of innovation and knowledge, becoming instead crossroads for peoples on either side of them. The former borderlands emerged as new imperial centers. What we now call the Middle East literally became a commercial middle ground between the Mediterranean and India. East Asia, principally China, finally connected indirectly with the Mediterranean via central and South Asia. Through China, whose traders reached Bali and other islands now in Indonesia, connections developed with Japan, Korea, and Southeast Asia. China, insulated from the west by the Himalayas and the Pamir Mountains, remained politically and culturally a mysterious land to those from the Mediterranean. Yet products made from silk revealed to the Greeks and Romans that an advanced society lay far to the east.

NOMADS AND TRADE ROUTES

The horse-riding nomads of Inner Eurasia made long-distance trade possible. For centuries, these scattered nomadic peoples had linked entire regions and facilitated trade and interactions between distant communities. Responding

Silk Roads
More than 5,000 miles of trade routes linking China, central Asia, and the Mediterranean. They were named for the silk famously traded along their land and sea routes, although ideas, people, and many other high-value commodities also moved along their lengths.

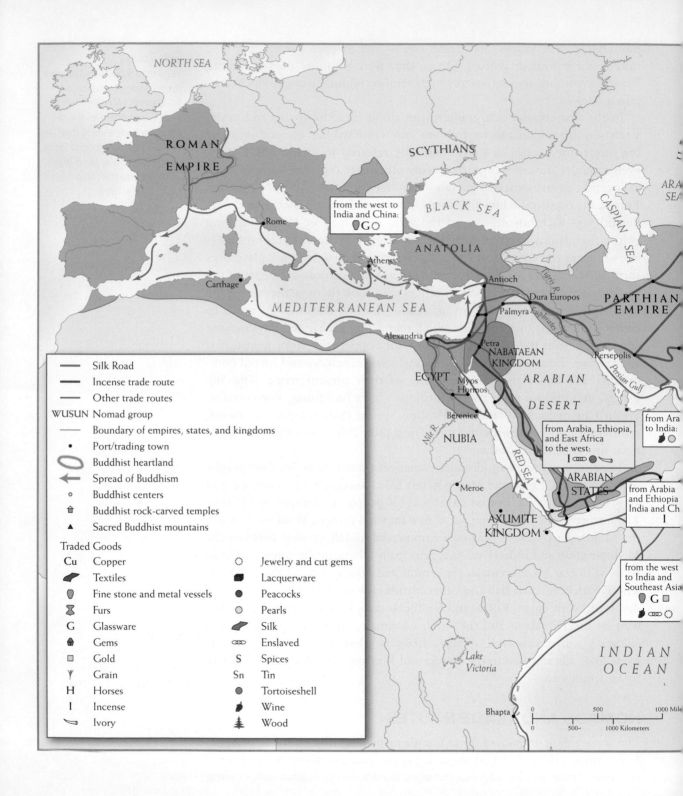

NORTH SEA

ROMAN
EMPIRE

SCYTHIANS

BLACK SEA

from the west to
India and China:
🝙 G ◌

ANATOLIA

ARAL
SEA

CASPIAN
SEA

Rome

Athens

Antioch

Dura Europos

Palmyra

Tigris R.

Euphrates R.

PARTHIAN
EMPIRE

Carthage

MEDITERRANEAN SEA

Alexandria

Petra
NABATAEAN
KINGDOM

Persepolis

Persian Gulf

EGYPT

Myos
Hormos

ARABIAN

from Arabia
to India:

DESERT

Berenice

Nile R.

NUBIA

Meroe

RED SEA

from Arabia, Ethiopia,
and East Africa
to the west:
I ⌘ ● 🝙

ARABIAN
STATES

from Arabia
and Ethiopia
India and Ch

I

AXUMITE
KINGDOM

from the west
to India and
Southeast Asia
🝙 G

Lake
Victoria

INDIAN
OCEAN

Bhapta

Silk Road

Incense trade route

Other trade routes

WUSUN Nomad group

Boundary of empires, states, and kingdoms

• Port/trading town

◯ Buddhist heartland

← Spread of Buddhism

◦ Buddhist centers

🛕 Buddhist rock-carved temples

▲ Sacred Buddhist mountains

Traded Goods

Cu	Copper	◌	Jewelry and cut gems
	Textiles		Lacquerware
	Fine stone and metal vessels	●	Peacocks
	Furs	○	Pearls
G	Glassware		Silk
	Gems	⌘	Enslaved
□	Gold	S	Spices
Y	Grain	Sn	Tin
H	Horses	●	Tortoiseshell
I	Incense		Wine
	Ivory	▲	Wood

0   500   1000 Miles

0   500   1000 Kilometers

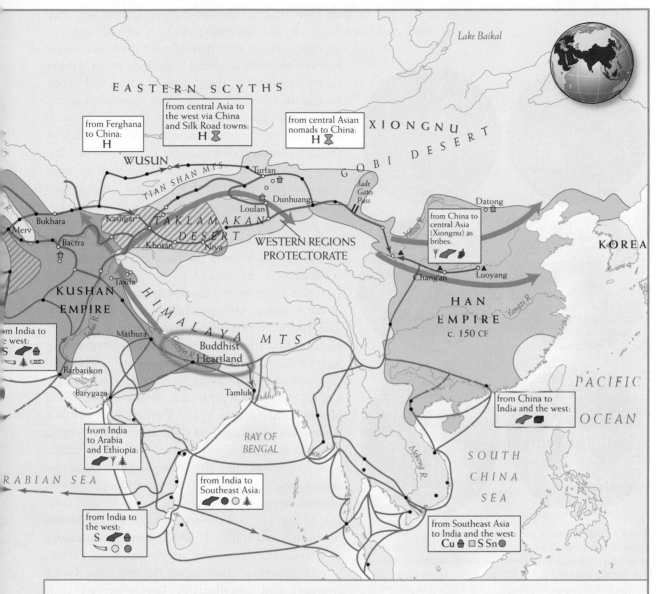

Map 6.2 Afro-Eurasian Trade and the Early Spread of Buddhism, c. 150 CE

During the period covered in this chapter, trade along land and sea routes increasingly brought the Afro-Eurasian world together. The early spread of Mahayana Buddhism happened along some of these same routes. This map highlights important commercial routes linking societies and the incredibly wide range of goods traded, as well as the early spread of Buddhism.

- What types of goods were flowing to the east? What goods flowed to the west? What might these flows suggest about the balance of trade in this period?

- Trace the route a trade good might take from Indonesia to Carthage, and from Luoyang to Rome. How do these routes differ? Based on the regions through which each route goes and the various features along the way (ports, Buddhist sites, and so on), what interactions do you imagine might have taken place along either route?

- Based on the location of various Buddhist sites on this map, how were Buddhism and trade interrelated?

Three Kushan Coins The blending of multiple religions into empires that were situated on trade routes is demonstrated on Kushan coinage, which includes a wide variety of deities over time. Kanishka I (r. 127–150 CE), who helped foster the spread of Mahayana Buddhism on the Silk Roads, minted coinage with an image of himself sacrificing at an altar on one side and the Buddha on the reverse (*top*). The same king also minted coins with his image encircled with the words "King of Kings" in Greek script on one side and the Greek sun god, Helios, recognizable by the radiate diadem, on the reverse (*middle*). Kanishka II, who ruled over the Kushans in the early third century CE, minted coins featuring the Hindu god Shiva with his bull, Nandi (horned head peeking out from behind Shiva's right leg), on the reverse (*bottom*). The simultaneous commerce of ideas and goods is easy to imagine given that the imagery on coins that facilitated the exchange reflected a range of gods.

to the drying out of their homelands in the second millennium BCE, they moved southward (see Chapter 3). Moving from place to place and maintaining close contact with their animals, the nomads were exposed to—and acquired resistance to—a greater variety of microbes than settled peoples did. Their relative immunity to disease made them ideal agents for linking distant settled communities. Nomads also raced into political vacuums and installed new regimes that linked northwest China and the Iranian plateau. Among the most important of these nomadic peoples were the Xiongnu (also spelled "Hsiung-nu") pastoralists, originally from the eastern part of the Asian steppe in modern Mongolia. By the third century BCE, their mastery of bronze technology made them the most powerful nomadic community in the area.

When Xiongnu power waned, a new empire, that of the Kushans, arose in their place around 50 CE. The Yuezhi, a nomadic group to the west of the Qin, unified the region's tribes, migrated southwestward, and established this Kushan Empire in Afghanistan and the Indus River basin. The Kushans' empire embraced a large and diverse territory and played a critical role in the formation of the Silk Roads. The Kushans had been an illiterate people, but they adopted Greek as their official language. Kushan coinage, like the Indo-Greek coinage discussed earlier, blended Greek and Indian elements. Mediterranean traders arriving in the Kushan markets to purchase silks from China, as well as Indian gemstones and spices, conducted their transactions in Greek. The coins they used—struck to Roman weight standards (themselves derived from Greek coinage) and inscribed in Greek—served their needs perfectly.

The Kushans also courted the local population by patronizing local religious cults. In Bactria, where they encountered the shrines of many different gods, the Kushan kings had their coins cast with images of various deities. They also donated generously to shrines of Zoroastrian, Vedic, and Buddhist cults. Wealth flowed into religious institutions, especially Buddhist monasteries. Under the Kushans, Buddhist monasteries were cosmopolitan organizations where Greco-Roman, Indic, and steppe nomadic cultures blended together.

Kushan rule stabilized the trading routes through central Asia that stretched from the steppes in the east to the Parthian Empire in the west. This territory became a major segment of the Silk Roads.

CARAVAN CITIES: SPICES AND TEXTILES

As nomads moved southwestward, they produced a new kind of commercial hub: **caravan cities**. Established at strategic locations (often at the edges of deserts or in oases or at the end points of major trade arteries), these cities became places where vast trading groups assembled before beginning their arduous journeys. Some caravan cities originating as Greek garrison towns became centers of Hellenistic culture, displaying such staples of the polis as public theaters. Caravan cities were among the most spectacular and resplendent urban centers of this era.

One of the most striking of these caravan cities was the Nabatean capital at Petra. The Nabateans were an Arabic-speaking people who eked out a living, primarily as sheepherders, in the Sinai Desert and the northwestern Arabian Peninsula. They also facilitated the movement of frankincense, myrrh, and other spices along the route—sometimes called the Incense or Spice Road—linking the Arabian Peninsula and Indian Ocean with the Mediterranean, where Greeks and Romans used these goods to make perfumes and incense. Because the Greeks and later the Romans needed large quantities of incense to burn in worshipping their gods, the trade passing through this region was extremely lucrative. Although originating in Nabatean herders' practice of carving shelters and cisterns for catching rainwater out of the solid stone of the forbidding landscape, the magnificent "Rock City" of Petra (*petros* in Greek means "rock") was made possible by the wealth accumulated from the spice trade. Houses, shrines, tombs, and even the vast theater—carved entirely from the sandstone terrain to seat 6,000 to 10,000 spectators—reflected Hellenistic influences. Petra's power and wealth lasted from the mid-second century BCE to the early second century CE. The caravan traders, the ruling elite of the rock city, controlled the supply of spices and fragrances from Arabia and India to the ever-expanding Roman Empire. Nabatean traders based in Petra traveled throughout the eastern Mediterranean, erecting temples wherever they established trading communities.

With Petra's decline during the Roman period, Palmyra became the most important caravan city at the western end of the Silk Roads. Rich citizens of Rome relied on the Palmyran traders to procure luxury goods for them, importing Chinese silks for women's clothing and incense for religious rituals, as well as gemstones, pearls, and many other precious items. Palmyran traders handled non-silken textiles as well, including cotton from India and

caravan cities
Cities (like Petra and Palmyra) that were located along land routes of the Silk Roads and served as hubs of commerce and cultural exchange between travelers and merchants participating in long-distance trade.

Palmyran Tomb Sculpture This tombstone relief sculpture shows a wealthy young Palmyran attended by a servant—probably an enslaved household worker. Palmyra was at the crossroads of the major cultural influences traversing Southwest Asia at the time. The style of the clothing—the flowing pants and top—and the couch and pillows reflect the trading contacts of the Palmyran elite, in this case with India to the east. The hairstyle and mode of self-presentation signal influences from the Mediterranean to the west.

cashmere wool from Kashmir or the nearby central Asian highlands. Administered by the chiefs of local tribes, Palmyra maintained considerable autonomy even under formal Roman control. Although the Palmyrans used a Semitic dialect in daily life, for state affairs and business they used Greek, a reminder of the continuing influence of Hellenism. Their merchants had learned Greek when the region came under Seleucid rule, and it remained useful when doing business with caravans from afar, long after the political influences of Hellenism had waned.

Palmyrans built a splendid marble city in the desert. A colonnade, theater, senate house, agora, and major temples formed the metropolitan area. Complexes of hostels, storage houses, offices, and temples served the needs of traders who passed through. The Palmyrans worshiped many deities, both local and Greek, and seemed concerned about their own afterlife. Like Petra, Palmyra had a cemetery as big as its residential area, with marble sculptures on the tombs depicting city life. Many tombs showed the master or the master and his wife reclining on Greek-style couches, holding drinking goblets. Sculptures of camel caravans and horses tell us that the deceased were caravan traders in this world who anticipated continuing their rewarding occupation in the afterlife.

Caravan cities such as Petra, and later Palmyra, linked the Mediterranean with the silk and incense routes that traversed Afro-Eurasia by land and sea. Goods came into the caravan cities via multiple land routes. One artery stretched from China, then across the Iranian plateau and the Syrian desert to reach the Mediterranean Sea, and another route cut south through modern

Afghanistan, into the Indus Valley, then along India's northwest coast and across the Indian Ocean to the Red Sea.

CHINA AND THE SILK ECONOMY

China's flourishing economy owed much to the fact that Chinese silks were the most sought-after commodity in long-distance trade. As thousands of precious silk bales made their way to Indian, central Asian, and Mediterranean markets, silk became the ultimate prestige commodity of the regions' ruling classes. Over time, the exchange between eastern and western portions of the Silk Roads was increasingly mediated by Persian, Xiongnu, Kushan, and other middlemen at the great oases and trading centers that grew up in central Asia. Local communities took profitable advantage of the silk trade from China based on their increased knowledge and contacts.

Not only was silk China's most valuable export, but it also served as a tool in diplomacy with the nomadic kingdoms on China's western frontiers and as a source of funds for the Chinese armies. The country's rulers used silk to pay off neighboring nomads and borderlanders, buying both horses and peaceful borders with the fabric. During the Zhou dynasty, it had served as a precious medium of exchange and trade.

People valued silk as a material for clothing; as a filament made by spinning the protein fibers extracted from the cocoons of silkworms, it is smooth yet strong. Whereas cloth spun from hemp, flax, and other fibers tends to be rough, silk looks and feels rich. Moreover, it is cool against the skin in hot summers and warm in the winter. Silk also has immense tensile strength, making it useful for bows, lute strings, and fishing lines. Artisans even wove silk into a tight fabric to make light body armor or light bags for transporting liquids (particularly useful for traders crossing arid expanses). Before the Chinese invented paper, silk was a popular writing material that was more durable than bamboo or wood. Texts written on silk often joined other funerary objects in the tombs of aristocratic lords and wealthy individuals.

As the long-distance silk trade grew, commerce within China also expanded. Because of reforms in the Warring States period, economic life in China after 300 BCE centered increasingly on independent farmers producing commercial crops for the marketplaces along land routes as well as rivers, canals, and lakes. As this market economy grew, merchants organized themselves based on family lineages and occupational guilds. Power now shifted away from agrarian elites and into the hands of urban financiers and traders. The traders benefited from the improvement in roads and waterways, which eased the transportation of grain, hides, horses, and silk from the villages to the new towns and cities. Bronze coins of various sizes and shapes, as well as cloth and silk used in barter, spurred long-distance trade. By the second century BCE, wealthy merchants were ennobled as local magnates and wore clothing that

Modern Destruction and Repatriation of Our World Cultural Heritage

From the mid-first millennium BCE, and to some extent for thousands of years prior, traders, soldiers, and others traveled along the land routes connecting Europe and Southwest Asia with central and East Asia. Situated along these timeworn routes, today's Turkey, Syria, Iraq, and Afghanistan were well positioned to become sites of military and cultural conflict. Alexander and his forces, after all, fought the Persians at the Granicus River and Issus in Turkey, and at Gaugamela in Iraq.

Contentious interactions along the routes of what were the ancient Silk Roads have continued to the present day, with sometimes devastating results to our world cultural heritage. In 2001, Taliban fighters trained their artillery on the majestic Bamiyan Buddhas in Afghanistan, obliterating the massive statues that had greeted pilgrims for one and a half millennia. Two years later, observers across the globe watched helplessly as pieces of neighboring Iraq's cultural heritage, including 5,000-year-old artifacts from the world's earliest civilization, were looted from the National Museum of Iraq in Baghdad. More destruction followed in 2015 in Mosul (ancient Nineveh) when Neo-Assyrian statues nearly three millennia old were smashed to the ground. In mid-2015, ISIS (the Islamic State in Iraq and Syria) destroyed many Roman-era buildings in the ancient caravan city of Palmyra, including temples (the Temple of Bel among them), a monumental arch, and the Tower of Elahbel. Meanwhile, U.S. president

Donald Trump drew criticism in early 2020 when he suggested that some of Iran's cultural sites were on a list of possible targets for American military strikes, a threat later walked back by others in his administration.

International law prohibits the intentional targeting of cultural heritage sites. The 1954 Hague Convention for the Protection of Cultural Property in the Event of Armed Conflict was developed in the aftermath of World War II to establish protections for "immovable and movable cultural heritage." The agreement included provisions to catalogue and protect this heritage in peacetime, to avoid directing hostilities toward it in wartime, and even to establish military units whose purpose

is to protect these sites and objects in times of hostility. Thanks to Robert M. Edsel's book *The Monuments Men: Allied Heroes, Nazi Thieves, and the Greatest Treasure Hunt in History* (2009) and the 2014 movie of the same name, many have heard of the pre–Hague Convention teams that searched for art plundered by the Nazis and attempted to preserve historical sites during World War II. Less familiar are the teams of modern-day servicepeople who continue this work. In the aftermath of the looting from the National Museum of Iraq in 2003, Lieutenant Colonel Matthew Bogdanos of the U.S. Marine Corps coordinated a team to track down the missing artifacts, with mixed success. Soon after,

Former Site of the Bamiyan Buddhas A 2019 photograph captures the gaping hole in the cliffside where one of the Bamiyan Buddhas stood for nearly 1,500 years.

Bogdanos worked with the president of the Archaeological Institute of America, Brian Rose, to develop a program to teach U.S. troops how to protect cultural heritage and spot stolen antiquities. Today, teams such as Rekrei (formerly Project Mosul) are attempting to crowdsource the digital preservation of cultural heritage by gathering photographs of at-risk and now-lost artifacts and historical sites. Still other initiatives empower local heritage professionals to do the same.

Two closely related issue are the proliferation of stolen artifacts on the global black market and a resurgence in demands for antiquities taken long ago to be repatriated (returned to their place of origin). In 1970, the United Nations Educational, Scientific, and Cultural Organization (UNESCO) convened in Paris a "Convention on the Means of Prohibiting and Preventing the Illicit Import, Export and Transfer of Ownership of Cultural Property." This agreement aimed to limit the removal of cultural property from its place of origin by banning uncertified imports and exports of such property and by requiring the repatriation of artifacts transferred after 1970. It articulated the international law that enables the prosecution of those who would attempt to sell or buy stolen artifacts.

In the case of antiquities stolen from their home countries before 1970, the best-known example is the fifth-century BCE Parthenon frieze, which was moved to England from the Athenian Acropolis in the early nineteenth century. A centerpiece of the British Museum's collection, the frieze has a home waiting for it in the Acropolis Museum in Athens. Global sentiment has shifted in recent years to favor the return of these antiquities. Priam's treasure (named for a famed king of Troy), excavated from the site of ancient Troy in modern-day Turkey, is a lesser-known example. This cache of objects, including a diadem that was described at the same time as the fabled Jewels of Helen, was transported to Berlin by the German archaeologist Heinrich Schliemann in the late nineteenth century, taken by the Russians in the aftermath of World War II, and resides today in the Pushkin Museum in Moscow. Legal debates rage regarding the rightful ownership of these treasures.

The present realities of destruction and the repatriation efforts raise important questions. Who owns the past, and whose responsibility is it to preserve a global cultural heritage? Such questions are made all the more pressing by the modern conflicts that rage in these same regions today.

Questions for Analysis

- How might the Taliban and ISIS justify their destruction of cultural heritage like the Bamiyan Buddhas and Neo-Assyrian artifacts in Mosul, respectively? To what extent does it reflect a colonialist mindset to suggest their justifications are invalid?
- What efforts have been exerted by the global community to protect and repatriate cultural heritage from along the Silk Roads?
- What do you think should be done about cultural heritage taken from a country prior to the 1970 UNESCO agreement?

Explore Further

1954 Hague Convention for the Protection of Cultural Property in the Event of Armed Conflict, http://www.unesco.org/new/en/culture/themes/armed-conflict-and-heritage/convention-and-protocols/1954-hague-convention/.

al Quntar, Salam, and Brian A. Daniels, "Responses to the Destruction of Syrian Cultural Heritage: A Critical Review of Current Efforts," *International Journal of Islamic Architecture* 5, no. 2 (2016): 381–97.

Bogdanos, Matthew, *Thieves of Baghdad: One Marine's Passion to Recover the World's Greatest Stolen Treasures* (2005).

Convention on the Means of Prohibiting and Preventing the Illicit Import, Export and Transfer of Ownership of Cultural Property 1970 (Paris, November 14, 1970), http://portal.unesco.org/en/ev.php-URL_ID=13039&URL_DO=DO_TOPIC&URL_SECTION=201.html.

Harmanşah, Ömür, "ISIS, Heritage, and the Spectacles of Destruction in the Global Media," *Near Eastern Archaeology* 78, no. 3 (September 2015): 170–77.

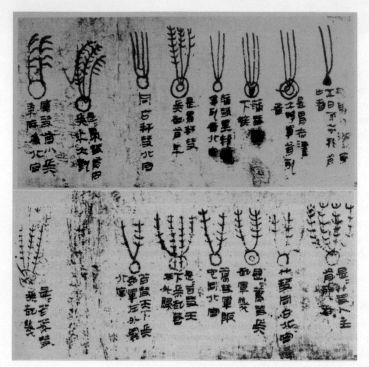

Silk Texts Before the invention of paper, silk was widely used as writing material because it was more mobile and durable than bamboo or wood for correspondence, maps, illustrations, and important texts included as funerary objects in the tombs of aristocrats. The Mawangdui silk texts shown here are from a Hunan tomb that was closed in 168 BCE and opened in 1973.

marked their official status. As commerce further expanded, regional lords opened local customs offices along land routes and waterways to extract a share of the money and products for themselves.

Though China still had little intellectual interaction with the rest of Afro-Eurasia, its long-distance commercial exchanges skyrocketed due to the Silk Road trade. Southern silk was only the first of many Chinese commodities that reached the world beyond the Taklamakan Desert. China also became an export center for lacquer, hemp, and linen. From Sichuan came iron, steel, flint, hard stone, silver, and animals, while jade came from the northwest. At the same time, China was importing Mediterranean, Indian, and central Asian commodities.

Despite its early development of commerce, China still had no major ports that could compare to the caravan cities of Petra and Palmyra. Most cities in the landlocked north were administrative centers where farmers and traders gathered under the regional states' political and military protection. The larger cities had gates that closed between sunset and sunrise; during the night, mounted soldiers patrolled the streets. Newer towns along the southeastern seacoast still looked upriver to trade with inland agrarian communities, which also produced silk for export. Facilitating oceanic trade became more of a concern for the state during this period, and merchant ships now enjoyed the protection of military boats. However, internal, interregional trade predominated, and it fed into the Silk Roads through decentralized networks.

THE SPREAD OF BUDDHISM ALONG THE TRADE ROUTES

In addition to silk traders, monks traveled along Afro-Eurasian trade arteries to spread the word of new religions. While Christians would later take advantage of these trade routes to spread their faith (see Chapter 8), Buddhism was the chief expansionist faith in this period. Under Kushan patronage during the first centuries CE, Buddhism reached out from India to China and central Asia, following the Silk Roads. Monks from the Kushan Empire accompanied traders traveling to China. There they translated Buddhist texts into Chinese and other languages, aided by Chinese converts. Buddhist ideas were slow to gain acceptance everywhere the monks proselytized. It took several centuries, and a new wave of nomadic migrations, for Buddhism to take root in China.

Buddhism fared less well when it followed the commercial arteries westward. The religion never became established on the Iranian plateau and made no substantial headway toward the Mediterranean. The main barrier was Zoroastrianism, which had been a state religion in the Persian Empire during the fifth and fourth centuries BCE (see Chapter 4); by the time Buddhism began to spread, Zoroastrianism had long been established in Iran. Iranian Hellenism had done little to weaken the power of Zoroastrianism, whose adherents formed city-based religious communities affiliated primarily with traders. These Zoroastrian traders continued to adhere to their own faith while traveling along the Silk Roads and did nothing to help Buddhism spread westward.

COMMERCE ON THE RED SEA AND INDIAN OCEAN

Using new navigational techniques and larger ships, seafarers eventually expanded the transport of Silk Road commodities via the Red Sea and the Indian Ocean. Although land routes were the tried-and-true avenues for migrants, traders, and wayfarers, they carried only what could be borne on the backs of humans and animals. Travel by land was slow and travelers were vulnerable to marauders. With time, some risk takers found ways of traversing waterways—eventually on an unprecedented scale and with an ease unimaginable to earlier merchants. These risk takers were Arabs, from the commercial middle ground of the Afro-Eurasian trading system.

Arab traders had long carried such spices as frankincense and myrrh to the Egyptians, who used them in religious and funerary rites, and later to the Greeks and Romans. Metals such as bronze, tin, and iron passed along overland routes from Anatolia, as did gold, silver, and chlorite from the Iranian plateau. Gold, ivory, and other goods from the northern part of India passed through Taxila (the capital of Gandhara) and the Hindu Kush Mountains into Persia as early as the sixth century BCE. Following the expansion of the Hellenistic world, however, ships increasingly conducted long-distance trade. Mastering the monsoons over time, they sailed down the Red Sea and across the Indian Ocean as they carried goods between the tip of the Arabian Peninsula and the ports of the Indian landmass.

Arab seafarers led the way into the Indian Ocean, forging links that joined East Africa, the eastern Mediterranean, and the Arabian Peninsula with India, Southeast Asia, and East Asia. Such voyages involved longer stays at sea and were far more dangerous than sailing in the Mediterranean. Yet, by the first century CE, Arab and Indian sailors were transporting Chinese silks, central Asian furs, and fragrances from Himalayan trees across the Indian Ocean. The city of Alexandria in Egypt soon emerged as a key transit point between periplus

"Sailing around" manual that preserved firsthand knowledge of navigation strategies and trading advice.

the Mediterranean Sea and the Indian Ocean. Boats carried Mediterranean exports of olives and olive oil, wine, drinking vessels, glassware, linen and wool textiles, and red coral up the Nile, stopping at Koptos and other port cities, from which camel caravans took the goods to ports on the Red Sea. For centuries, Mediterranean merchants had considered the Arabian Peninsula to be the end of the Spice Roads. But after Alexander's expedition and the establishment of colonies between Egypt and Afghanistan, they began to value the wealth and opportunities that lay along the shores of the Indian Ocean.

Arab sailors who ventured into the Indian Ocean benefited from new navigational techniques, especially celestial bearings (using the position of the stars to determine the position of the ship and the direction to sail). They used large ships called dhows, whose sails were rigged to easily capture the wind; these forerunners of modern cargo vessels were capable of long hauls in rough waters. Beginning about 120 BCE, mariners came to understand the seasonal rain-filled monsoon winds, which blow from the southwest between October and April and then from the northeast between April and October—knowledge that propelled the maritime trade connecting the Mediterranean with the Indian Ocean.

Mariners accumulated the new sailing knowledge in books—each called a **periplus** ("sailing around")—in which sea captains recorded the landing spots and ports between their destinations, as well as their precious cargoes. The *Periplus Maris Erythraei*, or *Periplus of the Red Sea*, was one such first-century BCE handbook. It offered advice to merchants traveling and trading along two major, connected routes: one on the Red Sea along the coastline of Egypt and the other on the Arabian Sea heading eastward to India. The author demonstrates keen observation and navigational skill in cataloguing the navigable routes, the marketable goods at each port, and anthropological insights on the inhabitants of the far-flung regions visited. The revolution in sailing techniques, like celestial bearing and the dhows, combined with practical knowledge, like that contained in the *Periplus Maris Erythraei*, dramatically reduced the cost of long-distance shipping and multiplied the ports of call around large bodies of water. Some historians have argued that there were now two sets of Silk Roads: one by land and one by sea.

Conclusion

Alexander's territorial gains were awesome in their scale, but his empire was as transitory as it was huge. Though it crumbled upon his death, Alexander's conquest had effects more profound than those of any military or political regime before. Alexander's armies ushered in an age of thinking and practices that transformed Greek achievements into a common culture—Hellenism—whose influences, both direct and indirect, touched far-flung societies for centuries thereafter.

Hellenism offered a common language, both literally and figuratively, that linked culture, institutions, and trade. However, many Greek-speaking peoples and their descendants in parts of central and Southwest Asia integrated local cultural practices with their own ways, creating diverse and rich cultures. Thus, the influences of culture flowed both ways. The economic story is equally complex. Following pathways forged by previous empires and kingdoms, Alexander's successors strengthened and expanded existing trade routes and centers of commercial activity, which ultimately led to the creation of the Silk Roads.

Although the effects of this Hellenistic age lasted longer than most cultural systems and had a wider appeal than previous philosophical and spiritual ideas, they did not overwrite everything that came before. Some, like the Jewish people of Judea and Alexandria, either fought against Hellenism with all their might or accommodated to it. Others, like the Romans and Carthaginians, took from the new common culture what they liked and discarded the rest.

In South Asia, the immediate successor to Alexander's military was the Mauryan Empire, which established its dominion over much of South Asia and even some of central Asia for close to a century and a half. Once Mauryan control receded, South Asia was opened up even more than before to currents moving swiftly across Afro-Eurasia, including the institutions and cultures of steppe nomads, seafarers, and Hellenists. The most telling South Asian responses occurred in the realm of spiritual and ethical norms, where Buddhist doctrines began to evolve toward a full-fledged world religious system.

Greater political integration helped fashion highways for commerce and enabled the spread of Buddhism. Nomads, like the Kushans, left their steppe lands and exchanged wares across great distances. As they found greater opportunities for business, their trade routes shifted farther south, radiating out of the oases of central Asia. Eventually merchants, rather than the trading nomads, seized the opportunities provided by new technologies, especially in sailing and navigation, and by thriving caravan cities. These commercial transformations connected distant parts of Afro-Eurasia. The Silk Roads and new sea-lanes connected ports and caravan cities from North Africa to South China, created new social classes, produced new urban settings, supported powerful new polities, and transported Hellenism and Buddhism well beyond their points of origin.

Focus On
The Creation of the Silk Roads and the Beginnings of Buddhism

The Mediterranean World

- The spread of Hellenism around the Mediterranean via Alexander's conquests and his successor kingdoms leads to a common language, cosmopolitan cities, new types of philosophy and religion, plantation slavery, and money-based economies.

Central and South Asia

- The Mauryan Empire, of Chandragupta and his grandson Aśoka, integrates the northern half of India in the aftermath of Alexander's withdrawal from the region.

- The Bactrian kingdom and Kushan Empire further solidify the spread of Hellenism into central Asia.

The Transformation of Buddhism

- The combined influences of Hellenism, Aśoka's adoption of the Buddhist faith, nomadism, and Indian Ocean seafaring transform Buddhism into a world religion.

Formation of Silk Roads

- Nomadic warriors from central Asia complete the final links of the overland Silk Roads, strengthening the ties that join peoples across Afro-Eurasia.

- Overland traders carry spices, transport precious metals, and convey Buddhist thought along the Silk Roads into China.

- Seafaring traders use new navigation techniques and larger ships called dhows to expand the transport of Silk Road commodities to the Mediterranean world via the Indian Ocean.

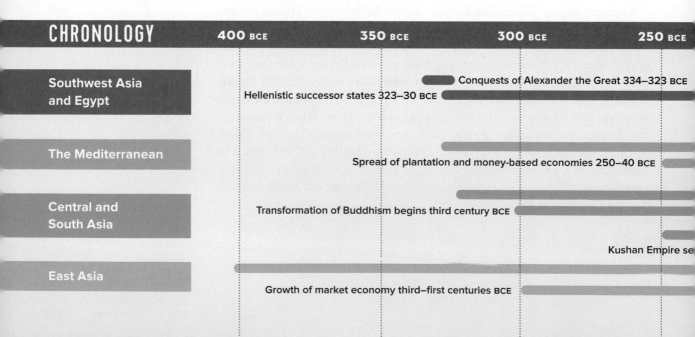

CHRONOLOGY	400 BCE	350 BCE	300 BCE	250 BCE
Southwest Asia and Egypt			Conquests of Alexander the Great 334–323 BCE	
	Hellenistic successor states 323–30 BCE			
The Mediterranean				
		Spread of plantation and money-based economies 250–40 BCE		
Central and South Asia		Transformation of Buddhism begins third century BCE		
				Kushan Empire se
East Asia				
		Growth of market economy third–first centuries BCE		

THINKING ABOUT GLOBAL CONNECTIONS

- **Thinking about Crossing Borders and Shrinking the Afro-Eurasian World** Alexander's conquests and the resulting Hellenistic kingdoms of his successors brought about a never-before-seen cultural unity across huge swaths of Afro-Eurasia. To what extent was this cultural diffusion—comparable in some ways to the globalization or "Americanization" of culture around the world in modern times—a positive development? In what ways might it have been seen by those living through it as a negative development?

- **Thinking about Transformation & Conflict and Shrinking the Afro-Eurasian World** Alexander and his successors brought about unity initially by brutal conquest, then later through diplomatic strategies and the spread of Hellenistic ideas. Likewise, as the conquest of Kalinga demonstrated, Aśoka brutally conquered territories before his change of heart and promotion of *dhamma*. Compare and contrast the role of military conflict and cultural movements (like Hellenism and *dhamma*) in bringing unity to the Hellenistic world and South Asia.

- **Thinking about Worlds Together, Worlds Apart and Shrinking the Afro-Eurasian World** The long-distance trade routes known as the Silk Roads, and sometimes the Incense Roads, brought intensified interactions among societies across Afro-Eurasia in the last centuries BCE. Which societies were closely involved in this exchange? Which appear to have been less involved? What accounts for these regions' involvement, or lack thereof, in Silk Road exchange?

Key Terms

Bactria p. 283	cosmopolitans p. 272	*Koine* Greek p. 272	*periplus* p. 300
bodhisattvas p. 286	Gandharan style p. 287	Mahayana Buddhism p. 285	Silk Roads p. 289
caravan cities p. 293	Hellenism p. 271	Mauryan Empire p. 280	

 Go to INQUIZITIVE to see what you've learned—and learn what you've missed—with personalized feedback along the way.

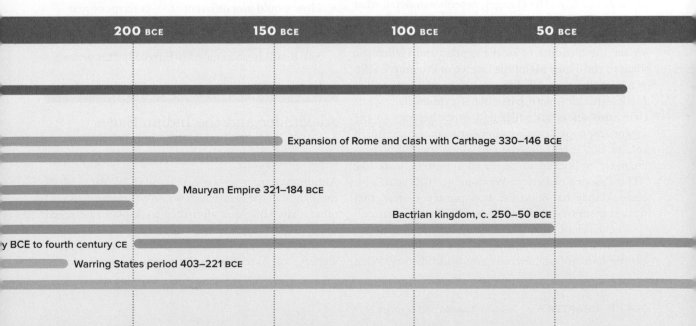

200 BCE   150 BCE   100 BCE   50 BCE

Expansion of Rome and clash with Carthage 330–146 BCE

Mauryan Empire 321–184 BCE

Bactrian kingdom, c. 250–50 BCE

y BCE to fourth century CE

Warring States period 403–221 BCE

Global Themes and Sources

Exploring Connectivity on the Silk Roads

In the aftermath of Alexander's conquests, Hellenistic successor states flourished in western Afro-Eurasia, Indo-Greek states like Bactria reigned in central Eurasia, the Mauryans developed the first "Indian" empire in South Asia, and a web of trade routes through each of these regions joined together to form the Silk Roads. Two powerful movements, Hellenism and Buddhism, thrived as a result of this connectivity and consolidation.

The sources in this section offer a glimpse into this world newly connected through expansive conquest and thickening exchange routes. While Arrian's *Anabasis* emphasizes Alexander's military campaigns as he marched his troops as far as the Ganges River, Arrian also includes in his narrative a number of nonmilitaristic encounters, such as Alexander and his Macedonian forces' contacts with Indian philosophers (which occurred around 325 BCE). The relationship between military conquest and the spread of ideas is also explored in Aśoka's Kalinga Edict (261 BCE). Aśoka, who ruled over an expanding Mauryan Empire in India two generations after Alexander had turned back from the Ganges, describes in detail what he refers to as "conquest through Dharma" when he converts to Buddhism. Just over seventy years later, we see the blending of local Egyptian and Hellenistic ideas in the Third Memphis Decree of Ptolemy V (196 BCE). In this text, local Egyptian priests honor their Hellenistic king with particular Egyptian flair, while that king offers tax relief and other benefits to the Egyptian peoples over whom he rules in the aftermath of a revolt. Farther to the east along the Silk Roads, changes in Buddhism begin to appear in texts like "The Practice of Perfect Wisdom" (c. 100 BCE). This early Mahayana Buddhist text preserves ideas that were transmitted and shaped by Silk Road exchange.

The level of connectivity required to investigate cause-and-effect relationships across far-flung regions can be hard to establish in early world history. What is particularly striking about the closing centuries of the first millennium BCE is that military conquest by Alexander, his successors, and Aśoka; the establishment of realms like the Bactrian kingdom and the Kushan Empire; and Silk Road exchange all bring a new degree of sustained connectivity that allows us to explore causality across regions. With empires and kingdoms from the Mediterranean to East Asia now linked to varying degrees by Silk Road exchange, we can begin to explore the direct effects of that connectivity, namely the spread of ideas like Hellenism and Buddhism.

Analyzing the Causes and Effects of Connectivity on the Silk Roads

- What evidence do you see for conquest and Silk Road connectivity in these texts?

- What evidence do you see for the effects (both short- and long-term) of conquests and Silk Roads, especially with respect to the spread of Hellenism and Buddhism?

- How would you differentiate—in terms of geographic scope, direction, magnitude, effect, and other factors—the role of conquest and the role of Silk Roads in shaping Afro-Eurasia in this period?

PRIMARY SOURCE 6.1

Alexander and the Indian Sages (c. 325 BCE), from *Anabasis of Alexander* (second century CE), Arrian

Although Arrian wrote his account of Alexander's campaigns in the east (which occurred around 325 BCE) more than 400 years after they took place, he relied on firsthand accounts from Alexander's Companions in order to compose his narrative. For this particular vignette of Alexander and the Indian sages, Arrian drew on the writings of Nearchus, who is mentioned at the end of this passage (7.3.6). Nearchus was a naval officer in Alexander's army who was famous for sailing from the Indus River to the Persian Gulf and for his composition of a text in which he recorded his firsthand knowledge of the region. In this particular passage, we can observe the ways that exploration and military expansion led to increased interaction between the peoples and ideas of the Mediterranean and the Indus region.

....

- What does the text reveal about the ideas of these Indian philosophers?

- How do Alexander and his Companions respond to the sages, to Dandamis, and to Calanus?

- What are the apparent causes for the interaction described here? What are some of the possible effects of this interaction on the Macedonian Greeks and on the Indians?

....

7.1.5 I have always liked the story of the Indian sages, some of whom Alexander chanced to come upon out of doors in a meadow, where they used to meet to discuss philosophy. On the appearance of Alexander and his army, these venerable men stamped with their feet and gave no other sign of interest. Alexander asked them through interpreters what they meant by this odd behavior, and they replied:

7.1.6 "King Alexander, every man can possess only so much of the earth's surface as this we are standing on. You are but human like the rest of us, save that you are always busy and up to no good, travelling so many miles from your home, a nuisance to yourself and to others. Ah well! You will soon be dead, and then you will own just as much of this earth as will suffice to bury you."

7.2.1 Alexander expressed his approval of these sage words; but in point of fact his conduct was always the exact opposite of what he then professed to admire. . . .

7.2.2 In Taxila, once, he met some members of the Indian sect of Wise Men whose practice it is to go naked, and he so much admired their powers of endurance that the fancy took him to have one of them in his personal train. The oldest man among them, whose name was Dandamis (the others were his

pupils), refused either to join Alexander himself or to permit any of his pupils to do so.

7.2.3 "If you, my lord," he is said to have replied, "are the son of God, why—so am I. I want nothing from you, for what I have suffices. I perceive, moreover, that the men you lead get no good from their world-wide wandering over land and sea, and that of their many journeyings there is no end. I desire nothing that you can give me; I fear no exclusion from any blessings which may perhaps be yours.

7.2.4 "India, with the fruits of her soil in due season, is enough for me while I live; and when I die, I shall be rid of my poor body—my unseemly housemate." These words convinced Alexander that Dandamis was, in a true sense, a free man; so he made no attempt to compel him. . . .

7.3.1 [N]o history of Alexander would be complete without the story of Calanus. In India Calanus had never been ill, but when he was living in Persia all strength ultimately left his body. In spite of his enfeebled state he refused to submit to an invalid regimen, and told Alexander that he was content to die as he was, which would be preferable to enduring the misery of being forced to alter his way of life.

7.3.2 Alexander, at some length, tried to talk him out of his obstinacy, but to no purpose; then, convinced that if he were any further opposed he would find one means or another of making away with himself, he yielded to his request, and gave instructions for the building of a funeral pyre. . . . Some say Calanus was escorted to the pyre by a solemn procession—horses, men, soldiers in armour, and people carrying all kinds of precious oils and spices to throw upon the flames; other accounts mention drinking-cups of silver and gold and kingly robes.

7.3.3 He was too ill to walk, and a horse was provided for him; but he was incapable of mounting it, and had to be carried on a litter, upon which he lay with his head wreathed with garlands in the Indian fashion, and singing Indian songs, which his countrymen declare were hymns of praise to their gods.

7.3.4 The horse he was to have ridden was of the royal breed of Nesaea, and before he mounted the pyre he gave it to Lysimachus, one of his pupils in philosophy. . . .

7.3.5 At last he mounted the pyre and with due ceremony laid himself down. All the troops were watching. Alexander could not but feel that there was a sort of indelicacy in witnessing such a spectacle—the man, after all, had been his friend; everyone else, however, felt nothing but astonishment to see Calanus give not the smallest sign of shrinking from the flames.

7.3.6 We read in Nearchus' account of this incident that at the moment the fire was kindled there was, by Alexander's orders, an impressive salute: the bugles sounded, the troops with one accord roared out their battle-cry, and the elephants joined in with their shrill war-trumpetings.

Source: Arrian, *The Campaigns of Alexander*, translated by Aubrey de Sélincourt (New York: Penguin Books, 1981), pp. 349–52.

Source: Arrian, *The Campaigns of Alexander*, translated by Aubrey de Sélincourt (New York: Penguin Books, 1981), pp. 349–52.

PRIMARY SOURCE 6.2

Kalinga Edict (261 BCE), Aśoka

King Aśoka (r. 268–231 BCE) proclaimed his adoption of Buddhism in inscriptions, called rock and pillar edicts, carved in stone throughout his Mauryan Empire in India. Wanting the message to be accessible to as many people as possible, Aśoka posted these inscriptions prominently at multiple sites (many of which, like Kandahar, were situated on the Silk Roads), using several languages (Aramaic, Greek, and Gandhari Prakrit) and different scripts (Aramaic, Greek, and Kharosthi). In the inscription of Edict 13, presented here, Aśoka describes his conversion to Buddhism after his forces brutally slaughtered the people of Kalinga in 261 BCE.

....

- According to this inscription, why does Aśoka adopt the "duties relating to Dharma" after the war in Kalinga?

- What does Aśoka hope will be the long-term effect of his adoption of Buddhism and his posting of these inscriptions? How exactly does Aśoka envision "conquest through Dharma" working?

- What specific claims does Aśoka make about how far his "conquest through Dharma" has spread?

....

The country of the Kalingas was conquered by king Piyadasi, Beloved of the Gods, eight years after his coronation. In this war in Kalinga, men and animals numbering one hundred and fifty thousand were carried away captive from that country, as many as one hundred thousand were killed there in action, and many times that number perished. After that, now that the country of the Kalingas has been conquered, the Beloved of the Gods is devoted to an intense practice of the duties relating to Dharma, to a longing for Dharma and to the inculcation of Dharma among the people. This is due to the repentance of the Beloved of the Gods on having conquered the country of the Kalingas.

Verily the slaughter, death and deportation of men which take place in the course of the conquest of an unconquered country are considered extremely painful and deplorable by the Beloved of the Gods. But what is considered even more deplorable by the Beloved of the Gods is the fact that injury to or slaughter or deportation of the beloved ones falls to the lot of the Brahmanas, the Sramanas, the adherents of other sects and the householders, who live in that country and among whom are established such virtues as obedience to superior personages, obedience to mother and father, obedience to elders and proper courtesy and firm devotion to friends, acquaintances, companions and relatives as well as to servants and the enslaved. And, if misfortune befalls the friends, acquaintances, companions and relatives of persons who are full of affection towards the former, even though they are themselves well provided for, the said misfortune as well becomes an injury to their own selves. In war, this fate is shared by all classes of men and is considered deplorable by the Beloved of the Gods.

Excepting the country of the Yavanas, there is no country where these two classes (the Brahmanas and the Sramanas) do not exist; and there is no place in any country where men are not indeed sincerely devoted to one sect or the other. Therefore, the slaughter, death or deportation of even a hundredth or thousandth part of all those people who were slain or who died or were carried away captive at that time in Kalinga, is now considered very deplorable by the Beloved of the Gods.

Now the Beloved of the Gods thinks that, even if a person should wrong him, the offence would be forgiven if it was possible to forgive it. And the forest-folk who live in the dominions of the Beloved of the Gods, even them he entreats and exhorts in regard to their duty. It is hereby explained to them that, in spite of his repentance, the Beloved of the Gods possesses power enough to punish them for their crimes, so that they should turn from evil ways and would not be killed for their crimes. Verily the Beloved of the Gods desires the following in respect of all creatures: non-injury to them, restraint in dealing with them, and impartiality in the case of crimes committed by them.

So, what is conquest through Dharma is now considered to be the best conquest by the Beloved of the Gods. And such a conquest has been achieved by the Beloved of the Gods not only here in his own dominions but also in the territories bordering on his dominions, as far away as at the distance of six hundred Yojanas, where the Yavana king named Antiyoka [Antiochus II of Syria] is ruling and where, beyond the kingdom of the said Antiyoka, four other kings named Turamaya [Ptolemy II Philadelphus of Egypt], Antikini [Antigonus II Gonatas of Macedon], Maka [Magas of Cyrene], and Alikasundara [Alexander II of Epirus, Greece] are also ruling, and, towards the south, where the Cholas and Pandyas are living as far as Tamraparni. Likewise here in the dominions of His Majesty, the Beloved of the Gods—in the countries of the Yavanas and Kambojas, of the Nabhakas and Nabhapanktis, of the Bhoja-paitryanikas and of the Andhras and Paulindas—everywhere people are conforming to the instructions in Dharma imparted by the Beloved of the Gods.

Even where the envoys of the Beloved of the Gods have not penetrated, there too men have heard of the practices of Dharma and the ordinances issued and the instructions in Dharma imparted by the Beloved of the Gods, and are conforming to Dharma and will continue to conform to it.

So, whatever conquest is achieved in this way, verily that conquest creates an atmosphere of satisfaction everywhere both among the victors and the vanquished. In the conquest through Dharma, satisfaction is derived by both the parties. But that satisfaction is indeed of little consequence. Only happiness of the people in the next world is what is regarded by the Beloved of the Gods as a great thing resulting from such a conquest.

And this record relating to Dharma has been written on stone for the following purpose, that my sons and great-grandsons should not think of a fresh conquest by arms as worth achieving, that they should adopt the policy of forbearance and light punishment towards the vanquished even if they conquer a people by arms, and that they should regard the conquest through Dharma as the true conquest. Such a conquest brings happiness to all concerned both in this world and in the next. And let all their intense joys be what is pleasure associated with Dharma. For this brings happiness in this world as well as in the next.

Source: *Inscriptions of Aśoka*, translated by D. C. Sircar (New Delhi: Publications Division, Ministry of Information and Broadcasting, Government of India, 1967), pp. 57–59.

Third Memphis Decree of Ptolemy V, from the Rosetta Stone (196 BCE)

The Rosetta Stone is widely known as an inscription that was key to the deciphering of hieroglyphs. What is less well known about the Rosetta Stone is what the text of the inscription actually said. The Rosetta Stone recorded a text known as the Third Memphis Decree of Ptolemy V (r. 204–181 BCE), a Hellenistic successor king in Egypt. It was the repeated occurrence of the cartouche containing his title, "Ptolemy, the everliving, the beloved of Ptah," that helped linguists begin to understand how hieroglyphs worked. The text describes the situation after Ptolemy V quashed a revolt against his control.

- **What evidence do you see in this text for Hellenistic influence on Egypt? For Egyptian influence on its Hellenistic king?**

- **What sorts of gifts and allowances does Ptolemy make, both to his own soldiers and to the Egyptian priests and temples?**

- **What would likely be the long-term effects of the cultural blending and Hellenistic rule in Egypt as a result of the specific developments this decree describes?**

1. On the twenty-fourth day of the month Gorpiaios; which correspondeth to the twenty-fourth day of the fourth month of the season Pert of the inhabitants of Ta-Mert [Egypt], in the twenty-third year of the reign of Horus-Ra the child . . .

2. . . . the King of the South and the North . . . the Son of the Sun, *Ptolemy, the ever-living, the beloved of Ptah* [in cartouche, italicized here to show its recurrence], the god who maketh himself manifest . . .

6. [O]n this day the superintendents of the temples, and the servants of the god, and those who are over the secret things of the god, and the libationers [who] go into the most holy place to array the gods in their apparel,

7. and the scribes of the holy writings, and the sages of the Double House of Life, and the other libationers [who] had come from the sanctuaries of the South and the North to Memphis, on the day of the festival, whereon

8. His Majesty . . . *Ptolemy, the ever-living, the beloved of Ptah* . . . entered into the Sehetch-Chamber, wherein they were wont to assemble, in Makha-Taui [place where Upper and Lower Egypt met], and behold they declared thus:—

9. Inasmuch as the King who is beloved by the gods, *Ptolemy, the ever-living, the beloved of Ptah* . . . hath given things of all kinds in very large quantities unto the lands of Horus and unto all

10. those who dwell in them, and unto each and every one who holdeth any dignity whatsoever in the,—now behold, he is like unto a God . . . and behold, His Majesty

11. possessed a divine heart which was beneficent towards the gods; and he hath given gold in large quantities, and grain in large quantities to the temples and he hath given very many lavish gifts in order to make Ta-Mert [Egypt] prosperous, and to make stable [her] advancement;

12. and he hath given unto the soldiers who are in his august service . . . according to their rank: [and of the taxes] some of them he hath cut off, and some of them [he hath lightened], thus causing the soldiers and those who live in the country to be prosperous

13. under his reign [and as regards the sums which were due to the royal house] from the people of Egypt, and likewise those [which were due] from every one who was in his august service, His Majesty remitted them altogether, howsoever great they were;

14. and he hath forgiven the prisoners who were in prison, and ordered that every one among them should be released from [the punishment] which he had to undergo. And His Majesty made an order saying:—In respect of the things [which are to be given to] the gods, and the money and the

15. grain which are to be given to the temples each year, and all the things [which are to be given to] the gods from the vineyards and from the corn-lands of the nome, all the things which were then due under the Majesty of his holy father

16. shall be allowed to remain [in their amounts] to them as they were then; and he hath ordered:— Behold, the treasury (?) shall not be made more full of contributions by the hands of the priests than it was up to the first year of the reign of His Majesty, his holy father. . . .

22. And His Majesty marched against the town of Shekam, which is in front of (?) the town of Uiset, which was in the possession of the enemy . . .

26. . . . and His Majesty captured the town by assault in a very short time, and he cut to pieces the rebels who were therein, and he made an exceedingly great slaughter among them, even like unto that which Thoth and Horus, the son of Isis and [the son of Osiris], made among those who rebelled against them. . . .

36. . . . And it has entered into the heart(s) of the priests of the temples of the South and of the North, and of each and every temple [that all the honours which are paid] to Ptolemy . . .

38. and to the Saviour-Gods, shall be [greatly increased]; and a statue of . . . *Ptolemy, ever-living, beloved of Ptah* . . . shall be set up [in every temple, in the most prominent place], and it shall be

39. called by his name "Ptolemy, the Saviour of Egypt." . . .

41. . . . [the priests have decreed] that this Decree shall [be inscribed] upon a stele of hard stone in the writing of the words of the gods, and the writing of the books, and in the writing of Haui-Nebui (i.e., Greeks), and it shall be set up in the sanctuaries in the temples which [are called] by his name.

Source: E. A. Wallis Budge, *The Nile, Notes for Travellers in Egypt*, 9th ed. (London: Thos. Cook and Son, 1907), pp. 228–40.

"The Practice of Perfect Wisdom" (c. 100 BCE)

"The Practice of Perfect Wisdom" may date to as early as 100 BCE. The text, which is preserved in the first forty-one verses of a much longer and later Buddhist text called the *Aṣṭasāhasrikā Prajñāpāramitā (Perfection of Wisdom in 8,000 Lines)*, is one of the earliest texts in Mahayana Buddhism. The transmission history of the "Practice of Perfect Wisdom" offers exciting evidence for the movement of Buddhist ideas on the Silk Roads. Scholars have identified an early Gandharan version of the text that was written on birch-bark scrolls in Kharosthi script (one of the scripts of Aśoka's edict in Primary Source 6.2). The text was also preserved in Chinese by Lokaksema, a monk who traveled from Gandhara (in Pakistan) to Luoyang (the Han capital) in the late second century CE. Its verses offer some of the earliest descriptions of what a bodhisattva is.

....

- **What elements of Buddhism do you recognize in this text? How do ideas about suffering and illusion fit in?**
- **What are the traits of a bodhisattva, as outlined in this text?**
- **In what ways does the Mahayana (or "Great Vehicle") Buddhism in this text differ from the basics of the Four Noble Truths and the Eightfold Path to achieve nirvana (according to the earliest form of Buddhism outlined in Chapter 5)? How might Silk Road connections and the transmission of these ideas from India to China have influenced the differences?**

....

[7.] The Bodhisattva, when he comprehends the dharmas [teachings] as he should

Does not retire into Blessed Rest. In wisdom then he dwells.

8. What is this wisdom, whose and whence, he queries,

And then he finds that all these dharmas are entirely empty.

Uncowed and fearless in the face of that discovery

Not far from Bodhi [enlightenment] is that Bodhi-being then.

9. To course in the skandhas [i.e., the five parts that make up a being: form, feeling, perception, conditioning, and consciousness], in form, in feeling, in perception,

Will and so on, and fail to consider them wisely;

Or to imagine these skandhas as being empty;

Means to course in the sign, the track of non-production ignored.

10. But when he does not course in form, in feeling, or perception,

In will or consciousness, but wanders without home,

Remaining unaware of coursing firm in wisdom,

His thoughts on non-production—then the best of all the calming trances cleaves to him.

11. Through that the Bodhisattva now dwells tranquil in himself,

His future Buddhahood assured by antecedent Buddhas.

Whether absorbed in trance, or whether outside it, he minds not.

For of things as they are he knows the essential original nature.

12. Coursing thus he courses in the wisdom of the Sugatas [Fortunate Ones],

And yet he does not apprehend the dharmas in which he courses.

This coursing he wisely knows as a no-coursing,

That is his practice of wisdom, the highest perfection.

13. What exists not, that non-existent the foolish imagine;

Non-existence as well as existence they fashion.

As dharmic facts existence and non-existence are both not real.

A Bodhisattva goes forth when wisely he knows this.

14. If he knows the five skandhas as like an illusion,

But makes not illusion one thing, and the skandhas another;

If, freed from the notion of multiple things, he courses in peace—

Then that is his practice of wisdom, the highest
 perfection.

15. Those with good teachers as well as deep insight,

Cannot be frightened on hearing the Mother's deep
 tenets.

But those with bad teachers, who can be misled by
 others,

Are ruined thereby, as an unbaked pot when in contact with moisture.

16. What is the reason why we speak of
 "Bodhisattvas"?

Desirous to extinguish all attachment, and to cut
 it off,

True non-attachment . . .

"Beings who strive for Bodhi" are they therefore
 called.

17. What is the reason why "Great Beings" are so
 called?

They rise to the highest place above a great number
 of people;

And of a great number of people they cut off mistak-
 en views.

That is why we come to speak of them as "Great
 Beings." . . .

19. This gnosis shows him all beings as like an
 illusion,

Resembling a great crowd of people, conjured up at
 the crossroads,

By a magician, who then cuts off many thousands of
 heads;

He knows this whole living world as a mock show,
 and yet remains without fear.

20. Form, perception, feeling, will and awareness

Are ununited, never bound, cannot be freed.

Uncowed in his thought he marches on to his Bodhi,

That for the highest of men is the best of all armours.

21. What then again is "the vessel that leads to the
 Bodhi"?

Mounted upon it one guides to Nirvana all beings.

Great is that vessel, immense, vast like the vastness of
 space.

Those who travel upon it are carried to safety, delight
 and ease.

22. Thus transcending the world, he eludes our
 apprehensions.

"He goes to Nirvana," but no one can say where he
 went to.

A fire's extinguished, but where, do we ask, has it
 gone to?

Likewise, how can we find him who has found the
 Rest of the Blessed?

23. The Bodhisattva's past, his future and his present
 must elude us,

Time's three dimensions nowhere touch him.

Quite pure he is, free from conditions, unimpeded.

That is his practice of wisdom, the highest
 perfection.

24. Wise Bodhisattvas, coursing thus, reflect on
 non-production,

And yet, while doing so, engender in themselves the
 great compassion,

Which is, however, free from any notion of a
 being.

Thereby they practice wisdom, the highest
 perfection.

25. But when the notion of suffering and beings
 leads him to think:

"Suffering I shall remove, the weal of the world I
 shall work!"

Beings are then imagined, a self is imagined,—

The practice of wisdom, the highest perfection, is
 lacking.

26. He wisely knows that all that lives is unproduced
 as he himself is;

He knows that all that is no more exists than he or
 any beings.

The unproduced and the produced are not
 distinguished,

That is the practice of wisdom, the highest
 perfection.

27. All words for things in use in this world must be
 left behind,

All things produced and made must be transcended—
The deathless, the supreme, incomparable gnosis is
    then won.
That is the sense in which we speak of perfect
    wisdom.
28. When free from doubts the Bodhisattva carries
    on his practice,

As skilled in wisdom he is known to dwell.
All dharmas are not really there, their essential
    original nature is empty.
To comprehend that is the practice of wisdom, per-
    fection supreme.

Source: *The Perfection of Wisdom in Eight Thousand Lines and Its Verse Summary*, translated by Edward Conze (1973; repr., San Francisco: Four Seasons Foundation, 1995), pp. 10–12.

Interpreting Visual Evidence

Coinage

The minting of coins was one of the many ways that rulers asserted their identity and conveyed propaganda about their rule. While minting coins was a statement of political authority, rulers often wanted to suggest not only the new ideals of their rule but also a cultural continuity. They chose for their coins words and images that blended the new with the old and the imported with the local.

The well-preserved gold octadrachm coin pictured below displays the image of Berenice II of Egypt (r. 246–221 BCE), one of the many female Egyptian rulers of this period. The coin's flip side shows a cornucopia brimming with fruit and the words *Berenike Basileia* (Queen Berenice). The next coin shown here was minted by King Menander (r. c. 165–130 BCE), known for his discussions with Indian sages on the nature of the Buddha. Menander stamped his own image on a silver coin, along with his name and his title,

Basileus Soter (King Savior). On the other side of the coin, the Greek goddess Athena is surrounded by an Indian writing known as Kharosthi script.

Several examples of coins from points farther east look a little different than these Hellenistic examples, but express similarly complex messages of identity and continuity. The knife-shaped coin with Chinese characters on it dates to 250–221 BCE and comes from northeastern China. It shows just how diverse coin types could be; even though the practice of government-issued coins was taking hold in many places, there was no one way to mint them. Even within China, coin types varied. The last coin pictured here is a bronze *ban liang* and was minted under the authority of Qin ruler King Huiwen (r. 338–311 BCE), an ancestor of Shi Huangdi, who later established the short-lived Qin dynasty in 221 BCE.

Questions for Analysis

1. Compare these coins with one another. To what extent do you think the "shrinking Afro-Eurasian world," described in this chapter, may have influenced their similarities and differences?

2. What messages might the images and words on the coins have conveyed to those who used them?

3. Coins of high value (like Berenice's gold octadrachm) are usually far better preserved than lower-value coins (like the bronze coin from the Qin dynasty). Why do you think that is the case?

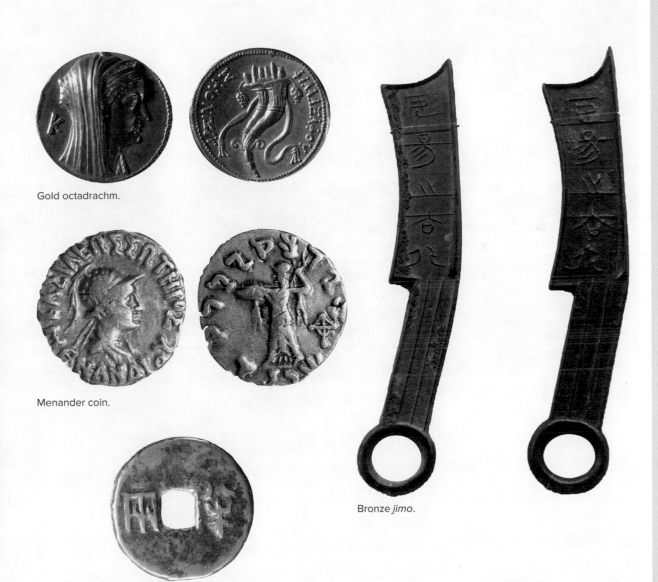

Gold octadrachm.

Menander coin.

Bronze *ban liang*.

Bronze *jimo*.

7

Han Dynasty China and Imperial Rome

300 BCE–300 CE

In third-century BCE China, the Eastern Zhou state of Qin absorbed the remaining Warring States (see Chapter 5) and set the stage for the Han dynasty. The chief minister of the Qin state, Li Si, urged his king to seize the opportunity presented by the disarray of his opponents: by combining his fearsome armies and his own personal virtues, the king could sweep away his rivals as if dusting ashes from a kitchen hearth. "This is the one moment in ten thousand ages," Li Si whispered to the man who would become Qin Shi Huangdi. The king listened carefully. He followed the advice and laid the foundations for a mighty empire. Although Shi Huangdi's Qin Empire collapsed in 207 BCE after a mere two decades, his political innovations set the stage for the much more powerful and longer-lasting Han Empire (206 BCE–220 CE), which became one of the most successful dynasties in Chinese history. Following the Qin model, the Han defeated other regional groups and established a Chinese empire that would last for four centuries.

Chapter Outline

- Globalizing Empires: The Han Dynasty and Imperial Rome
- The Han Dynasty (206 BCE–220 CE)
- The Roman Empire (c. 300 BCE–c. 300 CE)
- Conclusion

Core Objectives

- **IDENTIFY** the features that made Han China and imperial Rome globalizing empires.
- **DESCRIBE** the development of the Han dynasty from its beginnings through the third century CE.
- **EXPLAIN** the process by which Rome transitioned from a minor city-state to a dominating Mediterranean power.
- **COMPARE** Han China with imperial Rome in terms of political authority, economy, cultural developments, and military expansion.

At the other end of Afro-Eurasia, another great state, imperial Rome, also met its rivals in war, emerged victorious, and consolidated its power into a vast empire. The Romans achieved this feat by using violent force on a scale hitherto unseen in their part of the globe. The result was a state of huge size, astonishingly unified and stable. Living in the Roman Empire in the mid-70s CE, Pliny the Elder wrote glowingly about the unity of the imperial Roman state. In his eyes, all the benefits that flowed from Rome's extensive reach derived from the greatness of a peace that joined diverse peoples under one benevolent emperor. In this chapter, we will examine and compare the growth, politics, economies, and societies of the Han and Roman Empires.

Global Storylines

Comparing the Han and Roman Empires

- Flourishing at roughly the same time, Han China and the Roman Empire become powerful and enduring "globalizing empires."

- The Han dynasty, building on Qin foundations, establishes a bureaucratic imperial model and social order in East Asia.

- The Roman Empire becomes a Mediterranean superpower exerting far-reaching political, legal, economic, and cultural influence.

Globalizing Empires: The Han Dynasty and Imperial Rome

The Han and the Roman states became truly **globalizing empires**: they covered immense amounts of territory; included huge, diverse populations; and exerted influence far beyond their own borders. Their major innovation was not that they found new ways to plow resources into big armies and civil bureaucracies or that their rulers gave new justifications for their rule. Rather, what distinguished the Romans and the Han from their predecessors was their commitment to integrating conquered neighbors and rivals into their worlds—by extending laws, offering systems of representation, exporting belief systems, colonizing lands, and promoting trade within and beyond their empires.

Subject peoples became members of empires, not just the vanquished. Those who resisted not only waved away the benefits of living under imperial rule but also became the targets for military retribution.

Even today, geopolitical boundaries bear remarkable resemblances to those defined by these two empires at their peak. These states transcended the limits of previous territorial kingdoms and the first empires by deploying resources in new ways. The leaders of each empire laid out the political and cultural boundaries of regions that we now recognize as "China" and "Christendom."

To be "Han Chinese" meant that elites shared a common written language based on the Confucian classics, which qualified them for public office. It also meant that commoners from all walks of life shared the elites' belief system, which emphasized appropriate decorum and dress for each social level, the view that the agrarian-based Han Empire was a small-scale model of the entire cosmos, and ritual practices associated with ancestor worship. Consistent with Confucian ideals of the previous centuries, the Han practiced filial piety toward their elders, living and dead; for example, family members honored their ancestors with offerings at their tombs. In addition, the Han considered people who lived beyond Han boundaries uncivilized, even if some were ultimately folded into Han rule.

What it meant to be "Roman" changed over time as Rome's imperial reach expanded. In the fifth century BCE, being Roman meant being a citizen of the city of Rome, speaking Latin (the regional language of central Italy), and eating and dressing like Latin-speaking people. Ever important to the Romans was a sense of family, centered on the *domus* (or home), and an ongoing remembering of their ancestors. While wealthy, elite Romans would commission funerary parades to honor their familial dead, Romans of every social class honored their family's dead with graveside offerings of garlands and wine-soaked bread, especially during February's festival of the Parentalia.

THE BIG PICTURE

In what ways were Han China and imperial Rome similar? How were they different? What features made Han China and imperial Rome globalizing empires?

globalizing empires
Empires that cover immense territory; exert significant influence beyond their borders; include large, diverse populations; and work to integrate conquered peoples.

Han Tomb Doors Wealthy Han officials could afford elaborate burials that coincidentally provide much of our evidence for Han material culture, including figurines, vessels of all types, wall paintings, and even silk banners. One feature of these elite Han burials is the ornately carved tomb doors. Close inspection of the detailed imagery reveals robed men (village officials), trees (symbolizing a long-lasting family), flying birds, chariots, and a central monster mask that served as a protective spirit.

By the late second century BCE, the concept of Roman citizenship expanded to include not only citizens of the city but also anyone who had formal membership in the larger territorial state that the Romans were building. By the beginning of the third century CE, being Roman meant simply being a subject of the Roman emperors. This Roman identity became so deeply rooted that when the western parts of the empire disintegrated two centuries later, the inhabitants of the surviving eastern parts—who had no connection with Rome, did not speak Latin, and did not dress or eat like the original Romans—still considered themselves "Romans" in this broader sense.

The two empires differed in their patterns of development, types of public servants, and ideals for the best kind of government. For example, the civilian magistrate and the bureaucrat were typical of the Han Empire, whereas the citizen, the soldier, and the military governor were at the heart of the Roman Empire. In China, dynastic empires fashioned themselves according to the models of past empires. By contrast, Rome began as a collectively ruled city-state and pursued its road to domination as if creating something new. Nonetheless, like the Chinese, Romans were strongly traditional. Both new empires united huge landmasses and extraordinarily diverse populations.

While both China and Rome participated in Silk Road exchange, both economies were primarily agrarian. Yet free peasants worked the land in China, whereas a huge enslaved population worked the fields of the Roman Empire. At its height, the Han Empire included around 59 million inhabitants and covered 3 million square miles in China proper and, for a while, another 1 million square miles in central Asia. Just over a decade after the Han census and far to the west, the emperor Augustus oversaw a census that counted 4,937,000 Roman citizens (free adult men), which likewise amounted to around 60 million people, when women, children, and enslaved people were accounted for. The Roman Empire governed an area nearly as great as that of Han China, especially when counting the almost 1-million-square-mile area of the Mediterranean Sea, which was like a water highway for the Romans in the lands encircling it. An estimated two out of every three human beings on earth now fell directly under the authority of China or Rome. Their imperial control shaped the destiny and identity of the countless millions living within their respective realms.

Both empires left indelible legacies; following their collapses, both survived as models. Successor states in the Mediterranean sought to become the second

Rome, and after the Han dynasty fell, the Chinese people identified themselves and their language simply as "Han." Both empires raised life to a new level of bureaucratic and military complexity and offered a common identity on a grander scale than ever before. It was a vision that would never be lost.

The Han Dynasty (206 BCE–220 CE)

The Han dynasty oversaw an unprecedented blossoming of peace and prosperity in East Asia. Although supporters of the Han dynasty boasted of the regime's imperial uniqueness, in reality it owed much to its predecessor, the Qin state, which contributed vital elements of political unity and economic growth to its more powerful successor regime. (See Map 7.1.) Together, the Qin and Han created the political, social, economic, and cultural foundations that characterized imperial China thereafter.

Core Objectives

DESCRIBE the development of the Han dynasty from its beginnings through the third century CE.

A CRUCIAL FORERUNNER: THE QIN DYNASTY (221–207 BCE)

Although it lasted only fourteen years, the Qin dynasty integrated much of China and made important administrative and economic innovations. The Qin were but one of many militaristic regimes during the Warring States period (c. 403–221 BCE). What enabled the Qin to prevail over rivals was their expansion into the Sichuan region, which was remarkable for its rich mineral resources and fertile soils. There, a merchant class and the silk trade spurred economic growth, and public works fostered increased food production. These strengths enabled the Qin by 221 BCE to defeat the remaining Warring States and unify an empire that covered roughly two-thirds of modern China.

Supported by able ministers and generals, a large conscripted army, and a system of taxation that financed all-out war, the Qin ruler King Zheng assumed the mandate of heaven from the Zhou. Declaring himself **Shi Huangdi**, or "First August Emperor," in 221 BCE, Zheng harkened back to China's great mythical emperors of antiquity. Forgoing the title of king (*wang*), which had been used by leaders of the Zhou and Warring States, Zheng instead took the title of emperor (*di*), a term that had meant "ancestral ruler" for the Shang and Zhou.

Shi Huangdi centralized the administration of the empire. He forced the defeated rulers of the Warring States and their families to move to Xianyang, the Qin capital—where they would be unable to gather rebel armies. The First August Emperor then parceled out the territory of his massive state into thirty-six provinces, called **commanderies** (*jun*). Each commandery had a civilian and a military governor, as well as an imperial inspector. Regional

Shi Huangdi

Title taken by King Zheng in 221 BCE, when he claimed the mandate of heaven and consolidated the Qin dynasty. He is known for his tight centralization of power, including standardizing weights, measures, and writing; constructing roads, canals, and the beginnings of the Great Wall; and preparing a massive tomb for himself filled with an army of terra-cotta warriors.

commanderies

The thirty-six provinces (*jun*) into which Shi Huangdi divided territories. Each commandery had a civil governor, a military governor, and an imperial inspector.

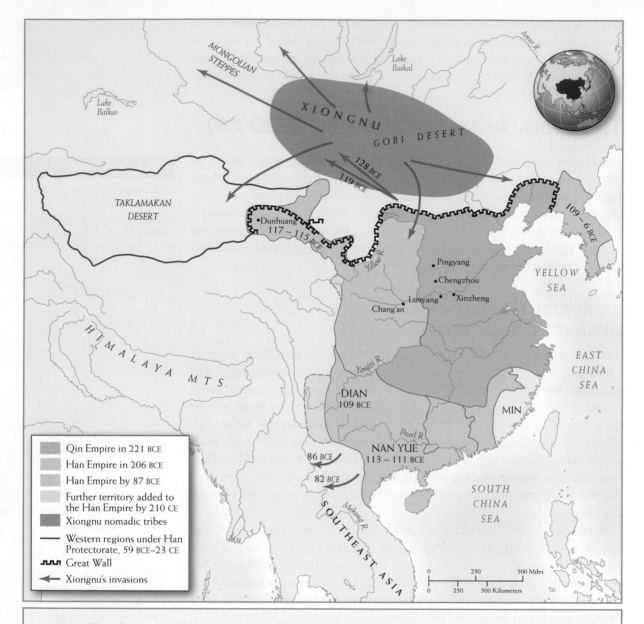

Map 7.1 The Qin and Han Dynasties, 221 BCE–220 CE

The short-lived Qin (221–207 BCE) and the much longer-lasting Han (206 BCE–220 CE) dynasties consolidated much of East Asia into one large regional empire.

- Based on the map, when and where did various phases of expansion take place from the Qin through the Han dynasty? What features shaped that expansion?

- Where was the Great Wall located, and against what was it defending?

- What impact did the pastoral Xiongnu have on the Han dynasty's effort to consolidate a large territorial state?

and local officials answered directly to the emperor, who could dismiss them at will. Civilian governors did not serve in their home areas, thus preventing them from building up power for themselves. These reforms provided China with a centralized bureaucracy and a hereditary emperor that later dynasties, including the Han, inherited.

The chief minister of the Qin Empire, Li Si, subscribed to the principles of Legalism developed during the Warring States period. This philosophy valued written law codes, administrative regulations, and inflexible punishments more highly than the rituals and ethics that Confucians emphasized or the spontaneity and natural order that the Daoists stressed. Determined to bring order to a turbulent world, Li Si advocated strict laws and harsh punishments applied to everyone regardless of rank that included beheading, mutilation, and loss of rank and office.

Other methods of control further facilitated Qin rule. Registration of the common people at the age of sixteen provided the basis for taxation and conscription both for military service and public works projects. The Qin emperor established standard weights and measures, as well as a standard currency. The Qin also improved communication systems and administrative efficiency by constructing roads radiating out from their capital to all parts of the empire. Just as crucial was the Qin effort to standardize writing. Banning regional variants of written characters, the Qin required scribes and ministers throughout the empire to adopt the "small seal script," which later evolved into the less complicated style of bureaucratic writing known as "clerical script" that became prominent during the Han dynasty. In 213 BCE, a Qin decree ordered officials to confiscate and burn all books in private possession, except for technical works on medicine, divination, and agriculture. Education and learning were now under the exclusive control of state officials.

The agrarian empire of the Qin yielded wealth that the state could tax, and increased tax revenues meant more resources for imposing order. The government issued rules on working the fields, taxed farming households, and conscripted laborers to build irrigation systems and canals so that even more land could come under cultivation. The Qin and, later, the Han dynasties relied on free farmers and conscripted the farmers' able-bodied sons into their huge armies. Working their own land and paying a portion of their crops in taxes, peasant families were the economic bedrock of the Chinese empire. Long-distance commerce thrived, as well. In the dynamic regional market centers of the cities, merchants peddled foodstuffs as well as weapons, metals, horses, dogs, hides, furs, silk, and salt—all produced in different regions and transported on the improved road system. Taxed both in transit and in the market at a higher rate than agricultural goods, these trade goods yielded even more revenue for the imperial government.

The Qin grappled with the need to expand and defend their borders, extending those boundaries in the northeast to the Korean Peninsula, in the

Intellectual Censorship This seventeenth-century painting depicts the infamous "Burning of the Books and Burying of the Scholars" edict enacted by Shi Huangdi at the suggestion of his adviser, Li Si. Unfortunately, even the state-approved texts were destroyed a mere six years later, during the fall of the Qin dynasty and sack of the capital.

south to present-day Vietnam, and in the west into central Asia. Relations between the settled Chinese and the nomadic Xiongnu to the north and west (see Chapter 6) teetered in a precarious balance until 215 BCE, when the Qin Empire pushed north into the middle of the Yellow River basin, seizing pasturelands from the Xiongnu and opening the region up for settlement. Qin officials built roads into these areas and employed conscripts and criminals to create a massive defensive wall that covered a distance of 3,000 miles along the northern border (the forerunner of the Great Wall of China—though north of the current wall, which was constructed more than a millennium later). In 211 BCE, the Qin settled 30,000 colonists in the steppe lands of Inner Eurasia.

Despite its military power, the Qin dynasty collapsed quickly, due to constant warfare and the heavy taxation and exhausting conscription that war required. When conscripted workers mutinied in 209 BCE, they found allies in descendants of Warring States nobles, local military leaders, and influential merchants. The rebels swept up thousands of supporters with their call to arms against the "tyrannical" Qin. Shortly before Shi Huangdi died in 210 BCE, even the educated elite joined former lords and regional vassals in revolt. The second Qin emperor committed suicide in 207 BCE, and his weak successor surrendered to the leader of the Han forces later that year. The resurgent Xiongnu confederacy also reconquered their old pasturelands as the dynasty fell.

BEGINNINGS OF THE WESTERN HAN DYNASTY

The civil war that followed the collapse of Qin rule opened the way for the formation of the Western Han dynasty. A commoner and former policeman named Liu Bang (r. 206–195 BCE) declared himself prince of his home area of Han. In 202 BCE, Liu proclaimed himself the first Han emperor. Claiming the mandate of heaven, the Han portrayed the Qin as evil; yet at the same time they adopted the Qin's bureaucratic system. In reality, Qin laws had been no crueler than those of the Han. Under Han leadership, China's armies swelled with some 50,000 crossbowmen who brandished mass-produced weapons made from bronze and iron. Armed with the crossbow, foot soldiers and mounted archers extended Han imperial lands in all directions. Following the Qin practice, the Han also relied on a huge conscripted labor force for special projects such as building canals, roads, and defensive walls.

The first part of the Han dynasty is known as the Western (or Former) Han dynasty (206 BCE–9 CE). The Han brought economic prosperity and the expansion of empire. This was especially the case under **Emperor Wu**, known also as Han Wudi, who presided over one of the longest and most eventful reigns in Chinese history (r. 141–87 BCE). Though he was called the "Martial Emperor" because of the state's many military campaigns, Emperor Wu rarely inspected his military units and never led them in battle. Wu followed the Daoist principle of *wuwei* (noninterference), striving to remain aloof from day-to-day activities and permitting the empire to function on its own if it did not require intervention. Still, he used a stringent penal code to eliminate powerful officials who got in his way. In a single year, his court system prosecuted over a thousand such cases.

HAN POWER AND ADMINISTRATION

Undergirding the Han Empire was the tight-knit alliance between the imperial family and the new elite—the scholar-gentry class—who shared a determination to impose order on the Chinese population. Although the first Han emperors had no choice but to compromise with the aristocratic groups who had helped overthrow the Qin, in time the Han created the most highly centralized bureaucracy in the world. No fewer than 23,500 individuals staffed the central and local governments. That structure became the source of the Han's enduring power. As under the Qin, the Han bureaucracy touched everyone because all males had to register, pay taxes, and serve in the military.

The Han court moved quickly to tighten its grip on regional administration. First it removed powerful princes, crushed rebellions, and took over the areas controlled by regional lords. According to arrangements instituted in 106 BCE by Emperor Wu, the empire consisted of thirteen provinces under imperial inspectors. As during the Qin dynasty, commanderies,

Qin Archer and Crossbow This kneeling archer was discovered in the tomb of Shi Huangdi, along with the thousands of other bowmen, cavalrymen, and infantry that composed the massive terra-cotta army. Notice his breastplate; its overlapping plates would have enhanced maneuverability. The wooden bow he was holding has disintegrated, but a replica appears above. The bronze arrowhead and trigger mechanism in this reproduction were found with the terra-cotta army.

Qin Coin After centuries of distinctive regional currencies, the Qin created this standardized bronze coin as part of their general unification policy.

each administered by a civilian and a military official, covered vast lands inhabited by countless ethnic groups totaling millions of people. These officials maintained political stability and ensured the efficient collection of taxes. However, given the immense numbers under their jurisdiction and the heavy duties they bore, in many respects the local administrative staff was still inadequate to the tasks facing it.

Government schools that promoted the scholar-official ideal became fertile sources for recruiting local officials. In 136 BCE, Emperor Wu founded what became the **Imperial University**, a college for classical scholars that supplied the Han need for well-trained bureaucrats. By the second century CE, the university boasted 30,000 students and faculty. Apart from studying the classics, Han scholars were naturalists and inventors. They made important medical discoveries, dealing with rational explanations of the body's functions and the role of wind and temperature in transmitting diseases. They also invented the magnetic compass and developed high-quality paper. Local elites encouraged their sons to master the classical teachings. This practice could secure future entry into the ruling class and firmly planted the Confucian classics at the heart of the imperial state.

Confucian thought slowly became the ideological buttress of the Han Empire. Under Emperor Wu, the bureaucracy deemed people's welfare to be the essential purpose of legitimate rule. By 50 BCE, *The Analects*, a collection of Confucius's sayings, was widely disseminated, and three Confucian ideals reigned as the official doctrine of the Han Empire: honoring tradition, respecting the lessons of history, and acknowledging the emperor's responsibility to heaven. Scholars used Confucius's words to tutor the princes. By embracing Confucian political ideals, Han rulers established an empire based on the mandate of heaven and crafted a careful balance in which the officials provided a counterweight to the emperor's autocratic strength. When the interests of the court and the bureaucracy clashed, however, the emperor's will was paramount.

THE ECONOMY AND THE NEW SOCIAL ORDER

Part of the Han leaders' genius was their ability to win the support of diverse social groups that had been squabbling for centuries. The basis of their success was their ability to organize daily life, create a stable social order, promote economic growth, and foster a state-centered religion. One important element in promoting political and social stability was that the Han allowed surviving Qin aristocrats to reacquire some of their former power. The Han also urged enterprising peasants who had worked the nobles' lands to become local leaders in the countryside. Successful merchants won permission to extend their influence in cities, and in local areas scholars found themselves in the role of masters when the state removed their lords.

Emperor Wu
(r. 141–87 BCE) Also known as Emperor Han Wudi, or the "Martial Emperor"; the ruler of the Han dynasty for more than fifty years, during which he expanded the empire through his extensive military campaigns.

Imperial University
Institution founded in 136 BCE by Emperor Wu (Han Wudi) not only to train future bureaucrats in the Confucian classics but also to foster scientific advances in other fields.

Out of a massive agrarian base flowed a steady stream of tax revenues and labor for military forces and public works. The Han court drew revenues from many sources: state-owned imperial lands, mining, and mints; tribute from outlying domains; household taxes on the nobility; and taxes on surplus grains from wealthy merchants. Emperor Wu established state monopolies in salt, iron, and wine to fund his expensive military campaigns. His policies encouraged silk and iron production—especially iron weapons and everyday tools—and controlled profiteering through price controls. He also minted standardized copper coins and imposed stiff penalties for counterfeiting.

Han cities were laid out in an orderly grid. Bustling markets served as public areas. Carriages transported rich families up and down wide avenues (and they paid a lot for the privilege: keeping a horse required as much grain as a family of six would consume). Court palaces became forbidden inner cities, off-limits to all but those in the imperial lineage or the government. Monumental architecture in China announced the palaces and tombs of rulers.

Domestic Life Daily life in Han China included new luxuries for the elite and reinforced traditional ideas about gender. Wealthy families lived in several-story homes with richly carved crossbeams and rafters and floors cushioned with embroidered pillows, wool rugs, and mats. Fine embroideries hung as drapes, and screens in the rooms secured privacy. Domestic space reinforced male authority as women and children stayed cloistered in inner quarters, preserving the sense that the patriarch's role was to protect them from a harsh society.

Nonetheless, some elite women, often literate, enjoyed respect as teachers and managers within the family while their husbands served as officials away from home. Ban Zhao, the younger sister of the historian Ban Gu (32–92 CE), was an exceptional woman whose talents reached outside the home. She became the first female Chinese historian and lived relatively unconstrained. After marrying a local resident, Cao Shishu, at the age of fourteen, she was called Madame Cao at court. Subsequently, she completed her elder brother's *History of the Former Han Dynasty* when he was imprisoned and executed. In addition to completing the first full dynastic history in China, Ban Zhao wrote *Lessons for Women*, in which she described the status of elite

Model of a Han Watchtower
Wealthy Han burials contained terra-cotta models of buildings—houses, animal pens, granaries—that would replicate one's life in the afterlife. Shown here is a model of a multistory watchtower standing just over 3 feet tall, the details of which give insight into Han building techniques in the first to third centuries CE. Archers with crossbows stand guard on an upper balcony, while a figure stands in greeting at the front gate.

women and presented the ideal woman in light of her virtue, her type of work, and the words she spoke and wrote. Women who were commoners led less protected lives. Many worked in the fields, and some joined troupes of entertainers to sing and dance for food at open markets.

Silk was abundant and available to all classes, though in winter only the rich wrapped themselves in furs while everyone else stayed warm in woolens and ferret skins. The rich also wore distinctive slippers lined with leather or silk. Wine and cooked meat came to the dinner tables of the wealthy on vessels fashioned with silver inlay or golden handles. Entertainment for those who could afford it included gambling, performing animals, tiger fights, foreign dancing girls, and even live music in private homes, performed by orchestras in the families' private employ. Although events like these had occurred during the Zhou dynasty, they had marked only public ritual occasions.

Social Hierarchy At the base of Han society was a free peasantry of farmers who owned and tilled their own land. The Han court upheld an agrarian ideal—which Confucians and Daoists supported—honoring the peasants' productive labors, while subjecting merchants to a range of controls (including regulations on luxury consumption) and belittling them for not doing physical labor. Confucians envisioned scholar-officials as working hard for the ruler to enhance a moral economy in which profiteering by greedy merchants would be minimal.

In reality, however, the first century of Han rule perpetuated the power of elites. At the apex were the imperial clan and nobles, followed, in order, by high-ranking officials and scholars, great merchants and manufacturers, and a regionally based class of local magnates. Below these elites, lesser

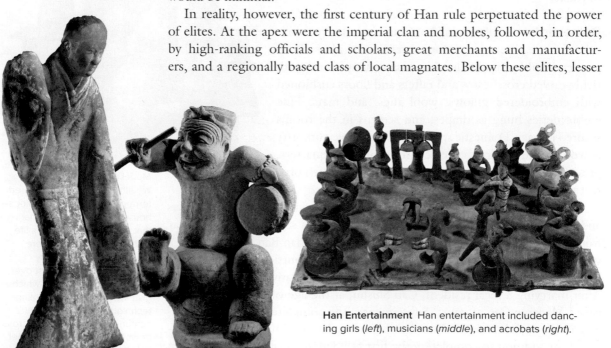

Han Entertainment Han entertainment included dancing girls (*left*), musicians (*middle*), and acrobats (*right*).

clerks, medium and small landowners, free farmers, artisans, small merchants, poor tenant farmers, and hired laborers eked out a living. The more destitute became enslaved government workers and relied on the state for food and clothing. At the bottom were convicts and people who were privately enslaved.

Between 100 BCE and 200 CE, scholar-officials linked the imperial center with local society. At first, their political clout and prestige complemented the power of landlords and large clans, but over time their autonomy grew as they gained wealth by acquiring private property. Following the fall of the Han, they emerged as the dominant aristocratic clans.

In the long run, the imperial court's struggle to limit the power of local lords and magnates failed. Rulers had to rely on local officials to enforce their rule, but those officials could rarely stand up to the powerful men they were supposed to be governing. And when central rule proved too onerous for local elites, they could rebel. Local uprisings against the Han that began in 99 BCE forced the court to relax its measures and left landlords and local magnates as dominant powers in the provinces. Below these privileged groups, powerless agrarian groups turned to Daoist religious organizations that crystallized into potent cells of dissent.

Religion and Omens Under Emperor Wu, Confucianism took on religious overtones. One treatise portrayed Confucius not as a humble teacher but as an uncrowned monarch, and even as a demigod and a giver of laws, which differed from the portrait in *The Analects* of a more modest, accessible, and very human Confucius.

Although Confucians at court championed classical learning, many local communities practiced forms of a remarkably dynamic popular Chinese religion. Imperial cults, magic, and sorcery reinforced the court's interest in astronomical omens—such as the appearance of a supernova, solar halos, meteors, and lunar and solar eclipses. Unpredictable celestial events, as well as earthquakes and famines, could be taken to mean that the emperor had lost the mandate of heaven. Powerful ministers exploited these occurrences to intimidate their ruler. People of high and low social position alike believed that witchcraft could manipulate natural events and interfere with the will of heaven. Religion in its many forms, from philosophy to witchcraft, was an essential feature of Han society from the elite to the poorer classes.

MILITARY EXPANSION AND THE SILK ROADS

The Han military machine was effective at expanding the empire's borders and enforcing stability around the borderlands. Peace was good for business, specifically for creating stable conditions that allowed the safe transit of goods over the Silk Roads. Emperor Wu did much to transform the military forces.

Following the Qin precedent, he made military service compulsory, resulting in a huge force: 100,000 crack troops in the Imperial Guard stationed in the capital and more than a million in the standing army.

Expanding Borders Han forces were particularly active along the borders. During the reign of Emperor Wu, Han control extended from southeastern China to northern Vietnam. When pro-Han Koreans appealed for Han help against rulers in their internal squabbles, Emperor Wu's expeditionary force defeated the Korean king and four Han commanderies sprang up in northern Korea. While incursions into Sichuan and the southwestern border areas were less successful due to mountainous terrain and malaria, a commandery nonetheless took root in southern Sichuan in 135 BCE, and soon it opened trading routes to Southeast Asia.

The Han Empire's most serious military threat, however, came from the Xiongnu and other nomadic peoples in the north. The Han inherited from the Qin a symbiotic relationship with these proud, horse-riding nomads: Han merchants brought silk cloth and thread, bronze mirrors, and lacquerware to exchange for furs, horses, and cattle. After humiliating defeats at the hands of the Xiongnu, the Han under Emperor Wu successfully repelled Xiongnu invasions around 120 BCE and ultimately penetrated deep into Xiongnu territory. The Xiongnu tribes were split in two, with the southern tribes surrendering and the northern tribes moving west, ultimately threatening Roman territory.

The Chinese Peace and the Silk Roads The retreat of the Xiongnu and other nomadic peoples introduced a glorious period of internal peace and prosperity some scholars have referred to as a ***Pax Sinica*** ("Chinese Peace," 149–87 BCE). During this period, long-distance trade flourished, cities ballooned, standards of living rose, and the population surged. As a result of their military campaigns, Emperor Wu and his successors enjoyed tribute from distant subordinate states, intervening in their domestic policy only if they rebelled. The Han instead relied on trade and markets to incorporate outlying lands as prosperous satellite states within the tribute system. The Xiongnu nomads even became key middlemen in Silk Road trade.

When the Xiongnu were no longer a threat from the north, the Han expanded westward. (See Map 7.2.) By 100 BCE, Emperor Wu had extended the northern defensive wall from the Tian Shan Mountains to the Gobi Desert. Along the wall stood signal beacons for sending emergency messages, and its gates opened periodically for trading fairs. The westernmost gate was called the Jade Gate, since jade from the Taklamakan Desert passed through it. Wu also built garrison cities at oases to protect the trade routes. Soldiers at these oasis garrison cities settled with their families on the frontiers. When its military power expanded beyond the Jade Gate, the Han government set

Pax Sinica
Modern term (paralleling the term *Pax Romana*) for the "Chinese Peace" that lasted from 149 to 87 BCE, a period when agriculture and commerce flourished, fueling the expansion of cities and the growth of the population of Han China.

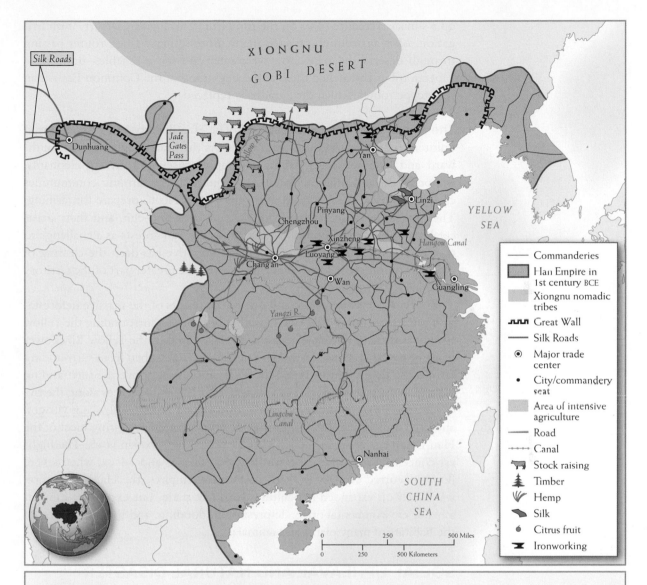

Map 7.2 *Pax Sinica*: The Han Dynasty in the First Century BCE

....

Agriculture, commerce, and industry flourished in East Asia under Han rule.

- According to the map, what were the main commodities in the Han dynasty, where were they located, and along what routes might they have moved to pass among the empire's regions?

- Locate the lines marking the commanderies into which Han territory was divided. What do you notice about their comparative size, resources, and other features?

- What do you notice about the location of major trade centers and the areas of intensive agriculture?

up a similar system of oases on the rim of the Taklamakan Desert. With irrigation, oasis agriculture attracted many more settlers. Trade routes passing through deserts and oases now were safer and more reliable—until fierce Tibetan tribes threatened them at the beginning of the Common Era—than the steppe routes, which they gradually replaced.

The Han Empire and Deforestation The Han dynasty had a significant, if unintended, impact on the environment. As the Han peoples moved southward and later westward, filling up empty spaces and driving elephants, rhinoceroses, and other animals into extinction, the farming communities cleared immense tracts of land of shrubs and forests to prepare for farming. The Han were especially fond of oak, pine, ash, and elm, and their artists celebrated them in paintings; farmers, however, saw forests as a challenge to their work. China's grand environmental narrative has been the clearing of old-growth forests that had originally covered the greater part of the territory of China.

But trees prevent erosion, and one of the results of the massive deforestation campaigns during the Han period in the regions surrounding the Yellow River was massive runoffs of soil into the river. In fact, the Yellow River owes its name to the immense quantities of mud that it absorbed from surrounding farmlands. This sediment raised the level of the river above the surrounding plain in many places. In spite of villagers' efforts to build levees along the river's banks, severe flooding occurred, threatening crops, destroying villages, and even undermining the legitimacy of ruling dynasties. During most of the Han Empire, a break in the levees took place every sixteen years. The highest concentration of flooding was between 66 BCE and 34 CE, when severe floods occurred every nine years. As in many empires, the Han's expansion was based on expanded agriculture and brisk trade, but expansion came at a major environmental price: deforestation, flooding, and the destruction of the habitats of many plants and animals.

SOCIAL UPHEAVAL AND NATURAL DISASTER

The strain of military expenses and the tax pressures those expenditures placed on small landholders and peasants were more than the Han Empire could bear. By the end of the first century BCE, heavy financial expenditures had drained the Chinese empire. A devastating chain of events exacerbated the empire's troubles: natural disasters led to crop failures, which led to landowners' inability to pay taxes that were based not on crop yield but on size of landholding. Wang Mang (r. 9–23 CE), a former Han minister and regent to a child emperor, took advantage of the crisis. Believing that the Han had lost the mandate of heaven, Wang Mang assumed the throne in 9 CE and established a new dynasty. He designed reforms to help the poor and to foster economic activity. He made efforts to stabilize the economy by confiscating gold from wealthy landowners and merchants, introducing a new currency, and attempting to minimize price fluctuations. By redistributing excess land, he hoped to allow all families to work their own parcels and share in cultivating a communal plot whose crops would become tax surplus for the state.

Wang Mang's regime, and his idealistic reforms, failed miserably. Violent resistance from peasants and large landholders, as well as the Yellow River's change in its course in 11 CE, contributed to his demise. When the Yellow River, appropriately called "China's Sorrow," changed course—as it has many times in China's long history—tremendous floods caused mass death, vast migrations, peasant impoverishment, and revolt. The floods of 11 CE likely affected half the Chinese population. Rebellious peasants, led by Daoist clerics, used this far-reaching disaster as a pretext to march on Wang's capital at Chang'an. The peasants painted their foreheads red in imitation of demon warriors and called themselves Red Eyebrows. By 23 CE, they had overthrown Wang Mang. The natural disaster was attributed by Wang's rivals to his unbridled misuse of power, and soon Wang became the model of the evil usurper.

THE LATER (EASTERN) HAN DYNASTY

After Wang Mang's fall, social, political, and economic inequalities fatally weakened the power of the emperor and the court. As a result, the Later (or Eastern) Han dynasty (25–220 CE), with its capital at Luoyang on the North China plain, followed a hands-off economic policy under which large landowners and merchants amassed more wealth and more property. Decentralizing the regime was also good for local business and long-distance trade, as the Silk Roads continued to flourish. Chinese silk became popular as far away as the Roman Empire. In return, China received from points west on the Silk Roads commodities including glass, jade, horses, precious stones, tortoiseshells, and fabrics. (See Current Trends in World History: Han China, the Early Roman Empire, and the Silk Roads.)

By the second century CE, landed elites enjoyed the fruits of their success in manipulating the Later (Eastern) Han tax system. It granted them so many land and labor exemptions that the government never again firmly controlled its human and agricultural resources as Emperor Wu had. As the court refocused on the new capital in Luoyang, local power fell into the hands of great aristocratic families. These elites acquired even more privately owned land and forced free peasants to become their rent-paying tenants, then raised their rents higher and higher.

Such prosperity bred greater social inequity—among large landholders, tenant farmers, and peasants working their small parcels—and a renewed source of turmoil. Simmering tensions between landholders and peasants boiled over in a full-scale rebellion in 184 CE. Popular religious groups championed new ideas among commoners and elites for whom the many-centuries-earlier Daoist sage Master Laozi, the voice of naturalness and spontaneity, was an exemplary model. Daoist masters challenged Confucian ritual conformity, and they advanced their ideas in the name of a divine order that would redeem all people, not just elites. Officials, along with other political outcasts, headed strong dissident groups and eventually formed local movements. Under their leadership, religious groups such as the Yellow Turbans—so called because they wrapped yellow scarves around their heads—championed Daoist upheaval across the empire. The Yellow Turbans drew on Daoist ideas to call for a just and ideal society. Their message received a warm welcome from a population that was increasingly hostile to Han rule.

Proclaiming the Daoist millenarian belief in a future "Great Peace," the Yellow Turbans demanded fairer treatment by the Han state and equal distribution of all farm lands. As agrarian conditions worsened, a widespread famine ensued. It was a catastrophe that, in the rebels' view, demonstrated the emperor's loss of the mandate of heaven. While Han military forces were successful in quashing the rebellion, significant damage had been done to Han rule. The economy disintegrated when people refused to pay taxes and provide forced labor, and internal wars engulfed the dynasty. After the 180s CE, three competing states replaced the Han: the Wei in the northwest, the Shu in the southwest, and the Wu in the south. A long-lasting unified empire did not return for several centuries.

The Roman Empire (C. 300 BCE– C. 300 CE)

At the other end of Afro-Eurasia from Han China, in a centuries-long process, Rome became a great power that ruled over as many as 60 million subjects. The Roman Empire at its height encompassed lands from the highlands of what is now Scotland in Europe to the lower reaches of the Nile River in modern-day Egypt and part of Sudan, and from the borders of the Inner Eurasian steppe in Ukraine and the Caucasus to the Atlantic shores of North Africa. (See Map 7.3.) Whereas the Han Empire dominated an enormous and unbroken landmass, the Roman Empire dominated lands around the Mediterranean Sea. Like the Han Chinese, though, the Romans acquired command over their world through violent military expansion. By the first century CE, almost unceasing wars against their neighbors had enabled the Romans to forge an unparalleled number of ethnic groups and minor states into a single, large political state.

FOUNDATIONS OF THE ROMAN EMPIRE

Core Objectives

EXPLAIN the process by which Rome transitioned from a minor city-state to a dominating Mediterranean power.

Three major factors influenced the beginnings of Rome's imperial expansion: migrations of foreign peoples, Rome's military might, and Roman political innovation.

Population Movements Between 450 and 250 BCE, migrations from northern and central Europe brought large numbers of Celts to settle in lands around the Mediterranean Sea. They convulsed the northern rim of the Mediterranean, staging armed forays into lands from what is now Spain in the west to present-day Turkey in the east. One of these migrations involved Gallic peoples from the region of the Alps and beyond who launched a series of violent incursions into northern Italy that ultimately—around 390 BCE—led to the seizure of Rome. The important result for the Romans was not their city's capture, which was temporary yet traumatic, but rather the permanent dislocation that the invaders inflicted on the city-states of the Etruscans. These Etruscans, themselves likely a combination of indigenous people and migrants from Asia Minor centuries before, spoke their own language and were centered in what is now Tuscany. Before the Gallic invasions, the Etruscans had dominated the Italian Peninsula. While the Etruscans with great difficulty drove the invading Gauls back northward, their cities never recovered nor did their ability to dominate other peoples in Italy, including their fledgling rival, the Romans. Thus, the Gallic migrations weakened Etruscan power, one of the most formidable roadblocks to Roman expansion in Italy.

Military Institutions and the War Ethos The Romans achieved unassailable military power by organizing the communities that they conquered in Italy into a system that generated manpower for their army. This development began around 340 BCE, when the Romans faced a concerted attack by their fellow Latin city-states. By then, the other Latins viewed Rome not as an ally in a system of mutual defense but as a growing threat to their own independence. After overcoming these nearby Latins, the Romans charged onward to defeat one community after another in Italy. Demanding from their defeated enemies a supply of men for the Roman army every year, Rome amassed a huge reservoir of military manpower.

In addition to their overwhelming advantage in manpower, the Romans cultivated an unusual war ethos. A heightened sense of honor drove Roman men to push themselves into battle again and again, and never to accept defeat. Guided by the example of great

A Loving Etruscan Wife and Husband This lid, dating to around 300 BCE, topped the sarcophagus of Thanchvil Tarnai (wife) and Larth Tetnies (husband). Their intimate pose on the marriage bed—wrapped in an eternal loving embrace with her right hand tenderly tucked behind his neck, their eyes locked and knees touching—suggests a perhaps unexpected degree of equality between husband and wife among the Etruscans of central Italy as Rome expanded to control the entire Italian Peninsula. The image on the side of the coffin that was meant to be seen depicted an Amazonomachy (Greeks fighting Amazons). Scholars have found traces of blue, red, pink, and purple pigments, revealing that the sarcophagus was once richly colored.

The Global View

NORTH SEA

BALTIC SEA

BRITANNIA

Londinium

ATLANTIC OCEAN

GERMANIA INFERIOR

BELGICA

GERMANI

GALLIA LUGDUNENSIS

Rhine R. LAURI

DECUMATES

IUTHUNGI

RAETIA

GALLIA AQUITANIA

GERMANIA SUPERIOR

NORICUM

Danube R.

GALLIA NARBONENSIS

PANNONIA

LUSITANIA

TARRACONENSIS

ITALIA

DALMATIA

ADRIATIC SEA

CORSICA

MINORCA

Rome

Corduba

MAJORCA

SARDINIA

BAETIA

M E D I T E R R A N E A N

MAURETANIA TINGITANA

SICILIA

MAURETANIA CAESARIENSIS

Carthage

Syracuse

NUMIDIA

AFRICA

GAETULI

GARAMANTES

Legend:

← Mediterranean Sea current

Roman expansion to 201 BCE

Roman expansion, 201–100 BCE

Roman expansion, 100–44 BCE

Roman expansion, 44 BCE–14 CE

Roman expansion, 14–96 CE

Roman expansion, 96–116 CE

GALLIA Roman province

GAETULI Border peoples

⊙ Important provincial capitals

Map 7.3 Roman Expansion to 120 CE

Roman expansion continued for several centuries before reaching its peak in the second century CE.

- According to the map, what were Rome's earliest provinces? What provinces were incorporated during the last phase of Rome's expansion? What sense, if any, can you make of the stages of Roman expansion, in terms of where and when the Romans expanded their territory?
- What features—geographical or otherwise—limited Roman expansion farther into Europe, Southwest Asia, and Africa?
- How did the sea current influence the movement of peoples and goods in the Mediterranean?

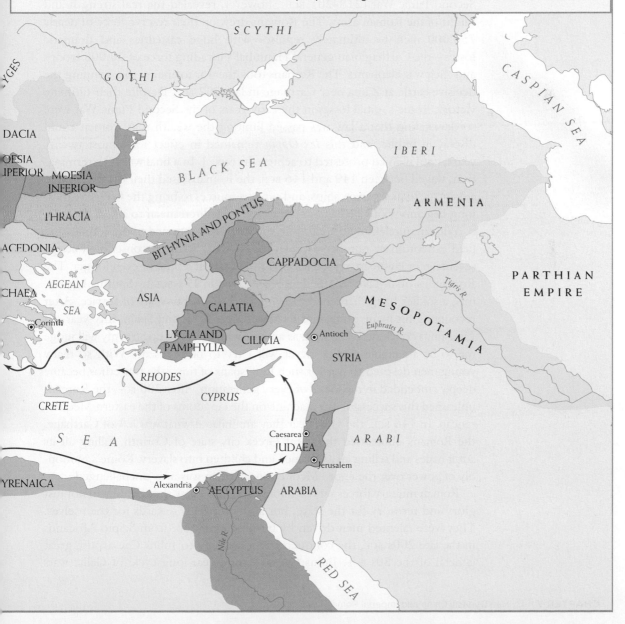

Punic Wars

Series of three wars fought between Rome and Carthage from 264 to 146 BCE that resulted in the end of Carthaginian hegemony in the western Mediterranean, the growth of Roman military might (army and navy), and the beginning of Rome's aggressive foreign imperialism.

warriors and shaped by a regime of training and discipline, in which minor infractions of duty were punishable by death, the Roman army trooped out to war in annual spring campaigns beginning in the month—still called March today—dedicated to and named for the Roman god of war, Mars.

By 275 BCE, Rome controlled the Italian Peninsula. It next entered into three great **Punic Wars** with Carthage, which had begun as a Phoenician colony and was now the major power centered in the northern parts of present-day Tunisia (see Chapters 4 and 5). The First Punic War (264–241 BCE) was a prolonged naval battle over the island of Sicily. With their victory, the Romans acquired a dominant position in the western Mediterranean. The Second Punic War (218–201 BCE), however, revealed the real strength and might of the Roman army. The Romans drew on their reserve force of nearly 750,000 men to ultimately repulse—with huge casualties and dramatic losses—the Carthaginian general Hannibal's invading force of 20,000 troops and their war elephants. The Romans took the war to enemy soil, winning the decisive battle at Zama near Carthage in late 202 BCE. Despite their ultimate victory, Rome's initial losses in the early years of the Second Punic War were so devastating that a law was passed limiting the wealth that women could display in public, and this *lex Oppia* remained in effect for almost twenty years, until women protested to achieve its repeal. In a final war of extermination, waged between 149 and 146 BCE, the Romans used their overwhelming advantage in manpower, ships, and other resources to bring the five-centuries-long hegemony of Carthage in the western Mediterranean to an end.

With an unrelenting drive to war, the Romans continued to draft, train, and field extraordinary numbers of men for combat. Soldiers, conscripted at age seventeen or eighteen, served for up to ten years at a time or even longer. The Roman historian Livy recorded a speech given in 171 BCE by Spurius Ligustinus, a soldier battle hardened from more than twenty years of service. After recounting his many campaigns in Macedonia, Syria, and Spain, fifty-year-old Ligustinus concluded: "So long as anyone who is calling up an army will judge me to be a suitable soldier, never will I try to be excused." With so many young men devoted to war for such long spans of time, the war ethos became deeply embedded in the ideals of every generation. After 200 BCE, the Romans unleashed this successful war machine on the kingdoms of the eastern Mediterranean. In 146 BCE, the same year they annihilated what was left of Carthage, the Romans obliterated the great Greek city-state of Corinth, killing all its adult males and selling all its women and children into slavery. Rome's monopoly of power over the entire Mediterranean basin was now unchallenged.

Roman military forces served under men who knew they could win not just glory and territory for the state, but also enormous rewards for themselves. They were talented men driven by burning ambition, from Scipio Africanus in the late 200s BCE, the conqueror of Carthage, to Julius Caesar, the great general of the 50s BCE. Julius Caesar's eight-year-long cycle of Gallic wars resulted in the deaths of more than 1 million Gauls and the enslavement of another million. Western Afro-Eurasia had never witnessed war on this scale; it had no equal anywhere, except in China.

Political Institutions and Internal Conflict The conquest of the Mediterranean placed unprecedented power and wealth into the hands of a few men in the Roman social elite. The rush of battlefield successes had kept Romans and their Italian allies preoccupied with the demands of army service overseas. Once this process of territorial expansion slowed, social and political problems that had been lying dormant began to resurface.

Following the traditional date of its founding in 509 BCE, the Romans had lived in a state that they called the "public thing," or **res publica** (hence the modern word *republic*). In this state, policy issued from the Senate—a body of permanent members, 300 to 600 of Rome's most powerful and wealthy citizens (by definition, male)—and from popular assemblies of the citizens. Every year the citizens elected the officials of state, principally two consuls who held power for a year and commanded the armies. The people also annually elected ten men who, as tribunes of the plebs ("the common people"), held the task of protecting the common people's interests against those of the rich and powerful. In severe political crises, Romans sometimes chose one man, a dictator, whose words, *dicta*, were law and who held absolute power over the state for no longer than six months. These institutions, originally devised for a city-state, were problematic for ruling a Mediterranean-sized empire.

res publica
Term (meaning "public thing") used by Romans to describe their Republic, which was advised by a Senate and was governed by popular assemblies of free adult males, who were arranged into voting units, based on wealth and social status, to elect officers and legislate.

Roman Farmers and Soldiers In the late Republic, most Roman soldiers came from rural Italy, where small farms were being absorbed into the landholdings of the wealthy and powerful. In the empire, soldiers were recruited from rural provincial regions. They sometimes worked small fields of their own and sometimes worked the lands of the wealthy—like the domain in the Roman province of Africa (in modern-day Tunisia) that is depicted in this mosaic.

Pax Romana

Latin term for "Roman Peace," referring to the period from 25 BCE to 235 CE, when conditions in the Roman Empire were relatively settled and peaceful, allowing trade and the economy to thrive.

Augustus

Latin term meaning "the Revered One"; title granted by the Senate to the Roman ruler Octavian in 27 BCE to signify his unique political position. Along with his adopted family name, *Caesar*, the military honorific *imperator*, and the senatorial term *princeps*, *Augustus* became a generic term for a leader of the Roman Empire.

Core Objectives

COMPARE Han China with imperial Rome in terms of political authority, economy, cultural developments, and military expansion.

By the second century BCE, Rome's power elites were exploiting the wealth from its Mediterranean conquests to acquire huge tracts of land in Italy and Sicily. They then imported enormous numbers of enslaved people from all around the Mediterranean to work this land. Free citizen farmers, the backbone of the army, were driven off their lands and into the cities. The result was a severe agrarian and recruiting crisis. In 133 and 123–121 BCE, two tribunes, the brothers Tiberius and Gaius Gracchus, tried—much as Wang Mang would in China more than a century later—to address these inequalities. The Gracchi brothers attempted to institute land reforms guaranteeing to all of Rome's poor citizens a basic amount of land that would qualify them for army service. But political enemies assassinated the elder brother, Tiberius, and orchestrated violent resistance that drove the younger brother, Gaius, to commit suicide while being chased by an angry mob.

Thereafter, poor Roman citizens looked not to state institutions but to army commanders, to whom they gave their loyalty and support, to provide them with land and income. These generals became increasingly powerful and started to compete with one another, ignoring the Senate and the traditional rules of politics. As generals sought control of the state and their supporters took sides, a long series of civil wars began that lasted from 90 BCE to the late 30s BCE. The Romans now turned inward on themselves the tremendous militaristic resources built up during the conquest of the Mediterranean.

EMPERORS, AUTHORITARIAN RULE, AND ADMINISTRATION

Julius Caesar's adopted son, Octavian (63 BCE–14 CE), ultimately reunited the fractured empire and emerged as undisputed master of the Roman world. Octavian's authoritarian one-man rule marked the beginning of the **Pax Romana** ("Roman Peace," 25 BCE–235 CE). This peace depended on the power of one man with enough authority to enforce an orderly competition among Roman aristocrats.

Octavian concentrated immense wealth and the most important official titles and positions of power in his own hands. Signaling the transition to a new political order in which he alone controlled the army, the provinces, and the political processes in Rome, Octavian assumed a new title, **Augustus** ("the Revered One")—much as the Qin emperor Zheng had assumed the new title of Shi Huangdi ("First August Emperor")—as well as the traditional republican roles of *imperator* ("commander in chief," or emperor), *princeps* ("first man"), and *Caesar* (a name connoting his adoptive heritage, but which over time became a title assumed by imperial successors).

Rome's subjects tended to see these emperors as heroic or even semidivine beings in life and to think of the good ones as becoming gods on their death. Yet emperors were always careful to present themselves as civil rulers whose power ultimately depended on the consent of Roman citizens and the might of the army. They contrasted themselves with the image of "king," a role the Romans had learned to detest from the monarchy they themselves had long ago overthrown to establish their Republic in 509 BCE. Nonetheless, the emperors' powers were immense.

Being a Roman emperor required finesse and talent, and few succeeded at it. Of the twenty-two emperors who held power in the most stable period of Roman history (between the first Roman emperor, Augustus, and the early third century CE), fifteen met their end by murder or suicide. As powerful as he might be, no individual emperor alone could govern an empire of such great size and population, encompassing a multitude of languages and cultures. He needed institutions and competent people to help him. In terms of sheer power, the most important institution was the army. Consequently, the emperors systematically transformed the army into a full-time professional force. Men now entered the imperial army not as citizen volunteers but as paid professionals who enlisted for life and swore loyalty to the emperor and his family. It was part of the emperor's image to present himself as a victorious battlefield commander, inflicting defeat on the "barbarians" who threatened the empire's frontiers.

For most emperors, however, governance was largely a daily chore of listening to complaints, answering petitions, deciding court cases, and hearing reports from civil administrators and military commanders. At its largest in the second century CE, the Roman Empire encompassed more than forty administrative units, called provinces. As in Han China, each had a governor appointed or approved by the emperor; but unlike Han China, which had its formal Confucian-trained bureaucracy with ranks of senior and junior officials, the Roman Empire of this period was relatively understaffed in terms of central government officials. The emperor and his provincial governors depended very much on local help, sometimes aided by elite enslaved men and freedmen (formerly enslaved men) serving as government bureaucrats. With a limited staff of full-time assistants and an entourage of friends and acquaintances, each governor was expected to guarantee peace. However, the state relied on private companies for some essential tasks, such as the collection of imperial taxes, in which the profit motives of the publicans (the men in the companies that took up government contracts) were at odds with the expectations of fair government among the empire's subjects.

A Roman Town Roman towns featured many of the standard elements of modern towns and cities. Streets and avenues crossed at right angles; roads were paved; sidewalks ran between streets and houses. The houses were often several stories high and had wide windows and open balconies. All these elements can be seen in this street from Herculaneum, eerily preserved by the deadly pyroclastic blast of gas and ash and the volcanic lava flow when nearby Mount Vesuvius erupted in August of 79 CE, burying the town and its inhabitants.

TOWN AND CITY LIFE

Due to the conditions of peace and the wealth it generated, urban settlements were clustered in core areas of the empire—central Italy, southern Spain, northern Africa, and the western parts of present-day Turkey. The towns, whose municipal charters echoed Roman forms of government, provided the backbone of local administration for the empire. Towns often were walled, and inside those walls the streets and avenues ran at right angles. A large, open-air, rectangular area called the *forum* dominated the town center. Around it clustered the main public buildings: the markets, the main temples of principal gods and goddesses, and the building that housed city administrators. Residential areas featured regular blocks of houses, close together and fronting on the streets. Larger towns contained large apartment blocks that were not much different from the four- and five-story buildings in any modern city. In the smaller towns, sanitary standards were reasonably good.

The imperial metropolis of Rome was another matter. With well over a million inhabitants, it was larger than any other urban center of its time; Xianyang and Chang'an—the Qin and Han capitals, respectively—each had a population of between 300,000 and 500,000. While Rome's inhabitants were privileged in terms of their access to government doles of wheat and

A Roman Municipal Charter These bronze tablets record the charter of Urso (the colony Genetiva Julia), founded in Spain by Julius Caesar in the 40s BCE. Charters like this one, set up for public display in the forum or central open area, displayed regulations for the conduct of public life in a Roman town, including rules governing family inheritance and property transfers, laws on the election of town officials, and definitions of their powers and duties. Of the more than seventy surviving clauses of the Urso charter, only one (number 133) specifically mentions women; this clause proclaims broadly that wives of colonists are bound by the law.

Deadly Roman Entertainment The huge amphitheater (*left*) is in the remains of the Roman city of Thysdrus in North Africa (the town of El Jem in modern-day Tunisia). The wealth of the Africans under the empire enabled them to build colossal entertainment venues that competed with the one in Rome in scale and grandeur. Roman gladiators would fight, sometimes to the death, in such venues. The mosaic from Rome (*right*) shows two gladiators at the end of a full combat in which Astacius has killed Astivus. The Greek letter theta, or "th" (the circle with a crossbar through it), beside the names of Astivus and Rodan indicates that these men are dead—*thanatos* being the Greek word for "death."

aqueduct-supplied water, their living conditions could be appalling, with people jammed into ramshackle high-rise apartments prone to collapse in a fire. Apart from crime and violence, poor sanitary conditions and the diseases that accompany them were constant threats to the population.

Towns large and small tended to have two major entertainment venues: a theater, adopted from Hellenistic culture and devoted to plays, dances, and other popular events; and an amphitheater, a Roman innovation with a much larger seating capacity that surrounded the oval performance area at its center. In the amphitheaters, Romans could stage exotic beast hunts and gladiatorial matches for the enjoyment of huge crowds of appreciative spectators. These public entertainment facilities of Roman towns stressed the importance of gatherings in which citizens participated in civic life, as compared with the largely private entertainment of the Han elite.

SOCIAL AND GENDER RELATIONS

In Rome's civil society, laws and courts governed formal relationships, including those based on patronage and the family. By the last century BCE, the Roman state's complex legal system featured a rich body of written law, courts, and well-trained lawyers. Deeply entrenched throughout the empire, this legal infrastructure long outlasted the Roman Empire. Also firmly embedded in Roman society was a system of personal relationships that linked the rich and powerful with the mass of average citizens. Men and women of wealth and high social status acted as patrons, protecting and supporting dependents or "clients" from the lower classes. From the emperor at the top

Claudia Antonia Tatiana of Aphrodisias Roman women of the upper class—like Claudia Antonia Tatiana of Aphrodisias (pictured here), Plancia Magna of Perge, Eumachia of Pompeii, Regilla of Athens, and Junia Rustica of Spain—accrued a great deal of money and power in ancient Rome. Such women could own a business, serve in a prominent civic priesthood, or become a major civic donor. Tatiana's clothing and hairstyle are typical of elite women in the Severan period (early third century CE). Just as women in the 1980s adopted the Princess Di haircut and many in the late 2010s sported popstar Ariana Grande's signature high ponytail, elite women across the Roman Empire often styled their hair after the empress's. In this case, Julia Domna's cantaloupe updo.

A Birthday Invitation This thin sheet of wood, one of the many Vindolanda Tablets (named for the fort in Roman Britain where they were found), records a birthday invitation written around 100 CE. It is remarkable not only that this mundane document has survived, but also that it was sent by a woman (Claudia Severa, wife of a garrison commander) to her friend (Sulpicia Lepidina, wife of a military prefect). The note gives an unexpected snapshot of interactions between military wives accompanying their husbands along the Roman frontier.

to the local municipal man at the bottom, the bonds between these groups in each city found formal expression in legal definitions of patrons' responsibilities to clients; at the same time, this informal social code raised expectations that the wealthy would be civic benefactors, sponsoring the construction of public libraries, bathhouses, and theaters.

While patronage was important, the family was at the very foundation of the Roman social order. Legally speaking, the authoritarian *paterfamilias* ("father of the family") had nearly total power over his dependents, including his wife, children, and grandchildren and the people he enslaved. Despite this patriarchal system, Roman women, even those of modest wealth and status, had much greater freedom of action and much greater control of their own wealth and property than did women in most Greek city-states. As in Han China, some women in the Roman world could be well educated, literate, well connected, and in control of their own lives—despite what the laws and ideas of Roman males might suggest.

THE ECONOMY AND NEW SCALES OF PRODUCTION

Rome achieved staggering transformations in agriculture and mining. The area of land surveyed and cultivated rose steadily throughout this period, as Romans spread into arid lands on the periphery of the Sahara Desert to the south and opened up heavily forested regions in present-day France and Germany to the north. Roman agriculture and mining relied on chattel slavery—the use of human beings purchased as private property (see Chapter 6). The massive concentration of wealth and enslaved people at the center of the Roman world led to the first large-scale commercial plantation

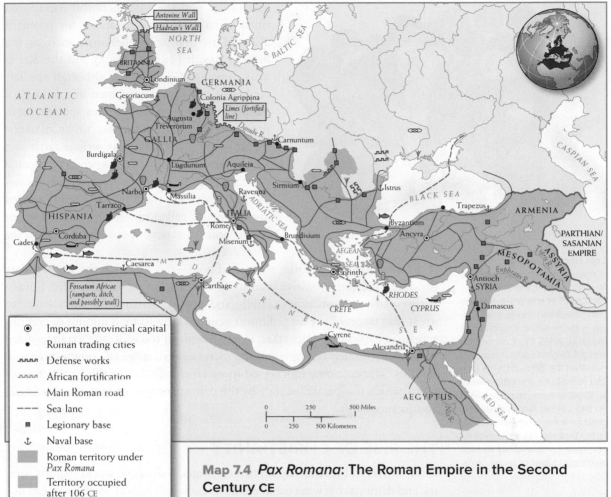

Map legend:

- ⊙ Important provincial capital
- • Roman trading cities
- ﹏ Defense works
- ﹏ African fortification
- — Main Roman road
- --- Sea lane
- ■ Legionary base
- ⚓ Naval base
- ▨ Roman territory under *Pax Romana*
- ▨ Territory occupied after 106 CE

Traded items
- ⬭ Metals
- ⚭ Enslaved people
- ⅄ Grain
- ▯ Marble
- ❧ Wine
- ◓ Ceramics
- ⌣ Oil
- ⬖ Amber
- ➤ Fish

Map labels: Antonine Wall, Hadrian's Wall, NORTH SEA, BALTIC SEA, BRITANNIA, Londinium, GERMANIA, Gesoriacum, Colonia Agrippina, Limes (fortified line), Augusta Treverorum, GALLIA, Rhine R., Danube R., Carnuntum, CASPIAN SEA, ATLANTIC OCEAN, Burdigala, Lugdunum, Aquileia, Sirmium, Istrus, BLACK SEA, Trapezus, ARMENIA, Narbo, Massilia, Ravenna, ADRIATIC SEA, Byzantium, Ancyra, PARTHIAN/ SASANIAN EMPIRE, Tarraco, HISPANIA, ITALIA, Rome, Brundisium, AEGEAN SEA, MESOPOTAMIA, Tigris R., Euphrates R., Corduba, Gades, Misenum, Caesarca, Corinth, Antioch, SYRIA, Damascus, Fossatum Africae (ramparts, ditch, and possibly wall), Carthage, MEDITERRANEAN SEA, CRETE, RHODES, CYPRUS, Cyrene, Alexandria, Nile R., RED SEA, AEGYPTUS

Scale: 0 — 250 — 500 Miles; 0 — 250 — 500 Kilometers

Map 7.4 *Pax Romana*: The Roman Empire in the Second Century CE

....

The Roman Empire enjoyed remarkable peace and prosperity in the second century CE. Economic production increased, and Roman culture expanded throughout the realm.

- According to the map, what commodities cluster in which regions? With what groups did Romans trade beyond their empire, and for what commodity in particular?

- What are some of the major sea-lanes and roads linking the different parts of the empire?

- What do you note about the locations of legionary bases and naval bases? What is the strategic value of their locations? How are the limits of empire delineated?

Coin Hoard Examining batches of coins buried for safekeeping reveals the range of coins in circulation at any one time. This coin hoard was found near Didcot in Oxfordshire, England. Buried around 165 CE, it contained about 125 gold coins minted between the 50s and 160s CE and represents the equivalent of about eleven years' pay for a Roman soldier. Gold coins were used for expensive transactions or to store wealth. Most ordinary purchases or payments were made with silver or brass coins.

agriculture and the first technical handbooks on how to run such operations for profit; it also led to dramatic rebellions, such as the Sicilian Revolt (135–132 BCE) and the Spartacus uprising (73–71 BCE), although the latter began among enslaved men in a school for gladiators. Slave-worked estates specialized in products destined for the big urban markets: wheat, grapes, and olives, as well as cattle and sheep. An impressive road system connected the far-flung parts of the empire. Milestones marked most of these roads, and complex ancient maps, called itineraries, charted major roads and distances between towns. (See Map 7.4.)

Rome mined copper, tin, silver, and gold—out of which the Roman state produced the most massive coinage system known in western Afro-Eurasia before early modern times. Public and private demand for metals was so great that traces of the air pollution generated by Roman mining operations remain in ice core samples taken from Greenland today. Rome's standardized currency facilitated taxation and the increased exchange of commodities and services. The economy functioned more efficiently due to this production of coins, which was paralleled only by the coinage output of Han dynasty China and its successors.

THE RISE OF CHRISTIANITY

Over centuries, Roman religion had cultivated a dynamic world of gods, spirits, and demons that was characteristic of earlier periods of Mediterranean history. **Christianity** took shape in this richly pluralistic world. Its foundations lay in a direct confrontation with Roman imperial authority: the trial of Jesus. After preaching the new doctrines of what was originally a sect of Judaism, Jesus was found guilty of sedition and executed by means of crucifixion—a standard Roman penalty—as the result of a typical Roman provincial trial overseen by a Roman governor, Pontius Pilatus.

No historical reference to Jesus survives from his own lifetime. Shortly after the crucifixion, Paul of Tarsus, a Jew and a Roman citizen from southeastern Anatolia, claimed to have seen Jesus in full glory outside the city of Damascus. Paul and the Mediterranean communities to whom he preached and wrote letters between 40 and 60 CE referred to Jesus as the Anointed One (the Messiah, in keeping with Jewish expectations) or the Christ—*ho Christos* in Greek (still the dominant language of the eastern Mediterranean region thanks to Hellenism). Only many decades later did accounts that came to be called the Gospels—such as Matthew, Mark, Luke, and John—describe Jesus's life and record his sayings. Jesus's preaching drew not only on Jewish models but also on the Egyptian and Mesopotamian image of the great king as shepherd of his people (see Chapter 3). With Jesus, this image of the good shepherd took on a new, personal closeness. Not a distant monarch but a preacher, Jesus had set out on God's behalf to gather a new, small flock.

Through the writings of Paul and the Gospels, both written in Greek, this image of Jesus rapidly spread beyond Palestine (where Jesus had preached only to Jews and only in the local language, Aramaic). Core elements of Jesus's message, such as the responsibilities of the well-off for the poor and the promised eventual empowerment of "the meek," appealed to many ordinary people in the wider Mediterranean world. But it was the apostle Paul who was especially responsible for reshaping this message for a wider audience. While Jesus's teachings were directed at villagers and peasants, Paul's message spoke to a world divided by religious identity, wealth, slavery, and gender differences: "There is neither Jew nor Greek, there is neither slave nor free, there is neither male nor female; for you are all one in Christ Jesus" (Galatians 3:28). This new message, universal in its claims and appeal, was immediately accessible to the dwellers of the towns and cities of the Roman Empire.

Just half a century after Jesus's crucifixion, the followers of Jesus saw in his life not merely the wanderings of a Jewish charismatic teacher, but a head-on collision between "God" and "the world." Jesus's teachings came to be understood as the message of a divine being—who for thirty years had moved (largely unrecognized) among human beings. Jesus's followers formed a church: a permanent gathering entrusted to the charge of leaders chosen by God and fellow believers. For these leaders and their followers, death offered a defining testimony for their faith. Early Christians hoped for a Roman trial and the opportunity to offer themselves as witnesses (*martyrs*) for their faith.

Persecutions of Christians were sporadic and were responses to local concerns. Not until the emperor Decius, in the mid-third century CE, did the state direct an empire-wide attack on Christians. But Decius died within a year of launching this assault, and Christians interpreted their persecutor's death as evidence of the hand of God in human affairs. By the last decades of the third century CE, Christian communities of various kinds, reflecting the different strands of their movement through the Mediterranean as well as the local cultures in which they settled, were present in every society in the empire.

THE LIMITS OF EMPIRE

The limitations of Roman force were a pragmatic factor in determining who belonged in, and was subject to, the empire as opposed to who was outside it and therefore excluded. The Romans pushed their authority in the west to the

Christianity
New religious movement originating in the Eastern Roman Empire in the first century CE, with roots in Judaism and resonance with various Greco-Roman religious traditions. The central figure, Jesus, was tried and executed by Roman authorities, and his followers believed he rose from the dead. The tradition was spread across the Mediterranean by his followers, and Christians were initially persecuted—to varying degrees—by Roman authorities. The religion was eventually legalized in 312 CE, and by the late fourth century CE it became the official state religion of the Roman Empire.

Han China, the Early Roman Empire, and the Silk Roads

This chapter offers detailed information allowing for a comparison of the globalizing empires of imperial Rome and Han China. To what extent, however, were these powerful, contemporary forces in contact with each other? Because the Roman Empire and Han China were separated by 5,000 miles, harsh terrain, and the powerful Parthian Empire, scholars have wondered about their interaction and knowledge of each other. (See Map 7.5.) In the nineteenth century, European archaeologists created the term "Silk Road," stressing the commercial linkages between these two great empires. (See Chapter 6 for more on the early Silk Roads.) Many twentieth-century historians have challenged this view, first, questioning the validity of the term due to its emphasis on silk exchange to the exclusion of other traded commodities, and, second, questioning the extent of direct, or even indirect, commercial exchanges between Han China and the Roman Empire. Some modern historians see the very idea of a Silk Road as part of a de-Europeanizing trend among global historians who are committed to elevating the Chinese as the true entrepreneurs of the age.

David F. Graf's recent exhaustively researched study offers an exciting new look at the Silk Roads and Chinese-Roman relations. He finds clear evidence that already by the reign of

Peutinger Table A medieval copy of a Roman-era itinerary (road map), the *Peutinger Table* charts the Romans' known world, stretching from Britain in the west to India in the east. This segment toward the western end of the map represents (from top to bottom) France, a strip of the Mediterranean Sea, and North Africa. Topographical features such as rivers and mountain ranges, as well as human-made features such as roads, towns, and ports, demonstrate the Romans' feet-on-the-ground understanding of the land they traversed.

Augustus, substantial amounts of Chinese silk were available in the Mediterranean world. Graf observes that the late first-century BCE poets Virgil and Ovid have many references to Chinese silk. Another first-century BCE poet, Horace, was more explicit about the use of Chinese silks, writing that "the sheer and transparent qualities of serica [Chinese] dresses became a symbol of degeneracy of the emperors and aristocratic women, drawing condemnation." In the late first century CE, natural historian Pliny the Elder commented somewhat disdainfully on

trade with the Seres (the Silk People): "Though mild in character, the Chinese still resemble wild animals in that they shun the company of the rest of humankind and wait for trade to come to them." While the *Peutinger Table*, a map (or itinerary) thought to reveal early first-century CE geographic knowledge, does not reach as far as China in the east, the Romans had sufficient information by the middle of the second century CE to enable mapmakers drawing on Ptolemy's *Geography* to locate China and the rest of East Asia on their map of the world.

The Han emperor most responsible for beginning to expand Chinese influence westward, opening up trade routes to China's west and gaining knowledge of western regions, was Emperor Wu (r. 141–87 BCE). In 139 BCE, Wu sent an official, Zhang Qian, accompanied by more than a hundred men, on a mission to the west. The primary goal of this mission was to secure alliances with central Asian states, most importantly the Yuezhi, against the Xiongnu nomads, who threatened the Han at this time. On his way to the Yuezhi, Zhang Qian was detained by a Xiongnu chieftain for ten years, during which he married a Xiongnu woman and had children with her. While in captivity, Zhang Qian gathered information on the commodities from this region and beyond, including Bactria, India, and Persia. He shared this information when he eventually escaped and returned to the Han capital at Chang'an. In short, Wu's diplomatic and military moves expanded China's understanding of the west and knowledge of routes through which silk could be shipped westward.

A second major Chinese initiative regarding the west occurred around the end of the first century CE and the beginning of the second. Here, the leading figure was General Ban Ch'ao (brother of Ban Zhao, who wrote the *Lessons for Women* excerpted at the end of this chapter). Ban Ch'ao held the office of Protector of the Western Territories between 91 and 101 CE. He brought the whole of the Tarim Basin under Chinese rule and established a set of forts on routes leading westward. He dispatched one of his adjuncts, Gan Ying, to travel westward and gather information on regions thus far unexplored by the Chinese. Gan Ying did not reach Rome, though his mission was to do so. Nevertheless, journeying only as far as the Black Sea or the Persian Gulf, he did acquire much information about Rome and its dependent states.

The Roman Empire was known to the Chinese as Da Qin. Gan Ying viewed Da Qin accurately in some respects and fantastically in others. In fact, Graf notes that the Chinese sources portrayed the Romans through their own spectacles, seeing Rome as "an idealized China, a Taoist utopia, a fictitious religious world divorced from reality." According to Chinese sources, the first direct contact with the Roman Empire occurred during the ninth year of the reign of Huandi (166 CE), when a private Roman merchant arrived at the Chinese commandery on the central Vietnamese coast with "gifts of elephant tusks, rhinoceros horn, and tortoise shell" during the reign of Marcus Aurelius. The Chinese court was unimpressed by these offerings, even wondering if the reports of Rome's power had been exaggerated.

Most of the Chinese silk that reached the Mediterranean regions came by sea via the route described in the *Periplus Maris Erythraei* (see Chapter 6), often through the Persian Gulf and Red Sea and then overland to ports along the coast of present-day Syria. But the overland route, which most scholars have called the Silk Road, was also in use at this time. The entry point for much Chinese silk was Palmyra. Trade through Palmyra reached its high point in the second century CE. To date, the largest quantity of silk found outside China and dated to ancient times was discovered in Palmyra. The polychrome silk weaving found in Palmyra can be traced back to

imperial Chinese workshops. The conclusion of the most recent scholarship on the Silk Roads and Chinese-Roman relations, according to Graf, is that "there was significant movement of peoples and goods along segments of the 'Silk Route' during the Roman imperial era," but the relations between the Chinese and the Romans were remote and "indirect."

Questions for Analysis

- What is the evidence for exchange between the Romans and the Han Chinese? What were the impediments to direct interaction between Rome and China?
- What did the Romans think about trade with China? What did the Chinese think of Rome?
- How does the evidence for interconnectivity between Rome and China influence your understanding of the comparative picture of these two globalizing empires?

Explore Further

Graf, David F., "The Silk Road between Syria and China," in *Trade, Commerce, and the State in the Roman World*, edited by Andrew Wilson and Alan Bowman (2018), pp. 443–529.

Hansen, Valerie, *The Silk Road: A New History* (2012).

Liu, Xinru, *The Silk Road in World History* (2010).

Sources: David F. Graf, "The Silk Road between Syria and China," in *Trade, Commerce, and the State in the Roman World,* edited by Andrew Wilson and Alan Bowman (Oxford: Oxford University Press, 2018), pp. 443–529 (quotations are from pp. 444, 460, 477–78).

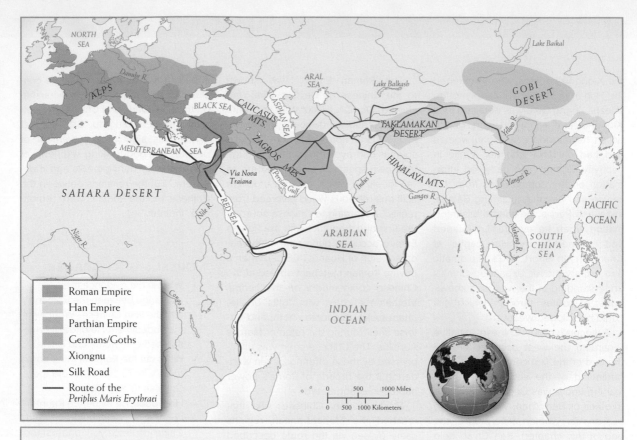

Map 7.5 Imperial Rome and Later (Eastern) Han China, C. 200 CE

Imperial Rome and the Later (Eastern) Han dynasty thrived simultaneously for about 200 years at the start of the first millennium CE. Despite their geographic spread and the Silk Roads running across Afro-Eurasia, the two empires did not have as much direct contact as one might expect.

- What major groups lived on the borders of imperial Rome and Han China?
- What were the geographical limits of the Roman Empire? Of Han China?
- Based on the map and your reading, what drew imperial Rome and Han China together? What kept them apart?

shores of the Atlantic Ocean, and to the south they drove it to the edges of the Sahara Desert. In both cases, there was little additional useful land available to dominate. Roman power was blocked, however, to the east by the Parthians and then the Sasanians and to the north by the Goths and other Germanic peoples.

The Parthians and Sassanians On Rome's eastern frontiers, powerful Romans, such as Marcus Crassus in the mid-50s BCE, Mark Antony in the early 30s BCE, and the emperor Trajan around 115 CE, wished to imitate the achievements of Alexander the Great and conquer the arid lands lying east of Judea and Syria. Crassus and Antony failed miserably, stopped by the Parthian Empire and its successor, the Sasanian Empire. The Romans, under Trajan, briefly annexed the provinces of Armenia and Mesopotamia but abandoned them soon thereafter. The Parthian people had moved south from present-day Turkmenistan and settled in the region comprising the modern states of Iraq and Iran. Parthian social order was founded on nomadic pastoralism and a war capability based on technical advances in mounted horseback warfare. Reliance on horses made the Parthian style of fighting highly mobile and ideal for warfare on arid plains and deserts. They perfected the so-called Parthian shot: the arrow shot from a bow with great accuracy at long distance and from horseback at a gallop. On the flat, open plains of Iran and Iraq, the Parthians had a decisive advantage over slow-moving, cumbersome mass infantry formations that had been developed for war in the Mediterranean. Eventually the expansionist states of Parthia and Rome became archenemies: they confronted each other in Mesopotamia for nearly four centuries.

The Sasanians expanded the technical advances in mounted horseback warfare that the Parthians had used so successfully in open desert warfare against the slow-moving Roman mass infantry formations. King Shapur I (r. 240–270 CE) exploited the weaknesses of the Roman Empire in the mid-third century CE, even capturing the Roman emperor Valerian. One early Christian writer, Lactantius, used Valerian's fate at the hands of the Sasanians—he was forced to serve in captivity as a footstool for the Sasanian king, then flayed and stuffed after death to stand in the Sasanian throne room as a warning to ambassadors—as a lesson for what happens to those who persecute Christians. As successful as the Parthians and the Sasanians were in fighting the Romans, however, they could never challenge Roman sway over Mediterranean lands. Their decentralized political structure limited their coordination and resources, and their horse-mounted style of warfare was ill suited to fighting in the more rocky and hilly environments of the Mediterranean world. (See Chapter 8 for more on the Sasanians.)

German and Gothic "Barbarians" In the lands across the Rhine and Danube, to the north, environmental conditions largely determined the limits of empire. The long and harsh winters, combined with excellent soil and growing conditions, produced hardy, dense population clusters scattered across vast distances. These illiterate, kin-based agricultural societies had changed little since the first millennium BCE.

As the Roman Empire fixed its northern frontiers along the Rhine and Danube Rivers, two factors determined its relationship with the Germans

Soldier versus Barbarian On the frontiers of the Roman Empire, the legionary soldiers faced the non-Roman "barbarians" from the lands beyond. In this piece of a stone-carved picture from Trajan's Column in Rome, we see a civilized and disciplined Roman soldier, to the left, facing a German "barbarian"—with uncut and unkempt hair, no formal armor, and a thatched hut for a home. Frontier realities were never so clear-cut, of course. Roman soldiers, often recruited from the "barbarian" peoples, were a lot more like them than was convenient to admit, and the "barbarians" were influenced by and closer to Roman cultural models than this picture indicates.

and Goths on the rivers' other side. First, these small societies had only one big commodity for which the empire was willing to pay: human bodies. So the slave trade out of the land across the Rhine and Danube became immense: gold, silver, coins, wine, arms, and other luxury items flowed across the rivers in one direction in exchange for enslaved people flowing into the empire. Second, the wars between the Romans and these societies were unremitting, as every emperor faced the expectation of dealing harshly with these so-called barbarians. Ironically, internal conflicts within the Roman Empire ultimately prompted increasing use of "barbarians" as soldiers and even as officers who served the empire.

While the Han Empire fell in the early third century CE, the Roman Empire would arguably continue to exist politically for more than two centuries (to at least the "traditional" collapse date of 476 CE), during which its history would become intertwined with the rise of Christianity, one of the world's universalizing religions.

Conclusion

China and Rome both constructed empires of unprecedented scale and duration, yet they differed in fundamental ways. Starting out with a less numerous and less dense population than China, Rome relied on enslaved people and "barbarian" immigrants to expand and diversify its workforce. While less than 1 percent of the Chinese population was enslaved, more than 10 percent of the population in the Roman Empire was enslaved. The Chinese rural economy was built on a huge population of free peasant farmers; this enormous labor pool, together with a remarkable bureaucracy, enabled the Han to achieve great political stability. In contrast, the millions of peasant farmers who formed the backbone of rural society in the Roman Empire were much more loosely integrated into the state structure. They never unified to revolt against their government and overthrow it, as did the mass peasant movements of Later (Eastern) Han China. In comparison with their counterparts in China, the peasants in the Roman Empire were not as well connected because they lived farther apart from one another, and they were not as united in purpose. Here, too, the Mediterranean environment accented separation and difference.

In contrast with the elaborate Confucian bureaucracy in Han China, the Roman Empire was relatively fragmented and underadministered. Moreover, no single philosophy or religion ever underpinned the Roman state in the way that Confucianism buttressed the dynasties of China. Both empires, however, benefited from the spread of a uniform language and imperial culture. The process was more comprehensive in China, which possessed a single language that the elites used, than in Rome, where officially a two-language world existed: Latin in the western Mediterranean, Greek in the east. Both states fostered a common imperial culture across all levels of society. Once entrenched, these cultures and languages lasted well after the end of empire.

Differences in human resources, languages, and ideas led the Roman and Han states to evolve in unique ways. In both places, however, faiths that filtered in from the margins—Christianity and Buddhism—eclipsed the classical and secular traditions that grounded the states' foundational ideals. Expanded communication networks accelerated the transmission of these new faiths. The new religions added to the cultural mix that outlasted the Roman Empire and the Han dynasty.

At their height, both states surpassed their forebears by translating unprecedented military power into the fullest form of state-based organization. Each state's complex organization involved the systematic control, counting, and taxing of its population. In both cases, the general increase of the population, the growth of huge cities, and the success of long-distance trade contributed to the new scales of magnitude, making these states the world's first two long-lasting global empires. The Han were not superseded in East Asia as the model empire until the Tang dynasty in the seventh century CE. In western Afro-Eurasia, the Roman Empire was not surpassed in scale or intensity of development until the rise of powerful European nation-states more than a millennium later.

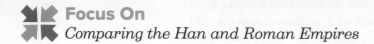

Focus On
Comparing the Han and Roman Empires

- Han China and imperial Rome assimilate diverse peoples and regard outsiders as uncivilized.

- Both empires develop professional military elites, codify laws, and value the role of the state (not just the ruler) in supporting their societies.

- Both empires serve as models for successor states in their regions.

- The empires differ in their ideals and the officials they value: Han China values civilian bureaucrats and magistrates; Rome values soldiers and military governors.

Key Terms

Augustus p. 338	Emperor Wu p. 323	*Pax Romana* p. 338	*res publica* p. 337
Christianity p. 344	globalizing empires p. 317	*Pax Sinica* p. 328	Shi Huangdi p. 319
commanderies p. 319	Imperial University p. 324	Punic Wars p. 336	

CHRONOLOGY

	300 BCE	200 BCE	100 BCE

East Asia

Qin Empire of Shi Huangdi 221–207 BCE

Emperor Wu expands Han Empire 141–87 BCE

The Mediterranean

Roman state expands through Italian Peninsula 340–265 BCE

Rome eliminates Carthage (Punic Wars) 264–146 BCE

Tiberius and Gaius Gracchus attempt agrarian reforms 133–121 BCE

- **Thinking about Worlds Together, Worlds Apart and Globalizing Empires** In the six centuries between 300 BCE and 300 CE, the Han dynasty and imperial Rome united huge populations and immense swaths of territory not only under their direct control but also under their indirect influence. In what ways did this expansive unity at each end of Afro-Eurasia have an impact on the connections between these two empires? In what ways did these two empires remain worlds apart?

- **Thinking about Changing Power Relationships and Globalizing Empires** Both the Han dynasty and the Roman Empire developed new models for heightened

authoritarian control placed in the hands of a single ruler. In what ways did this authoritarian control at the top shape power relationships at all levels of these two societies? What were some potential challenges to this patriarchal, centralized control?

- **Thinking about Transformation & Conflict and Globalizing Empires** Both the Han dynasty and the Roman Empire faced intense threats along their borders. In what ways did Han interactions with nomadic groups like the Xiongnu and Roman interactions with Parthians to the east and Germans and Goths to the north affect these globalizing empires?

 Go to INQUIZITIVE to see what you've learned—and learn what you've missed—with personalized feedback along the way.

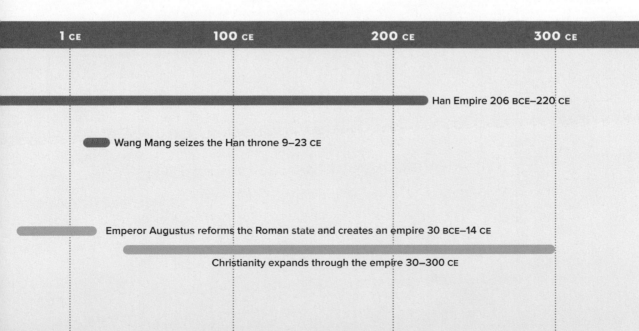

| 1 CE | 100 CE | 200 CE | 300 CE |

Han Empire 206 BCE–220 CE

Wang Mang seizes the Han throne 9–23 CE

Emperor Augustus reforms the Roman state and creates an empire 30 BCE–14 CE

Christianity expands through the empire 30–300 CE

Global Themes and Sources

Comparing Political and Domestic Order in Han China and Imperial Rome

The four passages included here illustrate views from the Han Chinese and the Romans on how to maintain order within their respective empires. The first two philosophical treatises, on rulership and government, provide a male point of view on legitimate political authority in each empire. The other two philosophical discussions (one written by a woman) describe how to bring harmony to the most basic unit of society in both the Han dynasty and the Roman Empire—the household.

In the first excerpt, the second-century BCE Han Chinese scholar Dong Zhongshu integrates a Confucian rationale into the justification for the legitimacy of Han rule. In the second text, Marcus Tullius Cicero, a leading Roman politician from the 60s through the 40s BCE, presents his view on the responsibilities of political officeholders in the Roman state. In the third selection, Ban Zhao, a female writer from Han China, offers *Lessons for Women* drawing on philosophical ideals. No exact parallel of Ban Zhao's text survives from the Roman Empire. While there are literary fragments, short handwritten notes, and possibly epitaphs (funeral inscriptions) composed by Roman women, we must turn to a male writer, the Stoic philosopher Musonius Rufus, for the fourth text, which gives a Roman perspective on women's education comparable to the *Lessons* of Ban Zhao.

These texts offer an opportunity to compare a range of issues. To begin with, you can compare the models for political order with those for domestic order *within* each empire. For example, examining the model for political harmony between ruler and people in Dong Zhongshu's text together with the model for domestic harmony in Ban Zhao's *Lessons for Women* clarifies the relationship between the public and the private sphere. In addition, you can identify and compare the expectations for political and domestic order in Han China with those of the Roman world. Beyond a mere identification of similarities and differences, you can use what you learned in this chapter to try to explain why those similarities and differences exist and begin to explore why they matter for understanding Han China and imperial Rome on their own terms.

Analyzing Political and Domestic Order in Han China and Imperial Rome

- According to these texts, what are the characteristics of a good ruler? Of good subjects? What are the traits of a good husband? A good wife?

- According to these texts, what brings political and domestic harmony? What brings discord?

- What elements in these texts suggest that they offer an elite, primarily male, perspective? To what extent do the ideas presented in these texts extend beyond elite men to women, children, and nonelites?

- What do these texts suggest about the similarities and differences in ideas about political and domestic harmony in Han China and late republican and imperial Rome? Why do you think those similarities and differences appear in these texts?

On the Responsibilities of Rulership (c. 100 BCE), Dong Zhongshu

Dong Zhongshu was an influential adviser during the reign of Emperor Wu (r. 141–87 BCE). In the late second century BCE, Dong wrote a philosophical treatise called *Chunqiu fanlu*, or *Luxuriant Dew of the Spring and Autumn Annals*. The excerpt provided here discusses the responsibilities of a ruler, the "spontaneous punishment" and "spontaneous reward" that derive from the nature of "he who rules," and the need to attend to the "three foundations." Dong's ideas about the importance of Confucianism were manifested in Emperor Wu's creation of the Imperial University for training bureaucrats.

....

- What are the duties of "he who rules the people," and what is at stake in the fulfillment of these duties?

- What are the "three foundations," and how does a good ruler attend to them?

- What evidence do you see of Confucian values in Dong Zhongshu's model of statecraft?

....

Section 1: He who rules the people is the basis of the state. Issuing edicts and initiating undertakings, he is the pivot of all living things. The pivot of all living things, he is the source of honor and dishonor. If he errs by a millimeter, a team of horses cannot retrieve him. This is why he who acts as the people's ruler is attentive toward the fundamental, careful of the beginning, respectful of the small, and cautious of the subtle. . . . He examines [his people's] past activities to verify their present dispositions. He reckons to what extent their accomplishments are derived from former worthies. He dispels their grievances and observes the causes of their disputes. He separates their factions and clans and observes the men they esteem. He relies upon his position to order his people and employs [correct] words to establish their reputations. . . . This is called "eliminating obstructions."

Section 2: He who rules the people is the foundation of the state. Now in administering the state, nothing is more important for transforming [the people] than reverence for the foundation. If the foundation is revered, the ruler will transform [the people] as if a spirit. If the foundation is not revered, the ruler will lack the means to unite the people. If he lacks the means to unite the people, even if he institutes strict punishments and heavy penalties, the people will not submit. This is called "throwing away the state.". . . Heaven, Earth, and humankind are the foundation of all living things. Heaven engenders all living things, Earth nourishes them, and humankind completes them. . . . These three assist one another just as the hands and feet join to complete the body. None can be dispensed with because without filial and brotherly

love, people lack the means to live; without food and clothing, people lack the means to be nourished; and without rites and music, people lack the means to become complete. If all three are lost, people become like deer, each person following his own desires and each family practicing its own customs. Fathers will not be able to order their sons, and rulers will not be able to order their ministers. Although possessing inner and outer walls, [the ruler's city] will become known as "an empty settlement.". . . Although no one endangers him, he will naturally be endangered; although no one destroys him, he will naturally be destroyed. This is called "spontaneous punishment." When it arrives, even if he is hidden in a stone vault or barricaded in a narrow pass, the ruler will not be able to avoid "spontaneous punishment."

One who is an enlightened master and worthy ruler believes such things. For this reason he respectfully and carefully attends to the three foundations. He reverently enacts the suburban sacrifice, dutifully serves his ancestors, manifests filial and brotherly love, encourages filial conduct, and serves the foundation of Heaven in this way. He takes up the plough handle to till the soil, plucks the mulberry leaves and nourishes the silkworms, reclaims the wilds, plants grain, opens new lands to provide sufficient food and clothing, and serves the foundation of Earth in this way. He establishes academies and schools in towns and villages to teach filial piety, brotherly love, reverence, and humility, enlightens [the people] with education, moves [them] with rites and music, and serves the foundation of humanity in this way.

If these three foundations are all served, the people will resemble sons and brothers who do not dare usurp authority, while the ruler will resemble fathers and mothers. He will not rely on favors to demonstrate his love for his people nor severe measures to prompt them to act. Even if he lives in the wilds without a roof over head, he will consider that this surpasses living in a palace. . . . Although no one assists him, he will naturally be powerful; although no one pacifies his state, peace will naturally come. This is called "spontaneous reward." When "spontaneous reward" befalls him, although he might relinquish the throne and leave the state, the people will take up their children on their backs and follow him as the ruler, so that he too will be unable to leave them. Therefore when the ruler relies on virtue to administer the state, it is sweeter than honey or sugar and firmer than glue or lacquer. This is why sages and worthies exert themselves to revere the foundation and do not dare depart from it.

Source: Dong Zhongshu, "Responsibilities of Han Rulership," in *Sources of Chinese Tradition*, vol. 1, *From the Earliest Times to 1600*, 2nd ed., edited by Wm. Theodore de Bary and Irene Bloom (New York: Columbia University Press, 1999), pp. 298–300.

PRIMARY SOURCE 7.2

The Role of the Roman State (mid-first century BCE), Cicero

Cicero was a powerful politician and rhetorician in the mid-first century BCE. He worked his way up through the various offices a Roman nobleman would hold in his political career. Cicero's first low-ranking political office led to a series of powerful speeches against a corrupt politician who had ruled brutally in Sicily. After that, his political and oratorical career thrived: his consulship in 63 BCE forestalled an attempted coup, and his many deliberative speeches shaped legislation for two decades. Cicero is writing from a deep well of experience when he outlines the role of the Roman state in his essay *De Officiis* (*On Offices*), excerpted here.

- **What are the duties of a state to its people?**
- **What are Cicero's views on private property, taxation, and bribery?**
- **To whom do Cicero's ideas on government and office holding apply?**

[73] The man in an administrative office, however, must make it his first care that everyone shall have what belongs to him and that private citizens suffer no invasion of their property rights by act of the state. It was a ruinous policy that Philippus proposed when in his tribuneship he introduced his agrarian bill. However, when his law was rejected, he took his defeat with good grace and displayed extraordinary moderation. But in his public speeches on the measure he often played the demagogue, and that time viciously, when he said that "there were not in the state two thousand people who owned any property." That speech deserves unqualified condemnation, for it favoured an equal distribution of property; and what more ruinous policy than that could be conceived? For the chief purpose in the establishment of constitutional state and municipal governments was that individual property rights might be secured. For, although it was by Nature's guidance that men were drawn together into communities, it was in the hope of safeguarding their possessions that they sought the protection of cities.

[74] The administration should also put forth every effort to prevent the levying of a property tax, and to this end precautions should be taken long in advance. Such a tax was often levied in the times of our forefathers on account of the depleted state of their treasury and their incessant wars. But, if any state (I say "any," for I would rather speak in general terms than forebode evils to our own; however, I am not discussing our own state but states in general)—if any state ever has to face a crisis requiring the imposition of such a burden, every effort must be made to let all the people realize that they must bow to the inevitable, if they wish to be saved. And it will also be the duty of those who direct the affairs of the state to take measures that there shall be an abundance of the necessities of life. It is needless to discuss the ordinary ways and means; for the duty is self-evident; it is necessary only to mention the matter.

[75] But the chief thing in all public administration and public service is to avoid even the slightest suspicion of self-seeking. "I would," says Gaius Pontius, the Samnite, "that fortune had withheld my appearance until a time when the Romans began to accept bribes, and that I had been born in those days! I should then have suffered them to hold their supremacy no longer." Aye, but he would have had many generations to wait; for this plague has only recently infected our nation. And so I rejoice that Pontius lived then instead of now, seeing that he was so mighty a man! It is not yet a hundred and ten years since the enactment of Lucius Piso's bill to punish extortion; there had been no such law before. But afterward came so many laws, each more stringent than the other, so many men were accused and so many convicted, so horrible a war was stirred up on account of the fear of what our courts would do to still others, so frightful was the pillaging and plundering of the allies when the laws and courts were suppressed, that now we find

ourselves strong not in our own strength but in the weakness of others.

* * *

[77] There is, then, to bring the discussion back to the point from which it digressed, no vice more offensive than avarice, especially in men who stand foremost and hold the helm of state. For to exploit the state for selfish profit is not only immoral; it is criminal, infamous. And so the oracle, which the Pythian Apollo uttered, that "Sparta should not fall from any other cause than avarice," seems to be a prophecy not to the Lacedaemonians alone, but to all wealthy nations as well. They who direct the affairs of state, then, can win the good-will of the masses by no other means more easily than by self-restraint and self-denial.

[78] But they who pose as friends of the people, and who for that reason either attempt to have agrarian laws passed, in order that the occupants may be driven out of their homes, or propose that money loaned should be remitted to the borrowers, are undermining the foundations of the commonwealth: first of all, they are destroying harmony, which cannot exist when money is taken away from one party and bestowed upon another; and second, they do away with equity, which is utterly subverted, if the rights of property are not respected. For, as I said above, it is the peculiar function of the state and the city to guarantee to every man the free and undisturbed control of his own particular property.

Source: Cicero, *De Officiis*, translated by Walter Miller (Cambridge, MA: Harvard University Press, 1913), pp. 249, 251, 253, 255.

PRIMARY SOURCE 7.3

Lessons for Women (c. 100 CE), Ban Zhao

A well-connected and highly educated woman, Ban Zhao wrote *Nujie*, or *Lessons for Women*, toward the end of the Han dynasty. Widowed at a young age, Ban Zhao was able to devote her attentions to literary and philosophical pursuits. Her father and brother were court historians writing the *Book of Han*, which she finalized herself following their deaths. Another brother was a prominent general who was Protector of the Western Territories (91–101 CE). Not only were Ban Zhao's life and literary career truly exceptional, but her articulation of a proper code for female behavior shaped expectations for mothers, wives, and daughters living during the Han dynasty and for hundreds of years later.

....

- According to Ban Zhao, what are the characteristics of a proper woman, and how are these reflected in a woman's behavior? How does Ban Zhao compare a woman's behavior with her husband's?

- What Chinese philosophical concepts inform Ban Zhao's *Lessons for Women*?

- How, if at all, does the fact that Ban Zhao was a woman influence your reading of this text?

....

Chapter I: Humility—Let a woman modestly yield to others; let her respect others; let her put others first, herself last. Should she do something good, let her not mention it; should she do something bad, let her not deny it. Let her bear disgrace; let her even endure when others speak or do evil to her. Always let her seem to tremble and to fear. (When a woman follows such maxims as these,) then she may be said to humble herself before others.

Let a woman retire late to bed, but rise early to duties; let her not dread tasks by day or by night. Let her not refuse to perform domestic duties whether easy or difficult. That which must be done, let her finish completely, tidily, and systematically. (When a woman follows such rules as these,) then she may be said to be industrious.

Let a woman be correct in manner and upright in character in order to serve her husband. Let her live in purity and quietness (of spirit), and attend to her own affairs. Let her love not gossip and silly laughter. Let her cleanse and purify and arrange in order the wine and the food for the offerings to the ancestors. (When a woman observes such principles as these,) then she may be said to continue ancestral worship.

No woman who observes these three (fundamentals of life) has ever had a bad reputation or has fallen into disgrace. If a woman fail to observe them, how can her name be honored; how can she but bring disgrace upon herself?

Chapter II: Husband and Wife—The Way of husband and wife is intimately connected with *Yin* and *Yang*, and relates the individual to gods and ancestors.

Truly it is the great principle of Heaven and Earth, and the great basis of human relationships. . . .

If a husband be unworthy then he possesses nothing by which to control his wife. If a wife be unworthy, then she possesses nothing with which to serve her husband. If a husband does not control his wife, then the rules of conduct manifesting his authority are abandoned and broken. If a wife does not serve her husband, then the proper relationship (between men and women) and the natural order of things are neglected and destroyed. . . .

Now examine the gentlemen of the present age. They only know that wives must be controlled, and that the husband's rules of conduct manifesting his authority must be established. They therefore teach their boys to read books and (study) histories. But they do not in the least understand that husbands and masters must (also) be served, and that the proper relationship and the rites should be maintained.

Yet only to teach men and not to teach women,—is that not ignoring the essential relation between them? According to the "Rites," it is the rule to begin to teach children to read at the age of eight years, and by the age of fifteen years they ought then to be ready for cultural training. Only why should it not be (that girls' education as well as boys' be) according to this principle?

Chapter III: Respect and Caution—As *Yin* and *Yang* are not of the same nature, so man and woman have different characteristics. The distinctive quality of the *Yang* is rigidity; the function of the *Yin* is yielding. Man is honored for strength; a woman is beautiful on account of her gentleness. . . .

Now for self-culture nothing equals respect for others. To counteract firmness nothing equals compliance. Consequently it can be said that the Way of respect and acquiescence is woman's most important principle of conduct. So respect may be defined as nothing other than holding on to that which is permanent; and acquiescence nothing other than being liberal and generous. Those who are steadfast in devotion know that they should stay in their proper places; those who are liberal and generous esteem others, and honor and serve (them). . . .

Chapter IV: Womanly Qualifications—A woman (ought to) have four qualifications: (1) womanly virtue; (2) womanly words; (3) womanly bearing; and (4) womanly work. Now what is called womanly virtue need not be brilliant ability, exceptionally different from others. Womanly words need be neither clever in debate nor keen in conversation. Womanly appearance requires neither a pretty nor a perfect face and form. Womanly work need not be work done more skillfully than that of others.

To guard carefully her chastity; to control circumspectly her behavior; in every motion to exhibit modesty; and to model each act on the best usage, this is womanly virtue.

To choose her words with care; to avoid vulgar language; to speak at appropriate times; and not to weary others (with much conversation), may be called the characteristics of womanly words.

To wash and scrub filth away; to keep clothes and ornaments fresh and clean; to wash the head and bathe the body regularly, and to keep the person free from disgraceful filth, may be called the characteristics of womanly bearing.

With whole-hearted devotion to sew and to weave; to love not gossip and silly laughter; in cleanliness and order (to prepare) the wine and food for serving guests, may be called the characteristics of womanly work.

Source: Pan Chao, *Lessons for Women*, in *Pan Chao. Foremost Woman Scholar of China*, translated by Nancy Lee Swann (New York: Century, 1932), pp. 83–86.

On Women's Education in Rome (first century CE), Musonius Rufus

Musonius Rufus was a Stoic philosopher who lived during the first century CE. As a proponent of Stoicism, he valued virtue, knowledge, and civic engagement. His discourses touch on everything from the food one should consume and the proper length of one's hair and beard to women's education and marriage. His optimism about the value of training women in philosophy can be offset against the views of the satirist Juvenal, his rough contemporary, who wrote, "Don't let the woman who shares your marriage bed adhere to a set style of speaking or hurl well rounded sentences. . . . Let there be things in books she does not understand."

- What are the qualities a woman must possess, according to Musonius Rufus? How do those expectations compare with those placed on men in this same text?

- Why does Musonius Rufus suggest it is a good idea for a woman to be educated and to study philosophy?

- How does the fact that this text represents the views of a male philosopher influence your reading of it? Do you think these views were widely held when he wrote this text? Why or why not?

(3) When he [Musonius Rufus] was asked whether women ought to study philosophy, he began to answer the question approximately as follows. Women have received from the gods the same ability to reason that men have. We men employ reasoning in our relations with others and so far as possible in everything we do, whether it is good or bad, or noble or shameful. Likewise women have the same senses as men, sight, hearing, smell, and all the rest. . . . In addition, it is not men alone who possess eagerness and a natural inclination towards virtue, but women also. Women are pleased no less than men by noble and just deeds, and reject the opposite of such actions. Since that is so, why is it appropriate for men to seek out and examine how they might live well, that is, to practice philosophy, but not women? Is it fitting for men to be good, but not women?

Let us consider in detail the qualities that a woman who seeks to be good must possess, for it will be apparent that she could acquire each of these qualities from the practice of philosophy.

In the first place a woman must run her household and pick out what is beneficial for her home and take charge of the household slaves.

In these activities I claim that philosophy is particularly helpful, since each of these activities is an aspect of life, and philosophy is nothing other than the science of living. . . . Next, a woman must be chaste, and capable of keeping herself free from illegal love affairs, and pure in respect to the other pleasures of indulgence, and not enjoy quarrels, not be extravagant, or preoccupied with her appearance. . . . There are still other requirements: she must control anger, and not

be overcome by grief, and be stronger than every kind of emotion. That is what the philosopher's rationale entails, and the person who knows it and practices it seems to me to be perfectly controlled, whether it is a man or a woman. So much for the subject of self-control.

Now, wouldn't the woman who practices philosophy be just, and a blameless partner in life, and a good worker in common causes, and devoted in her responsibilities towards her husband and her children, and free in every way from greed or ambition? Who could be like this more than the woman who practices philosophy, so long as she truly is a philosopher, since she must inevitably think that doing wrong is worse than being wronged, because it is more disgraceful to do wrong, and to think that being inferior is preferable to being ambitious, and in addition, to love her children more than her own life? What woman would be more just than someone who behaves like that? Surely it follows that an educated woman would be more courageous than an uneducated woman. . . . Wouldn't such a woman be a great help to her husband, and an ornament to her family, and a good example to all who know her? . . .

(4) . . . But it is easy to apprehend that there are not different sets of virtues for men and women. First, men and women both need to be sensible; what need could there be for a foolish man or woman? Second, both need to live just lives. An unjust man could not be a good citizen, and a woman could not run her household well, if she did not run it justly, since if she were unjust she would do wrong to her husband, as they say Eriphyle did to hers. Third, a wife ought to be chaste, and so should a husband, for the laws punish both parties in cases of adultery. Over-indulgence in food and drink and similar problems, excesses that bring disgrace to those who indulge in them, prove that moderation is essential for every human being, whether male or female, for it is only through moderation that we can avoid excess. . . .

It is reasonable, then, for me to think that women ought to be educated similarly to men in respect of virtue, and they must be taught starting when they are children, that this is good, and that bad, and that they are the same for both, and that this is beneficial and that harmful, and that one must do this, and not that. From these lessons reasoning is developed in both girls and boys, and there is no distinction between them. Then they must be told to avoid all base action. When these qualities have been developed both men and women will inevitably be sensible, and the well-educated person, whether male or female, must be able to endure hardship, accustomed not to fear death, and accustomed not to be humbled by any disaster, for this is how one can become manly.

***

(13a) He said that a husband and wife come together in order to lead their lives in common and to produce children, and that they should consider all their property to be common, and nothing private, not even their bodies. . . . In marriage there must be complete companionship and concern for each other on the part of both husband and wife, in health and in sickness and at all times. . . . When such caring for another is perfect, and the married couple provide it for one another, and each strives to outdo the other, then this is marriage as it ought to be and deserving of emulation, since it is a noble union.

Sources: Musonius Rufus, in *Women's Life in Greece and Rome*, 2nd ed., edited by Mary Lefkowitz and Maureen Fant (Baltimore: Johns Hopkins Press, 1992), pp. 50–54.

Interpreting Visual Evidence

Images of Power

While their empires were gained and maintained largely through military force, Shi Huangdi and Octavian Augustus also expressed their power through elaborate construction projects. Both men commissioned elaborate mausoleums in which they were buried. Shi Huangdi's massive mausoleum, located in Chang'an (modern-day Xi'an), contained not only the emperor's tomb but also as many as 8,000 life-sized terra-cotta warriors, their horses, and chariots. One ancient Chinese historian reported that the emperor's concubines and the craftsmen who designed the tomb were buried alive with the emperor, though the tomb itself has not been excavated. Augustus's mausoleum was constructed on the Field of Mars just outside the city walls of Rome and was meant to entomb him and his close relatives upon their deaths. While his mausoleum is much more modest than Shi Huangdi's, Augustus's burial site was just one component of his elaborate building program in Rome, which included a forum with its temple to Mars the Avenger, as well as an Altar of Peace and a massive sundial.

Power and authority could also be conveyed through portraiture. The so-called Prima Porta statue of Augustus, pictured here, depicts him as a triumphant general. The statue's iconography suggests several messages: for example, the breastplate shows

Shi Huangdi's terra-cotta army in Xi'an.

Emperor Augustus's mausoleum in Rome (*top*, aerial view; *bottom*, entrance).

his adopted son and heir, Tiberius, receiving back the military standards lost to the Parthians, and the Cupid on a dolphin calls to mind Augustus's divine ancestry reaching back to Venus. While there is no statue or other image from the Qin or Han period showing what Shi Huangdi looked like, the standard picture, dating to a much later period, shows him wearing an elaborate headpiece, a robe with a dragon on it, and a sword at his waist.

Questions for Analysis

1. Compare the mausoleums of Shi Huangdi and Augustus. What do you think each ruler was attempting to convey through his burial monument?

2. Looking at the images of these two rulers, what in the representations gives a visual cue of their authority? Why do you think there are no contemporary images of Shi Huangdi, but so many of Augustus?

3. What do these images of Shi Huangdi and Augustus and their burial monuments suggest about the nature of power in the Roman and Chinese worlds?

Augustus of Prima Porta.

Portrait of Shi Huangdi.

8

The Rise of Universalizing Religions

300-600 CE

Around 180 CE, twelve Christians, seven men and five women, stood trial before the provincial governor at Carthage. Their crime was refusal to worship the gods of the Roman Empire. While the governor argued for the simplicity of his religion with its devotion to "the protecting spirit of our lord the emperor," one Christian retorted that his own lord was "the king of kings and emperor of all nations." This distinction was an unbridgeable gap between the governor and the Christians. The governor condemned them all. "Thanks be to God!" cried the Christians, and straightaway they were beheaded. As the centuries unfolded, the governor's old Roman ideas of the supremacy of an emperor-lord would give way to the martyrs' devotion to their Lord God as emperor over all. As with Christianity's claim of an "emperor of all nations," a religion's capacity for universalizing—particularly its broad appeal across diverse peoples and cultures—became ever more important to its success.

From 300 to 600 CE, the entire Afro-Eurasian landmass experienced a surge of religious activity. In the west, Christianity became the state faith of the Roman Empire. In India, Vedic religion (Brahmanism) evolved into a more formal spiritual system called Hinduism. Buddhism

Chapter Outline

- Religious Change and Empire in Western Afro-Eurasia
- The Silk Roads
- Political and Religious Change in South Asia
- Political and Religious Change in East Asia
- Faith and Cultures in the Worlds Apart
- Conclusion

Core Objectives

- **DESCRIBE** the characteristics of universalizing religions, and **EXPLAIN** why universalizing religions developed to varying degrees in Afro-Eurasia but did not develop elsewhere in the world.

- **ANALYZE** the relationship between empires and universalizing religions across Afro-Eurasia in this period.

- **ASSESS** the connections between political unity and religious developments in sub-Saharan Africa and Mesoamerica in the fourth to sixth centuries CE.

- **COMPARE** the unifying political and cultural developments in sub-Saharan Africa and Mesoamerica with those that took place across Eurasia in this period.

universalizing religions

Religions that appeal to diverse populations; are adaptable to new cultures and places; promote universal rules and principles; proselytize new believers, often through missionaries; foster community; and, in some cases, do all of this through the support of an empire.

spread across northern India, central Asia, and China. Around the same time, the peoples living in sub-Saharan Africa reached beyond their local communities, creating common cultures across wider geographical areas. The Bantu-speaking peoples, residing in the southeastern corner of present-day Nigeria, began to spread their way of life throughout the entire southern half of the landmass. Similarly, across the Atlantic Ocean, the Maya established political and cultural institutions over a large portion of Mesoamerica. Across much of the world, spiritual concerns integrated scattered communities through shared faiths. (See Map 8.1.)

This integration was facilitated in Afro-Eurasia in part by the spread of what we might call universalizing religions. Two faiths in this era—Christianity and Buddhism—fit the model for this type of religion particularly well. Six main features characterize **universalizing religions**: their appeal to diverse populations (men and women, freeborn and enslaved, rich and poor); their adaptability as they moved from one cultural and geographical area to another; their promotion of universal rules and principles to guide behavior that transcended place, time, and specific cultural practices; their proselytizing of new believers by energetic and charismatic missionaries; the deep sense of community felt by their converts despite, and perhaps because of, their many demands on followers; and—in the case of Christianity, and to a lesser extent Buddhism—the support given to them by powerful empires. Even as the Roman Empire and the Han dynasty began to crumble, these universalizing traditions continued to flourish.

The peoples living in sub-Saharan Africa and the Americas, too, reached beyond their local communities, creating common cultures across wider geographical areas. As in Eurasia and North Africa, political and cultural transformations undergirded the emergence of these common belief systems. In Africa, the Bantu-speaking peoples, residing in the southeastern corner of present-day Nigeria, began to spread their way of life throughout the entire southern half of the landmass. Similarly, across the Atlantic Ocean, the Maya established political and cultural institutions over a large portion of Mesoamerica and laid the foundations of a common culture. As in Eurasia and North Africa, political and cultural transformations undergirded the emergence of these common belief systems.

Across Afro-Eurasia, universalizing religions were on the move. (See Map 8.2.) Religious leaders carrying written texts (books, scrolls, or tablets of wood or palm leaf) traveled widely. Christians from Persia went to China. Buddhists journeyed from South Asia to Afghanistan and used the caravan routes of central Asia to reach China. Voyages, translations, long-distance pilgrimages, and sweeping conversion campaigns remapped the spiritual landscape of the world. New religious leaders were the brokers of more universal but also more intolerant worldviews, premised on a distinct relationship between gods and their subjects. Religions and their brokers profoundly integrated societies. But they also created new ways to drive them apart.

Global Storyline

The Rise of Christianity, the Spread of Buddhism, and the Beginnings of Common Cultures

- Universalizing religions—notably Christianity and Buddhism—appeal to diverse, widespread populations and challenge the power of secular rulers and thinkers.

- Across Afro-Eurasia, these universalizing religions offer continuity even as powerful empires, specifically the Roman Empire in the west and the Han dynasty in China, are transformed.

- Along the Silk Roads, the merchants and rulers of Sasanian Persia, Sogdiana, and South Asia profoundly influence the exchange of goods, people, and ideas between east and west.

- In the "worlds apart," common cultural beliefs help unify new communities of Bantu speakers in sub-Saharan Africa and newly organized polities in Mesoamerica.

Religious Change and Empire in Western Afro-Eurasia

By the fourth century CE in western Afro-Eurasia, the Roman Empire was hardly the political and military juggernaut it had been 300 years earlier. Surrounded by peoples who coveted its wealth while resisting its power, Rome was fragmenting. So-called barbarians eventually overran the western part of the empire, but in many ways those areas still felt "Roman." Rome's endurance was a boon to the new religious activity that thrived in the turmoil of the immigrations and contracting political authority of the empire. Romans and so-called barbarians alike looked to the new faith of Christianity to maintain continuity with the past, eventually founding a central church in Rome to rule the remnants of empire.

THE APPEAL OF CHRISTIANITY

The spread of new religious ideas, including Christianity, in the Roman Empire changed the way people viewed their existence. Believing implied that an important otherworld loomed beyond the world of physical matter. Feeling contact with that other world gave worshippers a sense of worth; it guided them in this life, and they anticipated someday meeting their guides

THE BIG PICTURE

What are the characteristics of universalizing religions? What was the relationship between empire and universalizing religion in the Roman Empire, Sasanian Persia, China, and elsewhere along the Silk Roads?

The Global View

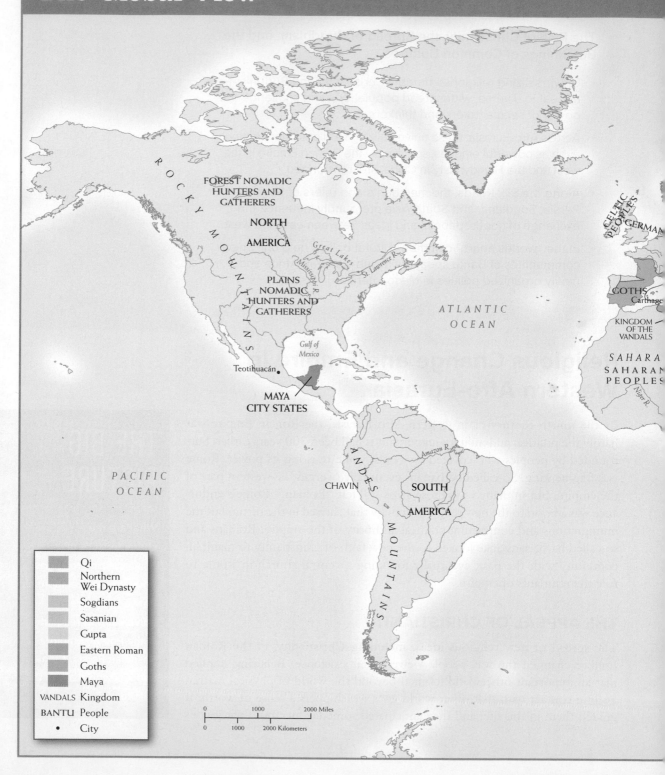

Qi
Northern
Wei Dynasty
Sogdians
Sasanian
Gupta
Eastern Roman
Goths
Maya
VANDALS Kingdom
BANTU People
• City

FOREST NOMADIC
HUNTERS AND
GATHERERS

NORTH
AMERICA

Great Lakes

Mississippi R.

St. Lawrence R.

ROCKY MOUNTAINS

PLAINS
NOMADIC
HUNTERS AND
GATHERERS

Gulf of
Mexico

Teotihuacán

MAYA
CITY STATES

ATLANTIC
OCEAN

PACIFIC
OCEAN

CHAVIN

ANDES MOUNTAINS

SOUTH
AMERICA

Amazon R.

CELTIC
PEOPLES

GERMAN

GOTHS

Carthage

KINGDOM
OF THE
VANDALS

SAHARA

SAHARAN
PEOPLES

Niger R.

0   1000   2000 Miles

0   1000   2000 Kilometers

ARCTIC OCEAN

FINNO-UGRIANS

PEOPLES
GOTHS
Rome
BLACK SEA
Constantinople
EASTERN ROMAN
EMPIRE
MEDITERRANEAN
SEA
Jerusalem
Alexandria

TURKIC

CASPIAN SEA

Samarkand
Merv   Panjikent
Bactra
Taxila

SOGDIANS

ARAL
SEA

TAKLAMAKAN
DESERT

GOBI DESERT

SEA
OF
JAPAN

NORTHERN
WEI DYNASTY
Luoyang
Chang'an   YELLOW
SEA

QI
EMPIRE

PACIFIC
OCEAN

PERSIAN
SASANIAN
EMPIRE

Ctesiphon
Persian Gulf

HIMALAYA MTS.

Indus R.
Ganges R.

GUPTA
EMPIRE

Yangzi R.

Mekong R.

DESERT

ARABS

RED SEA

ARABIAN
SEA

SOUTH
CHINA
SEA

Lake
Chad
BANTUS

Congo R.

Lake
Victoria
Lake
Tanganyika

KALAHARI
DESERT

INDIAN
OCEAN

AUSTRALIAN ABORIGINES

Map 8.1 Empires and Universalizing Religions, 300–600 CE

The period from 300 to 600 CE was a time of tumultuous political change accompanied by the spread of adaptable and accessible universalizing faiths.

- Comparing this map with those in Chapters 6 and 7, which polities are new? Which polities have disappeared? Which ones have expanded or contracted?

- Where on the map are the world's empires located? Why might that be the case?

- Looking at Map 8.2, what seems to be the relationship between these empires and religions or philosophies such as Christianity, Buddhism, Judaism, Hinduism, and Confucianism?

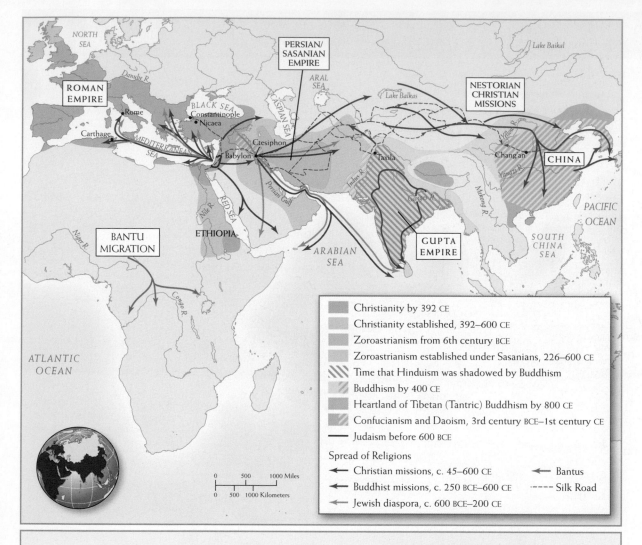

Map 8.2 The Spread of Universalizing Religions in Afro-Eurasia, 300–600 CE

The spread of universalizing religions and the shifting political landscape were intimately connected.

- Where did Hinduism, Buddhism, and Christianity emerge? Where did Zoroastrianism and Confucianism thrive? Which traditions coexisted, and where did they coexist?

- Along what routes did each religion expand? What comparisons can you draw about the directional spread and extent of these religions' expansion?

- What features appear to foster the diffusion of these traditions? What features appear to limit their expansion?

and spiritual friends there. No longer were the gods understood by believers as local powers to be placated by archaic rituals in sacred places. Many gods became omnipresent figures whom mortals could touch through loving attachment. As ordinary mortals now could hope to meet these divine beings in another, happier world, the sense of an afterlife glowed more brightly.

Christians' emphasis on obedience to their Lord God, rather than to a human ruler, sparked a Mediterranean-wide debate on the nature of religion as well as texts that explored these issues. Christians, like the Jews from whose tradition their sect had sprung, read and followed divinely inspired scriptures that told them what to believe and do, even when those actions went against the empire's laws. Christians spoke of their scriptures as "a divine codex." Bound in a compact volume or set of volumes, which reflected the revolutionary change from scrolls to books for knowledge transmission, this was the definitive code of God's law that outlined proper belief and behavior. By the late fourth century CE, Christians had largely settled on a combination of Jewish scriptures and newly authoritative Christian texts—including history, laws, prophecy, biography, poetry, letters, and ideas about the end of days—that would come to be known as the Bible.

Another central feature of early Christianity was the figure of the **martyr**. Martyrs were women and men whom the Roman authorities executed for persisting in their Christian beliefs instead of submitting to emperor worship, as we saw in this chapter's opening story of the twelve Scillitan martyrs—so-called for the town in North Africa from which they came. While other religions, including Judaism and later Islam, honored martyrs who died for their faith, Christianity claimed to be based directly on "the blood of martyrs," in the words of the North African Christian theologian Tertullian (writing around 200 CE).

The story of Vibia Perpetua, a well-to-do mother in her early twenties, offers a striking example of martyrdom. Perpetua and Felicitas, her maidservant (the Latin word *conserva* is perhaps more accurately translated as "slave," as scholars have recently suggested), refused to sacrifice to the Roman gods. Along with their companions, they were condemned in 203 CE to face wild beasts in the amphitheater of Carthage, a venue small enough that the condemned and the spectators would have had eye contact with one another throughout the fatal encounter. The prison diary that Perpetua dictated before her death offered to Christians and potential converts a powerful religious message that balanced heavenly visions and rewards with her concerns over responsibility to her father, brother, and infant son. The remembered heroism of women martyrs like Perpetua and Felicitas offset the increasingly male leadership—bishops and clergy—of the institutionalized Christian church.

Constantine: From Conversion to Creed Crucial in spurring Christianity's spread was the transformative experience of Constantine (c. 280–337 CE). Born near the Danubian frontier, he belonged to a class of professional soldiers whose careers took them far from the Mediterranean. Constantine's

martyr
Literally meaning "witness," a person executed by Roman authorities for maintaining his or her Christian beliefs rather than worshipping the emperor.

Mosaics of Christian Martyrdom Archaeologists have recently uncovered a sixth-century CE church dedicated to an as-yet-unidentified "glorious martyr" in modern Beit Shemesh, Israel. The inscription (*left*) records a donor's gift of the mosaic floor, marble work, and other elements of a martyrium (a holy site containing the relics of a martyr). A mosaic found in a Roman circus in North Africa (*right*) shows a criminal tied to a stake and being pushed on a cart toward a lunging leopard. Christian martyrs like Perpetua, Felicitas, and perhaps Beit Shemesh's "glorious martyr" were treated like criminals: they were executed, sometimes by being thrown to wild animals.

troops proclaimed him emperor after the death of his father, the emperor Constantius. In the civil war that followed, Constantine looked for signs from the gods. Before the decisive battle for Rome, which took place at a strategic bridge in 312 CE, he supposedly had a dream in which he saw an emblem bearing the words "In this sign you will conquer." The "sign," which he then placed on his soldiers' shields, was the first two letters of the Greek *christos*, a title for Jesus meaning "anointed one." Constantine's troops won the ensuing battle and, thereafter, Constantine's visionary sign became known all over the Roman world. Constantine showered imperial favor on this once-persecuted faith, not only legalizing Christianity (in 313 CE) but also praising the work of Christian bishops and granting them significant tax exemptions.

By the time that Constantine embraced Christianity, it had already made considerable progress within the Roman Empire. It had prevailed in the face of stiff competition and periodically intense persecution from the imperial authorities. Apart from the new imperial endorsement, Christianity's success could be attributed to the sacred aura surrounding its authoritative texts, the charisma of its holy men and women, the fit that existed between its doctrines and popular preexisting religious beliefs and practices, and its broad,

The Conversion of Constantine *Left:* In this painting, the seventeenth-century artist Rubens uses "period" details for historical accuracy: the *XP* (the first letters of the name of Christ in Greek) in the sky and beneath it the dragon standard of the Roman cavalry. While the traditional military standard was that of the eagle (center), Romans adopted the *draco* (dragon) standard from Sarmatian cavalrymen from the Eurasian steppe, who themselves may have adopted the symbol from China. *Right:* As shown on this early fourth-century CE coin, Constantine's famous *labarum* (standard) combined the Chi-Rho with the dragon. Later Christian iconography combined the spear with the dragon in the legend of Saint George, the patron saint of England, who was martyred in the Diocletianic persecution of 303 CE.

universalizing appeal to rich and poor, city dwellers and peasants, enslaved and free people, young and old, and men and women.

In 325 CE, hoping to bring unity to the diversity of belief within Christian communities, Constantine summoned all bishops to Nicaea (modern Iznik in western Turkey) for a council to develop a statement of belief, or **creed** (from the Latin *credo*, "I believe"). The resulting Nicene Creed balanced three separate divine entities—God "the father," "the son," and "the holy spirit"—as facets of one supreme being. Also at Nicaea the bishops agreed to hold Easter, the day on which Christians celebrate Christ's resurrection, on the same day in every church of the Christian world. Constantine's legacy to the Christian church was monumental. His conversion had happened in such a way that Christianity itself became the religion of the Roman Empire. Writing near the end of Constantine's reign, an elderly bishop in Palestine named Eusebius noted that the Roman Empire of his day would have surprised the martyrs of Carthage, who had willingly died rather than recognize any "empire of this world."

Christianity in the Cities and Beyond After 312 CE, the large churches built in every major city, many with imperial funding, signaled Christianity's growing strength. These gigantic meeting halls were called basilicas, from the Greek word *basileus*, meaning "king." They were modeled on Roman law-court buildings and could accommodate over a thousand worshippers. Inside

> **creed**
> From the Latin *credo*, meaning "I believe," an authoritative statement of belief. The Nicene Creed, formulated by Christian bishops at the Council of Nicaea in 325 CE, is an example of one such formal belief statement.

Basilica Interior The interior of a basilica was dominated by rows of ancient marble columns and was filled with light from upper windows, so that the eye was led directly to the apse of the church, where the bishop and clergy would sit under a dome, close to the altar.

a basilica's vast space, oil lamps shimmered on marble and brought mosaics to life. Rich silk hangings, swaying between rows of columns, increased the sense of mystery and directed the eye to the far end of the building—a splendidly furnished semicircular apse. Under the dome of the apse, which represented the dome of heaven, and surrounded by priests, the bishop sat and preached from his special throne, or *cathedra*. Worshippers had come into a different world. This was heaven on earth.

These basilicas became the new urban public forums, ringed with spacious courtyards where the city's poor would gather. In return for the tax exemptions that Constantine had granted them, bishops cared for the metropolitan poor. Bishops also became judges, as Constantine turned their arbitration process for disputes between Christians into a kind of small claims court. Offering the poor shelter, quick justice, and moments of unearthly splendor in grand basilicas, Christian bishops perpetuated "Rome" for centuries after the empire had disappeared.

The spread of Christianity outside the cities and into the hinterlands of Africa and Southwest Asia required the breaking of language barriers. In Egypt, Christian clergy replaced hieroglyphs with Coptic, a more accessible script based on Greek letters, in an effort to bridge the linguistic and cultural gap between town and countryside. In the crucial corridor that joined Antioch to Mesopotamia, Syriac, an offshoot of the Semitic language Aramaic, became a major Christian language. As Christianity spread farther north, to Georgia in the Caucasus and to Armenia, Christian clergy created written languages that are still used in those regions.

THE "FALL" OF ROME IN THE WEST

By the third and fourth centuries CE, the political and economic fabric of the old Roman world was unraveling. (See Map 8.3.) The so-called barbarian invasions of the late fourth and fifth centuries CE further contributed to that demise. These "invasions" were not so much an assault as a violent and chaotic immigration of young fighting men from the frontiers of the empire. Today the term *barbarian* implies uncultivated or savage, but its meaning in antiquity was "foreigner" (with overtones of inferiority). Inhabitants of the empire's western provinces had become accustomed to non-Roman soldiers from across the frontiers, and for them *barbarian* was synonymous with

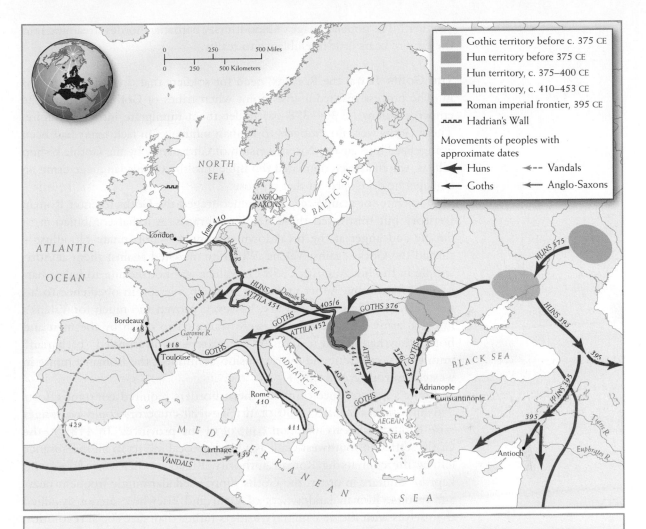

Map 8.3 Western Afro-Eurasia: War, Immigration, and Settlement in the Roman World, 375–450 CE

Invasions and migrations brought about the reconstitution of the Roman Empire at this time.

- Using the map, identify the people who migrated to or invaded the Roman Empire. Where were they from, and where did they go?
- How did these migrations and invasions reshape the political landscape of western Afro-Eurasia?
- Considering these effects, to what extent was the Roman depiction of these groups as "barbarians" a fair assessment?

"soldier." The popular image of bloodthirsty barbarian hordes streaming into the empire bears little resemblance to reality.

The Goths It was the Romans' need for soldiers that drew the barbarians in. The process reached a crisis point when tribes of Goths petitioned the emperor Valens (r. 364–378 CE) to let them immigrate into the empire. These Goths were no strangers to Roman influence: in fact, many had been evangelized into an anti-Nicene version of Christianity by the Gothic bishop Ulfilas, who had even translated the Bible into the Gothic language using an alphabet he developed for that purpose.

Desperate for manpower, Valens encouraged the Goths to enter Roman territory but mistreated these new immigrants. A lethal combination of famine and anger at the breakdown of supplies—not innate bloodlust—turned the Goths against Valens. When he marched against them at Adrianople in the hot August of 378 CE, Valens was not seeking to halt a barbarian invasion but rather intending to teach a lesson in obedience to his new recruits. The Gothic cavalry, however, proved too much for Valens's imperial army, and the Romans were trampled to death by the men and horses they had hoped to hire. As the pattern of disgruntled "barbarian" immigrants, civil war, and overextension continued, the Roman Empire in western Europe crumbled.

Rome's maintenance of its northern borders required constant efforts and high taxes. But after 400 CE the western emperors could no longer raise enough taxes to maintain control of the provinces. In 418 CE, the Goths settled in southwest Gaul as a kind of local militia to fill the absence left by the contracting Roman authority. Ruled by their own king, who kept his military in order, the Goths suppressed alarmingly frequent peasant revolts. Roman landowners of Gaul and elsewhere anxiously allied themselves with the new military leaders rather than face social revolution and the raids of even more dangerous armies. Although they practiced a different, "heretical" version of Christianity, the Goths came as Christian allies of the aristocracy, not as godless enemies of Rome.

Hunnish Jewelry This 3½-inch wolf-dragon, in gold embellished with garnets, formed the end of a torque (heavy necklace). Resting on the point of the wearer's collarbone, this symbol blended Roman and Chinese motifs. It was found in the Stavropol territory of modern Russia, in the land between the Black and Caspian Seas.

The Huns Romans and non-Romans also drew together to face a common enemy: the Huns. Led by their king Attila (r. 434–453 CE) for twenty years, the Huns threatened both Romans and Germanic peoples (like the Goths). While the Romans could hide behind their walls, the Hunnish cavalry regularly plundered the scattered villages and open fields in the plains north of the Danube.

Attila intended to be a "real" emperor of a warrior aristocracy. Having adopted (perhaps from the Chinese empire) the notion of a "mandate of heaven"—in his case, a divine right to rule the tribes of the north—he fashioned the first opposing empire that Rome ever had to face in northern Europe. Rather than selling his people's services to Rome, Attila extracted thousands of pounds of gold coins in tribute from the Roman emperors who hoped to stave off assaults by his brutal forces. Drained both militarily and economically by this Hunnish threat, the Roman Empire in the west disintegrated only twenty years after Attila's death.

In the last analysis, barbarians did not destroy the empire. They were only the last straw. The "fall" of the empire in western Europe was the result of a long process of overextension. Rome could never be as strong along its frontiers as it was around the Mediterranean, because those frontiers were too far away. Despite the famous Roman roads, travel time between the Rhine border and Rome was more than thirty days. Lacking the vast network of canals that enabled Chinese emperors to move goods and soldiers by water, Roman power could survive in the north only at the cost of constant effort and high taxes. But after 400 CE, the western emperors could no longer raise enough taxes to maintain control of the northern provinces, and invaders simply moved into the vacuum. In 476 CE, the last Roman emperor of the west, a young boy named Romulus Augustulus (namesake of both Rome's legendary founder and its first emperor), resigned to make way for a so-called barbarian king in Italy. (See Current Trends in World History: Fall of the Roman and Han Empires: A Comparative Perspective.)

The political unity of the Roman Empire in the west now gave way to a sense of unity through the church. The Catholic Church (*Catholic* meaning "universal," centered in the bishops' authority) became the one institution to which all Christians in western Europe, Romans and non-Romans alike, felt that they belonged. The bishop of Rome became the symbolic head of the western churches. Rome became a spiritual capital instead of an imperial one. By 700 CE, the great Roman landowning families of the Republic and early empire had vanished, replaced by religious leaders with vast moral authority.

CONTINUITY OF ROME IN THE EAST: BYZANTIUM

Elsewhere the Roman Empire was alive and well. From the borders of Greece to the borders of modern Iraq, and from the Danube River to Egypt and the borders of Saudi Arabia, the empire survived undamaged. The new Roman Empire of the east—to which historians gave the name **Byzantium**—had its own "New Rome," Constantinople. Founded in 324 CE by its namesake, Constantine, on the Bosporus straits separating Europe from Asia, this strategically located city was well situated to receive taxes in gold and to control the sea-lanes of the eastern Mediterranean.

Byzantium
Modern term for the Eastern Roman Empire (which would last until 1453), centered at its "New Rome," Constantinople, which was founded in 324 CE by Constantine on the site of the Greek city Byzantium.

Fall of the Roman and Han Empires: A Comparative Perspective

Both the Roman Empire and the Han Empire had an extraordinary number of similarities. Initially, they knew little about each other. With 5,000 miles of steppes, mountains, and deserts separating the empires, their knowledge of each other was based on traded commodities. Although they arose at slightly different times (the Han Empire at the end of the third century BCE and the Roman Empire at the end of the first century BCE), they both lasted approximately 400 years and had the same population (around 60 million, together more than half the world's population at the time). The rulers of both empires resided in capital cities that had the largest populations in the world. Both rulers were thought to have godlike powers, aspired to domination of their known world, and commanded huge militaries. Moreover, both empires were so powerful and long-lasting that subsequent Chinese and western European rulers sought to revive them. In China the imperial system, in spite of periods of considerable turmoil and fragmentation (especially from 300 to 600 CE), lasted more than 2,000 years, from the establishment of the Qin dynasty in 221 BCE to the abdication of the last Qing emperor on February 12, 1912, when the Chinese republic came into existence. In contrast, in western Europe, while political leaders sought to revive the fallen Roman Empire and claimed to

have done so first under Charlemagne and later under the Habsburgs as the Holy Roman Empire, these states were never true empires.

A variety of reasons exist for the endurance of China's imperial system and the failure of western European leaders to revive anything that resembled the Roman Empire. Three reasons stand out. First, China and Rome emerged as empires in markedly different ways. Second, during their four centuries of existence, their ruling elites created different political institutions and were guided by different ideologies. Third, their collapses were notably different.

The Road to Empire

The short-lived Qin Empire (221–207 BCE) cleared the way for the Han Empire and created the institutional foundations and solidified the ideological bases for the Han and subsequent dynasties. The Qin arose after the Shang and Zhou dynasties, which were important states but far from being true empires. Although the rulers of the Zhou dynasty, founded in 1045 BCE, remained on the throne until the third century BCE, the Zhou ceased to be a dynamic and powerful state in the eighth century BCE, giving way to the Spring and Autumn period (722–481 BCE) and the Warring States period (403–221 BCE). The Warring States period was crucial in establishing

the ideological foundations for China's imperial history. During this long period China experienced constant warfare, in which the size of armies and the number of casualties skyrocketed. According to China scholar Yuri Pines, the carnage of warfare led all the major Chinese intellectuals and scholar-officials, including Confucius, Mencius, Laozi, Mo Di, and the Legalists, to "endorse the idea that a single savior-like person would bring about unity and peace." These Axial Age philosophers in China created the ideological foundations for empire—foundations that compelled China's ruling elites to return over and over again to imperial rule through an emperor.

In contrast, the Roman state emerged as the dominant city-state in the Italian Peninsula beginning in the fifth century BCE. Rome warred continuously with other city-states on the peninsula right down to the first century CE (against Etruscans, Samnites, Greeks in southern Italy, and Italian allies). Additionally, Rome warred against other groups in the Mediterranean, from the Carthaginians in North Africa and Spain to the Hellenistic successor kingdoms to the east. Nonetheless, Rome's experience with warfare did not produce foundational philosophies. Moreover, its political ideology, drawn to some extent from the Greek city-states of the Axial Age, was based on republicanism. The empire emerged only at the end of the first century BCE.

Different Imperial Political Institutions and Ideologies

Geography was an important difference between Rome and Han China. The Roman Empire was not easy to govern territorially. Its ruler had to govern both sides of the Mediterranean Sea. In addition, Italy was a peninsula, Iberia was separated from northern Europe by the Pyrenees, and the British Isles were divided from mainland Europe by the English Channel. China had geographical barriers also. It was crisscrossed by rivers, mountains, and deserts that created diverse regional cultures. Thus, like the rulers of the Roman Empire, China's ruling elites had to impose their will on disparate ethnic and linguistic groups. Ideology, handed down from the Warring States period, proved immensely crucial in solidifying this unity. Equally important, however, was the role of the scholar-gentry class, who insisted that a detailed knowledge of the classics was the only way to enter the ruling class. Moreover, China was more closely governed than its Roman counterpart. The central and local governments were staffed by around 130,000 individuals, of whom 20,500 worked for the central administration. The far-flung Chinese bureaucracy made the Roman Empire seem undergoverned.

Rome was much more of a patchwork empire, governed in cooperation with local elites and nowhere as dependent on direct administration or a complex bureaucracy. Rome maintained its authority through its immense army and military coercion rather than ideological preeminence. Even considering Rome's late third-century CE system of more than 100 provinces managed as twelve dioceses, Rome never developed the kinds of administrative institutions that existed in the Han Empire.

The Decline and Fall of the Roman and Han Empires

While both the Roman and Han Empires lasted four centuries, their overthrows were decidedly different. Both succumbed to nomadic pastoral peoples—the Goths overwhelming the Roman state and the northern steppe peoples bringing the Han to their knees. European nomads entered the Roman Empire and destroyed Rome's power to rule in the west, while Christianity offered a degree of continuity. In the east, steppe peoples who invaded China did not destroy the Han imperial system but instead emulated it, even while maintaining their traditional political, social, and ideological practices in their homelands. Ultimately, western Europe and China diverged dramatically after the fall of the Roman and Han Empires. Europe ended up with

many fledgling states and vernacular languages, but one God, one papacy, and one dominant religion. In contrast, China had many minor gods, but one emperor, one dominant language, and a long-lasting Confucian bureaucracy.

Questions for Analysis

- What are some of the similarities and differences in the processes through which the Roman and Han Empires formed, were maintained, and fell?
- What might account for the differing outcomes in the aftermaths of the fall of the Han Empire and the fall of the Roman Empire in the west?

Explore Further

Pines, Yuri, *Envisioning Eternal Empire: Chinese Political Thought of the Warring States Era* (2009).

Pines, Yuri, *The Everlasting Empire: The Political Culture of Ancient China and Its Imperial Legacy* (2012).

Rosenthal, Jean-Laurent, and R. Bin Wong, *Before and Beyond Divergence: The Politics of Economic Change in China and Europe* (2011).

Scheidel, Walter (ed.), *Rome and China: Comparative Perspectives on Ancient World Empires* (2009).

Source: Yuri Pines, *Envisioning Eternal Empire: Chinese Political Thought of the Warring States Era* (Honolulu: University of Hawaii Press, 2009), p. 26.

Constantinople was one of the most spectacularly successful cities in Afro-Eurasia, soon boasting a population of over half a million and 4,000 new palaces. Every year, more than 20,000 tons of grain arrived from Egypt, unloaded on a dockside over a mile long. A gigantic hippodrome echoing Rome's Circus Maximus straddled the city's central ridge, flanking an imperial palace whose opulent enclosed spaces stretched down to the busy shore. As they had for centuries before in Rome, emperors would sit in the imperial box, witnessing chariot races as rival teams careened around the stadium. The hippodrome also featured displays of eastern imperial might, as ambassadors came from as far away as central Asia, northern India, and Nubia.

Similarly, the future emperor Justinian came to Constantinople as a young man from an obscure Balkan village, to seek his fortune. When he became emperor in 527 CE, he considered himself the successor of a long line of forceful Roman emperors—and he was determined to outdo them. Most important, Justinian reformed Roman laws. Within six years a commission of lawyers had created the *Digest*, a massive condensation and organization of the pre-existing body of Roman law. Its companion volume was the *Institutes*, a teacher's manual for schools of Roman law. These works were the foundation of what later ages came to know as "Roman law," followed in both eastern and western Europe for more than a millennium.

Reflecting the marriage of Christianity with empire was Hagia Sophia, a church grandly rebuilt by Justinian on the site of two earlier basilicas. The basilica of Saint Peter in Rome, the largest church built by Constantine two centuries earlier, would have reached only as high as the lower galleries of Hagia Sophia. Walls of multicolored marble, gigantic columns of green and purple granite, audaciously curved semicircular niches placed at every corner, and a spectacular dome lined with gleaming gold mosaics inspired awe in those who entered its doors. Hagia Sophia represented the flowing together of Christianity and imperial culture that for another 1,000 years would mark the Eastern Roman Empire centered in Constantinople.

Hagia Sophia The domed ceiling of Justinian's Hagia Sophia in Constantinople soared high above worshippers. Intricate mosaics decorated many of the walls and ceilings. The mosaic adorning the southwestern entryway, shown here, depicts Jesus sitting in the lap of the Virgin Mary. On the right, Constantine presents to Jesus and Mary his new city of Constantinople; on the left, Justinian offers his Hagia Sophia.

Internal discord, as well as contacts between east and west, intensified during Justinian's reign. Justinian quelled riots at the heart of Byzantium, like the weeklong Nika riots in 532 CE in which thousands died when a group of senators used the unrest and high emotions of the chariot races as a cover for revolt. He also undertook wars to reclaim parts of the western Mediterranean and to hold off the threat from Sasanian Persia in the east (see next section). Perhaps the grisliest reminder of this increased connectivity was a sudden onslaught in 541–542 CE of the bubonic plague from the east. One-third of the population of Constantinople died within weeks. Justinian himself survived, but thereafter he ruled an empire whose heartland was decimated. Nonetheless, Justinian's contributions—to the law, to Christianity, to the maintenance of imperial order—helped Byzantium last almost a millennium after Rome in the west had fallen away.

The Silk Roads

Although exchange along the Silk Roads had been taking place for centuries (see Chapter 6), the sharing of knowledge between the Mediterranean world and China began in earnest during this period. Wending their way across the difficult terrains of central Asia, a steady parade of merchants, scholars, ambassadors, missionaries, and other travelers transmitted commodities, technologies, and ideas between the Mediterranean worlds and China, and across the Himalayas into northern India, exploiting the commercial routes of the Silk Roads. Ideas, including the beliefs of the universalizing religions described in this chapter, traveled along with goods on these exchange routes. Christianity spread through the Mediterranean and beyond, and as we shall see later in this chapter, Buddhism and the Vedic religion (Brahmanism) also continued to spread.

The great oasis cities of central Asia played a crucial role in the effective functioning of the Silk Roads. While the Sasanians controlled the city of Merv in the west, nomadic rulers became the overlords of Sogdiana and extracted tribute from the cities of Samarkand and Panjikent in the east. The tribal confederacies in this region maintained the links between west and east by patrolling the Silk Roads between Iran and China. They also joined north to south as they passed through the mountains of Afghanistan into the plains of northern India. As a result, central Asia between 300 and 600 CE was the hub of a vibrant system of religious and cultural contacts covering the whole of Afro-Eurasia. (See Map 8.4.)

SASANIAN PERSIA

Beginning at the Euphrates River and stretching for eighty days of slow travel across the modern territories of Iraq, Iran, Afghanistan, and much of central Asia, the Sasanian Empire of Persia (224–651 CE) encompassed all the land routes of western Asia that connected the Mediterranean world with East Asia. In the early third century CE, the Sasanians had replaced the Parthians

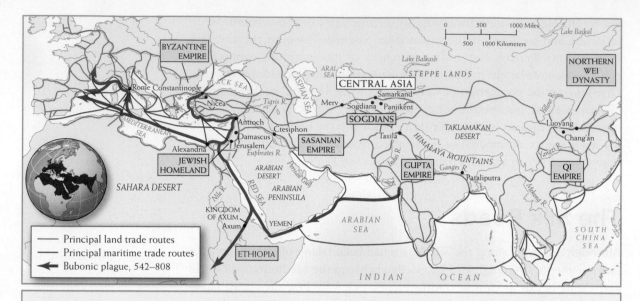

Map 8.4 Exchanges across Afro-Eurasia, 300–600 CE

Southwest Asia remained the crossroads of Afro-Eurasia in a variety of ways. Trade goods flowing between west and east passed through this region, as did universalizing religions.

- Trace the principal trade routes and maritime routes. Locate the cities of Merv, Samarkand, and Panjikent. How do the locations of these cities compare with the locations of some of the major cities of the west in the Mediterranean and the east in India and China?
- Based on your reading of the chapter and their location on the map, what role did the kingdom of Sogdiana and the Sasanian Empire play in trade in this era?
- What was the relationship between trade routes and the spread of the bubonic plague?

as rulers of the Iranian plateau and Mesopotamia. The Sasanian ruler called himself the "King of Kings of Iranian and non-Iranian lands," a title suggestive of the Sasanians' aspirations to universalism. The ancient irrigated fields of what is modern Iraq became the economic heart of this empire. Its capital, Ctesiphon, arose where the Tigris and the Euphrates rivers come close to each other, only 20 miles south of modern Baghdad.

Symbolizing the king's presence at Ctesiphon was the 110-foot-high vaulted Great Arch of Khusro, named after Justinian's rival, Khusro I Anoshirwan (Khusro of the Righteous Soul). As his name implied, Khusro Anoshirwan (r. 531–579 CE) exemplified the model ruler: strong and just. His image in the east as an ideal monarch was as glorious as that of Justinian in the west as an ideal Christian Roman emperor. For both Persians and Arab Muslims of later ages, the Arch of Khusro was as awe-inspiring as Justinian's Hagia Sophia was to Christians.

The Sasanian Empire controlled the trade crossroads of Afro-Eurasia and posed a military threat to Byzantium. Its Iranian armored cavalry was a fighting machine adapted from years of competition with the nomads of central Asia. These fearless horsemen fought covered from head to foot in flexible armor (small plates of iron sewn onto leather) and chain mail, riding "blood-sweating horses" draped in thickly padded cloth. Their lethal swords were light and flexible owing to steel-making techniques imported from northern India. With such cavalry, Khusro in 540 CE sacked Antioch, a city of great significance to early Christianity. The campaign was a warning, at the height of Justinian's glory, that Mesopotamia could reach out once again to conquer the eastern Mediterranean shoreline. Under Khusro II the confrontation between Persia and Rome escalated into the greatest war that had been seen for centuries. Between 604 and 628 CE, Persian forces under Khusro II conquered Egypt and Syria and even reached Constantinople before being defeated in northern Mesopotamia.

Politically united by Sasanian control, Southwest Asia also possessed a cultural unity. Syriac was the dominant language. While the Sasanians themselves were devout Zoroastrians (see Chapter 4), Christianity and Judaism enjoyed tolerance in Mesopotamia. Nestorian Christians—so named by their opponents for their acceptance of a hotly contested understanding of Jesus's divine and human nature, promoted by a former bishop of Constantinople named Nestorius—exploited Sasanian trade and diplomacy to spread their faith as far as Chang'an in China and the western coast of southern India. Protected by the Sasanian King of Kings, the Jewish rabbis of Mesopotamia compiled the monumental Babylonian Talmud at a time when their western peers, in Roman Palestine, were feeling cramped under the Christian state. The Sasanian court also embraced offerings from northern India, including the *Panchatantra* stories (moral tales played out in a legendary kingdom of the animals), polo, and the game of chess. In this regard Khusro's was truly an empire of crossroads, where the cultures of central Asia and India met those of the eastern Mediterranean.

THE SOGDIANS AS LORDS OF THE SILK ROADS

The Sogdians, who controlled the oasis cities of Samarkand and Panjikent, served as human links between the two ends of Afro-Eurasia. Their religion was a blend of Zoroastrian and Mesopotamian beliefs, touched with Brahmanic influences. Their language was the common tongue of the early Silk Roads, and their shaggy camels bore the commodities that passed through their entrepôts (transshipment centers). Moreover, their mansions, such as those excavated at Panjikent, show strong influences from the warrior aristocracy culture of Iran. The palace walls display gripping frescoes of armored riders, reflecting the revolutionary change to cavalry warfare from

Multicultural Celebration in Afrasiab This seventh-century CE wall painting was found in what archaeologists have described as an aristocratic house in Afrasiab (modern Samarkand, Uzbekistan), centrally located along the Silk Roads. The procession on the south wall (pictured here) depicts riders on elephants, horses, and camels. The full set of nearly life-size frescoes stretches almost 38 feet in length in what has been called the "Hall of Ambassadors" because it includes groups from China, central Asia, and Korea.

Rome to China. The Sogdians were known as merchants as far away as China. Their commercial skills enabled them to become the richest country in central Asia, building large houses and decorating the walls of their homes with elaborate paintings.

Through the Sogdians, products from Southwest Asia and North Africa found their way to the eastern end of the landmass. Carefully packed for the long trek on jostling camel caravans, Persian and Roman goods rode side by side. Along with Sasanian silver coins and gold pieces minted in Constantinople, these exotic products found eager buyers as far east as China and Japan.

BUDDHISM ON THE SILK ROADS

South of the Hindu Kush Mountains, in northern India, nomadic groups made the roads into central Asia safe to travel, enabling Buddhism to spread northward and eastward via the mountainous corridor of Afghanistan into China. Buddhist monks were the primary missionary agents, the bearers of a universal message who traveled across the roads of central Asia, carrying holy books, offering salvation to commoners, and establishing themselves more securely in host communities than did armies, diplomats, or merchants.

At Bamiyan, a valley of the Hindu Kush—two gigantic statues of the Buddha, 121 and 180 feet in height, were carved from a cliffside during the fourth and fifth centuries CE (and stood there for 1,500 years until dynamited by the Taliban in 2001). Travelers found welcoming cave monasteries here and at oases all along the way from the Taklamakan Desert to northern China, where—2,500 miles from Bamiyan—travelers also encountered five huge Buddhas carved from cliffs in Yungang, China. While those at Bamiyan stood tall with royal majesty, the Buddhas of Yungang sat in postures of meditation. In the cliff face and clustered around the feet of the Bamiyan Buddhas various elaborately carved cave chapels housed intricate paintings with Buddhist imagery. Surrounding the Yungang Buddhas, over fifty caves sheltered more than 50,000 statues representing Buddhist deities and patrons. The Yungang Buddhas, seated just inside the Great Wall, welcomed travelers to the market in China and marked the eastern end of the central Asian Silk Road system.

Bamiyan and Yungang Buddhas Compare the Buddhas at Bamiyan (*left*) and Yungang (*right*). Note the Gandharan dress and standing pose of the Bamiyan Buddha, whose majesty and ornamentation the pilgrim Xuanzang described in the mid-seventh century CE. The Buddha in Yungang, one of five created under the emperors of the Northern Wei, sits at the foothills of the Great Wall, marking the eastern destination of the central Asian Silk Roads.

(See Map 8.5.) The Bamiyan and Yungang Buddhas are a reminder that by the fourth century CE religious ideas were creating world empires of the mind, transcending kingdoms of this world and bringing a universal message contained in their holy scriptures.

Political and Religious Change in South Asia

South Asia, especially the area of modern India, enjoyed a surge of religious enthusiasm during the Gupta dynasty, the largest political entity in South Asia from the early fourth to the mid-sixth century CE. Its kings facilitated commercial and cultural exchange, much as the Roman Empire had done in the west. Chandragupta I (r. c. 320–335 CE, not to be confused with Chandragupta Maurya from Chapter 6), calling himself "King of Kings, Great King," together with his son, expanded Gupta territory to the entire northern Indian plain and made a long expedition to southern India. The development of Hinduism out of the *varna*-bound Vedic Brahmanic religion and the continued spread of Buddhism helped unify a diverse region and the diverse peoples who lived there.

Core Objectives

ANALYZE the relationship between empires and universalizing religions in South Asia and China.

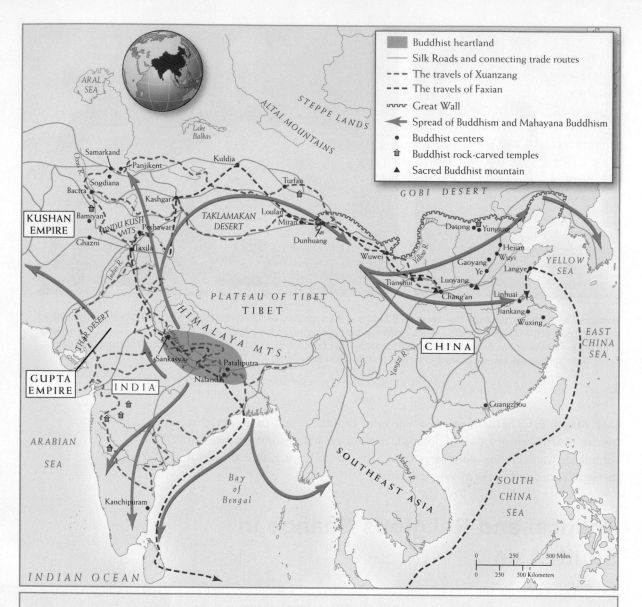

Map 8.5 Buddhist Landscapes, 300–600 CE

....

Buddhism spread from its heartland in northern India to central and East Asia at this time. Trade routes, along with the merchants and pilgrims who traveled along them, fostered that spread.

- Trace the trade routes and the routes showing the spread of Buddhism. According to the map, what role did increasingly extensive trade routes play in spreading Buddhism?
- Locate the Buddhist centers and rock-carved temples, especially at Bamiyan, Dunhuang, and Yungang. How might their location on trade routes have influenced the spread of this universalizing faith?
- Trace the travels of Faxian and Xuanzang. How are their routes similar and different, and what do they suggest about growing connections between East Asia and South Asia?

THE HINDU TRANSFORMATION

During this period, the ancient Brahmanic Vedic religion spread widely in South Asia. Because Buddhism and Jainism had many devotees in cities and commercial communities (see Chapter 5), conservative Brahmans turned their attention to rural India and brought their religion into accord with rural life and agrarian values. This refashioned Brahmanic religion emerged as the dominant faith in Indian society in the form of what we today call **Hinduism**.

In the religion's new, more accessible form, believers became vegetarians, abandoning the animal sacrifices that had been important to their earlier rituals. Their new rituals were linked to self-sacrifice—denying themselves meat rather than offering up slaughtered animals to the gods, as they had done previously. Three major deities—Brahma, Vishnu, and Shiva—formed a trinity representing the three phases of the universe—birth, existence, and destruction, respectively—and the three expressions of the eternal self, or *atma*. Vishnu was the most popular of the three and was thought by believers to reveal himself through various avatars (or incarnations).

Poets during the reign of Chandragupta II (r. c. 380–415 CE), grandson of Chandragupta I and a generous patron of the arts, expressed the religious sentiments of the age. Working with the motifs and episodes from two early epics, the *Mahabharata* and the *Ramayana* (see Chapter 4), these poets addressed new problems and praised new virtues. What had once been lyric dramas and narrative poems written to provide entertainment now served as collective memories of the past and underscored Brahmanic religious beliefs about ideal behavior. The heroes and deeds that the poets praised in classical Sanskrit served as models for kings and their subjects.

A central part of the *Mahabharata* revolves around the final battle between two warring confederations of Vedic tribes. The hero Arjuna, the best warrior of one of these confederations, is unwilling to fight against his enemies because many of them are his cousins. At a crucial moment on the battlefield, Krishna—an avatar of Vishnu, who was Arjuna's charioteer and religious teacher—intervenes, commanding Arjuna to slay his foes, even those related to him. Krishna reminds Arjuna that he belongs to the Kshatriya *varna*, the warriors put on earth to govern and to fight against the community's enemies. The *Bhagavad Gita*, which preserves this tale of Krishna and Arjuna, became part of the authoritative literature of Hindu spirituality. It prescribed religious and ethical teachings and behaviors, called *dharma* in Hinduism, for people at every level of society.

Gold Coin of Chandragupta II
The Gupta dynasty, based in the Middle and Lower Ganges plains, was known for its promotion of indigenous Indian culture. Here, Chandragupta II, the most famous king of the dynasty, is shown riding a horse in the style of the invaders from the central Asian steppes.

Hinduism
Ancient Brahmanic Vedic religion that emerged as the dominant faith in India in the third century CE. It reflected rural and agrarian values and focused on the trinity of Brahma (birth), Vishnu (existence), and Shiva (destruction).

Hindu Statue This huge statue of a three-headed god, located in a cave on a small island near Mumbai, represents the monotheistic theology of Hinduism. Brahma, the creator; Vishnu, the keeper; and Shiva, the destroyer, are all from one *atma*, the single soul of the universe.

Hindus also adopted the deities of other religions, even regarding the Buddha as an avatar of Vishnu. Thus, the Hindu world of gods became larger and more accessible than the earlier Vedic one, enabling more believers to share a single faith. Hindus did not wish to approach the gods only through the sacrificial rituals at which Brahmans alone could officiate. Individuals, therefore, also developed an active relationship with particular gods through personal devotion, in a practice called *bhakti*. This individualized, personal *bhakti* devotion attracted Hindus of all social strata, while the mythological literature wove the deities into a heavenly order presided over by the trinity of Brahma, Vishnu, and Shiva as universal gods. During this period Hindus lived side by side with Buddhists, competing for followers by building ornate temples and sculptures of gods and by holding elaborate rituals and festivals.

While the stories of human-divine interaction, the larger number of gods, and the development of *bhakti* devotion made Hinduism more personal than the old Vedic Brahmanism had been, Hinduism was still very much rooted in the hierarchical *varna* system. Although Hinduism was more accessible to a wider audience than Brahmanism had been, there were limits to how universalizing this tradition could be since the *varna* system, with which it was closely intertwined, did not extend outside South Asia.

THE TRANSFORMATION OF THE BUDDHA

During the Gupta period, the two main schools of Buddhism—the newer Mahayana (Greater Vehicle) school and the older Hinayana (Lesser Vehicle) school—acquired universalizing features that were different from what the Buddha had preached centuries earlier. The historical Buddha was a sage who was believed to enter *nirvana*, ending the pain of consciousness. In the earliest Buddhist doctrine, god and supernatural powers were not a factor (see Chapter 5). But by 200 CE, a crucial transformation had occurred: the Buddha's followers started to view him as a god. Mahayana Buddhism not only recognized the Buddha as a god but extended worship to the many bodhisattvas who bridged the gulf between the Buddha's perfection and the world's sadly imperfect peoples (see Chapter 6). It was especially in the Mahayana school that Buddhism became a universalizing religion, whose adherents worshipped divinities, namely the Buddha and the bodhisattvas, rather than recognizing them merely as great men.

Some Buddhists fully accepted the Buddha as god but could not accept the divinity of bodhisattvas; these adherents belonged to the more monkish school of **Hinayana Buddhism**, later called Theraveda in Sri Lanka and Southeast Asia. Rejecting Sanskrit authoritative scripture on the supernatural power of bodhisattvas, they remained loyal to the early Buddhist texts, which were probably based on the words of the Buddha himself. Hinayana temples barred all colorful idols of the bodhisattvas and other heavenly beings; they contained images of only the Buddha. Buddhism, with its vibrant competing Mahayana and Hinayana schools, spread along the Silk Roads far beyond its South Asian point of origin.

CULTURE AND IDEOLOGY INSTEAD OF AN EMPIRE

Unlike China and Rome, India during the Gupta period did not have a centralized empire that could establish a code of laws and an overarching administration. Instead, what emerged to unify South Asia was a distinctive form of cultural synthesis—called by scholars the **Sanskrit cosmopolis**—based on Hindu spiritual beliefs and articulated in the Sanskrit language.

Spearheading this development from 300 to 1300 CE were priests and intellectuals well versed in the Sanskrit language and literary and religious texts. As Sanskrit spread, it stepped beyond religious scriptures and became the public language of politics, although local languages retained their prominence in day-to-day administration and everyday life. Kings and emperors used Sanskrit to express the ideals of royal power and responsibility. Rulers issued inscriptions in it, recording their genealogies and their prestigious acts. Poets celebrated ruling dynasties and recorded important moments in the language.

The emergence of Sanskrit as the common language of the elites in South and Southeast Asian societies also facilitated the spread of Brahmanism. Possessing an unparalleled knowledge of the language, Brahmans circulated their ideals on morality and society in Sanskrit texts, the most influential of which was the **Code of Manu**. This document records a discourse given by a sage, Manu, to a gathering of wise men seeking answers on how to organize their communities after the destruction wrought by a series of floods. The text lays out a set of laws designed to address the problems of assimilating strangers into expanding towns and refining the hierarchical Brahmanic order as the agricultural frontier expanded. Above all, the Code of Manu offered guidance for living within the *varna* and *jati* system, including whom to marry, which profession to follow, and even what to eat. The Code of Manu

Hinayana Buddhism
(termed "Lesser Vehicle" Buddhism by the Mahayana/ "Greater Vehicle" school; also called Theraveda Buddhism) A more traditional, conservative branch of Buddhism that accepted the divinity of the Buddha but not of bodhisattvas.

Sanskrit cosmopolis
Cultural synthesis based on Hindu spiritual beliefs expressed in the Sanskrit language that unified South Asia in place of a centralized empire.

Code of Manu
Brahmanic code of law that took shape in the third to fifth centuries CE and expressed ideas going back to Vedic times. Framed as a conversation between Manu (the first human and an ancient lawgiver) and a group of wise men, it articulated the rules of the hierarchical *varna* system.

Varna **Hierarchies** The dazzlingly diverse population of India, as depicted in this palace scene from a Gupta dynasty fresco, from Cave 17 at Ajanta, depended on the ancient system of *varnas* and *jatis* to lend it law and order.

provided mechanisms for absorbing new groups into the system of *varnas* and *jatis*, thus propelling Hinduism into every aspect of life, far beyond the boundaries of imperial control.

During this period, settlers from northern India pushed southward into lands formerly outside the domain of the Brahmans. In these territories Brahmans encountered Buddhists and competed with them to win followers. The mixing of these two groups and the intertwining of their ideas and institutions ultimately created a common "Indic" culture organized around a shared vocabulary addressing concepts such as the nature of the universe and the cyclical pattern of life and death. Much of this mixing of ideas took place in schools, universities, and monasteries. The Buddhists already possessed large monasteries, such as Nalanda in northeast India, where 10,000 residential faculty and students assembled, and more than 100 smaller establishments in southeast India housing at least 10,000 monks. In these settings Buddhist teachers debated theology, cosmology, mathematics, logic, and botany. Brahmans also established schools where similar intellectual topics were discussed and where Buddhist and Brahmanic Hindu ideas were fused.

The resulting Indic cultural unity covered around 1 million square miles and a highly diverse population. Although India did not have a single governing entity like China and did not adhere to one religious system as in the Christian Roman Empire, it was developing a distinctive culture based on the intertwining of two shared, accessible, and—to varying degrees—universalizing religious traditions.

Political and Religious Change in East Asia

With the fall of the Han dynasty, China experienced a period of political disunity and a surge of new religious and cultural influences. In the first century CE, Han China was the largest state in the world, with as great a population as the Roman Empire had at its height. Its emperor extracted an annual income of millions of pounds of rice and bolts of cloth and conscripted millions of workers whose families paid tribute through their labor. Later Chinese regarded the end of the Han Empire as a disaster just as great as western Europeans regarded the end of the Roman Empire. In post-Han China, new influences arrived via the Silk Roads through contact with nomadic "barbarians" and the proselytizing of Buddhist monks, and new forms of Daoism responded to a changing society.

THE WEI DYNASTY IN NORTHERN CHINA

After the fall of the Han in 220 CE, several small kingdoms—at times as many as sixteen of them—competed for control. Civil wars raged for roughly three centuries, a time called the Six Dynasties period (220–589 CE), when no single state was able to conquer more than half of China's territory. The most successful regime was that of the Tuoba, a people originally from Inner Mongolia. In 386 CE, the Tuoba founded the Northern Wei dynasty, which lasted 150 years and administered part of the Han territory. Although technically Mongolian "barbarians," the Northern Wei had lived for generations within the Chinese orbit as tributary states.

The Northern Wei maintained many Chinese traditions of statecraft and court life: they taxed land and labor on the basis of a census, conferred official ranks and titles, practiced court rituals, preserved historical archives, and promoted classical learning and the use of classical Chinese for record keeping and political discourse. Though they were nomadic warriors, they adapted their large standing armies to city-based military technology, which required drafting huge numbers of workers to construct dikes, fortifications, canals, and walls.

Among the challenges facing the Northern Wei rulers was the need to consolidate authority over their own highly competitive nomadic people. One strategy was to make their own government more "Chinese." Under Emperor Xiaowen (r. 471–499 CE), for example, the Tuoba royal family adopted the Chinese family name of Yuan and required all court officials to speak Chinese and wear Chinese clothing. However, the Tuoba warrior families resisted these policies. Xiaowen also rebuilt the old Han imperial capital of Luoyang based on classical architectural models dating from the Han dynasty and made it the seat of his government.

Emperor Xiaowen in Buddhist Procession Emperor Xiaowen's son dutifully commissioned this massive carving (nearly 7 feet by 12 feet) of his father with his retinue in the Longmen Caves in Luoyang. This relief showing Xiaowen (fourth figure from the right) in procession to honor the Buddha was accompanied by another that depicted the empress in procession. Displayed at the entrance to a magnificent Buddhist cave temple, the reliefs are a testament to the Northern Wei's adoption of Chinese aesthetics and their devotion to Buddhism in the early sixth century CE.

Wei rulers sought stronger relationships with the Han Chinese families of Luoyang that had not fled south. The Wei offered them political power as officials in the Wei bureaucracy and more land. For example, the Dowager Empress Fang (regent for Xiaowen 476–490 CE) attempted progressive land reforms that offered land to all young men—whether Han or Wei—who agreed to cultivate it. But even this plan failed to bridge the cultural divides between the "civilized" Han Chinese of Luoyang and the "barbarian" Tuoba Wei, because the latter showed no interest in farming.

Members of the Wei court supported Buddhist temples and monumental cave sites in an appeal to their Tuoba roots while also honoring Confucian traditions dating to the ancient Zhou period. But Emperor Xiaowen's bid for unification was unsuccessful; his death cut short his efforts. Several decades of intense fighting among military rulers in the north followed, ultimately leading to the downfall of the Northern Wei dynasty.

CHANGING DAOIST TRADITIONS

Daoism, a popular Chinese religion under the Han and a challenge to the Confucian state and its scholar-officials, lost its political edge and adapted to the new realities in this period of disunity. Two new traditions of Daoist thought flourished in this era of self-doubt. The first was organized and community oriented, and involved heavenly masters who as mortals guided local religious groups or parishes. Followers sought salvation through virtue, confession, and ceremonies, including a mystical initiation rite. A second Daoist tradition was more individualistic, attempting to reconcile Confucian classical learning with Daoist religious beliefs in the occult and magic. It used trance and meditation to control human physiology. Through such mental and physical efforts, a skilled practitioner could accumulate

Mogao Caves at Dunhuang
This scene comes from Mogao Cave 285 (c. 540 CE, during the Northern Wei dynasty) at Dunhuang on the Silk Roads. Winged apsaras (heavenly spirits) float above a landscape of brilliant blue-hued mountains and deer-filled forests. On the left, five robbers, who have been blinded by troops in a previous scene, wander aimlessly, but in the central scene, their sight having been restored after adopting Buddhism, they sit peacefully at the foot of the Buddha. Hundreds of beautifully painted caves were created at Mogao over several centuries through the painstaking devotion of monks and with the sponsorship of wealthy donors, whose names are often inscribed on the walls.

enough religious merit to prolong his life. The concept of religious merit and demerit in Daoist circles echoed the Buddhist notion of karmic retribution (the cosmic assessment of one's acts in this life that determines one's rebirth into a better or worse next life). For the Daoists, however, eternal life was the ultimate goal, and not the Buddhists' ideal of release from the cycle of life, death, and rebirth.

BUDDHISM IN CHINA

Buddhism's universalizing message appealed to many people living in the fragmented Chinese empire. By the third and fourth centuries CE, travelers from central Asia who had converted to Buddhism had become frequent visitors in the streets and temples of the competing capitals: Chang'an, Luoyang, and Nanjing. Spreading the faith required intermediaries, endowed with texts and explanations, to convey its message. Kumarajiva (344–413 CE), a renowned Buddhist scholar and missionary, was the right man, in the right place, at the right time to spread Buddhism in China—where it already coexisted with other faiths.

Kumarajiva's influence on Chinese Buddhist thought was critical. Not only did he translate previously unknown Buddhist texts into Chinese, but he also clarified Buddhist terms and philosophical concepts. He and his disciples established a Mahayana branch known as Madhyamika (Middle Way) Buddhism, which used irony and paradox to show that reason was limited. For example, they contended that all reality was transient because nothing

Xuanzang This painting portrays the Chinese pilgrim Xuanzang accompanied by a tiger on his epic travels in South Asia to collect important Buddhist scriptures.

remained unchanged over time. They sought enlightenment by means of transcendental visions and spurned experiences in the material world of sights and sounds.

Kumarajiva represented the beginning of a profound cultural shift. After 300 CE, Buddhism began to expand in northwestern China, taking advantage of imperial disintegration and the decline of Daoism and state-sponsored Confucian classical learning. The Buddhists stressed devotional acts, such as daily prayers and mantras, which included seated meditations in solitude requiring mind and breath control, as well as the saving power of the Buddha and the saintly bodhisattvas who postponed their own salvation for the sake of others. They even encouraged the Chinese to join a new class—the clergy. The idea that persons could be defined by faith rather than kinship was not new in Chinese society, but it had special appeal in a time of serious crisis like that of the turbulent Six Dynasties period. In the south, the immigrants from the north found that membership in the Buddhist clergy and monastic orders offered a way to restore their lost prestige.

Even more important, in the northern states— now part Chinese, part "barbarian"—Buddhism provided legitimacy. With Buddhists holding prominent positions in government, medicine, and astronomy, the Wei ruling houses could espouse a philosophy that was just as legitimate as that of the Han Chinese. As a Tuoba who ruled at the height of the Northern Wei in the early sixth century CE, Emperor Xuanwu was an avid Buddhist who made Mahayana Buddhism the state religion during his reign.

In 643 CE, the Chinese Buddhist Xuanzang brought back to Chang'an (then the world's largest city) an entire library of Buddhist scriptures—527 boxes of writings and 192 birch-bark tablets—that he had collected on a pilgrimage to Buddhist holy sites in South Asia. He lodged them in the Great Wild Goose Pagoda and immediately began to translate every line into Chinese. Although the importation of these texts from India was profoundly important, Buddhism did not seek to be the same in all places and at all times. On the contrary, as the expression of a cosmic truth as timeless and varied as the world itself, Buddhism showed a high level of adaptability, easily absorbing the gods and the wisdom of every country it touched.

By 400 CE, China had more than 1,700 Buddhist monasteries and about 80,000 monks and nuns. By contrast, in 600 CE (after two centuries of monastic growth), Gaul and Italy—the two richest regions of western Europe—had, altogether, only 320 monasteries, many with fewer than 30 monks. Yet, in the two ends of Afro-Eurasia, the principal bearers of the new religions were monks. Set apart from "worldly" affairs in their refuges, they enjoyed the pious support of royal courts and warriors whose lifestyles differed sharply from their own. Through their devoted faith in the divine and the support of secular rulers, these two universalizing religions—Buddhism and Christianity—would continue to grow, flourish, and revitalize themselves.

Faith and Cultures in the Worlds Apart

In most areas of sub-Saharan Africa and Mesoamerica, it was not easy for ideas, institutions, peoples, and commodities to circulate broadly. Thus, we do not see the development of universalizing faiths like those in Eurasia. Rather, belief systems and their associated deities remained local. Nonetheless, sub-Saharan Africans and peoples living in Mesoamerica revered prophetic figures who, they believed, communicated with deities and brought to humankind divinely prescribed rules of behavior. Peoples in both regions honored beliefs and rules that were passed down orally across generations. These unifying spiritual traditions guided behavior and established social customs.

Core Objectives

ASSESS the connections between political unity and religious developments in sub-Saharan Africa and Mesoamerica in the fourth to sixth centuries CE.

BANTUS OF SUB-SAHARAN AFRICA

Today, most of Africa south of the equator is home to peoples who speak some variant of more than 400 Bantu languages. Although scholars using oral traditions and linguistic evidence can trace a clear narrative of the Bantu people no farther back than 1000 CE, it appears that the first Bantu speakers lived in the southeastern part of modern Nigeria, where about 4,000 or 5,000 years ago they likely shifted from hunting, gathering, and fishing to practicing settled agriculture. Preparing just 1 acre of tropical rain forest for farming required removing 600 tons of moist vegetation. To accomplish this arduous task, Bantus used mainly machetes, billhooks, and controlled burning. Bantus cultivated woodland plants such as yams and mushrooms, as well as palm oils and kernels. Yet the difficulties in preparing the land for settled agriculture did not keep the Bantus from being the most expansionist of African peoples. (See Map 8.6.)

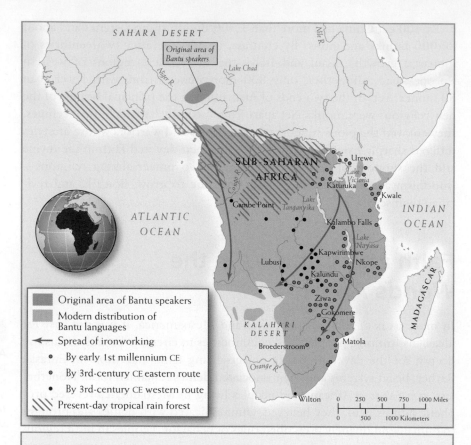

Map 8.6 Bantu Migrations in Africa

The migration of Bantu speakers throughout much of sub-Saharan Africa in the first millennium CE dramatically altered the cultural landscape.

- According to the map, where did the Bantu speakers originate? Into which areas did the Bantu speakers migrate? Why might they have migrated in that direction?

- Trace the spread of ironworking with the Bantu speakers. How might ironworking have enabled Bantu speakers to dominate the peoples already living in the regions to which they migrated?

- What range of topography and ecological zones did the Bantu speakers encounter as they moved southward and eastward? How might that have influenced their spread into new regions?

Bantu Migrations Following riverbeds and elephant trails, Bantu migrants traveled out of West Africa in two great waves. One wave moved across the Congo forest region to East Africa. Their knowledge of iron smelting enabled them to deploy iron tools for agriculture. Because their new habitats supported a mixed economy of animal husbandry and sedentary agriculture, this group became relatively prosperous. A second wave of migrants moved southward through the rain forests in present-day Congo, eventually reaching the Kalahari Desert. The tsetse fly–infested environment did not permit them to rear livestock, so they were limited to subsistence farming. These Bantus learned to use iron later than those who had moved to the Congo region in the east.

Precisely when these **Bantu migrations** began is unclear, but once underway, the travelers moved rapidly. Genetic and linguistic evidence reveals that they absorbed most of the hunting and gathering populations who originally inhabited these areas. What enabled the Bantus to prevail and prosper was their skill as settled agriculturalists. They adapted their farming techniques and crops to widely different environments, including the tropical rain forests of the Congo River basin, the savanna lands of central Africa, the high grasslands around Lake Nyanza (formerly Lake Victoria), and the highlands of Kenya.

For the Bantu of the rain forests of central Africa (the western Bantu), the introduction of the banana plant from tropical South and Southeast Asia was decisive. Linguistic evidence suggests that it first arrived in the Upper Nile region and then traveled into the rest of Africa with small groups migrating from one favorable location to another; the earliest proof of its presence is a record from the East African coast dating to 525 CE. The banana adapted well to the equatorial rain forests, withstanding the heavy rainfalls, requiring less clearing of rain forests, reducing the presence of the malaria-carrying *Anopheles* mosquito, and providing more nutrients than the indigenous yam crop. Exploiting banana cultivation, the western Bantu filled the equatorial rain forests of central Africa between 500 and 1000 CE.

Bantu Cultures, East and West The widely different ecological zones into which the Bantu-speaking peoples spread made it difficult to establish the same political, social, and cultural institutions. In the Great Lakes area of the East African savanna lands and the savanna lands of central Africa, where communication was relatively easy, the eastern Bantu speakers developed centralized polities whose kings ruled by divine right. They moved into heavily forested areas similar to those they had left in southeastern Nigeria. These locations supported a way of life that remained fundamentally unaltered until European colonialism in the twentieth century.

The western Bantu-speaking communities of the lower Congo River rain forests formed small-scale societies based on family and clan connections. They organized themselves socially and politically into age groups, the most important of which were the ruling elders. Within these age-based networks, individuals who demonstrated talent in warfare, commerce, and

Bantu migrations
Waves of population movement from West Africa into eastern and southern Africa during the first millennium CE, bringing new agricultural practices to these regions and absorbing much of the hunting and gathering population.

politics provided leadership. Certain rights and duties were imposed on different social groups based mainly on their age. Males moved from child to warrior to ruling elder, and females transitioned from child to married child-bearer. Bonds among age groups were powerful, and movement from one to the next was marked by meaningful and well-remembered rituals. So-called big men, supported by followers attracted by their valor and wisdom as opposed to inheritance, promoted territorial expansion. Individuals who could attract a large community of followers, marry many women, and sire many children could lead their bands into new locations and establish dominant communities.

These rain forest communities held a common belief that the natural world was inhabited by spirits, many of whom were their own heroic ancestors. These spiritual beings intervened in mortals' lives and required constant appeasement. Diviners helped men and women understand the spirits' ways, and charms warded off the misfortune that aggrieved spirits might wish to inflict. Diviners and charms also protected against the injuries that living beings—witches and sorcerers—could inflict. In fact, much of the misfortune that occurred in the Bantu world was attributed to these malevolent forces. The Bantu migrations ultimately filled up more than half the African landmass. The Bantus spread a political and social order based on family and clan structures that rewarded individual achievement—and maintained an intense relationship to the world of nature that they believed was imbued with supernatural forces.

MESOAMERICANS

Core Objectives

COMPARE the unifying political and cultural developments in sub-Saharan Africa and Mesoamerica with those that took place across Eurasia in this period.

As in sub-Saharan Africa, the process of settlement and expansion in Mesoamerica differed from that in the large empires of Afro-Eurasia. Mesoamerica had no integrating artery of a giant river and its floodplain, and so it lacked the extensive resources that a state could harness for monumental ambitions. Nonetheless, some remarkable polities developed in the region, ranging from the city-state of Teotihuacán to the more widespread influence of the Maya. (See Map 8.7.)

Teotihuacán Around 300 BCE, people in the central plateau and the southeastern districts of Mesoamerica where the dispersed villages of Olmec culture had risen and fallen (see Chapter 5) began to gather in larger settlements. Soon, political and social integration led to city-states. Teotihuacán, in the heart of the fertile valley of central Mexico, became the largest center of the Americas before the Aztecs almost 1,500 years later.

Fertile land and ample water from the valley's marshes and lakes fostered high agricultural productivity despite the inhabitants' technologically rustic methods of cultivation. The local food supply sustained a metropolis of

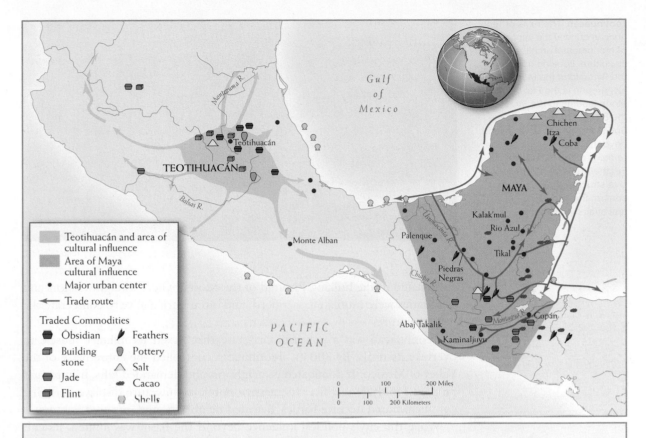

Map 8.7 Mesoamerican Worlds, 200–700 CE

....

At this time, two groups dominated Mesoamerica: one was located at the city of Teotihuacán, in the center, and the other, the Maya, was in the south.

- Locate the traded commodities on the map. What do you note about the distribution of these commodities?
- Where are the trade routes located? What might have fostered interaction between Teotihuacán and the Maya?

between 100,000 and 200,000 residents, living in more than 2,000 apartment compounds lining the city's streets. At one corner rose the massive pyramids of the sun and the moon—the focus of spiritual life for the city dwellers. Marking the city's center was the huge royal compound; the grandeur and refinement of its stepped stone temple, the Pyramid of the Feathered Serpent, were famous throughout Mesoamerica.

The feathered serpent was central to the spiritual lives of Teotihuacán's people. It was a symbol of fertility that governed reproduction and life. The feathered serpent's temple was the core of a much larger structure. From it radiated the awesome promenade known as the Street of the Dead, which

Teotihuacán The ruins of Teotihuacán convey the importance of monumental architecture to its culture. Looking down from the Pyramid of the Moon, in the foreground is the Plaza of the Moon leading to the Street of the Dead. The Pyramid of the Sun stands in the distance and beyond it, out of sight, are the remains of the Pyramid of the Feathered Serpent. These massive structures were meant to confirm the importance of spiritual affairs in urban life.

culminated in the hulking Pyramid of the Moon, where foreign warriors and dignitaries were mutilated, sacrificed, and often buried alive to consecrate the holy structure.

Teotihuacán was a powerful city-state that flexed its military muscle to overtake its rivals. By 300 CE, Teotihuacán controlled the entire basin of the Valley of Mexico. It dominated its neighbors and demanded gifts, tribute, and humans for ritual sacrifice. Its massive public architecture displayed art that commemorated decisive battles, defeated neighbors, and captured fighters.

While the city's political influence beyond the basin was limited, its cultural and economic diffusion were significant. Making use of porters, Teotihuacán's merchants traded their ceramics, ornaments of marine shells, and all sorts of decorative and valued objects (especially of green obsidian) far and wide. At the same time, Teotihuacán imported pottery, feathers, and other goods from distant lowlands.

This kind of expansion left much of the political and cultural independence of neighbors intact, with only the threat of force keeping them in check. In the fifth century CE, however, invaders burned Teotihuacán and smashed the carved figurines of the central temples and palaces, targeting Teotihuacán's institutional and spiritual core.

The Maya In the Caribbean region of Yucatán and its interior, the Maya people flourished from about 250 CE to their zenith in the eighth century. The Maya lived in an inhospitable region—hot, infertile, lacking navigable river systems, and vulnerable to hurricanes. Yet the Maya established hundreds, possibly thousands, of agrarian villages scattered across the diverse ecological zones of present-day southern Mexico to western El Salvador. Villages were linked by their shared Mayan language and through tribute payments, chiefly from lesser settlements to sacred towns. Until recently, scholars believed that at their peak the Maya may have numbered as many as 10 million. Today, as scholars reevaluate their assumptions based on new LIDAR (light detection and ranging) imaging, many conclude that population estimates may have been too low. LIDAR mapping tools are revealing Maya settlements that are much more elaborate than those that were previously excavated in the jungles of Guatemala, Belize, Honduras, and El Salvador; as a result, population estimates may need to increase many times over.

Maya Political and Social Structure The Maya established a variety of kingdoms around major ritual centers—such as Palenque, Copán, and Piedras Negras—and their hinterlands. Such hubs were politically independent but culturally and economically interconnected through commerce. Some larger settlements, such as Tikal and Kalak'mul, became sprawling centers with dependent provinces. In 2018, scientists using jungle-penetrating laser scanning determined that many of the Maya centers were much larger and more densely settled than had been previously thought and that they had defensive walls, had extensive irrigation systems, and were connected by roads.

Maya culture encompassed about a dozen kingdoms that shared many features. Ambitious rulers in these larger states frequently engaged in hostilities with one another. Highly stratified, with an elaborate class structure, each kingdom was topped by a shamanistic king who legitimated his position via his lineage, reaching back to a founding father and, ultimately, the gods. The vast pantheon of gods included patrons of each subregion, as well as a creator god and deities for rain, maize, war, and the sun.

Palenque Deep in the Lacandon jungle lies the ruin of the Maya city of Palenque. Its pyramid, on the left, overlooks the site; on the right, the Tower of the Palace shadows a magnificent courtyard where religious figures and nobles gathered. There is no mistaking how a city like Palenque could comma its hinterland with reli authority.

Gods were neither especially cruel nor benevolent; rather, they focused on the dance that sustained the axis connecting the underworld and the skies. What humans had to worry about was making sure that the gods got the attention and reverence they needed.

This was the job of Maya rulers. Kings sponsored elaborate public rituals to reinforce their divine heritages, including ornate processions down their cities' main boulevards to honor gods and their descendants, the rulers. Lords and their wives performed ritual blood sacrifice to feed their ancestors. A powerful priestly elite, scribes, legal experts, military advisers, and skilled artisans were vital to the hierarchy.

Most of the Maya people remained tied to the land, which could sustain a high population only through dispersed settlements. Poor soil quality and limited water supply prevented large-scale agriculture. Through terraces, the draining of fields, and slash-and-burn agriculture, the Maya managed a subsistence economy of diversified agrarian production. Villagers cultivated maize, beans, and squash, rotating them to prevent the depletion of soil nutrients. Farmers supplemented these staples with root crops such as sweet potato and cassava. Cotton—the basic fiber used for clothing—frequently grew amid rows of other crops as part of a diversified mix.

Maya Writing, Mathematics, and Architecture A common set of beliefs, codes, and values connected the dispersed Maya villages. Sharing a similar language, the Maya developed writing and an important class of scribes, who were vital to the society's integration. Rulers rewarded scribes for writing grand epics about dynasties and their founders, major battles, marriages, deaths, and sacrifices. Such writings offered to Maya shared common histories, beliefs, and gods—always associated with the narratives of ruling families.

The best-known surviving Maya text is the *Popol Vuh*, a "Book of Community." It narrates one community's creation myth, extolling its founders (twin heroes) and the experiences—wars, natural disasters, human ingenuity—that enabled a royal line to rule the Quiché kingdom. The text begins with the gods' creation of the earth and ends with the rituals the kingdom's tribes must follow to avoid a descent into social and political anarchy, which had occurred several times throughout their history.

The Maya also had skilled mathematicians, who devised a calendar and studied astronomy. They accurately charted regular celestial movements and marked the passage of time by precise lunar and solar cycles. The Maya kept sacred calendars, by which they rigorously observed their rituals at the proper times. Each change in the cycle had particular rituals, dances, performances, and offerings to honor the gods with life's sustenance.

Cities reflected a ruler's ability to summon his subjects to contribute to the kingdom's greatness. Plazas, ball courts, terraces, and palaces sprawled out from neighborhoods. Activity revolved around grand royal palaces and massive ball courts, where competing teams treated enthusiastic audiences to contests that were more religious ritual than game. The Maya also excelled at building monumental structures. In Tikal, for instance, surviving buildings include six massive, steep funerary pyramids featuring elaborately carved and painted masonry walls, vaulted ceilings, and royal burial chambers; the tallest temple soars more than 220 feet high (40 feet higher than Justinian's Hagia Sophia).

Maya Bloodletting and Warfare

Maya elites were obsessed with spilling blood as a way to honor rulers and ancestors as well as gods. This gory rite led to frequent warfare, especially among rival dynasties, the goal of which was to capture victims for these rituals. Rulers would also shed their own blood at intervals set by the calendar. Royal wives drew blood from their tongues and men had their penises perforated. Such bloodletting by means of elaborately adorned and sanctified instruments was reserved for those of noble descent. Carvings and paintings portray blood cascading from rulers' mutilated bodies.

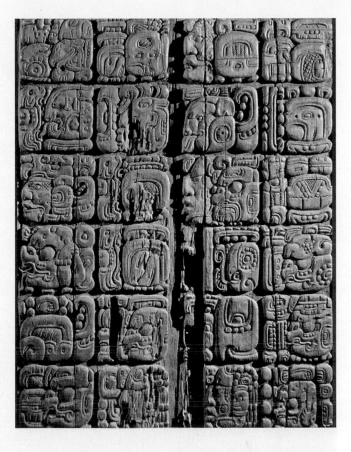

Wood Tablet This detail of a wood-carved tablet from a temple in the city of Tikal (c. 741 CE) is a fine example of the ornate form of scribal activity, which combined images and portraits with glyphs that tell a narrative.

Internal warfare eventually doomed the Maya, especially after devastating confrontations between Tikal and Kalak'mul during the fourth through seventh centuries CE. With each outbreak, rulers drafted larger armies and sacrificed greater numbers of captives. Crops perished. People fled. After centuries of misery, it must have seemed as if the gods themselves were abandoning the Maya people. The cycle of violence destroyed the cultural underpinnings of elite rule that had held the Maya world together. There was no single catastrophic event, no great defeat by a rival power. The Maya people simply abandoned their spiritual centers, and cities became ghost towns. As populations declined, jungles overtook temples. Eventually, the hallmark of Maya unity—the ability to read a shared script—vanished. While vibrant religious traditions thrived in sub-Saharan Africa and in Mesoamerica, they served more to reinforce the political and social situations from which they came rather than to spread a universalizing message far beyond their original context.

Conclusion

Maya Court Procession Brilliantly painted scenes from the late eighth-century CE Temple of the Murals in Bonampak, Mexico, include images of tribute processions, brutal conflicts, and bloody rituals associated with the installation of a ruler. In Room 1, pictured here, the upper panel shows Maya dignitaries, while the lower panel features singers and musicians playing rattles and drums.

The breakdown of two imperial systems—Rome around the Mediterranean, and Han China in East Asia—introduced an era in which religion and shared culture rather than military conquest and political institutions linked large areas of Afro-Eurasia.

The Roman Empire gave way to a new religious unity, first represented by Christian dissenters and then co-opted by the emperor Constantine. In western Europe, the sense of unity unlimited by imperial frontiers gave rise to a universal, or "Catholic," church—the "true" Christian religion that believers felt all peoples should share. In the eastern Mediterranean, where the Roman Empire survived, Christianity and empire coalesced to reinforce one another. Christians here held that beliefs about God and Jesus found their most correct expression within the Eastern Roman Empire and in its capital, Constantinople.

Similarly, in East Asia, the weakening of the Han dynasty enabled Buddhism to dominate Chinese culture. Without a unified state in China, Confucian officials lost their influence, while Buddhist priests and monks enjoyed patronage from regional rulers, local warriors, and commoners. In India, Brahman elites exploited population movements beyond the reach of traditional rulers as they established ritual forms for daily life on every level of society, while melding aspects of their own Vedic faith with those of Buddhism to create a new Hindu synthesis.

Not all regions felt the spread of universalizing religions, however. In most of sub-Saharan Africa, belief systems were much more localized. Similarly, in Mesoamerica, where long-distance transportation was harder and political authority more diffuse, religion was a unifying force but nothing like

Core Objectives

EXPLAIN why universalizing religions developed to varying degrees in Afro-Eurasia but did not develop elsewhere in the world.

the widespread universalizing religions of Afro-Eurasia. Nevertheless, spiritual life was no less profound. Here, a strong sense of a shared worldview, a shared sense of purpose, and a shared sense of faith enabled common cultures to develop. Indeed, the Bantus and the Maya became large-scale common cultures—but ruled at the local level.

Thus, the period 300–600 CE saw the emergence of three great cultural units in Afro-Eurasia, each defined in religious terms: Christianity in the Mediterranean and parts of Southwest Asia, Hinduism in South Asia, and Buddhism in East Asia. They illustrate the ways in which peoples were converging under larger religious tents, while also becoming more distinct. Universalizing religions, whether Christian or Buddhist, and codes of behavior, such as the Brahmanic Code of Manu, gave people a new way to define themselves and their loyalties.

Focus On
The Rise of Christianity, the Spread of Buddhism, and the Beginnings of Common Cultures

Europe and Southwest Asia

- Christianity moves from a minority, persecuted faith to a state religion in the Roman Empire.

- The Sasanian state in Iran provides fertile ground for a tolerant mixture of Zoroastrianism, Nestorian Christianity, Judaism, Buddhism, and Brahmanic religion.

South Asia and East Asia

- Brahmanism, or Hinduism, becomes the dominant religion among the Vedic peoples of South Asia.

- Buddhism spreads out of South Asia along the Silk Roads through central Asia and into East Asia (now fractured politically, but with the Buddhist-leaning Northern Wei having a dominant influence).

Sub-Saharan Africa and Mesoamerica

- Large parts of sub-Saharan Africa are influenced by the spread of Bantu-speaking, ironworking migrants who adapt to a range of ecological zones.

- In Mesoamerica, urban kingdoms thrive in Teotihuacán (central Mexico) and among the Maya (of Yucatán).

Key Terms

Bantu migrations p. 397	creed p. 373	martyr p. 371	universalizing
Byzantium p. 377	Hinayana Buddhism p. 389	Sanskrit cosmopolis	religions p. 366
Code of Manu p. 389	Hinduism p. 387	p. 389	

CHRONOLOGY

	1 CE	100 CE	200 CE	300 CE	400 CE

The Mediterranean and Southwest Asia

Emperor Constantine legalizes Christianity in Roman Empire 313 CE ●

Central Asia

South Asia

Transformation of Brahmanism into Hinduism begins or second century CE

East Asia

Six Dynasties period 220–589 CE

Sub-Saharan Africa

Bantu migrations from western Africa to south, central, and east 1 CE–1000 CE

Mesoamerica

Maya culture dominates Yucatán Peninsula and surrounding area third–ninth centuries CE

- **Thinking about Crossing Borders and Universalizing Religions** Why did borders seem to infuse vitality into Christianity and Buddhism in the fourth through sixth centuries CE? Which religions in this period did not seem to cross borders and why? What effect did this have on those religions?

- **Thinking about Changing Power Relationships and Universalizing Religions** Universalizing religions, like Christianity and Buddhism, were successful in part because of their diverse personalized appeal to men and women, rich and poor, and the upper and lower classes. How might this diverse appeal enable a uni-

versalizing religion like Christianity to undermine and alter traditional power relationships? In what ways did Buddhism do the same?

- **Thinking about Worlds Together, Worlds Apart and Universalizing Religions** Why did universalizing religions like Christianity and Buddhism develop in some parts of the world but not in others in the period 300 to 600 CE? How did these universalizing religions allow for continuity in Eurasia, even as empires fell away? In the "worlds apart," how might the lack of universalizing religion have influenced continuity, as political entities rose and fell over time?

 Go to INQUIZITIVE to see what you've learned—and learn what you've missed—with personalized feedback along the way.

500 CE	600 CE	700 CE	800 CE	900 CE	1000 CE

Sasanian Empire flourishes in Iran and Mesopotamia third–sixth centuries CE

"Barbarian" invasions of Roman Empire fourth–fifth centuries CE

Byzantine Empire flourishes in eastern Mediterranean fifth–seventh centuries CE

Byzantine and Sasanian wars sixth–seventh centuries CE

Buddhism spreads through central Asia fourth–sixth centuries CE

Sogdian merchant communities dominate Silk Road trade through central Asia fourth–sixth centuries CE

Gupta Empire 320–550 CE

Buddhism gains in popularity fourth–sixth centuries CE

City of Teotihuacán dominates Valley of Mexico fourth–fifth centuries CE

Global Themes and Sources

Continuity and Change in Pilgrimage

Pilgrimage went hand in hand with the spread of universalizing religions along the trade routes that stretched across Eurasia. Christians and Buddhists traveled the religious geography of their faith, visiting sacred sites and relics and hearing stories of holy women and men. The pilgrimages described here are arranged chronologically by journey (not date of composition) and grouped by tradition (Christianity, then Buddhism), in order to track changes within a tradition over time in this all-important practice, as well as to see the similarities and differences in how pilgrimage worked for each. The account from Hinduism was written in the mid-first millennium CE, roughly at the same time the Christian and Buddhist pilgrims were traveling, but describes a legendary character's travel to holy sites and people almost 1,500 years earlier. It thus offers a Hindu perspective on pilgrimage that can be contrasted with the pilgrimages within the universalizing traditions of Christianity and Buddhism.

The church historian Socrates (not to be confused with the ancient Greek philosopher of the same name) recounts the faith-inspired travels of Helena, the mother of the emperor Constantine, as well as those of individuals who traveled into Africa and India to spread the Gospel. That historical account (reported almost 200 years after the fact) can be compared with the first-person travel diary kept by a woman named Egeria who journeyed to holy sites across the eastern Mediterranean in the late fourth century CE, recording the places she visited and her experiences at each location. At roughly the same time Egeria was traveling, an elderly Chinese Buddhist monk named Faxian was making his way from Chang'an in China to South Asia to look for Buddhist scriptures and to visit sites sacred to Buddhism. More than 200 years later, another Buddhist monk, named Xuanzang, traveled west along the Silk Roads to Samarkand, where he turned south into India, visiting Buddhist sites along the way before returning to China. The passage from the *Bhagavata Purana* describes the travels of Vidura, a major character in the *Mahabharata* whose legendary storyline extends back to 1000 BCE.

Taken together, these sources offer an excellent opportunity to track how certain aspects of pilgrimage endure while others change over time. Religiously motivated travel and monasticism were central to the spread of universalizing religious traditions in the mid-first millennium CE. Consequently, the similarities and differences in pilgrimage, over time and across traditions, make it possible to track the relative importance of this religious tourism within the larger context of the ever-expanding influence of Christianity and Buddhism.

Analyzing Continuity and Change in Pilgrimage

- What do these pilgrims—Helena, Egeria, Faxian, Xuanzang, and Vidura—see and do when they visit a holy site? To what extent does pilgrimage within Christianity and Buddhism seem to change over time? In what ways is there continuity in the practice of pilgrimage?

- What appears to be the role of storytelling in pilgrimage? What do these excerpts suggest about the relationship between monasteries and holy sites? Between pilgrims and written text?

- How do the similarities and differences over time and across traditions—in terms of where religious travelers go, what they do, how and to whom they report their experiences—indicate the extent to which a tradition was a universalizing faith?

Recovery of the Cross of Christ by Helena (c. 325 CE), from *Ecclesiastical History* (fifth century CE), Socrates

Socrates wrote his *Ecclesiastical History* in the early fifth century CE to describe the important years from 305 CE (when Constantine, the emperor who legalized Christianity, began to consolidate his imperial power) through 439 CE (when Theodosius II, who oversaw a major codification of Roman law, was emperor in the east and the Vandals and Huns were threatening the western empire). In the passages here, Socrates offers the story of how Helena, the mother of Constantine, reputedly found the cross on which Jesus was crucified, as well as how Christianity spread into Africa and India during Constantine's reign. Helena's travels to Jerusalem and the voyage of Meropius and Frumentius to India illustrate early attempts by Christians to mark sacred space and to spread their tradition beyond the boundaries of the Roman Empire.

- **What does Helena find when she travels to Jerusalem, and how does she verify its legitimacy to her satisfaction? What are the impediments to her success?**

- **How are Helena's finds marked? What might be the significance of this building activity in the short and long term?**

- **What does the text reveal about how Christianity spread into new territories?**

Chapter 18: Helena, the emperor's mother . . . being divinely directed by dreams went to Jerusalem. Finding that which was once Jerusalem, desolate . . . she sought carefully the sepulcher of Christ, from which he arose after his burial; and after much difficulty, by God's help she discovered it. What the cause of the difficulty was I will explain in a few words. Those who embraced the Christian faith, after the period of his passion, greatly venerated this tomb; but those who hated Christianity, having covered the spot with a mound of earth, erected on it a temple to Venus, and set up her image there, not caring for the memory of the place. This succeeded for a long time; and it became known to the emperor's mother. Accordingly she having caused the statue to be thrown down, the earth to be removed, and the ground entirely cleared, found three crosses in the sepulcher: one of these was that blessed cross on which Christ had hung, the other two were those on which the two thieves that were crucified with him had died. With these was also found the tablet of Pilate, on which he had inscribed in various characters, that the Christ who was crucified was king of the Jews. Since, however, it was doubtful which was the cross they were in search of, the emperor's mother was not a little distressed; but from this trouble the bishop of Jerusalem, Macarius, shortly relieved her. And he solved the doubt by faith, for he sought a sign from God and obtained it. The sign was this: a certain woman of the neighborhood, who had been long afflicted with disease, was now just at the point of death; the bishop therefore arranged it so that each of the crosses should be brought to the dying woman, believing that she would be healed on touching the precious cross. Nor was he disappointed in his expectation: for the two crosses having been applied which were not the Lord's, the woman still continued in a dying state; but when the third, which was the true cross, touched her, she was immediately healed, and recovered her former strength. In this manner then was the genuine cross discovered. The emperor's mother erected over the place of the sepulcher a magnificent church, and named it *New Jerusalem*, having built it facing that old and deserted city. There she left a portion of the cross, enclosed in a silver case, as a memorial to those who might wish to see it: the other part she sent to the emperor, who being persuaded that the city would be perfectly secure where that relic should be preserved, privately enclosed it in his own statue, which stands on a large column of porphyry in the forum called Constantine's at Constantinople. I have written this from report indeed; but almost all the inhabitants of Constantinople affirm that it is true. Moreover the nails with which Christ's hands were fastened to the cross (for his mother having found these also in the sepulcher had sent them) Constantine took and had made into bridle-bits and a helmet, which he used in his military expeditions. The emperor supplied all materials for the construction of the churches, and wrote to Macarius the bishop to expedite these edifices. When the emperor's mother had completed the *New Jerusalem*, she reared another church not at all inferior, over the cave at Bethlehem where Christ was born according to the flesh: nor did she stop here, but built a third on the mount of his Ascension. . . . She was also very munificent to the churches and to the poor; and having lived a life of piety, she died when about eighty years old. Her remains were conveyed to New Rome, the capital, and deposited in the imperial sepulchers. . . .

Chapter 19: We must now mention in what manner Christianity was spread in this emperor's reign: for it was in his time that the nations both of the Indians in the interior, and of the Iberians first embraced the Christian faith. . . . When the apostles went forth by lot among the nations, Thomas received the apostleship of the Parthians; Matthew was allotted Ethiopia; and Bartholomew the part of India contiguous to that country: but the interior of India, in which many barbarous nations using different languages lived, was not enlightened by Christian doctrine before the times of Constantine. I now come to speak of the cause which led them to become converts to Christianity. A certain philosopher, Meropius, a Tyrian by race, determined to acquaint himself with the country of the Indians, being stimulated to this by the example of the philosopher Metrodorus, who had previously traveled through the region of India. Having taken with him therefore two youths to whom he was related, who were by no means ignorant of the Greek language, Meropius reached the country by ship. . . . It so happened that a little before that time the treaty between the Romans and Indians had been violated. The Indians, therefore, having seized the philosopher and those who sailed with him, killed them all except his two youthful kinsmen; but sparing them from compassion for their tender age, they sent them as a gift to the king of the Indians. He being pleased with the personal appearance of the youths, constituted one of them, whose name was Edesius, cupbearer at his table; the other, named Frumentius, he entrusted with the care of the royal records. . . . Thus Frumentius controlled all things and made it a task to enquire whether among the Roman merchants trafficking with that country, there were any Christians to be found: and having discovered some, he informed them who he was, and exhorted them to select and occupy some appropriate places for the celebration of Christian worship. In the course of a little while he built a house of prayer; and having instructed some of the Indians in the principles of Christianity, they fitted them for participation in the worship.

Source: Socrates Scholasticus, *Ecclesiastical History*, in *Nicene and Post-Nicene Fathers of the Christian Church*, vol. 2, translated by A. C. Zenos (Grand Rapids, MI: Wm. B. Eerdmans, 1957), pp. 21–23.

PRIMARY SOURCE 8.2

Diary of a Pilgrimage (late fourth century CE), Egeria

Egeria was a nun who traveled from Spain to the eastern Mediterranean (modern Turkey, Syria, Israel, and Egypt) to visit sites important to early Christianity. Her writing is striking not only because it was composed by a far-traveling woman but also because it is the earliest recorded Christian pilgrimage account. Egeria's rich descriptions of the places she visits, the people she meets, and the religious rituals performed at each site demonstrate how pilgrimage could enliven the faith of the adherents of universalizing traditions.

- **What details does Egeria offer that give you a sense of what her travel was like?**
- **What does Egeria do at the places she visits? How are people, place, and story a significant part of that experience?**
- **How has pilgrimage changed from Helena's time to Egeria's time, just two generations later? How has it remained the same? What do you think accounts for these similarities and differences?**

Chapter 22: After I had returned to Antioch, I remained there for a whole week, until whatever was necessary for our journey had been prepared. I then set out from Antioch and, after journeying for several days, arrived in the province called Cilicia, the capital city of which is Tarsus, the same Tarsus in which I had already been on my trip down to Jerusalem.

Since the shrine of Saint Thecla is located a three-day journey from Tarsus, in Isauria, it was a great pleasure for me to go there, particularly since it was so near at hand.

Chapter 23: I set out from Tarsus and I came to a certain city by the sea, still in Cilicia, called Pompeiopolis. From there I crossed over in the regions of Isauria, and I stayed at a city called Corycus. On the third day I arrived at a city called Seleucia of Isauria. On arriving there, I went to the bishop, a very holy man and a former monk. I also saw there in the same city a very beautiful church. Since it is around fifteen hundred feet from the city to the shrine of Saint Thecla, which lies beyond the city on a rather flat hill, I thought it best to go out there to make the overnight stop which I had to make.

At the holy church there is nothing but countless monastic cells for men and women. I met there a very dear friend of mine, and a person to whose way of life everyone in the East bears witness, the holy deaconess Marthana, whom I had met in Jerusalem, where she had come to pray. She governs these monastic cells of *aputactitae*, or virgins. Would I ever be able to describe how great was her joy and how great mine when she saw me? But to return to the subject: There are many cells all over the hill, and in the middle there is a large wall which encloses the church where the shrine is. It is a very beautiful shrine. The wall is set there to guard the church against the Isaurians, who are evil men, who frequently rob and who might try to do something against the monastery which is established there. Having arrived there in the name of God, a prayer was said at the shrine and the complete Acts of Saint Thecla was read. I then gave unceasing thanks to Christ our God, who granted to me, an unworthy woman and in no way deserving, the fulfillment of my desires in all things. And so, after spending two days there seeing the holy monks and the *aputactitae*, both men and women, who live there, and after praying and receiving Communion, I returned to Tarsus and to my journey.

I made a three-day stop before setting out on my journey from there, in the name of God. On the same day I arrived at the resting station called Mansocrenae, located at the base of Mount Tarsus, and I stopped there. The next day I climbed Mount Tarsus and travelled by a route, already known to me, through several provinces that I had already crossed on my journey down, that is, Cappadocia, Galatia, and Bithynia. Then I arrived at Chalcedon, where I stopped because of the very famous shrine of Saint Euphemia, already known to me from before. On the following day, after crossing the sea, I arrived in Constantinople, giving thanks to Christ our God who deigned to bestow such favor on me, an unworthy and undeserving person. Not only did He deign to fulfill my desire to go there, but He granted also the means of visiting what I desired to see, and of returning again to Constantinople.

After arriving there, I did not cease giving thanks to Jesus our God, who had deigned to bestow His grace upon me, in the various churches, that of the apostles and the numerous shrines that are here. As I send this letter to Your Charity and to you, reverend ladies, it is already my intention to go, in the name of Christ our God, to Asia, that is, to Ephesus, to pray at the shrine of the holy and blessed apostle John. If, after this, I am still living, I will either tell Your Charity in person—if God will deign to grant that—about whatever other places I shall have come to know, or certainly I will write you of it in letters, if there is anything else I have in mind.

You, my sisters, my light, kindly remember me, whether I live or die.

Source: Egeria, *Ancient Christian Writers: Diary of a Pilgrimage*, translated by George E. Gringras (Mahwah, NJ: Newman Press, 1970), pp. 86–89.

PRIMARY SOURCE 8.3

A Record of Buddhistic Kingdoms (early fifth century CE), Faxian

Faxian's journeys blended two elements of universalizing tradition: pilgrimage and texts. He was motivated to travel to the homeland of Buddhism to gather or copy as many Buddhist texts as possible so he could bring them back to China. His description of his travels—from China to India to Sri Lanka and back again—offers a view of the varied worship practices within different schools of Buddhism, as well as the many different regions where Buddhism flourished.

- What specific details does Faxian offer about the sites he visits? What do you think is the purpose of that level of detail?

- How are the holy sites visited by Faxian marked out?

- What role do other monks and monasteries play in Faxian's travel?

Chapter 31: From this place, after travelling to the west for four yojanas [Vedic unit of measure, approximately 8 miles], (the pilgrims) came to the city of Gayâ; but inside the city all was emptiness and desolation. Going on again to the south for twenty *le* [Chinese unit of measure, roughly one-third of a mile], they arrived at the place where the Bodhisattva for six years practised with himself painful austerities. All around was forest.

Three *le* west from here they came to the place where, when Buddha had gone into the water to bathe, a deva [divine being] bent down the branch of a tree, by means of which he succeeded in getting out of the pool.

Two *le* north from this was the place where the Grâmika girls presented to Buddha the rice gruel made with milk; and two *le* north from this (again) was the place where, seated on a rock under a great tree, and facing the east, he ate (the gruel). The tree and the rock are there at the present day. The rock may be six cubits in breadth and length, and rather more than two cubits in height. In Central India the cold and heat are so equally tempered that trees will live in it for several thousand and even for ten thousand years.

Half a yojana from this place to the north-east there was a cavern in the rocks, into which the Bodhisattva entered, and sat cross-legged with his face to the west. (As he did so), he said to himself, "If I am to attain to perfect wisdom (and become Buddha), let there be a supernatural attestation of it." On the wall of the rock there appeared immediately the shadow of a Buddha, rather more than three feet in length, which is still bright at the present day. At this moment heaven and earth were greatly moved, and devas in the air spoke plainly, "This is not the place where any Buddha of the past, or he that is to come, has attained, or will

attain, to perfect Wisdom. Less than half a yojana from this to the south-west will bring you to the patra tree, where all past Buddhas have attained, and all to come must attain, to perfect Wisdom." When they had spoken these words, they immediately led the way forwards to the place, singing as they did so. . . .

At the place mentioned above . . . men subsequently reared topes [or stupas, Buddhist shrines with relics] and set up images, which all exist at the present day.

Where Buddha, after attaining to perfect wisdom, for seven days contemplated the tree, and experienced the joy of vimukti; where, under the patra tree, he walked backwards and forwards from west to east for seven days; where the devas made a hall appear, composed of the seven precious substances, and presented offerings to him for seven days; where the blind dragon Muchilinda encircled him for seven days; where he sat under the nyagrodha tree, on a square rock, with his face to the east, and Brahma-deva came and made his request to him; where the four deva kings brought to him their alms-bowls; where the 500 merchants presented to him the roasted flour and honey; and where he converted the brothers Kaśyapa and their thousand disciples;—at all these places topes were reared.

At the place where Buddha attained to perfect Wisdom, there are three monasteries, in all of which there are monks residing. The families of their people around supply the societies of these monks with an abundant sufficiency of what they require, so that there is no lack or stint. The disciplinary rules are strictly observed by them. The laws regulating their demeanour in sitting, rising, and entering when the others are assembled, are those which have been practised by all the saints since Buddha was in the world down to the present day. The places of the four great topes have been fixed, and handed down without break, since Buddha attained to nirvâna. Those four great topes are those at the places where Buddha was born; where he attained to Wisdom; where he (began to) move the wheel of his Law; and where he attained to pari-nirvâna.

***

Chapter 36: From Vârânasî (the travellers) went back east to Pâṭaliputtra. Faxian's original object had been to search for (copies of) the Vinaya [texts governing monastic communities in Buddhism]. In the various kingdoms of North India, however, he had found one master transmitting orally (the rules) to another, but no written copies which he could transcribe. He had therefore travelled far and come on to Central India. Here in the mahâyâna monastery, he found a copy of the Vinaya, containing the Mahâsânghika rules,—those which were observed in the first Great Council, while Buddha was still in the world. . . . [The account then describes a range of texts collected by Faxian.]

In consequence (of this success in his quest) Faxian stayed here for three years, learning Sanskrit books and the Sanskrit speech, and writing out the Vinaya rules.

Source: Faxian, *A Record of Buddhistic Kingdoms, Being an Account by the Chinese Monk Fâ-Hien of His Travels in India and Ceylon* (A.D. 399–414) *in Search of the Buddhist Books of Discipline*, translated by James Legge (Oxford: Clarendon Press, 1886), pp. 87–90, 98–99.

PRIMARY SOURCE 8.4

Travels of Xuanzang (seventh century CE)

Like Faxian, the Chinese monk Xuanzang traveled along the Silk Roads encountering many varieties of Buddhism as it was practiced in different regions and many texts produced within those different Buddhist communities. And like Faxian's writings, Xuanzang's vivid descriptions of the places he visits offer wide-eyed wonder and storytelling leavened with practical analyses of distances between cities, the sizes of structures and communities, and the local cultures he encounters. Read closely, however, for the subtle differences in the ways that Xuanzang describes the world through which he moves more than 200 years after Faxian.

• **What does Xuanzang note about the sites that he visits? Why do you think he offers these details?**

• **How do monasteries and convents fit into Xuanzang's travel? What does this text reveal about the development of stupas and the placement of relics within them?**

• **How does Xuanzang's travel compare with that of his fellow Buddhist Faxian, more than 200 years earlier? What are the similarities and differences over time in how pilgrimage is described and what a pilgrim does?**

Po-Ho [Balkh, in northern Afghanistan]. This country is about 800 *li* from east to west, and 400 *li* from north to south; on the north it borders on the Oxus. The capital is about 20 *li* in circuit. It is called generally the little Râjagriha [site in northeastern India, important in Buddhism and Jainism, first capital of Magadha kingdom]. This city, though well (*strongly*) fortified, is thinly populated. The products of the soil are extremely varied, and the flowers, both on the land and water, would be difficult to enumerate. There are about 100 convents and 3000 monks, who all study the religious teaching of the Little Vehicle [i.e., Hinayana Buddhism].

Outside the city, towards the south-west, there is a convent called Navasanghârâma, which was built by a former king of this country. The Masters (of Buddhism), who dwell to the north of the great Snowy Mountains, and are authors of Sâstras, occupy this convent only, and continue their estimable labours in it. There is a figure of Buddha here, which is lustrous with (reflects the glory of) noted gems, and the hall in which it stands is also adorned with precious substances of rare value. This is the reason why it has often been robbed by chieftains of neighbouring countries, covetous of gain.

This convent also contains (possesses) a statue of Pisha-men (Vaiśravaṇa) Dêva, by whose spiritual influence, in unexpected ways, there is protection afforded to the precincts of the convent. . . .

Within the convent, in the southern hall of Buddha, there is the washing-basin which Buddha used. It contains about a peck, and is of various colours, which dazzle the eyes. It is difficult to name the gold and stone of which it is made. Again, there is a tooth of Buddha about an inch long, and about eight or nine tenths of an inch in breadth. Its colour is yellowish white; it is pure and shining. Again, there is the sweeping brush of Buddha, made of the plant "Ka-she" (kâśâ). It is about two feet long and about seven inches round. Its handle is ornamented with various gems. These three relics are presented with offerings on each of the six fast-days by the assembly of lay and cleric believers. Those who have the greatest faith in worship see the objects emitting a radiance of glory.

To the north of the convent is a stûpa, in height about 200 feet, which is covered with a plaster hard as the diamond, and ornamented with a variety of precious substances. It encloses a sacred relic (she-li), and at times this also reflects a divine splendour.

To the south-west of the convent there is a Vihâra [monastery]. Many years have elapsed since its foundation was laid. It is the resort (of people) from distant quarters. There are also a large number of men of conspicuous talent. As it would be difficult for the several possessors of the four different degrees (fruits) of holiness to explain accurately their condition of saintship, therefore the Arhats [people who have reached nirvana] . . . , when about to die, exhibit their spiritual capabilities (miraculous powers), and those who witness such an exhibition found stûpas in honour of the deceased saints. These are closely crowded together here, to the number of several hundreds. Besides these there are some thousand others, who, although they had reached the fruit of holiness (i e., Arhatship), yet having exhibited no spiritual changes at the end of life, have no memorial erected to them.

At present the number of priests is about 100; so irregular are they morning and night in their duties, that it is hard to tell saints from sinners.

To the north-west of the capital about 50 *li* or so we arrive at the town of Ti-wei; 40 *li* to the north of this town is the town of Po-li. In each of these towns there is a stûpa about three chang (30 feet) in height. In old days, when Buddha first attained enlightenment after advancing to the tree of knowledge, he went to the garden of deer; at this time two householders meeting him, and beholding the brilliant appearance of his person, offered him from their store of provisions for their journey some cakes and honey. The lord of the world, for their sakes, preached concerning the happiness of men and Dêvas, and delivered to them, his very first disciples, the five rules of moral conduct and the ten good qualities (shen, virtuous rules). When they had heard the sermon, they humbly asked for some object to worship (offer gifts). On this Tathâgata delivered to them some of his hair and nail-cuttings. Taking these, the merchants were about to return to their own country, when they asked of Buddha the right way of venerating these relics. Tathâgata forthwith spreading out his Sanghâti on the ground as a square napkin, next laid down his Uttarâsanga and then his Sankakshikâ; again over these he placed as a cover his begging-pot, on which he erected his mendicant's staff. Thus he placed them in order, making thereby (the figure of) a stûpa. The two men taking the order, each went to his own town, and then, according to the model which the holy one had prescribed, they prepared to build a monument, and thus was the very first Stûpa of the Buddhist religion erected.

Source: *Buddhist Records of the Western World, Translated from the Chinese of Hiuen Tsiang (A.D. 629)*, vol. 1, translated by Samuel Beal (London: Trübner, 1884), pp. 43–48.

PRIMARY SOURCE 8.5

Travels of Vidura in Distant Vedic Past (c. 1000 BCE[?]), from the *Bhaguvata Purana* (recorded c. 500 CE)

The excerpt of the *Bhagavata Purana* offered here tells the story of Vidura, the brother of the king Dhṛtarāṣṭra, and the sacred journey Vidura takes through India. The increasing popularity of accessible *bhakti* devotion at the time this text reached its written form can be traced in the personal relationship that several of the characters, including Vidura, have with Krishna, who is the human incarnation of the Hindu god Vishnu. Even with those hints of personal connection, Vidura's pilgrimage stands in striking contrast to those in the other texts offered here.

- Why does Vidura go on pilgrimage? What does Vidura do when he visits holy sites?

- What in the text suggests Vidura's personalized relationship with Krishna?

- How is Vidura's pilgrimage similar to travels by the Christians Helena and Egeria and the Buddhists Faxian and Xuanzang? How is it different? What do you think accounts for these similarities and differences?

SB 3.1. (10) When Vidura was invited by his elder brother [Dhṛtarāṣṭra] for consultation, he entered the house and gave instructions which were exactly to the point. His advice is well-known, and instructions by Vidura are approved by expert ministers of state. (11) [Vidura said:] You must now return the legitimate share to Yudhiṣṭhira who has no enemies and who has been forebearing through untold sufferings due to your offenses. He is waiting with his younger brothers, among whom is the revengeful Bhīma, breathing heavily like a snake. Surely you are afraid of him. (13) You are maintaining offense personified, Duryodhana, as your infallible son, but he is envious of Lord Kṛṣṇa [i.e., Krishna]. And because you are thus maintaining a nondevotee of Kṛṣṇa, you are devoid of all auspicious qualities. Relieve yourself of this ill fortune as soon as possible and do good to the whole family! (14) While speaking thus, Vidura, whose personal character was esteemed by respectable persons, was insulted by Duryodhana, who was swollen with anger and whose lips were trembling. Duryodhana was in company with Karna, his younger brothers and his maternal uncle Śakuni. (15) "Who asked him to come here, this son of a kept mistress? He is so crooked that he spies in the interest of the enemy against those on whose support he has grown up. Toss him out of the palace immediately and leave him with his only breath." (16) Thus being pierced by arrows through his ears and afflicted to the core of his heart, Vidura placed his bow on the door and quit his brother's palace. He was not sorry, for he considered the acts of the external energy to be supreme. (17) By his piety, Vidura achieved the advantages of the pious Kauravas [i.e., children of Dhṛtarāṣṭra]. After leaving Hastināpura, he took shelter of many places of pilgrimages, which are the Lord's lotus feet. With a desire to gain a high order of pious life, he traveled to holy places where thousands of transcendental forms of the Lord are situated. (18) He began to travel along, thinking only of Kṛṣṇa, through various holy places like Ayodhyā, Dvārakā and Mathurā [all cities in India]. He traveled where the grove, hill, orchard, river and lake are all pure and sinless and where the forms of the Unlimited decorate the temples. Thus he performed the pilgrim's progress. (19) While so traversing the earth, he simply performed duties to please the Supreme Lord Hari. His occupation was pure and independent. He was constantly sanctified by taking his bath in holy places, although he was in the dress of a mendicant and had no hair dressing nor a bed on which to lie. Thus he was always unseen by his various relatives. (20) Thus, when he was in the land of Bhāratavarṣa [i.e., India] traveling to all the places of pilgrimage, he visited Prabhāsakṣetra. At that time Mahārāja Yudhiṣṭhira was the emperor and held the world under one military strength and one flag. (21) At the place of pilgrimage at Prabhāsa, it came to his knowledge that all his relatives had died due to violent passion, just as an entire forest burns due to fire produced by the friction of bamboos. After this he proceeded west, where the river Sarasvatī flows. (22) On the bank of the river Sarasvatī there were eleven places of pilgrimage, namely (1) Trita, (2) Uśanā, (3) Manu, (4) Pṛthu, (5) Agni, (6) Asita, (7) Vāyu, (8) Sudāsa, (9) Go, (10) Guha and (11) Śrāddhadeva. Vidura visited all of them and duly performed rituals. (23) There were also many other temples of various forms of the Supreme Personality of Godhead Viṣṇu, established by great sages and demigods. These temples were marked with the chief emblems of the Lord, and they reminded one always of the original Personality of Godhead, Lord Kṛṣṇa. (24) Thereafter he passed through very wealthy provinces like Surat, Sauvīra and Matsya and through western India, known as Kurujāṅgala. At last he reached the bank of the Yamunā, where he happened to meet Uddhava, the great devotee of Lord Kṛṣṇa. (25) Then, due to his great love and feeling, Vidura embraced him [Uddhava] who was a constant companion of Lord Kṛṣṇa and formerly a great student of Bṛhaspati. Vidura then asked him for news of the family of Lord Kṛṣṇa, the Personality of Godhead. (26) [Please tell me] whether the original Personalities of Godhead, who incarnated Themselves at the request of Brahmā [who is born out of the lotus flower from the Lord] and who have increased the prosperity of the world by elevating everyone, are doing well in the house of Śūrasena. (27) [Please tell me] whether the best friend of the Kurus, our brother-in-law Vasudeva, is doing well. He is very munificent. He is like a father to his sister, and he is always pleasing to his wives. (33) As the Vedas are the reservoir of sacrificial purposes, so the daughter of King Devaka-bhoja conceived the Supreme Personality of Godhead in her womb, as did the mother of the demigods. Is she [Devakī] doing well? (45) O my friend, please, therefore, chant the glories of the Lord, who is meant to be glorified in the places of pilgrimage. He is unborn, and yet He appears by His causeless mercy upon the surrendered rulers of all parts of the universe. Only for their interest did He appear in the family of His unalloyed devotees the Yadus.

Source: *Śrīmad Bhāgavatam*, Third Canto, "The Status Quo" (Part 1, Chapters 1–8), translated by His Divine Grace A. C. Bhaktivedanta Sawmi Prabhupāda (Los Angeles: The Bhaktivedanta Book Trust, 1972), pp. 9–11, 13–16, 19–23, 25–28, 34, 47.

Interpreting Visual Evidence

Representations of Holiness

One of the features of universalizing religions discussed in this chapter is that they offered individuals a more personal connection with the divine. This accessibility is visible in the religious art from the period.

As the images here show, artists expressed what it means to be holy in various ways. The Yungang Caves in northeastern China were situated at the eastern end of the Silk Roads. The large statues and interior painting and carvings pictured here were created between 450 and 525 CE, during the Northern Wei dynasty. Many different Buddhas reside in individual niches on the walls surrounding the large central Buddha statue. Thousands of miles away, in the crumbling Western Roman Empire, the Archbishop's Chapel from Ravenna (c. 500 CE) in northern Italy preserved depictions of martyrs and other religious figures, notably Perpetua and Felicitas. These women appear here not as violently bloodied witnesses to their faith but rather as a serenely modest matron and her humble (and enslaved) maidservant.

The two relief sculptures pictured here provide additional perspectives on sacred subjects. The Hindu relief depicts the Kalyanasundara, or "beautiful marriage," of Parvati and Shiva (the Hindu god of destruction and rejuvenation). This particular relief was carved in

the mid-sixth century CE in Cave 1 at Elephanta on an island in the harbor of modern-day Mumbai. Its imagery recurs in numerous versions throughout the ancient Hindu temples of India and beyond. In this carving, Parvati, a reincarnation of Shiva's first wife, Sati, is married to Shiva as a reward for her patient devotion. The final image is a limestone relief from Yaxchilán, Mexico, and shows a royal Maya bloodletting ritual. In the image (dated by the glyphs to October 26, 709 CE), the queen pierces her tongue with a thorny rope in a reenactment of the bloodletting by the gods in the Maya creation narrative.

Yungang Caves.

Perpetua and Felicitas.

Kalyanasundara of Parvati and Shiva.

Questions for Analysis

1. Compare these visual representations of what it means to be holy. To what extent do they convey a message that is particular to their tradition?

2. What might account for the similarities in these depictions of what it means to be holy?

3. Given what you know about the features of these universalizing traditions, what in these images might suggest human access to holiness or the possibility of a personal connection to the divine?

4. How does the location of these images (where they were created and displayed) contribute to an understanding of how universalizing these traditions were?

Royal bloodletting ritual.

9

New Empires and Common Cultures

600–1000 CE

In 754 CE al-Mansur, ruler of the new Muslim Abbasid dynasty, decided to relocate his capital city from Damascus (the capital of Islam's first dynasty) closer to the Abbasids' home region on the Iranian plateau. Islam was barely a century old, yet it flourished under this second dynasty. The caliph al-Mansur chose, for both practical and symbolic reasons, to build his capital near an unimposing village called Baghdad. Not only did the site lie between Mesopotamia's two great rivers, at the juncture of the canals that linked them, but it was also close to the ancient capital of the earlier Sasanian Empire and the site of ancient Sumerian and Babylonian power. By building at Baghdad, al-Mansur could reaffirm Mesopotamia's centrality in the world and promote the universalizing ambitions of Islam.

Al-Mansur's choice had enduring effects. Baghdad became a vital crossroads for commerce. Overnight, the city exploded into a bustling world entrepôt. Chinese goods arrived by land and sea; commodities from Inner Eurasia flowed in over the Silk Roads; and cargo-laden camel caravans wound across Baghdad's western desert, linking the capital with Syria, Egypt, North Africa, and southern Spain. The unity that the Abbasids imposed from Baghdad intensified the movement of peoples, ideas, innovations, and commodities.

While Islam was gaining ground in central Afro-Eurasia, Chinese might was surging in East Asia under the Tang dynasty. Yet Islam and Tang China were clearly different worlds. The Islamic state had a universalizing religious mission: to bring humankind under the

Core Objectives

- **DESCRIBE** and **EXPLAIN** the spread of Islam, Buddhism, and Christianity from 600 to 1000 CE.
- **COMPARE** the organizational structures of the Abbasids, Tang China, and Christendom.
- **COMPARE** the internal divisions within the Islamic, Tang, and Christian worlds.
- **EVALUATE** the relationships between religion, empire, and commercial exchange across Afro-Eurasia during this period.

authority of the religion espoused by the Prophet Muhammad. In contrast, the Tang state had no such grandiose religious goals; the ruling elites supported religious variety within China, and they did not use Buddhism to expand their control into areas outside China. Instead, the Tang rulers expected that their neighbors would copy Chinese institutions and pay tribute as symbols of respect to the greatness of the Tang Empire. Though not as expansive as Islam and the Tang Empire, Christianity also strived in this period to extend its domain and add to its converts. With Islam's warriors, traders, and scholars crossing into Europe, Chinese influences taking deeper root in East Asia, and Christendom extending itself across Europe, religion and empire once again intertwined to serve as the social foundation across much of Afro-Eurasia.

Global Storyline

Religion and Empires: Islam, the Tang Dynasty, Christendom, and Common Cultures

- The universalizing religion of Islam, based on the message of the Prophet Muhammad, originates on the Arabian Peninsula and spreads rapidly across Afro-Eurasia.

- The expanding Tang dynasty in East Asia consolidates its bureaucracy, struggles with religious pluralism, and extends its influence into central and East Asia.

- Christianity splits over religious and political differences, leading to a divide between Roman Catholicism in the west and Greek Orthodoxy in the east.

The Origins and Spread of Islam

Islam began on the Arabian Peninsula. Despite its remoteness and sparse population, by the sixth century CE Arabia was brushing up against exciting outside currents: long-distance trade, religious debate, and imperial politics. The Hijaz—the western region of Arabia bordering the Red Sea—knew the outside world through trading routes reaching up the coast to the Mediterranean. Mecca, located in the Hijaz, was an unimposing village of simple mud huts. Mecca's inhabitants included both merchants and the caretakers of a revered sanctuary called the Kaaba, a dwelling place of deities. In this remote region, one of the world's major prophets emerged, and the universalizing faith he founded soon spread from Arabia through the trade routes stretching across Southwest Asia and North Africa.

THE BIG PICTURE

What cultural, political, and economic factors influenced the expansion of Islam, Buddhism, and Christianity from 600 to 1000 CE?

A VISION, A TEXT, A NEW COMMUNITY

Born in Mecca around 570 CE into a well-respected tribal family, Muhammad enjoyed only limited financial success as a trader. Then came a revelation that would convert this merchant into a proselytizer of a new faith. In 610 CE, while the forty-year-old Muhammad was on a month-long spiritual retreat in a cave near Mecca, he believed that God came to him in a vision and commanded him to recite a series of revelations.

The early revelations were short and powerful, emphasizing a single, all-powerful God (Allah) and providing instructions for Muhammad's fellow Meccans to carry this message to nonbelievers. Muhammad's early preaching had a clear message. He urged his small band of followers to act righteously, to set aside false deities, to submit themselves to the one and only true God, and to care for the less fortunate—for the Day of Judgment was imminent. Muhammad's most insistent message was the oneness of God, a belief that has remained central to the Islamic faith ever since.

These teachings, compiled into an authoritative version after the Prophet's death, constituted the foundational text of Islam: the Quran. Accepted as the word of God, the Quran's verses were understood to have flowed flawlessly through God's perfect instrument, the Prophet Muhammad. Muhammad believed that he was a prophet in the tradition of Moses, other Hebrew prophets, and Jesus and that he communicated with the same God that they did. The Quran and Muhammad proclaimed the tenets of a new faith intended to unite a people and to expand the faith's spiritual frontiers. Islam's message already had universalizing elements, though how far it was to be extended, whether to the tribesmen living in the Arabian Peninsula or well beyond, was not at all clear at first.

In 622 CE, Muhammad and a small group of followers, opposed by Mecca's leaders because of their radical religious beliefs and their challenge to the

Mecca At the great mosque at Mecca, which many consider the most sacred site in Islam, hundreds of thousands of worshippers gather for Friday prayers. Many are performing their religious duty to go on a pilgrimage to the holy places in the Arabian Peninsula.

ruling elite's authority, escaped to Yathrib (later named Medina). The perilous 200-mile journey, known as *the hijra* ("breaking off of relations" or "departure"), yielded a new form of communal unity: the *umma* ("band of the faithful"). So significant was this moment that Muslims date the beginning of the Muslim era from this year.

Medina became the birthplace of a new faith called Islam ("submission"—in this case, to the will of God) and a new community called Muslims ("those who submit"). The city of Medina had been facing tribal and religious tensions, and by inviting Muhammad and his followers to take up residence there, its elders hoped that his leadership and charisma would bring peace and unity to their city. Early in his stay Muhammad drew on the pragmatic business mindset he no doubt had acquired from years of working as a merchant to put forth the Constitution of Medina. This document laid down rules intended to promote harmony among the different groups in the city (including its Muslim and Jewish inhabitants), in part by requiring the community's people to refer all unresolvable disputes to God and Muhammad. Now the residents were expected to replace traditional family, clan, tribal, and religious affiliations with loyalty to Muhammad as the one and true Prophet of God.

Over time, the core practices and beliefs of every Muslim would crystallize as the **five pillars of Islam**. Muslims were expected to (1) *proclaim* the phrase "there is no God but God and Muhammad is His Prophet"; (2) *pray* five times daily facing Mecca; (3) *fast* from sunup until sundown during the month of Ramadan; (4) *travel on a pilgrimage* (or *hajj*) to Mecca at least once in a lifetime if their personal resources permitted; and (5) *pay alms in*

five pillars of Islam
Five practices that unite all Muslims: (1) proclaiming that "there is no God but God and Muhammad is His Prophet"; (2) praying five times a day; (3) fasting during the daylight hours of the holy month of Ramadan; (4) traveling on pilgrimage to Mecca; and (5) paying alms to support the poor.

the form of taxation that would alleviate the hardships of the poor. These clear-cut expectations gave the imperial system that soon developed a doctrinal and legal structure and a broad appeal to diverse populations.

MUHAMMAD'S SUCCESSORS AND THE EXPANDING *DAR AL-ISLAM*

In 632 CE, in his early sixties, the Prophet passed away; but Islam remained vibrant thanks to the energy of its early followers—especially Muhammad's first four successors, the "rightly guided caliphs" (the Arabic word *khalīfa* means "successor"). These caliphs ruled over Muslim peoples and the expanding state. They institutionalized the new faith. They set the new religion on the pathway to imperial greatness by linking religious uprightness with territorial expansion, empire building, and an appeal to all peoples. (See Current Trends in World History: The Origins of Islam in the Late Antique Period: A Historiographical Breakthrough.)

Driven by religious fervor and a desire to acquire the wealth of conquered territories, Muslim soldiers embarked on military conquests and sought to found a far-reaching territorial empire. This expansion of the Islamic state was one aspect of the struggle that they called *jihad*, between the *dar al-Islam* ("the world of Islam") and the *dar al-harb* ("the world of warfare"). Within fifteen years, their skill in desert warfare and their inspired military leadership enabled Muslim soldiers to expand the *dar al-Islam* into Syria, Egypt, and Iraq—centerpieces of the former Byzantine and Sasanian Empires. The Byzantines saved the core of their empire by pulling back to the highlands of Anatolia, where they could defend their frontiers. In contrast, the Sasanians hurled their remaining military resources against the Muslim armies, only to be annihilated.

A political vacuum opened in the new and growing Islamic empire with the assassination of Ali, the last of the "rightly guided caliphs." Ali was arguably the first male convert to Islam and had proved a fierce leader in the early battles for expansion. The Umayyads, a branch of one of the Meccan clans, laid claim to Ali's legacy. Having been governors of the province of Syria under Ali, the Umayyads relocated the capital to the Syrian city of Damascus and introduced a hereditary monarchy, the Umayyad caliphate, in 661 CE to resolve leadership disputes. Although tolerant of conquered populations, Umayyad dynasts did not permit non-Arabic-speaking converts to hold high political offices, an exclusive policy that contributed to their ultimate demise.

DIFFICULTIES IN DOCUMENTATION

Little can be gleaned about Muhammad himself and the evolution of Islam from Arabic-Muslim sources known to have been written in the seventh century CE. Non-Muslim sources, especially Christian and Jewish texts, which are

The Origins of Islam in the Late Antique Period: A Historiographical Breakthrough

The recent explosion of historical writing on the origins of Islam owes an enormous debt to the creation of the field of Late Antiquity, in particular the 1971 publication of Peter R. Brown's pioneering work *The World of Late Antiquity, AD 150 to 750*. Although the study itself predated the surge in globally oriented studies, it was part of a powerful globalist impulse to create new chronologies and new geographies. Its impact compelled scholars of classical and Islamic history to expand their research boundaries as well as their linguistic abilities.

Late Antiquity, according to Brown, was characterized by cultural Hellenism, centered in the Mediterranean basin. While Christianity was a decidedly new religion, Christian theologians and philosophers like Origen, Athanasius, and Augustine employed Hellenic thought to assimilate Christianity to the Hellenism of the Greco-Roman world. Brown similarly recognized Islam's incorporation of Mediterranean ideas. The Arabs, spilling out of the Arabian Peninsula, created an empire like that of the Roman-Byzantine and Sasanian Empires, even assimilating many Byzantine and Sasanian practices and preserving and adding to Greek learning, a heritage that they passed on to Europe at the time of the Renaissance. According to Brown, "The religion of Islam . . . [was] the most rapid crisis in the religious history of the Late Antique period." In another work, he added that "early Islam trembled on the brink of becoming (like its ancestors—Judaism and Christianity) a Mediterranean civilization." For Brown, the true end of the Late Antique period came only in 750 CE with the foundation of the Abbasid dynasty. Islam's new capital at Baghdad (rather than the more Mediterranean-oriented Umayyad capital in Damascus), along with its thrust eastward into Iran and farther east into Khurasan, turned Islam away from the Mediterranean basin and its Greco-Roman culture and institutions.

Brown's challenge to Islamicists was to determine whether Islam in the first century of its existence was in fact an extension of Late Antiquity. In truth, historians of Islam were slow to accept the challenge, noting that other than the Quran itself, what we know about Islam's first two centuries comes from Muslim sources written in the eighth, ninth, and even tenth centuries CE. But in reality, there was a substantial non-Muslim literature on the origins of Islam that in spite of biases against Islam contained vital information on its origins.

Nearly four decades after Brown issued his challenge, classicists and Islamicists started exploring the beginnings of Islam using non-Muslim sources, including Greek, Armenian, Aramaic, Latin, Hebrew, Samaritan, Pahlavi, Syriac, and Arabic texts. Now scholars have revised our understanding of Muhammad's career, the emergence of a monotheistic creed in the Arabian Peninsula, and the Arabs' aspiration to create a universal empire. One of these scholars, Aziz al-Azmeh, has asserted that the birth of Islam was not a rupture with earlier traditions often unsympathetic to Muhammad and early Islam, are more abundant and contain useful data on the Prophet and the early messages of Islam. These non-Muslim sources raise questions about Muhammad's birthplace, his relationship to the most powerful of the clans during his stay in Mecca, and even the date of his death. Many of these sources, as well as the Quran itself, stress the end-times content of Muhammad's preachings and the actions of his followers. The conclusion that scholars derive from these sources is that it was only during the eighth century CE, in the middle of the Umayyad period, that Islam lost its end-of-the-world emphasis and settled into a long-term religious and political system.

but "an integral part of late antiquity." An important finding from these new sources is that when Islam originated, Jews and Christians were welcomed and some became Muhammad's early followers. Moreover, as the Arabs poured out of the Arabian Peninsula into Syria, Iraq, and Egypt, they did not see themselves as carrying a new religion. As monotheists, they welcomed alliances with Christians, Jews, and Zoroastrians. Islam did not emerge as a separate confessional religion, with many of the features that exist today, until the reign of the Umayyad ruler Abd al-Malik Ibn Marwan (r. 685–705). Much of the evidence comes from non-Muslim sources, but evidence also appears on coins minted in the name of Abd al-Malik and, especially, on the Dome of the Rock, a building constructed in 692 in Jerusalem by Abd al-Malik. The coins and the building bear numerous inscriptions, many of them from the Quran, that proclaim the distinctiveness of Islam from Christianity and Judaism.

Questions for Analysis

- How did Brown's *World of Late Antiquity* pose a challenge to scholars of early Islam?
- Why do you think scholars of Islam were slow to respond to Brown's challenge?
- How has the understanding of Islam's beginnings changed with the contributions of recent scholarship?

Explore Further

al-Azmeh, Aziz, *The Emergence of Islam in Late Antiquity: Allah and His People* (2014).

Bowersock, G. W., *The Crucible of Islam* (2017).

Donner, Fred M., *Muhammad and the Believers at the Origins of Islam* (2010).

Grabar, Oleg, *The Shape of the Holy: Early Islamic Jerusalem* (1996).

Hoyland, Robert G., *In God's Path: The Arab Conquests and the Creation of an Islamic Empire* (2015).

Robinson, Chase F., *'Abd al-Malik* (2005).

Shoemaker, Stephen J., *The Death of a Prophet: The End of Muhammad's Life and the Beginnings of Islam* (2012).

Sources: Peter R. Brown, *The World of Late Antiquity, AD 150 to 750* (London: Thames & Hudson, 1971; reprint as Norton Paperback, 1989), p. 189; Peter R. Brown, *Society and the Holy in Late Antiquity* (Berkeley: University of California Press, 1982), p. 68; Aziz al-Azmeh, *The Emergence of Islam in Late Antiquity: Allah and His People* (Cambridge, England: Cambridge University Press, 2014), pp. 2–3.

The only Muslim source that we have on Muhammad and early Islam is the Quran itself, which, according to Muslim tradition, was compiled during the caliphate of Uthman (r. 644–656 CE). Recent scholarship has questioned this claim, suggesting a later date, sometime in the early eighth century CE, for the standardization of the Quran. Some scholars even contend that the text by then had additions to, and redactions of, Muhammad's message. The Quran, in fact, is quiet on some of the most important events of Muhammad's life. It mentions the name of Muhammad only four times. For more information, scholars have depended on biographies of Muhammad, one of the first of which was compiled by Ibn Ishaq (704–767 CE);

this work is not available to present scholars, but it was used by later Muslim authorities, notably Ibn Hisham (d. 833 CE), who wrote *The Life of Muhammad*, and Islam's most illustrious historian, Muhammad Ibn al-Jarir al-Tabari (838–923 CE). Although the works of these later writers come from the ninth and tenth centuries CE, Muslim tradition ever since has held these sources to be reliable on Muhammad's life and the evolution of Islam after the death of the Prophet.

THE ABBASID REVOLUTION

As the Umayyads spread Islam beyond Arabia, some peoples resisted what they experienced as Arab Umayyad religious impurity and repression. In particular, these peoples believed that the continuing discrimination against them despite their conversion to Islam was humiliating and unfair. The Arab Umayyad conquerors enslaved large numbers of non-Arabs. These enslaved people could leave their servile status only through manumission. Even so, the non-Arab freed peoples who converted found that they, too, were still regarded as lesser persons, although they lived in Arab households and had become Muslims. This situation existed even though the Arabs totaled about 250,000 to 300,000 during the Umayyad era, while non-Arab populations were 100 times as populous, totaling between 25 and 30 million. The area where protest against Arab domination reached a crescendo was in the east, notably in Khurasan, which included portions of modern-day Turkmenistan, Uzbekistan, Tajikistan, and Afghanistan. In Khurasan, most of the Arab conquerors did not live separately from the local populations but instead lived in close contact with them and intermarried local, ethnically different women. Ultimately, a new coalition emerged under the Abbasi family, which claimed descent from the Prophet. Disgruntled provincial authorities and their military allies, as well as non-Arab converts, joined the movement.

After amassing a sizable military force, the Abbasid coalition trounced the Umayyad ruler in 750 CE and began its caliphate, which would last 500 years. The center of the Muslim state then shifted to Baghdad in Iraq (as we saw at the start of this chapter), signifying the eastward sprawl of the faith and its empire. This shift represented a success for non-Arab groups within Islam without eliminating Arab influence at the dynasty's center—the capital, Baghdad, in Arabic-speaking Iraq.

Islam's appeal to converts during the Abbasid period was diverse. Some turned to it for practical reasons, seeking reduced taxes or enhanced power. Others, particularly those living in ethnically and religiously diverse regions, welcomed the message of a single all-powerful God and a single community united by a clear code of laws. Islam, drawing its original impetus from the teachings and actions of a prophetic figure, followed the trajectory of

Christianity and Buddhism and became a faith with a universalizing message and appeal. It owed much of its success to its ability to merge the contributions of vastly different geographic, economic, and intellectual territories into a rich yet unified culture. (See Map 9.1.)

The Caliphate An early challenge for the Abbasid rulers was to determine how traditional, or "Arab," they could be and still rule so vast an empire. They chose to keep the bedrock political institution of the early Islamic state—the **caliphate** (the line of political rulers reaching back to Muhammad). Although the caliphs exercised political authority over the Muslim community, they were not understood to have inherited Muhammad's prophetic powers or any authority in religious doctrine. That power was reserved for religious scholars, called *ulama*.

Abbasid rule borrowed practices from successful predecessors in its mixture of Persian absolute authority and the royal seclusion of the Byzantine emperors who lived in palaces far removed from their subjects. This blend of absolute authority and decentralized power involved a delicate and ultimately unsustainable balancing act. As the empire expanded, it became increasingly decentralized politically, enabling wily regional governors and competing caliphates in Spain and Egypt to grab power. Even as Islam's political center diffused, though, its spiritual center remained fixed in Mecca, where many of the faithful gathered to fulfill their pilgrimage obligation.

The Army The Abbasids, like all rulers, relied on force to integrate their empire. Yet they struggled with what the nature of that military force should be: a citizen conscript, all-Arab force or a professional, even non-Arab, army. In the early stages, leaders conscripted military forces from local Arab populations, creating citizen armies. Ultimately, however, the Abbasids recruited professional soldiers from Turkish-speaking communities in central Asia and from the non-Arab, Berber-speaking peoples of North and West Africa. Their reliance on foreign—that is, non-Arab—military personnel represented a major shift in the Islamic world. Not only did the change infuse the empire with dynamic new populations, but soon these groups gained political authority. Having begun as an Arab state and then incorporated strong Persian influence, the Islamic empire now embraced Turkish elements from the pastoral belts of central Asia.

Islamic Law (the *Sharia*) and Theology Islamic law, or the **sharia**, began to take shape in the Abbasid period. The work of generations of religious scholars, the *sharia* covers all aspects of practical and spiritual life, providing legal principles for marriage contracts, trade regulations, and religious prescriptions such as prayer, pilgrimage rites, and ritual fasting. The most influential early scholar of the *sharia* was an eighth-century CE Palestinian-born

caliphate
Islamic state, headed by a caliph—chosen either by election from the community (Sunni) or from the lineage of Muhammad (Shiite)—with political authority over the Muslim community.

sharia
Body of Islamic law that has developed over centuries, based on the Quran, the sayings of Muhammad (*hadith*), and the legal opinions of Muslim scholars (*ulama*).

NORTH SEA

EUROPE

ATLANTIC

OCEAN

• Aachen

FRANKISH

EMPIRE

Tours
732 ✗

721 ✗
720 ✗ 720
720
714

Danube R.

PYRENEES

KINGDOM
OF THE
VISIGOTHS

• Toledo
712

• Lisbon
711

• Cordoba
711

711 ✗

Carthage
697

720/720

720

B Y Z A N T I N E   E M P I R E

Constantinople

BLACK

717

ANATOLIA

Rhodes
654 ✗

TAURUS MTS.

670, 674, 717

654

654

M E D I T E R R A N E A N   S E A

ATLAS MOUNTAINS

N O R T H

A F R I C A

SAHARA DESERT

Tripoli
647

Barca
643

Alexandria
642 ✗

Al-Fustat
(Cairo)

Jerusalem
638

EGYPT

Nile R.

Niger R.

	Muslim lands by 634 CE
	Muslim lands by 656 CE
	Muslim lands by 756 CE
←	Muslim raid
✗	Muslim victory, with date
✗	Muslim defeat, with date
656	Date of Muslim conquest
◄	Further expansion of Islam
	Byzantine Empire, 610 CE
	Sasanian Empire, 610 CE
	Frankish Empire, 610 CE
•	City

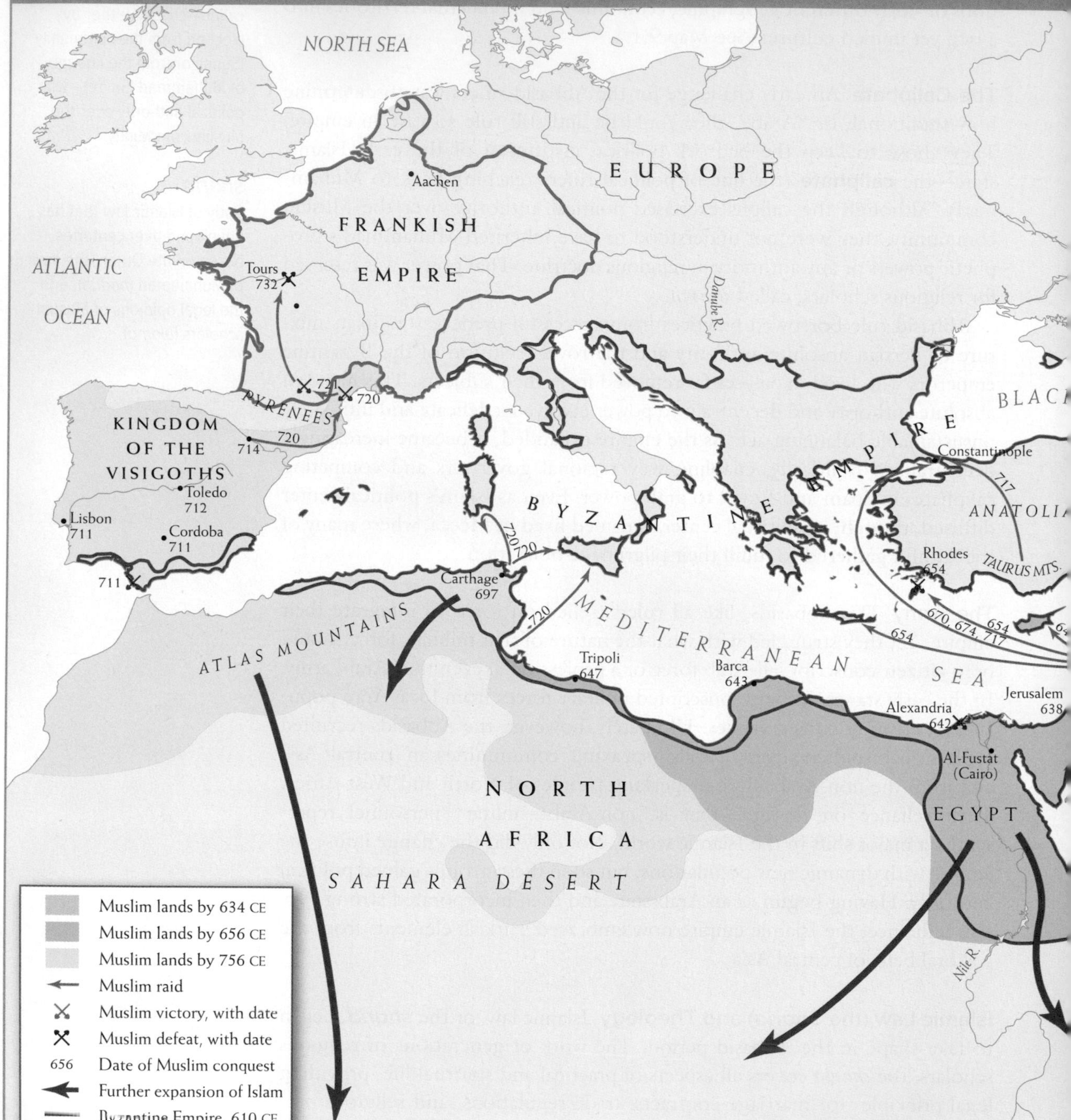

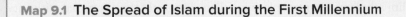

Map 9.1 The Spread of Islam during the First Millennium

Islam emerged in the Arabian Peninsula in the seventh century CE. Within 150 years, leaders of this religious community had conquered a vast amount of territory.

- What regions did the Muslims take over by 634 CE? By 756 CE?
- What were the limits to Muslim expansion during the first 150 years, according to the map? How would you explain these limits?
- Beyond the initial areas of Islamic conquest, where did Islam continue to expand? What do you think drew Islam into these regions?

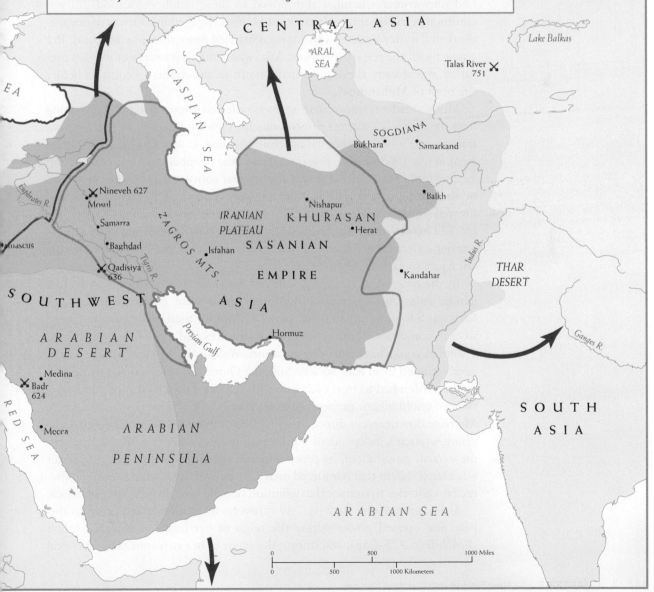

Arab, al-Shafi'i, who insisted that Muhammad's laws as laid out in the Quran, in addition to his sayings and actions as written in later reports (*hadith*), provided all the legal guidance that Islamic judges needed. This shift gave *ulama* (Muslim scholars) a central place in Islam since only their spiritual authority, and not the political authority of the caliphs, was qualified to define religious law. The *ulama*'s ascendance opened a sharp division within Islam: between the secular realm of the caliphs and the religious sphere of religious judges, experts on Islamic law, teachers, and holy men.

Gender in Early Islam Pre-Islamic Arabia was one of the last regions in Southwest Asia where patriarchy had not triumphed. Instead, men still married into women's families and moved to those families' locations, as was common in tribal communities. Some women engaged in a variety of occupations and, if they became wealthy, even married more than one husband. But contact with the rest of Southwest Asia, where men's power over women prevailed, was already altering women's status in the Arabian Peninsula before the birth of Muhammad.

Muhammad's relations with women reflected these changes. As a young man, he married a woman fifteen years his senior—Khadija, an independent trader—and took no other wives before she died. It was Khadija to whom he went in fear following his first revelations. She wrapped him in a blanket and assured him of his sanity. She was also his first convert. Later in life, however, he took younger wives, some of whom were widows of his companions, and insisted on their veiling (partly as a sign of their modesty and privacy). He married his favorite wife, Aisha, when she was only nine or ten years old. As a major source for collecting Muhammad's sayings, Aisha became an important figure in early Islam.

By the time Islam reached Southwest Asia and North Africa, where strict gender rules and women's subordinate status were entrenched, the new faith was adopting a patriarchal outlook. Muslim men could divorce freely; women could not. A man could take four wives and numerous concubines; a woman could have only one husband. Well-to-do women, always veiled, lived secluded from male society. Still, the Quran did offer women some protections. Men had to treat each wife with respect if they took more than one. Women could inherit property (although only half of what a man inherited). Marriage dowries went directly to the bride rather than to her guardian, indicating women's independent legal standing; and while a woman's adultery drew harsh punishment, its proof required eyewitness testimony. The result was a legal system that reinforced men's dominance over women but empowered magistrates to oversee the definition of male honor and proper behavior.

Al-Khayzurān Bint Atta (d. 789) provides a fascinating exception to this rule. She exerted power during the reign of her husband, Abbasid caliph al-Mahdi (r. 775–785), and during the reign of her two sons. The historical tradition is somewhat hostile to her, depicting her as manipulative and overly domineering in her rise from an total enslavement, to *umm walad* (unsellable mother of her enslaver's child), to wife, and then to mother of caliphs. Her reported ruthlessness even included maneuvering her younger son, Harun al-Rashid (r. 786–809), into power by having her elder son murdered. Al-Khayzurān's reputed influence over al-Rashid is perhaps matched by that of Zubaidah (d. 831), the woman he married. Zubaidah was a well-educated woman, who went on pilgrimage multiple times and even donated money for the construction of several wells along the *hajj* route between Baghdad and Mecca. Either al-Khayzurān or Zubaidah, or a blend of both, may well have been the inspiration for the learned Scheherazade, whose stories to a jilted king compose *One Thousand and One Nights*. Together they demonstrate how extraordinary women could assert power even within a community becoming ever more patriarchal in outlook.

THE BLOSSOMING OF ABBASID CULTURE

The arts flourished during the Abbasid period, a blossoming that left its imprint throughout society. Within a century of Abbasid rule, Arabic had superseded Greek as the Muslim world's preferred language for poetry, literature, medicine, science, and philosophy. Arabic spread beyond native speakers to become the language of the educated classes. Arabic scholars preserved and extended Greek and Roman thought, in part through the transmission of treatises by Aristotle, Hippocrates, Galen, Ptolemy, and Archimedes, among others. To house such manuscripts, patrons of the arts and sciences—including the caliphs—opened magnificent libraries.

Core Objectives

EVALUATE the relationships between religion, empire, and commercial exchange across Afro-Eurasia during this period.

The Muslim world absorbed scientific breakthroughs from China and other areas: Muslims incorporated the use of paper from China, adopted siege warfare from China and Byzantium, and assimilated knowledge of plants from the ancient Greeks. From Indian sources, scholars borrowed a numbering system based on the concept of zero and units of ten—what we today call Arabic numerals. Arab mathematicians were pioneers in arithmetic, geometry, algebra, and trigonometry. Since much of Greek science had been lost in the west and later was reintroduced via the Muslim world, the Islamic contribution to the west was of immense significance. Thus, this intense borrowing, translating, storing, and diffusing of ideas brought worlds together.

ISLAM IN A WIDER WORLD

As Islam spread and decentralized, it generated dazzling and often competitive dynasties in Spain, North Africa, and points farther east. Each dynastic state revealed the Muslim talent for achieving high levels of artistry far from its heartland. But growing diversity led to a problem: Islam fragmented

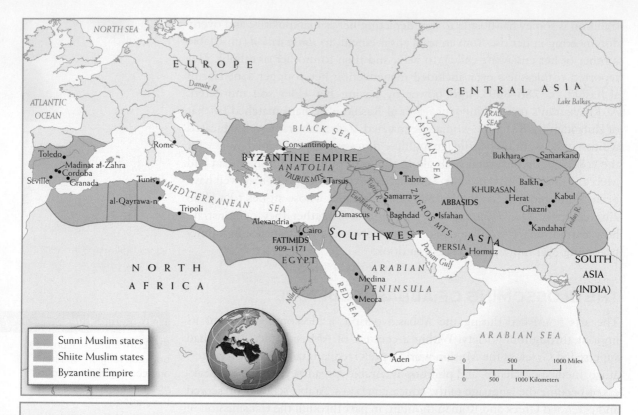

Map 9.2 **Political Fragmentation in the Islamic World, 750–1000 CE**

By 1000 CE, the Islamic world was politically fractured and decentralized. The Abbasid caliphs still reigned in Baghdad, but they wielded very limited political authority.

- What are the regions where major Islamic powers emerged?
- What areas were Sunni? Which were Shiite?
- Looking back to empires in the Mediterranean and Southwest Asia in earlier periods, how would you compare the area controlled by Islam with the extent of the Roman Empire (Chapter 7), Hellenistic kingdoms (Chapter 6), and the Persian Empire (Chapter 4)? What do you think accounts for the differences?

politically. No single political regime could hold its widely dispersed believers together. (See Map 9.2.)

Cities in Spain One extraordinary Muslim state arose in Spain under Abd al-Rahman III (r. 912–961 CE), the successor ruler of a Muslim kingdom founded there over a century earlier. Abd al-Rahman brought peace and stability to a violent frontier region where civil conflict had disrupted commerce and intellectual exchange. His evenhanded governance promoted amicable relations among Muslims, Christians, and Jews, and his diplomatic

The Great Mosque of Cordoba The great mosque of Cordoba was built in the eighth century ce by the Umayyad ruler Abd al-Rahman I and added to by other Muslim rulers, including al-Hakim II (who succeeded Abd al-Rahman III), considered by many historians to have been the most powerful and effective of the Spanish Umayyad caliphs.

relations with Christian potentates as far away as France, Germany, and Scandinavia generated impressive commercial exchanges between western Europe and North Africa. He expanded and beautified the capital city of Cordoba, and his successor made the Great Mosque of Cordoba one of Spain's most stunning sites. In the nearby city of Madinat al-Zahra, Abd al-Rahman III surrounded the city's administrative offices and mosque with verdant gardens of lush tropical and semitropical plants, tranquil pools, fountains that spouted cooling waters, and sturdy aqueducts that carried potable water to the city's inhabitants.

Talent in Central Asia In the eastern regions of the Islamic empire, Abbasid rulers in Baghdad surrounded themselves with learned men from Sogdiana, the central Asian territory where Greek learning had flourished. The Barmaki family, who for several generations held high administrative offices under the Abbasids, came from the central Asian city of Balkh. Loyal servants of the caliph, the Barmakis made sure that wealth and talent from the crossroads of Asia were funneled into Baghdad. Devoted patrons of the arts, the Barmakis promoted and collected Arabic translations of Persian, Greek, and Sanskrit manuscripts. They also encouraged central Asian scholars to enhance their learning by moving to Baghdad. These scholars included the Islamic cleric al-Bukhari (d. 870 CE), who was a renowned collector of *hadith*; the mathematician al-Khwarizmi (c. 780–850 CE), who modified Indian digits into Arabic numerals and wrote the first book on algebra; and the philosopher al-Farabi (d. 950 CE), from a Turkish military family, who also made his way to Baghdad, where he studied eastern Christian teachings and promoted the Platonic ideal of a philosopher-king. Even when the Abbasid caliphate began to decline, intellectual vitality continued under the patronage of local rulers. The best example of this is, perhaps, the polymath Ibn Sina (known in the west as Avicenna; 980–1037 CE), whose *Canon of Medicine* stood as the standard medical text in both Southwest Asia and Europe for centuries.

Trade in Sub-Saharan Africa Carried by traders and scholars, Islam also crossed the Sahara Desert and penetrated well into Africa, where merchants exchanged weapons and textiles for gold, salt, and enslaved people. (See Map 9.3.) Trade did more than join West Africa to North Africa. It generated prodigious wealth, which allowed centralized political kingdoms to develop. The most celebrated was Ghana, which lay at the terminus of North Africa's major trading routes and was often hailed in Arab sources for its gold, as well as its pomp and power. Seafaring Muslim traders carried Islam into East Africa via the Indian Ocean. As early as the eighth century CE, coastal trading communities in East Africa were exporting ivory and possibly exporting enslaved people. By the tenth century, the East African coast featured a mixed African-Arab culture. The region's evolving Bantu language absorbed Arabic words and before long gained a new name, Swahili (derived from the Arabic plural of the word meaning "coast").

Green Revolution in the Islamic World New crops, especially food crops, leaped across political and cultural borders during this period, offering expanding populations more diverse and nutritious diets and the ability to feed increased numbers. Most of these crops originated in Southeast Asia, made their way to India, and dispersed throughout the Muslim world and into China. They included new strains of rice, taro, sour oranges, lemons, limes, and most likely coconut palm trees, sugarcane, bananas, plantains, and mangoes. Sorghum and possibly cotton and watermelons arrived from Africa.

Once Muslims conquered the Sindh in northern India in 711 CE, the crop innovations pioneered in Southeast Asia made their way to the west. Soon a "green revolution" in crops and diet swept through the Muslim world. Sorghum supplanted millet and the other grains of antiquity because it was hardier, had higher yields, and required a shorter growing season. Citrus trees added flavor to the diet and provided refreshing drinks during the summer heat. Increased cotton cultivation led to a greater demand for textiles.

For over 300 years, farmers from northwest India to Spain, Morocco, and West Africa made impressive use of the new crops. They increased agricultural output, slashed fallow periods, and grew as many as three crops on lands that formerly had yielded one. (See Map 9.4.) As a result, farmers could feed larger communities; even as cities grew, the countryside became more densely populated and even more productive.

Map 9.3 Islam and Trade in Sub-Saharan Africa, 700–1000 CE

....

Islamic merchants and scholars, not Islamic armies, carried Islam into sub-Saharan Africa. Trace the trade routes in Africa, making sure to follow the correct direction of trade.

- According to the map key and icons, what commodities were Islamic merchants seeking below the Sahara?
- What were the major trade routes and the direction of trade in Africa?
- How did trade and commerce shape the geographic expansion of the Islamic faith?

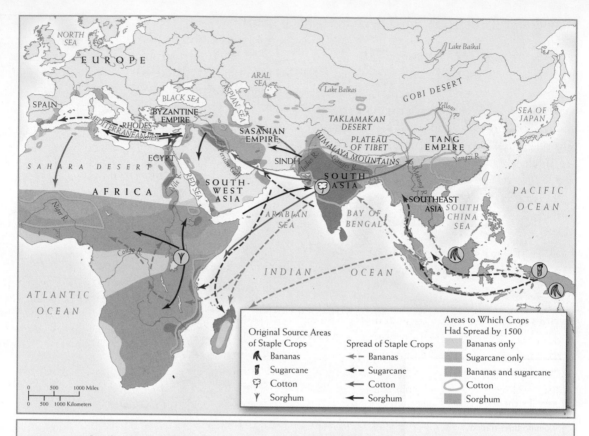

Map 9.4 Agricultural Diffusion in the First Millennium

The second half of the first millennium saw a revolution in agriculture throughout Afro-Eurasia. Agriculturalists across the landmass increasingly cultivated similar crops.

- Where did the staple crops originate? In what direction and where did most of them flow?
- What role did the spread of Islam and the growth of Islamic empires (see Map 9.1) play in the process?
- What role did Southeast Asia and the Tang dynasty play in the spread of these crops?

OPPOSITION WITHIN ISLAM: SHIISM AND THE FATIMIDS

Islam's whirlwind rise generated internal tensions from the start. It is hardly surprising that a religion that extolled territorial conquests and created a large empire in its first decades would also spawn dissident religious movements that challenged the existing imperial structures. Muslims shared a reverence for a basic text and a single God but often had little else in common. Religious and political divisions only grew deeper as Islam spread into new corners of Afro-Eurasia.

Sunnis and Shiites Early division within Islam was fueled by disagreements about who should succeed the Prophet, how the succession should take place, and who should lead Islam's expansion into the wider world. **Sunnis** (from the Arabic word meaning "tradition") accepted that the political succession from the Prophet to the four "rightly guided caliphs" and then to the Umayyad and Abbasid dynasties was the correct one. The vast majority of Muslims today are Sunni. Dissidents, like the Shiites, contested the Sunni understanding of political and spiritual authority. **Shiites** ("members of the party of Ali") felt that the proper successors should have been Ali, who had married the Prophet's daughter Fatima, and then his descendants. Ali was one of the early converts to Islam and one of the band of Meccans who had migrated with the Prophet to Medina. The fourth of the "rightly guided caliphs," he ruled over the Muslim community from 656 to 661 CE, dying at the hands of an assassin who struck him down as he was praying in a mosque in Kufa, Iraq. Shiites believed that Ali's descendants, whom they called *imams*, had religious and prophetic power as well as political authority—and thus should be spiritual leaders.

Shiism appealed to regional and ethnic groups whom the Umayyads and Abbasids had excluded from power; it became Islam's most potent dissident force and created a permanent divide within Islam. Shiism was well established in the first century of Islam's existence, and over time the Sunnis and Shiites diverged even more than these early political disputes over succession might have indicated. Both groups had their own versions of the *sharia*, their own collections of *hadith*, and their own theological tenets.

The Fatimids Repressed in what is present-day Iraq and Iran, Shiite activists made their way to North Africa, where they joined with dissident Berber groups to topple several rulers. In 909 CE, a Shiite religious and military leader, Abu Abdallah, overthrew the Sunni ruler there. Thus began the Fatimid regime.

After conquering Egypt in 969 CE, the Fatimids set themselves against the Abbasid caliphs of Baghdad, refusing to acknowledge their legitimacy and claiming to speak for the whole Islamic world. The Fatimid rulers established their capital at al-Qahira (or Cairo). Early on they founded al-Azhar Mosque, which attracted scholars from all over Afro-Eurasia and spread Islamic learning outward. They also built other elegant mosques and centers of learning. The Fatimid regime lasted until the late twelfth century, though its rulers made little headway in persuading the Egyptian population, most of whom remained Sunnis, to embrace their Shiite beliefs.

By 1000 CE Islam, which had originated as a radical religious revolt in a small corner of the Arabian Peninsula, had grown into a vast political and religious empire. It had become the dominant force in the middle regions of Afro-Eurasia. Like its rival in this part of the world, Christianity, it aspired to

Sunnis
Majority sect within modern Islam that follows a line of political succession from Muhammad, through the first four caliphs (Abu Bakr, Umar, Uthman, and Ali), to the Umayyads and beyond, with caliphs chosen by election from the *umma* (not from Muhammad's direct lineage).

Shiites
Minority tradition within modern Islam that traces political succession through the lineage of Muhammad and breaks with Sunni understandings of succession at the death of Ali (cousin and son-in-law of Muhammad and fourth caliph) in 661 CE.

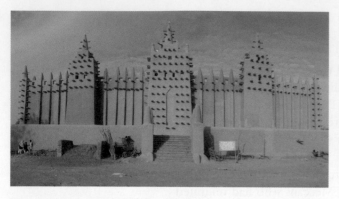

The Jenne Mosque and al-Azhar Mosque The Jenne Mosque (*left*) arose in the kingdom of Mali when that kingdom was at the height of its power. The mosque speaks to the depth and importance of Islam's roots in the Malian kingdom. The mosque of al-Azhar (*right*) is Cairo's most important ancient mosque. Built in the tenth century CE by the Fatimid conquerors and rulers of Egypt, it quickly became a leading center for worship and learning, frequented by Muslim clerics and admired in Europe.

universality. But unlike Christianity, it was linked from its outset to political power. Muhammad and his early followers created an empire to facilitate the expansion of their faith, while their Christian counterparts inherited an empire when Constantine embraced the new faith. A vision of a world under the jurisdiction of Muslim caliphs, adhering to the dictates of the *sharia*, drove Muslim armies, merchants, and scholars to territories thousands of miles away from Mecca and Medina. Yet as Islam's reach stretched thin, political fragmentation within the Muslim world meant that Islam could not extend to much of western Europe and China.

The Tang State

Core Objectives

COMPARE the organizational structures of the Abbasids, Tang China, and Christendom.

The rise of the powerful Tang Empire (618–907 CE) in China paralleled Islam's explosion out of Arabia and its impact throughout Afro-Eurasia. Once again the landmass had two centers of power, as Islam replaced the Roman Empire in counterbalancing the power and wealth of China. Like the Umayyads and the Abbasids, the Tang dynasty promoted a cosmopolitan culture. Under Tang rule Buddhism, medicine, and mathematics from India gave China's chief cities an international flavor. China became a hub for East Asian integration and spread its influence to Korea and Japan.

TERRITORIAL EXPANSION UNDER THE TANG DYNASTY

The Tang dynasty expanded the boundaries of the Chinese state and reestablished its dominance in East and central Asia. After the fall of the Han, China had faced a long period of political fragmentation (see Chapter 8).

As had happened several times before, yet another sudden change in the course of the Yellow River caused extensive flooding on the North China plain and set the stage for the emergence of the Tang dynasty. Revolts ensued as the population faced starvation. Li Yuan, the governor of a province under the short-lived Sui dynasty (589–618 CE), marched on Chang'an and took the throne in 618 CE. He promptly established the Tang dynasty and began building a strong central government by increasing the number of provinces and doubling the number of government offices. By 624 CE, the initial steps of establishing the Tang dynasty were complete, but Li Yuan's ambitious son, Li Shimin, forced his father to abdicate and took the throne in 627 CE.

An expanding Tang state required a large and professionally trained army, capable of defending far-flung frontiers and squelching rebellious populations. Toward these efforts the Tang built a military organization of aristocratic cavalry and peasant soldiers. The cavalry regularly clashed on the northern steppes with encroaching nomadic peoples, who also fought on horseback; at its height the Tang military had 700,000 horses. At the same time, between 1 and 2 million peasant soldiers garrisoned the south and toiled on public works projects.

Much like the Islamic forces, the Tang's frontier armies increasingly relied on pastoral nomadic soldiers from the Inner Eurasian steppe. Notable were the Uighurs, Turkish-speaking peoples who had moved into western China and by 750 CE constituted the empire's most potent military force. These warriors mobilized fearsome cavalries, fired longbows at distant range, and wielded steel swords and knives in hand-to-hand combat. The Tang military also pushed the state into Tibet, the Red River valley in northern Vietnam, Manchuria, and Bohai (near the Korean Peninsula).

At the empire's height, Tang armies controlled more than 4 million square miles of territory (see Map 9.5)—an area as large as the entire Islamic world in the ninth and tenth centuries CE. Once the Tang administrators brought South China's rich farmlands under cultivation (by draining swamps, building an intricate network of canals and channels, and connecting lakes and rivers to the rice lands), the state was able to collect taxes from roughly 10 million families, representing 57 million individuals. Most of these taxes took the form of agricultural labor, which propelled the expansion of cultivated frontiers throughout the south.

ORGANIZING THE TANG EMPIRE

The Tang Empire emulated the Han in many ways, but its rulers also introduced new institutions. The heart of the agrarian-based Tang state was the magnificent capital city of Chang'an, whose population reached 1 million, half of whom lived within its impressive city walls. The outer walls enclosed a 30-square-mile area. Internal security arrangements made it one of the safest urban locales for its age. Its more than 100 quarters were separated from

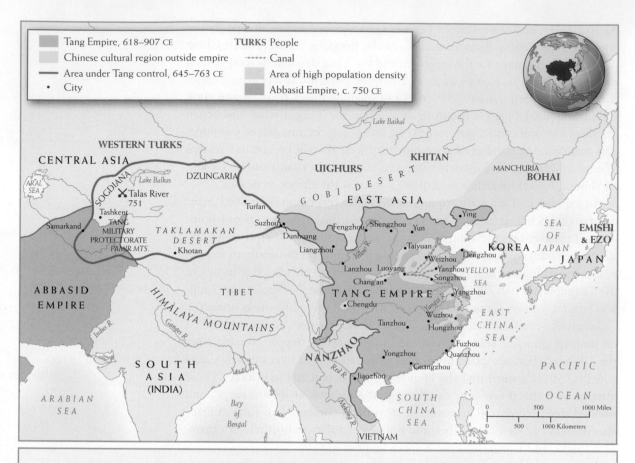

Map 9.5 The Tang State in East Asia, 750 CE

The Tang dynasty, at its territorial peak in 750 CE, controlled a state that extended from central Asia to the East China Sea.

- Which parts of the Tang dynasty benefited from the canal system that had been enhanced by its short-lived predecessor, the Sui?
- How did the area under Tang control change over time? Based on your reading of the chapter and the information on the map, what factors shaped the area controlled by the Tang?
- What foreign areas were under Tang control? What areas were heavily influenced by Tang government and culture?

each other by interior walls with gates that were closed at night, after which no one was permitted on the streets. Horsemen patrolled the streets until the gates reopened in the morning. Chang'an had a large foreign population, estimated at one-third of its total, and a diverse religious life. Zoroastrian fires burned as worshippers sacrificed animals and chanted temple hymns. Nestorian Christians from Syria found a welcoming community, and Buddhists could boast ninety-one of their own temples in Chang'an in 722 CE.

Confucian Administrators Despite the Tang's reliance on the fruits of agriculture and a military force, the day-to-day control of the empire required an efficient and loyal civil service. Entry into the Tang ruling group required knowledge of Confucian ideas and all the commentaries on the Confucian classics. It also required skill in the intricate classical Chinese language, in which this literature was written.

The Tang state introduced the world's first fully written **civil service examinations**, which tested sophisticated literary skills and knowledge of the Confucian classics. The Tang also allowed the use of Daoist classics as texts for the exams, believing that the early Daoists represented another important stream of ancient wisdom. Candidates for office, whom local elites recommended, gathered in the capital triennially to take qualifying exams. They had been trained since the age of three in the classics and histories, either by their families or in Buddhist temple schools. Most failed, but those who were successful underwent further trials to evaluate their character and determine the level of their appointments. New officials were selected from the pool of graduates on the basis of social conduct, eloquence, skill in calligraphy and mathematics, and legal knowledge.

Although in theory official careers were open to anyone of proven talent, in practice they were closed to certain groups. Women were not permitted to serve, nor were sons of merchants or those who could not afford a classical education. Over time, though, Tang civil examinations forced aristocrats to compete with commoner southern families, whose growing wealth gave them access to educational resources that made them the equals of the old elites. Through examinations, this new elite eventually outdistanced the sons of the northern aristocracy in the Tang government, in effect by out-studying them.

The system underscored education as the primary avenue for success. Even impoverished families sought the best classical education they could afford for their sons. Although few succeeded in the civil examinations, many boys and even some girls learned the fundamentals of reading and writing. The Buddhists played a crucial role in extending education across society: as part of their charitable mission, their temple schools introduced many children to primers based on classical texts. Many Buddhist monks, in fact, entered the clergy only after not qualifying for or failing the civil examinations.

China's Female Emperor Not all Tang power brokers were men. The wives and mothers of emperors wielded influence in the court—usually behind the scenes, but sometimes publicly. The most striking example is Empress Wu.

Born into a noble family, Wu Zhao played music and mastered the Chinese classics as a young girl. Because she was witty, intelligent, and beautiful, Wu was recruited before age thirteen to Li Shimin's court and became his favorite concubine. When Li Shimin died, his son assumed power and became Emperor Gaozong. Wu became the new emperor's favorite concubine and

civil service examinations
Set of challenging exams instituted by the Tang to help assess potential bureaucrats' literary skill and knowledge of the Confucian classics.

Christianity in China Nestorian Christianity made a lasting impression on the Tang Empire. *Left:* This mural created in Xinjiang, China, by a Tang artist records a procession on Palm Sunday (the Sunday before Easter, when Christians remember Jesus's triumphal entry into Jerusalem prior to his trial and crucifixion). *Right:* The 9-foot-tall Nestorian Stele, also called the Xi'an Stele, records details about the Nestorian community in China in the seventh and eighth centuries CE, including theological doctrine and missionary visits as well as church leadership and interactions between Nestorians and Tang emperors.

gave birth to the sons he required to succeed him. As the mother of the future emperor, Wu enjoyed heightened political power. Subsequently, she took the place of Gaozong's empress, Wang, by accusing her of killing Wu's newborn daughter. Emperor Gaozong believed his favorite concubine, Wu, and married her. Following Gaozong's death, Wu Zhao made herself Empress Wu (r. 684–705 CE). She expanded the military and recruited her administrators from the civil examination candidates to oppose her enemies at court.

Wu ordered scholars to write biographies of famous women, and she empowered her mother's clan by assigning high political posts to her relatives. Later, she moved her court from Chang'an to Luoyang, where she tried to establish a new "Zhou dynasty," seeking to imitate the widely admired era of Confucius. Empress Wu elevated Buddhism over Daoism as the favored state religion, invited the most gifted Buddhist scholars to her capital at Luoyang, built Buddhist temples, and subsidized spectacular cave sculptures. In fact, Chinese Buddhism achieved its highest officially sponsored development in this period.

Eunuchs Tang rulers protected themselves, their possessions, and especially their women with loyal and well-compensated **eunuchs** (men surgically

eunuchs
Surgically castrated men who rose to high levels of military, political, and personal power in several empires (for instance, the Tang and the Ming Empires in China; the Abbasid and Ottoman Empires; and the Byzantine Empire).

The Tang Court *Left:* This tenth-century CE painting of elegant ladies of the Tang imperial court enjoying a feast and music tells us a great deal about the aesthetic tastes of elite women in this era. It also shows the secluded "inner quarters," where court ladies passed their daily lives far from the hurly burly of imperial politics. *Right:* Castrated males, known as eunuchs, guarded the women and protected the royal family of Tang emperors. By the late eighth century CE, eunuchs were fully integrated into the government and wielded a great deal of military and political power.

castrated as youths and thus sexually impotent). By the late eighth century CE, more than 4,500 eunuchs were fully entrenched in the Tang Empire's institutions, wielding significant power not only within the imperial household but at the court and beyond. For instance, the Chief Eunuch controlled the military. Through him, the military power of court eunuchs extended to every province and garrison station in the empire, forming an all-encompassing network. This eunuch bureaucracy mediated between the emperor and the provincial governments.

Under Emperor Xianzong (r. 805–820 CE), eunuchs acted as a third pillar of the government, working alongside the official bureaucracy and the imperial court. Yet by 838 CE, the delicate balance of power among throne, eunuchs, and civil officials had evaporated. Eunuchs became an unruly political force in late Tang politics, and their competition for influence produced political instability.

AN ECONOMIC REVOLUTION

At its height, Tang China's economic achievements included agricultural production based on an egalitarian land allotment system, an increasingly fine handicrafts industry, a diverse commodity market, and a dynamic urban life. The earlier short-lived Sui dynasty had started this economic progress by reunifying China and building canals, especially the Grand Canal linking the north and south. The Tang continued by centering their efforts on the Grand Canal and the Yangzi River, which flows from west to east. These waterways aided communication and transport throughout the empire. The south grew richer, largely through the backbreaking labor of immigrants from the north. Fertile land along the Yangzi became China's new granary, and areas south of the Yangzi became its demographic center.

Green Revolution in Tang China The same agricultural revolution that was sweeping through South Asia and the Muslim world also took East Asia by storm. China received the same crops that Muslim cultivators were carrying westward. Rice was critical. New varieties entered from the south, and groups migrating from the north (after the collapse of the Han Empire) eagerly took them up. Soon Chinese farmers became the world's most intensive wet-field rice cultivators. Early- and late-ripening seeds supported two or three plantings a year. Champa rice, introduced from central Vietnam, was especially popular for its drought resistance and rapid ripening.

Because rice needs ample water, Chinese hydraulic engineers went into the fields to design water-lifting devices, which peasant farmers used to construct hillside rice paddies. This new rice cultivation was also the partial impetus for the canal building already mentioned. Engineers dug canals linking rivers and lakes, and they even drained swamps, alleviating the malaria that had long troubled the region. Their efforts yielded a booming and constantly moving rice frontier.

Trade in Luxuries Chinese merchants took full advantage of the Silk Roads to trade with India and the Islamic world; when rebellions in northwest China and the rise of Islam in central Asia jeopardized the land route, the "silk road by the sea" became the avenue of choice. From all over Asia and Africa, merchant ships arrived in South China ports bearing spices, medicines, and jewelry in exchange for Chinese silks and porcelains. In the large cities of the Yangzi delta, workshops produced rich brocades (silk fabrics), fine paper, intricate woodblock prints, unique iron casts, and exquisite porcelains. Art collectors all across Afro-Eurasia especially valued Tang "tricolor pottery," decorated with brilliant hues. Chinese artisans transformed locally grown cotton into highest-quality clothing. Painting and dyeing technology improved, and the resulting superb silk products generated significant tax revenue. These Chinese luxuries dominated the trading networks that reached Southwest Asia, Europe, and Africa via the Silk Roads and the Indian Ocean.

ACCOMMODATING WORLD RELIGIONS

The early Tang emperors tolerated remarkable religious diversity. Nestorian Christianity, Zoroastrianism, and Manichaeanism (a radical Christian sect) had entered China from Persia during the time of the Sasanian Empire. Islam came later. These spiritual impulses—together with Buddhism and the indigenous teachings of Daoism and Confucianism—spread throughout the Tang Empire and at first were widely used to enhance state power.

The Growth of Buddhism Buddhism, in particular, thrived under Tang rule. Initially, Emperor Li Shimin distrusted Buddhist monks because they avoided serving the government and paying taxes. Yet after Buddhism gained acceptance as one of the "three ways" of learning—joining Daoism and Confucianism—Li endowed huge monasteries, sent emissaries to India to collect texts and relics, and commissioned Buddhist paintings and statuary. Caves along the Silk Roads, such as those at Dunhuang, provided ideal venues for monks to paint the inside walls where religious rites and meditation took place.

Anti-Buddhist Campaigns By the mid-ninth century CE, however, the growing influence of China's hundreds of thousands of Buddhist monks and nuns threatened Confucian and Daoist leaders, who responded by arguing that Buddhism's values conflicted with native traditions. One Confucian-trained scholar-official, Han Yu, even attacked Buddhism as a foreign doctrine of barbarian peoples who were different in language, culture, and knowledge. Although Han Yu was exiled for his objections, two decades later the state began suppressing Buddhist monasteries and confiscating their wealth, fearing that religious loyalties would undermine political ones. Increasingly intolerant Confucian scholar-administrators argued that the Buddhist monastic establishment threatened the imperial order.

One of the Four Sacred Mountains This monastery on Mount Song is famous because in 527 CE an Indian priest named Bodhidharma arrived there to initiate the Zen school of Buddhism in China.

By the mid-ninth century CE, the Tang state openly persecuted Buddhism. Emperor Wuzong (814–846 CE), for instance, closed more than 4,600 monasteries and destroyed 40,000 temples and shrines. More than 260,000 Buddhist monks and nuns endured a forced return to secular life, after which the state parceled out monastery lands to taxpaying landlords and peasant farmers. To expunge the cultural impact of Buddhism, classically trained literati revived ancient prose styles and the teachings of Confucius and his followers. Their efforts reversed some of the early Buddhist successes in China.

Although Buddhism remained important, the Tang era represented the triumph of homegrown ideologies (Confucianism and Daoism) over a foreign universalizing religion (Buddhism). In addition, by permanently dismantling huge monastic land holdings, the Tang ensured that no religion would rival its power. Successor dynasties continued to keep religious establishments weak and fragmented, although Confucianism maintained a more prominent role within society as the basis of the ruling classes' ideology and as a quasi-religious belief system for a wider portion of the population. The result was persistent religious diversity within China.

TANG INTERACTIONS WITH KOREA AND JAPAN

While China was opening up to the cultures of its western regions, its own culture was reaching out to the east—to Korea and, eventually, to Japan. (See Map 9.6.) Chinese influence, both indirect and direct, had reached into Korea for more than a millennium, and later into Japan, but not without local resistance and the flourishing of entirely indigenous and independent political and religious developments.

Early Korea Interactions with China played a fundamental role in the history of the Korean Peninsula. Unification in 668 CE under the Silla—one of three rival states in Korea—enabled Koreans to establish an autonomous government, but their opposition to the Chinese did not deter them from modeling their government on the Tang imperial state. The Silla rulers dispatched annual emissaries bearing tribute payments to the Chinese capital and regularly sent students and monks. As a result, literary Chinese—not their own dialect—became the written language of Korean elites. Chinese influence extended to the way in which the Silla state organized its court and bureaucracy and to the construction of the Silla capital city of Kumsong, which imitated the Tang capital of Chang'an. Silla's fortunes became entwined with the Tang's to such an extent, however, that once the Tang declined, Silla also began to fragment and ultimately surrendered to the Koryo kingdom in 935 CE.

Early Japan Like Korea, Japan also felt influences emanating from China, and it responded by thwarting and accommodating them at the same time

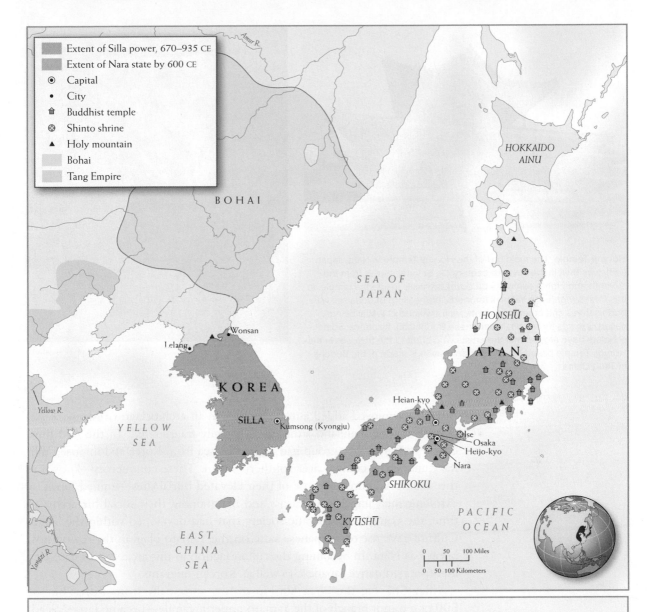

Map 9.6 Tang Borderlands: Korea and Japan, 600–1000 CE

The Tang dynasty held great power over emerging Korean and Japanese states, although it never directly ruled either region.

- Based on the map, what connections do you see between Korea and Japan and the Tang Empire?
- What, if any, relationship do you see between the proliferation of Buddhist temples and Shinto shrines?

Horyuji Temple The main hall of the Horyuji Temple in Nara, Japan (*left*), was built in the seventh century CE. Several murals from the seventh and eighth centuries CE cover the walls inside the temple. In this fresco (*right*), the Yakushi (or medicine/healing) Buddha sits with bodhisattvas and other attendants, while winged celestial beings, called *apsaras* (or *tennin*, in Japanese Buddhism), fly above. Some scholars have argued that the artists who created the frescoes in the Horyuji Temple based the images on drawings made of the Buddha in Tang China.

But Japan enjoyed added autonomy: it was an archipelago of islands, separated from the mainland although internally fragmented. In the mid-third century CE, a warlike group had arrived by sea from Korea and imposed military and social control over southern Japan. These conquerors—known as the "Tomb Culture" because of their elevated burial sites—unified Japan by extolling their imperial ancestors and maintaining their social hierarchy. In time, the complex aristocratic society that had developed within the Tomb Culture gave rise to a Japanese state on the Yamato plain in the region now known as Nara. In becoming the ruling faction in this area, the Yamato clan incorporated native Japanese as well as Korean migrants.

After 587 CE, the Soga kinship group—originally from Korea but by 500 CE a minor branch of the Yamato imperial family—became Japan's leading family and controlled the Japanese court through intermarriage. Soon they were attributing their cultural innovations to their own Prince Shotoku (574–622 CE), of Soga and Yamato descent. Contemporary Japanese scribes claimed that Prince Shotoku, rather than Korean immigrants, introduced Buddhism to Japan and that his illustrious reign sparked Japan's rise as an exceptional island kingdom. Shotoku promoted both Buddhism and Confucianism, thus enabling Japan, like its neighbor China, to accommodate numerous religions.

Indeed, religious influences flowed into Japan, contributing to spiritual diversity while bolstering the Yamato rulers. Although Prince Shotoku and later Japanese emperors turned to Confucian models for government, they also dabbled in occult arts and Daoist purification rituals. In addition, governmental edicts promoted Buddhism as the state religion of Japan. Association with Buddhism gave the Japanese state extra status by lending it the prestige of a universalizing religion whose appeal stretched to Korea, China, and India. State-sponsored spiritual diversity led native Shinto cults—which believed that after death a person's soul (or spirit) became a Shinto *kami*, or local deity, provided that it was nourished and purified through proper rituals and festivals—to formalize a creed of their own. The introduction of Confucianism and Buddhism motivated Shinto adherents to assemble their diverse religious practices into a well-organized belief system. Shinto priests now collected ancient liturgies, and Shinto rituals (such as purification rites to ward off demons and impurities) gained recognition in the state's official Department of Religion.

Political integration under Prince Shotoku did not mean political stability, however. In 645 CE, the Nakatomi kinship group seized the throne and eliminated the Soga and their allies. Via intermarriage with the imperial clan, the Nakatomi became the new spokesmen for the Yamato tradition. Thereafter, Nakatomi no Kamatari (614–669 CE) enacted a series of reforms that reflected Confucian principles of government allegedly enunciated by Shotoku. These reforms enhanced the power of the ruler, no longer portrayed simply as an ancestral kinship group leader but now depicted as an exalted "emperor" (*tenno*) who ruled by the mandate of heaven, as in China, and exercised absolute authority.

THE FALL OF TANG CHINA

Hence, at the eastern end of Afro-Eurasia, the Tang, as well as the Silla of Korea and the Yamato state of Japan, interacted with one another and blended both religious and political authority to maintain stability. The peak of Chinese power in East Asia occurred just as the Abbasids were expanding into Tang portions of central Asia. Yet, despite the Abbasid Empire's spread, China in 750 CE was still the most powerful and best-administered empire in the world. When Muslim forces drove the Tang from Turkistan in 751 CE at the Battle of Talas River, however, their success emboldened groups such as the Sogdians and Tibetans to challenge the Tang and even take their capital. As a result, the Tang gradually retreated into the old heartlands along the Yellow and Yangzi Rivers. Thereafter, misrule, court intrigues, economic exploitation, and popular rebellions weakened the empire, but the dynasty held on for over a century more until northern invaders toppled it in 907 CE.

The Emergence of European Christendom

Core Objectives

COMPARE the internal divisions within the Islamic, Tang, and Christian worlds.

European historians debate whether or not to label this period in Europe "the Dark Ages." Scholars who have spurned the term "Dark Ages," in favor of the term "Late Antiquity," emphasize the political and cultural continuities between Rome and its successor states, especially in the eastern Mediterranean, and the new dynamic institutions that arose in Rome's wake. Scholars who favor the term "Dark Ages" stress what they see as a sharp cultural, political, and economic decline accompanying the Roman Empire's fall, especially in the western Mediterranean. "The Dark Ages," as a label for this period, has been resurrected by environmental historians, who argue that the period was indeed dark, as a result of a colder and drier climate. Agricultural production declined, famines occurred year after year, and infectious diseases spread across Afro-Eurasia (for example, the plague during the reign of Justinian; see Chapter 8). This harsher climate and the diseases that accompanied it between 400 and 900 CE caused dying and mortality on a large scale. The drought that was wreaking havoc in Europe is the same one that helped spur Arab tribal peoples, carrying the banner of Islam, to pour out of their severely affected lands in the Arabian Peninsula in search of better lands and a better life, as other nomadic groups had done.

Although western Europe lacked a highly developed political empire like that of the Abbasids or the Tang dynasty, Christianity increasingly unified the peoples of Europe. In fifth-century CE western Europe, the mighty Roman military machine gave way to a multitude of warrior leaders whose principal allegiances were local. The political ideal of the Roman Empire certainly influenced western Europeans, but the true inheritor of Rome in the west was the Roman Catholic Church, with its priests, missionaries, and monks. In northern Europe, a frontier mentality and the Viking threat shaped Christianity. In eastern Europe and Byzantium, a form of Christianity known as Greek Orthodoxy had become dominant by 1000 CE. Together, these two major strands of the faith—the western Roman Catholic Church and eastern Greek Orthodoxy—constituted the realm of Christendom, the entire portion of the world in which Christianity prevailed as a unifying institution. (See Map 9.7.)

CHARLEMAGNE'S FLEDGLING EMPIRE

Far removed from the old centers of high culture, Charlemagne (r. 768–814 CE), ruler of the Franks, expanded his western European kingdom through constant warfare and plunder. In 802 CE, Harun al-Rashid, the Abbasid ruler of Baghdad, sent the gift of an elephant to Charlemagne, already the king of the Franks for three decades and recently crowned by the pope in Rome as

Map 9.7 Christendom, 600–1000 CE

The end of the first millennium saw much of Europe divided between two versions of Christianity, each with different traditions. On the map, locate Rome and Constantinople, the two seats of power in Christianity.

- According to the map, what were the two major regions where Christianity held sway? In what directions did Roman Catholic Christianity and Greek Orthodox Christianity spread?

- Where were important churches and monasteries heavily concentrated? Why do you think they were focused in those regions?

- The map suggests that missionaries played important roles in spreading Roman Catholicism and Greek Orthodoxy. Why do you think this was the case?

Scenes from the Life of Charlemagne A thirteenth-century stained glass window from Chartres Cathedral in France depicts several scenes from the life of Charlemagne. This portion of the massive window captures several scenes of the Frankish king in action: in the center, from top to bottom, are Charlemagne commissioning the construction of a church, going on a trip to Spain, and offering relics to the church at Aachen. On the left are scenes of Charlemagne at prayer and gazing to the heavens, and on the right are images of him besieging a city and being visited by a saint in his dreams.

"Holy Roman Emperor" (on Christmas Day in 800 CE). While the Franks interpreted the caliph's gift as an acknowledgment of Charlemagne's power, al-Rashid more likely sent the rare beast as a gracious reminder of his own formidable sway. In al-Rashid's eyes, Charlemagne's "empire" was a minor principality. Although Charlemagne claimed the lofty title of emperor and ultimately controlled much of western Europe, compared with the Islamic world's rulers and vast domain, he was a political lightweight.

Charlemagne's empire had a population of less than 15 million; he rarely commanded armies larger than 5,000; and his tax system was rudimentary. At a time when the caliph's palace at Baghdad covered nearly 250 acres, Charlemagne's palace at Aachen was merely 330 by 655 feet. Baghdad itself was almost 40 square miles in area, whereas there was no "town" outside the palace at Aachen. The palace was essentially a large country house set in open countryside, where Charlemagne and his Franks hunted wild boar from horseback.

Charlemagne and his men were representatives of the warrior class that dominated post-Roman western Europe. After Roman control faded away, war became once again the duty and joy of the aristocrats. Although the Franks vigorously engaged in trade, even that trade was based on war. Europe's principal export at this time was Europeans, and the massive sale of prisoners of war, in markets at Alexandria, Tunis, and southern Spain, financed the Frankish Empire. The main victims of this trade were Slavic-speaking peoples, tribal hunters and cultivators from eastern Europe. This trade in Slavs gives us the modern—and troubled—term *slave*.

Yet Charlemagne's seemingly uncivilized and inhospitable empire offered fertile ground for Christianity to sink down roots. As Christianity grew in western and northern Europe, the rough frontier mentality fueled its expansionist ambitions.

CHRISTIANITY IN WESTERN EUROPE

Christians of the west, including those in northern Europe, felt that theirs was the one truly universal religion. Their goal was to bring rival groups into a single Roman "catholic" (from the Greek for "universal") church that was replacing a political unity lost in western Europe when the Roman Empire fell. Drawing on Augustine of Hippo's centuries-old ideas (c. 410 CE), the western Christians believed that the "city of God" would take earthly shape in the form of a catholic church, and that this catholic church was not just for Romans—it was for all times and for all peoples.

The arrival of Christianity in northern Europe provoked a cultural revolution. Preliterate societies now encountered a sacred text—the Bible—in a language that seemed utterly strange. Latin had become a sacred language, and books themselves were vehicles of the holy. The bound codex, which had replaced the clumsy scroll, was still messy: it had no divisions between words, no punctuation, no paragraphs, no chapter headings. Readers who knew Latin as a spoken language could understand the script. But Irishmen, Saxons, and Franks could not, for they had never spoken Latin. Consequently, manuscript copyists in the newly Christian north lavished great care on the few parchment texts—like the Gospels in the Book of Kells (c. 800 CE)—that were prepared with words separated, sentences correctly punctuated and introduced by uppercase letters, and chapter heading marked.

Those producing these stunning Bibles were starkly different from ordinary men and women. They were monks and nuns. Christian **monasticism** had originated in Egypt, but it suited well the missionary tendencies of Christianity in northern Europe. The root of "monastic" and "monk" is the Greek *monos*, "alone": a monastic was a man or a woman who chose to live alone, without the support of marriage or family. In Muslim (and Jewish) communities, religious leaders emphasized what they had in common with those around them. Accordingly, many Islamic scholars, theologians, and mystics were married men, even merchants and courtiers. In the Christian west, the opposite was true: warrior societies honored small groups of monks and nuns who were utterly unlike themselves: unmarried, unfit for warfare, and intensely literate in an incomprehensible tongue.

Monasticism appealed to a deep sense that the very men and women who had little in common with ordinary people were best suited to mediate between believers and God. Laypersons (common believers, not clergy) gave gifts to the monasteries and offered them protection. In return, they gained the prayers of monks and nuns and the reassurance that although they themselves were warriors and men of blood, the monks' and nuns' interventions on their behalf would keep them from going to hell. Payment for human sin, the atoning power of Jesus's crucifixion, and the efficacy of monastic prayers were significant theological emphases for western Roman Catholics.

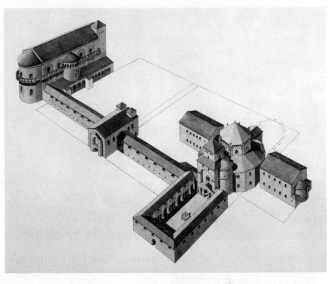

Charlemagne's Palace and Chapel Though not large by Byzantine or Islamic standards, Charlemagne's palace and chapel were heavy with symbolic meaning. A royal hall for banqueting in Frankish, "barbarian" style was linked by a covered walkway to the Imperial domed chapel, which was meant to look like a miniature version of Hagia Sophia in Constantinople. Outside the chapel was a courtyard, like the one outside the shrine of Saint Peter in Rome.

monasticism
From the Greek word *monos* (meaning "alone"), the practice of living without the ties of marriage or family, forsaking earthly luxuries for a life of prayer and study. While Christian monasticism originated in Egypt, a variant of ascetic life had long been practiced in Buddhism.

Monasticism *Left:* The great monasteries of the age of Charlemagne, such as the Saint Gallen Monastery, were like Roman legionary settlements. Placed on the frontiers of Germany, they were vast stone buildings, around which entire towns would gather. Their libraries, the largest in Europe, were filled with parchment volumes, carefully written out and often lavishly decorated in a "northern," Celtic style. *Right:* Monasticism was also about the lonely search for God at the very end of the world, which took place in these Irish monasteries on the Atlantic coast. The cells, made of loose stones piled in round domes, are called "beehives."

The Catholic Church of northern Europe was a religion of monks, whose communities represented an otherworldly alternative to the warrior societies of the time. By 800 CE, most regions of northern Europe held great monasteries, many of which were far larger than the local villages. Supported by thousands of serfs donated by kings and local warlords, the monasteries became powerhouses of prayer that kept the regions safe.

Northern Christianity also gained new ties to an old center: the city of Rome. The Christian bishop of Rome had always enjoyed much prestige but often took second place to other bishops in Carthage, Alexandria, Antioch, and Constantinople. Though people spoke of him with respect as *papa* ("the grand old man"), many others shared that title.

By the ninth century CE, this picture had changed. Believers from the distant north saw only one *papa* left in western Europe: Rome's pope. New Christians in northern borderlands wanted to find a religious leader for their hopes, and the Catholic Church of western Europe united behind the symbolic center of Rome and its popes. Charlemagne fed this desire when, in 800 CE, he went out of his way to celebrate Christmas Day by visiting the shrine of Saint Peter in Rome. There, Pope Leo III acclaimed him as the new "emperor" of the west. A "modern" Rome—inhabited by popes, famous for shrines of the martyrs, and protected by a "modern" Christian monarch from the north—was what Charlemagne's subjects wanted.

VIKINGS AND CHRISTENDOM

Vikings from Scandinavia exposed the weakness of Charlemagne's Christian empire. When al-Rashid's elephant died in 813 CE, the Franks viewed it as an omen of coming disasters. The great beast keeled over when his handlers marched him out to confront a Viking army from Denmark. Charlemagne died the next year. In the next half century, Charlemagne's empire of borderland peoples met its match on the wide border between the European landmass and the Atlantic. (See Map 9.8.)

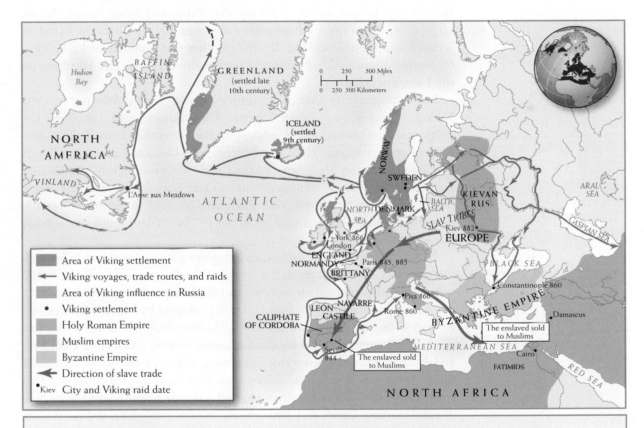

Map 9.8 The Age of Vikings and the Slave Trade, 800–1000 CE

Vikings from Scandinavia dramatically altered the history of Christendom.

- In what directions did the Vikings carry out their voyages, trade routes, and raids?
- What were the geographical limits of the Viking explorations in each direction?
- In what direction did the slave trade move, and what role did the Vikings and the Holy Roman Emperors play in expanding it?

Vikings

Warrior group from Scandinavia that used its fighting skills and sophisticated ships to raid and trade deep into eastern Europe, southward into the Mediterranean, and westward to Iceland, Greenland, and North America.

The **Vikings**' motives were announced in their name, which derives from the Old Norse *vik*, "to be on the warpath." The Vikings sought to loot the now-wealthy Franks and replace them as the dominant warrior class of northern Europe. They succeeded in their plundering and enslaving because of a deadly technological advantage: ships of unparalleled sophistication. Light and agile, Viking ships traveled far up the rivers of northern Europe and could even be carried overland from one river system to another. Under sail, the same boats could tackle open water and cross the North Atlantic. In the ninth century CE, the Vikings set their ships on both courses. They sacked the great monasteries along the coasts of Ireland and Britain and overlooking the Rhine and Seine Rivers. At the same time, Norwegian adventurers colonized the uninhabited island of Iceland, and then Greenland. By 982 CE, they had even reached continental North America and established a settlement at L'Anse aux Meadows on the Labrador coast.

More long-lasting than their settlements in North America was the Viking incursion into eastern Europe. The Vikings sailed east along the Baltic and then turned south, edging up the rivers that crossed the watershed of central Russia. Here the Dnieper, the Don, and the Volga Rivers flow south into the Black Sea and the Caspian. Consequently, the Vikings created an avenue of commerce that linked Scandinavia and the Baltic directly to Constantinople and Baghdad. Muslim geographers bluntly called this route "the Highway of the Slaves" because so much of the trade was in human cargo.

In 860 CE, more than 200 Viking longships gathered ominously beneath the walls of Constantinople in the straits of the Bosporus. What they found was not poorly defended monasteries or Charlemagne's rustic Aachen, but a city with a population exceeding 100,000 protected by well-engineered late Roman walls. For nearly two centuries, Constantinople had resisted almost yearly campaigns launched by the successive Islamic empires of Damascus and later Baghdad. These campaigns were deflected by Constantinople's highly professional generals, a line of skillfully constructed fortresses that controlled the roads across Anatolia, and a deadly technological advantage in naval warfare: Greek fire. This combination of petroleum and potassium, when sprayed from siphons, would explode in a great sheet of flame on the water. The experience and weaponry of Byzantium were too much for the Vikings, and their raid of the most significant city in eastern Christendom was a spectacular failure. Despite their inability to take Byzantium, the Vikings asserted an enduring influence through their forays across the North Atlantic, their brutal interactions with Christian communities in northern Europe, and their expansion into eastern Europe, especially the slave trade they facilitated there.

GREEK ORTHODOX CHRISTIANITY

Outlasting so many military emergencies bolstered the morale of the eastern Christians and led to a flowering of Christianity in this region. Not just Constantinople but Justinian's Hagia Sophia—its heart—had survived significant threats. That great building and the solemn Greek divine liturgy that reverberated within its domed spaces symbolized the branch of Christian belief that dominated in the east: **Greek Orthodoxy**. Greek Orthodox theology held that Jesus became human less to atone for humanity's sins (as emphasized in Roman Catholicism) and more to facilitate *theosis* (a transformation of humans into divine beings). This was a truly distinct message from that which prevailed in the Roman Catholicism of the west.

In the tenth century CE, as Charlemagne's empire collapsed in western Europe, large areas of eastern Europe became Greek Orthodox, not Roman Catholic. In addition, Greek Christianity gained a spiritual empire in Southwest Asia. The conversion of Russian peoples, Balkan Slavs, and Arab peoples to Greek Orthodox Christianity was a complex process. It reflected a deep admiration for Constantinople on the part of Russians, Bulgarians, Arabs, and Slav princes. It was an admiration as intense as that of any western Catholic for the Roman popes. This admiration amounted to awe, as shown by the famous story of the conversion to Greek Christianity of the rulers of Kiev (descendants of Vikings). Unimpressed by the religious practice and structures of Catholic Franks, these Russian Christians were overwhelmed by what to their eyes was the almost heavenly splendor of the churches they encountered in Greece and Constantinople.

By the year 1000 CE, then, there were two Christianities: the new and confident "borderland" **Roman Catholicism** of western Europe and an ancient Greek Orthodoxy. Western Roman Catholics believed that their church was destined to expand everywhere. Greek Orthodox Christians were less euphoric but believed that their church would forever survive the regular ravages of invasion. This was a significant difference in attitude; Greek Orthodox Christians considered the Franks barbarous and grasping, and western Roman Catholics contemptuously called the eastern Christians "Greeks" and condemned them for "Byzantine" cunning.

Thus, like Islam, the Christian world was divided, with differences in heritage, theology, customs, and levels of urbanization. At that time, the

Oseberg Ship The Viking ship was a triumph of design. It could be rowed up the great rivers of Europe, or its sails could take it across the Atlantic. The Oseberg ship pictured here contained the early ninth-century CE burial of a high-status Viking woman.

Greek Orthodoxy
Branch of eastern Christianity, originally centered in Constantinople, that emphasizes the role of Jesus in helping humans achieve union with God.

Roman Catholicism
Western European Christianity, centered on the papacy in Rome, that emphasizes the atoning power of Jesus's death and aims to expand as far as possible.

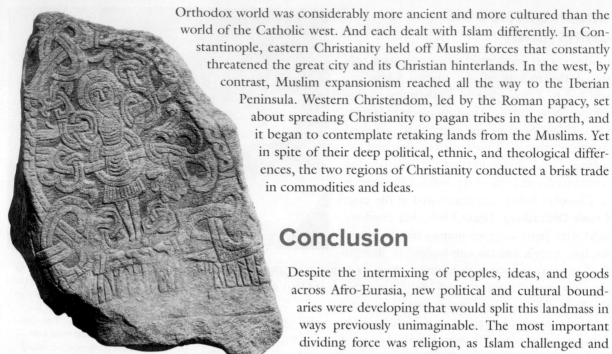

Orthodox world was considerably more ancient and more cultured than the world of the Catholic west. And each dealt with Islam differently. In Constantinople, eastern Christianity held off Muslim forces that constantly threatened the great city and its Christian hinterlands. In the west, by contrast, Muslim expansionism reached all the way to the Iberian Peninsula. Western Christendom, led by the Roman papacy, set about spreading Christianity to pagan tribes in the north, and it began to contemplate retaking lands from the Muslims. Yet in spite of their deep political, ethnic, and theological differences, the two regions of Christianity conducted a brisk trade in commodities and ideas.

Conclusion

Despite the intermixing of peoples, ideas, and goods across Afro-Eurasia, new political and cultural boundaries were developing that would split this landmass in ways previously unimaginable. The most important dividing force was religion, as Islam challenged and slowed the spread of Christianity and as Buddhism challenged the ruling elite of Tang China. As a consequence, Afro-Eurasia's major cultural zones began to compete in terms of religious and cultural doctrines. The Islamic Abbasid Empire pushed back the borders of the Tang Empire. But the conflict grew particularly intense between the Islamic and Christian worlds, where the clash involved faith as well as frontiers.

The Tang Empire revived Confucianism, insisting on its political and moral primacy as the foundation of a new imperial order, and it embraced the classical written language as another unifying element. By doing so, the Tang counteracted universalizing foreign religions—notably Buddhism but also Islam—spreading into the Chinese state. The same adaptive strategies influenced new systems on the Korean Peninsula and in Japan.

In some circumstances, faith followed empire and relied on rulers' support or tolerance to spread the word. This was the case especially in East Asia. At the opposite extreme, empire followed faith—as in the case of Islam, whose believers endeavored to spread their empire in every direction. The Islamic empire and its successors represented a new force: expanding political power backed by one God whose instructions were to spread his message. In the worlds of Christianity, a common faith absorbed elements of a common culture (shared books, a language for the learned classes). But in the west, political rulers never overcame inhabitants' intense allegiance to local authority.

Jelling Stone Carved on the side of this great stone, Christ appears to be almost swallowed up in an intricate pattern of lines. For the Vikings, complicated interweaving like serpents or twisted gold jewelry was a sign of majesty: hence, in this, the first Christian monument in Denmark, Christ is part of an ancient pattern of carving, which brought good luck and victory to the king.

While universalizing religions expanded and common cultures grew, debate raged within each religion over foundational principles. In spite of the diffusion of basic texts in "official" languages, regional variations of Christianity, Islam, and Buddhism proliferated as each belief system spread. The period from 600 to 1000 CE demonstrated that religion, reinforced by prosperity and imperial resources, could bring peoples together in unprecedented ways. But it could also, as the next chapter will illustrate, drive them apart in bloody confrontations.

Focus On
Religion and Empires: Islam, the Tang Dynasty, Christendom, and Common Cultures

The Islamic Empire

- Warriors from the Arabian Peninsula defeat Byzantine and Sasanian armies and establish an Islamic empire stretching from Morocco to South Asia.

- The Abbasid state takes over from the Umayyads, crystallizes the main Islamic institutions of the caliphate and Islamic law, and promotes cultural achievements in religion, philosophy, and science.

- Disputes over Muhammad's succession lead to a deep and enduring split between Sunnis and Shiites.

Tang China

- The Tang dynasty dominates East Asia and exerts a strong influence on Korea and Japan.

- Tang rulers balance Confucian and Daoist ideals with Buddhist thought and practice.

- A common written language and shared philosophy, rather than a single universalizing religion, integrate the Chinese state.

Christian Europe

- Charlemagne establishes an empire in part of western Europe, while the Vikings raid and trade from their homeland in Scandinavia westward to North America, southward to the Mediterranean, and eastward to the Caspian Sea.

- Monks, nuns, and Rome-based popes spread Christianity throughout western Europe.

- Constantinople-based Greek Orthodoxy survives the spread of Islam.

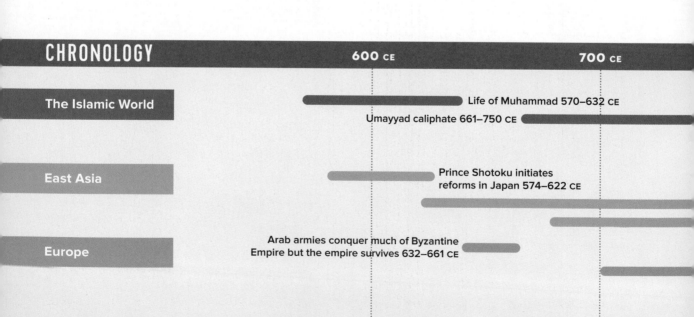

CHRONOLOGY

	600 CE	700 CE

The Islamic World
Life of Muhammad 570–632 CE
Umayyad caliphate 661–750 CE

East Asia
Prince Shotoku initiates reforms in Japan 574–622 CE

Europe
Arab armies conquer much of Byzantine Empire but the empire survives 632–661 CE

- **Thinking about Crossing Borders and Faith & Empire** As Islam spread outside its initial Arabian context, the faith underwent a range of developments. As Christianity and Buddhism continued to spread, these traditions underwent changes as well. Compare the shifts that took place within Islam as it expanded (600–1000 CE) with those within Buddhism and Christianity, not only in their earlier periods (see Chapter 8) but also during the period from 600 to 1000 CE.

- **Thinking about Changing Power Relationships and Faith & Empire** As each of the empires discussed in this chapter matured, divisions developed within the faiths that initially had helped to bring unity to their respective regions. In the Abbasid world, a split developed between Sunni and Shiite Muslims. In Tang China, Buddhism and Confucianism vied for political influence. Christendom divided into the Roman Catholic west and the Greek Orthodox east. What was the exact nature of each religious disagreement? How do these divisions compare in terms of the root of the internal rifts and their impact in the political realm?

- **Thinking about Worlds Together, Worlds Apart** The empires described in this chapter reached across wide swaths of territory and interacted with vibrant societies on their margins. The peoples of Europe struggled with the onslaught of the fierce Vikings. The peoples of Tang China interacted with neighboring Korea and Japan. How does the interaction of Europe and the Vikings compare with the relations of the Tang and the external influences that they experienced? To what extent did the Abbasids contend with similar exchanges?

Key Terms

caliphate p. 429

civil service
    examinations p. 443

eunuchs p. 444

five pillars of Islam p. 424

Greek Orthodoxy p. 459

monasticism p. 455

Roman Catholicism
    p. 459

sharia p. 429

Shiites p. 439

Sunnis p. 439

Vikings p. 458

 Go to **INQUIZITIVE** to see what you've learned—and learn what you've missed—with personalized feedback along the way.

800 CE	900 CE	1000 CE

Abbasid caliphate 750–1258 CE

Fatimid Shiite regime founded in Egypt 969 CE ●

Tang dynasty in China 618–907 CE

Silla unify Korean state 668–935 CE

Catholic Church based in Rome begins converting much of northern Europe into Christian communities eighth century CE

Charlemagne unites much of western Europe into a short-lived Christian kingdom 768–814 CE

Vikings raid much of Europe and establish strong commercial links across eastern Europe ninth and tenth centuries CE

Global Themes and Sources

Women and Community in the Context of New Empires

Within each of the new empires discussed in this chapter, belief systems addressed the diverse and influential roles—as daughters, wives, mothers, caregivers, and more—that women played in family and community. In historical contexts ranging from the early Islamic states and western Christendom to Tang China and Viking Scandinavia, practical concerns as well as religious and philosophical ideals influenced the realities that governed women's lives.

Muslim ideas about women and family originated in the Arabian Peninsula and spread as the Umayyad and Abbasid Empires extended their reach from Southwest Asia into central Asia and across North Africa and into Spain. As Christendom expanded across western Europe, so too did the influence of both the monastics at the heart of Christianity and Christian ideas about women's roles. Although Tang authorities vacillated in their official support of Buddhism, there was no doubt about the enduring importance of Confucian thought in political and social matters, including its ideas about family and filial piety. And as Vikings set out from Scandinavia into the British Isles, Iceland, and beyond, as well as into the interior of central Europe, Viking expectations for women went with them and were shaped by the new ideas, including Christianity, that they encountered.

The four sources included here offer an opportunity to explore the factors shaping women's lives, as well as the ways that women shaped the expanding empires described in this chapter. Working with sources about women in this, and every, historical context presents challenges. We must account for the (sometimes hostile) male authorship and audience of the sources, balance ideal expectations for women against the realities of lived experience, and work around the sources' frequent focus on elite and exceptional women, for instance, Empress Wu of the Tang or Khadija, the wife of Muhammad, rather than on unnamed nonelite women. By examining primary sources to identify societal expectations regarding women, we can better understand the broader historical context of each empire. Conversely, each of these empires provides a context for exploring the role of women within the diverse communities that spanned Eurasia from 600 to 1000 CE.

Analyzing Women in the Context of New Empires

- What do these texts (and the empires they represent) reveal about societal expectations for women's behavior and for men's behavior toward women? What might account for any similarities and differences?

- Which women and men are included, explicitly and implicitly, in the expectations laid out in these texts? Who is excluded? What do these inclusions and exclusions suggest about the historical contexts of these texts?

- Based on the historical sources, how did the belief systems of Islam, Christianity, and Confucianism offer contexts for gender expectations and family structures?

- In what ways do the expectations about women's behavior and their role in the community challenge your impression of women's roles in the historical contexts of Abbasid Islam, western Christendom, Tang China, and the Viking world?

- How might an increasingly connected world have modified gender roles as the belief systems that created those roles came into contact with one another?

PRIMARY SOURCE 9.1

Surah 4, An-Nisa, from the Quran (seventh century CE)

Surah 4 ("On Women") of the Quran outlines rules about marriage, inheritance, and the treatment of orphans, among other family-oriented topics. Recorded in the seventh century CE, the Quran, along with *hadith* (sayings of Muhammad), formed the basis for later *sharia* (law) that regulated community matters. As you read the source, imagine the community shaped by the expectations laid out in this excerpt from the Quran.

- Who is the presumed audience of these rules? How do you know?

- What are the rules with respect to women? The rules with respect to orphans? The rules about inheritance?

- What are the benefits of abiding by the rules? The penalties for breaking them?

- What conclusions might you draw about the wider context of the early Islamic world, given the ideals laid out in this text for how to treat women and children?

4.1 O people! be careful of (your duty to) your Lord, Who created you from a single being and created its mate of the same (kind) and spread from these two, many men and women; and be careful of (your duty to) Allah, by Whom you demand one of another (your rights), and (to) the ties of relationship; surely Allah ever watches over you.

4.2 And give to the orphans their property, and do not substitute worthless (things) for (their) good (ones), and do not devour their property (as an addition) to your own property; this is surely a great crime.

4.3 And if you fear that you cannot act equitably towards orphans, then marry such women as seem good to you, two and three and four; but if you fear that you will not do justice (between them), then (marry) only one or what your right hands possess; this is more proper, that you may not deviate from the right course.

4.4 And give women their dowries as a free gift, but if they of themselves be pleased to give up to you a portion of it, then eat it with enjoyment and with wholesome result.

4.5 And do not give away your property which Allah has made for you a (means of) support to the weak of understanding, and maintain them out of (the profits of) it, and clothe them and speak to them words of honest advice.

4.6 And test the orphans until they attain puberty; then if you find in them maturity of intellect, make over to them their property, and do not consume it extravagantly and hastily, lest they attain to full age; and whoever is rich, let him abstain altogether, and whoever is poor, let him eat reasonably; then when you make over to them their property, call witnesses in their presence; and Allah is enough as a Reckoner.

4.7 Men shall have a portion of what the parents and the near relatives leave, and women shall have a portion of what the parents and the near relatives leave, whether there is little or much of it; a stated portion.

4.8 And when there are present at the division the relatives and the orphans and the needy, give them (something) out of it and speak to them kind words.

4.9 And let those fear who, should they leave behind them weakly offspring, would fear on their account, so let them be careful of (their duty to) Allah, and let them speak right words.

4.10 (As for) those who swallow the property of the orphans unjustly, surely they only swallow fire into their bellies and they shall enter burning fire.

4.11 Allah enjoins you concerning your children: The male shall have the equal of the portion of two females; then if there are more than two females, they shall have two-thirds of what the deceased has left, and if there is one, she shall have the half; and as for his parents, each of them shall have the sixth of what he has left if he has a child, but if he has no child and (only) his two parents inherit him, then his mother shall have the third; but if he has brothers, then his mother shall have the sixth after (the payment of) a bequest he may have bequeathed or a debt; your parents and your children, you know not which of them is the nearer to you in usefulness; this is an ordinance from Allah: Surely Allah is Knowing, Wise.

4.12 And you shall have half of what your wives leave if they have no child, but if they have a child, then you shall have a fourth of what they leave after (payment of) any bequest they may have bequeathed or a debt; and they shall have the fourth of what you leave if you have no child, but if you have a child then they shall have the eighth of what you leave after (payment of) a bequest you may have bequeathed or a debt; and if a man or a woman leaves property to be inherited by neither parents nor offspring, and he (or she) has a brother or a sister, then each of them two shall have the sixth, but if they are more than that, they shall be sharers in the third after (payment of) any bequest that may have been bequeathed or a debt that does not harm (others); this is an ordinance from Allah: and Allah is Knowing, Forbearing.

4.13 These are Allah's limits, and whoever obeys Allah and His Apostle, He will cause him to enter gardens beneath which rivers flow, to abide in them; and this is the great achievement.

4.14 And whoever disobeys Allah and His Apostle and goes beyond His limits, He will cause him to enter fire to abide in it, and he shall have an abasing chastisement.

Source: Sura 4, translated by Marmaduke Pickthall, revised by Jane Dammen McAuliffe, in *The Norton Anthology of World Religions*, vol. 2, *Islam*, edited by Jack Miles et al. (New York: W. W. Norton, 2015), pp. 87–89.

PRIMARY SOURCE 9.2

Law of Adamnan (700 CE)

The *Law of Adamnan* demonstrates both the brutal realities of tribal warfare as Christianity spread into Ireland and the efforts of Christian clergy and lay leaders to do something about it. This text describes how a monk named Adamnan of Iona was inspired by his mother and an angel to develop a law protecting noncombatants that was then signed by kings, nobles, and religious authorities. As you read the *Law of Adamnan*, consider how the source describes the impact of the Christian context on the treatment of women.

- According to the text, what were the lives of women and children like before Adamnan's Law?

- What protections for women, children, and clergy does Adamnan's Law create? What are the penalties for not treating women and children the way the law demands?

- What rationale, explicit and implicit, does the source offer to explain the reasoning for these new protections?

1. Five ages before the birth of Christ, to wit, from Adam to the Flood, from the Flood to Abraham, from Abraham to David, from David to the Captivity in Babylon, from the Babylonian Captivity to the birth of Christ. During that time women were in bondage and in slavery, until Adamnan, son of Ronan, son of Tinne, son of Aed, son of Colum, son of Lugaid, son of Setne, son of Fergus, son of Conall, son of Niall, came.

2. *Cumalach* [slave] was a name for women till Adamnan came to free them. . . .

3. The work which the best women had to do, was to go to battle and battlefield, encounter and camping, fighting and hosting, wounding and slaying. On one side of her she would carry her bag of provisions, on the other her babe. Her wooden pole upon her back. Thirty feet long it was, and had on one end an iron hook, which she would thrust into the tress of some woman in the opposite battalion. Her husband behind her, carrying a fence-stake in his hand, and flogging her on to battle. For at that time it was the head of a woman, or her two breasts, which were taken as trophies.

4. Now after the coming of Adamnan no woman is deprived of her testimony, if it be bound in righteous deeds. For a mother is a venerable treasure, a mother is a goodly treasure, the mother of saints and bishops and righteous men, an increase in the Kingdom of Heaven, a propagation on earth.

5. Adamnan suffered much hardship for your sake, O women, so that ever since Adamnan's time one half of your house is yours, and there is a place for your chair in the other half; so that your contract and your safeguard are free; and the first law made in Heaven and on earth for women is Adamnan's Law. . . .

***

33. Here begins the speech of the angel to Adamnan: . . . On Pentecost eve a holy angel of the Lord came to him, and again at Pentecost after a year, and seized a staff, and struck his side and said to him; "Go forth into Ireland, and make a law in it that women be not in any manner killed by men, through slaughter or any other death, either by poison, or in water, or in fire, or by any other beast, or in a pit, or by dogs, but that

they shall die in their lawful bed. Thou shalt establish a law in Ireland and Britain for the sake of the mother of each one, because a mother has borne each one, and for the sake of Mary mother of Jesus Christ, through whom all are. Mary besought her Son on behalf of Adamnan about this Law. For whoever slays a woman shall be condemned to a twofold punishment, that is, his right hand and his left foot shall be cut off before death, and then he shall die, and his kindred shall pay seven full *cumals* [1 *cumal* (unit of measure) = 3 cows], and one-seventh part of the penance. If, instead of life and amputation, a fine has been imposed, the penance is fourteen years, and fourteen *cumals* shall be paid. But if a host has done it, every fifth man up to three hundred shall be condemned to that punishment; if few, they shall be divided into three parts. The first part of them shall be put to death by lot, hand and foot having been first cut off; the second part shall pay fourteen full *cumals*; the third shall be cast into exile beyond the sea, under the rule of a hard regimen; for the sin is great when any slays the mother and sister of Christ's mother and the mother of Christ, and her who carries a spindle and who clothes every one. But he who from this day forward shall put a woman to death and does not do penance according to the Law, shall not only perish in eternity, and be cursed for God and Adamnan, but all shall be cursed that have heard it and do not curse him, and do not chastise him according to the judgement of this Law." . . .

34. This is the enactment of Adamnan's Law in Ireland and Britain. . . . The enactment of this Law of Adamnan is a perpetual law on behalf of clerics and women and innocent children until they are capable of slaying a man, and until they take their place in the tribe, and their (first) expedition is known.

Source: Adamnan, *Anecdota Oxoniensia: Cáin Adamnáin: An Old-Irish Treatise on the Law of Adamnan*, edited and translated by Kuno Meyer (Oxford: Clarendon Press, 1905), pp. 3, 5, 23, 25.

<hr>

PRIMARY SOURCE 9.3

Analects for Women (800 CE), Song Ruoxin and Song Ruozhao

In the late eighth century CE, two young women, Song Ruoxin and Song Ruozhao, composed their *Analects for Women* while in attendance at the court of the Tang emperor. This text, which expands on Ban Zhao's ideas from almost 700 years earlier, adapted Confucian thought to create a set of advice for women living around 800 CE in Tang China. As you read the text, watch for clues that suggest a Confucian context.

- Who is the presumed audience of this text? How do you know?
- What are the responsibilities of a Tang woman, according to this text? What would her life be like?
- In what ways does the text adapt Confucian values such as *ren* (benevolence), *li* (proper conduct/ritual), and *xiao* (filial piety) to women's experience?

[Ban Zhou] said: I am the wife of a virtuous man, the daughter of an eminent family. I observe all the four proprieties and am well-read in history. As I pause from women's work and read, (I find that) there have been many heroines praiseworthy and some virtuous women admirable. I feel sorry that posterity has not followed their model. I thus write this work entitled *The Analects for Women* in the hope of teaching women to inherit the good and guard against the evil. Those who follow these teachings will be regarded as virtuous women, whose names will rank among those of their predecessors and be passed down to future generations.

Book One: On Deportment

The first thing for any woman to learn is the principle of deportment: that of purity and chastity. If you are pure, then chastity will follow; if you are chaste, then you will be honored. Don't turn your head and look while walking. Don't show your teeth while speaking. Don't move your knees while sitting. Don't sway your dress while standing. Don't laugh out loud when happy. Don't shout when angry. Indoors or out, men and women should be in separate groups. . . . Don't give your name to a man who is not your relative. Don't become friendly with a woman who is not from a good family. Only by being decorous and proper will you be a [proper] person.

Book Five: On Serving the Parents

While still at home, every woman should revere her parents. Every morning get up early and ask after their health. When it's cold, start a fire. Use a fan to cool them when it is hot. Serve food when they are hungry, and bring tea when they are thirsty. If your parents rebuke you, don't become flustered; listen attentively and think about what they have said day and night. If there is anything that is not done accordingly, correct it as you were told. Don't take what they have said as commonplace, but obey their instructions, and never argue with them. If there is something you don't understand, don't hesitate to ask them.

When parents get old, be concerned for them morning and evening, making shoes, darning socks, and sewing clothes for them. . . . When parents suffer from any illness, don't leave their bedside. . . . Steep the medicine and try it yourself. Pray for the help of the spirits and Buddha, and hope for recovery. In case misfortune should occur or death take them, let pain penetrate to the marrow of your bones, wail and lament, never forgetting the three years of suckling. Clothe the dead and don mourning clothes. Prepare for burial and arrange the sacrifices. Do obeisance and burn joss sticks. Continue to cultivate dignity so that your parents can rise to Heaven. . . .

Book Seven: On Serving One's Husband

When a woman is married, her husband will be her master among relatives. The affinity to the former life becomes the marriage of the present life. To compare one's husband to Heaven is not meaningless. The husband [should be] firm and the wife yielding. An affectionate couple rely on each other. At home, treat your husband as respectfully as you would a guest. When he speaks to you, listen attentively. If your husband has some evil ways, remonstrate repeatedly. Don't learn from those ignorant women who bring evil on themselves. . . .

Book Eleven: On Conciliation and Yielding

The rules for managing a household for a wife are to prize harmony and filial piety above all else. When your mother-in-law rebukes you, don't feel hurt. When your father-in-law has any criticism, listen to it quietly. In the upper rooms and in the lower chambers, with nephews and nieces, you should behave harmoniously. Whether [disagreements are] right or wrong, don't get involved. [Whether an issue involves] good or bad,

don't argue. Shameful family matters should never be exposed to the public. . . .

Book Twelve: On Preserving Chastity

Women of old, both chaste and virtuous, have had their names recorded in the annals of history and passed down to the present day. Women nowadays who have not learned from them should not consider it too difficult to begin. The first [principle] is that of preserving chastity; the second, that of purity and virtuousness. If there is a daughter in a family, don't [let her] leave the inner chambers. When there are guests, don't go beyond the main hall. Don't spread gossip, or speak in vile language. . . . If there occurs the misfortune of the husband dying at a young age, wear mourning clothes for three years, and remain firm in your will to preserve your chastity. Protect your family and manage your property. Clean and sweep your husband's tomb. In life or in death, it is one life shared.

Source: Song Ruoxin and Song Ruozhao, "Book of Analects for Women: Consort Song (Tang)," translated by Heying Jenny Zhan and Roger Bradshaw, *Journal of Historical Sociology* 9, no. 3 (1996): 261, 263–65, 267–68.

Unn the Deep-Minded, from the *Laxdale Saga* (c. 900 CE)

Viking sagas—such as the Gísla saga, the Njáls saga, and the Grettis saga—record the travels and interactions of Vikings. Women often feature as major characters in these tales. While the *Laxdale Saga* focuses on the four marriages of Guðrún and ends with her death as a Christian nun in Iceland, the saga opens in northern Scotland with the unusual life of another woman, Unn (also called Aud, in other sagas), who lived around 900 CE. Unn is certainly an exceptional character, but her matchmaking and wealth accumulation offer a glimpse into the power that a Viking woman could wield within her community.

- **What are some of Unn's accomplishments, and what makes her exceptional, according to the *Laxdale Saga*?**
- **How is Unn able to achieve all that she does?**
- **What can you learn about the context of Viking family and community, and women's roles within each, by examining Unn's life in the *Laxdale Saga*?**

Unn the Deep-minded was in Caithness [northern Scotland] when her son Thorstein fell. When she heard that Thorstein was dead, and her father had breathed his last, she deemed she would have no prospering in store there. So she had a ship built secretly in a wood, and when it was ready built she arrayed it, and had great wealth withal; and she took with her all her kinsfolk who were left alive; and men deem that scarce may an example be found that any one, a woman only, has ever got out of such a state of war with so much wealth and so great a following. From this it may be seen how peerless among women she was. Unn had with her many men of great worth and high birth. . . . When she was ready, Unn took her ship to the Orkneys; there she stayed a little while, and there she married off Gro, the daughter of Thorstein the Red. . . . After that Unn steered her ship to the Faroe Isles, and stayed there for some time. There she married off another daughter of Thorstein, named Olof, and from her sprung the noblest race of that land, who are called the Gate-Beards.

. . . Unn now got ready to go away from the Faroe Isles, and made it known to her shipmates that she was going to Iceland. She had with her Olaf "Feilan," the son of Thorstein, and those of his sisters who were unmarried. After that she put to sea, and, the weather being favourable, she came with her ship to the south of Iceland to Pumice-Course (Vikrarskeid). There they had their ship broken into splinters, but all the men and goods were saved.

. . . Then she went about all the Broadfirth-Dales, and took to her lands as wide as she wanted. After that Unn steered her ship to the head of the bay, and there her high-seat pillars were washed ashore, and then she deemed it was easy to know where she was to take up her abode. She had a house built there: it was afterwards called Hvamm, and she lived there. . . .

After that Unn gave to more men parts of her land-take. . . . [The text then recounts the men to whom Unn doles out parcels of land, describing their female relatives in great detail.]

Olaf "Feilan" was the youngest of Thorstein's children. He was a tall man and strong, goodly to look at, and a man of the greatest mettle. Unn loved him above all men, and made it known to people that she was minded to settle on Olaf all her belongings at Hvamm after her day. Unn now became very weary with old age, and she called Olaf "Feilan" to her and said: "It is on my mind, kinsman, that you should settle down and marry." . . . That same summer Olaf "Feilan" married Alfdis. Their wedding was at Hvamm. Unn spent much money on this feast. . . . The wedding feast was very crowded; yet there did not come nearly so many as Unn had asked, because the Islefirth people had such a long way to come. Old age fell now fast upon Unn, so that she did not get up till mid-day, and went early to bed. No one did she allow to come to her for advice between the time she went to sleep at night and the time she was aroused, and she was very angry if any one asked how it fared with her strength. . . . Unn went into the hall and a great company with her, and when all seats were taken in the hall, everyone was much struck by the lordliness of the feast. Then Unn said: "Bjorn and Helgi, my brothers, and all my other kindred and friends, I call witnesses to this, that this dwelling with all its belongings that you now see before you, I give into the hands of my kinsman, Olaf, to own and to manage." After that Unn stood up and said she would go to the bower where she was wont to sleep, but bade everyone have for pastime whatever was most to his mind, and that ale should be the cheer of the common folk. . . . But the day after Olaf went to the sleeping bower of Unn, his grandmother, and when he came into the chamber there was Unn sitting up against her pillow, and she was dead. Olaf went into the hall after that and told these tidings. Everyone thought it a wonderful thing, how Unn had upheld her dignity to the day of her death. So they now drank together Olaf's wedding and Unn's funeral honours, and the last day of the feast Unn was carried to the [burial mound] that was made for her. She was laid in a ship in the cairn, and much treasure with her, and after that the cairn was closed up.

Source: *Laxdaela Saga*, translated by Muriel A. C. Press (London: J. M. Dent, 1899; Project Gutenberg, 2006), pp. 6–12, http://www.gutenberg.org/files/17803/17803-h/17803-h.htm.

Interpreting Visual Evidence

Transmission of Religious Knowledge

A major development in the period from 600 to 1000 CE was the production of authoritative versions of religious texts. The images gathered here show the variety of forms these texts took—ranging from scroll to codex, handwritten manuscript to printed text—and the diverse materials used in making them.

The Lindisfarne Gospel was created around 700 CE by a Christian monk named Eadfrith on a remote island off England. A beautifully "illuminated" (decorated) page opens each Gospel, followed by Latin text, to which a monk named Aldred in the tenth century CE added an Old English translation between the lines. Pictured here are two pages: one showing the beginning of the Gospel of Matthew and the other showing the last page of the codex, on which Aldred added some information about the gospels.

The "Diamond Sutra," shown in the next image, was printed in 868 CE, during the Tang dynasty, in Dunhuang, China. Using carved wooden blocks, this text with illustrations was printed on separate sheets of paper, then glued onto a scroll nearly 16 feet long. It is the oldest surviving printed text that has a date on it. In this text, written in Chinese, the Buddha instructs an elderly student that one must cut through, as with a diamond, the illusion that masks all perception.

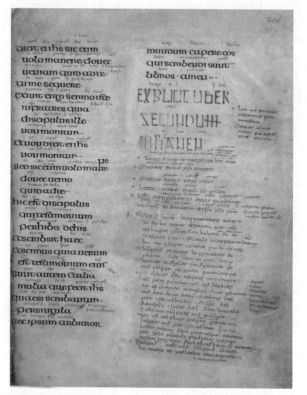

The Lindisfarne Gospel (700 CE, with tenth-century CE interlinear comments).

Early manuscripts of the Quran show a variety of geometric embellishments and beautifully flowing Arabic calligraphy. Pictured here are a ninth-century CE manuscript page from Tunis and a tenth-century CE Persian folio of the Quran in the Kufic lettering style. The image of the Persian Quran shows not only how the pages were laid out but also the construction of the codex.

From a world apart, the Maya Dresden Codex dates to around 1100 CE but records a text originally written perhaps 300 years before. It includes astronomical tables and ritual instructions on both sides of the bark paper, which is nearly 12 feet long. As many as six different scribes used around 350 glyphs and numerical symbols in composing this text.

Finally, the palm-leaf manuscript pictured here dates to around 1300 CE and preserves a copy of a Jain text, the *Kalpa Sutra*, the content of which dates to as early as the fourth century BCE. In the scene here, Vimalaprava, a Jain monk, offers instruction to a prince. Like many of the Hindu and Buddhist texts that circulated in Southeast Asia, this later copy of the *Kalpa Sutra* was written in Sanskrit in ink on palm leaves that were then stacked between wooden slats and strung together.

The "Diamond Sutra" (868 CE).

Quran from Tunis (ninth century CE).

Quran from Persia (tenth century CE).

The Dresden Codex (c. 1100 CE).

The *Kalpa Sutra* (c. 1300 CE).

Questions for Analysis

1. Compare the various texts. What are the similarities and differences in terms of content, form, and decoration, and what do you think accounts for them?

2. Consider the languages in which these texts are written. What role does translation seem to play in the transmission of these texts and the preservation of the ideas they contain?

3. Given what you know from this chapter about the Abbasid caliphate, Tang China, Charlemagne's Europe, and the Vikings, what role do you think empires played in the preservation, or destruction, of religious texts?

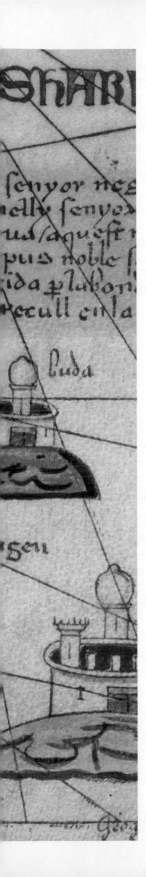

10

Becoming "The World"

1000–1300 CE

In the late 1270s two Nestorian Christian monks, Bar Sāwmā and Markōs, voyaged from the court of the Mongol leader Kublai Khan in what is now Beijing into the heart of the Islamic world and beyond. They were not Europeans. They were Uighurs, a Turkish people of central Asia, many of whom had converted to Christianity centuries earlier. The monks hoped to make a pilgrimage to Jerusalem in order to visit the tombs of the martyrs enshrined there and along the way.

On their journey westward, Bar Sāwmā and Markōs traveled a world bound together by economic and cultural exchange. The two monks lingered at the magnificent trading hub of Kashgar in what is now western China, where caravan routes converged in a market for jade, exotic spices, and precious silks. Unable to continue on to Jerusalem due to the route's dangers (including murderous robbers), the monks parted ways at Baghdad. Later, in 1287, Bar Sāwmā was appointed an ambassador by the Buddhist Mongol il-Khan of Persia, Arghūn, to drum up support among European leaders for an attack on Jerusalem to wrest it from Muslim control. He visited Constantinople (where the Byzantine emperor gave him gold and silver), Rome (where he met with the pope at the shrine of Saint Peter), Paris (where he saw that city's vibrant university), and Bordeaux (where he was welcomed by the English king, Edward I). In the end, neither monk ever reached Jerusalem or returned to China. Bar Sāwmā ended his days

Core Objectives

- **IDENTIFY** technological advances of this period, especially in ship design and navigation, and **EXPLAIN** how they facilitated the expansion of Afro-Eurasian trade.

- **DESCRIBE** the varied social and political forces that shaped the Islamic world, India, China, and Europe, and **EVALUATE** the degree to which these forces integrated cultures and geographic areas.

- **COMPARE** the internal integration and external interactions of sub-Saharan Africa with those of the Americas, and with the connected Eurasian world.

- **ASSESS** the impacts that the Mongol Empire had on Afro-Eurasian peoples and places.

in Baghdad, and Markōs became patriarch of the Nestorian branch of Christianity, centered in modern-day Iran. Yet their voyages exemplified the crisscrossing of people, money, goods, and ideas along the trade routes and sea-lanes that connected the world's regions.

Three related themes dominate the period from 1000 to 1300 CE, at the end of which a monk like Bar Sāwmā could make such a journey. First, trade along sea-based routes increased and coastal trading cities began to expand dramatically. Second, greater trade and religious integration generated the world's four major cultural "spheres," whose inhabitants were linked by shared institutions and beliefs: the Islamic world, India, China, and Europe. Sub-Saharan Africa and the Americas also thrived during this period; however, they remained more fragmented, experiencing more limited political and economic integration. Third, the Mongol Empire, stretching from China to Persia and as far as eastern Europe, ruled over huge swaths of land in many of the world's major cultural spheres. Each of these three themes contributes to an understanding of how Afro-Eurasia became a "world" unified through trade, migration, and even religious conflict.

Global Storyline

The Emergence of the World We Know Today

- Advances in maritime technology lead to increased sea trade, transforming coastal cities into global trading hubs and elevating Afro-Eurasian trade to unprecedented levels.

- Intensified trade and religious integration shape four major cultural "spheres": the Islamic world, India, China, and Europe.

- Sub-Saharan Africa is drawn into Eurasian exchange, resulting in a true Afro-Eurasia–wide network, while the Americas experience more limited political, economic, and cultural integration.

- The Mongol Empire integrates many of the world's major cultural spheres.

Development of Maritime Trade

By the tenth century CE, sea routes were becoming more important than land networks for long-distance trade. Improved navigational aids, better map-making, refinements in shipbuilding, and new political support for shipping made seaborne trade easier and slashed its cost. These developments also fostered the growth of maritime commercial hubs (called anchorages), which further facilitated the expansion of maritime trade.

A new navigational instrument spurred this boom: the magnetic needle compass. This Chinese invention initially identified promising locations for houses and tombs, but eleventh-century sailors from Guangzhou (Canton) used it to find their way on the high seas. The use of this device eventually spread among navigators. The compass not only allowed sailing under cloudy skies but also improved mapmaking.

An array of new ship types—dhows, junks, and cogs—allowed for more impressive mastery of the seas. Dhows, ships with triangular sails called lateens, maximized the power of the monsoon trade winds on the Arabian Sea and the wider Indian Ocean. Sailing the South China Sea were junks, large, flat-bottomed ships with internal sealed bulkheads, stern-mounted rudders, as many as four decks, six masts with a dozen sails, and the space to carry as many as 500 men. And, in the Atlantic, cogs, with their single mast and square sail, linked Genoa to locations as distant as the Azores and Iceland. The numbers testify to the power of the maritime revolution: while a porter could carry about 10 pounds over long distances, and animal-drawn wagons could

THE BIG PICTURE

How did the major cultural spheres of the Afro-Eurasian world from 1000 to 1300 CE develop their unique identities while becoming unified through trade, migration, and religion?

Belitung Dhow This museum display in Singapore cleverly depicts a reconstruction of the Belitung dhow (albeit without the signature triangular sail) rising on a wave of Changsha bowls excavated from the actual wreck on the floor of the Java Sea.

move 100 pounds of goods over small distances, the Arab dhows could transport up to 5 tons of cargo, Atlantic cogs as much as 200 tons, and Chinese junks more than 500 tons. One particularly fascinating recent archaeological discovery that demonstrates the connectivity brought by these ships is the Belitung dhow. Shipwrecked in the Java Sea off the coast of the Indonesian island of Belitung in the early ninth century CE, this 50-foot ship likely hailed from the southern coast of the Arabian Peninsula (modern-day Oman or Yemen), based on analysis of the wood from which it was constructed. But the sunk ship was filled with more than 60,000 artifacts from Tang dynasty China. The artifacts offer evidence for the kind of direct, long-distance maritime trade between China and the Abbasid world that was bringing the world closer together by 1000 CE.

Although it may seem ironic to assert after invoking a shipwreck as evidence, the business of shipping, on the whole, became less dangerous in the period from 1000 to 1300 CE thanks not only to these innovations in shipbuilding but also to local political support. Maritime traders enjoyed the protection of political authorities such as the Song rulers in China, who maintained a standing navy that protected traders and lighthouses that guided trading fleets in and out of harbors. The Fatimid caliphate in Egypt profited from maritime trade and defended merchant fleets from pirates, using armed convoys of ships to escort commercial fleets and regulate the ocean traffic. This system of protection soon spread to North Africa and southern Spain.

Long-distance trade spawned the growth of commercial cities. These cosmopolitan **entrepôts** served as transshipment centers, located on land between borders or in ports where ships could drop anchor. In these cities, traders exchanged commodities and replenished supplies. Beginning in the late tenth century CE, several regional centers became major anchorages of the maritime trade: in the west, the Egyptian port city of Alexandria on the Mediterranean (and Cairo, just up the Nile); near the tip of the Indian subcontinent, the port of Quilon (now Kollam); in the Malaysian Archipelago, the city of Melaka; and in the east, the Chinese city of Quanzhou. (See Map 10.1.) These hubs thrived under the political stability of powerful rulers who recognized that trade would generate wealth for their regimes.

Cairo and Alexandria were the Mediterranean's main maritime commercial centers. Cairo was home to numerous Muslim and Jewish trading firms, and Alexandria was their lookout post on the Mediterranean. The Islamic legal system prevalent in Egypt promoted a favorable business environment. With the clerics' blessing, Muslim traders formed partnerships between those who had capital to lend and those who needed money to expand their businesses: owners of capital entrusted their money or commodities to agents who, after completing their work, returned the investment and a share of the profits to the owners—and kept the rest as their reward. The English word *risk* derives from the Arabic *rizq*, the extra allowance paid to merchants in lieu of interest.

Core Objectives

IDENTIFY technological advances of this period, especially in ship design and navigation, and EXPLAIN how they facilitated the expansion of Afro-Eurasian trade.

entrepôts

Multiethnic trading stations, often supported and protected by regional leaders, where traders exchanged commodities and replenished supplies in order to facilitate long-distance trade.

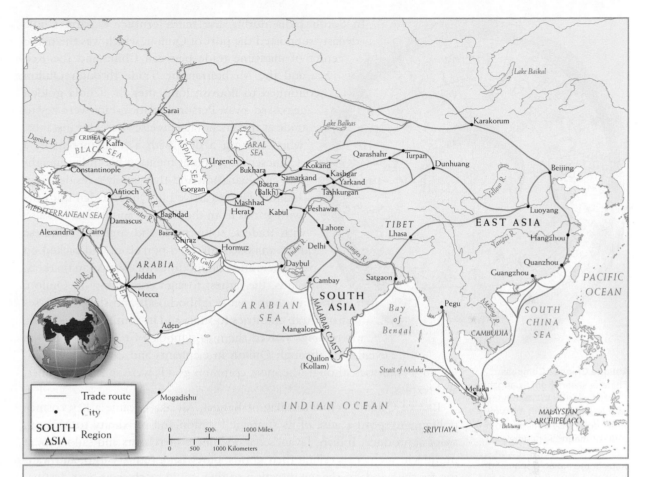

Map 10.1 Afro-Eurasian Trade, 1000–1300 CE

During the early second millennium, Afro-Eurasian merchants increasingly turned to the Indian Ocean to transport their goods. Locate the global hubs of Quilon, Alexandria, Cairo, Melaka, and Quanzhou on this map.

- What regions do each of these global hubs represent?
- Based on the map, why would sea travel have been preferable to overland travel?
- According to the text, what revolutions in maritime travel facilitated this development?

Through Alexandria, Europeans acquired silks from China, especially the coveted *zaytuni* (satin) fabric from Quanzhou. But many more goods passed through the Egyptian anchorage: from the Mediterranean, olive oil, glassware, flax, corals, and metals; from India, gemstones and aromatic perfumes; and from elsewhere, minerals and chemicals for dyeing or tanning, and raw materials such as timber and bamboo. Paper and books (including hand-copied Bibles, Talmuds, and Qurans) traveled along this network as well.

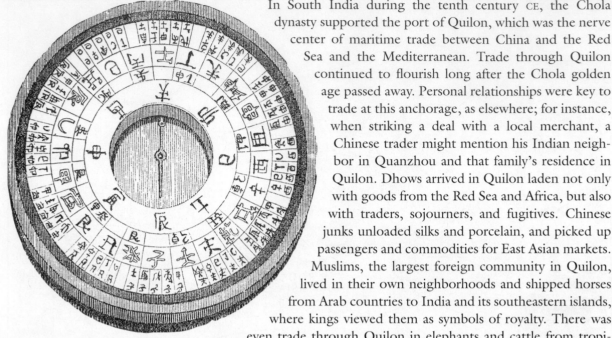

Antique Chinese Compass
Chinese sailors from Guangzhou (Canton) started to use magnetic needle compasses in the eleventh century. By the thirteenth century, magnetic needle compasses were widely used on ships in the Indian Ocean and were starting to appear in the Mediterranean.

In South India during the tenth century CE, the Chola dynasty supported the port of Quilon, which was the nerve center of maritime trade between China and the Red Sea and the Mediterranean. Trade through Quilon continued to flourish long after the Chola golden age passed away. Personal relationships were key to trade at this anchorage, as elsewhere; for instance, when striking a deal with a local merchant, a Chinese trader might mention his Indian neighbor in Quanzhou and that family's residence in Quilon. Dhows arrived in Quilon laden not only with goods from the Red Sea and Africa, but also with traders, sojourners, and fugitives. Chinese junks unloaded silks and porcelain, and picked up passengers and commodities for East Asian markets. Muslims, the largest foreign community in Quilon, lived in their own neighborhoods and shipped horses from Arab countries to India and its southeastern islands, where kings viewed them as symbols of royalty. There was even trade through Quilon in elephants and cattle from tropical countries, though the most common goods were spices, perfumes, and textiles.

East of Quilon, across the Bay of Bengal, Melaka became a key cosmopolitan entrepôt because of its strategic location and proximity to Malayan tropical produce. Indian, Javanese, and Chinese merchants and sailors spent months in such ports selling their goods, purchasing return cargo, and waiting for the winds to change direction so they could reach their next destination. During peak season, Southeast Asian ports were crowded with colorfully dressed foreign sailors, local Javanese artisans who produced finely textured batik handicrafts, and traders eager for profit. The traders converged from all over Asia to flood the markets with their merchandise and to search for pungent herbs, aromatic spices, and agrarian staples such as quick-ripening strains of rice to ship out.

In China, the Song government set up offices of seafaring affairs in its three major ports: Quanzhou, Guangzhou (Canton), and a third near present-day Shanghai. In return for a portion of the taxes on the goods passing through these entrepôts, these offices registered cargoes, sailors, and traders, while guards kept a keen eye on the traffic. All foreign traders in Song China were guests of the governor, who doubled as the chief of seafaring affairs. Every year, the governor conducted a wind-calling ritual. Traders of every origin—Arabs, Persians, Jews, Indians, and Chinese—witnessed the ceremony, then joined together for a sumptuous banquet. Although most foreign merchants did not reside apart from the rest of the city, they did maintain buildings

Mazu As much as sailors used compasses, they could still appeal for divine help at shrines devoted to Mazu, the goddess of seafarers. While many Mazu temples of varying size dotted the shorelines of the East and South China Seas, the shrine at Guangzhou now includes a 48-foot-tall statue of Mazu gazing out into the harbor. Mazu's origin-story is rooted in the life of a young girl named Lin Mo (living in the late 900s ce) who miraculously saved her family from stormy seas.

for religious worship according to their faiths. A mosque from this period still stands on a busy street in Quanzhou. Hindu traders living in Quanzhou worshipped in a Buddhist shrine where statues of Hindu deities stood alongside those of Buddhist gods. Each of these bustling ports teemed with a cosmopolitan mix of peoples, goods, and ideas that flowed through growing maritime networks thanks to improved ships and better navigational tools.

The Islamic World in a Time of Political Fragmentation

While the number of Muslim traders began to increase in commercial hubs from the Mediterranean to the South China Sea, it was not until the ninth and tenth centuries CE that Muslims became a majority within their own Abbasid Empire (see Chapter 9), and even then rulers struggled to unite the diverse Islamic world. From the outset, Muslim rulers and clerics dealt with large non-Muslim populations, even as these groups were converting to Islam. Rulers accorded non-Muslims religious toleration as long as the non-Muslims accepted Islam's political dominion. Jewish, Christian, and Zoroastrian communities within Muslim lands were free to choose their own religious leaders and to settle internal disputes in their own religious courts. They did, however, have to pay a special tax, the *jizya*, and defer to their Muslim rulers. While tolerant, Islam was an expansionist, universalizing faith.

jizya
Special tax that non-Muslims were forced to pay to their Islamic rulers in return for which they were given security and property and granted cultural autonomy.

Intense proselytizing—especially by Sufi missionaries (whose ideas are discussed later in this chapter)—carried the sacred word to new frontiers and, in the process, reinforced the spread of Islamic institutions that supported commercial exchange.

ENVIRONMENTAL CHALLENGES AND POLITICAL DIVISIONS

Severe climate conditions—freezing temperatures and lack of rainfall—afflicted the Eastern Mediterranean and the Islamic lands of Mesopotamia, the Iranian plateau, and the steppe region of central Asia in the late eleventh and early twelfth centuries. The Nile's low water levels devastated Egypt, the breadbasket for much of the area. At least one-quarter of the summer floods that normally brought sediment-enriching deposits to Egypt's soils and guaranteed abundant harvests failed in this period. Driven in part by drought, Turkish nomadic pastoralists poured out of the steppe lands of central Asia in search of better lands, wreaking political and economic havoc everywhere they invaded.

At the same time these climate-driven Turkish pastoralists were migrating and the Islamic faith was increasing its reach across Afro-Eurasia, the political institutions of Islam were fragmenting. (See Map 10.2.) From 950 to 1050 CE, it appeared that Shiism would be the vehicle for uniting the Islamic world. The Fatimid Shiites had established their authority over Egypt and much of North Africa (see Chapter 9), and the Abbasid state in Baghdad was controlled by a Shiite family, the Buyids. Each group created universities, in Cairo and Baghdad respectively, ensuring that leading centers of higher learning were Shiite. But divisions also sapped Shiism, and Sunni Muslims began to challenge Shiite power and establish their own strongholds. In Baghdad, the Shiite Buyid family surrendered to the invading Seljuk Turks, a Sunni group, in 1055. A century later, the last of the Shiite Fatimid rulers gave way to a new Sunni regime in Egypt.

The Seljuk Turks who took Baghdad had been migrating into the Islamic heartland from the Asian steppes as early as the eighth century CE, bringing superior military skills and an intense devotion to Sunni Islam. When they flooded into the Iranian plateau in 1029, they contributed to the end of the magnificent cultural flourishing of the early eleventh century. When Seljuk warriors ultimately took Baghdad in 1055, they established a nomadic state in Mesopotamia in place of the once powerful Abbasid state that now lacked the resources to defend its lands and its peoples, weakened by famines and pestilence. The Seljuk invaders destroyed institutions of learning and public libraries and looted the region's antiquities. Once established in Baghdad, they founded outposts in Syria and Palestine, then moved into Anatolia after defeating Byzantine forces in 1071.

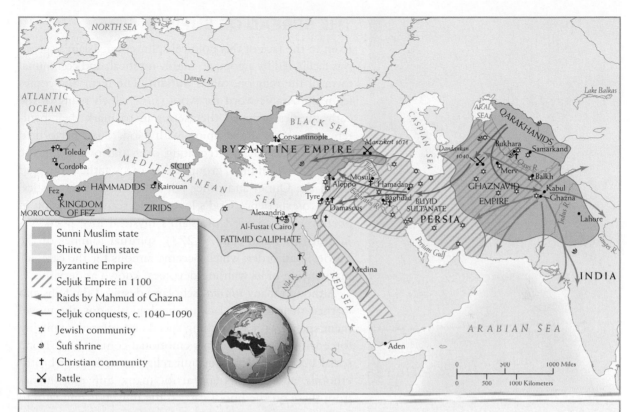

Map 10.2 The Islamic World, 900–1200 CE

The Islamic world experienced political disintegration in the first centuries of the second millennium.

- According to the map key, what were the two major types of Islamic states in this period? What were some of the major political entities?
- What were the sources of instability in this period, according to the map?
- What do you note about the locations of Jewish and Christian communities, as well as Sufi shrines, across the Islamic world?

By the thirteenth century the Islamic heartland had fractured into three regions. In the east (central Asia, Iran, and eastern Iraq), the remnants of the old Abbasid state persevered, with a succession of caliphs claiming to speak for all of Islam yet deferring to their Turkish military commanders. In the core of the Islamic world—Egypt, Syria, and the Arabian Peninsula—where Arabic was the primary language, military men of non-Arab origin held the reins of power. Farther west in North Africa, Arab rulers prevailed, but the influence of Berbers, some from the northern Sahara, was extensive. Islam was a vibrant faith, but its polities were splintered.

THE SPREAD OF SUFISM

Even in the face of this political splintering, Islam's spread was facilitated by a popular, highly mystical, and communal form of the religion, called **Sufism**. The term *Sufi* comes from the Arabic word for wool (*suf*), which many of the early mystics wrapped themselves in to mark their penitence. Seeking closer union with God, Sufis performed ecstatic rituals such as repeating over and over again the name of God. In time, groups of devotees gathered to read aloud the Quran and other religious tracts. Sufi mystics' desire to experience God's love found ready expression in poetry. Most admired of Islam's mystical love poets was Jalal al-Din Rumi (1207–1273), spiritual founder of the Mevlevi Sufi order, which became famous for the ceremonial dancing of its whirling devotees, known as dervishes.

Although many *ulama* (scholars) despised the Sufis and loathed their seeming lack of theological rigor, the movement spread with astonishing speed and offered a unifying force within Islam. Sufism's emotional content and strong social bonds, sustained in Sufi religious orders, or brotherhoods, added to its appeal for many. Sufi missionaries from these brotherhoods carried the universalizing faith to India, to Southeast Asia, across the Sahara Desert, and to many other distant locations. It was through these brotherhoods that Islam became truly a religion for the people. As trade increased and more converts appeared in the Islamic lands, urban and peasant populations came to understand the faith practiced by the political, commercial, and scholarly upper classes even while they remained attached to their Sufi brotherhood ways. Over time, Islam became even more accommodating, embracing Persian literature, Turkish ruling skills, and Arabic-language contributions in law, religion, literature, and science.

WHAT WAS ISLAM?

Buoyed by Arab dhows on the high seas and carried on the backs of camels following commercial routes, Islam had been transformed from Muhammad's original vision of a religion for Arab peoples (see Chapter 9). By 1300, its influence spanned Afro-Eurasia and reached multitudes of non-Arab converts. While Arabic remained the primary language of religious devotion, Persian became the language of Islamic philosophy and art and Turkish the language of Islamic law and administration. Islam attracted city dwellers and rural peasants alike, as well as its original audience of desert nomads. Muslim scholars formed universities, such as al-Qarawiyyin in Fez, Morocco (859 CE),

Dervishes The dance of Sufi mystics was an important means of reaching union with God. This illustration from a fifteenth-century publication of Firdawsi's *Shah Namah* depicts whirling dervishes with one hand stretching toward heaven and the other reaching toward the earth. Their richly colored robes and long streaming hair differ from the white garb and tall hats of modern dervishes.

Sufism
Emotional and mystical form of Islam that appealed to the common people.

and al-Azhar in Cairo, Egypt (970 CE). Islam's extraordinary universal appeal generated an intense cultural flowering around 1000 CE.

That cultural blossoming in all fields of high learning was marked by diversity in both language and ideas. Representing the new Persian ethnic pride was Abu al-Qasim Firdawsi (920–1020 CE), a devout Muslim who believed in the importance of pre-Islamic Sasanian traditions. In the epic poem *Shah Namah* (Book of Kings), he celebrated the origins of Persian culture and narrated the history of the Iranian highland peoples from the dawn of time to the Muslim conquest. Indicative of the enduring prominence of the Islamic faith and the Arabic language in thought was the legendary Ibn Rushd (1126–1198), known as Averroës in the western world. Steeped in the writings of Aristotle, Ibn Rushd's belief that faith and reason were compatible even influenced the thinking of the Christian world's leading philosopher and theologian, Thomas Aquinas (1225–1274).

The Islamic world's achievements in science were truly remarkable. Its scholars were at the pinnacle of scientific knowledge throughout the world in this era. Ibn al-Shatir (1304–1375), working on his own in Damascus, produced non-Ptolemaic models of the universe that later researchers noted were mathematically equivalent to those of Copernicus. Even earlier, the Maragha school of astronomers (1259 and later) in western Iran had produced a non-Ptolemaic model of the planets. Some historians of science believe that Copernicus must have seen an Arabic manuscript written by a thirteenth-century Persian astronomer that contained a table of the movements of the planets. In addition, scholars in the Islamic world produced works in medicine, optics, and mathematics as well as astronomy that were in advance of the achievements of Greek and Roman scholars.

During this period, the Islamic world became one of the four cultural spheres that would play a major role in world history, laying the foundation for what would become known as the Middle East up through the middle of the twentieth century. Islam became the majority religion of the inhabitants of Southwest Asia and North Africa, Arabic language use became widespread, and the Turks began to establish themselves as a dominant force, ultimately creating the Ottoman Empire, which would last into the twentieth century. The Islamic world became integral in transregional trade and in the creation and transmission of knowledge.

India as a Cultural Mosaic

With its pivotal location along land- and sea-based trade routes, India became an intersection for the trade, migration, and culture of Afro-Eurasian peoples. With 80 million inhabitants in 1000 CE, it had the second-largest population in the region, not far behind China's 120 million. Turks ultimately spilled

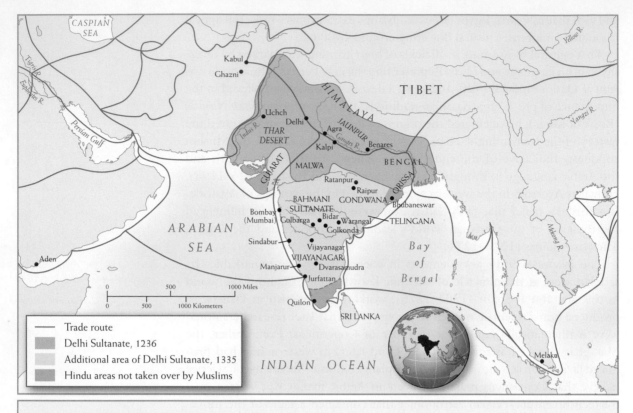

Map 10.3 South Asia in 1300

As the fourteenth century began, India was a blend of many cultures. Politically, the Turkish Muslim regime of the Delhi Sultanate dominated the region.

- What region was controlled by the Delhi Sultanate in 1236? How did the area controlled by the Delhi Sultanate change in just 100 years?
- How does the map suggest that trade routes helped spread the Muslims' influence in India?
- Where on the map do Hindu areas resist Muslim political control? Based on your reading, what factors may have accounted for Hinduism's continued appeal despite the Muslims' political power?

into India as they had into the Islamic heartlands, bringing their newfound Islamic beliefs. But the Turkish newcomers encountered an ethnic and religious mix of which they were just one part. (See Map 10.3.)

SHIFTING POLITICAL STRUCTURES

Before the Turks arrived, India was splintered among rival chiefs called *rajas*. These leaders gained support from Brahmans by doling out land grants to them. Since much of the land was uncultivated, the Brahmans first built temples, then converted the indigenous hunting and gathering peoples to the Hindu traditions, and finally taught the converts how to cultivate the land. In this way, Brahmans simultaneously spread their faith and expanded the agrarian tax base for themselves and the *rajas*. They also repaid the *rajas'* support by compiling elaborate genealogies for them, endowing them with lengthy and legitimizing ancestries. In return, the *rajas* demonstrated that they, too, were well versed in Sanskrit culture, including equestrian skills and courtly etiquette, and were prepared to patronize artists and poets.

When Turkish warlords began entering India, the *rajas* had neither the will nor resources to resist them after centuries of fighting off invaders. For example, Mahmud of Ghazna (r. 998–1030 CE) launched many expeditions from the Afghan heartland into northern India and, eager to win status within Islam, made his capital, Ghazna, a center of Islamic learning. Mahmud's expansion in the early eleventh century marked the height of what came to be known as the Ghaznavid Empire (977–1186 CE). Later, in the 1180s, Muhammad Ghuri led another wave of Islamic Turkish invasions from Afghanistan across the Delhi region in northern India. Wars raged between the Indus and Ganges Rivers until, one by one, all the way to the lower Ganges Valley, the fractured kingdoms of the *rajas* toppled. The Turks introduced their own customs while accepting local social structures, such as the hierarchical *varna* system. The Turks constructed grand mosques and built impressive libraries where scholars could toil and share their wisdom with the court.

While the Ghaznavids were impressive, the most powerful and enduring of the Turkish Muslim regimes of northern India was the **Delhi Sultanate** (1206–1526), whose rulers brought political integration but also strengthened the cultural diversity and tolerance that were already a hallmark of the Indian social order. Sultans recruited local artisans for numerous building projects, and palaces and mosques became displays of the Indian architectural tastes adopted by Turkish newcomers. But Islam never fully dominated South Asia because the sultans did not force their subjects to convert. Nor did they display much interest in the flourishing commercial life along the Indian coast. The sultans permitted these areas to develop on their own: Persian Zoroastrian traders settled on the coast around modern-day Mumbai, while farther south, Arab traders controlled the Malabar coast. The Delhi Sultanate was a rich and powerful regime that brought political integration but did not enforce cultural homogeneity.

WHAT WAS INDIA?

During the eleventh, twelfth, and thirteenth centuries, India became the most diverse and, in some respects, the most tolerant region in Afro-Eurasia. India in this era arose as an impressive but fragile mosaic of cultures, religions,

Delhi Sultanate (1206–1526)
A Turkish Muslim regime in northern India that, through its tolerance for cultural diversity, brought political integration without enforcing cultural homogeneity.

Hindu Temple When Buddhism started to decline in India, Hinduism was on the rise. Numerous Hindu temples were built, many of them adorned with ornate carvings like this small tenth-century CE temple in Bhubaneshwar in East India.

and ethnicities. When the Turks arrived, the local Hindu population, having had much experience with foreign invaders and immigrants, assimilated these intruders as they had done earlier peoples. Before long, the newcomers thought of themselves as Indians who, however, retained their Islamic beliefs and steppe ways. They continued to wear their distinctive trousers and robes and flaunted their horse-riding skills. At the same time, the local population embraced some of their conquerors' ways, donning the tunics and trousers that characterized central Asian peoples.

Diversity and cultural mixing became most visible in the multiple languages that flourished in India. Although the sultans spoke Turkish languages, they regarded Persian literature as a high cultural achievement and made Persian their courtly and administrative language. Meanwhile, most of their Hindu subjects spoke local languages, adhered to the regulations of the *varna* system of hierarchies, and practiced diverse forms of Hindu worship. The rulers in India did what Muslim rulers in Southwest Asia and the Mediterranean did with Christian and Jewish communities living in their midst: they collected the *jizya* tax and permitted communities to worship as they saw fit and to administer their own communal law. Ultimately, Islam proved in India that it did not have to be an intolerant conquering religion to prosper.

Although Buddhism had been in decline in India for centuries, it, too, became part of the cultural intermixing of this period. As Vedic Brahmanism evolved into Hinduism (see Chapter 8), it absorbed many Buddhist doctrines and practices, such as nonviolence (*ahimsa*) and vegetarianism. The two religions became so similar in India that Hindus simply considered the Buddha to be one of their deities—an incarnation of the great god Vishnu. Many Buddhist moral teachings mixed with and became Hindu stories. Artistic motifs reflected a similar process of adoption and adaptation. Goddesses, some beautiful and others fierce, appeared alongside Buddhas, Vishnus, and Shivas as their consorts. The Turkish invaders' destruction of major monasteries in the thirteenth century deprived Buddhism of local spiritual leaders. Lacking dynastic support, Buddhists in India were more easily assimilated into the Hindu population or converted to Islam.

Once the initial disruptive effects of the Turkish invasions were absorbed, India remained a highly diverse and tolerant region during this period. Most important, India also emerged as one of the four major cultural spheres, enjoying a tremendous level of integration as Turkish-Muslim rulers and their traditions and practices were successfully intermixed with the native Hindu society, leading to a more integrated and peaceful India.

Song China: Insiders versus Outsiders

The preeminent world power in 1000 CE was still China, despite its recent turmoil. In 907 CE the Tang dynasty splintered into regional kingdoms, mostly led by military generals. In 960 CE one of these generals, Zhao Kuangyin, ended the fragmentation, reunified China, and assumed the mandate of heaven for the Song dynasty (960–1279 CE). The following three centuries witnessed many economic and political successes, but northern nomadic tribes kept the Song dynasty from completely securing its reign. (See Map 10.4 and Map 10.5.) Ultimately, one of those nomadic groups, the Mongols, would bring the Song dynasty to an end, but not before Song influence had fanned out into Southeast Asia, helping to create new identities in the polities that developed there.

Core Objectives

DESCRIBE the varied social and political forces that shaped the Islamic world, India, China, and Europe, and **EVALUATE** the degree to which these forces integrated cultures and geographic areas.

ECONOMIC AND POLITICAL DEVELOPMENTS

Chinese merchants, like those from India and the Islamic world, participated in Afro-Eurasia's powerful long-distance trade. Yet China's commercial successes could not have occurred without the country's strong agrarian base—especially its vast wheat, millet, and rice fields, which fed a population that reached 120 million. Crop cultivation benefited from breakthroughs in metalworking that produced stronger iron plows, which Song farmers harnessed to sturdy water buffalo to extend the agricultural frontier.

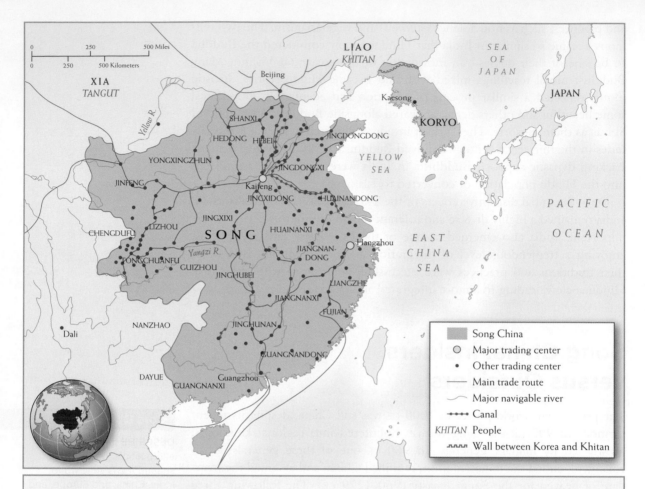

Map 10.4 East Asia in 1000 CE

Several states emerged in East Asia between 1000 and 1300 CE, but none were as strong as the Song dynasty in China. Using the key to the map, try to identify the factors that contributed to the Song state's economic dynamism.

- What do you note about the location of the major trading centers?
- What do you note about the distribution of the other trading centers?
- According to the map, what external factors kept the Song dynasty from completely securing its reign?

Manufacturing also flourished. With the use of piston-driven bellows to force air into furnaces, Song iron production in the eleventh century equaled that of Europe in the early eighteenth century. In the early tenth century CE, Chinese alchemists mixed saltpeter with sulfur and charcoal to produce a product that would burn and could be deployed on the battlefield: gunpowder. Song entrepreneurs were soon inventing a remarkable array of

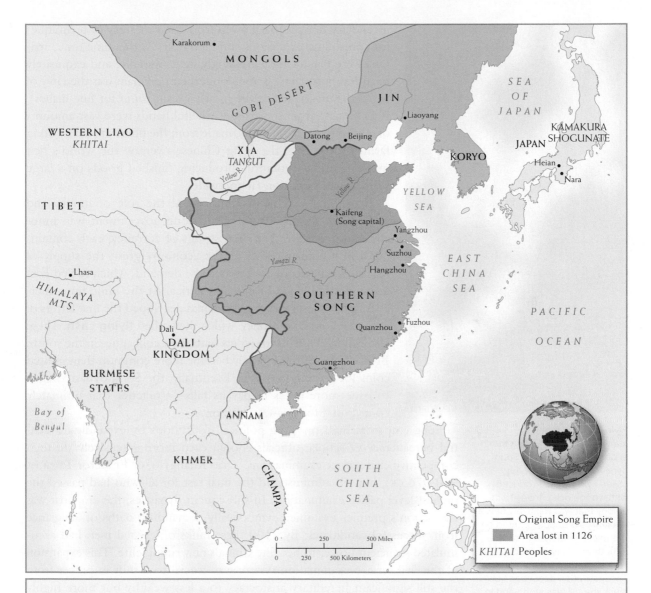

Map 10.5 East Asia in 1200

The Song dynasty regularly dealt with "barbarian" neighbors with a balance of military response and outright bribery.

- What were the major "barbarian" tribes on the borders of Song China during this period?
- Approximately what percentage of Song China was lost to the Jin in 1126?
- Apart from so-called barbarians, what other polities existed on the borders of Song China?

Flying Cash Among the many innovations fueling the economic boom of the Song dynasty was paper money, called flying cash. Produced with woodblock printing technology that was relatively new at the time, the images printed on this example include, from top to bottom, coins, an inscription, and laborers at a warehouse. The inscription describes how much the bill was worth and in what regions it could be used as payment.

flying cash
Letters of exchange—early predecessors of paper money—first developed by guilds in the northern Song province Shanxi that eclipsed coins by the thirteenth century.

incendiary devices that flowed from their mastery of techniques for controlling explosions and high heat. At the same time, artisans were producing increasingly light, durable, and exquisitely beautiful porcelains. Before long, their porcelain was the envy of all Afro-Eurasia (hence the modern term *china* for fine dishes). Also flowing from the artisans' skillful hands were vast amounts of clothing and handicrafts, made from the fibers grown by Song farmers. In effect, the Song Chinese oversaw the world's first manufacturing revolution, producing finished goods on a large scale for consumption far and wide.

Expanding commerce transformed the role of money and its wide circulation. By now the Song government was annually minting nearly 2 million strings of currency, each containing 1,000 copper coins. As the economy grew, the supply of metal currency could not match the demand, which fueled East Asia's desire for gold from East Africa. At the same time, merchant guilds in northwestern Shanxi developed the first letters of exchange, or paper money, which they called **flying cash**. These letters linked northern traders with their colleagues in the south. Before long, printed money became more common than minted coins for trading purposes. Eventually, the Song dynasty began to issue more notes to pay its bills—a practice that ultimately contributed to runaway inflation.

Song emperors built on Tang political institutions by expanding a central bureaucracy of scholar-officials chosen even more extensively through competitive civil service examinations. Zhao Kuangyin, or Emperor Taizu (r. 960–976 CE), himself administered the final test for all who had passed the highest-level palace examination. In subsequent dynasties, the emperor was the nation's premier examiner, symbolically demanding oaths of allegiance from successful candidates. By 1100 these ranks of learned men had accumulated sufficient power to become China's new ruling elite. This expansion of the civil service examination system was crucial to a shift in power from the still significant hereditary aristocracy to a less wealthy but more highly schooled class of scholar-officials.

CHINA'S NEIGHBORS: NOMADS, JAPAN, AND SOUTHEAST ASIA

China's prosperity influenced its neighbors and its interactions with them. As Song China flourished, nomads on the outskirts eyed the Chinese successes closely. To the north, nomadic societies formed their own dynasties and adopted Chinese institutions. These non-Chinese nomads sought both to conquer and to copy China proper. Despite its sophisticated weapons, the Song army could not match its enemies on the steppe when the nomads united against it. Steel tips improved the arrows that Song soldiers shot from their crossbows, and flamethrowers and "crouching tiger" catapults sent incendiary bombs streaking into their enemies' ranks. But none of these breakthroughs was secret. Warrior neighbors on the steppe mastered the new arts of war more fully than did the Song military. Consequently, China drew on its economic success (and the innovation of paper money) to "buy off" the borderlanders. This short-term solution, however, led to economic instability (particularly inflation) and military weakness, especially as the Song forces were cut off, via the steppe nomads, from their supply of horses for warfare purposes.

Feeling the pull of China's economic and political gravity, cultures around China consolidated their own internal political authority and defined their own identities in order to keep from being swallowed up by China. At the same time, they increased their commercial transactions with China. In Japan, for instance, leaders distanced themselves from Chinese influences, but they also developed a strong sense of their islands' distinctive identity. Even so, the long-standing dominance of Chinese ways remained apparent at virtually every level of Japanese society, and was most pronounced at the imperial court in the capital city of Heian (present-day Kyoto), which was modeled after the Chinese capital city of Chang'an. Outside Kyoto, however, a less China-centered way of life existed and began to impose itself on the center. Here, local notables, mainly military leaders and large landowners, began to challenge the imperial court for dominance. This challenge was accompanied

Core Objectives

DESCRIBE the social and political forces that shaped Song China, and **EVALUATE** the degree to which they integrated the cultures of East Asia.

Angkor Wat Mistaken by later European explorers for a remnant of Alexander the Great's conquests, the enormous temple complexes built by the Khmer people in Angkor borrowed their intricate layout and stupa (a moundlike structure containing religious relics) architecture from the Brahmanic Indian temples of the time. As their capital, Angkor was a microcosm of the world for the Khmer, who aspired to represent the macrocosm of the universe in the magnificence of Angkor's buildings and their geometric layout.

Chinese and Barbarian After losing the north, the Chinese grew resentful of outsiders. They drew a dividing line between their own agrarian society and the nomadic warriors, calling them "barbarians." Such identities were not fixed, however. Chinese and so-called barbarians were mutually dependent.

by the arrival of an important new social group in Japanese society—samurai warriors. By the beginning of the fourteenth century, Japan had multiple sources of political and cultural power: an imperial family with prestige but little authority; an endangered and declining aristocracy; powerful landowning notables based in the provinces; and a rising and increasingly ambitious class of samurai.

During the Song period, Southeast Asia became a crossroads of Afro-Eurasian influences. The Malay Peninsula became home to many entrepôts for traders shuttling between India and China, because it connected the Bay of Bengal and the Indian Ocean with the South China Sea. (See Map 10.6.) Consequently, Southeast Asia was characterized by a fusion of religions and cultural influences: Vedic Brahmanism in Bali and other islands, Islam in Java and Sumatra, and Mahayana Buddhism in Vietnam and other parts of mainland Southeast Asia. Important Vedic and Buddhist kingdoms emerged in Southeast Asia. The most powerful and wealthy of these kingdoms was the Khmer Empire (889–1431 CE), with its capital at Angkor, in present-day Cambodia. Public works and magnificent temples dedicated to the revived Vedic gods from India went hand in hand with the earlier influence of Indian Buddhism. One of the greatest temple complexes in Angkor—Angkor Wat—exemplified the Khmers' heavy borrowing from Vedic Indian architecture and the revival of the Hindu pantheon within the Khmer royal state. Kingdoms like the Khmer Empire functioned as political buffers between the strong states of China and India and brought stability and further commercial prosperity to the region.

WHAT WAS CHINA?

Paradoxically, the increasing exchange between outsiders and insiders within China hardened the lines that divided them and gave residents of China's interior a highly developed sense of themselves as a distinct people possessing a superior culture. Exchanges with outsiders nurtured a "Chinese" identity among those who considered themselves true insiders and referred to themselves as "Han." Song Chinese grew increasingly suspicious and resentful toward the outsiders living in their midst. They called these outsiders "barbarians" and treated them accordingly.

Print culture crystallized the distinct Chinese identity. Of all Afro-Eurasian societies in 1300, the Chinese were the most advanced in their use of printing, book publishing, and circulation, in part due to the invention

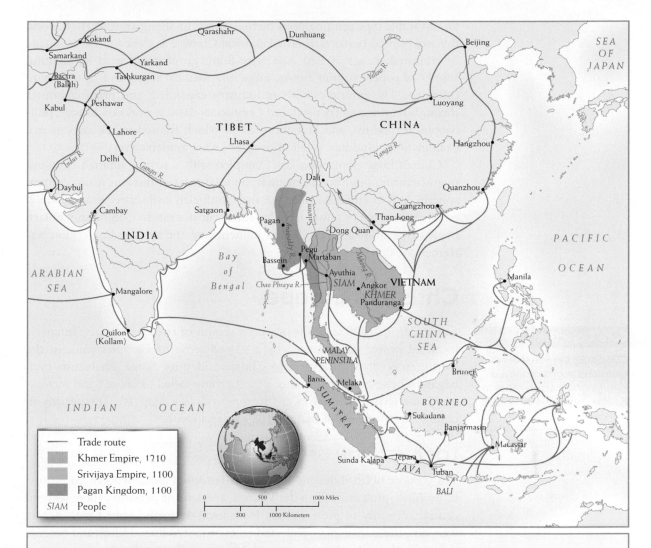

Map 10.6 Southeast Asia, 1000–1300 CE

....

Cross-cultural influences affected Southeast Asian societies during this period.

- What geographic features (rivers, mountains, islands, straits, etc.) shape Southeast Asia?
- What makes Southeast Asia unique geographically compared to other regions of the world?
- Based on the map, why were the kingdoms of Southeast Asia exposed to so many cross-cultural influences?

of a movable type printing press by the artisan Bi Sheng around 1040. Song dynasty printed books established classical Chinese as the common language of educated classes in East Asia. The Song government used its plentiful supply of paper to print books, especially medical texts, and to distribute calendars. The private publishing industry expanded, and printing houses throughout the country produced Confucian classics, works on history, philosophical treatises, and literature—all of which figured in the civil service examinations. Buddhist publications, too, were available everywhere.

China's huge population base, coupled with a strong agrarian base and manufacturing innovations, made it the wealthiest of the four major cultural spheres, and its common language and Confucian civil service system, which enabled a transfer of power from hereditary aristocrats to Confucian scholars, made it the most unified. China's influence on the surrounding region was tremendous.

Christian Europe

Core Objectives

COMPARE the role that religions and migration played in forging unified identities in Europe, India, and the Islamic worlds.

Europe, from 1000 to 1300 CE, was a region of strong contrasts. Intensely localized power was balanced by a shared sense of Europe's place in the world, especially with respect to Christian identity. Some inhabitants even began to believe in the existence of something called "Europe" and increasingly referred to themselves as "Europeans" (see Map 10.7), especially in contrast to the world of Islam to the east and south.

LOCALIZATION OF POWER

The collapse of Charlemagne's empire had exposed much of northern Europe to invasion, principally from the Vikings, and left the peasantry there with no central authority to protect them from local warlords. Armed with deadly weapons, these strongmen collected taxes, imposed forced labor, and became the unchallenged rulers of society. Peasants toiled under the authority of these landholding lords, who controlled every detail of their subjects' lives. The Franks (in northern France) were the trendsetters for this development in eleventh- and twelfth-century Europe.

manorialism
System in which the manor (a lord's home, its associated industry, and surrounding fields) served as the basic unit of economic power; an alternative to the concept of feudalism (the hierarchical relationships of king, lords, and peasantry) for thinking about the nature of power in western Europe from 1000 to 1300 CE.

The peasantry's subjugation to this knightly class was at the heart of a system scholars have called feudalism (emphasizing the power of the local lords over the peasantry), but a more accurate term for the system is **manorialism**, which emphasizes instead the manor's role as the basic unit of economic power. The manor comprised the lord's fortified home (or castle), the surrounding fields controlled by the lord but worked by peasants (as free tenants or as serfs tied to the land), and the village in which those peasants lived. Although manorialism was driven by agriculture, limited manufacturing and trade augmented the manor economy. This system harnessed agrarian energy

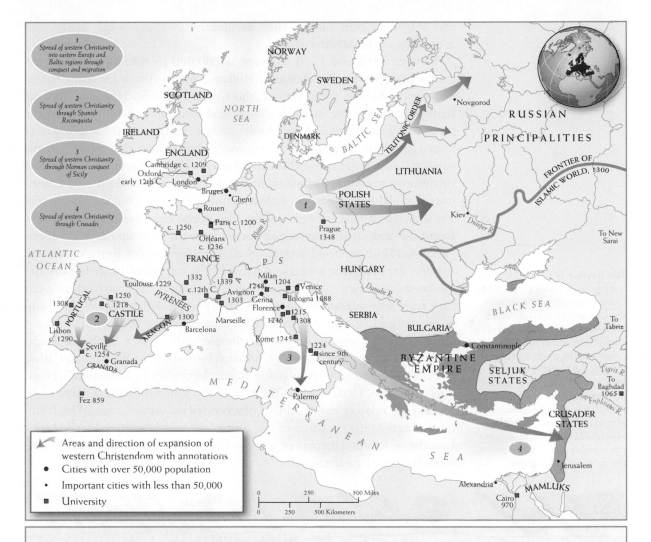

Map 10.7 Western Christendom in 1300

Catholic Europe expanded geographically and integrated culturally during this era.

- According to this map, into what areas did western Christendom successfully expand?
- What were the different means by which western Christianity expanded?
- Which are the earliest universities on the map? What might account for the flourishing of universities where they were located?

and helped western Europe shed its identity as a somewhat "barbarian" appendage of the Mediterranean.

Between 1100 and 1200, as many as 200,000 pioneering peasants emigrated from present-day Belgium, Holland, and northern Germany to the frontiers of Europe (now Poland, the Czech Republic, Hungary, and the Baltic states). Despite its harsh climate and landscape, the area offered the promise of freedom from feudal lords' arbitrary justice and the imposition of forced labor that the peasants had experienced in western Europe. In a fragile balance between the native elites and liberty-seeking newcomers, castles and villages echoing the landscape of manorial France now replaced local economies that had been based on gathering honey, hunting, and the slave trade. For a thousand miles along the Baltic Sea, forest clearings dotted with new farmsteads and small towns edged inward from the coast up the river valleys.

Russian lands modeled themselves after Byzantium, not Rome or western Europe. Set in a giant borderland between the steppes of Inner Eurasia and the booming centers of Europe, Russia's cities lay at the crossroads of overland trade and migration. These cities were not agrarian centers, but hubs of expanding long-distance trade. Kiev became one of the region's greatest urban centers, a small-scale Constantinople with its own miniature Hagia Sophia (see Chapter 8). Russian Christians looked not to the Roman Catholic faith associated with the popes in Rome, but rather to Byzantium's Hagia Sophia and the Orthodoxy of the east as the source of religious authority. Russian Christianity remained that of a borderland—vivid oases of high culture set against the backdrop of vast forests and widely scattered settlements. Like the agricultural manors of western Europe, these Russian cities demonstrate the highly localized nature of power in Europe in this period.

The Bayeux Tapestry This tapestry was allegedly prepared by Queen Matilda, wife of William the Conqueror, and her ladies to celebrate the successful invasion of England in 1066. These embroidering women captured the intense brutality of the invasion not only in the central narrative thread showing spears flying, long shields studded with arrows, and cavalry galloping in on great horses, but also in the margins where chain mail is being ripped off corpses.

WHAT WAS CHRISTIAN EUROPE?

Christianity in this era—primarily the Roman Catholicism of the west, but also the Orthodoxy of the east—became a universalizing faith that transformed the region becoming known as "Europe." The Christianity of post-Roman Europe had been a religion of monks, and its most dynamic centers were great monasteries. Members of the laity were expected to revere and support their monks, nuns, and clergy, but not to imitate them. By 1200, all this had changed. The internal colonization of western Europe—the clearing of woods and founding of villages—ensured that parish churches arose in all but the wildest landscapes. Now the clergy reached more deeply into the private lives of the laity. Marriage and divorce, previously considered family matters, became the domain of the church.

New understandings of religious devotion and innovative institutions for learning developed in the west. For instance, the followers of Francis of Assisi (1182–1226) emerged as an order of preachers who brought a message of repentance. Franciscans encouraged the laity—from the poorest to the elite—to feel remorse for their wrongdoings, to confess their sins to local priests, and to strive to be better Christians. At nearly the same time, intellectuals were beginning to gather in Paris to form one of the first European universities, a sort of trade guild of scholars. These professional thinkers endeavored to prove that Christianity was the only religion that fully addressed the concerns of all rational human beings. Such was the message of Thomas Aquinas, who wrote *Summa contra Gentiles* (Summary of Christian Belief against Non-Christians) in 1264. The growing number of churches, new religious orders, and universities began to change what it meant to live in a "Christian Europe."

RELATIONS WITH THE ISLAMIC WORLD

In the late eleventh century, western Europeans launched the Crusades, a wave of attacks against the Muslim world. The First Crusade began in 1095, when Pope Urban II appealed to the warrior nobility of France to put their violence to good use: they should combine their role as pilgrims to Jerusalem

Crusader Kneeling, this Crusader promises to serve God (as he would serve a feudal lord) by going to fight on a Crusade (as he would fight for any lord to whom he had sworn loyalty). The two kinds of loyalty—to God and to one's lord—were deliberately intertwined in promoting the Crusades. Both were about war. But fighting for God was unambiguously good, while fighting for a lord was not always so clear-cut.

with that of soldiers in order to free the Christian "holy land" from Muslim rule. Such a just war, the clergy proposed, was a means for absolution, not a source of sin.

Starting in 1097, an armed host of around 60,000 men set out from north-western Europe to seize Jerusalem. The crusading forces included knights in heavy armor as well as people drawn from Europe's impoverished masses, who joined the movement to help besiege cities and construct a network of castles as the Christian knights drove their frontier forward. The fleets of Venice, Genoa, and Pisa helped transport later Crusaders and supplied the kingdoms they created as they moved eastward. Later Crusaders, espe-cially those from the upper class, brought their wives, who found a degree of autonomy away from their homeland. Eleanor of Aquitaine, for example, led her own army. Melisende (r. 1131–1152), born Armenian royalty in the Crusader state of Edessa, ruled as queen of Jerusalem after her father's death, despite occasional attempts by her husband and later her son to challenge her authority. Regarded as wise and experienced in affairs of the state, she was popular with local Christians. As a result, the society of the Crusader states remained more open to women and the lower classes than in Europe. There are even accounts of a children's crusade (1212), inspired by the visions of a boy. Over time, the Crusades drew together a range of peoples from varied walks of life in common purpose.

No fewer than nine Crusades were fought over the two centuries that fol-lowed Urban II's call; but none of the coalitions, in the end, created lasting Christian kingdoms in the lands the Crusaders "reconquered." Most knights returned home, their epic pilgrimages completed. The remaining fragile net-work of Crusader lordships barely threatened the Islamic heartland. The real prosperity and the capital cities of Muslim kingdoms lay inland, away from the coast—at Cairo, Damascus, and Baghdad. The assaults' long-term effect was to harden Muslim feelings against the Franks and the millions of non-western Christians who had previously lived peacefully in Egypt and Syria.

Even so, a range of sources offer Muslim and Christian perspectives that show tolerance of, and curiosity about, each other. For example, Usāmah Ibn Munqidh (1095–1188), a learned Syrian leader, describes his shock at the Frankish Crusaders' backward medical practices and the freedom they offered their wives, in addition to well-meaning exchanges such as a partic-ular Frank's confusion about the direction in which Muslims pray. Similarly, Jean de Joinville (1224–1317), a French chronicler of Louis X of France who led the Seventh Crusade, marveled at the order within the sultan's camp and the role of musicians in calling the Muslim forces to hear the sultan's orders.

Other campaigns of Christian expansion, like the Iberian efforts to drive out the Muslims, were more successful. Beginning with the capture of Toledo in 1061, the Christian kings of northern Spain slowly pushed back the Muslims. Eventually they reached the heart of Andalusia in southern

Iberia and conquered Seville, adding more than 100,000 square miles of territory to Christian Europe. Another force, from northern France, crossed Italy to conquer Muslim-held Sicily, ensuring Christian rule in that strategically located mid-Mediterranean island. Unlike the Crusaders' fragile foothold at the edge of the Middle East, these two conquests were a turning point in relations between Christian and Muslim power in the Mediterranean. Christianity—and in particular the rise of the Roman Catholic Church, the spread of universities, and the fight against the Muslims in their native and spiritual homelands—was a force that helped create a cultural sphere known as Europe, whose peoples would become known as European, at the western end of the Afro-Eurasian landmass during this period.

Worlds Coming Together: Sub-Saharan Africa and the Americas

From 1000 to 1300 CE, sub-Saharan Africa and the Americas became far more internally integrated—culturally, economically, and politically—than before. Islam's spread and the growing trade in gold, enslaved people, and other commodities brought sub-Saharan Africa more fully into the exchange networks of the Eastern Hemisphere, but the Americas remained isolated from Afro-Eurasian networks for several more centuries.

Core Objectives

COMPARE the internal integration and external interactions of sub-Saharan Africa with those of the Americas, and with the connected Eurasian world.

SUB-SAHARAN AFRICA COMES TOGETHER

During this period, sub-Saharan Africa's relationship to the rest of the world changed dramatically. While sub-Saharan Africa had never been a world entirely apart before 1000 CE, its integration with Eurasia now became much stronger. Increasingly, its hinterlands found themselves touched by the commercial and migratory impulses emanating from the Indian Ocean and Arabian Sea transformations. (See Map 10.8.)

West Africa and the Mande-Speaking Peoples Once trade routes bridged the Sahara Desert (see Chapter 9), the flow of commodities and ideas linked sub-Saharan Africa to North Africa and Southwest Asia. As the savanna region became increasingly connected to developments in Eurasia, Mande-speaking peoples became the primary agents for integration within and beyond West Africa. Exploiting their expertise in commerce and political organization, the Mande edged out rivals. The Mande homeland was a vast area, 1,000 miles wide, between the bend in the Senegal River to the west and the bend of the Niger River to the east, and stretching more than 2,000 miles from the Senegal River in the north to the Bandama River in the south.

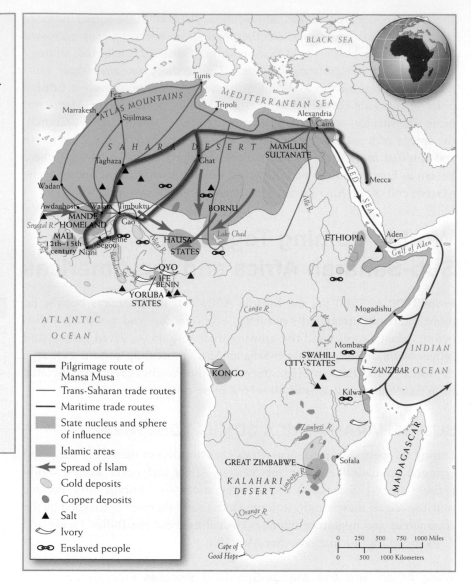

Map 10.8 Sub-Saharan Africa, 1300

Increased commercial contacts influenced the religious and political dimensions of sub-Saharan Africa at this time. Compare this map with Map 9.3.

- Where had strong Islamic communities emerged by 1300? By what routes might Islam have spread to those areas?

- According to this map, what types of activity were taking place in sub-Saharan West Africa?

- What goods were traded in sub-Saharan Africa, and along what routes did those exchanges take place?

Map labels:

BLACK SEA

MEDITERRANEAN SEA

Tunis
Fez
Marrakesh
ATLAS MOUNTAINS
Sijilmasa
Tripoli
Alexandria
Cairo

S A H A R A   D E S E R T

MAMLUK SULTANATE

Taghaza
Ghat
Mecca

Wadan
Awdaghost
Walata
Timbuktu
BORNU
Senegal R.
MANDE HOMELAND
Gao
MALI 12th–15th century
Jenne
Segou
Niani
Lake Chad
Nile R.
RED SEA
ETHIOPIA
Aden
Gulf of Aden

HAUSA STATES

OYO
IFE
BENIN
YORUBA STATES

Bani R.
Bandama R.

ATLANTIC OCEAN

Congo R.

Mogadishu

Mombasa
SWAHILI CITY-STATES
ZANZIBAR
INDIAN OCEAN
Kilwa

KONGO

Zambezi R.
GREAT ZIMBABWE
Sofala
KALAHARI DESERT
Limpopo R.
MADAGASCAR

Orange R.

Cape of Good Hope

Legend:

— Pilgrimage route of Mansa Musa
— Trans-Saharan trade routes
— Maritime trade routes
State nucleus and sphere of influence
Islamic areas
→ Spread of Islam
Gold deposits
Copper deposits
▲ Salt
Ivory
Enslaved people

0   250   500   750   1000 Miles
0   500   1000 Kilometers

By the eleventh century, the Mande-speaking peoples were spreading their cultural, commercial, and political hegemony from the savanna grasslands southward into the woodlands and tropical rain forests stretching to the Atlantic Ocean. Those dwelling in the rain forests organized small-scale societies led by local councils, while those in the savanna lands developed centralized forms of government under sacred kingships. Mande speakers believed that their kings had descended from the gods and that they enjoyed the gods' blessing.

As the Mande extended their territory to the Atlantic coast, they gained access to tradable items that residents of Africa's interior were eager to have—notably kola nuts and malaguetta peppers, for which the Mande exchanged iron products and manufactured textiles. Mande-speaking peoples, with their far-flung commercial networks and highly dispersed populations, dominated trans-Saharan trade in salt from the northern Sahel, gold from the Mande homeland, and enslaved people. By 1300, Mande-speaking merchants had followed the Senegal River to its outlet on the Atlantic coast and then pushed their commercial frontiers farther inland and down the coast. Thus, even before European explorers and traders arrived in the mid-fifteenth century, West African peoples had created dynamic networks linking the hinterlands with coastal trading hubs.

Mali Empire
West African empire, founded by the legendary king Sundiata in the early thirteenth century. It facilitated thriving commerce along routes linking the Atlantic Ocean, the Sahara, and beyond.

The Mali Empire In the early thirteenth century, the **Mali Empire** became the Mande successor state to the kingdom of Ghana (see Chapter 9). The origins of the Mali Empire and its legendary founder are enshrined in *The Epic of Sundiata*. Sundiata's triumph, which occurred in the first half of the thirteenth century, marked the victory of new cavalry forces over traditional foot soldiers. Horses now became prestige objects for the savanna peoples, symbols of state power.

Under the Mali Empire, commerce was in full swing. With Mande trade routes extending to the Atlantic Ocean and spanning the Sahara Desert, West Africa was no longer an isolated periphery of the central Muslim lands. Mansa Musa (r. 1312–1332), perhaps Mali's most famous sovereign, made a celebrated *hajj*, or pilgrimage to Mecca, in 1324–1325. He traveled through Cairo and impressed crowds with the size of his retinue—including soldiers, wives, consorts, and as many as 12,000 enslaved people—and his displays of wealth, especially many dazzling items made of gold. Mansa Musa's lengthy three-month stopover in Cairo, one of Islam's primary cities, astonished the Egyptian elite and awakened much of the world to the fact that Islam had spread far below the Sahara and that a sub-Saharan state could mount such an impressive display of power and wealth.

The Mali Empire boasted two of West Africa's largest cities. Jenne, an entrepôt dating back to 200 BCE, was a vital assembly point for caravans laden with salt, gold, and enslaved people preparing for journeys west to the Atlantic coast and north over the Sahara. More spectacular was the city of Timbuktu; founded around 1100 as a seasonal camp for nomads, it grew in

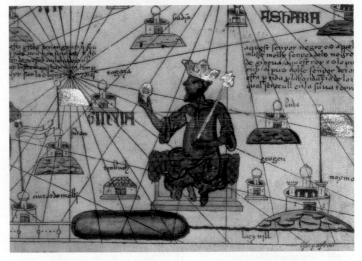

West African Gold This detail from the 1375 *Catalan Atlas* shows Mansa Musa, the king of Mali, on his throne, surrounded by images of gold. When Mansa Musa traveled on pilgrimage to Mecca (1324–1325), his caravan brought immense quantities of gold—nearly 100 camels, each bearing 300-pound sacks of gold—and spent it so generously that the contemporary writer al-Umari (1301–1349) reported that the influx of gold deflated its value in the Mediterranean economy.

Great Zimbabwe Massive stone walls, at points as high as 36 feet, surrounded the "Great Enclosure" that makes up part of the ruins of Great Zimbabwe. The city, covering almost 3 square miles, was a center of the gold trade between the East African coastal peoples and traders sailing on the Indian Ocean. Great Zimbabwe flourished during the thirteenth, fourteenth, and fifteenth centuries.

size and importance under the patronage of various Mali kings. By the fourteenth century, it was a thriving commercial, intellectual, and religious center famed for its three large mosques, which are still standing.

Trade between East Africa and the Indian Ocean Africa's eastern and southern regions were also integrated into long-distance trading systems. Because of the monsoon winds, East Africa was a logical end point for much of the Indian Ocean trade. Swahili peoples living along that coast became brokers for trade from the Arabian Peninsula, the Persian Gulf territories, and the western coast of India. Merchants in the city of Kilwa on the coast of present-day Tanzania brought ivory, gold, enslaved people, and other items from the interior and shipped them to destinations around the Indian Ocean.

Shona-speaking peoples grew rich by mining the gold ore in the highlands between the Limpopo and Zambezi Rivers. By 1000 CE, the Shona had founded up to fifty small religious and political centers, each one erected from stone to display its power over the peasant villages surrounding it. Around 1100, one of these centers, Great Zimbabwe, stood supreme among the Shona. Built on the fortunes made from gold, its most impressive landmark was a massive elliptical building made of stones fitted so expertly that they needed no grouting.

Enslaved African people were as valuable as African gold in shipments to Indian Ocean as well as Mediterranean markets. After Islam spread into Africa and sailing techniques improved, the slave trade across the Sahara Desert and Indian Ocean boomed. Although the Quran mitigated the severity of slavery by requiring Muslim enslavers to treat their workers kindly and praising those who freed the enslaved, the African slave trade flourished under Islam. Africans became enslaved either by being taken as prisoners of war or by being sold into slavery as punishment for committing a crime. Enslaved people might work as soldiers, seafarers on dhows, domestic servants, or plantation workers. Conditions for plantation laborers on the agricultural estates of lower Iraq were so oppressive that they led, in the ninth century CE, to one of the most significant slave wars documented in world history (the Zanj rebellion). Yet in this era, plantation slave labor, like that which later became prominent in the Americas in the nineteenth century, was the exception, not the rule.

THE AMERICAS

During this period, the Americas were untouched by the connections reverberating across Afro-Eurasia. Apart from limited Viking contacts in North America (see Chapter 9), navigators still did not cross the large oceans that separated the Americas from other lands. Yet, here, too, commercial and expansionist impulses fostered closer contact among peoples who lived there.

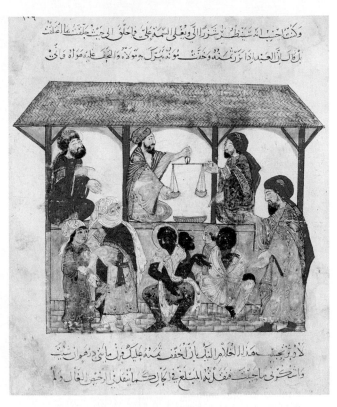

Enslaved, Bought, and Sold
Enslaved men and women were a common commodity in the marketplaces of the Islamic world. Turkish conquests during the years from 1000 to 1300 CE put many prisoners on the slave market.

Andean States of South America Growth and prosperity in the Andean region gave rise to South America's first empire. The **Chimú Empire** developed early in the second millennium in the fertile Moche Valley bordering the Pacific Ocean. (See Map 10.9.) Ultimately, the Moche people expanded their influence across numerous valleys and ecological zones, from pastoral highlands to rich valley floodplains to the fecund fishing grounds of the Pacific coast. As their geographic reach grew, so did their wealth.

The Chimú economy was successful because it was highly commercialized. Agriculture was its base, and complex irrigation systems turned the arid coast into a string of fertile oases capable of feeding an increasingly dispersed population. Cotton became a lucrative export to distant markets along the Andes. Parades of llamas and porters lugged these commodities up and down the steep mountain chains that form the spine of South America. A well-trained bureaucracy oversaw the construction and maintenance of canals, and a hierarchy of provincial administrators watched over commercial hinterlands.

The Chimú Empire's biggest city was Chan Chan, which had been growing ever larger since its founding around 900 CE. By the time the Chimú Empire was thriving, Chan Chan held a core population of 30,000 inhabitants. A sprawling walled metropolis covering nearly 10 square miles, with extensive roads circulating through its neighborhoods, Chan Chan boasted ten huge palaces at its center. Protected by thick walls 30 feet high, these

Chimú Empire
South America's first empire, centered at Chan Chan, in the Moche Valley on the Pacific coast from 1000 through 1470 CE, whose development was fueled by agriculture and commercial exchange.

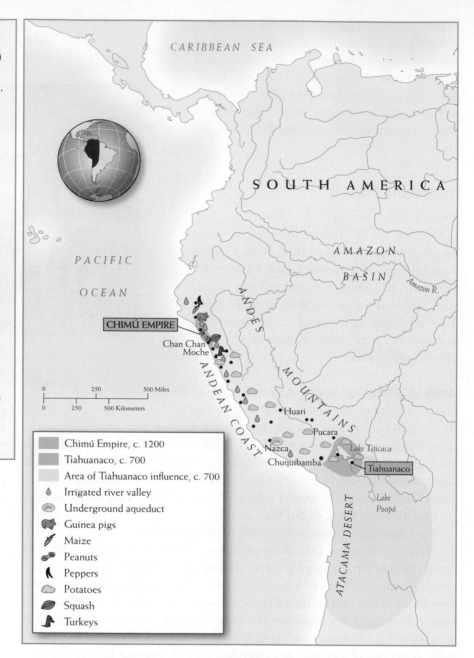

Map 10.9 Andean States, c. 700–1400 CE

Although the Andes region of South America was isolated from Afro-Eurasian developments before 1500, it was not stagnant. Indeed, political and cultural integration brought the peoples of this region closer together.

- Where are the areas of Chimú Empire and Tiahuanaco influence on the map?
- What was the ecology and geography of each region, and how might that have shaped each region's development?
- What crops and animals did the Chimú and Tiahuanaco benefit from?

CARIBBEAN SEA

SOUTH AMERICA

PACIFIC OCEAN

AMAZON BASIN

Amazon R.

ANDES MOUNTAINS

CHIMÚ EMPIRE

Chan Chan
Moche

ANDEAN COAST

Huari

Pucara

Nazca

Lake Titicaca

Chuquibamba

Tiahuanaco

Lake Poopó

ATACAMA DESERT

0   250   500 Miles
0   250   500 Kilometers

Chimú Empire, c. 1200
Tiahuanaco, c. 700
Area of Tiahuanaco influence, c. 700
Irrigated river valley
Underground aqueduct
Guinea pigs
Maize
Peanuts
Peppers
Potatoes
Squash
Turkeys

opulent residence halls symbolized the rulers' power. Within the compound, emperors erected burial complexes for storing their accumulated riches: fine cloth, gold and silver objects, splendid *Spondylus* shells, and other luxury goods. Around the compound spread neighborhoods for nobles and artisans; farther out stood rows of commoners' houses. The Chimú regime, centered

Chan Chan The image shows some of the remains of Chan Chan. The city covered 15 square miles and was divided into neighborhoods for nobles, artisans, and commoners, with the elites living closest to the hub of governmental and spiritual power.

at Chan Chan, lasted until Inca armies invaded in the 1460s and incorporated the Pacific state into their own immense empire.

Toltecs in Mesoamerica Additional hubs of regional trade developed farther north. By 1000 CE, Mesoamerica had seen the rise and fall of several complex societies, including Teotihuacán and the Maya (see Chapter 8). Caravans of porters bound the region together, working the intricate roads that connected the coast of the Gulf of Mexico to the Pacific and the southern lowlands of Central America to the arid regions of modern Texas. (See Map 10.10.) The **Toltecs** filled the political vacuum left by the decline of Teotihuacán and tapped into the commercial network radiating from the rich valley of central Mexico.

The Toltecs grew to dominate the valley of Mexico between 900 and 1100 CE. They were a combination of migrant groups, farmers from the north and refugees from the south fleeing the strife that followed Teotihuacán's demise. These migrants settled northwest of Teotihuacán as the city waned, making their capital at Tula. They relied on a maize-based economy supplemented by beans, squash, and dog, deer, and rabbit meat. Their rulers made sure that enterprising merchants provided them with status goods such as ornamental pottery, rare shells and stones, and precious skins and feathers.

Tula was a commercial hub, a political capital, and a ceremonial center. While its layout differed from Teotihuacán's, many features revealed borrowings from other Mesoamerican peoples. Temples consisted of giant pyramids topped by colossal stone soldiers, and ball courts where subjects and conquered peoples alike played their ritual sport were found everywhere.

Toltecs
Mesoamerican peoples who filled the political vacuum left by Teotihuacán's decline; established a temple-filled capital and commercial hub at Tula.

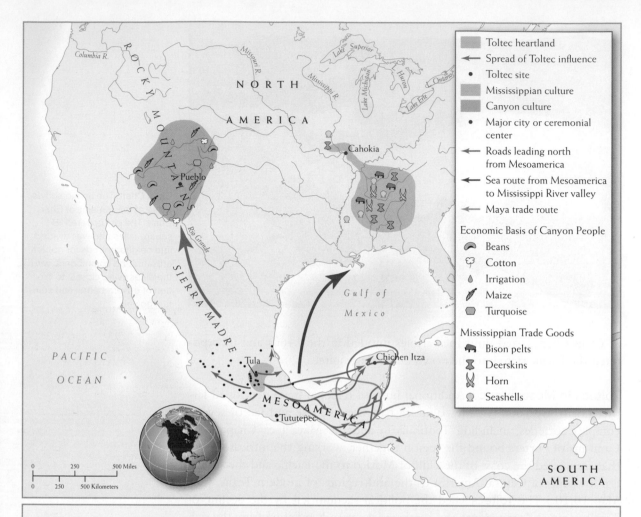

Map 10.10 Commercial Hubs in Mesoamerica and North America, 1000 CE

....

Both Cahokia and Tula were commercial hubs of vibrant regional trade networks.

- What routes linked Tula and the Toltecs with other regions?
- What goods circulated in the regions of Pueblo and Cahokia?
- Based on the map, what appear to be some of the differences between Canyon culture, Mississippian culture, and the Toltecs?

The architecture and monumental art reflected the mixed and migratory origins of the Toltecs in a combination of Maya and Teotihuacáno influences. At its height, the Toltec capital teemed with 60,000 people, a huge metropolis by contemporary European standards (if small by Song Chinese and Abbasid standards).

Cahokians in North America As in South America and Mesoamerica, cities took shape at the hubs of trading networks across North America. The largest was **Cahokia**, along the Mississippi River near modern-day East St. Louis, Illinois. A city of about 15,000, it approximated the size of London at the time. Farmers and hunters had settled in the region around 600 CE, attracted by its rich soil, its woodlands that provided fuel and game, and its access to trade via the Mississippi. Eventually, fields of maize and other crops fanned out toward the horizon. The hoe replaced the trusty digging stick, and satellite towns erected granaries to hold the growing harvests.

By 1000 CE, Cahokia was an established commercial center for regional and long-distance trade. The hinterlands produced staples for Cahokia's urban consumers, and in return its crafts rode inland on the backs of porters and to distant markets in canoes. Woven fabrics and ceramics from Cahokia were exchanged for mica from the Appalachian Mountains, seashells and sharks' teeth from the Gulf of Mexico, and copper from the upper Great Lakes. Cahokia became more than an importer and exporter: it was the exchange hub for an entire regional network trading in salt, tools, pottery, woven stuffs, jewelry, and ceremonial goods.

Dominating Cahokia's urban landscape were enormous earthen mounds of sand and clay (thus the Cahokians' nickname of "mound people"). It was from these artificial hills that the people honored spiritual forces. Building these types of structures without draft animals, hydraulic tools, or even wheels was labor-intensive, so the Cahokians recruited neighboring people to help. A palisade around the city protected the metropolis from marauders.

Ultimately, Cahokia's success bred its downfall. As woodlands fell to the axe and the soil lost its nutrients, timber and food became scarce. In contrast to the sturdy dhows of the Arabian Sea and the bulky junks of the China seas, Cahokia's river canoes could carry only limited cargoes. Cahokia's commercial networks met their limits. When the creeks that fed its water system could not keep up with demand, engineers changed their course, but to no avail. By 1350 the city was practically empty. But Cahokia represented the growing networks of trade and migration in North America and the ability of North Americans to organize vibrant commercial societies.

Two forces contributed to greater integration in sub-Saharan Africa and the Americas from 1000 to 1300 CE: commercial exchange (of salt, gold,

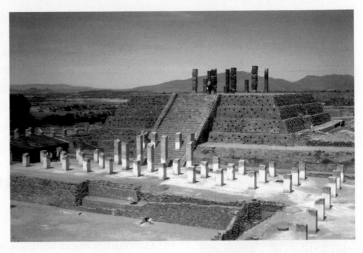

Toltec Temple Tula, the capital of the Toltec Empire, carried on the Mesoamerican tradition of locating ceremonial architecture at the center of the city. The Pyramid of the Morning Star cast its shadow over all other buildings. And above them stood columns of the Atlantes, carved Toltec god-warriors, the figurative pillars of the empire itself. The walls of this pyramid were likely embellished with images of snakes and skulls. The north face of the pyramid has the image of a snake devouring a human.

Cahokia
Commercial city on the Mississippi River for regional and long-distance trade of commodities such as salt, shells, and skins and of manufactured goods such as pottery, textiles, and jewelry; marked by massive artificial hills, akin to earthen pyramids, used to honor spiritual forces.

ivory, and enslaved people in sub-Saharan Africa and shells, pottery, textiles, and metals in the Americas) and urbanization (at Jenne, Timbuktu, and Great Zimbabwe in sub-Saharan Africa and at Chan Chan, Tula, and Cahokia in the Americas). By 1300, trans-Saharan and Indian Ocean exchange had brought Africa into full-fledged Afro-Eurasian networks of exchange and, as we will see in Chapter 12, transatlantic exchange would soon bring the Americas into a global network.

The Mongol Transformation of Afro-Eurasia

Core Objectives

ASSESS the impacts that the Mongol Empire had on Afro-Eurasian peoples and places.

Commercial networks were clearly one way to integrate the world. But just as long-distance trade could connect people, so could conquerors. The Inner Eurasian steppes had already unleashed horse-riding warriors such as the Kushans and Xiongnu (see Chapters 6 and 7). Now, the Mongols created an empire that straddled east and west, expanding their reach not only through brutal conquest but also through intensified trade and cultural exchange. (See Map 10.11.)

WHO WERE THE MONGOLS?

The Mongols were a combination of forest and steppe peoples. Residing in circular, felt-covered tents, which they shared with some of their animals, they lived by hunting and livestock herding. They changed campgrounds with the seasons. Life on the steppes was such a constant struggle that only the strong survived. Their food, primarily animal products, provided high levels of protein, which built up their muscle mass and their strength. Always on the march, their society resembled a perpetual standing army with bands of well-disciplined military units led by commanders chosen for their skill.

Wielding heavy compound bows made of sinew, wood, and horn, Mongol archers were deadly accurate at over 200 yards—even at full gallop. Their small but sturdy horses, capable of withstanding extreme cold, bore saddles with high supports in front and back, enabling the warriors to maneuver at high speeds. With their feet secure in iron stirrups, the archers could rise in their saddles to aim their arrows without stopping. These expert horsemen often remained in the saddle all day and night, even sleeping while their horses continued on. Each warrior kept many horses, replacing tired mounts with fresh ones so that the armies could cover up to 70 miles per day.

Mongol tribes solidified their conquests by extending kinship networks, building an empire out of an expanding confederation of familial tribes. The tents, or households, were interrelated mostly by marriage: they were alliances sealed by the exchange of daughters. Conquering men married conquered women, and conquered men were selected to marry the conquerors' women. Chinggis Khan (the founder of the Mongol dynasty) may have had more than 500 wives, most of them daughters of tribes that he conquered or that allied with him.

Elite women could play important political roles. Chinggis Khan's mother, Hoelun, and his first wife, Börte, were instrumental in his rise to power, but even before playing the role of khan maker, women had figured large in Mongol tribal politics. In the generation after Chinggis, Sorghaghtani Beki, a Nestorian Christian and the mother of Kublai Khan (the first official Mongol ruler of China), helped engineer her sons' rule. Illiterate herself, she made sure that each son acquired a second language to aid in administering conquered lands. Despite her own Christian faith, Sorghaghtani gathered Confucian scholars to prepare Kublai Khan to rule China. Chabi, Kublai's senior wife, offered patronage to Tibetan monks who set about converting the Mongol elite in China to Tibetan Buddhism. While some elite Mongol women played a role in fostering religious diversity, others took part in battles. Khutulun, a niece of Kublai Khan, became famous for besting men in wrestling matches and claiming their horses as spoils.

Yet the political influence wielded by these later *khātūns* (Mongol queens) and other elite women of the Mongol ruling class is only one part of the story. Women in Mongol society were responsible for bearing and rearing children, shearing and milking livestock, and processing animal pelts for clothing. They organized camp logistics in times of peace and war. Although women were often bought and sold, Mongol wives had the right to own property and to divorce. More recent studies of Mongol women have emphasized the economic influence they wielded as they acquired this wealth and property of their own. Central to making sense of Mongol women is recognizing that theirs was a changing story. Mongol family dynamics and gender roles changed due not only to the dramatic and relatively swift transformation of the Mongols from a pastoral steppe society to a settled empire, but also to the regional differences in ideas about women's roles in the varied regions into which the Mongols spread.

CONQUEST AND EMPIRE

The Mongols' need for grazing lands contributed to their desire to conquer distant fertile belts and rich cities. The Mongols depended on settled peoples for grain and manufactured goods, including iron for tools, wagons, weapons, bridles, and stirrups. Their first expansionist forays followed caravan routes.

The Mongol expansion began in 1206 under a united cluster of tribes. These tribes were unified by a gathering of clan heads who chose one of those

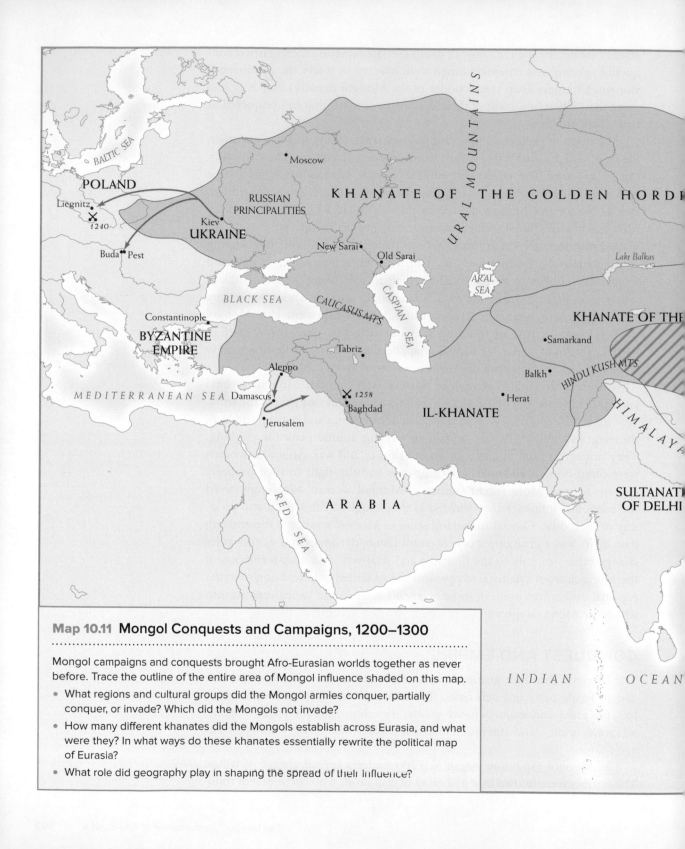

Map 10.11 Mongol Conquests and Campaigns, 1200–1300

Mongol campaigns and conquests brought Afro-Eurasian worlds together as never before. Trace the outline of the entire area of Mongol influence shaded on this map.

- What regions and cultural groups did the Mongol armies conquer, partially conquer, or invade? Which did the Mongols not invade?
- How many different khanates did the Mongols establish across Eurasia, and what were they? In what ways do these khanates essentially rewrite the political map of Eurasia?
- What role did geography play in shaping the spread of their influence?

Map labels:
BALTIC SEA
POLAND
Liegnitz
1240
Buda • Pest
Moscow
RUSSIAN PRINCIPALITIES
Kiev
UKRAINE
KHANATE OF THE GOLDEN HORDE
URAL MOUNTAINS
New Sarai • Old Sarai
Lake Balkas
ARAL SEA
CASPIAN SEA
BLACK SEA
CAUCASUS MTS.
Constantinople
BYZANTINE EMPIRE
Tabriz
KHANATE OF THE
Samarkand
Aleppo
Balkh
HINDU KUSH MTS.
Damascus
1258
Herat
MEDITERRANEAN SEA
Baghdad
Jerusalem
IL-KHANATE
HIMALAYA
RED SEA
ARABIA
SULTANATE OF DELHI
INDIAN OCEAN

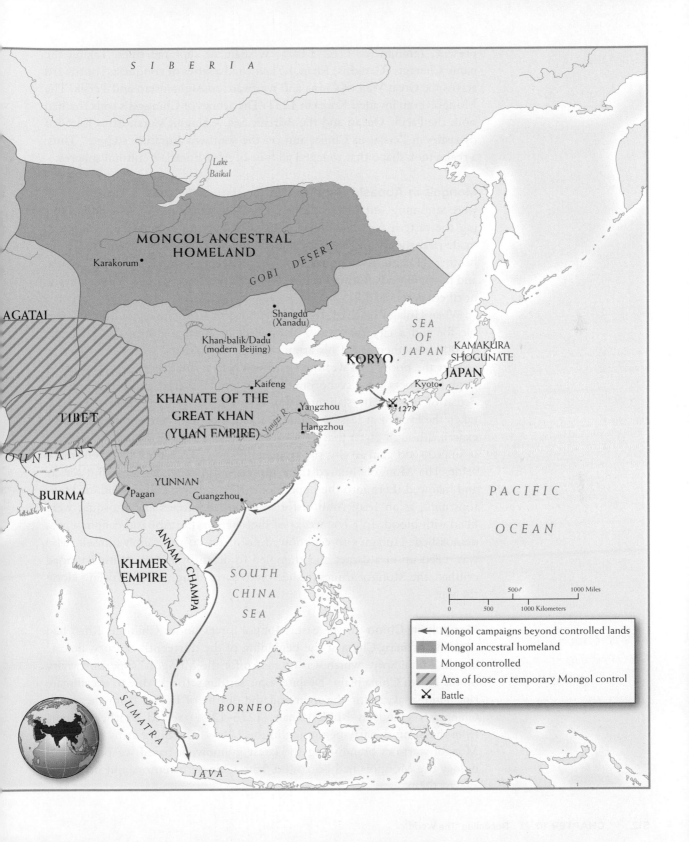

SIBERIA

Lake
Baikal

MONGOL ANCESTRAL
HOMELAND

GOBI DESERT

Karakorum

AGATAI

Shangdu
(Xanadu)

Khan-balik/Dadu
(modern Beijing)

TIBET

KHANATE OF THE
GREAT KHAN
(YUAN EMPIRE)

Kaifeng

Yangzhou

Hangzhou

Yangzi R.

KORYO

SEA
OF
JAPAN

KAMAKURA
SHOGUNATE

Kyoto

JAPAN

1279

OUNTAINS

BURMA

YUNNAN

Pagan

Guangzhou

KHMER
EMPIRE

ANNAM

CHAMPA

SOUTH
CHINA
SEA

PACIFIC

OCEAN

SUMATRA

BORNEO

JAVA

0   500   1000 Miles

0   500   1000 Kilometers

⟵ Mongol campaigns beyond controlled lands

Mongol ancestral homeland

Mongol controlled

Area of loose or temporary Mongol control

✕ Battle

present, Temüjin (c. 1162–1227), as khan, or supreme ruler. Taking the name Chinggis (Genghis) Khan, he launched a series of conquests southward across the Great Wall of China and westward to Afghanistan and Persia. The Mongols even invaded Korea in 1231. The armies of Chinggis's sons reached both the Pacific Ocean and the Adriatic Sea. Chinggis's grandsons founded dynasties in Persia, in China, and on the southern Eurasian steppes. Thus, a realm took shape that touched all four of Afro-Eurasia's cultural spheres.

Mongols in Abbasid Baghdad In the thirteenth century, Mongol tribes were streaming out of the steppes, crossing the whole of Asia and entering the eastern parts of Europe. Mongke Khan, a grandson of Chinggis, made clear the Mongol aspiration to world domination: he commanded his brother, Hulagu, to conquer Iran, Syria, Egypt, Byzantium, and Armenia, and he appointed another brother, Kublai, to rule over China, Tibet, and the northern parts of India.

When Hulagu reached Abbasid Baghdad in 1258, he encountered a feeble foe and a city that was a shadow of its former glorious self. Merely 10,000 horsemen faced his army of 200,000 soldiers, who were eager to acquire the booty of a wealthy city. Even before the battle had taken place, Baghdadi poets were composing elegies for their dead and mourning the defeat of Islam. The slaughter was vast. Hulagu himself claimed to have taken the lives of at least 2 million people (two thousand thousands, to be exact), although given that he was boasting to a French king in an attempt to impress and gain an ally, the exaggerated numbers cannot be taken at face value. The Mongols hunted their adversaries in wells, latrines, and sewers and followed them into the upper floors of buildings, killing them on rooftops until, as an Iraqi Arab historian observed, streets and mosques were filled with blood. In a few weeks of sheer terror, the Abbasid caliphate was demolished. Hulagu's forces showed no mercy to the caliph himself, who was rolled up in a carpet and trampled to death by horses. With Baghdad crushed, the Mongol armies pushed on to Syria, slaughtering Muslims along the way.

Mongols in China In the east, Mongol forces under Chinggis Khan had entered northern China at the beginning of the thirteenth century, defeating the Khitai army, which was no match for the Mongols' superior cavalry on the North China plain. Despite some serious setbacks due to the climate (including malaria for the men and the deaths of horses from the heat), Chinggis's grandson Kublai Khan (1215–1294) seized southern China from the Song dynasty beginning in the 1260s. The Song army fell before Mongol warriors brandishing the latest gunpowder-based weapons, technology the Mongols had borrowed from Chinese inventors and now used against them.

Hangzhou, the last Song capital, fell in 1276. Kublai Khan's most able commander, Bayan, led his crack Mongol forces in seizing town after town, moving ever closer to the capital, while the Dowager Empress tried to buy them off, proposing substantial tribute payments, but Bayan was uncompromising. Once conquered, the Dowager Empress and Hangzhou were treated well by the Mongols. In fact, Hangzhou was still one of the greatest cities in the world when it was visited by the Venetian traveler Marco Polo in the 1280s and by the Muslim traveler Ibn Battuta in the 1340s. Both men agreed that neither Europe nor the Islamic world had anything like it.

Kublai Khan founded his Yuan dynasty with a capital at Khan-balik (also called Dadu, which became present-day Beijing). The Mongol conquest of both north and south changed China's political and social landscape. But Mongol rule did not impose rough steppe-land ways on the "civilized" urbanite Chinese. While non-Chinese outsiders took political control, they were a conquering elite that ruled over a vast Han majority. The result was a divided ruling system in which incumbent Chinese elites governed locally, while the newcomers managed the unifying central dynasty and collected taxes for the Mongols.

Southeast Asia also felt the whiplash of Kublai Khan's conquest. Circling Song defenses in southern China, the Mongols galloped southwest and conquered states in Yunnan and in Burma. From there, in the 1270s, the armies headed directly back east into the soft underbelly of the Song state. In this sweep, portions of mainland Southeast Asia became annexed to China for the first time. Kublai Khan used the conquered Chinese fleets to push his expansionism onto the high seas—meeting with failure during his unsuccessful

Mongol Warriors This miniature painting is one of the illustrations for *History* by Rashid al-Din, the most outstanding scholar under the Mongol regimes. Note the relatively small horses and strong bows used by the Mongol soldiers.

A Most Unusual Nomad State

Although nomadic pastoralists and sedentary agriculturalists depended on each other to flourish, their deep commitments to their institutions and ways of life made cooperation difficult. Pastoralists endeavored to be as self-sufficient as possible. They scorned peoples who dug in the soil. On the other hand, as we noted in Chapter 3, sedentary peoples, most notably their literate members, regarded herders as uncivilized barbarians. The Chinese, for instance, saw the steppe peoples who lived to the north of them, and who often invaded their state, as greedy, violent raiders from barbarian lands.

The Mongols were the quintessential pastoral nomads. Very little is known of their early history, largely because they were a small, fragmented, and powerless people living along the borderlands of southern Siberia, eastern Mongolia, and northwestern Manchuria. To their east lived the Tatars, and to their west the Uighurs and Khitai, far more powerful pastoral peoples from whom the Mongols learned many

of their political and military skills. The Mongols first surface in Chinese sources during the Tang dynasty (618–907 CE). The Chinese, who feared the military capabilities of steppe peoples and were regularly invaded and even conquered by those peoples, had little fear of the Mongols at this time, regarding them as an insignificant community far from the empire's northern frontier. The Mongols were well known, however, for raiding, looting, and violence toward outsiders and among themselves.

Few individuals have had a greater impact on world history than the founder of the Mongol state, Temüjin (c. 1162–1227). His youthful travails hardened him as a warrior and made him a leader. Having lost his father at a young age and being the eldest of his siblings, he, along with his mother, endured a harsh existence. But as an adult, he unified warring Mongol clans and defeated the Mongols' enemies, either assimilating them to the Mongol way of life or exterminating them if they refused his leadership. In 1206,

as a result of his spectacular military successes, he took the name Chinggis Khan, meaning "supreme ruler." Not only did he bring most of Inner Asia under his rule, but his armies pushed southward into Manchuria and northern China and west toward central Asia and the Islamic states. At his death in 1227, he divided his vast territorial conquests among the four sons of his first wife, Börte. These men and their successors created four Mongol states, called khanates, loosely linked as an empire: Yuan China; the Khanate of the Golden Horde; the northern steppe (Khanate of the Chagatai); and Persia, known as the Il-Khanate.

The Mongols established their rule over settled societies in China, Iran, central Asia, and Russia, but then had to decide how to rule over sedentary populations. Specifically, the issue facing Mongol rulers was whether to foster close relations with the ruling classes of the conquered societies or stay apart, relying on military force. In truth, the Mongol Empire was fragmented and each state was

1274 and 1281 invasions of Japan from Korea. An ill-fated Javanese expedition to extend Mongol reach beyond the South China Sea in 1293 was Kublai Khan's last.

In the end, the Mongol Empire reached its outer limits. In the west, the Egyptian Mamluks stemmed the advancing Mongol armies and prevented Egypt from falling into their hands. In the east, the waters of the South China Sea and the Sea of Japan foiled Mongol expansion into Java and Japan. Better at conquering than governing, the Mongols struggled to rule their vast possessions in makeshift states. Bit by bit, they yielded control to local ruled in manifestly different ways. Yet one quality underlay all the Mongol states—the dominant presence of the Mongol military and the high prestige that was attached to being a Mongol. Commonly, pastoral nomads who conquered sedentary peoples kept their distance from those settled societies with their cities, bureaucracies, artisans, and priests, instead extracting tribute from them while maintaining their own distinctive way of life. For example, Chinggis forbade his followers to live in towns, and the Golden Horde Mongols lived separately from the peoples they conquered, maintaining their pastoral norms, content to receive tribute payments.

Early on, some of Chinggis's followers wanted to annihilate the northern Chinese population and turn the region into pure pastureland. Ogodei, Chinggis's third son and successor as the Great Khan, was opposed to Chinggis's merciless and destructive practices and ordered his followers not to kill or loot indiscriminately. One of Ogodei's successors, Kublai, became the founder of the Yuan dynasty (1279–1368) in China, claiming for himself the Chinese mandate of heaven. Even so, Kublai cherished his Mongol identity, never learned Chinese, and never consulted a book in Chinese. Moreover, the Yuan rulers divided the populations under their rule into four ranked tiers: the first was the Mongols themselves; the second, the non-Han Chinese of the western parts of Inner Asia, mainly nomads like themselves; the third, the northern Chinese, conquered early in the Mongol expansion; and the fourth, the southern Chinese, once ruled by the Song dynasty and the center of Confucian culture. In such a fashion, the Yuan dynasty, although centered in China proper—the heartland of urbanization and high culture—did not allow itself to be swallowed up by the Han population or its culture.

Thus, the Mongol Empire, which lasted for more than two centuries, made an uneasy accommodation with sedentary populations, with its rulers partially embracing the institutions of the sedentary peoples, but never fully renouncing their pastoral, nomadic ways.

Questions for Analysis

- How did nomads and sedentary peoples view one another?
- Why might one consider the Mongols in general, and Temüjin in particular, to be unlikely conquerors?
- In what ways did different Mongol leaders negotiate the difference between pastoral and sedentary ways?

Explore Further

Di Cosmo, Nicola, Allen J. Frank, and Peter Golden (eds.), *The Cambridge History of Inner Asia: The Chinggisid Age* (2009).

Khazanov, Anatoly M., *Nomads and the Outside World,* 2nd ed., trans. Julia Crookurden, with a foreword by Ernest Gellner (1994).

Mote, Frederick W., *Imperial China, 900–1800* (1999).

Rossabi, Morris, *A History of China* (2014).

Tanner, Harold M., *China: A History* (2009).

administrators and rulers who governed as their surrogates. There was also frequent feuding among the Mongol rulers themselves. In China and in Persia, Mongol rule collapsed in the fourteenth century. Ultimately, the Mongols would meet a deadly adversary even more brutal than they were: the plague of the fourteenth century (see Chapter 11).

Mongol conquest reshaped Afro-Eurasia's social landscape. Islam would never again have a unifying authority like the caliphate or a powerful center like Baghdad. China, too, was divided and changed by the Mongols' introduction of Persian, Islamic, and Byzantine influences into China's

architecture, art, science, and medicine. The Yuan policy of benign tolerance brought elements from Christianity, Judaism, Zoroastrianism, and Islam
into the Chinese mix. The Mongol thrust also facilitated the flow of fine
goods, traders, and technology from China to the rest of the world. Finally,
the Mongol conquests encouraged an unprecedented Afro-Eurasian interconnectedness, surpassing even the Hellenistic connections that Alexander's
conquests had brought in the late fourth century BCE (see Chapter 6). Out
of Mongol conquest and warfare would come centuries of trade, migration,
and increasing contacts among Africa, Europe, and Asia.

Conclusion

Between 1000 and 1300 CE, Afro-Eurasia was forming large cultural spheres.
As trade and migration spanned longer distances, these spheres prospered
and became more integrated. In central Afro-Eurasia, Islam was firmly established, its merchants, scholars, and travelers acting as commercial and cultural
intermediaries as they spread their universalizing faith. As seaborne trade
expanded, India, too, became a commercial crossroads. Merchants in its port
cities welcomed traders arriving from Arab lands to the west, from China,
and from Southeast Asia. China also boomed, pouring its manufactures into
trading networks that reached throughout Eurasia and even into Africa.
Christian Europe had two centers—at Rome and at Constantinople—both
of which were at war with Islam.

Neither sub-Saharan Africa nor the Americas saw the same degree of integration, but trade and migration in these areas had profound effects. Certain
African cultures flourished as they encountered the commercial energy of
trade on the Indian Ocean. Africans' trade with one another linked coastal
and interior regions in an ever more integrated world. American peoples also
built cities that dominated cultural areas and thrived through trade. American cultures shared significant features: reliance on trade, maize, and the
exchange of goods such as shells and precious feathers. And larger areas honored the same spiritual centers.

By 1300, trade, migration, and conflict were connecting Afro-Eurasian
worlds in unprecedented ways. When Mongol armies swept into China, into
Southeast Asia, and into the heart of Islam, they applied a thin coating of
political integration to these widespread regions and built on existing trade
links. At the same time, most people's lives remained quite localized, driven
by the need for subsistence and governed by spiritual and governmental representatives acting at the behest of distant authorities.

Still, locals noticed the evidence of cross-cultural exchanges everywhere—
in the clothing styles of provincial elites, such as Chinese silks in Paris or
quetzal plumes in northern Mexico; in enticements to move (and forced

removals) to new frontiers; in the news of faraway conquests or advancing armies. Worlds were coming together within themselves and across territorial boundaries, while remaining apart as they sought to maintain their own identities and traditions. In Afro-Eurasia especially, as the movement of goods and peoples shifted from ancient land routes to sea-lanes, these contacts were more frequent and far-reaching. Never before had the world seen so much activity connecting its parts, nor had there ever been so much cultural similarity within those parts. By the time the Mongol Empire arose, the regions composing the globe were those that we now recognize as the cultural spheres of today's world.

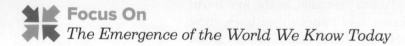

TRACING THE GLOBAL STORYLINE

Focus On
The Emergence of the World We Know Today

The Islamic World

- The Islamic world undergoes a burst of expansion, prosperity, and cultural diversification but remains politically fractured.

- Arab merchants and Sufi mystics spread Islam over great distances and make it more appealing to other cultures, helping to transform Islam into a distinct cultural sphere.

- Islam travels across the Sahara Desert; the powerful gold- and enslaved people-supplying empire of Mali arises in West Africa.

China

- The Song dynasty reunites China after three centuries of fragmented rulership, reaching into the past to reestablish a sense of a "true" Chinese identity as the Han through a widespread print culture and denigration of outsiders.

- Agrarian success and advances in manufacturing—including the production of both iron and porcelain—fuel an expanding economy, complete with paper money.

India

- India remains a mosaic under the canopy of Hinduism despite cultural interconnections and increasing prosperity.

- The invasion of Turkish Muslims leads to the Delhi Sultanate, which rules over India for three centuries, strengthening cultural diversity and tolerance.

Christian Europe

- Roman Catholicism becomes a "mass" faith and helps create a common European cultural identity.

- Feudalism organizes the relationship between elites and peasants, while manorialism forms the basis of the economy.

- Europe's growing confidence is manifest in its efforts, including the Crusades and the reconquering of Iberia, to drive Islam out of "Christian" lands.

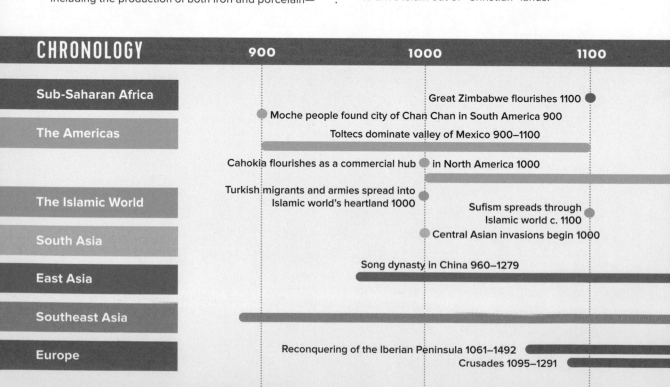

CHRONOLOGY

	900	1000	1100
Sub-Saharan Africa			Great Zimbabwe flourishes 1100 ●
The Americas	Moche people found city of Chan Chan in South America 900		
	Toltecs dominate valley of Mexico 900–1100		
	Cahokia flourishes as a commercial hub ● in North America 1000		
The Islamic World	Turkish migrants and armies spread into Islamic world's heartland 1000	Sufism spreads through Islamic world c. 1100	
South Asia		Central Asian invasions begin 1000	
East Asia	Song dynasty in China 960–1279		
Southeast Asia			
Europe	Reconquering of the Iberian Peninsula 1061–1492		
	Crusades 1095–1291		

THINKING ABOUT GLOBAL CONNECTIONS

- **Thinking about Worlds Together, Worlds Apart** From 1000 to 1300 CE, a range of social and political developments contributed to the consolidation of four cultural spheres that still exist today: Europe, the Islamic world, India, and China. In what ways did these spheres interact with one another? In what ways was each sphere genuinely distinct from the others? To what extent were sub-Saharan Africa and the Americas folded into these spheres and with what result?

- **Thinking about Transformation & Conflict and Becoming the World** As the four cultural spheres of Afro-Eurasia consolidated, shocking examples of conflict between them began to take place. Whether from Pope Urban II's call in 1095 to reclaim the "holy land" from Muslims or the Mongol Hulagu's brutal sack of Baghdad in 1258, this period was marked by large-scale warfare between rival cultural spheres. To what extent was such conflict inevitable? In what ways did conflict transform the groups involved?

- **Thinking about Crossing Borders and Becoming the World** Major innovations facilitated economic exchange in the Indian Ocean and in Song China. The magnetic needle compass, better ships, and improved maps shrank the Indian Ocean to the benefit of traders. Similarly, paper money in Song China changed the nature of commerce. How did these developments shift the axis of Afro-Eurasian exchange? What evidence suggests that bodies of water and the routes across them became more significant than overland exchange routes in binding together Afro-Eurasia? What might be the longer-term implications of these developments?

Key Terms

Cahokia p. 507	entrepôts p. 476	Mali Empire p. 501	Sufism p. 482
Chimú Empire p. 503	flying cash p. 490	manorialism p. 494	Toltecs p. 505
Delhi Sultanate p. 485	*jizya* p. 479		

 Go to INQUIZITIVE to see what you've learned—and learn what you've missed—with personalized feedback along the way.

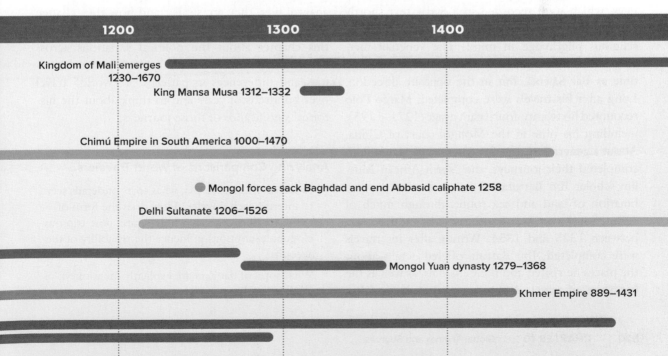

1200 — 1300 — 1400

Kingdom of Mali emerges 1230–1670
King Mansa Musa 1312–1332

Chimú Empire in South America 1000–1470

Mongol forces sack Baghdad and end Abbasid caliphate 1258
Delhi Sultanate 1206–1526

Mongol Yuan dynasty 1279–1368

Khmer Empire 889–1431

Global Themes and Sources

Comparing "World" Travelers over Time

The maritime revolution described in this chapter, along with the Silk Roads across Inner Eurasia, facilitated travel for trade, diplomacy, and religious pilgrimage on a scale previously unseen. While earlier travelers, like the Spanish nun Egeria or the Buddhist monks Faxian and Xuanzang (see Global Themes and Sources in Chapter 8), had covered great distances and for reasons similar to those of some of the travelers whose accounts you'll read here, the sheer distances traveled by Bar Sāwmā or Ibn Battuta eclipse the journeys of their centuries-earlier counterparts. Like the earlier pilgrims, however, several travelers who moved between the worlds of Afro-Eurasia in this period left records of their stunning journeys or were written about by others.

As we saw at the start of this chapter, Bar Sāwmā traveled primarily along land routes from Yuan dynasty China all the way to modern-day France in the late thirteenth century. A Nestorian Christian monk, Bar Sāwmā appears to have made his journeys, which were recorded in a Syriac text shortly after his death in 1294, with both diplomacy and religious pilgrimage in mind. The Venetian merchant Marco Polo was traveling at nearly the same time as Bar Sāwmā, but in the opposite direction. Long after his travels were completed, Marco Polo recounted his twenty-four-year voyage (1271–1295), including his time in the Mongol court of China. About a generation after Bar Sāwmā and Marco Polo completed their journeys, the North African Muslim scholar Ibn Battuta set out to traverse a combination of land and sea routes through much of Africa, Southwest Asia, Southeast Asia, and East Asia between 1325 and 1354. Writing after his travels were completed, Ibn Battuta offered details about the places he visited and their customs, as well as the hardships of travel. A rough contemporary of Ibn Battuta, a Syrian Islamic historian by the name of al-Umari who lived in the first half of the fourteenth century, provides the fourth passage here, a description of the pilgrimage of yet another famous traveler, Mansa Musa, the king of Mali, in 1324–1325. The final "world" traveler represented here is the Chinese naval commander Zheng He, whose voyages came later (1405–1433; see Chapter 11) but can be usefully compared with those of Bar Sāwmā, Marco Polo, Ibn Battuta, and Mansa Musa. In a series of expeditions, Zheng He's fleet sailed from China through Southeast Asia, to Sri Lanka, into the northern Indian Ocean, and even to the Persian Gulf and the Red Sea, leaving stone inscriptions at many of the sites it visited.

The records of these travelers—Bar Sāwmā, Marco Polo, Ibn Battuta, Mansa Musa, and Zheng He—allow us not only to study the realities of pilgrimage and exploration in this period, but also to analyze how they are similar and how they change over time. Together with what you've learned in this chapter about the political situations across Afro-Eurasia, you can begin to explain the similarities and differences in patterns of "world" travel over hundreds of years and to think about the historical significance of those journeys.

Analyzing Comparisons of World Travelers

- Based on these excerpts, what sorts of details seem to interest each traveler? How does the form of each text (life of revered holy figure, post-trip travelogue, inscription) influence the reliability of the account?

- What sorts of dangers are explicitly mentioned, or implied, in these texts?

- What in the texts suggests the exchange of goods and ideas?

- Compare these travel accounts with those from the Global Themes and Sources feature of Chapter 8. What are some of the similarities and differences in the "world" travels of these two groups of individuals? What accounts for those changes and continuities over time?

Pilgrimage to Jerusalem (c. 1300), Bar Sāwmā

This passage illustrates the realities of travel for Bar Sāwmā and his travel companion, Markōs, in the late thirteenth century. Setting out from the Mongol capital Khan-balik, they enter the territory of Mar Denha (or Mar Catholicus), the patriarch of the Nestorian Church, who, after greeting them warmly, sends them on their way to visit holy sites. Just in this one passage, we can see the territory these pilgrims covered, starting in Khan-balik, arriving at Maraghah (in the territory of modern Azerbaijan), continuing on to Baghdad, and then into Armenia and Georgia. Many of the interactions and travel issues they describe resonate with those of the Spanish nun Egeria. (Titles of sites have been set in all capitals, as in the original translation.)

- What are some of the practical travel issues Bar Sāwmā and his travel companion face?

- How do Bar Sāwmā and his companion interact with people and places on their travels?

- How do those travel issues and interactions compare with those of the Spanish nun Egeria, 900 years earlier?

And having enjoyed the conversation of those brethren they set out to go to ADHÔRBÎJÂN . . . so that they might travel from there to BAGHDÂD, to MÂR DENHÂ, the Catholicus. . . . Now it happened that Mâr Catholicus had come to MÂRÂGHÂH [a town of ADHÔRBÎJÂN, the capital of HÛLÂGÛ KHÂN], and they met him there. And at the sight of him their joy grew great, and their gladness was

increased. . . . And when [Mar Catholicus] asked them, "Whence [come] ye?" they replied, "From the countries of the East, from KHÂN BÂLÎK, the city of the King of Kings [KÛBLÂI] KHÂN. We have come to be blessed by you, and by the Fathers (i.e. Bishops), and the monks, and the holy men of this quarter of the world. And if a road [openeth] to us, and God hath mercy upon us, we shall go to JERUSALEM."

. . . [Catholicus] comforted them and said unto them, "Assuredly, O my sons, the Angel of Providence shall protect you on this difficult journey, and he shall be a guide unto you until the completion of your quest." . . .

[After a few days, Bar Sāwmā and his companion] request [of Mar Catholicus]: "If we have found mercy (i.e. favour) in the eyes of Mâr our Father, let him permit us to go to BAGHDÂD, in order that we may receive a blessing from the holy sepulchers (or relics?) of MÂR MÂRÊ, . . . the Apostle, the teacher of the East, and those of the Fathers that are there. And from there we would go to the monasteries that are in the country of BÊTH GARMAI and in NISIBIS that we may be blessed there also, and demand assistance."

And when the Catholicus saw the beauty of their object, and the innocence of their minds, and the honesty of their thoughts, he said unto them, "Go ye, my sons, and may Christ, the Lord of the Universe, grant unto you your petition." . . . And he wrote for them a *pêthîkhâ* (i.e. a letter of introduction) to these countries so that they might be honourably entreated whithersoever they went; and he sent with them a man to show them the way, and to act as a guide along the roads.

And they arrived in Baghdad, and thence they went to the Great Church of KÔKÊ [at Ctesiphon]. . . . And they went to the monastery of MÂR MÂRÎ, the Apostle, and received a blessing from the sepulchers (or relics?) of that country. And from there they turned back and came to the country of BÊTH GARMAI, and they received blessings from the shrine (or tomb) of MÂR EZEKIEL [the prophet, near Dâkôk], which was full of helps and healings. And from there they went to ARBÎL, and thence to MÂWSIL (i.e. Môṣul on the Tigris). And they went [to] SHÎGAR (SINJÂR), and NISIBIS, and MERDÂ (MARDÎN); and were blessed by the shrine [containing] the bones of MÂR AWGÎN, the second CHRIST. And thence they went to GÂZARTÂ of BÊTH ZABHDAI, and they were blessed by all the shrines and monasteries, and the religious houses, and monks, and the Fathers (i.e. Bishops) in their dioceses. . . .

And when they arrived at the city of Animto [i.e. ANÎ, the ancient capital of Christian ARMENIA, situated on an affluent of the river Araxes], and saw the monasteries and the churches therein, they marvelled at the great extent of the buildings and at their magnificence. And thence they went towards BÊTH GÛRGÂYÊ (i.e. the country of Georgia), so that they might travel by a clear (or safe?) road, but when they arrived there they heard from the inhabitants of the country that the road was cut because of the murders and robberies which had taken place along it.

Chapter 4. And the two monks turned back and came to Mâr Catholicus, who rejoiced [at the sight of] them, and said unto them, "This is not the time for a journey to JERUSALEM. The roads are a disturbed state, and the ways are cut. Now behold, ye have received blessings from all the Houses of God, and the shrines (or relics?) which are in them, and it is my opinion that when a man visits them with a pure heart, the service thus paid to them is in no way less than that of a pilgrimage to Jerusalem."

Source: Rabban Bar Sāwmā. *The Monks of Kublai Khan, Emperor of China, or The History of the Life and Travels of Rabban Sāwmā*, translated by E. A. Wallis Budge (London: Religious Tract Society, 1928), pp. 140–43, 145–46.

<hr />

PRIMARY SOURCE 10.2

The Mongol Capital at Kanbalu (Khan-balik) (c. 1300), Marco Polo

In the last quarter of the thirteenth century, the Venetian merchant Marco Polo, together with his father and uncle, undertook a magnificent trek eastward on the Silk Roads. They ultimately arrived at Khan-balik,

the capital of the Mongol Yuan dynasty (and the place from which Bar Sāwmā set out, in the previous passage). There, they encountered Kublai Khan. Long after his journey was completed, Marco Polo offered this thorough description of the city, which would ultimately become Beijing. While some scholars have questioned the veracity of Polo's travels, arguing that he may never have made it all the way to China, the detail offered in this passage suggests firsthand experience.

....

- What does Marco Polo emphasize in his description of Kanbalu (Khan-balik)?

- What different groups of people live in greater Khan-balik? How are they organized and distributed?

- Why do you think Marco Polo focuses on the issues that he describes?

....

The city of Kanbalu is situated near a large river in the province of Cathay, and was in ancient times eminently magnificent and royal. The name itself implies "the city of the sovereign;" but his majesty having imbibed an opinion from the astrologers, that it was destined to become rebellious to his authority, resolved upon the measure of building another capital, upon the opposite side of the river, where stand the palaces just described: so that the new and the old cities are separated from each other only by the stream that runs between them. The new-built city received the name of Tai-du, and all the Cathaians, that is, all those of the inhabitants who were natives of the province of Cathay, were compelled to evacuate the ancient city, and to take up their abode in the new. Some of the inhabitants, however, of whose loyalty he did not entertain suspicion, were suffered to remain, especially because the latter, although of the dimensions that shall presently be described, was not capable of containing the same number as the former, which was of vast extent.

This new city is of a form perfectly square, and twenty-four miles in extent, each of its sides being neither more nor less than six miles. It is enclosed with walls of earth, that at the base are about ten paces thick, but gradually diminish to the top, where the thickness is not more than three paces. In all parts the battlements are white. The whole plan of the city was regularly laid out by line, and the streets in general are consequently so straight, that when a person ascends the wall over one of the gates, and looks right forward, he can see the gate opposite to him on the other side of the city. In the public streets there are, on each side, booths and shops of every description. All the allotments of ground upon which the habitations throughout the city were constructed are square, and exactly on a line with each other; each allotment being sufficiently spacious for handsome buildings, with corresponding courts and gardens. One of these was assigned to each head of a family; that is to say, such a person of such a tribe had one square allotted to him, and so of the rest. Afterwards the property passed from hand to hand. In this manner the whole interior of the city is disposed in squares, so as to resemble a chessboard, and planned out with a degree of precision and beauty impossible to describe. The wall of the city has twelve gates, three on each side of the square, and over each gate and compartment of the wall there is a handsome building; so that on each side of the square there are five such buildings, containing large rooms, in which are disposed the arms of those who form the garrison of the city, every gate being guarded by a thousand men. It is not to be understood that such a force is stationed there in consequence of the apprehension of danger from any hostile power whatever, but as a guard suitable to the honour and dignity of the sovereign. Yet it must be allowed that the declaration of the astrologers has excited in his mind a degree of suspicion with regard to the Cathaians. . . .

Outside of each of the gates is a suburb so wide that it reaches to and unites with those of the other nearest gates on both sides, and in length extends to the distance of three or four miles, so that the number of inhabitants in these suburbs exceeds that of the city itself. Within each suburb there are, at intervals, as far perhaps as a mile from the city, many hotels, or caravanserais, in which the merchants arriving from various parts take up their abode; and to each description of people a separate building is assigned, as we should say, one to the Lombards, another to the Germans, and a third to the French. . . .

Guards, in parties of thirty or forty, continually patrol the streets during the course of the night, and make diligent search for persons who may be from their homes at an unseasonable hour, that is, after the third stroke of the great bell. When any are met with under such circumstances, they immediately apprehend and confine them, and take them in the morning for examination before officers appointed for that purpose, who, upon the proof of any delinquency, sentence them, according to the nature of the offence, to a severer or lighter infliction of the bastinade beating with a cudgel, usually on the soles of the feet, which sometimes, however, occasions their death. It is in this manner that crimes are usually punished amongst these people, from a disinclination to the shedding of blood, which their *baksis* or learned astrologers instruct them to avoid.

Source: Marco Polo, *The Travels of Marco Polo, The Venetian*, ed. Thomas Wright (London: George Bell and Sons, 1904), pp. 181–86.

The Holy Sites of Jerusalem (c. 1360), Ibn Battuta

Ibn Battuta's travels dwarf those of any other world traveler in this period. What began as a *hajj* became a journey of tens of thousands of miles. Traveling for more than a quarter century, Ibn Battuta was particularly interested in the role and practice of Islam in each place he visited. While he was sometimes called into action to serve as a learned Muslim *qadi* (judge) in the places he visited, his travels often took the form of engaged and devoted religious tourism, as when he visited Jerusalem, as described in the passage here.

- **What do you make of Ibn Battuta's itinerary? What sites does he visit? What, and how, does he learn about the history of each site?**

- **How does Ibn Battuta describe mosques? Churches? What do you think accounts for the differences in his descriptions?**

- **How do Ibn Battuta's descriptions of holy sites compare with those in Bar Sāwmā's account?**

From Gaza I travelled to the city of Abraham [Hebron], the mosque of which is of elegant, but substantial, construction, imposing and lofty, and built of squared stones. At one angle of it there is a stone, one of whose faces measures twenty-seven spans. It is said that Solomon commanded the *jinn* to build it. Inside it is the sacred cave containing the graves of Abraham, Isaac, and Jacob, opposite which are three graves, which are those of their wives. I questioned the imám, a man of great piety and learning, on the authenticity of these graves, and he replied: "All the scholars whom I have met hold these graves to be the very graves of Abraham, Isaac, Jacob and their wives. No one questions this except introducers of false doctrines; it is a tradition which has passed from father to son for generations and admits of no doubt.". . .

On the way from Hebron to Jerusalem, I visited Bethlehem, the birthplace of Jesus. The site is covered by a large building; the Christians regard it with intense veneration and hospitably entertain all who alight at it.

We then reached Jerusalem (may God ennoble her!), third in excellence after the two holy shrines of Mecca and Medína, and the place whence the Prophet was caught up into heaven. Its walls were destroyed by the illustrious King Saladin and his successors, for fear lest the Christians should seize it and fortify themselves in it. The sacred mosque is a most beautiful building, and is said to be the largest mosque in the world. Its length from east to west is put at 752 "royal" cubits and its breadth at 435. On three sides it has many entrances, but on the south side I know of one only, which is that by which the imám enters. The entire mosque is an open court and unroofed, except the mosque al-Aqsá, which has a roof of most excellent workmanship, embellished with gold and brilliant colours. Some other parts of the mosque are roofed as well. The Dome of the Rock is a building of extraordinary beauty, solidity, elegance, and singularity of shape. It stands on an elevation in the centre of the mosque and is reached by a flight of marble steps. It has four doors. The space round it is also paved with marble, excellently done, and the interior likewise. Both outside

and inside the decoration is so magnificent and the workmanship so surpassing as to defy description. The greater part is covered with gold so that the eyes of one who gazes on its beauties are dazzled by its brilliance, now glowing like a mass of light, now flashing like lightning. In the centre of the Dome is the blessed rock from which the Prophet ascended to heaven, a great rock projecting about a man's height, and underneath it there is a cave the size of a small room, also of a man's height, with steps leading down to it. Encircling the rock are two railings of excellent workmanship, the one nearer the rock being artistically constructed in iron, and the other of wood.

Among the grace-bestowing sanctuaries of Jerusalem is a building, situated on the farther side of the valley called the valley of Jahannam [Gehenna] to the east of the town, on a high hill. This building is said to mark the place whence Jesus ascended to heaven. In the bottom of the same valley is a church venerated by the Christians, who say that it contains the grave of Mary. In the same place there is another church which the Christians venerate and to which they come on pilgrimage. This is the church of which they are falsely persuaded to believe that it contains the grave of Jesus. All who come on pilgrimage to visit it pay a stipulated tax to the Muslims, and suffer very unwillingly various humiliations. Thereabouts also is the place of the cradle of Jesus, which is visited in order to obtain blessing.

Source: Ibn Battúta, *Ibn Battúta: Travels in Asia and Africa, 1325–1354*, translated and edited by H. A. R. Gibb (London: George Routledge & Sons, Ltd., 1929), pp. 55–57.

PRIMARY SOURCE 10.4

The *Hajj* of Mansa Musa (1324–1325), al-Umari

Al-Umari was a historian who lived in the first half of the fourteenth century. While his personal life reflected the vicissitudes of court politics in Mamluk-controlled Syria (complete with a period of imprisonment when he fell out of favor), his well-researched history was much appreciated by his contemporaries. The passage included here, in which al-Umari describes the famed *hajj* of Mansa Musa, shows that al-Umari himself traveled to Cairo to gather information from local informants about Mansa Musa's sojourn in the city.

- What are the layers of reporting in this passage? How does the traveling historian al-Umari come by his information on Mansa Musa?

- How does Mansa Musa's *hajj* influence the peoples with whom he and his retinue come into contact?

- How typical was Mansa Musa's *hajj*? Even if it was atypical, what can you generalize about the role of *hajj* in the Mediterranean and Indian Ocean worlds based on Mansa Musa's and Ibn Battuta's experiences?

The emir Abū 'l-Ḥasan 'Alī b. Amīr Ḥajib told me that he was often in the company of sultan Mūsā the king of this country when he came to Egypt on the Pilgrimage. He was staying in [the] Qarāfa [district of Cairo] and Ibn Amīr Ḥajib was governor of Old Cairo and Qarāfa at that time. A friendship grew up between them and this sultan Mūsā told him a great deal about himself and his country and the people of the Sūdān who were his neighbours. One of the things which he told him was that his country was very extensive and contiguous with the Ocean. By his sword and his armies he had conquered 24 cities each with its surrounding district with villages and estates. It is a country rich in livestock—cattle, sheep, goats, horses, mules—and different kinds of poultry—geese, doves, chickens. The inhabitants of his country are numerous, a vast concourse, but compared with the peoples of the Sūdān who are their neighbours and penetrate far to the south they are like a white birth-mark on a black cow. He has a truce with the gold-plant people, who pay him tribute.

Ibn Amīr Ḥajib said that he asked him about the gold-plant, and he said: "It is found in two forms. One is found in the spring and blossoms after the rains in open country (ṣaḥrā'). It has leaves like the *najīl* grass and its roots are gold (*tibr*). The other kind is found all the year round at known sites on the banks of the Nīl and is dug up." . . .

Sultan Mūsā told Ibn Amīr Ḥajib that gold was his prerogative and he collected the crop as a tribute except for what the people of that country took by theft.

"This sultan Mūsā, during his stay in Egypt both before and after his journey to the Noble Ḥājib, maintained a uniform attitude of worship and turning towards God. It was as though he were standing before Him because of His continual presence in his mind. He and all those with him behaved in the same manner and were well-dressed, grave, and dignified. He was noble and generous and performed many acts of charity and kindness. He had left his country with 100 loads of gold which he spent during his Pilgrimage on the tribes who lay along his route from his country to Egypt, while he was in Egypt, and again from Egypt to the Noble Hijāz and back."

From the beginning of my coming to stay in Egypt I heard talk of the arrival of this sultan Mūsā on his Pilgrimage and found the Cairenes eager to recount what they had seen of the Africans' prodigal spending. . . .

This man flooded Cairo with his benefactions. He left no court emir (*amīr muqarrab*) nor holder of a royal office without the gift of a load of gold. The Cairenes made incalculable profits out of him and his suite in buying and selling and giving and taking. They exchanged gold until they depressed its value in Egypt and caused its price to fall. . . .

Merchants of Miṣr and Cairo have told me of the profits which they made from the Africans, saying that one of them might buy a shirt or cloak (*thawb*) or robe (*izār*) or other garment for five dinars when it was not worth one. Such was their simplicity and trustfulness that it was possible to practice any deception on them. They greeted anything that was said to them with credulous acceptance. But later they formed the very poorest opinion of the Egyptians because of the obvious falseness of everything they said to them and their outrageous behaviour in fixing the prices of the provisions and other goods which were sold to them. . . .

Muhanna' b. 'Abd al-Bāqī al-'Ujrumī the guide informed me that he accompanied sultan Mūsā when he made the Pilgrimage and that the sultan was very open-handed towards the pilgrims and the inhabitants of the Holy Places. He and his companions maintained great pomp and dressed magnificently during the journey. He gave away much wealth in alms. "About 200 mithqals of gold fell to me" said Muhanna' "and he gave other sums to my companions." Muhanna' waxed eloquent in describing the sultan's generosity, magnanimity, and opulence.

Gold was at a high price in Egypt until they came in that year. The mithqal did not go below 25 *dirhams* and was generally above, but from that time its value fell and it cheapened in price and has remained cheap till now. The mithqal does not exceed 22 *dirhams* or less. This has been the state of affairs for about twelve years until this day by reason of the large amount of gold which they brought into Egypt and spent there.

Source: al-Umari, *Corpus of Early Arabic Sources for West African History*, translated by J. F. P Hopkins (Cambridge: Cambridge University Press, 1981), pp. 267, 269–71.

The Galle Trilingual Stone Inscription (1411), Zheng He

No discussion of world travelers in this increasingly connected Afro-Eurasian world would be complete without evidence from Zheng He's travels, although he lived in a slightly later period than the other travelers discussed here (namely, during the Ming dynasty, which took the mandate of heaven from the Mongol Yuan dynasty of China in the aftermath of the Black Death; see Chapter 11). The seven far-reaching naval expeditions undertaken by Zheng He from 1405 to 1433 illustrate Ming patronage of voyages of exploration that demonstrated the dynasty's might. This trilingual inscription (in Chinese, Persian, and Tamil), set up in 1411 by Zheng He and his companions at Sri Lanka (called Ceylon in the source), demonstrates the pragmatic religious devotion of those voyaging for nonreligious aims.

- What range of goods does Zheng He's embassy offer? Why are these specific commodities offered?

- Why do Zheng He, who was born and raised a Muslim, and his companions make offerings to Buddha?

- How do Zheng He's reasons for travel and what he does at this holy site compare with the reasons and actions of the other travelers in this section?

His Majesty, the Emperor of the Great Ming dynasty has despatched the eunuchs Ching-Ho [Zheng He], Wang Ch'ing-Lien, and others to set forth his utterance before Buddha, the World Honoured one, as follows:

"Deeply do we reverence you, Merciful and Honoured One, whose bright perfection is wide-embracing, and whose way of virtue passes all understanding, whose law enters into all human relations, and the years of whose great Kalpa (period) are like the sand of the river in number, you whose controlling influence ennobles and converts, whose kindness quickens, and whose strength discerns, whose mysterious efficacy is beyond compare! Whereas Ceylon's mountainous isle lies in the south of the ocean, and its Buddhist temples are sanctuaries of your gospel, where your miraculous responsive power imbues and enlightens. Of late, we have dispatched missions to announce our mandate to foreign nations, and during their journey over the ocean they have been favoured with the blessing of your beneficent protection. They escaped disaster or misfortune and journeyed in safety to and fro. In everlasting recognition of your supreme virtue, we, therefore, bestow offerings in recompense, and do now reverently present before Buddha, the Honoured One, oblations of gold and silver, gold embroidered jewelled banners of variegated silk, incense burners, and flower vases, silks of many colours in lining and exterior, lamps and candles with other gifts, in order to manifest the high honour of our worship. Do you, Lord Buddha, bestow on them, your regard!"

List of Alms bestowed at the shrine of the Buddhist temple in the Mountain of Ceylon as offerings:

1000 pieces of gold; 5000 pieces of silver; fifty rolls of embroidered silk in many colours, fifty rolls of silk taffeta in many colours; four pairs of jewelled banners, gold embroidered, and of variegated silk; two pairs of the same picked in red; one pair of the same in yellow; one pair in black; five antique brass incense burners; five pairs of antique brass flower vases picked in gold on lacquer, with gold stands; five pairs of yellow brass candle-sticks, picked in gold on lacquer, with gold stand; five yellow brass lamps picked in gold on lacquer, with gold stands; five incense vessels in vermilion red, lacquered gold picked on lacquer, with gold stands; six pairs of golden lotus flowers; 2500 catties of scented oil; ten pairs of wax candles; ten sticks of fragrant incense.

The date being the seventh year of Yung-Lo (1410 a.d.) marked Chi ch'ou in the sixty years' cycle, on the Chia Hsu day of the sixty days cycle in the second moon, being the first day of the month. A reverent oblation.

Source: "Appendix I. Translation of the Chinese Inscription," translated by Edmund Backhouse, in "The Galle Trilingual Stone," *Spolia Zeylanica* 8 (Issued from the Colombo Museum; Ceylon: H. M. Richards, Acting Government Printer, 1913), pp. 125–26. Bracketed notes added by the author.

Interpreting Visual Evidence

Imagining the World

During this period when Afro-Eurasia was "becoming the world," cartographers began producing "world" maps. In 1154 al-Idrisi, a Muslim cartographer sponsored by King Roger II of Sicily, produced his *Tabula Rogeriana*. Al-Idrisi's map was accompanied by a commentary that contained information about the ten regions (numbered west to east; but note that the map was drawn so that the south is at the top) and seven climate zones (numbered south to north and following the scheme set forth by the second-century CE Greco-Roman geographer Ptolemy). In 1375, a Jewish mapmaker named Abraham Cresques, from the island of Majorca off the east coast of Spain, produced the second map included here, which is known as the *Catalan Atlas*. Cresques's map is a mixture of practical information

and storytelling. The crisscrossed lines that mark compass bearings, suggestive of a nautical chart, reflect the influence of the compass on European mapmaking beginning around 1300. The ornate depictions of the Mali king Mansa Musa and the caravan of Marco Polo offer historical information. In 1459, a monk named Fra Mauro, from Venice, created his *Mappa Mundi* (Map of the World), the third map pictured here. Fra Mauro's map is striking in its detail and information. Not only does it carefully mark out shorelines, rivers, cities, and other geographic features, but it also includes banners with detailed information and even drawings of the different types of ships (such as the North Atlantic cogs, Chinese junks, and Arabian dhows, discussed in this chapter) that sailed the different seas.

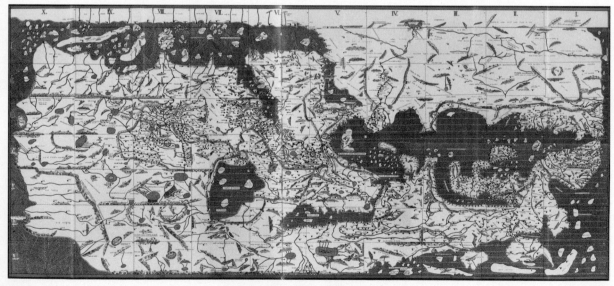

Al-Idrisi's *Tabula Rogeriana*.

Cresques's *Catalan Atlas*.

1. Compare these maps in terms of their representations of land, water, perspective, and other features. What accounts for the maps' similarities and differences?

2. Based on the features and information on the maps, where did the cartographers get the data to create them? How might these maps have been used, and by whom?

3. What do these maps suggest about how these cartographers and their patrons understood the known world? Why are certain parts of the world emphasized and others left off?

Fra Mauro's *Mappa Mundi*.

11

Crises and Recovery in Afro-Eurasia

1300–1500

When Mongol armies besieged the Genoese trading outpost of Caffa on the Black Sea in 1346, they not only damaged trading links between East Asia and the Mediterranean but also unleashed a devastating disease: the bubonic plague. Defeated Genoese merchants and soldiers withdrew, unknowingly taking the germs with them aboard their ships. By the time they arrived in Messina, Sicily, half the passengers were dead. The rest were dying. People waiting on shore for the ships' cargoes were horrified at the sight and turned the ships away. Desperately, the captains went to the next port, only to face the same fate. Despite these efforts at isolation, Europeans could not keep the plague (later called the Black Death) from reaching their shores. As it spread from port to port, it eventually contaminated all of Europe, killing nearly two-thirds of the population.

This story illustrates the magnitude and complexity of the Mongol invasions. They devastated polities, ravaged trade routes, and unwittingly unleashed the bubonic plague. The invasions left behind a series of khanates ruled by local warlords, rather than a centralized state. But Mongol invasions also intensified cultural and political contacts. The channels of exchange—the land trails and sea-lanes of human voyagers—became accidental conduits for deadly microbes. Indeed, these germs devastated societies far more decisively than did Mongol warfare. They were the real "murderous hordes" of world history.

Chapter Outline

- Collapse and Consolidation
- The Islamic Heartland
- Western Christendom
- Ming China
- Conclusion

Core Objectives

- **DESCRIBE** the nature and origins of the crises spanning Afro-Eurasia during the fourteenth century.

- **ASSESS** the impact of the Black Death on China, the Islamic world, and Europe.

- **COMPARE** the ways in which regional rulers in post-plague Afro-Eurasia attempted to construct unified states, and **ANALYZE** the extent and nature of their successes.

- **EXPLAIN** the role that religious belief systems played in rebuilding the Islamic world, Europe, and Ming China in the fourteenth and fifteenth centuries.

- **EXAMINE** the way art and architecture reflected the political realities of the Islamic world, Europe, and Ming China after the Black Death.

- **COMPARE** how Ottoman, Iberian, and Ming rulers extended their territories and regional influence.

So staggering was the Black Death's toll that population densities did not recover for 200 years. Most severely affected were regions that the Mongols had brought together: settlements and commercial hubs along the old Silk Roads and around the Mediterranean and South China Seas. While segments of the Indian Ocean trading world experienced death and disruption, South Asian societies, which had escaped the Mongol conquest, also escaped the great loss of life and political disruptions associated with the Black Death.

Out of the rubble of Mongol conquest and disease emerged the green shoots of a new world. This chapter explores the ways in which Afro-Eurasian peoples restored what they thought was valuable from old traditions after these crises, while discarding what they thought had failed them in favor of radically new institutions and ideas. Much of the recovery had striking similarities across Afro-Eurasia, as societies reaffirmed their most deeply held and long-standing beliefs. Chinese rulers looked to Confucian thought and well-known dynastic institutions to provide guidance going forward. In the Muslim heartland, a small band of Turkish-speaking warriors—the Ottomans—channeled the energies of a revived Islam to expand their own territory and the Muslim world. Europeans also invoked their traditions. In the Iberian Peninsula, political elites used a resurgent Catholicism to spread their political power and drive Muslim communities out of Europe. Europeans also created new dynastic monarchies and looked to their distant past in Greek and Roman culture for inspiration.

Global Storyline

The Black Death, Recovery, and Conquest

- The spread of the Black Death and the collapse of the Mongol Empire set off crises across Afro-Eurasia, with major demographic, political, economic, and cultural consequences.

- Across Afro-Eurasia, continuity in religious beliefs and cultural institutions accompanies changes in political structures in Europe, the Muslim world, and China.

- In central Eurasia, new rulers—most notably the Ottomans—rebuild dynasties in place of the Mongols, using a blend of religion, military expansion, administrative control, and cultural tolerance.

- In western Christendom, new monarchies establish political order, and the Renaissance brings a cultural rebirth to societies devastated by plague.

- In East Asia, the Ming dynasty replaces the Mongol Yuan dynasty, using an elaborate Confucian bureaucracy to oversee infrastructure and long-distance exchange.

Collapse and Consolidation

Although the Mongol invasions overturned political systems, the plague devastated society itself. The pandemic killed millions, disrupted economies, and threw communities into chaos. Rulers could explain to their people the assaults of "barbarians," but it was much harder to make sense of an invisible enemy. Nonetheless, in response to the upheaval, new ruling groups moved to reorganize their states. By making strategic marriages and building powerful armies, these rulers enlarged their territories, formed alliances, and built dynasties.

SPREAD OF THE BLACK DEATH

The spread of the Black Death was the fourteenth century's most significant historical development. (See Map 11.1.) Originating in Inner Asia, the disease afflicted peoples from China to Europe and killed 25 to 65 percent of infected populations.

How did the **Black Death** move so far and so fast? One explanation may lie in climate changes. The cooler climate of this period—scholars refer to a "Little Ice Age"—may have weakened populations and left them vulnerable to disease. In Europe, for instance, beginning around 1310, harsh winters and rainy summers shortened growing seasons and ruined harvests. Exhausted soils no longer supplied the resources required by growing urban and rural populations, while nobles squeezed the peasantry in an effort to maintain their luxurious lifestyle. The ensuing famine lasted from 1315 to 1322, during which time millions of Europeans died of starvation or of diseases against which the malnourished population had little resistance. Climate change and famine crippled populations on the eve of the Black Death. Climate change also spread drought across central Asia, where bubonic plague had lurked for centuries. So when steppe peoples migrated in search of new pastures and herds, they carried the germs with them and into contact with more densely populated agricultural communities. Rats also joined the exodus from the arid lands and transmitted fleas to other rodents, which then skipped to humans.

The resulting epidemic was terrifying, for its causes were unknown at the time. Infected victims died quickly—sometimes overnight—and in agony, coughing up blood and oozing pus and blood from black sores the size of eggs.

But it was the trading network that spread the germs across Afro-Eurasia into famine-struck western Europe. This wider Afro-Eurasian population was vulnerable because its members had no immunity to the disease. The first outbreak in a heavily populated region occurred in the 1320s in southwestern

THE BIG PICTURE

What crises affected fourteenth-century Afro-Eurasia and what was the range of responses to those crises?

Black Death
Plague pandemic that ravaged Europe, East Asia, and North Africa in the fourteenth century, killing large numbers of people, including perhaps as much as one-third of the European population.

Plague Victim The plague was highly contagious and quickly led to death. Here a physician and his helper cover their noses to avoid the unbearable stench emanating from the patient.

China. From there, the disease spread through China and then continued its death march along the major trade routes westward. Many of these routes terminated at the Italian port cities, where ships with dead and dying people aboard arrived in 1347. From there, what Europeans called the Pestilence or the Great Mortality engulfed the western end of the landmass. Societies in China, the Muslim world, and Europe suffered the disastrous effects of the Black Death.

Plague in China China was ripe for the plague pandemic. Its population had increased under the Song dynasty (960–1279) and subsequent Mongol rule. But by 1300, hunger and scarcity spread as resources were stretched thin. The weakened population was especially vulnerable. For seventy years, the Black Death ravaged China, reduced the size of the already small Mongol population, and shattered the Mongols' claim to a mandate from heaven. In 1331, plague may have killed 90 percent of the population in Bei Zhili (modern Hebei) Province. From there it spread throughout other provinces, reaching Fujian and the coast at Shandong. By the 1350s, most of China's large cities had suffered severe outbreaks.

Even as the Black Death was engulfing China, bandit groups and dissident religious sects were undercutting the power of the last Mongol Yuan rulers. Popular religious movements warned of impending doom. Most prominent was the Red Turban movement, which blended China's diverse cultural and religious traditions, including Buddhism, Daoism, and other faiths. Its leaders emphasized strict dietary restrictions, penance, and ceremonial rituals and made proclamations that the world was drawing to an end.

Plague in the Islamic World The plague devastated parts of the Muslim world as well. The Black Death reached Baghdad by 1347. By the next year, the plague overtook Egypt, Syria, and Cyprus, causing as many as 1,000 deaths a day according to a Tunisian report. Animals, too, were afflicted.

Core Objectives

ASSESS the impact of the Black Death on China, the Islamic world, and Europe.

One Egyptian writer commented: "The country was not far from being ruined. . . . One found in the desert the bodies of savage animals with the bubos under their arms. It was the same with horses, camels, asses, and all the beasts in general, including birds, even the ostriches." In the eastern Mediterranean, plague left much of the Islamic world in a state of near political and economic collapse. The great Arab historian Ibn Khaldûn (1332–1406), who lost his mother and father and a number of his teachers to the Black Death in Tunis, underscored the desolation. "Cities and buildings were laid waste, roads and way signs were obliterated, settlements and mansions became empty, dynasties and tribes grew weak," he wrote. "The entire world changed."

Plague in Europe In Europe, the Black Death made landfall on the Italian Peninsula; then it seized France, the Netherlands, Belgium, Luxembourg, Germany, and England in its deathly grip. Overcrowded and unsanitary cities were particularly vulnerable. All levels of society—the poor, craftspeople, aristocrats—were at risk, although flight to the countryside offered some protection from infection. Nearly 50 million of Europe's 80 million people perished between 1347 and 1351. After 1353, the epidemic waned, but the plague returned every seven years or so for the rest of the century and sporadically through the fifteenth century. Consequently, the European population continued to decline, until by 1450 many areas had only one-quarter the number of a century earlier.

In the face of the Black Death, some Europeans turned to debauchery, determined to enjoy themselves before they died. Others, especially in urban settings in Flanders, the Netherlands, and parts of Germany, claimed to find God's grace outside what they saw as a corrupt Catholic Church. Semimonastic orders like the Beghards and Beguines, which had begun in the century or so before the plague, expanded in its wake. These laypeople (unordained men and women) argued that people should trust their own "interior instinct" more than the Gospel as then preached. By contrast, the Flagellants were so convinced that man had incurred God's wrath that they whipped themselves to atone for human sin.

For many who survived the plague, disappointment with the clergy smoldered. Famished peasants resented priests and monks for living lives of luxury. In addition, they despaired at the absence of clergy when they were so greatly needed. While many clerics had perished attending to their parishioners during the Black Death, others had fled to rural retreats far from the ravages of the plague, leaving their followers to fend for themselves.

The Black Death wrought devastation throughout Afro-Eurasia. The Chinese population plunged from around 115 million in 1200 to 75 million or less in 1400, as the result of the Mongol invasions of the thirteenth century

SCANDINAVIA
1349

NORTH SEA

Novgorod

Moscow

MUSCOVY
1351

Edinburgh
1350

BRITAIN

Dublin
1349

London
1348

Oxford
1348

Bremen
1349

Lübeck
1349

Danzig

Cologne
1349

Cracow

Kiev

Rostov

KHANATE OF THE
GOLDEN HORDE

New Sarai

ARAL
SEA

Amiens
1348

EUROPE

Paris
1348

Venice
1347

Buda
1349

Avignon
1347

Genoa
1347

Florence
1347

Constantinople
1347

Caffa
1346

BLACK

SEA

CASPIAN
SEA

Bordeaux
1348

Siena
1347

Marseille

Barcelona
1348

Pisa
1347

Naples

Trebizond

Tabriz

Bukhara

Samar

Lisbon
1349

Madrid

Palermo 1347

Messina
1347

Athens
1347

ANATOLIA

Maraghah

SPAIN
1348

Algiers

Tunis

Aleppo
1347

IL-KHANATE

Ceuta

Fez

MEDITERRANEAN

SEA

Damascus
1347

Baghdad
1347

Isfahan

PERSIA

Marrakesh
1349

Tripoli
1348

Alexandria
1347

Jerusalem
1347

Basra

Shiraz

Hormuz

Cairo
1347

ARABIA

Persian Gulf

Medina

Mecca
1348

RED SEA

ARABIAN
SEA

AFRICA

Aden
1351

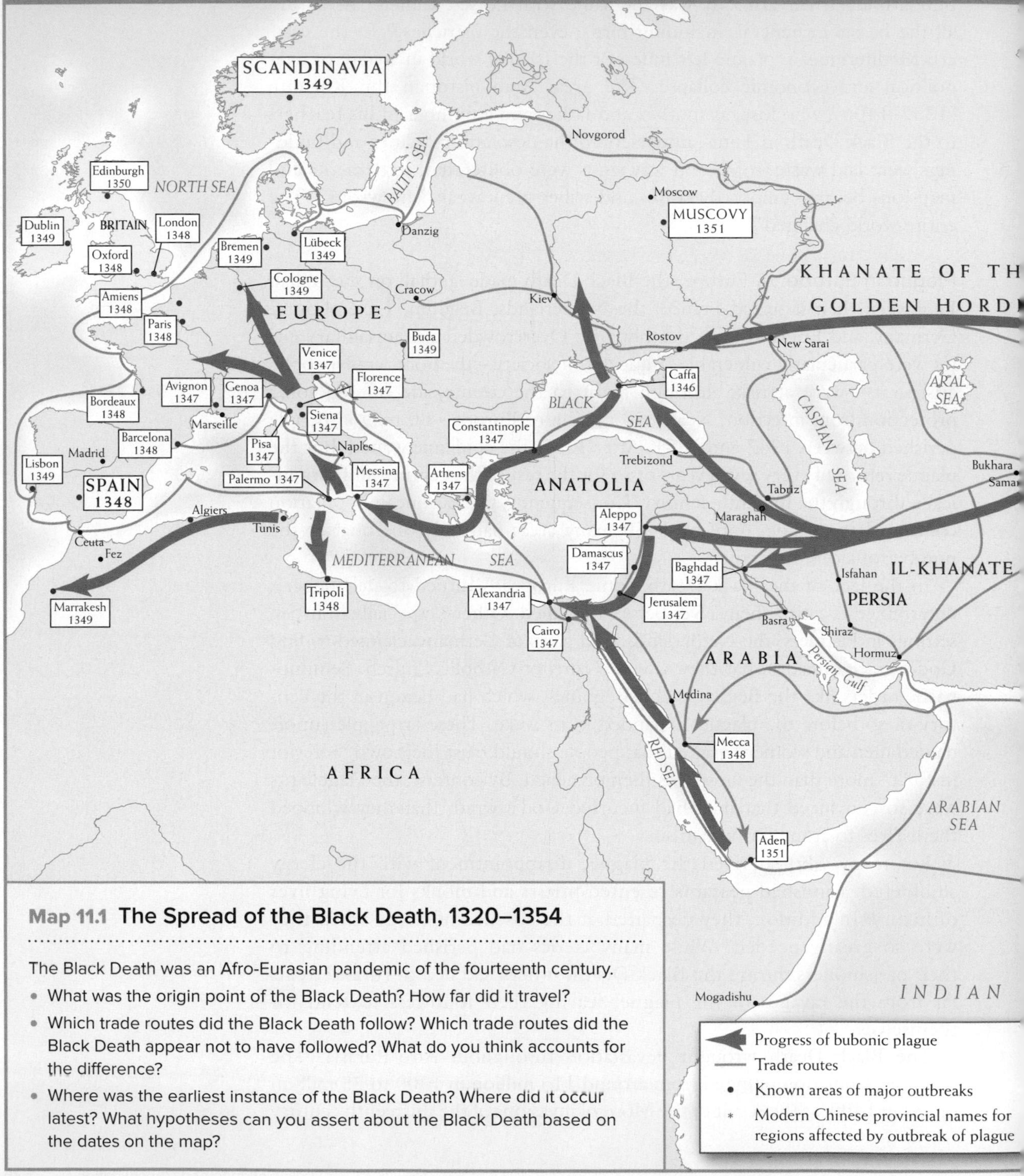

Map 11.1 The Spread of the Black Death, 1320–1354

The Black Death was an Afro-Eurasian pandemic of the fourteenth century.

- What was the origin point of the Black Death? How far did it travel?
- Which trade routes did the Black Death follow? Which trade routes did the Black Death appear not to have followed? What do you think accounts for the difference?
- Where was the earliest instance of the Black Death? Where did it occur latest? What hypotheses can you assert about the Black Death based on the dates on the map?

Mogadishu

INDIAN

Progress of bubonic plague
— Trade routes
• Known areas of major outbreaks
* Modern Chinese provincial names for regions affected by outbreak of plague

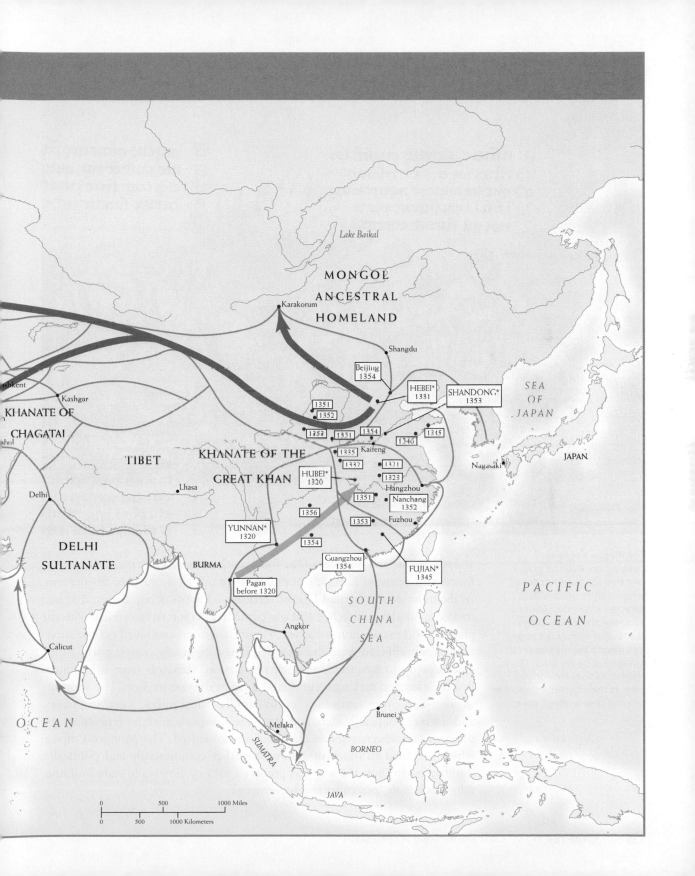

Lake Baikal

MONGOL
ANCESTRAL
HOMELAND

Karakorum

Shangdu

Beijing
1354

HEBEI*
1331

SHANDONG*
1353

SEA
OF
JAPAN

shkent

Kashgar

KHANATE OF
CHAGATAI

1351
1352

1353   1351   1354

1346   1345

JAPAN

TIBET

KHANATE OF THE

GREAT KHAN

1335   Kaifeng

1332

Nagasaki

Lhasa

HUBEI*
1320

1371

1323

Delhi

Hangzhou

DELHI

SULTANATE

YUNNAN*
1320

1351

1356

Nanchang
1352

1353   Fuzhou

BURMA

1354

FUJIAN*
1345

Guangzhou
1354

PACIFIC

OCEAN

Pagan
before 1320

SOUTH
CHINA
SEA

Calicut

Angkor

OCEAN

Melaka

Brunei

SUMATRA

BORNEO

JAVA

0   500   1000 Miles

0   500   1000 Kilometers

E nfuere alerent chafcû loz
M estiez loz en ezt ǂ besoing
M out loz cômêt agerreloing
L i filȝ le roi furent ploze
L uoz qil furent enteze

S arqeus ozent trop fcu
S iles mistrêt enȝ amba
V elez leur frere haute
E nteze furent riche

r lpais furent ǂ enfieloz
B zien dim an œdit lautor

N la pluo belle teîtfer
S ouȝ ael na cuer qil p
n ela pluo belle teînfa
L et biautre nela refp

The Plague Pandemic's Destruction Bubonic plague tore through the countries of western Christendom. Italy, depicted in this detail from a fourteenth-century Italian illuminated manuscript page, was among the regions most devastated by the Black Death. Neighbors buried neighbors, parents buried children, and the rich and poor suffered alike.

and the disease and disorder of the fourteenth century. Over the course of the fourteenth century, Europe's population shrank by more than 50 percent. In the most densely settled Islamic territory—Egypt—a population that had totaled around 6 million in 1400 was cut in half. When farmers fell ill with the plague, food production collapsed. Famine followed and killed off the survivors. Worst afflicted were the crowded cities, especially coastal ports. Some cities lost up to two-thirds of their population. Refugees from urban areas fled their homes, seeking security and food in the countryside. The shortage of food and other necessities led to rapidly rising prices, work stoppages, and unrest. Political leaders added to their unpopularity by repressing the unrest. Everywhere, regimes trembled and collapsed. The Mongol Empire, which had held so much of Eurasia together commercially and politically, disintegrated. Thus, the way was prepared for experiments in state building, religious beliefs, and cultural achievements.

REBUILDING STATES

dynasty
Hereditary ruling family that passed control from one generation to the next.

Starting in the late fourteenth century, Afro-Eurasians began the task of reconstructing both their political order and their trading networks. By then the plague had died down, though it continued to afflict peoples for centuries. However, the rebuilding of military and civil administrations—no easy task—also required political legitimacy. With their people deeply shaken by the extraordinary loss of life, rulers needed to revive confidence in themselves and their regimes, which they did by fostering beliefs and rituals that confirmed their legitimacy and by increasing their control over subjects.

The basis for power was a political institution well known to Afro-Eurasians for centuries, the **dynasty**—the hereditary ruling family that passed control from one generation to the next. Like those of the past, the new dynasties sought to establish their legitimacy in three ways. First, ruling families insisted that their power derived from a divine calling: Ming emperors in China claimed for themselves what previous dynastic rulers had asserted—the "mandate of heaven"—while European monarchs claimed to rule by "divine right." From their base in Anatolia, Ottoman warrior-princes asserted that they now carried the banner of Islam. In these ways, ruling households affirmed that God or the heavens intended for them to hold power. Second, leaders attempted to prevent squabbling among potential heirs by establishing clear rules about succession to the throne. Many European states tried to standardize succession by passing titles to the eldest male heir, thus ensuring political stability at a potential time of crisis, but in practice there were countless complications and quarrels. In the Islamic world, successors could be designated by the current ruler or elected by the community; here, too, struggles over succession were frequent. Third, ruling families elevated their power through conquest or alliance—by ordering armies to forcibly extend their domains or by marrying their royal offspring to rulers of other states or members of other elite households, a technique widely practiced in Europe. Once it established legitimacy, the typical royal family would consolidate power by enacting coercive laws and punishments and sending emissaries to govern distant territories. A ruling family would also establish standing armies and new administrative structures to collect taxes and to oversee building projects that proclaimed royal power.

As we will see in the next three sections of this chapter, the innovative state building that followed the plague's devastating wake would not have been as successful had it not drawn on older traditions. The peoples of the Islamic world held fiercely to their religion as successor states, notably the Ottoman Empire, absorbed numerous Turkish-speaking groups. In Europe, a cultural flourishing based largely on ancient Greek and Roman models gave rise to thinkers who proposed new views of governance. The Ming renounced the Mongol expansionist legacy and emphasized a return to Han rulership, consolidating control of Chinese lands and concentrating on internal markets rather than overseas trade. Many of these regimes lasted for centuries, long enough to set deep roots for political institutions and cultural values that molded societies long after the Black Death.

The Islamic Heartland

Core Objectives

COMPARE the ways in which regional rulers in post-plague Afro-Eurasia attempted to construct unified states, and ANALYZE the extent and nature of their successes.

The devastation of the Black Death followed hard on the heels of the Mongol destruction of Islam's most important city, Baghdad, and Islam's old political order. The double shock of conquest and disease shattered whatever was left of Islamic unity and cleared the way for new Islamic states to emerge. The old, Arabic-speaking Islamic world remained vital in Islam's geographic heartland, but it now had to yield authority to new rulers and religious men. This new Islamic world included large Turkish- and Persian-speaking populations as well. The implosion of the Abbasid caliphate in Baghdad made way for powerful, more militarized, expansionist successors capable of extending Islam's reach into Christian heartlands in the west and the Delhi Sultanate in the east.

The recovery from conquest and disease was slow. Eventually, the Ottomans, the Safavids, and the Mughals emerged as the dominant states in the Islamic world in the early sixteenth century. They exploited the rich agrarian resources of the Indian Ocean regions and the Mediterranean basin, and they benefited from a brisk seaborne and overland trade. By the mid-sixteenth century the Mughals controlled the northern Indus River valley; the Safavids occupied Persia; and the Ottomans ruled Anatolia, the Arab world, and much of southern and eastern Europe. Here we will explore in depth the Ottoman Empire, which emerged first and endured the longest of the three. (See Chapter 12 for a fuller discussion of the Mughals and Chapter 14 for more on the Safavids.)

THE OTTOMAN EMPIRE

Ottoman Empire
A Turkish warrior band that transformed itself into a vast, multicultural, bureaucratic empire that lasted from the early fourteenth century through the early twentieth century and encompassed Anatolia, the Arab world, and large swaths of southern and eastern Europe.

The rise of the **Ottoman Empire** owed as much to innovative administrative techniques and religious tolerance as to military strength. Although the Mongols considered Anatolia to be a borderland region of little economic importance, their military forays in the late thirteenth century opened up the region to new political forces. The ultimate victors here were the Ottoman Turks. They transformed themselves from warrior bands roaming the borderlands between the Islamic and Christian worlds into rulers of a settled state and, finally, into sovereigns of a far-flung, highly bureaucratic empire. (See Map 11.2.)

Under their chief, Osman (r. 1299–1326), the Turkish Ottomans formalized a stern and disciplined warrior ethos. In addition to deploying their fierce warriors, knowns as *ghazis*, Osman and his son Orhan (r. 1326–1362), both Sunni Muslims, proved skilled at working with those who held different religious beliefs, including Byzantine Christians, Sufi dervishes, and Shiites. Osman and Orhan offered genuine opportunities for others to exercise power and gain wealth. While other Turkish warrior bands fought for booty

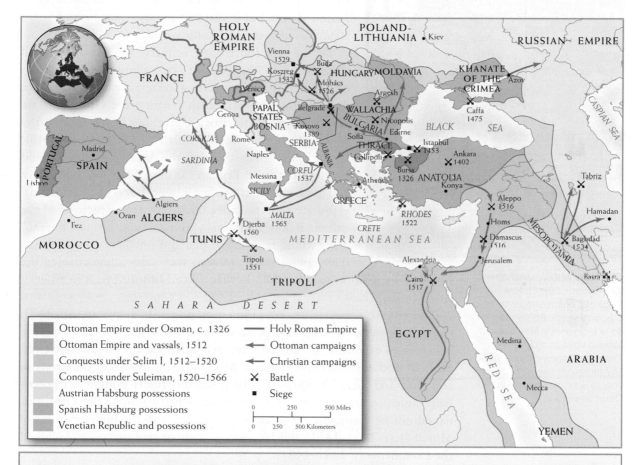

Map 11.2 The Ottoman Empire, 1300–1566

This map charts the expansion of the Ottoman state from the time of its founder, Osman, through the reign of Suleiman, the empire's most illustrious ruler.

- Where did the Ottoman Empire originate under Osman? Into what regions did the Ottomans expand between the years 1326 and 1566?
- What were the geographic limits of the Ottoman Empire?
- What governments were able to resist Ottoman expansion?

The Siege of Constantinople
A depiction of the Turkish siege of Constantinople from Burgundian spy Bertrandon de la Broquiere's 1453 book of travels, *Voyage d'Outre-Mer*. The use of heavy artillery in the fifty-three-day siege of Constantinople was instrumental to the Ottoman victory.

under charismatic military leaders, they failed because, unlike the Ottomans, they did not integrate these religious groups and the range of artisans, merchants, bureaucrats, and clerics whose support was essential in the Ottoman rise to power. The Ottomans triumphed over their rivals by adapting techniques of administration from neighboring groups and by attracting those groups to their rule. In time, not only did the Ottoman state win the favor of Islamic clerics, but it also became the champion of Sunni Islam throughout the Islamic world.

By the mid-fourteenth century, the Ottomans had expanded into the Balkans, becoming the most powerful force in the eastern Mediterranean and western Asia. By the early sixteenth century, the Ottoman state controlled a vast territory, stretching in the west to the Moroccan border, in the north to Hungary and Moldavia, in the south through the Arabian Peninsula, and in the east to the Persian border. What was impressive and new within the Islamic world was the Ottomans' elaborate administrative hierarchy, atop which stood the sultan. Below him was a military and civilian bureaucracy whose task was to demand obedience and revenue from subjects. The bureaucracy's discipline enabled the sultan to expand his realm, which in turn forced him to invest in an even larger bureaucracy.

The empire's spectacular expansion was primarily a military affair. To recruit followers, the Ottomans promised wealth and glory to new subjects. This was an expensive undertaking, but territorial expansion generated vast financial and administrative rewards. Moreover, by spreading the spoils of conquest and lucrative administrative positions, rulers bought off potentially unhappy subordinates. Still, without military might, the Ottomans would not have enjoyed the successes associated with the brilliant reigns of Murad II (r. 1421–1451) and his appropriately named successor, Mehmed the Conqueror (r. 1451–1481).

Mehmed's most spectacular triumph was the conquest of Constantinople, an ambition for Muslim rulers ever since the birth of Islam. Mehmed left no doubt that this was his primary goal: shortly after his coronation, he vowed to capture Constantinople, the ancient Roman and Christian capital of the Byzantine Empire, and a city of immense strategic and commercial importance, which had withstood Muslim efforts at conquest for centuries. First, Mehmed built a fortress of his own to prevent European vessels from reaching the capital. Then, by promising his soldiers free access to booty and portraying the city's conquest as a holy cause, he amassed a huge army that outnumbered the defending force of 7,000 by more than ten times. For fifty-three days his troops bombarded Constantinople's massive walls with artillery that included enormous cannons built by Hungarian and Italian engineers. On May 29, 1453, Ottoman troops overwhelmed the surviving defenders and took Constantinople—which Mehmed promptly renamed Istanbul.

The Tools of Empire Building The Ottomans adopted Byzantine administrative practices to unify their enlarged state and incorporated many of Byzantium's powerful families into it. Their dynastic power, however, was not only military; it also rested on a firm religious foundation. At the center of this empire was the sultan, who combined a warrior ethos with an unwavering devotion to Islam. Describing himself as the "shadow of God" on earth, the sultan claimed the role of caretaker for the Islamic faith. Throughout the empire, he devoted substantial resources to the construction of elaborate mosques and to the support of Islamic schools. As self-appointed defender of the faith, the sultan assumed the role of protector of the holy cities on

The Süleymaniye Mosque Built by Sultan Suleiman to crown his achievements, the Süleymaniye Mosque was designed by the architect Sinan to dominate the city. Four tall minarets called the faithful to prayer. Location mattered to Suleiman. The Bosporus Strait, the vital route connecting the Mediterranean with the Black Sea, is visible beyond the mosque, and Justinian's Hagia Sophia (not visible here) is located just across a park from the mosque.

Topkapi Palace

Palace complex located in Istanbul that served as both the residence of the sultan, along with his harem and larger household, and the political headquarters of the Ottoman Empire.

the Arabian Peninsula and of Jerusalem, while working to unite the realm's diverse lands and peoples and constantly striving to extend the borders of Islam. During the reign of Suleiman (r. 1520–1566), the Ottomans reached the height of their territorial expansion. Under his administration, the Ottoman state ruled 20 to 30 million people. By the time Suleiman died, the Ottoman Empire bridged Europe and the Arab world.

Istanbul's **Topkapi Palace** exhibited the Ottomans' view of governance, the sultans' emphasis on religion, and the continuing influence of Ottoman familial traditions. Laid out by Mehmed II, the palace complex projected a vision of Istanbul as the center of the world. As a way to promote the sultan's magnificent power, architects designed the complex so that the buildings containing the imperial household were nestled behind layers of outer courtyards, in a mosaic of mosques, courts, and special dwellings for the sultan's harem. The harem had its own hierarchy of thousands of women, from the sultan's mother and consorts to the enslaved women who waited on them, and it became a formidable political force at the heart of Ottoman power.

The growing importance of Topkapi Palace as the command post of empire represented a crucial transition in the history of Ottoman rulers. Not only was the palace the place where future bureaucrats received their training; it was also the place where the chief bureaucrat, the grand vizier, carried out the day-to-day running of the empire. Whereas the early sultans had led their soldiers into battle personally and had met face-to-face with their kinsmen, the later rulers withdrew into the sacredness of the palace, venturing out only occasionally for grand ceremonies. Still, every Friday, subjects lined up outside the palace to introduce their petitions, ask for favors, and seek justice. If they were lucky, the sultans would be there to greet them—but they did so behind grated glass, issuing their decisions by tapping on the window. The palace thus projected a sense of majestic, distant wonder, a home fit for semidivine rulers.

Diversity and Control The Ottoman Empire's endurance into the twentieth century owed much to the ruling elite's ability to gain the support and employ the talents of exceedingly diverse populations. After all, neither conquest nor conversion eliminated cultural differences among the empire's distant provinces. Thus, for example, the Ottomans' language policy was one of flexibility and tolerance. Although Ottoman Turkish was the official language of administration, Arabic was the primary language of the Arab provinces, the common tongue of street life. Within the empire's European lands, many people spoke their own languages. From the fifteenth century onward, the Ottoman Empire was perhaps more multilingual than any of its rivals.

In politics, as in language, the Ottomans showed flexibility and tolerance. The imperial bureaucracy permitted extensive regional autonomy. In fact, Ottoman military cadres perfected a technique for absorbing newly conquered territories into the empire by parceling them out as revenue-producing units

The Topkapi Palace A view of the inner courtyard of the Topkapi Palace complex. Note the grand construction with entrances leading to the Council Hall, the Treasury, and the Tower of Justice. This courtyard was the site of important Ottoman ceremonies, such as the accession of sultans, the distribution of janissaries' salaries, and the reception of foreign emissaries.

among loyal followers and kin. Regional appointees could collect local taxes, part of which they earmarked for Istanbul and part of which they pocketed for themselves. This approach was a common administrative device for many world dynastic empires ruling extensive domains.

Like other empires, the Ottoman state was always in danger of losing control over its provincial rulers. Local potentates—the group that the imperial center allowed to rule in their distant regions—found that great distances enabled them to operate independently from central authority. These rulers kept larger amounts of tax revenues than Istanbul deemed proper. So, to limit their autonomy, the Ottomans established the janissaries, a corps of infantry soldiers and bureaucrats who owed direct allegiance to the sultan. The system at its high point involved conscription of Christian youths from the empire's European lands. This conscription, called the **devshirme**, required each village to hand over a certain number of males between the ages of eight and eighteen. Uprooted from their families and villages, these young men—selected for their fine physiques and good looks—were converted to Islam and sent to farms to build up their bodies and learn Turkish. A select few were moved on to Topkapi Palace to learn Ottoman military, religious, and administrative techniques. Some of these men—such as the architect Sinan, who designed the Süleymaniye Mosque—later enjoyed exceptional careers in the arts and sciences. Recipients of the best education available in the Islamic world, trained in Ottoman ways, instructed in the use of modern weaponry, and deprived of family connections, the *devshirme* recruits were prepared to serve the sultan (and the empire as a whole) rather than the interests of any particular locality or ethnic group.

Thus, the Ottomans established their legitimacy via military skill, religious backing, and a loyal bureaucracy. They artfully balanced the decentralizing tendencies of the outlying regions with the centralizing forces of the imperial capital. Relying on a careful mixture of religious faith, imperial patronage, and cultural tolerance, the sultans curried loyalty and secured political stability. Indeed, the Ottoman Empire was so strong and stable that it dominated the coveted and highly contested trading crossroads between Europe and Asia for many centuries. Thus, its consolidation had powerful consequences

devshirme
The Ottoman system of taking non-Muslim children in place of taxes in order to educate them in Muslim ways and prepare them for service in the sultan's bureaucracy.

for Europeans' efforts to rebuild their societies after the plague; above all, it closed off their traditional overland trade routes to India and China.

Western Christendom

No region suffered more from the Black Death than western Christendom, and arguably no region made a more spectacular comeback. From 1100 to 1300, Europe had enjoyed a surge in population, rapid economic growth, and significant technological and intellectual innovations, only to see these achievements halted in the fourteenth century by famine and the Black Death. Europeans responded by creating new political and cultural forms. New dynastic states arose, competing with one another, and a movement called the Renaissance revived Europe's connections with its Greek and Roman past and produced masterpieces of art, architecture, and other forms of thought.

THE CATHOLIC CHURCH, STATE BUILDING, AND ECONOMIC RECOVERY

Core Objectives

EXPLAIN the role that religious belief systems played in rebuilding the Islamic world, Europe, and Ming China in the fourteenth and fifteenth centuries.

In the aftermath of famine and plague, the peoples of western Christendom, like those in the Muslim world, looked to their religious beliefs and institutions as foundations for recovery. The faith of many had been severely tested, and religious authorities had to struggle to reclaim their power. To begin with, the late medieval western church found itself divided at the top (at one point during this period there were three popes) and challenged from below, both by individuals pursuing alternative kinds of spirituality and by increasing demands on the clergy and church administration. Disappointment with the clergy smoldered. The peasantry despaired at the absence of clergy when they were so greatly needed during the famines and Black Death. With groups like the Beghards and Beguines challenging the clergy's right to define religious doctrine and practices, the church fought back, identifying all that was suspect and demanding strict obedience to the true faith. This response included the persecution of Jews, Muslims in the Iberian Peninsula, gays, sex workers, "witches," and others considered by the church to be heretical. During this period the church also expanded its charitable and bureaucratic functions, providing alms to the urban poor and registering births, deaths, and economic transactions. Crucially, when faced with challenges to its authority, the church associated itself with secular rulers, lending moral authority to kings who claimed to rule "by divine right."

At the same time, the high death toll of the fourteenth and fifteenth centuries emboldened those who survived to seek higher wages or reductions in their feudal obligations. When landlords resisted or kings tried to impose new taxes, there were uprisings, including a 1358 peasant revolt in France that was dubbed the Jacquerie (the term derived from "Jacques Bonhomme," a name that contemptuous "masters" used for all peasants). Armed with only knives and staves, the peasantry went on a rampage, killing hated nobles and clergy and burning and looting all the property they could get their hands on. At issue was the peasants' insistence that they should no longer be tied to their land or have to pay for the tools they used in farming.

A better-organized uprising took place in England in 1381. Although the English Peasants' Revolt began as a protest against a tax levied to raise money for a war on France, it was also fueled by postplague labor shortages: serfs demanded the freedom to move about, and free farmworkers called for higher wages and lower rents. When landlords balked at these demands, aggrieved peasants assembled at the gates of London. The protesters demanded abolition of the feudal order, but the king ruthlessly suppressed them. Nonetheless, in both France and England a free peasantry gradually emerged as labor shortages made it impossible to keep peasants bound to the soil.

Europe's political rulers aligned themselves with church leaders to rebuild their states and consolidate their power. One royal family, the Habsburgs, drew on their Catholic religious traditions and established a powerful, long-lasting dynasty that would rule large parts of central Europe for centuries to follow.

The Imperial Crown Creating new emblems of authority and a culture of grandeur was important to rising monarchies of Afro-Eurasia. In an effort to distance themselves from their time-worn, conquering reputations, they invested heavily in palaces and elaborate courtly cultures. Above all, the crown and the throne became the symbols of imperial regality, as wearing the crown or sitting on the throne conferred supremacy. It was important, therefore, for these emblems to exude wealth and ostentation. This is the crown of the Holy Roman Emperor. Studded with pearls and large sapphires, emeralds, and amethysts, it combined piety (note the cross and the inlaid plaques of biblical scenes) with authority.

This family provided continuous emperors from 1445 to 1806 for the federation of states known as the Holy Roman Empire, and for a time they ruled Spain and its New World colonies. Yet even at the height of its power in the early sixteenth century, the Habsburg monarchy never succeeded in restoring an integrated empire to western Europe.

In 1450, western Christendom had no central government, no official tongue, and only a few successful commercial centers, mostly in the Mediterranean basin. (See Map 11.3.) The feudal system of a lord's control over the peasantry (see Chapter 10), which was now in decline, left a legacy of political fragmentation and enduring elite privileges, which made the consolidation of a unified Christian Europe even more difficult to achieve. Europe's linguistic diversity reflected its political fragmentation. No single ruler or language united peoples, even when they shared a religion. Europe saw Latin lose ground as rulers chose various regional dialects (such as French, Spanish, or English) to be their official state languages, in contrast with China, whose written literary Chinese script remained a key administrative tool for the new dynasts, and the Islamic world, where Arabic was the common language of faith and Turkish the language of administration.

Those who sought to rule the emerging states faced numerous obstacles. For example, rival claimants to the throne financed threatening private armies. Also, the clergy demanded and received privileges in the form of access to land and relief from taxation; they often meddled in politics, and the church became a formidable economic powerhouse. And once the printing press became more widely available in Europe in the 1460s, printers circulated anonymous pamphlets criticizing the court and the clergy. Some states had consultative political bodies—such as the Estates-General in France, the Cortes in Spain, and Parliament in England—in which princes formally asked representatives of their people for advice and, in the case of the English Parliament, for consent to new forms of taxation. Such political bodies gave no voice to common men and no representation to women. But they did allow the collective expression of grievances against overbearing policies.

Out of the chaos of famine, disease, and warfare, the diverse peoples of Europe found a political way forward. This path involved the formation of centralized dynastic monarchies. While not new to this period, the political institution of **monarchy** was particularly instrumental to western Christendom in the fifteenth century. Often in competition with the new monarchies, a handful of European city-states, in which a narrow group of wealthy and influential voters selected their leaders, survived right up to the nineteenth century and in some cases into the twentieth. Consolidation of these states occurred sometimes through strategic marriages but more often through warfare, both between princely families and with local aristocratic allies and foreign mercenaries.

One striking example of this political turmoil was the Hundred Years' War (1337–1453), in which the French sought to throw off English domination.

monarchy
Political system in which one individual holds supreme power and passes that power on to his or her next of kin.

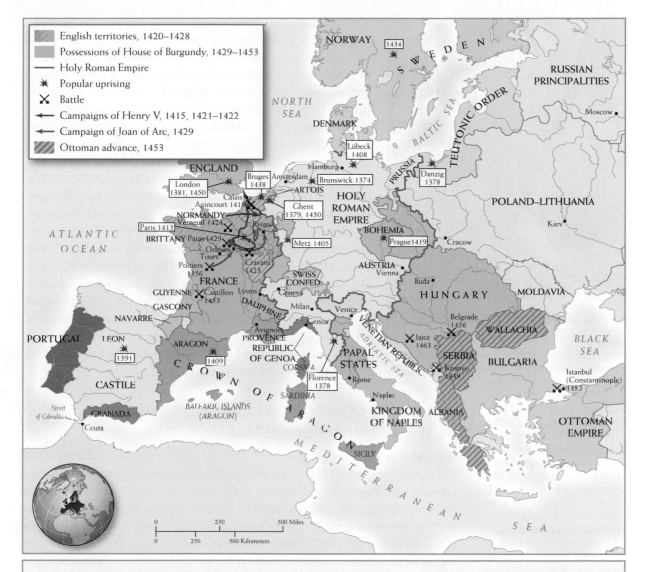

Map 11.3 legend:
- English territories, 1420–1428
- Possessions of House of Burgundy, 1429–1453
- Holy Roman Empire
- ✳ Popular uprising
- ✕ Battle
- ← Campaigns of Henry V, 1415, 1421–1422
- ← Campaign of Joan of Arc, 1429
- Ottoman advance, 1453

Map 11.3 Western Christendom, 1400–1500

Europe was a region divided by dynastic rivalries during the fifteenth century. Locate the most powerful regional dynasties on the map: Portugal, Castile, Aragon, France, Burgundy, England, and the Holy Roman Empire.

- Using the scale, contrast the sizes of political units in this map with those in Maps 11.2 (Ottoman Empire) and 11.4 (Ming China). Explain the significance of the differences.

- Where did popular uprisings take place? Based on your reading, why did those regions experience popular unrest?

- Based on the map, why might the Venetian Republic have been particularly engaged, both in trade and intermittent warfare, with the Ottomans?

The Black Death raged in the early years of this intermittent conflict. A central figure toward the end of the war was the peasant girl Joan of Arc, whose visions of various saints inspired her to support the French monarch Charles VII and see him crowned at Reims Cathedral. While Joan was a charismatic leader of troops, commanding as many as 8,000 at the decisive battle at Orléans, eventually the French nobility turned on her, and she was captured by the English. Joan was tried for heresy and burned at the stake in Rouen in 1431. Joan's brief, but remarkable, part in the Hundred Years' War illustrates the role an exceptional woman, even a peasant girl, could play on the predominantly male, elite political stage.

Elsewhere, in southern Europe, where economies rebounded through seaborne trade with Southwest Asia, political stabilization was swifter. The stabilization of Italian city-states such as Venice and Florence, and of monarchical rule in Portugal and Spain, led to an economic and cultural flowering known as the Renaissance. In northern and western Europe, the process took longer. In England and France, in particular, internal feuding, regional warfare, and religious fragmentation delayed recovery for decades (see Chapter 12).

Joan of Arc Joan of Arc became an icon of French identity. Inspired by divine visions of the archangel Michael as well as Saint Margaret and Saint Catharine, she was famous for leading troops to battle in the drive to repel English forces during the Hundred Years' War. But for many French nobles, she was a troublemaker; they captured her and gave her to the English, who burned her at the stake in 1431. She was nineteen years old. It was only later, as the French monarchy consolidated itself and cast about for popular symbols, that she was rebranded from popular rebel to martyr for the nation.

POLITICAL CONSOLIDATION AND TRADE IN THE IBERIAN PENINSULA

War and overseas trade played a central role in the emergence of new dynasties in Portugal and Spain. Through the fourteenth century, Portuguese Christians devoted themselves to fighting the Moors, who were Muslim occupants of North Africa, the western Sahara, and the Iberian Peninsula. After the Portuguese crossed the Strait of Gibraltar and seized the Moorish fortresses at Ceuta, in Morocco, their ships could sail between the Mediterranean and the Atlantic without Muslim interference. With that threat diminished, the Portuguese perceived their neighbor Castile (a region in what is now Spain) as their chief foe. Under João I (r. 1385–1433), Portugal defeated the Castilians, becoming the dominant power on the Iberian Peninsula. No longer preoccupied with Castilian competition, the Portuguese sought new territories and trading opportunities in the North Atlantic and along the West African coast. João's son Prince Henrique, known later as Henry the Navigator, further expanded the royal family's domain by supporting expeditions down the coast of Africa and offshore to the Atlantic islands of Madeira and the Azores. The west and central coasts of Africa and the islands of the North and South Atlantic, including the Cape Verde Islands, São Tomé, Principe, and Fernando Po, soon became Portuguese ports of call.

Portuguese monarchs granted the Atlantic islands to nobles as hereditary possessions on condition that the grantees colonize them, and soon the colonizers were establishing lucrative sugar plantations. In gratitude, noble families and merchants threw their political weight behind the king. Subsequent monarchs continued to cultivate local aristocrats' support for monarchical authority, thus ensuring smooth succession to the crown for members of the royal family.

In Spain, a new dynasty also emerged, though the road was difficult. Medieval Spain comprised rival kingdoms that quarreled ceaselessly. Within those kingdoms, several religions coexisted: Muslims, Jews, and Christians lived side by side in relative harmony, and Muslim armies still occupied strategic posts in the south. Over time, marriages and the formation of kinship ties among nobles and between royal lineages yielded a new political order. One by one, the major houses of the Spanish kingdoms intermarried, culminating in the wedding of Isabella of Castile and Ferdinand of Aragon in 1469. This marriage linked Castile, wealthy and populous, to Aragon, which enjoyed an extended trading network in the Mediterranean. Together, the monarchs brought unruly nobles and distant towns under their control. They topped off their achievements by marrying their children into other European royal families—especially the Habsburgs, central Europe's most powerful dynasty. Thus, Spain's two most important provinces were joined, and Spain later became a state to be reckoned with.

The new Spanish rulers sent Christian armies south to push Muslim forces out of the Iberian Peninsula. By the mid fifteenth century, only Granada, a strategic linchpin overlooking the straits between the Mediterranean and the Atlantic, remained in Muslim hands. After a long and costly siege, Christian forces captured the fortress there in 1492. This was a victory of enormous symbolic importance, as joyous as the fall of Constantinople to Mehmed and the Ottomans in 1453 was depressing (for Christians).

The Inquisition and Westward Exploration Isabella and Ferdinand sought to drive all non-Catholics out of Spain. Terrified by Ottoman incursions into Europe, they launched the **Inquisition** in 1481, taking aim especially against *conversos*—converted Jews and Muslims, whom they suspected were Christians only in name. When Granada fell, the crown ordered the expulsion of all Jews from Spain. After 1499, a more tolerant attempt to convert the Moors (Muslims) by persuasion gave way to forced conversion—or emigration. All told, almost half a million people were forced to flee the Spanish kingdoms. This lack of tolerance meant that Spain, like other European states in this era, became increasingly homogeneous. With fewer groups vying for influence within their territories, rulers' attention turned outward, fueling rivalries between the various European states.

So strong was the tide of Spanish fervor by late 1491 that the monarchs listened now to a Genoese navigator whose pleas for patronage they had

Inquisition
General term for a tribunal of the Roman Catholic Church that enforced religious orthodoxy. Several inquisitions took place over centuries, seeking to punish heretics, witches, Jews, and those whose conversion to Christianity was called into doubt.

Ferdinand and Isabella Entering Granada This altar relief, sculpted by Felipe Vigarny in the early sixteenth century, depicts the triumphant entrance of King Ferdinand and Queen Isabella into the city of Granada after their conquest of this last Muslim stronghold in Spain.

Renaissance
Term meaning "rebirth" used by historians to characterize the cultural flourishing of European nations between 1430 and 1550, which emphasized a break from the church-centered medieval world and a new concept of humankind as the center of the world.

previously rejected. Christopher Columbus promised them unimaginable riches that could finance their military campaigns and bankroll a crusade to liberate Jerusalem from Muslim hands. Off he sailed with a royal patent that guaranteed the monarchs a share of all he discovered. Soon the Spanish economy was reorienting itself toward the Atlantic, and Spain's merchants, missionaries, and soldiers were preparing for conquest and profiteering in what the Spanish had perceived, just a few years before, as a blank space on the map.

THE RENAISSANCE

Just as the Ming invoked Han Chinese traditions and the Ottomans looked to Sunni Islam to point the way forward, European elites drew on their own traditions for guidance as they rebuilt after the devastation of the plague. They found inspiration in ancient Greek and Roman institutions and ideas. Europe's extraordinary political and economic revival also involved a powerful outpouring of cultural achievements, led by Italian scholars and artists and financed by bankers, churchmen, and nobles. Much later, scholars coined the word **Renaissance** ("rebirth") to characterize the cultural flourishing of the Italian city-states, France, the Netherlands, England, and the Holy Roman Empire in the period 1430–1550. What was being "reborn" was ancient Greek and Roman art and learning—knowledge that could help people understand an expanding world and support the rights of secular individuals to exert power in it.

Although Christians generally portrayed the "fall" of Constantinople as a calamity, in fact the Muslim conquest brought benefits to western Europe. Many Christian survivors fled to ports in the west, bringing with them classical and Arabic manuscripts previously unknown in Europe. The well-educated, Greek-speaking émigrés generally became teachers and translators, thereby helping to revive Europeans' interest in classical antiquity and spreading knowledge of ancient Greek (which had virtually died out in medieval times). These manuscripts and teachers would play a vital role in Europe's Renaissance.

Although the Renaissance was largely funded by popes, Christian kings, and powerful wealthy merchants, it challenged the authority of traditional religious elites, breaking the medieval church's monopoly on answers to the big questions. Religious topics and themes, such as David and Goliath, Judith and Holofernes, and various scenes from Jesus's story (the annunciation of his birth to Mary, Jesus's adoration by the magi, and his baptism and crucifixion), dominated much of Renaissance art, but these themes took on new meaning as warnings to overbearing rulers and reminders to the obscenely wealthy, who sponsored many of these works, of their place in the cosmos and the civic responsibility that stemmed from their wealth. These religious themes were also joined by classical topics, such as scenes from mythology and the ancient past. The movement valued secular forms of learning, rather than just Christian doctrine, and a more human-centered understanding of the cosmos.

The Renaissance was all about new exposure to the old—to classical texts and ancient art and architectural forms. Although some Greek and Roman texts were known in Europe and the Islamic world, the use of the printing press made others accessible to western scholars for the first time. Scholars now realized that the pre-Christian Greeks and Romans had developed powerful means of representing and caring for the human body. Having studied the world directly, without the need to square their observations with biblical information, the ancients had much to teach about geography, astronomy, and architecture and about how to govern states and armies. For Renaissance scholars it was no longer enough to understand Christian doctrine and to concern themselves with the next world. One had to go back to the original, classical sources in order to understand the human condition. This in turn required the learning of languages and history. Scholarship that attempted to return to Greek and Roman sources became known as **humanism**.

Because political and religious powers were not united in Europe (as they were in China and the Islamic world), scholars and artists seeking sponsors for their work could play one side against the other or, alternatively, could suffer both clerical and political persecution. Michelangelo, a leading painter, sculptor, architect, and engineer of the age, completed commissions for the famous Florentine bankers and political leaders of the Medici family, for the Florentine Wool Guild, and for Pope Julius II. Peter Paul Rubens painted for the courts of France, Spain, England, and the Netherlands, as well as selling paintings on the open market. These two painters, renowned for showing a great deal of flesh, frequently offended conservative church officials. Even so, most support for the arts came either from the church or from individual clergymen, and virtually all secular donors were devout believers who commissioned works with religious themes. The Dutch scholar Desiderius Erasmus ridiculed corrupt popes and the clergy under the patronage of English, Dutch, and French supporters while remaining a Catholic, an ordained cleric,

Core Objectives

EXAMINE the way art and architecture reflected the political realities of the Islamic world, Europe, and Ming China after the Black Death.

humanism
The Renaissance aspiration to develop a greater understanding of the human experience than the Christian scriptures offered by reaching back into ancient Greek and Roman texts.

Renaissance Masterpieces *Left:* Leonardo da Vinci's *The Last Supper* depicts Christ's disciples reacting to his announcement that one of them will betray him. *Right:* Michelangelo's *David* stands over 13 feet high and was conceived as an expression of Florentine civic ideals.

and an opponent of Reformation doctrines. Conflicts within the Catholic Church, between the church and secular leaders, and among secular leaders and wealthy private citizens enabled artists to present challenging images and ideas with an unusual independence.

Gradually, a network of educated men and women took shape that was not wholly dependent on the church, the state, or a single princely patron. Classical knowledge gave individuals the means to challenge political, clerical, and aesthetic authority. Moreover, rivalries between Europe's relatively small states and city-states allowed many of these scholars to dodge the authorities by fleeing to neighboring communities. Of course, they could also use their learning to defend the older elites: for example, numerous lawyers and scholars continued to work for the popes in defending the papacy. At the same time, men like Erasmus and later Martin Luther (the leading figure of the Reformation in the sixteenth century) looked to secular princes to support their critical scholarship. In Florence, Niccolò Machiavelli wrote the most famous treatise on authoritarian power, *The Prince* (1513). Machiavelli argued that political leadership required mastering the rules of modern statecraft, even if in some cases this meant disregarding moral imperatives. Holding and exercising power were vital ends in themselves, he claimed; traditional ideas of civic virtue should not deter rulers, like those of the Medici family, from maintaining control over society.

The Printing Press Over time one major technological advance, the invention of the **printing press**, would serve to increase the spread of knowledge

printing press
A machine used to print text or pictures from type or plates, dramatically increasing the speed at which information could be copied and disseminated. The spread of printing press technology in the 1450s created a revolution in communication around the world.

more than any other phenomenon. The earliest advances in printing were made in China, where wood block printing first appeared around 220 CE, followed by movable type around 1040, and then the first metal movable type was used in Korea around 1300. In the 1450s, Johannes Gutenberg, the son of a German goldsmith, applied a technology to printing that was similar to the technology used to stamp metal coins. The first printed newspapers, leaflets, pamphlets, and books were printed on large wood frame presses that used rows of movable type to stamp the ink on the printed pages. Now hundreds of copies could be made in a few hours, hundreds of hours faster than handwritten and hand-bound copies of books could be produced. A second key factor that made this communication revolution possible was readily available cheap paper, made from old rags turned into pulp at local mills. Rising literacy rates, which increased the demand for books, were a third factor.

Invention of the Printing Press Around 1450, the German goldsmith Johannes Gutenberg invented the printing press. It was not a complex or elaborate device. Consider the simplicity of this mechanical device, with few moving parts and the use of a modest screw to push plates together. Nonetheless, its ability to reproduce thousands of pages per day—as opposed to only dozens at the hands of scribes—slashed the cost of printing and made information cheap. Just as important, the device itself was inexpensive and easy to build. Within a few decades, printing presses were in operation throughout western Europe, reading books became commonplace, and religious and secular authorities lost what control was left to them over the creation and flow of information.

Artistic and intellectual experiments, specifications for innovative weapons, and humanist writings were rapidly exported from Renaissance Italy to other parts of Europe. Major news like Columbus's first voyage and the resulting encounters and conquests spread rapidly around Europe, as did major criticisms of this new form of European imperialism. Rulers also used this revolution in communication to expand and centralize their own power through widely distributed printed propaganda and the creation of standardized national languages. The powerful impact of printing was immediate, and its role in communication would continue to grow and evolve for the centuries ahead both in Europe and globally.

With Renaissance ideas challenging traditional authority and rulers facing a range of internal and external obstacles, the new monarchies of Europe were not all immediately successful in consolidating power and unifying peoples. In France and England, for example, the great age of monarchy had yet to dawn. Even when stable states did arise in Europe, they were fairly small compared with the Ottoman and Ming Empires. In the mid-sixteenth century, Portugal and Spain, Europe's two most expansionist states, had populations of 1 million and 9 million, respectively. England, excluding Wales, had a mere 3 million in 1550. Only France, with 17 million, had a population close to the Ottoman Empire's 25 million. And these numbers paled in comparison with Ming China's population of nearly 200 million in 1550 and Mughal India's 110 million in 1600. But in Europe, small could be advantageous. Portugal's relatively small population meant that the crown had fewer groups to control. In the world of finance, the most successful merchants were those inhabiting the smaller Italian city-states and, a bit later, the cities of the northern Netherlands. The Florentines developed sophisticated banking techniques, created extensive networks of agents throughout Europe and the Mediterranean, and served as bankers to the popes. At the same time, the Renaissance—which flourished in the city-states and newly stabilized monarchies—made elite European culture more cosmopolitan and independent from government authority, even if it could not unify the states and peoples who cultivated it.

Ming China

Like the Europeans, the Chinese saw their stable worldview and political order crumble under the catastrophes of human and microbial invasions. Moreover, like the Europeans, people in China had long regarded outsiders as "barbarians" and balked at being ruled by them. Together, the Mongols and the Black Death upended the political and intellectual foundations of what had appeared to be the world's most integrated society. The Mongols brought the Yuan dynasty to power; then the plague devastated China and prepared the way for the emergence of a new dynasty. The **Ming dynasty**, ruled by ethnically Han Chinese, defined itself against its foreign predecessors. Ming emperors sought to reinforce everything Chinese. (See Current Trends in World History: Ming Fashion.) In particular, they supported China's vast internal agricultural markets in an attempt to minimize dependence on merchants and foreign trade.

RESTORING ORDER

In the chaotic fourteenth century, as plague and famine ravaged China and the Mongol Yuan dynasty collapsed, only a strong military movement capable of overpowering other groups could restore order. That intervention began at the hands of a poor young man who had trained in the **Red Turban movement**: Zhu Yuanzhang, a successful warlord who had led a rebellion against the waning power of the Mongols and any others who would assert control in their wake.

It soon became clear that Zhu had a much grander design for China than the ambitions of most warlords. When he took Nanjing in 1356, he renamed it Yingtian ("in response to heaven"). Buoyed by subsequent successful military campaigns, Zhu (r. 1368–1398) took the imperial title of Hongwu ("expansive and martial") Emperor and proclaimed the founding of the Ming ("brilliant") dynasty in 1368. Soon thereafter, his troops met little resistance when they seized the Yuan capital of Khan-balik (soon renamed Beijing), causing the Mongol emperor to flee to his homeland in the steppe. It would, however, take the Hongwu Emperor almost another twenty years to reunify the entire country.

Ming dynasty
Successor to the Mongol Yuan dynasty that reinstituted and reinforced Han Chinese ceremonies and ideals, including rule by an ethnically Han bureaucracy.

Red Turban movement
Diverse religious movement in China during the fourteenth century that spread the belief that the world was drawing to an end as Mongol rule was collapsing.

CENTRALIZATION UNDER THE MING

The Hongwu Emperor and successive Ming emperors had to rebuild a devastated society from the ground up. Although in the past China had experienced natural catastrophes, wars, and social dislocation, the plague's legacy was devastation on an unprecedented scale. It left the new rulers with the formidable challenge of rebuilding the great cities, restoring respect for ruling elites, and reconstructing the bureaucracy.

Imperial Grandeur and Kinship The rebuilding began with the Hongwu Emperor, whose capital at Nanjing reflected imperial grandeur. When the dynasty's third emperor, the Yongle ("perpetual happiness") Emperor, relocated the capital to Beijing, he flaunted an even more grandiose style, employing around 100,000 artisans and 1 million laborers to build this new capital. The city had three separate walled enclosures. Inside the outer city walls sprawled the imperial city; within its walls lay the palace compound, the Forbidden City. Traffic within the walled sections navigated through broad boulevards leading to the different gates, above which imposing towers soared. The palace compound, where the imperial family resided, had more than 9,000 rooms. Anyone standing in the front courts, which measured more than 400 yards on a side and boasted marble terraces and carved railings, would gasp at the awe-inspiring projection of power. That was precisely the effect the Ming emperors wanted (just as the Ottoman sultans did in building Topkapi Palace).

Marriage and kinship buttressed the power of the Ming imperial household, much as dynastic strategies did in Europe. The Ming dynasty's founder married the adopted daughter of a leading Red Turban rebel (her father, according to legend, was a convicted murderer), thereby consolidating his power and eliminating a threat. Empress Ma, as she was known, became the Hongwu Emperor's principal wife and was praised for her compassion. Emerging as the kinder face of the regime, she tempered the harsh and sometimes cruel disposition of her spouse. He had numerous other consorts as well, including Korean and Mongol women, who bore him twenty-six sons and sixteen daughters. (His household was similar to, although on a smaller scale than, the Ottoman sultan's harem at Topkapi Palace.)

Building a Bureaucracy Faced with the challenge of reestablishing order out of turmoil, the Hongwu Emperor initially sought to rule through his kinsmen—by giving imperial princes generous stipends, command of large garrisons, and significant autonomy in running their domains. However, when the princes' power began to threaten the court, the Hongwu Emperor slashed their stipends, reduced their privileges, and took control of their garrisons. No longer dependent on these men, he established an imperial

Ming Fashion

Ming rulers liked to represent themselves as custodians of "civilized" Han traditions, in contrast to the "barbarian" ways of the previous Mongol Yuan dynasty. However, from governmental practices to clothing fashions, there were visible signs everywhere that the Ming, despite their rhetoric, followed in the footsteps of the Yuan and became more and more linked to an ever-growing, interconnected world. As trade with neighboring and faraway lands continued unabated and merchants and travelers kept moving, it proved to be impossible for the Ming to keep outside influences at arm's length. At the same time, the rhetoric of a return to Han traditions did generate moves to invoke antiquity in the realm of fashion. Status-conscious elites with newfound wealth eagerly purchased clothes in what they believed to be the ancient Han style, hoping to set themselves apart from the common people. Their flirtation with antiquity, however, often ended up being more of a reinvention to satisfy the surging demands of the market than a genuine return to earlier conventions.

Founder Zhu Yuanzhang set the tone of the Ming by trying to rid the

An example of headwear used by Ming officials, reputedly following the style of earlier dynasties. The beams attached to the crown of the cap indicate the official's rank, so the cap is known as a "beamed cap."

country of the close-fitting tunics worn by the Mongols. He advocated instead the wearing of the reputedly Tang-style garment of earlier times. While this measure did meet with some success, the vibrant clothing industry was hardly free of its fascination with the "exotic," such as horsehair skirts from Korea for men. These skirts were a

rare commodity when they first arrived, probably via trade missions. But by the late fifteenth century, local weavers had become so skilled in making them, and consumers so eager to obtain them, that craftworkers were caught stealing the tails of horses to satisfy the soaring demand for the raw materials. Indeed, undoubtedly to the chagrin of the first Ming emperor and his descendants, much of the Yuan style and even terminology in both male and female clothing persisted during the Ming era.

The retro movement in fashion, as mentioned, had more to do with the demands of a changing Ming society than with the official advocacy for restorationism. Nowhere was this more apparent than in the myriad styles of hats for men—a convenient yet highly visible way to make a statement of social standing. Invoking the names of earlier dynasties, styles included the Han cap, the Jin cap, the Tang cap, and so on. The most interesting, however, was the Chunyang hat, which allegedly drew upon both Han and Tang styles in its design but had actually become a symbol of the so-called new and strange fashion that so often attracted commentary in Ming writings. In fact,

bureaucracy beholden only to him and to his successors. Its officials won appointments through their outstanding performance on a reinstated civil service examination.

In addition, the Hongwu Emperor took other steps to install a centralized system of rule. He assigned bureaucrats to oversee the manufacture of porcelain, cotton, and silk products as well as tax collection. He reestablished the Confucian school system as a means of selecting a cadre of loyal officials (not unlike the Ottoman janissaries and administrators). He

The "paddy-field gown" for women might have had its origins in Buddhist robes.

girls dress in silk gauze, and the sing-song girls look down on brocaded silks and embroidered gowns." Respectable women, we are told, looked to the clothing and style of the courtesans of the prosperous southern region of the country for ideas and inspiration for fashion. Indeed, much of our visual knowledge of Ming women's clothing comes from paintings that likely depicted highly trained courtesans or the female "entertainers" that were ubiquitous in Ming urban centers. These paintings reveal the different and consistently evolving styles of clothing for Ming women, including the "paddy-field gowns"—which might have owed their origins to Buddhist robes—that were the focus of much criticism from those who frowned on the growing penchant for the exotic, the strange, the outrageous, and the irreverent in the realm of fashion. If nothing else, this debate about clothing certainly tells us that despite the often conservative stance and policies of the Ming regime, the everyday life of many Ming subjects was a constant exercise in negotiating the multiple impacts of both the old and the new, as well as the familiar and the foreign, in different arenas of their rapidly changing society.

it was favored by the young, who had nothing but disdain for ancient styles!

Nor was the rage for fashion reserved for only men, or even for just the privileged. One Ming writer lamented, perhaps with a hint of exaggeration, "Nowadays the very servant

Questions for Analysis

- What are some examples of Ming "retro" fashion? Why did the Ming elite cultivate an "ancient" Han style?
- How do we know about changes in women's fashion in the Ming era? Are there any dangers in using these sources to understand the dress of all Ming women?
- Flipping back through the illustrations in this chapter, what do you see of the clothing from other regions? What questions does the analysis of Ming clothing presented here raise for you as you reexamine the images of Ottomans and western Europeans?

Explore Further

Clunas, Craig, and Jessica Harrison-Hall (eds.), *Ming: 50 Years That Changed China* (2014).

Finnane, Antonia, *Changing Clothes in China: Fashion, History, Nation* (2008).

also set up local networks of villages to rebuild irrigation systems and to supervise reforestation projects to prevent flooding—with the astonishing result that the amount of land reclaimed nearly tripled within eight years. For water supply and flood control, over 40,000 reservoirs underwent repairs or new construction. Historians estimate that the Hongwu Emperor's reign oversaw the planting around Nanjing of about 1 billion trees, which were later used in building a maritime expedition fleet in the early fifteenth century.

The Forbidden City The Yongle Emperor relocated the capital to Beijing, where he began the construction of the Forbidden City, or imperial palace. The palace was designed to inspire awe in all who saw it.

The imperial palace not only projected the image of a power center; it *was* the center of power. Every official received his appointment by the emperor through the Ministry of Personnel. The Hongwu Emperor also eliminated the post of prime minister (he executed the man who held the post) and ruled directly. Ming bureaucrats had to kneel before the emperor. The drawback of this centralized control, of course, was that the Ming emperor had to keep tabs on this immense system. The Hongwu Emperor constantly moved his bureaucrats around, sometimes fortifying the administration, sometimes undermining it lest it become too autonomous. Over time, the Hongwu Emperor nurtured a bureaucracy far more extensive than that of the Ottomans. The Ming thus established the most highly centralized system of government of all the monarchies of this period.

RELIGION UNDER THE MING

Just as the Ottoman sultans projected themselves as Muslim rulers, calling themselves the shadow of God, and European monarchs claimed to rule by divine right, the Ming emperors enhanced their legitimacy by drawing on ancient Chinese religious traditions. Citing the mandate of heaven, the emperor revised and strengthened the elaborate rites and ceremonies that had supported dynastic power for centuries. Official rituals, such as those related to the gods of soil and grain, reinforced political and social classes, portraying the rulers as the moral and spiritual benefactors of their subjects. In lavish ceremonies, the emperor engaged in sacrificial rites, cultivating his image as mediator between the human and the spiritual worlds. The message was clear: the gods were on the side of the Ming household.

MING RULERSHIP

Conquest and defense helped establish the Ming empire, and bureaucracy kept it functioning. The empire's scale required complex administration. (See Map 11.4.) To many outsiders (especially Europeans, whose region was in a state of constant war), Ming stability and centralization appeared to be political wizardry.

Ming rulers worried in particular about maintaining the support of ordinary people in the countryside. The emperor wished to be seen as the special guardian of his subjects. He wanted their allegiance as well as their taxes and labor. But during hard times, poor farmers were reluctant to provide resources—taxes or services—to distant officials. A popular Chinese proverb was "The mountain is high and the emperor is far away." For these reasons, and because he distrusted state bureaucrats, the Hongwu Emperor preferred to entrust the management of rural communities to local leaders, whom he appointed as village chiefs, village elders, or tax captains. Within these communities, the dynasty created a social hierarchy based on age, sex, and kinship. While women's labor remained critical for the village economy, the government reinforced a gender hierarchy by promoting women's chastity and constructing commemorative arches for widows who honored their husbands by refraining from remarrying.

Like the European and Islamic states, the Ming Empire faced periodic unrest and rebellion. Rebels often proclaimed their own brand of religious beliefs and local elites resented central control. Outright terror helped stymie these threats to central authority. In a massive wave of carnage, the Hongwu Emperor slaughtered anyone who posed a threat to his authority, from the highest of ministers to the lowliest of scribes. From 1376 to 1393, four of his purges condemned close to 100,000 subjects to execution.

Yet, despite the emperor's immense power, the Ming Empire remained undergoverned. Indeed, as the population multiplied, there

Ming Deities A pantheon of deities were worshipped during the Ming dynasty, demonstrating the rich religious culture of the period and the elaborate way in which faith reinforced hierarchy.

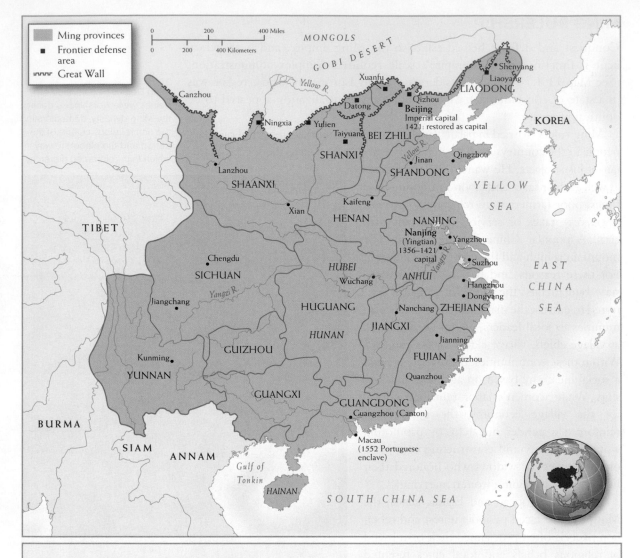

Map 11.4 Ming China, 1500–1600

The Ming state was one of the largest empires at this time—and the most populous. Using the scale, determine the length of its coastline and its internal borders.

- What were the two Ming capitals and the three main seaport trading cities? How far are they from one another?

- According to the map, where did the Ming rulers expect the greatest threat to their security?

- How many provinces are outlined on the map? How far is Beijing from some of the more distant provinces? What sorts of challenges did that create for the centralized style of Ming rule, and how does the chapter suggest those challenges were resolved?

were too few loyal officials to handle local affairs. By the sixteenth and early seventeenth centuries, for example, some 10,000 to 15,000 officials shouldered the responsibility of managing a population exceeding 200 million people. Nonetheless, the Hongwu Emperor bequeathed to his descendants a set of tools for ruling that drew on subjects' direct loyalty to the emperor and on the intricate workings of an extensive bureaucracy. His legacy enabled his successors to balance local sources of power with the needs of dynastic rulership.

TRADE AND EXPLORATION UNDER THE MING

Gradually, the political stability brought by the Ming dynasty allowed trade to revive. Now the new dynasty's merchants reestablished China's preeminence in long-distance commercial exchange. Chinese silk and cotton textiles, as well as fine porcelains, ranked among the world's most coveted luxuries. When a Chinese merchant ship sailed into a port, trading partners and onlookers crowded the docks to watch the unloading of precious cargoes. Although Ming rulers' support for overseas ventures wavered and eventually declined, this period saw important developments in Chinese trade and exploration.

Overseas Trade: Success and Suspicion During the Ming period, Chinese traders based in the three main ports—Hangzhou, Quanzhou, and Guangzhou (Canton)—were as energetic as their Muslim counterparts in the Indian Ocean. These and other ports were home to prosperous merchants and the point of convergence for vast sea-lanes. Leaving the mainland ports, Chinese vessels carried precious wares to offshore islands, the Pescadores, and Taiwan. From there, they sailed on to the ports of Southeast Asia. As entrepôts for global goods, East Asian ports flourished. Former fishing villages developed into major urban centers.

The Ming dynasty viewed overseas expansion with suspicion, however. The Hongwu Emperor feared that too much contact with the outside world would cause instability and undermine his rule. In fact, he banned private maritime commerce in 1371. But enforcement was lax, and by the late fifteenth century maritime trade had once again surged. Because much of the thriving business took place in defiance of official edicts, constant friction occurred between government officials and maritime traders. Although the Ming government ultimately agreed to issue licenses for overseas trade in the mid-sixteenth century, its policies continued to vacillate. To Ming officials, unlike their counterparts in Portugal and Spain, the sea represented problems of order and control rather than opportunities.

The Expeditions of Zheng He One spectacular exception to the early Ming attitude toward maritime trade was a series of officially sponsored expeditions in the early fifteenth century. It was the ambitious third Ming emperor, the

Core Objectives

COMPARE how Ottoman, Iberian, and Ming rulers extended their territories and regional influence.

Zheng He

Ming naval commander who, from 1405 to 1433, led seven massive naval expeditions to impress other peoples with Ming might and to establish tributary relations with Southeast Asia, Indian Ocean ports, the Persian Gulf, and the east coast of Africa.

Yongle Emperor, who took this initiative. One of his loyal followers was a Muslim whom the Ming army had captured as a boy. The youth was castrated and sent to serve at the court (as a eunuch, he could not continue his family line and so theoretically owed allegiance solely to the emperor). Given the name **Zheng He** (1371–1433), he grew up to be an important military leader. The emperor entrusted him with venturing out to trade, collect tribute, and display China's power to the world.

From 1405 to 1433, Zheng He commanded the world's greatest armada and led seven naval expeditions. His larger ships stretched 400 feet in length (Columbus's *Santa Maria* was 85 feet), carried hundreds of sailors on four tiers of decks, and maneuvered with sophisticated rudders, nine masts, and watertight compartments. The first expedition set sail with 28,000 men aboard a flotilla of sixty-two large ships and over 200 lesser ones. Zheng He and his entourage aimed to establish tributary relations with far-flung territories—from Southeast Asia to the Indian Ocean ports, to the Persian Gulf, and to the east coast of Africa. (See Map 11.5.) These expeditions sought not territorial expansion but rather control of trade and tribute. When the Yongle Emperor died in 1424, the expeditions lost their most enthusiastic patron.

Zheng He's Ships and Exotic Cargo The largest ship in Zheng He's armada had nine staggered masts and twelve silk sails. This graphic demonstrates just how large and complex Zheng He's ships were, compared with Christopher Columbus's *Santa Maria*. With ships so large, Zheng He's fleet could return to China with magnificent and exotic cargo, like the giraffes brought as tribute from Bengal in 1414 and Malindi in 1415. These tribute giraffes were recorded in several paintings, some inscribed with a poem attributed to his contemporary Shen Du that described the giraffes as *qilin*, mythical creatures that appear during the rule of a great leader.

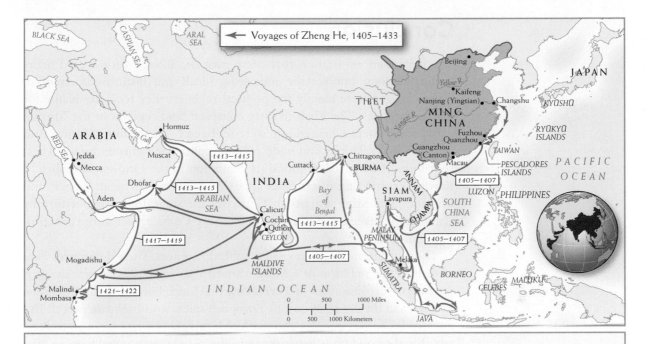

Map 11.5 Voyages of Zheng He, 1405–1433

Zheng He's voyages are some of the most famous in world history. Many have speculated about how history might have been different if the Chinese emperors had allowed the voyages to continue.

- What routes did Zheng He's armada follow?
- Referring to other maps in this chapter and earlier chapters, with what peoples did Zheng He's armada come into contact?
- Using the scale on the map, estimate how far Zheng He's armada sailed. How does this distance compare with the distances covered by other world travelers you've encountered in this text?

Moreover, by the mid-fifteenth century, there was a revival of military threats from the north. Recalling how the maritime-oriented Song dynasty had been overrun by invaders from the north (see Chapter 10), Ming officials withdrew imperial support for seagoing ventures and instead devoted their energies to overland ventures and defense.

Even though maritime commerce continued without official patronage, the Ming decision to forgo overseas ventures was momentous. Although China remained the wealthiest, most densely settled region of the world, with fully developed state structures and thriving markets, the empire's wariness of overseas projects deprived merchants and would-be explorers of vital support in an age when others were beginning to look outward and overseas.

Conclusion

The dying and devastation that came with the Black Death caused many transformations, but certain underlying ideals and institutions endured. What changed were mainly the political regimes; they took the blame for the catastrophes. The Yuan dynasty collapsed, and regimes in the Muslim world and western Christendom were replaced by new political forms. And yet, universal religions and wide-ranging cultural systems endured. A fervent form of Sunni Islam found its champion in the Ottoman Empire. In Europe, centralizing monarchies appeared in Spain, Portugal, France, and England. The Ming dynasts in China set the stage for a long tenure by claiming the mandate of heaven and stressing China's place at the center of their universe.

The new states and empires had notable differences. These differences were evident in the ambition of a Ming warlord who established a new dynasty, the military expansionism of Turkish warrior bands bordering the Byzantine Empire, and the desire of various European rulers to consolidate power. But interactions among peoples also mattered; this era saw an eagerness to reestablish and expand trade networks and a desire to convert unbelievers to "the true faith"—be it a form of Islam or an exclusive Christianity.

All the dynasties surveyed in this chapter faced similar problems. They had to establish legitimacy, ensure smooth succession, deal with religious movements, and forge working relationships with nobles, townspeople, merchants, and peasants. Yet each state developed a distinctive identity. They all combined political innovation, traditional ways of ruling, and ideas borrowed from neighbors. European monarchies achieved significant internal unity, often through warfare with competing states. Ottoman rulers perfected techniques for ruling an ethnically and religiously diverse empire: they moved military forces swiftly, allowed local communities a degree of autonomy, and trained a bureaucracy dedicated to the Ottoman and Sunni Islamic way of life. The Ming fashioned an imperial system based on a Confucian bureaucracy and intense subordination to the emperor so that they could manage a mammoth population. The rising monarchies of Europe and the Ottoman state all blazed with religious fervor and sought to eradicate or subordinate the beliefs of other groups.

The new states displayed unprecedented political and economic powers. All demonstrated military prowess, a desire for stable political and social hierarchies and secure borders, and a drive to expand. Each legitimized its rule via dynastic marriage and succession, state-sanctioned religion, and administrative bureaucracies. Each supported vigorous commercial activity. The Islamic regimes, especially, engaged in long-distance commerce and, by conquest and conversion, extended their holdings.

For western Christendom, the Ottoman conquests were decisive. They provoked Europeans to establish commercial connections to the east, south, and west. The consequences of their new toeholds would be momentous—just as the Chinese decision to turn away from overseas exploration and commerce meant that China's contact with the outside world would be overland and more limited. As we shall see in Chapter 12, both decisions were instrumental in determining which worlds would come together and which would remain apart.

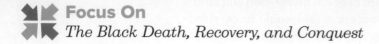

Focus On
The Black Death, Recovery, and Conquest

Collapse and Consolidation

- Bubonic plague originates in Inner Asia and afflicts people from China to Europe.

- Climate change and famine leave people vulnerable to infection, while commerce facilitates the spread of disease.

- The plague kills 25 to 65 percent of infected populations and leaves societies in turmoil.

The Islamic Heartland

- Ottomans overrun Constantinople and become the primary Sunni regime in the Islamic world.

- The Ottomans establish their legitimacy with military prowess, religious backing, and a loyal bureaucracy.

- Sultans manage the decentralizing tendencies of outlying provinces with flexibility and tolerance, relying on religious faith, patronage, and bureaucracy.

Western Christendom

- New dynastic monarchies that claim to rule by divine right appear in Portugal, Spain, France, and England.

- The Inquisition takes aim against *conversos*—converted Jews and Muslims.

- A rebirth of classical learning, known as the Renaissance, originates in Italian city-states and spreads throughout western Europe.

Ming China

- The Ming dynasty replaces the Mongol Yuan dynasty and rebuilds a strong state from the ground up, claiming a mandate from heaven.

- An elaborate, centralized bureaucracy oversees the revival of infrastructure and long-distance trade.

- The emperor and bureaucracy concentrate on developing internal markets and overland trade at the expense of overseas commerce.

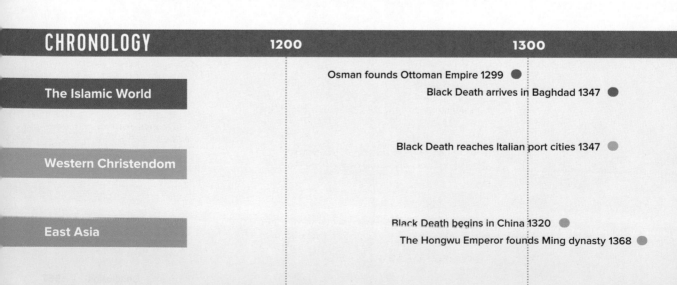

CHRONOLOGY

	1200	1300
The Islamic World		Osman founds Ottoman Empire 1299 ● Black Death arrives in Baghdad 1347 ●
Western Christendom		Black Death reaches Italian port cities 1347 ●
East Asia		Black Death begins in China 1320 ● The Hongwu Emperor founds Ming dynasty 1368 ●

THINKING ABOUT GLOBAL CONNECTIONS

- **Thinking about Exchange Networks** By the fourteenth century, most of the Afro-Eurasian landmass was bound together by multiple exchange networks that functioned on many levels—political, cultural, and commercial. How did these exchange networks facilitate the spread of the plague? In what ways did the spread of the Black Death correspond with and diverge from existing political, cultural, and commercial networks?

- **Thinking about Changing Power Relationships** Fourteenth-century famine and plague, and the accompanying political, economic, and natural crises, together triggered powerful, often differing, responses

in western Europe, the Ottoman lands, and Ming China. How did men and women at different levels of society respond to the fourteenth-century crises? How did their responses reshape their societies? Pay special attention to the relationships among ordinary men and women, elites, and imperial bureaucracies in all three regions.

- **Thinking about Environmental Impacts** Climate change laid the groundwork for the devastation of the Black Death. What environmental developments in Europe, central Asia, and China set the stage for the Black Death?

Key Terms

Black Death p. 533
devshirme p. 545
dynasty p. 539
humanism p. 553

Inquisition p. 551
Ming dynasty p. 556
monarchy p. 548

Ottoman Empire p. 540
printing press p. 554
Red Turban movement p. 556

Renaissance p. 552
Topkapi Palace p. 544
Zheng He p. 564

 Go to INQUIZITIVE to see what you've learned—and learn what you've missed—with personalized feedback along the way.

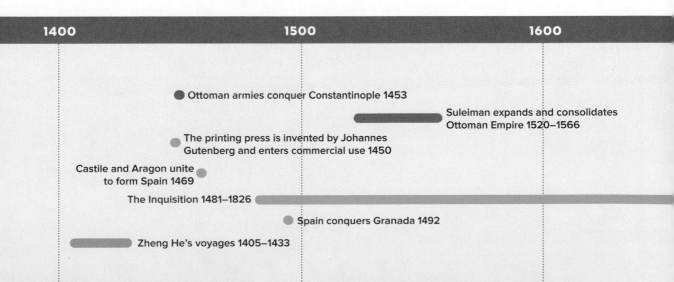

1400   1500   1600

Ottoman armies conquer Constantinople 1453

Suleiman expands and consolidates Ottoman Empire 1520–1566

The printing press is invented by Johannes Gutenberg and enters commercial use 1450

Castile and Aragon unite to form Spain 1469

The Inquisition 1481–1826

Spain conquers Granada 1492

Zheng He's voyages 1405–1433

Global Themes and Sources

Causes and Effects of the Black Death

··

The devastation wrought by the plague in Afro-Eurasia and the upheaval that followed were unprecedented and far-reaching in their impact. Families were broken as parents, spouses, and children deserted one another for fear of contagion. Religious responses varied from hopelessness to ecstatic devotion. The plague affected the economy as well, causing skyrocketing prices, diminished availability of goods and labor, and unmet demand for certain products and services. Dramatic population losses demonstrate its demographic impact: beginning in southwestern China in the 1320s, the Pestilence or Great Mortality, as it came to be known in Europe, wiped out between 25 and 65 percent of the populations it afflicted.

The plague traveled along the trade routes of Inner Eurasia, taking advantage of the connectivity that had bound the Afro-Eurasian world together and facilitated the movement of people, goods, and ideas. The plague also took advantage of an already weakened population that had experienced a "Little Ice Age" and a resulting famine in the early years of the fourteenth century. Modern scholars have scrutinized sources to determine answers to such questions as what the precise death tolls were, why the plague's effects were so much more devastating in some regions than in others, and what kind of disease it was—septicemic (blood-borne and spread by fleas on rats and other animals), pneumonic (airborne, spread by the coughing that accompanied the spewing of blood that so many of the sources report), or a combination of the two. No less fascinating, however, are the attempts by writers of the fourteenth and early fifteenth centuries to understand the plague's causes and immediate effects.

The sources here offer a mix of perspectives. Some come from authors who experienced plague firsthand and others from authors who lived in the plague's aftermath and considered its causes and its effects.

There are regional accounts from two different cultural spheres: the Islamic world, particularly Syria and Egypt, and Europe. Ibn al-Wardi, from Aleppo in Syria, recorded his thoughts on what was causing the plague and described immediate responses to, and effects of, the disease. His understanding offers only the most short-term perspective because he died from the plague in 1349 and thus did not live to see the long-term aftermath. The Florentine Baldassarre de Buonaiuti experienced the plague in one of the European cities hit the hardest by the disease. There are echoes of Baldassarre in the introduction to Boccaccio's famed *Decameron*, in which elite youth withdraw from the city and entertain one another with stories, having locked themselves away in a country villa to escape the sickness in the city. In his later years, Baldassarre recollected the events of 1348 in his *Florentine Chronicle*. The plague offered Ibn Khaldûn an opportunity to ruminate on the patterns of civilization in his *Muqaddimah* (c. 1375). Written in Cairo, his historiographical masterpiece gives a North African perspective on the effects of the plague a full generation after its impact. Finally, a student of Ibn Khaldûn, al-Maqrizi, gives yet another Cairene, Islamic perspective, a generation later.

These sources, with their different perspectives—Christian and Islamic, contemporary and from the plague's aftermath, by chronicler and by philosophical historian, European as well as Southwest Asian and North African—encourage us to think about the complexity of cause and effect. We can see how those who lived in proximity to this catastrophic event described the causes of what they, or their recent relatives, had lived through. The sources allow us to consider the short- and long-term effects of the disease as experienced in the fourteenth and fifteenth centuries. And, together with the material in the chapter, the sources give us an opportunity to reflect both on the complexity of causation, teasing out the primary and secondary causes for how the plague played out, and on the larger historical significance of the plague and its aftermath.

Analyzing the Causes and Effects of the Black Death

- How do the responses to, and the effects of, plague in the Muslim world (as reported by al-Wardi, Ibn Khaldûn, and al-Maqrizi) compare with those in Florence (as reported in *The Florentine Chronicle*)?

- What patterns in explaining causation and effects of plague do you detect in these sources? How do the various causes and effects explicitly or implicitly discussed in each text build on one another?

- Based on your reading of these sources, what do you think is the short- and long-term historical significance of the effects of the plague?

PRIMARY SOURCE 11.1

Plague in Southwest Asia (1349), Ibn al-Wardi

Al-Wardi wrote two major works, one a natural history of the Islamic world and the other a history, from which this excerpt on the plague's devastation is taken. His is the most thorough extant contemporary Muslim description of the Black Death. Al-Wardi's discussion of the plague is rendered all the more poignant by the fact that he became one of its victims as the plague swept through Aleppo in 1349.

- **What role does religion and/or God play in al-Wardi's account of the plague? How do the Sunni-Shiite division and other rifts factor into al-Wardi's account?**

- **How does al-Wardi describe the plague's progress across Afro-Eurasia, and what does that description suggest about al-Wardi's understanding of causation?**

- **What are some of the attempted remedies described by al-Wardi, and what do those remedies suggest about the understanding of the plague's causes?**

God is my security in every adversity. My sufficiency is in God alone. Is not God sufficient protection for His servant? Oh God, pray for our master, Muḥammad, and give him peace. Save us for his sake from the attacks of the plague and give us shelter.

The plague frightened and killed. It began in the land of darkness. Oh, what a visitor! It has been current for fifteen years. China was not preserved from it nor could the strongest fortress hinder it. The plague afflicted the Indians in India. It weighed upon the Sind. It seized with its hand and ensnared even the lands of the Uzbeks. How many backs did it break in what is Transoxiana! The plague increased and spread further. It attacked the Persians, extended its steps toward the land of Khiṭai, and gnawed away at the Crimea. It pelted Rūm with live coals and led the outrage to Cyprus and the islands. The plague destroyed mankind in Cairo. Its eye was cast upon Egypt, and behold, the people were wide-awake. It stilled all movement in Alexandria. . . .

Then, the plague turned to Upper Egypt. It, also, sent forth its storm to Barqah. The plague attacked Gaza, and it shook Asqalān severely. The plague oppressed Acre. The scourge came to Jerusalem and paid the *zakāt* [with the souls of men]. It overtook those people who fled to the al-'Aqsā Mosque, which stands beside the Dome of the Rock. If the door of mercy had not been opened, the end of the world would have occurred in a moment. It, then, hastened its pace and attacked the entire maritime plain. The plague trapped Sidon and descended unexpectedly upon Beirut, cunningly. Next, it directed the shooting of its arrows to Damascus. There the plague sat like a king on a throne and swayed with power, killing daily one thousand or more and decimating the population. It destroyed mankind with its pustules. May God the Most High spare Damascus to pursue its own path and extinguish the plague's fires so that they do not come close to her fragrant orchards.

Oh God, restore Damascus and protect her from insult.

Its morale has been so lowered that people in the city sell themselves for a grain. . . .

The plague and its poison spread to Sarmīn. It reviled the Sunni and the Shī'ī. It sharpened its spearheads for the Sunni and advanced like an army. The plague was spread in the land of the Shīʿī with a ruinous effect. To Antioch the plague gave its share. Then, it left there quickly with a shyness like a man who has forgotten the memory of his beloved. . . . The plague subjected Dhulūl and went straight through the lowlands and the mountains. It uprooted many people from their homes. Then, the plague sought Aleppo, but it did not succeed. By God's mercy the plague was the lightest oppression. . . . How amazingly does it pursue the people of each house! One of them spits blood, and everyone in the household is certain of death. It brings the entire family to their graves after two or three nights. . . .

Oh God, it is acting by Your command. Lift this from us. It happens where You wish; keep the plague from us. Who will defend us against this horror other than You the Almighty? . . .

Oh, if you could see the nobles of Aleppo studying their inscrutable books of medicine. They multiply its remedies by eating dried and sour foods. The buboes which disturb men's healthy lives are smeared with Armenian clay. Each man treated his humours and made life more comfortable. They perfumed their homes with ambergris and camphor, cyperus and sandal. They wore ruby rings and put onions, vinegar, and sardines together with the daily meal. They ate less broth and fruit but ate the citron and similar things.

If you see many biers and their carriers and hear in every quarter of Aleppo the announcements of death and cries, you run from them and refuse to stay with them. In Aleppo the profits of the undertakers have greatly increased. . . .

We ask God's forgiveness for our souls' bad inclination; the plague is surely part of His punishment. We take refuge from His wrath in His pleasure and from His chastisement in His restoring. . . .

Among the things which exasperated the Muslims and brought suffering is that our enemy, the damned people of Sis, are pleased by our trial. They act as if they are safe from the plague—that there is a treaty so that it will not approach them or that they have triumphed over it. Our Lord does not create us as an enticement for those who disbelieve. . . .

This plague is for the Muslims a martyrdom and a reward, and for the disbelievers a punishment and a rebuke. When the Muslim endures misfortune, then patience is his worship. It has been established by our Prophet, God bless him and give him peace, that the plague-stricken are martyrs. This noble tradition is true and assures martyrdom. And this secret should be pleasing to the true believer. If someone says it causes infection and destruction, say: God creates and recreates.

Source: Michael Dols, "Ibn al-Wardi's Risalah al-Naba an al-Waba, a Translation of a Major Source for the History of the Black Death in the Middle East," in *Near Eastern Numismatics, Iconography, Epigraphy, and History: Studies in Honor of George C. Miles*, edited by Dickran K. Kouymjian (Beirut: American University of Beirut, 1974), pp. 447–54.

PRIMARY SOURCE 11.2

The Florentine Chronicle, Rubric 643 (late fourteenth century), Baldassarre de Buonaiuti

Marchione di Coppo Stefani (the pseudonym for Baldassarre de Buonaiuti) wrote his chronicle in the late fourteenth century after he retired from Florentine business and politics. When he was about twelve years old, in 1348, the Black Death swept through Florence. Buonaiuti's later recollection of the plague balances the practical effects of the pestilence, such as inflation, with the pathos of the plague—namely, family members deserting one another and abandoned sick people calling out for help.

- How does Buonaiuti describe the plague and its ferocity? What details does he report to support that description?

- While Buonaiuti may not directly assert an explanation for the causes of the plague, what are some indirect indicators for what those experiencing the plague thought were its causes?

- What are the effects of the plague on family? On religion? On the economy? On the population?

Concerning a Mortality in the City of Florence in Which Many People Died

In the year of the Lord 1348 there was a very great pestilence in the city and district of Florence. It was of such a fury and so tempestuous that in houses in which it took hold previously healthy servants who took care of the ill died of the same illness. Almost none of the ill survived past the fourth day. Neither physicians nor medicines were effective. Whether because these illnesses were previously unknown or because physicians had not previously studied them, there seemed to be no cure. There was such a fear that no one seemed to know what to do. When it took hold in a house it often happened that no one remained who had not died. And it was not just that men and women died, but even sentient animals died. Dogs, cats, chickens, oxen, donkeys, sheep showed the same symptoms and died of the same disease. And almost none, or very few, who showed these symptoms, were cured. The symptoms were the following: a bubo in the groin, where the thigh meets the trunk; or a small swelling under the armpit; sudden fever; spitting blood and saliva (and no one who spit blood survived it). It was such a frightful thing that when it got into a house, as was said, no one remained. Frightened people abandoned the house and fled to another. Those in town fled to villages. Physicians could not be found because they had died like the others. And those who could be found wanted vast sums in hand before they entered the house. And when they did enter, they checked the pulse with face turned away. They inspected the urine from a distance and with something odoriferous under their nose. Child abandoned the father, husband the wife, wife the husband, one brother the other, one sister the other. In all the city there was nothing to do but to carry the dead to a burial. And those who died had neither confessor nor other sacraments. And many died with no one looking after them. And many died of hunger because when someone took to bed sick, another in the house, terrified, said to him: "I'm going for the doctor." Calmly walking out the door, the other left and did not return again. Abandoned by people, without food, but accompanied by fever, they weakened. There were many who pleaded with their relatives not to abandon them when night fell. But [the relatives] said to the sick person, "So that during the night you did not have to awaken those who serve you and who work hard day and night, take some sweetmeats, wine or water. They are here on the bedstead by your head; here are some blankets." And when the sick person had fallen asleep, they left and did not return. . . .

No one, or few, wished to enter a house where anyone was sick, nor did they even want to deal with those healthy people who came out of a sick person's house. And they said to them: "He is stupefied, do not speak to him!" saying further: "He has it because there is a bubo in his house." They call the swelling a bubo. Many died unseen. So they remained in their beds until they stank. And the neighbors, if there were any, having smelled the stench, placed them in a shroud and sent them for burial. . . .

At every church, or at most of them, they dug deep trenches. . . . And those who were responsible for the dead carried them on their backs in the night in which they died and threw them into the ditch, or else they paid a high price to those who would do it for them. The next morning, if there were many [bodies] in the trench, they covered them over with dirt. And then more bodies were put on top of them, with a little more dirt over those; they put layer on layer just like one puts layers of cheese in a lasagna.

The *beccamorti* [literally, vultures] who provided their service, were paid such a high price that many were enriched by it. Many died from [carrying away the dead], some rich, some after earning just a little, but high prices continued. Servants, or those who took care of the ill, charged from one to three florins per day and the cost of things grew. . . .

Some fled to villas, others to villages in order to get a change of air. Where there had been no [pestilence], there they carried it; if it was already there, they caused it to increase. None of the guilds in Florence was working. All the shops were shut, taverns closed; only the apothecaries and the churches remained open. If you went outside, you found almost no one. And many good and rich men were carried from home to church on a pall by four *beccamorti* and one tonsured clerk who carried the cross. Each of them wanted a florin. This mortality enriched apothecaries, doctors, poultry vendors, *beccamorti*, and greengrocers who sold poultices of mallow, nettles, mercury and other herbs necessary to draw off the infirmity. And it was those who made these poultices who made a lot of money. . . .

This pestilence began in March, as was said, and ended in September 1348. And people began to return to look after their houses and possessions. And there were so many houses full of goods without a master that it was stupefying. . . .

Now it was ordered by the bishop and the Lords [of the city government] that they should formally inquire as to how many died in Florence. When it was seen at the beginning of October that no more persons were dying of the pestilence, they found that among males, females, children and adults, **96,000** died between March and October.

Source: Marchione di Coppo Stefani, *Cronaca Fiorentina*, edited by Niccolo Rodolico, vol. 30 of *Rerum Italicarum Scriptores* (Citta di Castello: S. Lapi, 1903–1913). As translated by Duane Osheim.

Berbers, Arabs, and Plague in the Maghrib, from the *Muqaddimah* (c. 1375), Ibn Khaldûn

Born in Tunis, Ibn Khaldûn came from a family that had been active in the political development of Spain and the Maghrib (North Africa) in the century before his birth. Ibn Khaldûn followed in his family's tradition of public service. In his forties, however, he stepped back from public life and composed a grand multivolume history, in the introduction to which, the *Muqaddimah*, he outlines a far-reaching analytical philosophy of history. Essential to his analysis is a theory of causation and considerations about the rise and fall of civilizations. (Ibn Khaldûn offers dates according to the Muslim calendar, which marks time from Muhammad's migration from Mecca to Medina in 622 CE. CE equivalents are provided in brackets.)

- What are the causes of population shifts of Berbers and Arabs in the Maghrib, according to Ibn Khaldûn?
- What does Ibn Khaldûn say were the effects of the plague on civilization?
- How does Ibn Khaldûn use earlier writers of history, al-Masûdî and al-Bakrî, to explore the purpose of history? How does the plague fit into Ibn Khaldûn's ideas about history writing?

History refers to events that are peculiar to a particular age or race. Discussion of the general conditions of regions, races, and periods constitutes the historian's

foundation. Most of his problems rest upon that foundation, and his historical information derives clarity from it. It forms the topic of special works, such as the *Murúj adh-dhahab* of al-Mas‘ûdî. In this work, al-Mas‘ûdî commented upon the conditions of nations and regions in the West and in the East during his period (which was) the three hundred and thirties [the nine hundred and forties]. He mentioned their sects and customs. He described the various countries, mountains, oceans, provinces, and dynasties. He distinguished between Arabic and non-Arabic groups. His book, thus, became the basic reference work for historians, their principal source for verifying historical information.

Al-Mas‘ûdî was succeeded by al-Bakri who did something similar for routes and provinces, to the exclusion of everything else, because, in his time, not many transformations or great changes had occurred among the nations and races. However, at the present time—that is, at the end of the eighth [fourteenth] century—the situation in the Maghrib, as we can observe, has taken a turn and changed entirely. The Berbers, the original population of the Maghrib, have been replaced by an influx of Arabs, (that began in) the fifth [eleventh] century. The Arabs outnumbered and overpowered the Berbers, stripped them of most of their lands, and (also) obtained a share of those that remained in their possession. This was the situation until, in the middle of the eighth [fourteenth] century, civilization both in the East and the West was visited by a destructive plague which devastated nations and caused populations to vanish. It swallowed up many of the good things of civilization and wiped them out. It overtook the dynasties at the time of their senility, when they had reached the limit of their duration. It lessened their power and curtailed their influence. It weakened their authority. Their situation approached the point of annihilation and dissolution. Civilization decreased with the decrease of mankind. Cities and buildings were laid waste, roads and way signs were obliterated, settlements and mansions became empty, dynasties and tribes grew weak. The entire inhabited world changed. The East, it seems, was similarly visited, though in accordance with and in proportion to (the East's more affluent) civilization. It was as if the voice of existence in the world had called out for oblivion and restriction, and the world had responded to its call. God inherits the earth and whomever is upon it.

When there is a general change of conditions, it is as if the entire creation had changed and the whole world been altered, as if it were a new and repeated creation, a world brought into existence anew. Therefore, there is need at this time that someone should systematically set down the situation of the world among all regions and races, as well as the customs and sectarian beliefs that have changed for their adherents, doing for this age what al-Mas'ūdī did for his. This should be a model for future historians to follow. In this book of mine, I shall discuss as much of that as will be possible for me here in the Maghrib. I shall do so either explicitly or implicitly in connection with the history of the Maghrib, in conformity with my intention to restrict myself in this work to the Maghrib, the circumstances of its races and nations, and its subjects and dynasties, to the exclusion of any other region. (This restriction is necessitated) by my lack of knowledge of conditions in the East and among its nations, and by the fact that secondhand information would not give the essential facts I am after.

Source: Ibn Khaldûn, *The Muqaddimah, an Introduction to History*, vol. 1, translated by Franz Rosenthal (New York: Pantheon Books, 1958), pp. 63–65.

PRIMARY SOURCE 11.4

Plague in Syria and Egypt in 1348–1350 (early fifteenth century), al-Maqrizi

Al-Maqrizi wrote his extensive historical works in Cairo in the early fifteenth century. His roots in Cairo were deep, but his family also had connections in Damascus, and he lived there for about ten years in his forties. Given that al-Maqrizi was such a prolific historian, it is surprising that much of what is known about him is based on writings about him by contemporaries and later biographers. Interestingly for our purposes, he was a student of Ibn Khaldûn in Cairo.

• What part of the population seems to have been hardest hit by the plague? Why might the death toll from plague have been higher during Ramadan?

• What was the effect of the plague on religious practices?

• What impact did the plague have on the workforce in terms of wages, available workers, and employment opportunities?

News reached [Cairo from Syria] that the plague in Damascus had been less deadly than in Tripoli, Hama, and Aleppo. From . . . [October 1348] death raged with intensity. 1200 people died daily and, as a result, people stopped requesting permits from the administration to bury the dead and many cadavers were abandoned in gardens and on the roads.

In New and Old Cairo, the plague struck women and children at first, then market people, and the numbers of the dead augmented. . . . The [ravages of the] plague intensified in . . . [November] in [New] Cairo and became extremely grave during *Ramadan* [December], which coincided with the arrival of winter. . . . The plague continued to spread so considerably that it became impossible to count how many died. . . .

In [January 1349], new symptoms developed and people began spitting up blood. One sick person came down with internal fever, followed by an unrestrained need to vomit, then spat blood and died. Those around him in his house fell ill, one after the other and in one or two nights they all perished. Everyone lived with the overwhelming preoccupation that death was near. People prepared themselves for death by distributing alms to the poor, reconciled with one another, and multiplied their acts of devotion.

None had time to consult doctors or drink medicinal syrups or take other medications, so rapidly did they die. By [January 7th,] bodies had piled up in the streets and markets; [town leaders] appointed burial brigades, and some pious people remained permanently at places of prayer in New and Old Cairo to recite funeral orations over the dead. The situation worsened beyond limits, and no solution appeared possible. Almost the entire royal guard disappeared and the barracks in the sultan's citadel contained no more soldiers.

Statistics of the dead from funerals in Cairo during . . . [November and December] attained 900,000. . . . There were 1,400 litters on which they carried the dead and soon even they did not suffice. So they began carrying dead bodies in boxes, on doors taken from stores and on plain boards, on each of which they placed two to three bodies.

People began searching for *Quran* readers for funerals, and many individuals quit their trades to recite prayers at the head of burial procession[s]. A group of people devoted themselves to applying a coat of clay to the inner sides of the graves. Others volunteered to wash corpses, and still others to carry them. Such volunteers received substantial wages. For example, a *Quran* reader earned 10 *dirhams*: the moment he finished with one funeral, he ran off to another. A body carrier demanded six *dirhams* in advance, and still it was hard to find any. A grave digger wanted 50 *dirhams* per grave. But most of them died before they had a chance to spend their earnings.

Family celebrations and marriages no longer took place. . . . No one had held any festivities during the entire duration of the epidemic, and no voice was heard singing. In an attempt to revive these activities, the *wazir* [prime minister] reduced by a third the taxes paid by the woman responsible for collecting dues on singers. The call to prayer was suspended at many locations, and even at the most important ones, there remained only a single *muezzin* [caller to prayer].

The drum batteries before most of the officers' quarters no longer functioned, and the entourage of a commander [who controlled a thousand men] was reduced now from about fifteen to three soldiers.

Most of the mosques and *zawiyas* [*Sufi* lodges] were closed. It was also a known fact that during this epidemic no infant survived more than one or two days after his birth, and his mother usually quickly followed him to the grave.

At [the end of February], all of Upper Egypt was afflicted with the plague. . . . According to information that arrived . . . from . . . other regions, lions, wolves, rabbits, camels, wild asses and boars, and other savage beasts, dropped dead, and were found with scabs on their bodies.

The same thing happened throughout Egypt. When harvest time arrived, many farmers had already perished [and no field hands remained to gather crops]. Soldiers and their young slaves or pages headed for the fields. They tried to recruit workers by promising them half of the proceeds, but they could not find anyone to help them gather the harvest. They threshed the grain with their horses [hoofs], and winnowed the grain themselves, but, unable to carry all the grain back, they had to abandon much of it.

Most craft workshops closed, since artisans devoted themselves to disposing of the dead, while others, not less numerous, auctioned off property and textiles [which the dead left behind]. Even though the prices of fabric and other such commodities sold for a fifth of their original value . . . they remained unsold. . . . Religious texts sold by their weight, and at very low prices.

Workers disappeared. You could not find either water carriers, or launderers or servants. The monthly salary of a horse groom rose from 30 to 80 *dirhams*. . . . This epidemic, they say, continued in several countries for 15 years.

Source: al-Maqrizi, *The Guide to the Knowledge of Dynasties and Kings*, excerpted in *The Middle East and Islamic World Reader*, edited by Marvin Gettleman and Stuart Schaar (New York: Grove Press, 2012), pp. 52–53.

Interpreting Visual Evidence

Marking Boundaries, Inspiring Loyalty

The fourteenth century witnessed the emergence of dynastic states across Afro-Eurasia that endured for centuries. The size of these new states and the ethnic and religious diversity of their populations posed formidable challenges to those in power. Rulers had to distinguish those who belonged to the community—and owed taxes or military service—from those who did not. They used a careful mixture of privilege and punishment to create a sense of unity among their subjects while at the same time justifying their own right to rule and reinforcing traditional social hierarchies. The three images below show different ways rulers approached this problem.

The first painting, from around 1500, is by the Spanish artist Pedro Berruguete. It portrays a scene

Spanish painting by Berruguete.

The *devshirme* system.

from two centuries earlier in which Spanish authorities burned people at the stake for their alleged heretical beliefs. Notice in the foreground members of the Dominican Order, who were instrumental in the administration of the Inquisition, and soldiers loyal to the crown. The second image, a miniature painting from 1558, depicts the *devshirme* system in the Ottoman Empire. Authorities took non-Muslim children from their families in Europe as a human tribute in place of cash taxes, which poor regions could not pay. The children would then be educated in Ottoman Muslim ways and prepared for service in the sultan's civil and military bureaucracy. The final image, a painting on silk by Ch'iu Ying, represents a group of Confucian scholars waiting for the results of their civil service examination. Candidates spent three days and two nights taking examinations as they sought to enter the Ming bureaucracy.

Chinese painting by Ch'iu Ying.

Questions for Analysis

1. Assess the combinations of privilege and punishment conveyed by these images. What kinds of assistance or special privileges did leaders grant, to whom did they offer this assistance, and what kinds of punishments did they impose?

2. Describe the original context for these images. Who might have created these images, for whom were they created, and who might have seen them?

3. Interpret the role religion plays in these images. How does the artist present the relationship between religion and social order?

4. Comparing the three paintings, how did Berruguete's painting reframe the relationship between royal authorities and traditional elites?

Further Readings

Chapter 1: Becoming Human

Arsuaga, Juan Luis, *The Neanderthal's Necklace: In Search of the First Thinkers*, trans. Anthony Klatt (2002). A stimulating overview of prehistory that focuses on the Neanderthals and compares them with *Homo sapiens*.

Barham, Lawrence, and Peter Mitchell, *The First Africans: African Archaeology from the Earliest Toolmakers to Most Recent Foragers* (2008). New findings on the evolution of hominids and hominins in Africa.

Barker, Graeme, *Agricultural Revolution in Prehistory: Why Did Foragers Become Farmers?* (2006). The most recent truly global and up-to-date study of this momentous event in world history.

Bellwood, Peter, *First Farmers: The Origins of Agricultural Societies* (2005). A state-of-the-art global history of the origins of agriculture including recent archaeological, linguistic, and microbiological data.

Bender, Michael L., *Paleoclimate* (2013). A definitive overview of the world's climate over the entire life of our universe, written by a renowned geoclimatologist.

Bogucki, Peter, *The Origins of Human Society* (1999). An authoritative overview of prehistory.

Brooke, John L., *Climate Change and the Course of Global History: A Rough Journey* (2014). An excellent overview of the impact of climate on history; particularly useful for the hominin period and the emergence of *Homo sapiens*.

Callaway, Ewen, "Oldest *Homo sapiens* Fossil Claim Rewrites Our Species' History," *Nature News*, June 7, 2017, doi:10.1038/nature.2017.22114. Describes and contextualizes Hublin's (see below) early *Homo sapiens* finds at Jebel Irhoud in Morocco.

Cauvin, Jacques, *The Birth of the Gods and the Origins of Agriculture*, translated by Trevor Watkins from the original 1994 French publication (2000). An important work on the agricultural revolution of Southwest Asia and the evolution of symbolic thinking at this time.

Cavalli-Sforza, Luigi Luca, *Genes, Peoples, and Languages*, translated by Mark Seielstad from the original 1996 French publication (2000). An expert's introduction to the use of gene research for revealing new information about the evolution of human beings in the distant past.

Childe, V. Gordon, *What Happened in History* (1964). A classic work by one of the pioneers in studying the early history and evolution of human beings. Though superseded in many respects, it is still an important place to start one's reading and a work of great power and emotion.

Christian, David, *Maps of Time: An Introduction to Big History* (2004). Offers an outline of Big History from the formation of the universe and planets, to the beginnings of life on earth, to humans, to the modern era; emphasizes the value of examining both collective learning and human extensification/intensification of the earth's resources for making sense of human history at the grandest scale.

Clark, J. Desmond, and Steven A. Brandt (eds.), *From Hunters to Farmers: The Causes and Consequences of Food Production in Africa* (1984). Excellent essays on the agricultural revolution.

Cohen, Mark Nathan, *The Food Crisis in Prehistory: Overpopulation and the Origins of Agriculture* (1977). An older, but pioneering, work on the role of population growth in bringing about the domestication of plants and animals. Although disputed in recent studies, Cohen's work is an important starting point for studying this transformational development.

Coon, Carleton Stevens, *The Story of Man: From the First Human to Primitive Culture and Beyond*, 2nd ed. (1962). An important early work on the evolution of humans, emphasizing the distinctiveness of "races" around the world.

Cunliffe, Barry (ed.), *The Oxford Illustrated Prehistory of Europe* (1994). The definitive work on early European history.

Dalton, Rex, "Peking Man Older Than Thought," *Nature,* March 11, 2009, doi:10.1038/news.2009.149. Describes the use of aluminum-beryllium dating techniques to push back the date for *Homo erectus* (Peking Man) to 770,000 years ago and the implications of this revised date.

Ehrenberg, Margaret, *Women in Prehistory* (1989). What was the role of women in hunting and gathering societies, and how greatly were women affected by the agricultural revolution? The author offers a number of stimulating generalizations.

Ehret, Christopher, *The Civilizations of Africa: A History to 1800* (2002). Although this is a general history of Africa, the author, a linguist and an expert on early African history, offers new information and new overviews of African peoples in very ancient times.

Fagan, Brian, *People of the Earth: An Introduction to World Prehistory* (1989). An authoritative overview of early history, widely used in classrooms.

Fage, J. D., and Roland Oliver (eds.), *The Cambridge History of Africa*, 8 vols. (1975–1984). A pioneering work of synthesis by two of the first and foremost scholars of the history of Africa. Volume 1 deals with African prehistory.

Frison, George C., *Survival by Hunting: Prehistoric Human Predators and Animal Prey* (2004). An archaeologist applies his knowledge of animal habitats, behavior, and hunting strategies to an examination of prehistoric hunting practices in the North American Great Plains and Rocky Mountains.

Gebauer, Anne Birgitte, and T. Douglas Price (eds.), *Transition to Agriculture in Prehistory* (1992). Excellent essays on the agricultural revolution, especially those written by the two editors.

Gibbons, Ann, "World's Oldest *Homo sapiens* Fossils Found in Morocco," *Science*, June 7, 2017, doi:10.1126/science.aan6934. An accessible discussion of Jebel Irhoud fossils that explains how they "fit" the picture of other hominid finds.

Gokhman, David, et al., "Reconstructing Denisovan Anatomy Using DNA Methylation Maps," *Cell* 179 (2019): 180–92. Describes the process by which Gokhman and his team used aDNA to predict possible ways that genetic variations would manifest as physical differences between hypothetical Denisovan skeletons and those of *Homo sapiens* and Neanderthals.

Greshko, Michael, "Earliest Evidence for Humans on the 'Roof of the World' Found," *National Geographic*, November 29, 2018. Discusses evidence (including more than 3,600 stone artifacts) that humans occupied Nwya Devu, a site in the central Tibetan Plateau, 30,000 to 40,000 years ago.

Harari, Yuval Noah, *Sapiens: A Brief History of Humankind* (2015). A largely successful overview of human history from the hominins to the present.

Hershkovitz, Israel, et al., "The Earliest Modern Humans Outside Africa," *Science* 359 (January 26, 2018): 456–59. Reviews the scientific evidence for the *Homo sapiens* fossils found at Mount Carmel, pushing back the date of *Homo sapiens* migration out of Africa closer to 180,000 years ago.

Hublin, Jean-Jacques, et al., "New Fossils from Jebel Irhoud, Morocco and the Pan-African Origin of *Homo sapiens*," *Nature* 546 (June 8, 2017): 289–92, doi:10.1038/nature22336. The report from Hublin's team that explains the significance of the Jebel Irhoud site and of the identification of the fossils found there as *Homo sapiens*.

"Inter-Group Violence among the Early Holocene Hunter-Gatherers of West Turkana, Kenya," *Nature* 529 (January 21, 2016): 394–98. Describes a spectacular discovery of the remains of hunters and gatherers who engaged in warfare.

Johanson, Donald, Lenora Johanson, and Blake Edgar, *Ancestors: In Search of Human Origins* (1999). A good overview of human evolution, with insightful essays on *Homo erectus* and *Homo sapiens*.

Johanson, Donald C., and Kate Wong, *Lucy's Legacy: The Quest for Human Origins* (2009). Describes Johanson's initial finding and classification of Lucy, and also reviews new discoveries in paleoanthropology since that important find.

Jones, Steve, Robert Martin, and David Pilbeam (eds.), *The Cambridge Encyclopedia of Human Evolution* (1992). A superb guide to a wide range of subjects, crammed with up-to-date information on the most controversial and obscure topics of human evolution and early history.

Ki-Zerbo, J. (ed.), *Methodology and African Prehistory*, vol. 1 of *General History of Africa* (1981). The first volume of UNESCO's general history of Africa, written for the most part by scholars of African heritage.

Klein, Richard G., and Blake Edger, *The Dawn of Human Culture* (2002). A fine and reliable guide to the tangled history of human evolution.

Leakey, Richard, *The Origin of Humankind* (1994). A readable and exciting account of human evolution, written by the son of the pioneering archaeologists Louis and Mary Leakey, a scholar of equal stature to his parents.

Lewin, Roger, *The Origin of Modern Humans* (1993). Yet another good overview of human evolution, with useful chapters on early art and the use of symbols.

Lewis-Kraus, Gideon, "Is Ancient DNA Research Revealing New Truths—or Falling into Old Traps?" *New York Times Magazine,* January 17, 2019. Offers an accessible review of David Reich's groundbreaking paleogenetic claims, while leveling challenges against the findings and methods of David Reich and others who use aDNA to chart ancient genomes.

Loewe, Michael, and Edward Shaughnessy (eds.), *The Cambridge History of Ancient China: From the Origins of Civilization to 221 B.C.* (1999). A good review of the archaeology of ancient China.

Mathieson, Iain, et al., "Genome-Wide Patterns of Selection in 230 Ancient Eurasians," *Nature* 522 (November 23, 2015), published online. New DNA research on the skeletons of 230 West-Eurasians who lived between 6500 and 300 BCE shows the three waves of migrations into Europe in its distant past. These migrations came from Africa via Southwest Asia, Anatolia, and the Russian steppes.

Mellaart, James, *Çatal Höyük: A Neolithic Town in Anatolia* (1967). A detailed description of one of the first towns associated with the agricultural revolution in Southwest Asia.

Meredith, Martin, *Born in Africa: The Quest for Human Origins* (2011). A well-written and authoritative overview of the evolution of humankind from the earliest hominins to *Homo sapiens.*

Mithen, Steven, *The Prehistory of the Mind: The Cognitive Origins of Art and Science* (1996). A stimulating discussion of the impact of biological and cultural evolution on the cognitive structure of the human mind.

Olson, Steve, *Mapping Human History: Genes, Race, and Our Common Origins* (2003). Using the findings of genetics and attacking the racial thinking of an earlier generation of archaeologists, the author writes powerfully about the unity of all human beings.

Price, T. Douglas (ed.), *Europe's First Farmers* (2000). A discussion of the agricultural revolution in Europe.

Price, T. Douglas, and Anne Birgitte Gebauer (eds.), *Last Hunters—First Farmers: New Perspectives on the Prehistoric Transition to Agriculture* (1996). An exciting collection of essays by some of the leading scholars in the field studying the transition from hunting and gathering to settled agriculture.

Reich, David, *Who We Are and How We Got Here: Ancient DNA and the New Science of the Human Past* (2018). Offers an overview of the new findings of paleobiologists working with ancient DNA.

Richter, Daniel, et al., "The Age of the Hominin Fossils from Jebel Irhoud, Morocco, and the Origins of the Middle Stone Age," *Nature* 546 (June 8, 2017): 293–96, doi:10.1038/nature22335. Reviews the methods used by scientists to determine the date of the *Homo sapiens* fossils at Jebel Irhoud.

Sahlins, Marshall, "Notes on the Original Affluent Society," in *Man the Hunter,* edited by Richard B. Lee and Irven DeVore (1968), pp. 85–89. Sahlins coined the widely used and now famous expression "affluent society" for hunters and gatherers.

Scarre, Chris (ed.), *The Human Past: World Prehistory and the Development of Human Societies* (2005). An encyclopedia and an overview rolled up into one mammoth volume, written by leading figures in the field of early human history.

Shaw, Thurstan, et al. (eds.), *The Archaeology of Africa: Food, Metals, and Towns* (1993). Up-to-date research on the earliest history of human beings in Africa.

Shreeve, James, "Mystery Man," *National Geographic* 228 (October 2015): 30–57. An authoritative and up-to-date account of the extraordinary discovery of fossil remains of a hominid species, now named *Homo naledi.*

Smith, Bruce D., *The Emergence of Agriculture* (1995). How early humans domesticated wild animals and plants.

Stringer, Christopher, and Robin McKie, *African Exodus: The Origins of Modern Humanity* (1996). Detailed data on why Africa was the source of human origins and why *Homo sapiens* is a recent wanderer out of Africa.

Tattersall, Ian, *The Fossil Trail: How We Know What We Think We Know about Human Evolution* (1995). A passionately written book about early archaeological discoveries and the centrality of Africa in human evolution.

———, *Masters of the Planet: The Search for Our Human Origins* (2012). The most recent survey of human evolution.

———, *The World from Beginnings to 4000 BCE* (2008). A brief up-to-date overview of humanity's early history by a leading authority.

Van Oosterzee, Penny, *Dragon Bones: The Story of Peking Man* (2000). Describes how the late nineteenth-century unearthing of sites in China containing fossils of animals used for medicinal purposes led to the discovery of the fossils of Peking Man.

Wei-Haas, Maya, "DNA Reveals First Look at Enigmatic Human Relative," *National Geographic,* September 19, 2019. Reviews paleogeneticist David Gokhman's work in using ancient DNA to reconstruct the physical traits of Denisovans.

Weiss, Mark L., and Alan E. Mann, *Human Biology and Behavior: An Anthropological Perspective* (1996). The authors stress the contribution that biological research has made and continues to make to the unraveling of the mystery of human evolution.

Wrangham, Richard, *Catching Fire: How Cooking Made Us Human* (2009). The author shows how fire made it possible for humans to have a more varied and richer diet but also one that provided energy for the one organ—the brain—that consumes the most energy.

Chapter 2: Rivers, Cities, and First States, 3500–2000 BCE

Adams, Robert McCormick, *The Evolution of Urban Society* (1966). A classic study of the social, political, and economic processes that led to the development of the first urban civilizations.

Algaze, Guillermo, *Ancient Mesopotamia at the Dawn of Civilization* (2008). A compelling analysis of the complex environmental and social factors underlying the rise of the world's first urban culture in southern Mesopotamia.

———, *The Uruk World System: The Dynamics of Expansion of Early Mesopotamian Civilization* (1993). A compelling argument for the colonization of the Tigris-Euphrates basin by the proto-Sumerians at the end of the fourth millennium BCE.

Andrews, Carol, *Egyptian Mummies* (1998). An illustrated summary of Egyptian mummification and burial practices.

Bagley, Robert, *Ancient Sichuan: Treasures from a Lost Civilization* (2001). Describes the remarkable findings in southwestern China, particularly at Sanxingdui, that have challenged earlier accounts of the Shang dynasty's central role in the rise of early Chinese civilization.

Bar-Yosef, Ofar, and Anatoly Khazanov (eds.), *Pastoralism in the Levant: Archaeological Materials in Anthropological Perspectives* (1992). Classic study of the role of nomads in the development of societies in the Levant during the Neolithic period.

Bruhns, Karen Olsen, *Ancient South America* (1994). The best basic text on pre-Columbian South American cultures.

Butzer, Karl W., *Early Hydraulic Civilization in Egypt: A Study of Cultural Ecology* (1976). The best work on how the Egyptians dealt with the Nile floods and the influence that these arrangements had on the overall organization of society.

Cunliffe, Barry, *By Steppe, Desert, and Ocean: The Birth of Eurasia* (2015). A work that stresses the connections among the societies of China, India, Mesopotamia, Egypt, and Europe.

———, *Europe between the Oceans, 9000 BC–AD 1000* (2008). A very up-to-date and spectacularly illustrated account of early Europe.

Feng, Li, *Early China: A Social and Cultural History* (2013). An important new study on the origins of Chinese culture.

Fukuyama, Francis, *The Origins of Political Order: From Prehistoric Times to the French Revolution* (2011). A superb overview of the powerful political elements that were behind the great river-basin societies in ancient times.

Habu, Junko, *Ancient Jomon of Japan* (2004). Study of prehistoric Jomon hunters and gatherers on the Japanese archipelago that incorporates several different aspects of anthropological studies, including hunter and gatherer archaeology, settlement archaeology, and pottery analysis.

Horden, Peregrine, and Nicholas Purcell, *The Corrupting Sea: A Study of Mediterranean History* (2000). A global overview of the history of the Mediterranean over three millennia.

Jacobsen, Thorkild, *The Treasures of Darkness: A History of Mesopotamian Religion* (1976). Best introduction to the religious and philosophical thought of ancient Mesopotamia.

Kemp, Barry J., *Ancient Egypt: Anatomy of a Civilization* (1989). A synthetic overview of the culture of the pharaohs.

Kramer, Samuel Noah, *The Sumerians: Their History, Culture and Character* (1963). Classic study of the Sumerians and their culture by a pioneer in Sumerian studies.

Liverani, Mario, *The Ancient Near East: History, Society, and Economy* (2014). An important and recent history of Southwest Asia, incorporating the latest scholarship.

Manning, J. G., *The Open Sea: The Economic Life of the Ancient Mediterranean World from the Iron Age to the Rise of Rome* (2018). A survey of the main economic systems of the Mediterranean from the first millennium BCE to the rise of the Roman Empire.

Middleton, Guy D., *Understanding Collapse: Ancient History and Modern Myths* (2017). An important corrective to those who stress climate change as the primary factor undermining the societies in Mesopotamia, Egypt, and the Indus Valley.

Pollock, Susan, *Ancient Mesopotamia: The Eden That Never Was* (1999). An analysis of the social and economic development of Mesopotamia from the beginnings of settlement until the reign of Hammurabi.

Possehl, Gregory L., *Indus Age: The Beginnings* (1999). The second of four volumes analyzing the history of the Indus Valley civilization.

Postgate, J. N., *Early Mesopotamia: Society and Economy at the Dawn of History* (1992). A study of the economic and political development of the Sumerian civilization.

Preziosi, Donald, and L. A. Hitchcock, *Aegean Art and Architecture* (1999). One of the best general guides to the figurative and decorative art produced both by the Minoans and Mycenaeans and by related early societies in the region of the Aegean.

Ratnagar, Shereen, *Trading Encounters: From the Euphrates to the Indus in the Bronze Age*, 2nd ed. (2004). A comprehensive presentation of the evidence for the relationship between the Indus Valley and its western neighbors.

———, *Understanding Harappa: Civilization in the Greater Indus Valley* (2001). An overview, written by a leading Indian archaeologist, on the many features of Harappan civilization, including major settlements, trade, and writing.

Rice, Michael, *Egypt's Legacy: The Archetypes of Western Civilization, 3000–300 BC* (1997). The author argues for the decisive influence of Egyptian culture on the whole of the Mediterranean and its later historical development.

Roaf, Michael, *Cultural Atlas of Mesopotamia and the Ancient Near East* (1990). A comprehensive compendium of the historical and cultural development of the Mesopotamian civilization from the Neolithic background through the Persian Empire.

Scott, James C., *Against the Grain: A Deep History of the Earliest States* (2017). A work by a well-known and prolific sociologist who is intent on demonstrating that the rise of cities and territorial states imposed burdens of exploitation and suffering on most of humankind and destroyed the egalitarianism of pre-city-state life.

Shaw, Ian (ed.), *The Oxford History of Ancient Egypt* (2000). The most up-to-date and comprehensive account of the history of Egypt down to the Greek invasion.

Singh, Ajit, et al., "Counter-intuitive Influence of Himalayan River Morphodynamics on Indus Civilisation Urban Settlements," *Nature Communications* 8, article no. 1617 (2017), doi:10.1038/s41467-017-01643-9. Demonstrates how data from NASA's shuttle topography mission are being used to understand paleochannels of now-dried-up rivers and how those rivers influenced early Indus settlement patterns.

Tallet, Pierre, and Gregory Marouard, "The Harbor of Khufu on the Red Sea Coast at Wadi al-Jarf, Egypt," *Near Eastern Archaeology* 77, no. 1 (2014): 4–14. Accessible description of the archaeological work undertaken at an Egyptian site, arguably the world's oldest harbor. Includes excellent maps and photos of excavated materials, such as storage jars, ship debris, sandstone anchors, and the papyri that contain Merer's records.

Thorp, Robert, *The Chinese Neolithic: Trajectories to Early States* (2005). Uses the latest archaeological evidence to describe the development of early Bronze Age cultures in northern and northwestern China from about 2000 BCE.

Tignor, Robert L., *Egypt: A Short History* (2011). An overview of the history of Egypt from the rise of the pharaohs to the present.

Van de Mieroop, Marc, *A History of Ancient Egypt* (2011). A historian of ancient Southwest Asia undertakes to view Egypt through the lens of his interest in ancient cities and territorial states.

Wachsmann, Shelley, *Seagoing Ships and Seamanship in the Bronze Age Levant* (1998). Provides a compelling, in-depth, and well-documented review of the evidence for ships from several Bronze Age seafaring peoples (including Egyptians, Mycenaeans, and Sea Peoples) and also discusses activities such as shipbuilding, navigation, and piracy.

Wright, Rita P., *The Ancient Indus: Urbanism, Economy, and Society* (2010). A reconstruction of the Indus society with updated archaeological data.

Chapter 3: Nomads, Territorial States, and Microsocieties, 2000–1200 BCE

Allan, Sarah, *The Shape of the Turtle: Myth, Art, and Cosmos in Early China* (1991). Explains the roles of divination and sacrifice in artistic representations of the Shang cosmology.

Allen, James P., *Middle Egyptian: An Introduction to the Language and Culture of Hieroglyphs* (2000). An introduction to the system of writing and its use in ancient Egypt.

Anthony, David W., *The Horse, the Wheel, and Language: How Bronze-Age Riders from the Eurasian Steppes Shaped the Modern World* (2007). A superb analysis of the origins and spread of the Indo-European peoples.

Arnold, Dieter, *Building in Ancient Egypt: Pharaonic Stone Masonry* (1996). Details the complex construction of monumental stone architecture in ancient Egypt.

Baines, John, and Jaromir Málek, *Atlas of Ancient Egypt* (1980). Useful compilation of information on ancient Egyptian society, religion, history, and geography.

Beal, Richard H., *The Organization of the Hittite Military* (1992). A detailed study based on textual sources of the world's first chariot-based army.

Behringer, Wolfgang, *A Cultural History of Climate* (2010). A general history of the impact of climate on many different societies.

Bell, Barbara, "The Dark Ages in Ancient History. I. The First Dark Age in Egypt," *American Journal of Archaeology* 75 (January 1971): 1–26. An environmental analysis of the decline of the Old Kingdom and the emergence of the First Intermediate Period.

Bogucki, Peter, and Pam J. Crabtree (eds.), *Ancient Europe 8000 BC–AD 1000: Encyclopedia of the Barbarian World*, 2 vols. (2004). An indispensable handbook on the economic, social, artistic, and religious life in Europe during this period.

Breasted, James Henry (trans.), *Ancient Records of Egypt: Historical Documents from the Earliest Times to the Persian Conquest*, 5 vols. (1906). Breasted's five-volumes offer a collection of translated Egyptian inscriptions arranged by dynasty that give insight into a wide range of issues, including trade, military campaigns, royal edicts, biographical information of pharaohs, and religion.

Bruhns, Karen Olsen, *Ancient South America* (1994). The best basic text on pre-Columbian South American cultures.

Bryant, Edwin, *The Quest for the Origins of Vedic Culture: The Indo-Aryan Migration Debate* (2001). Insight into the highly charged debate on who the Indo-European speakers were, where they originated, and where they migrated to.

Castleden, Rodney, *The Mycenaeans* (2005). One of the best current surveys of all aspects of the Mycenaean Greeks.

Chadwick, John, *The Decipherment of Linear B,* 2nd ed. (1968). Not only a retelling of the story of the decipherment of the Linear B script, but also an introduction to the actual content and function of the tablets themselves.

Childs-Johnson, Elizabeth, "Fu Zi, the Shang Woman Warrior," in Lily Xiao Hong Lee, A. D. Stefanowska, and Sue Wiles (eds.), *Biographical Dictionary of Chinese Women, Antiquity through Sui, 1600 B.C.E.–618 C.E.* (2007), pp. 19–25. Offers a biography of Fu Hao (Fu Zi) that summarizes much Chinese-language scholarship as well as a thorough discussion of the items found in her tomb.

Cline, Eric H., *1177 B.C.: The Year Civilization Collapsed* (2014). An engaging account, drawing on a wide array of archaeological and literary evidence, that discusses the many factors—including internal political turmoil, invasions (like those of the Sea Peoples), and disruption of international trade—that contributed to a "systems collapse" at the end of the Mediterranean Bronze Age.

———, *Sailing the Wine-Dark Sea: International Trade and the Late Bronze Age Aegean* (1994). An excellent account of the trade and contacts between the Aegean and other areas of the Mediterranean, Europe, and the Near East during the late Bronze Age.

Cunliffe, Barry, *Facing the Ocean: The Atlantic and Its Peoples, 8000 BC–AD 1500* (2001). An in-depth, highly useful treatment of western Europe during this period.

——— (ed.), *Prehistoric Europe: An Illustrated History* (1997). A state-of-the-art treatment of first farmers, agricultural developments, and material culture in prehistoric Europe.

Curry, Andrew, "Slaughter at the Bridge," *Science* 351 (March 25, 2016): 1384–89. New information on a battle among hunting and gathering warriors in northern Europe in the thirteenth century BCE.

Davis, W. V., and L. Schofield, *Egypt, the Aegean and the Levant: Interconnections in the Second Millennium BC* (1995). A discussion of the complex interactions in the eastern Mediterranean during the "international age."

Doumas, Christos, *Thera: Pompeii of the Ancient Aegean* (1983). A study of the tremendous volcanic eruption and explosion that destroyed the Minoan settlement on the island of Thera.

Drews, Robert, *Coming of the Greeks: Indo-European Conquests in the Aegean and the Near East* (1988). A good survey of the evidence for the "invasions" or "movements of peoples" that reconfigured the world of the eastern Mediterranean and Near East.

Finley, M. I., *The World of Odysseus*, 2nd rev. ed. (1977; reprint, 2002). The classic work that describes what might be recovered about the social values and behaviors of men and women in the so-called Dark Ages of early Greek history.

Frankfort, Henri, *Ancient Egyptian Religion: An Interpretation* (1948; reprint, 2000). A classic study of Egyptian religion and culture during the pharaonic period.

Frayne, Douglas R., *The Royal Inscriptions of Mesopotamia, Early Periods*, vol. 4., *Old Babylonian Period, 2003–1595 BC.* (1990). A standard and still-useful study of this period in Babylonian history.

Keightley, David N., *The Ancestral Landscape: Time, Space, and Community in Late Shang China, ca. 1200–1045 BC* (2000). Provides insights into the nature of royal kinship that undergirded the Shang court and its regional domains.

Kemp, Barry J., *Ancient Egypt: Anatomy of a Civilization* (2006). A definitive presentation of the history, culture, and religion of ancient Egypt.

Klein, Jacob, "The Marriage of Martu: The Urbanization of 'Barbaric' Nomads," in Meir Malul (ed.), *Mutual Influences of Peoples and Cultures in the Ancient Near East* (1996). A crucial text in the corpus of scholarship on Sumerian literature.

Kristiansen, Kristian, *Europe before History* (1998). The finest recent survey of all the major developmental phases of European prehistory.

McIntosh, Jane, *Handbook to Life in Prehistoric Europe* (2006). Highlights the archaeological evidence that enables us to re-create the day-to-day life of different prehistoric communities in Europe.

Pines, Yuri, *The Everlasting Empire: The Political Culture of Ancient China and Its Imperial Legacy* (2012). How imperial unity became the norm in ancient China.

Preziosi, Donald, and L. A. Hitchcock, *Aegean Art and Architecture* (1999). One of the best general guides to the figurative and decorative art produced both by the Minoans and Mycenaeans and by related early societies in the region of the Aegean.

Quirke, Stephen, *Ancient Egyptian Religion* (1992). A highly readable presentation of ancient Egyptian religion that summarizes the roles and attributions of the many Egyptian gods.

The Rigveda, the Earliest Religious Poetry of India, trans. Stephanie W. Jamison and Joel P. Brereton (2014). A new translation of the earliest literature of South Asia, correcting errors made in earlier translations.

Robins, Gay, *The Art of Ancient Egypt* (1997). The most comprehensive survey to date of the art of pharaonic Egypt.

———, *Women in Ancient Egypt* (1993). An interesting survey of the place of women in ancient Egyptian society.

Romer, John, *Ancient Lives: Daily Life in Egypt of the Pharaohs* (1990). A discussion of the economic and social lives of everyday ancient Egyptians.

Roth, Martha T., *Law Collections from Mesopotamia and Asia Minor* (1995). An assemblage of law codes from Southwest Asia, including Hammurabi's famous legal edicts.

Sandars, N. K., *The Sea Peoples: Warriors of the Ancient Mediterranean* (1985). A readable discussion of a very complex period of Levantine history.

Simpson, William Kelly (ed.), *The Literature of Ancient Egypt: An Anthology of Stories, Instructions, and Poetry* (1972). A compilation of the most important works of literature from ancient Egypt.

Thapar, Romila, *The Past before Us: Historical Tradition of Early North India* (2013). A comprehensive evaluation of ancient Indian literature.

Thorp, Robert L., *China in the Early Bronze Age: Shang Civilization* (2005). Reviews the archaeological discoveries near Anyang, site of two capitals of the Shang kings.

Van De Mieroop, Marc, *King Hammurabi of Babylon: A Biography* (2004). A useful biography of an important Babylonian ruler and lawgiver.

Warren, Peter, *The Aegean Civilizations: From Ancient Crete to Mycenae*, 2nd ed. (1989). An excellent textual and pictorial guide to all the basic aspects of the Minoan and Mycenaean societies.

Wilson, John A., *The Culture of Ancient Egypt* (1951). A classic study of the history and culture of pharaonic Egypt.

Yadin, Yigael, *The Art of Warfare in Biblical Lands in the Light of Archaeological Discovery* (1963). A well-illustrated presentation of the machinery of war in the second and first millennia BCE.

Yoffee, Norman (ed.), *The Cambridge World History*, vol. 3, *Early Cities in Comparative Perspective* (2014). One of nine volumes that trace world history through individual articles written by experts.

Chapter 4: First Empires and Common Cultures in Afro-Eurasia, 1250–325 BCE

Ahlström, Gosta W., *The History of Ancient Palestine from the Paleolithic Period to Alexander's Conquests* (1993). An excellent survey of the history of the region by a renowned expert, with good attention to the recent archaeological evidence.

Assmann, Jan, *The Invention of Religion: Faith and Covenant in the Book of Exodus*, trans. Robert Savage (2018). An exposition by an expert on the evolution of early religions and a claim for the importance of the book of Exodus as the foundational work of monotheism.

Astour, Michael, "New Evidence on the Last Days of Ugarit," *American Journal of Archaeology* 69 (1965). An early and important article on the destruction of important cities in the Levant in the twelfth century BCE.

Aubet, Maria Eugenia, *The Phoenicians and the West,* 2nd ed. (2001). The basic survey of the Phoenician colonization of the western Mediterranean and Atlantic, with special attention to recent archaeological discoveries.

Behringer, Wolfgang, *A Cultural History of Climate,* trans. Patrick Camiller (2010). A summary view of the place of climate in historical change, written by an expert in historical climatology.

Benjamin, Craig (ed.), *The Cambridge World History,* vol. 4, *A World with States, Empires, and Networks, 1200 BCE–900 CE* (2015). An important overview of developments in the world, with individual chapters written by experts.

Briant, Pierre, *From Cyrus to Alexander: A History of the Persian Empire,* trans. Peter T. Daniels (2002). A complex and comprehensive history of the Persian Empire by its finest modern scholar.

Bright, John, *A History of Israel,* 4th ed. (2000). An updated version of a classic and still very useful overview of the whole history of the Israelite people down to the end of the period covered in this chapter.

Cook, J. M., *The Persian Empire* (1983). An older but still useful, and highly readable, standard history of the Persian Empire.

Fagan, Brian, *The Long Summer: How Climate Changed Civilization* (2004). An accessible overview of the role of climate in historical change, written by one of the leading historians of ancient history and an individual who has brought together considerable evidence about climate change and historical development.

Falkenhausen, Lothar von, *Chinese Society in the Age of Confucius (1000–250 BC): The Archaeological Evidence* (2006). A timely reassessment of early Chinese history that compares the literary texts on which it has traditionally been based with the new archaeological evidence.

Frahm, Eckart (ed.), *A Companion to Assyria* (2017). The work of expert Assyriologists and hence the most up-to-date study of these ancient states.

Frye, Richard N., *The Heritage of Persia* (1963). This classic study of ancient Iran gives the political and literary history of the Persians and their successors.

Fukuyama, Francis, *The Origins of Political Order: From Prehuman Times to the French Revolution* (2011). Argues that the first real kings in Chinese history and the first real states and dynasties did not appear until the Qin and Han.

Grayson, A. K., "Assyrian Civilization," in *Cambridge Ancient History,* vol. 3, pt. 2, pp. 194–228 (1992). The Neo-Assyrian and Neo-Babylonian Empires and other states of the Near East, from the eighth to the sixth century BCE.

Hornung, Erik, *Akhenaten and the Religion of Light,* translated from the German by David Lorton (1999). An important, brief biography of Egypt's most controversial pharaoh.

———, *History of Ancient Egypt: An Introduction,* translated from the German by David Lorton (1999). An accessible overview of the history of ancient Egypt by a leading Egyptologist.

Isserlin, Benedikt J., *The Israelites* (1998). A very well-written and heavily illustrated history of all aspects of life in the regions of the Levant inhabited by the Israelites, equally good on the latest scholarship and the archaeological data.

Keay, John, *India: A History* (2010). A useful, readable overview of the sweep of Indian history.

Lancel, Serge, *Carthage: A History,* trans. Antonia Nevill (1997). By far the best single-volume history of the most important Phoenician colony in the Mediterranean (the first three chapters are especially relevant to materials covered in this chapter).

Lemche, Niels Peter, *Ancient Israel: A New History of Israelite Society* (1988). A quick, readable, and still up-to-date summary of the main phases and themes.

Lewis, Mark Edward, *Writing and Authority in Early China* (1999). A work that traces the changing uses of writing to command assent and obedience in early China.

Liu, Guozhong, *Introduction to the Tsinghua Bamboo-Strip Manuscripts,* trans. Christopher J. Foster and William N. French (2016). An important essay on the implications of these texts for our understanding of early Western Zhou history.

Liverani, Mario, *The Ancient Near East: History, Society and Economy* (2014). Parts 5 and 6 are especially relevant to the materials covered in this chapter.

Luckenbill, Daniel David, *Ancient Records of Assyria and Babylonia,* vol. 1, *Historical Records of Assyria from the Earliest Times to Sargon* (1926). Luckenbill's English translations of Neo-Assyrian documents (mostly inscriptions), arranged chronologically by king's reign, provide insight into Neo-Assyrian politics, religion, building programs, and much more. A short introduction accompanies each translation.

Markoe, Glenn E., *Phoenicians* (2000). A thorough survey of the Phoenicians and their society as it first developed in the Levant and then expanded over the Mediterranean, with excellent illustrations of the diverse archaeological sites.

Matthews, Victor H., and Don C. Benjamin, *Social World of Ancient Israel, 1350–587* BCE (1993). A thematic overview of the main occupational groups and social roles that characterized ancient Israelite society.

Oates, Joan, and David Oates, *Nimrud: An Assyrian Imperial City Revealed* (2001). A fine and highly readable summary of the state of our knowledge of the Neo-Assyrian Empire from the perspective of the early capital of Ashurnasirpal II.

Oded, Bustenay, *Mass Deportations and Deportees in the Neo-Assyrian Empire* (1979). A detailed textual examination of the deportation strategy of the Neo-Assyrian kings. Good for in-depth research of the question.

Potts, D. T., *The Archaeology of Elam: Formation and Transformation of an Ancient Iranian State* (1999). The definitive study of the archaeology of western Iran from the Neolithic period through the Persian Empire.

Quinn, Josephine C., and Nicholas C. Vella (eds.), *The Punic Mediterranean* (2014). A valuable and readable collection of chapters on various aspects of how the Phoenician colonization of the Mediterranean led to the formation of new cultural identities.

Radner, Karen, *Ancient Assyria: A Very Short Introduction* (2015). A highly readable and up-to-date survey of all the important aspects

of Neo-Assyrian government and society.

———, "The Neo-Assyrian Empire," in Michael Gehler and Robert Rollinger (eds.), *Imperien und Reiche in der Weltgeschichte* (2014), pp. 101–20. An outstanding overview by one of the most learned historians of ancient Assyria.

Shaughnessy, Edward L., *Sources of Western Zhou History: Inscribed Bronze Vessels* (1992). Detailed work on the historiography and interpretation of the thousands of ritual bronze vessels discovered by China's archaeologists.

Stein, Burton, *A History of India*, 2nd ed., edited by David Arnold (2010). One of the standard general histories of India, brought up to date by a leading historian of the subcontinent.

Tanner, Harold M., *China: A History* (2009). A readable and up-to-date overview of the sweep of Chinese history.

Thapar, Romila, *The Aryan: Recasting Constructs* (2011). On the rise of the theory of an Aryan race and the beginnings of Indian history.

———, *From Lineage to State* (1984). The only book on early India that uses religious literature historically and analyzes major lineages to reveal the transition from tribal society to state institutions.

Tignor, Robert L., *Egypt: A Short History* (2010). A succinct treatment of the entire history of Egypt from the pharaohs to the present, with three chapters on the ancient period.

Trautmann, Thomas, *India: Brief History of a Civilization* (2011). A highly readable survey of Indian history with emphasis on its early history.

Tubb, Jonathan N., *Canaanites* (1998). This well-illustrated book is the best recent survey of one of

the main ethnic groups dominating the culture of the Levant.

Wunsch, Cornelia, "The Egibi Family," in Gwendolyn Leick (ed.), *The Babylonian World* (2007), pp. 232–42. An Assyriologist and expert on the Egibi family archive reviews the family connections and the wide-ranging business dealings reflected in this unique and valuable collection of Neo-Babylonian records.

Chapter 5: Worlds Turned Inside Out, 1000–350 BCE

Adams, William Y., *Nubia: Corridor to Africa* (1977). The authoritative historical overview of Nubia, the area of present-day Sudan just south of Egypt and a geographic connecting point between the Mediterranean and sub-Saharan Africa.

Allan, Sarah, *Buried Ideas. Legends of Abdication and Ideal Government in Early Chinese Bamboo-Slip Manuscripts* (2016). Four recently discovered Warring States texts challenge long-standing ideas about Chinese intellectual history.

Armstrong, Karen, *Buddha* (2001). A readable and impressive account of the life of the Buddha.

———, *The Great Transformation: The Beginning of Our Religious Traditions* (2006). A thorough investigation of a key moment in the evolution of religious thought, explaining the traditions that arose in the ninth century BCE in four regions of the civilized world as a response to the violence of the period.

Aubet, Maria Eugenia, *The Phoenicians and the West*, 2nd ed. (2001). The basic survey of the Phoenician colonization of the western Mediterranean and Atlantic, with special attention to recent archaeological discoveries.

Barker, Graeme, and Tom Rasmussen, *The Etruscans* (1998). The most up-to-date introduction to this important pre-Roman society in the Italian Peninsula, with strong emphasis on broad social and material patterns of development as indicated by the archaeological evidence.

Beckwith, Christopher I., *The Greek Buddha: Pyrrho's Encounter with Early Buddhism in Central Asia* (2015). A pioneering work on the introduction of Buddhist views into the Greek philosophical scene.

Bellah, Robert N., "What Is Axial about the Axial Age?" *European Journal of Sociology* 46, no. 1 (2005): 69–89. A useful categorical analysis of the four cases of axial "breakthrough"—ancient Israel, Greece, India, and China.

Benjamin, Craig (ed.), *The Cambridge World History*, vol. 4, *A World with States, Empires, and Networks, 1200 BCE–900 CE* (2015). Essays by experts on these centuries in world history. Especially important for thinking about the Axial Age is the chapter by Bjorn Wittrock, "The Axial Age in World History," pp. 101–19.

Bresson, Alain, *The Making of the Ancient Greek Economy: Institutions, Markets, and Growth in the City-States*, trans. Steven Rendall (2015). The most conceptually sophisticated and factually up-to-date account of the economic regimes of the Greek city-states.

Bruhns, Karen Olsen, *Ancient South America* (1994). A very useful overview of recent debates and conclusions about pre-Columbian archaeology in South America, including both the Andes and the lowland and coastal regions.

Burkert, Walter, *Greek Religion*, trans. John Raffan (1985). The best one-volume introduction to early Greek religion, placing the Greeks in their larger Mediterranean and Near Eastern contexts.

Cartledge, Paul (ed.), *The Cambridge Illustrated History of Ancient Greece* (2002). An excellent history of the Greek city-states down to the time of Alexander the Great.

Chakravarti, Uma, *The Social Dimensions of Early Buddhism* (1987). A description of the life of the Buddha drawn from early Buddhist texts.

Cho-yun, Hsu, *Ancient China in Transition* (1965). An account of the political, economic, social, and intellectual changes that occurred during the Warring States period.

Coarelli, Filippo (ed.), *Etruscan Cities* (1975). A brilliantly and lavishly illustrated guide to the material remains of the Etruscans: their cities, their magnificent tombs, and their architecture, painting, sculpture, and other art.

Coe, Michael, et al. (eds.), *The Olmec World: Ritual and Rulership* (1996). A collection of field-synthesizing articles with important illustrations, based on one of the most comprehensive exhibitions of Olmec art in the world.

Confucius, *The Analects (Lun Yü)*, trans. D. C. Lau (1979). An outstanding translation of the words of Confucius as recorded by his major disciples. Includes valuable historical material needed to provide the context for Confucius's teachings.

Eisenstadt, S. N. (ed.), *The Origins and Diversity of the Axial Age* (1986). An important, original analysis of the great ancient civilizations and a systematic exploration of the conditions under which they developed.

Elman, Benjamin A., and Martin Kern (eds.), *Statecraft and Classical Learning: The Rituals of Zhou in East Asian History* (2010). Traces the long-term political rise of classical learning and state rituals in East Asia from the decline of the Eastern Zhou kingdom to the rise of later imperial dynasties in China, Japan, and Korea.

Falkenhausen, Lothar von, *Chinese Society in the Age of Confucius (100–250 BC)* (2006). The larger Chinese society under the influence of Confucian thought.

Finley, M. I., and H. W. Pleket, *The Olympic Games: The First Thousand Years* (2005). A fine description of the most famous of the Greek games; it explains how they exemplify the competitive spirit that marked many aspects of the Greek city-states.

Garlan, Yvon, *Slavery in Ancient Greece*, trans. Janet Lloyd (1988). A treatment of the emergence, development, and institutionalization of "chattel slavery" in the Greek city-states.

———, *War in the Ancient World: A Social History*, trans. Janet Lloyd (1976). A discussion of the emergence of the forms of warfare, including male citizens fighting in hoplite phalanxes and the development of siege warfare, that were typical of the Greek city-states.

Iliffe, John, *Africans: The History of a Continent*, 2nd ed. (2007). A first-rate scholarly survey of Africa from its beginnings, with a strong emphasis on demography.

Jaspers, Karl, *The Origin and Goal of History*, trans. Michael Bullock (1953). A book that reckons with the philosophy of the history of humankind and heightens our awareness of the present by locating it within the framework of the obscurity of prehistory.

Kagan, Donald, *The Peloponnesian War* (2004). A vivid description of the war that pitted the major Greek city-states, including Athens and Sparta, against one another over the latter half of the fifth century BCE.

Lancel, Serge, *Carthage: A History*, trans. Antonia Nevill (1997). By far the best single-volume history of the most important Phoenician colony in the Mediterranean.

Lewis, Mark Edward, *Sanctioned Violence in Early China* (1990). An analysis of the use of sanctioned violence as an element of statecraft from the Warring States period to the formation of the Qin and Han Empires in the second half of the first millennium BCE.

———, *Writing and Authority in Early China* (1999). A revisionist account of the central role of writing and persuasion in models for the invention of a Chinese world empire.

Ling, Trevor, *The Buddha: Buddhist Civilization in India and Ceylon* (1972). An overview of Buddhism in India and Ceylon.

Lloyd, G. E. R., *Early Greek Science: Thales to Aristotle* (1970). An especially clear and concise introduction to the main developments and intellectuals that marked the emergence of critical secular thinking in the early Greek world.

Lloyd, G. E. R., and Nathan Sivin, *The Way and the Word: Science and Medicine in Early China and Greece* (2002). A comprehensive rethinking of the social and political settings in ancient China and city-state Greece that contributed to the different views of science and medicine that emerged in each place.

Morris, Ian, and Walter Scheidel (eds.), *The Dynamics of Ancient Empires: State Power from Assyria to Byzantium* (2010). A work by experts on ancient empires and city-states. The essay by Ian Morris on Athens is especially useful.

Mote, Frederick, *Intellectual Foundations of China* (1971). An early but still useful description of the seminal figures in China's early intellectual life.

Murray, Oswyn, *Early Greece*, 2nd ed. (1993). One of the best introductions to the emergence of the Greek city-states down to the end of the Archaic Age.

Ober, Josiah, *The Rise and Fall of Classical Greece* (2015). A compelling general interpretation of the rise of the Greek city-states in the sixth and fifth centuries BCE and their subsequent demise in the fourth century BCE.

Osborne, Robin, *Archaic and Classical Greek Art* (1998). An outstanding book that clearly explains the main innovations in Greek art, setting them in their historical context.

———, *Greece in the Making, 1200–479 BC* (1999). The standard history of the whole early period of the Greek city-states, characterized by an especially fine and judicious mix of archaeological data and literary sources.

Pallottino, Massimo, *The Etruscans,* rev. ed., trans. J. Cremona (1975). A fairly traditional but still classic survey of all aspects of Etruscan history and political and social institutions.

Pines, Yuri, Paul R. Goldin, and Martin Kern (eds.), *Ideology of Power and Power of Ideology in Early China* (2015). A new assessment of state ideology and political legitimation under the Eastern Zhou dynasty during the Warring States era.

Provan, Iain, *Convenient Myths: The Axial Age, Dark Green Religion, and the World That Never Was* (2013). An illumination of two deeply rooted myths—the first being Karl Jaspers's construct of world religions spontaneously emerging from a shared set of values, the second being David Suzuki's assertion that organized religion severed society's previous connection with nature—and their dangers.

Rayor, Diane J., and André Lardinois, *Sappho: A New Translation of the Complete Works* (2014). Offers commentary about the identification and reconstruction of the Sapphic fragments, as well as authentic and readable translations of the Greek.

Redford, Donald B., *From Slave to Pharaoh: The Black Experience of Ancient Egypt* (2004). A description of Egypt's twenty-fifth dynasty, which was made up of Sudanese conquerors.

The Sayings of Lao Tzu, trans. Lionel Giles (1904). A translated collection of Master Lao's sayings, which offer a third-century BCE expression of Daoist philosophy.

Schaberg, David, *A Patterned Past: Form and Thought in Early Chinese Historiography* (2002). A comprehensive study of the intellectual content of historical anecdotes by the followers of Confucius collected around the fourth century BCE.

Schaps, David, *The Invention of Coinage and the Monetization of Ancient Greece* (2004). A new analysis that offers a broad overview of the emergence of coined money in the Near East and the eastern Mediterranean and its effects on the spread of money-based markets.

Sharma, J. P., *Republics in Ancient India, c. 1500 B.C.–500 B.C.* (1968). Relying on information from early Buddhist texts, this book first revealed that South Asia had not only monarchies but also alternative polities.

Shaw, Thurston, *Nigeria: Its Archaeology and Early History* (1978). An important introduction to the early history of Nigeria by one of that country's leading archaeologists.

Shinnie, P. L., *Ancient Nubia* (1996). An excellent account of the history of the ancient Nubians, who, we are discovering, had great influence on Egypt and on the rest of tropical Africa.

Snodgrass, Anthony, *Archaic Greece: The Age of Experiment* (1981). A good introduction to the archaeological evidence of Archaic Greece.

Taylor, Christopher, Richard Hare, and Jonathan Barnes, *Greek Philosophers* (1999). A fine, succinct, one-volume introduction to the major aspects of the three big thinkers who dominated the high period of classical Greek philosophy: Socrates, Plato, and Aristotle.

Torok, Laszlo, *Meroe: Six Studies on the Cultural Identity of an Ancient African State* (1995). A good collection of essays on Meroe.

Welsby, Derek A., *The Kingdom of Kush: The Napatan and Meroitic Empires* (1996). A fine book on these two important Nubian kingdoms.

Chapter 6: Shrinking the Afro-Eurasian World, 350–100 BCE

al Quntar, Salam, and Brian A. Daniels, "Responses to the Destruction of Syrian Cultural Heritage: A Critical Review of Current Efforts," *International Journal of Islamic Architecture* 5, no. 2 (2016): 381–97. Describes the work of the Safeguarding the Heritage of Syria and Iraq (SHOSI) project to empower local "heritage activists" to document, protect, and raise awareness of the threats to Syrian cultural heritage

Bogdanos, Matthew, *Thieves of Baghdad: One Marine's Passion to Recover the World's Greatest Stolen Treasures* (2005). U.S. Marine Corps colonel, lawyer, and National Humanities Medal–winner Bogdanos offers a compelling first-person narrative of his team's work to track down thousands of antiquities looted from Baghdad's National Museum in the aftermath of the U.S. invasion in 2003.

Bradley, Keith, *Slavery and Rebellion in the Roman World, 140 B.C.–70 B.C.* (1989). A description of the rise of large-scale plantation slavery in Sicily and Italy, and a detailed account of the three great slave wars.

Bresson, Alain, *The Making of the Ancient Greek Economy: Markets and Growth in the City-States*, trans. Steven Rendall (2015). An up-to-date and theoretically well-informed analysis of the market economics of the Greek city-states in the Hellenistic era.

Briant, Pierre, *Alexander the Great and His Empire: A Short Introduction*, translated by Amélie Kuhrt from a work originally published in 1974 and revised in 2005 (2010). A classic account of Alexander the Great's life.

Browning, Iain, *Palmyra* (1979). A narrative of the history of the important desert city that linked eastern and western trade routes.

Carney, Elizabeth, *Olympias: Mother of Alexander the Great* (2006). Carney explores the hostile ancient sources that describe the role of Olympias in late fourth-century BCE political intrigue to peel back the gender-based critique and offer a more nuanced and sympathetic understanding of her actions and motivations.

Casson, Lionel, *The Periplus Maris Erythraei* (1989). An introduction to a typical ancient sailing manual, this one of the Red Sea and Indian Ocean.

———, *Ships and Seamanship in the Ancient World* (1995). The classic account of the ships and sailors that powered commerce and war on the high seas.

Colledge, Malcolm, *The Art of Palmyra* (1976). A well-illustrated introduction to the unusual art of Palmyra with its mixture of eastern and western elements.

Convention on the Means of Prohibiting and Preventing the Illicit Import, Export and Transfer of Ownership of Cultural Property 1970 (Paris, November 14, 1970), http://portal.unesco.org/en/ev.php-URL_ID=13039&URL_DO=DO_TOPIC&URL_SECTION=201.html. This document records the UNESCO agreement that limits illegal trade in cultural property, with the goals of both reducing the black market for art, artifacts, and manuscripts and returning improperly removed items to their rightful place of origin. It includes several post-2000 reports from member states.

Fowler, Barbara H., *The Hellenistic Aesthetic* (1989). How the artists in this new age saw and portrayed their world in new and different ways.

Green, Peter, *Alexander to Actium: The Historical Evolution of the Hellenistic Age* (1990). The best general guide to the whole period in all of its various aspects, and well illustrated.

Habicht, Christian, *Athens from Alexander to Antony*, trans. Deborah L. Schneider (1997). The authoritative account of what happened to the great city-state of Athens in this period.

Hansen, Valerie, *The Silk Road: A New History* (2012). A recent work on the Silk Roads; authoritative on the eastern terminus of this vital trade route.

Harmanşah, Ömür, "ISIS, Heritage, and the Spectacles of Destruction in the Global Media," *Near Eastern Archaeology* 78, no. 3 (September 2015): 170–77. Considers the voyeuristic element of the world's consumption of images of ISIS's destruction of cultural heritage, characterizing ISIS's behavior not as iconoclasm but rather as "iconoclash."

Herodotus, *The Histories*, 4 vols., trans. Tom Holland (2013). A basic work, which many scholars regard as the first world history.

Holt, Frank L., *Thundering Zeus: The Making of Hellenistic Bactria* (1999). A basic history of the most eastern of the kingdoms spawned by the conquests of Alexander the Great.

Hopkirk, Peter, *Foreign Devils on the Silk Road* (1984). A historiography of the explorations and researches on the central Asian Silk Roads in the nineteenth and early twentieth centuries.

Juliano, Annette L., and Judith A Lerner (eds.), *Nomads, Traders and Holy Men along China's Silk Road* (2003). A description of the travelers along the Silk Roads in human terms, focusing on warfare, markets, and religion.

Kosmin, Paul J., *The Land of the Elephant Kings: Space, Territory, and Ideology in the Seleucid Empire* (2014). The best current analysis of the relationships of Seleucid kings, both with their own subjects and, especially, with the Mauryan kingdom of India and the nomadic peoples of central Asia.

Kuzima, E. E., *The Prehistory of the Silk Road* (2008). Valuable information on the early history of the Silk Roads.

Lane Fox, Robin, *Alexander the Great* (1973). Still the most readable and in many ways the sanest biography of the world conqueror.

Lewis, Naphtali, *Greeks in Ptolemaic Egypt* (1986). An account of the relationships between Greeks and Egyptians as seen through the lives of individual Greek settlers and colonists.

Liu, Xinru, *Ancient India and Ancient China* (1988). The first work to connect political and economic developments in India and China with the evolution and spread of Buddhism in the first half of the first millennium.

———, *The Silk Road in World History* (2010). A study of the history of the great trade and communications routes that connected the different regions of Afro-Eurasia between the third century BCE and the thirteenth century CE.

Long, Antony A., *Hellenistic Philosophy: Stoics, Epicureans, Sceptics*, 2nd ed. (1986). One of the clearest guides to the main new trends in Greek philosophical thinking in the period.

Manning, J. G., *The Last Pharaohs: Egypt under the Ptolemies, 305–30 BC* (2010). An important work on the way the Ptolemy dynasty merged Greek and Egyptian institutions.

Martin, Luther H., *Hellenistic Religions: An Introduction* (1987). An introduction to the principal new Hellenistic religions and cults that emerged in this period.

Mendels, Doron, *The Rise and Fall of Jewish Nationalism* (1992). A sophisticated account of the various phases of Jewish resistance in Judea to foreign domination.

Miller, James Innes, *The Spice Trade of the Roman Empire, 29 B.C. to A.D. 641* (1969). A first-rate study of the spice trade in the Roman Empire.

Penrose, Walter Duvall, Jr., *Postcolonial Amazons: Female Masculinity and Courage in Ancient Greek and Sanskrit Literature* (2016). A theoretically inflected exploration of Greek (Athenian and non-Athenian) ideas about female masculinity and a range of warrior women—from Artemisia of Caria (who fought on the side of the Persians against the Greeks), to Hellenistic warrior queens, to Persian and Indian female bodyguards—to historicize Greek legends of the Amazons.

Pomeroy, Sarah B., *Women in Hellenistic Egypt: From Alexander to Cleopatra* (1990). A highly readable investigation of women and family in the best-documented region of the Hellenistic world.

Ray, Himanshu P., *The Wind of Change: Buddhism and the Maritime Links of Early South Asia* (1994). Ray's study of Buddhism and maritime trade stretches from the Arabian Sea to the navigations between South Asia and Southeast Asia.

Rosenfield, John, *The Dynastic Art of the Kushans* (1967). Instead of focusing on the Gandharan Buddhist art itself, Rosenfield selects sculptures of Kushan royals and those representing nomadic populations in religious shrines to display the central Asian aspect of artworks of the period.

Rostovtzeff, Michael Ivanovich, *Caravan Cities*, trans. D. and T. Talbot Rice (1932). Though published more than seven decades ago, this small volume contains accurate descriptions of the ruins of many caravan cities in modern Jordan and Syria.

———, *The Social and Economic History of the Hellenistic World* (1941). A monumental achievement; one of the great works of history written in the twentieth century. An unsurpassed overview of all aspects of the politics and social and economic movements of the period. Despite its age, there is still nothing like it.

Schoff, Wilfred H. (ed. and trans.), *The Periplus of the Erythraean Sea* (1912). An invaluable tool for mapping names and places from the Red Sea to Indian coastal areas during this period.

Shipley, Graham, *The Greek World after Alexander, 323–30 BC* (2000). A more up-to-date survey than Peter Green's work (above), with more emphasis on the historical detail in each period.

Tarn, W. W., *Greeks in Bactria and India* (1984). The most comprehensive coverage of Greek sources on Hellenistic states in Afghanistan and northwest India.

Thapar, Romila, *Ashoka and the Decline of the Mauryas* (1973). Using all available primary sources, including the edicts of Aśoka and Greek authors' accounts, Thapar gives the most authoritative analysis of the first and the most important empire in Indian history.

Vainker, Shelagh, *Chinese Silk: A Cultural History* (2004). A work that traces the cultural history of silk in China from its early origins to the twentieth century and considers its relationship to the other decorative arts. The author draws on the most recent archaeological evidence to emphasize the role of silk in Chinese history, trade, religion, and literature.

Wood, Frances, *The Silk Road: Two Thousand Years in the Heart of Asia* (2004). Illustrated with drawings, manuscripts, paintings, and artifacts to trace the Silk Roads to their origins as far back as Alexander the Great, with an emphasis on their importance to cultural and religious movements.

Young, Gary K., *Rome's Eastern Trade: International Commerce and Imperial Policy, 31 BC–AD 305* (2001). This study examines the taxation and profits of eastern trade from the perspective of the Roman government.

Chapter 7: Han Dynasty China and Imperial Rome, 300 BCE–300 CE

Barbieri-Low, Anthony J., and Robin D. S. Yates, *Law, State, and Society in Early Imperial China: A Study with Critical Edition and Translation of the Legal Texts from Zhangjiashan Tomb No. 247*, 2 vols. (2015). A new account of changes in Western (Former) Han dynasty law in terms of its moralization via instituting Confucianism.

Bodde, Derk, *China's First Unifier: A Study of the Ch'in Dynasty as Seen in the Life of Li Ssu (280?–208 B.C.)* (1938). A classic account of the key Legalist adviser, Li Si, who formulated the Qin policy to enhance its autocratic power.

Bowman, Alan K., *Life and Letters on the Roman Frontier: Vindolanda and Its Peoples* (1994). An introduction to the exciting discovery of writing tablets at a Roman army base in northern Britain.

Bradley, Keith, *Slavery and Society at Rome* (1994). The best single overview of the major aspects of the slave system in the Roman Empire.

Chevallier, Raymond, *Roman Roads*, trans. N. H. Field (1976). A guide to the fundamentals of the construction, maintenance, administration, and mapping of Roman roads.

Coarelli, Fillipo (ed.), *Pompeii*, trans. Patricia Cockram (2006). A lavishly illustrated large volume that allows the reader to sense some of the wondrous wealth of the buried city of Pompeii.

Colledge, Malcolm A. R., *The Parthians* (1967). A bit dated but still a fundamental introduction to the Parthians, the major power on the eastern frontier of the Roman Empire.

Cornell, Tim, *The Beginnings of Rome: Italy and Rome from the Bronze Age to the Punic Wars, c. 2000 to 264 B.C.* (1995). The single best one-volume history of Rome through its early history to the first war with Carthage.

Cornell, Tim, and John Matthews, *Atlas of the Roman World* (1982). A history of the Roman world; much more than simply an atlas. It is provided not only with good maps and a gazetteer, but also with marvelous color illustrations and a text that guides the reader through the basics of Roman history.

Csikszentmihalyi, Mark, *Readings in Han Chinese Thought* (2006). A volume presenting a representative selection of primary sources to illustrate the growth of ideas in early imperial times; a useful introduction to the key strains of thought during this crucial period.

Di Cosmo, Nicola, and Michael Maas (eds.), *Empires and Exchanges in Eurasia in Late Antiquity* (2018). Expert historians examine commercial and other connections between the west and the east during the Late Antique period.

Dien, Albert E., "The Qin Army and Its Antecedents," in Liu Yang (ed.), *China's Terracotta Warriors: The First Emperor's Legacy* (2013). An account of the Qin army in light of its Warring States precedents.

Dixon, Suzanne, *The Roman Family* (1992). The best one-volume guide to the nature of the Roman family and family relations.

Garnsey, Peter, and Richard Saller, *The Roman Empire: Economy, Society, and Culture*, 2nd ed. (2014). A perceptive and critical introduction to three basic aspects of social life in the empire.

Giardina, Andrea (ed.), *The Romans*, trans. Lydia Cochrane (1993). Individual studies of important typical figures in Roman society, from the peasant and the bandit to the merchant and the soldier.

Goldsworthy, Adrian, *The Roman Army at War: 100 B.C.–A.D. 200* (1996). A summary history and analysis of the Roman army in action during the late Republic and early Empire.

Goodman, Martin, *The Roman World: 44 B.C.–A.D. 180* (1997). A newer basic history text covering the high Roman Empire.

Graf, David F., "The Silk Road between Syria and China," in Andrew Wilson and Alan Bowman (eds.), *Trade, Commerce, and the State in the Roman World* (2018), pp. 443–529. An exhaustive overview of relations between the Roman Empire and Han China, based on the most recent research of historians.

Hansen, Valerie, *The Silk Road: A New History* (2012). An important study of the Silk Roads, based on much original research.

Harper, Kyle, *The Fate of Rome: Climate, Disease, and the End of an Empire* (2017). A vigorous and persuasive argument that climate played a significant role in the decline of the Roman Empire.

Harris, William, *Ancient Literacy* (1989). A basic survey of what is known about communication in the form of writing and books in the Roman Empire.

Hopkins, Keith, *Death and Renewal: Sociological Studies in Roman History*, vol. 2 (1983). Innovative studies in Roman history, including one of the best on gladiators and another on death and funerals.

———, *A World Full of Gods: Pagans, Jews and Christians in the Roman Empire* (1999). A somewhat unusual but interesting and provocative look at the world of religions in the Roman Empire.

Hughes, J. Donald, *Environmental Problems of the Greeks and Romans: Ecology in the Ancient Mediterranean*, 2nd ed. (2014). A much improved and expanded edition of a classic work on the environment in Greek and Roman antiquity and a state-of-the-art summary of our current knowledge.

Juliano, Annette L., and Judith A. Lerner (eds.), *Nomads, Traders and Holy Men along China's Silk Road* (2003). A description of the travelers along the Silk Roads in human terms, focusing on warfare, markets, and religion.

Kern, Martin, and Michael Hunter (eds.), *The Analects: A Western Han Text?* (2013). Challenges the assumption that the Confucian *Analects* was compiled before the Han Dynasty.

Knapp, Robert C., *Invisible Romans* (2011). A highly readable introduction to the lower orders of Roman imperial society: the poor, the enslaved, freedmen, prostitutes, gladiators, bandits, and pirates (among others).

Kraus, Theodore, and Leonard von Matt, *Pompeii and Herculaneum: The Living Cities of the Dead*, trans. Robert E. Wolf (1975). A huge, lavishly illustrated compendium of all aspects of life in the buried cities of Pompeii and Herculaneum as preserved in the archaeological record.

Liang, Cai, *Witchcraft and the Rise of the First Confucian Empire* (2014). A new account of the rise of the Confucians at the Western (Former) Han court during the famous witchcraft trials circa 91–87 BCE.

Liu, Xinru, *The Silk Road in World History* (2010). A short overview of the Silk Roads, written by a scholar whose specialty is India, and of the manifold connections involving East Asia, South Asia, Southwest Asia, North Africa, and Europe.

Loewe, Michael, *The Government of the Qin and Han Empires: 221 BCE–220 CE* (2006). A useful overview of the government of the early empires of China. Topics include the structure of central government, provincial and local government, the armed forces, officials, government communications, the laws of the empire, and control of the people and the land.

Millar, Fergus, *The Crowd in the Late Republic* (1998). An innovative study of the democratic power of the citizens in the city of Rome itself.

———, *The Emperor in the Roman World, 31 B.C.–A.D. 337* (1992). Everything you might want to know about the Roman emperor, with special emphasis on his civil role as the administrator of an empire.

Potter, David S., *The Roman Empire at Bay, A.D. 180–395*, 2nd ed. (2014). A new basic text covering the later Roman Empire, including the critical transition to a Christian state.

Potter, David S., and David J. Mattingly (eds.), *Life, Death, and Entertainment in the Roman Empire* (1999). A good introduction to basic aspects of Roman life in the empire, including the family, feeding the cities, religion, and popular entertainment.

Qian, Sima, *Records of the Grand Historian: Qin Dynasty*, trans. Burton Watson, 3rd ed. (1995). The classic work of Chinese history in a readable translation. The Han dynasty's Grand Historian describes the slow rise and meteoric fall of the Qin dynasty from the point of view of the succeeding dynasty, which Sima Qian witnessed or heard of during his lifetime.

Scheidel, Walter (ed.), *Rome and China: Comparative Perspectives on Ancient World Empires* (2009). Historians of the Roman and Han Empires offer a series of essays that compare these two empires.

——— (ed.), *The Science of Roman History: Biology, Climate, and the Future of the Past* (2018). Experts apply biology, climatology, and other scientific subjects to the study of the Roman Empire.

Southern, Pat, *The Roman Army: A Social and Institutional History* (2006). A fundamental guide to all aspects of the Roman army.

Todd, Malcolm, *The Early Germans*, rev. ed. (2004). A basic survey of the peoples in central and western Europe at the time of the Roman Empire.

Vainker, Shelagh, *Chinese Silk: A Cultural History* (2004). A work that traces the cultural history of silk in China from its early origins to the twentieth century and considers its relationship to the other decorative arts. The author draws on the most recent archaeological evidence to emphasize the role of silk in Chinese history, trade, religion, and literature.

Wells, Peter S., *The Barbarians Speak: How the Conquered Peoples Shaped Roman Europe* (1999). The cultures of the peoples of central and northern Europe at the time of the Roman Empire and their impact on Roman culture.

Wood, Frances, *The Silk Road: Two Thousand Years in the Heart of Asia* (2004). A work illustrated with drawings, manuscripts, paintings, and artifacts to trace the Silk Roads to their origins as far back as Alexander the Great. The author stresses the importance of the Silk Roads to cultural and religious movements.

Woolf, Greg (ed.), *The Cambridge Illustrated History of the Roman World* (2005). A good guide to various aspects of Roman history, culture, and provincial life.

———, *Rome: An Empire's Story* (2012). An up-to-date narrative of the Roman Empire told according to major themes that are particularly relevant to world history.

Chapter 8: The Rise of Universalizing Religions, 300–600 CE

Bowersock, Glen W., *Empires in Collision in Late Antiquity* (2013). Brilliant, short studies of the relations between Ethiopia, Arabia, and Byzantium as a background to the origins of Islam.

Bowersock, Glen W., Peter Brown, and Oleg Grabar (eds.), *Late Antiquity: A Guide to the Postclassical World* (1999). Essays and items for the entire period 150–750 CE. The volume covers the Roman, East Roman, Sasanian, and early Islamic worlds.

Brown, Peter, *The Rise of Western Christendom: Triumph and Diversity*, A.D. *200–1000*, 2nd ed. (2003). The rise and spread of Christianity in Europe and Asia, with up-to-date bibliographies on all topics, maps, and time charts.

———, "The Silk Road in Late Antiquity," in V. H. Maier and J. Hickman (eds.), *Reconfiguring the Silk Road* (2014). The Silk Roads from the perspective of their western outlets and influences.

———, *Through the Eye of a Needle: Wealth, the Fall of Rome, and the Making of Christianity in the West, 350–550* (2012). Christianity and Roman society before and after the end of the empire.

———, *Treasure in Heaven: The Holy Poor in Early Christianity* (2016). On the social role of early Christian monasticism in Syria and Egypt.

———, *The World of Late Antiquity: From Marcus Aurelius to Muhammad, ad 150–750* (1989). A social, religious, and cultural history of the late Roman and Sasanian empires, with illustrations and a time chart.

Bühler, G. (trans.), *The Laws of Manu* (1886). The classic translation of one of India's most important historical, legal, and religious texts.

Canepa, Matthew P., *The Two Eyes of the Earth: Art and Ritual of Kingship between Rome and Sasanian Iran* (2009). An interesting look at how two great global powers, Rome and Iran, shared images of rulership.

Clynes, Tom, "Laser Scans Reveal Maya 'Megalopolis' below Guatemalan Jungle," *National Geographic News*, February 1, 2018, https://news.nationalgeographic.com/2018/02/maya-laser-lidar-guatemala-pacunam/. Highlights the use of LIDAR laser technology to uncover extensive Maya ruins, including additional pyramids, intercity road systems, defensive walls, irrigation systems, quarries, and other structures.

Coe, Michael D., *The Maya*, 6th ed. (1999). A work by the world's most famous Mayanologist, with recent evidence, analyses, and illustrations.

Cowgill, George L., "The Central Mexican Highlands and the Rise of Teotihuacan to the Decline of Tula," in Richard Adams and Murdo Macleod (eds.), *The Cambridge History of the Native Peoples of the Americas*, vol. 2,

Mesoamerica, pt. 1 (2000). A thorough review of findings about urban states in central Mexico.

Fash, William L., *Scribes, Warriors and Kings: The City of Copan and the Ancient Maya* (2001). A fascinating and comprehensive study of one of the most elaborate of the Maya city-kingdoms.

Fisher, Greg (ed.), *Arabs and Empires before Islam* (2015). A collection of up-to-date studies on the relationships of various Arab groups with imperial powers, especially Rome and Persia.

————. *Between Empires: Arabs, Romans, and Sasanians in Late Antiquity* (2011). Arab, Roman, and Sasanian empires compared.

Fowden, Elizabeth Key, *The Barbarian Plain: Saint Sergius between Rome and Iran* (1999). The study of a major Christian shrine and its relations to Romans, Persians, and Arabs.

Fowden, Garth, *Empire to Commonwealth: The Consequences of Monotheism in Late Antiquity* (1993). A study of the relationship between empire and world religions in western Asia.

Fried, Johannes, *The Middle Ages*, trans. Peter Lewis (2015). An impressive overview of the Late Antique period and the Early Middle Ages.

Gombrich, Richard F., and Sheldon Pollack (eds.), *Clay Sanskrit Library* (2005–2006). All major works from the Gupta and post-Gupta periods, in both Sanskrit and English versions. During the Gupta period, classical Sanskrit literature reached its apex, with abundant drama, poetry, and folk stories.

Gordon, Charles, *The Age of Attila* (1960). The last century of the Roman Empire in western Europe, vividly illustrated from contemporary sources.

Haldon, John, *The Empire That Would Not Die: The Paradox of Eastern Rome's Survival* (2010). Incorporates much new climatological evidence.

Hansen, Valerie, *The Silk Road: A New History* (2012). A detailed history of the Silk Roads, based largely on Chinese sources.

Harper, Prudence, *The Royal Hunter: The Art of the Sasanian Empire* (1978). The ideology of the Sasanian Empire as shown through excavated hoards of precious silverware.

Heather, Peter, *The Fall of the Roman Empire: A New History of Rome and the Barbarians* (2006). A military and political narrative based on up-to-date archaeological material.

Herrmann, Georgina, *Iranian Revival* (1977). The structure and horizons of the Sasanian Empire as revealed in its monuments.

Hillgarth, Jocelyn (ed.), *Christianity and Paganism, 350–750: The Conversion of Western Europe*, rev. ed. (1986). A collection of contemporary sources.

Holcombe, Charles, *In the Shadow of the Han: Literati Thought and Society at the Beginning of the Southern Dynasties* (1994). A clear and concise account of the evolution of thought in China after the fall of the Han dynasty in 220 CE. The book presents the rise of Buddhism and Daoism as popular religions as well as elite interests in classical learning in a time of political division and barbarian conquest in North and South China.

La Vaissière, Étienne de, *Sogdian Traders: A History*, trans. James Ward (2005). A summary of historical facts about the most important trading community and its commercial networks on the Silk Roads, from the early centuries CE to its demise in the ninth century CE.

Little, Lester (ed.), *Plague and the End of Antiquity: The Pandemic of 541–750* (2008). A series of debates over the nature and impact of the first great pandemic attested in global history.

Liu, Xinru, and Lynda Norene Shaffer, *Connections across Eurasia: Transportation, Communication, and Cultural Exchanges on the Silk Roads* (2007). A survey of trade and religious activities on the Silk Roads.

Lopez, Ariel G., *Shenoute of Atripe and the Uses of Poverty: Rural Patronage, Religious Conflict, and Monasticism in Late Antique Egypt* (2013). Places a leading Egyptian abbot in his full social context.

Maas, Michael, *The Age of Attila: The Cambridge Companion to the Age of Attila* (2013). Essays on this important age in the Late Antique period.

———— (ed.), *The Cambridge Companion to the Age of Justinian* (2005). A survey of all aspects of the eastern Roman Empire in the sixth century CE.

————, *Readings in Late Antiquity: A Source Book* (1999). Well-chosen extracts that illustrate the interrelation of Romans and non-Romans, and of Christians, Jews, and pagans.

Moffett, Samuel, *A History of Christianity in Asia*, vol. 1 (1993). Particularly valuable on Christians in China and India.

Munro-Hay, Stuart, *Aksum: An African Civilization of Late Antiquity* (1991). The origins of the Christian kingdom of Ethiopia.

Murdock, George P., *Africa: Its Peoples and Their History* (1959). A vital introduction to the peoples of Africa and their history.

Oliver, Roland, *The African Experience: From Olduvai Gorge to the Twenty-First Century* (1999). An important overview, written by one of the pioneering scholars of African history and one of the leading authorities on the Bantu migrations.

Payne, Richard. *A State of Mixture: Christians, Zoroastrians, and Iranian Political Culture in Late Antiquity* (2015). A new view of Christianity in Sasanian Iran.

Pines, Yuri, *Envisioning Eternal Empire: Chinese Political Thought of the Warring States Era* (2009). A critical comparative work that focuses on the Warring States period and discusses how the rise of an imperial ideology was formative in the Chinese commitment to imperial rule.

————, *The Everlasting Empire: The Political Culture of Ancient China and Its Imperial Legacy* (2012). Stresses the critical role that the Warring States period played in the formulation of an enduring imperial ideology.

Pourshariati, Parvaneh, *The Decline and Fall of the Sasanian Empire: The Sasanian-Parthian Confederacy and the Arab Conquest of Iran* (2008). An innovative perspective on the demise of the Sasanians and the relevance of their decline for the Arab conquest of Iran.

Pregadio, Fabrizio, *Great Clarity: Daoism and Alchemy in Early Medieval China* (2006). An examination of the religious aspects of Daoism. The book focuses on the relation of alchemy to the Daoist traditions of the third to sixth centuries CE and shows how alchemy was integrated into the elaborate body of doctrines and practices of Daoists at that time.

Rea, Jennifer A., and Liz Clarke, *Perpetua's Journey: Faith, Gender, and Power in the Roman Empire* (2018). An innovative graphic history that includes a new translation of the martyrdom text and

scholarly essays on Perpetua's historical context.

Rosenthal, Jean-Laurent, and R. Bin Wong, *Before and Beyond Divergence: The Politics of Economic Change in China and Europe* (2011). A spirited attempt to understand why Europe outperformed China in the period leading up to the twenty-first century.

Scheidel, Walter (ed.), *Rome and China: Comparative Perspectives on Ancient World Empires* (2009). The essays by Walter Scheidel and Nathan Rosenstein expertly compare the Roman and Han Empires.

Tannous, Jack, *The Making of the Medieval Middle East: Religion, Society, and Simple Believers* (2018). An essential study of how Southwest Asia, Egypt, and North Africa, the birthplace of Judaism and Christianity, became an Islamic area.

Tempels, Placide, *Bantu Philosophy* (1959). A highly influential effort to argue for the underlying cultural unity of all the Bantu peoples.

Vansina, Jan, *Paths in the Rainforests: Toward a History of Political Tradition in Equatorial Africa* (1990). The best work on Bantu history.

Walker, Joel, *The Legend of Mar Kardagh: Narrative and Christian Heroism in Late Antique Iraq* (2006). Christians and Zoroastrians in northern Iraq and in Iran.

Yarshater, Ehsan, *Encyclopedia Iranica* (1982–). A guide to all aspects of the Sasanian Empire and to religion and culture in the regions between Mesopotamia and central Asia.

Zürcher, E., *The Buddhist Conquest of China: The Spread and Adaptation of Buddhism in Early Medieval China*, 3rd ed. (2007). A reissue of the classic account of the assimilation of Buddhism in China during the medieval period, with particular focus on the religious and philosophical

success of Buddhism among Chinese elites in South China.

Chapter 9: New Empires and Common Cultures, 600–1000 CE

Ahmed, Leila, *Women and Gender in Islam* (1992). A superb overview of the relations between men and women throughout the history of Islam.

al-Azmeh, Aziz, *The Emergence of Islam in Late Antiquity: Allah and His People* (2014). A detailed and comprehensive treatment of the origins of Islam, written by a scholar aware of all historical sources of this period.

Aneirin, *Y Gododdin: Britain's Oldest Heroic Poem,* ed. and trans. A. O. H. Jarman (1988). A sixth-century CE Welsh text that describes the battle of the last Britons against the invading Anglo-Saxons.

Arberry, Arthur J., introduction to *The Koran Interpreted: A Translation,* trans. Arthur J. Arberry (1986). One of the most eloquent appreciations of this classical work of religion.

Augustine, *The City of God,* trans. H. Bettenson (1976). An excellent translation of Augustine's monumental work of history, philosophy, and religion.

Berkey, Jonathan P., *The Formation of Islam: Religion and Society in the Near East, 600–1800* (2005). A recent overview of the history of Islam before the modern era. It is particularly sensitive to the influence of external elements on the history of the Muslim peoples.

Bol, Peter, *This Culture of Ours: Intellectual Transitions in T'ang and Sung China* (1994). A study tracing the transformation of the shared culture of the Chinese learned elite from the seventh to the twelfth centuries.

Bowersock, G. W., *The Crucible of Islam* (2017). A classicist treatment of the origins of Islam.

———, *The Throne of Adulis: Red Sea Wars on the Eve of Islam* (2013). A vital study of the kingdom of Himyar, in present-day Yemen, a center of Judaism and Christianity before the rise of Islam in the Arabian Peninsula.

Brooke, John L., *Climate Change and the Course of Global History: A Rough Journey* (2014). An overview of a changing climate and its impact on historical developments.

Brown, Peter, *The Rise of Western Christendom: Triumph and Diversity*, AD 200–1000, 2nd ed. (2003). A description of the changes in Christianity in northern Europe and the emergence of the new cultures and political structures that coincided with this development.

Bulliet, Richard W., *Conversion to Islam in the Medieval Period: An Essay in Quantitative History* (1979). A study of the rate at which the populations overrun by Arab conquerors in the seventh century CE embraced the religion of their rulers.

———, *Cotton, Climate, and Camels in the Early Islamic State* (2009). A fascinating account of economic development on the Iranian plateau, with an emphasis on climate.

Cook, Michael, *The Koran: A Very Short Introduction* (2000). A useful overview of Islam's holy book.

———, *Muhammad* (1983). A brief but careful life of the Prophet that takes full account of the prolific and often controversial preexisting scholarship.

Creswell, K. A. C., *A Short Account of Early Muslim Architecture*, revised and supplemented by James W. Allan (1992). The definitive treatment of the subject, brought up to date.

Crone, Patricia, *The Nativist Prophets of Early Islam: Rural Revolt and Local Zoroastrianism* (2012). The rise of protest movements in Islam that led to the Abbasid takeover from the Umayyads.

Cross, S. H., and O. P. Sherbowitz-Westor (trans.), *The Russian Primary Chronicle* (1953). A vivid record of the Viking settlement of Kiev, of the conversion of Kiev, and of the princes of Kiev in the tenth and eleventh centuries.

Donner, Fred M., *The Early Islamic Conquests* (1981). The best account of the Arab conquests in the Persian and Byzantine Empires in the seventh century CE.

———, *Muhammad and the Believers at the Origins of Islam* (2010). An Islamicist reexamines early historical sources on the origins of Islam and contends that the early Muslim believers did not separate from Christianity and Judaism until more than a half century had elapsed from Muhammad's first proclamations.

Duncan, John, *The Origins of the Chosŏn Dynasty* (2000). A historical account of the early Korean dynasties from 900 to 1400 CE.

Elman, Benjamin, *Precocious China: Civil Examinations, 1400–1900* (2013). Summary of civil exams in China from medieval times.

Fage, J. D., *Ghana: A Historical Introduction* (1966). A brief but authoritative history of Ghana from earliest times to the twentieth century.

Fisher, Humphrey J., *Slavery in the History of Muslim Black Africa* (2001). A general history of the relations between North Africa and Black Africa, focusing on one of the most important aspects of contact—the slave trade.

Fowden, Garth, *Before and after Muhammad: The First Millennium Refocused* (2014). The author sets Islam in its larger Greek and Christian context; part of the work of the Late Antique scholarly community.

Grabar, Oleg, *The Shape of the Holy: Early Islamic Jerusalem* (1996). The best account of the architecture of early Islam, including the building and the purposes of the Dome of the Rock, one of Islam's early and iconic places of worship.

Graham-Campbell, James, *Cultural Atlas of the Viking World* (1994). A positioning of the Vikings against their wider background in both western and eastern Europe.

Haider, Najam, *The Origins of the Shi'a: Identity, Ritual, and Sacred Space in Eighth-Century Kufah* (2011). A definitive study on the origin of Shiism.

Hawting, G. R., *The First Dynasty of Islam: The Umayyad Caliphate*, A.D. 661–750 (2000). The essential scholarly treatment of Islam's first dynasty.

Herrmann, Georgina, *Iranian Revival* (1977). The structure and horizons of the Sasanian Empire as revealed in its monuments.

Hillgarth, J. N. (ed.), *Christianity and Paganism, 350–750: The Conversion of Western Europe*, rev. ed. (1986). A collection of contemporary sources.

Hodges, Richard, and David Whitehouse, *Mohammed, Charlemagne, and the Origins of Europe* (1983). A spirited comparison of Islam and the rise of Europe.

Hodgson, Marshall G. S., *The Venture of Islam: Conscience and History in a World Civilization*, 3 vols. (1977). A magnificent history of the Islamic peoples. Its first volume, *The Classical Age of Islam*, is basic reading for anyone interested in the history of the Muslim world.

Holdsworth, May, *Women of the Tang Dynasty* (1999). An account of women's lives during the Tang dynasty.

Hourani, Albert, *History of the Arab Peoples* (2002). The best overview of Arab history.

Hoyland, Robert G., *In God's Path: The Arab Conquests and the Creation of an Islamic Empire* (2015). An overview of new findings about the origins of Islam.

Jones, Gwynn, *The Norse Atlantic Saga* (1986). The Viking discovery of America.

Kennedy, Hugh, *The Prophet and the Age of the Caliphate: The Islamic Near East from the Sixth to the Eleventh Century* (2004). A very good synthesis of the rise and spread of Islam.

Lee, Peter, et al. (eds.), *Sources of Korean Tradition*, vol. 1 (1996). A unique view of Korean history through the eyes and words of the participants or witnesses themselves, as provided in translations of official documents, letters, and policies.

Levtzion, Nehemia, *Ancient Ghana and Mali* (1980). The best introduction to the kingdoms of West Africa.

Levtzion, Nehemia, and Jay Spaulding, *Medieval West Africa: Views from Arab Scholars and Merchants* (2003). An indispensable source book on early West African history.

Levy-Rubin, Milka, *Non-Muslims in the Early Islamic Empire: From Surrender to Co-existence* (2011). The exploitation of non-Muslims in early Islam and their later conversion and rise to prominence.

Lewis, Bernard (trans.), *Islam from the Prophet Muhammad to the Capture of Constantinople*, vol. 2, *Religion and Society* (1974). A fine collection of original sources that portray various aspects of classical Islamic society.

———, *The Middle East: Two Thousand Years of History from the Rise of Christianity to the Present Day* (1995). A stimulating introduction to an area that has seen the emergence of three of the great world religions.

Lewis, David Levering, *God's Crucible: Islam and the Making of Europe, 570–1215* (2008). An exciting and well-written overview of the high period of Islamic power and cultural attainments.

Middleton, John, *The Swahili: The Social Landscape of a Mercantile Community* (2000). An exciting synthesis of the Swahili culture of East Africa.

Miyazaki, Ichisada, *China's Examination Hell* (1981). A study of China's examination system.

Nurse, Derek, and Thomas Spear, *The Swahili: Reconstructing the History and Language of an African Society, 800–1500* (1984). A work that explores the history of the Muslim peoples who lived along the coast of East Africa.

Peters, F. E., *Muhammad and the Origins of Islam* (1994). A work that explores the early history of Islam and highlights the critical role that Muhammad played in promoting a new religion and a powerful Arab identity.

Pourshariati, Parveneh, *Decline and Fall of the Sasanian Empire* (2008). Fundamental analysis of the end of the Sasanian Empire and the reasons for the success of the Arab/Muslim invasions.

Robinson, Chase F., *'Abd al-Malik* (2005). A short biography of the powerful Umayyad ruler who played a critical role in distinguishing Islam from the other monotheisms in the region, namely, Christianity, Judaism, and Zoroastrianism.

———, *The Formation of the Islamic World, Sixth to Eleventh Centuries*, vol. 1 of *The New Cambridge History of Islam* (2010). The first volume of an authoritative and up-to-date six-volume overview of the history of Islam from the sixth century CE to the present.

Schirokauer, Conrad, David Lurie, and Suzanne Gay, *A Brief History of Japanese Civilization*, 2nd ed. (2005). A balanced account; chapters focus on developments in art, religion, literature, and thought as well as on Japan's economic, political, and social history in medieval times.

Shoemaker, Stephen J., *The Death of a Prophet: The End of Muhammad's Life and the Beginnings of Islam* (2012). A careful revision of the standard biographies of Muhammad, based on non-Muslim sources.

Smith, Julia, *Europe after Rome: A New Cultural History, 500–1000* (2005). A vivid analysis of society and culture in so-called Dark Age Europe.

Totman, Conrad, *History of Japan* (2004). A recent and readable summary of Japanese history from ancient to modern times.

Twitchett, Denis, *The Birth of the Chinese Meritocracy: Bureaucrats and Examinations in T'ang China* (1976). A description of the role of the written civil examinations that began during the Tang dynasty.

———, *Financial Administration under the T'ang Dynasty* (1970). A pioneering account—based on rare Dunhuang documents that survived from medieval times in Buddhist grottoes in central Asia—of the political and economic system undergirding the Chinese imperial state.

Whittow, Mark, *The Making of Byzantium, 600–1025* (1996). A study on the survival and revival of the eastern Roman Empire as a major power in eastern Europe and Southwest Asia.

Wood, Ian, *The Missionary Life: Saints and the Evangelization of Europe, 400–1050* (2001). The horizons of Christians on the frontiers of Europe.

Chapter 10: Becoming "The World," 1000–1300 CE

Allsen, Thomas, *Commodity and Exchange in the Mongol Empire: A Cultural History of Islamic Textiles* (1997). A study that uses golden brocade, the textile most treasured by Mongol rulers, as a lens through which to analyze the vast commercial networks facilitated by the Mongol conquests and control.

———, *Culture and Conquest in Mongol Eurasia* (2001). A work that emphasizes the cultural and scientific exchanges that took place across Afro-Eurasia as a result of the Mongol conquest.

Bagge, Svere, Michael Gelting, and Thomas Lindkvist (eds.), *Feudalism: New Landscapes of Debate* (2011). A collection of essays on interpretations of feudalism by experts on the topic.

Bartlett, Robert, *The Making of Europe: Conquest, Colonization and Cultural Change, 950–1350* (1993). The modes of cultural, political, and demographic expansion of feudal Europe along its frontiers, especially in eastern Europe.

Bay, Edna G., *Wives of the Leopards: Gender, Politics, and Culture in the Kingdom of Dahomey* (1998). A work that stresses the role of women in an important West African society and dips into the early history of this area.

Beach, D. N., *Shona and Zimbabwe, 900–1850: An Outline of Shona History* (1980). A good place to start for exploring the history of Great Zimbabwe.

Broadbridge, Anne F., *Women and the Making of the Mongol Empire* (2018). By examining the lives of women in Chinggis Khan's orbit, this study uncovers not only details about the lives of well-known elite Mongol women but also a larger picture of the roles of women in kinship strategies binding Mongol tribes, the economy fueling nomadic life, and the political machinations driving conquest.

Brooks, George E., *Landlords and Strangers: Ecology, Society, and Trade in Western Africa, 1000–1630* (1993). A survey assembled from primary sources of early West African history that stresses transregional connections.

Bulliet, Richard W., *Cotton, Climate, and Camels in Early Islamic Iran* (2009). An analysis of the upswing of the Iranian plateau economy after the Muslim conquest and its subsequent decline as a result of climate change.

Buzurg ibn Shahriyar of Ramhormuz, *The Book of the Wonders of India: Mainland, Sea and Islands,* ed. and trans. G. S. P. Freeman-Greenville (1981). A collection of stories told by sailors, both true and fantastic; they help us imagine the lives of sailors of the era.

Chappell, Sally A. Kitt, *Cahokia: Mirror of the Cosmos* (2002). A thorough and vivid account of the "mound people"; it explores not just what we know of Cahokia but how we know it.

Christian, David, *A Short History of Russia, Central Asia, and Mongolia*, vol. 1, *Inner Eurasia from Prehistory to the Mongol Empire* (1998). Essential reading for students interested in interconnections across the Afro-Eurasian landmass.

Curtin, Philip, *Cross-Cultural Trade in World History* (1984). A groundbreaking book on intercultural trade with a primary focus on Africa, especially the cross-Saharan trade and Swahili coastal trade.

Dawson, Christopher, *Mission to Asia* (1980). Accounts of China and the Mongol Empire brought back by Catholic missionaries and diplomats after 1240.

De Nicola, Bruno, *Women in Mongol Iran: The Khātūns, 1206–1335* (2017). Drawing on a wide range of source material, De Nicola explores the political, economic, and religious influence of women in Mongol society from the pre-imperial steppe nomadic context to the settled empire, in particular the Il-Khanate of Persia.

Di Cosmo, Nicola, Allen J. Frank, and Peter Golden (eds.), *The Cambridge History of Inner Asia: The Chinggisid Age* (2009). A definitive study of the Mongol period, written by the leading scholars of this period.

Ellenblum, Ronnie, *The Collapse of the Eastern Mediterranean: Climate Change and the Decline of the East, 950–1072* (2012). An analysis of the impact of freezing temperatures and drought on the societies of the eastern Mediterranean.

Flecker, Michael, "A 9th-Century Arab or Indian Shipwreck in Indonesian Waters," *International Journal of Nautical Archaeology* 29, no. 2 (2000): 199–217. Offers an early detailed description of the Belitung dhow's excavation, likely place of origin, construction, and cargo.

———, "A 9th-Century Arab or Indian Shipwreck in Indonesian Waters: Addendum," *International Journal of Nautical Archaeology* 37, no. 2 (2008): 384–86.

An update on the origin of the Belitung dhow that, based on a comparative analysis of wood fibers, argues that the ship's timbers suggest it was built in Oman or Yemen (on the southern coast of the Arabian Peninsula), not India as was earlier considered to be a possibility.

———, "A 9th-Century Arab Shipwreck in Indonesia," in Regina Krahl et al. (eds.), *Shipwrecked: Tang Treasures and Monsoon Winds* (2010), pp. 100–119. Flecker's most recent consideration of the Belitung dhow, published in a collection of essays to accompany an exhibition focused on the important shipwreck.

Foltz, Richard C., *Religions of the Silk Road: Overland Trade and Cultural Exchange from Antiquity to the Fifteenth Century* (1999). A study of the populations and the cities of the Silk Roads as transmitters of culture across long distances.

Franklin, Simon, and Jonathan Shepherd, *The Emergence of Rus: 750–1200* (1996). The formation of medieval Russia between the Baltic and Black Seas.

Gibb, Hamilton A. R., *Saladin: Studies in Islamic History*, ed. Yusuf Ibish (1974). A sympathetic portrait of one of Islam's leading political and military figures.

Glahn, Richard von, "Re-examining the Authenticity of Song Paper Money Specimens," *Journal of Song-Yuan Studies* 36 (2006): 79–106. Provides a close examination, including descriptions, images, and translations, of many examples of paper money from the Song and Yuan dynasties. The article offers a detailed discussion (on pp. 93–94) of the flying cash example reproduced in Chapter 10.

Goitein, S. D., *Letters of Medieval Jewish Traders* (1973). The classic study of medieval Jewish trading communities based on the commercial papers deposited in the Cairo Geniza (a synagogue storeroom) during the tenth and eleventh centuries CE; it explores not only commercial activities but also the personal lives of the traders around the Indian Ocean basin.

———, *A Mediterranean Society: An Abridgment in One Volume*, rev. and ed. Jacob Lassner (1999). A portrait of the Jewish merchant community with ties across the Afro-Eurasian landmass, based largely on the documents from the Cairo Geniza (of which Goitein was the primary researcher and interpreter).

———, "New Light on the Beginnings of the Karim Merchant," *Journal of Social and Economic History of the Orient* 1 (1958). Goitein's description of Egyptian trade.

Goitein, S. D., and Mordechai A. Friedman, *India Traders of the Middle Ages: Documents from the Cairo Geniza* (2008). Collection of documents (translated into English) and authoritative essays that explore the eleventh- and twelfth-century trade conducted by several prominent Jewish families along the Mediterranean and Indian Ocean routes.

Harris, Joseph E., *The African Presence in Asia: Consequences of the East African Slave Trade* (1971). One of the few books that looks broadly at the impact of Africans and African slavery on the societies of Asia.

Hartwell, Robert, "Demographic, Political, and Social Transformations of China, 750–1550," *Harvard Journal of Asiatic Studies* 42 (1982): 365–442. A pioneering study of the demographic changes that overtook China during the Tang and Song dynasties, which are described in light of political reform movements and social changes in this crucial era.

Historical Relations across the Indian Ocean: Report and Papers of the Meeting of Experts Organized by UNESCO at Port Louis, Mauritius, from 15 to 19 July, 1974 (1980). Excellent essays on the connections of Africa with Asia across the Indian Ocean.

Hitti, Philip, *An Arab-Syrian Gentleman and Warrior in the Period of the Crusades: Memoirs of Usāmah ibn-Munqidh* (1929). The Crusaders seen through Muslim eyes.

Hodgson, Natasha, *Women, Crusading, and the Holy Land in Historical Narrative* (2007). A book dealing with the Crusades and focusing on the place of women in them.

Holt, P. M., *The Age of the Crusades: The Near East from the Eleventh Century to 1517* (1984). The Crusades period as seen from the eastern Mediterranean and through the lens of a leading British scholar of the area.

Huff, Toby E., *The Rise of Early Modern Science* (2009). A bold attempt to look at the rise of scientific work in the Islamic world, premodern China, and Europe, seeking to explain why the scientific revolution occurred in Europe rather than the Islamic world or China.

Hymes, Robert, and Conrad Schirokauer (eds.), *Ordering the World: Approaches to State and Society in Sung Dynasty China* (1993). A collection of essays that traces the intellectual, social, and political movements that shaped the Song state and its elites.

Ibn Battuta, *The Travels of Ibn Battuta*, trans. H. A. R. Gibb (2002). A readable translation of the classic book, originally published in 1929.

Ibn Fadlan, Ahmad, *Ibn Fadlan's Journey to Russia: A Tenth Century*

Traveler from Baghdad to the Volga River, translated with commentary by Richard Frye (2005). A coherent summary of the observations of an envoy who traveled from Baghdad to Russia.

Irwin, Robert, *The Middle East in the Middle Ages: The Early Mamluk Sultanate, 1250–1582* (1986). Egypt under Mamluk rule.

Jeppie, Shamil, and Souleymane Bachir Diagne (eds.), *The Meanings of Timbuktu* (2008). New materials on the ancient Muslim city of Timbuktu by scholars who have been preserving its manuscripts and writing about its historical importance.

Khazanov, Anatoly M., *Nomads and the Outside World*, 2nd ed., trans. Julia Crookurden, with a foreword by Ernest Gellner (1994). A classic overview of nomadism, based on years of research, covering all the nomadic communities of Afro-Eurasia.

Lambourn, Elizabeth A., *Abraham's Luggage: A Social Life of Things in the Medieval Indian Ocean World* (2018). Uses Abraham Ben Yiju's 173-item luggage list to unpack a fascinating social and economic history of a North African Jewish trader living in southern India.

Lancaster, Lewis, Kikun Suh, and Chai-shin Yu (eds.), *Buddhism in Koryo: A Royal Religion* (1996). A description of Buddhism at its height in the Koryo period, when the religion made significant contributions to the development of Korean culture.

Levtzion, Nehemia, and Randall L. Pouwels (eds.), *The History of Islam in Africa* (2000). A useful general survey of the place of Islam in African history.

Lewis, Bernard (trans.), *Islam: From the Prophet Muhammad to the Capture of Constantinople*, vol. 2, *Religion and Society* (1974). A fine collection of original sources that portray various aspects of classical Islamic society.

Lopez, Robert S., *The Commercial Revolution of the Middle Ages, 950–1350* (1976). An account focusing on the development around the Mediterranean of commercial practices such as the use of currency, accounting, and credit.

Lyons, Malcolm C., and D. E. P. Jackson, *Saladin: The Politics of the Holy War* (1984; reprint, 2001). The fundamental revisionist work on one of the more important historical figures of the time.

Maalouf, Amin, *The Crusades through Muslim Eyes*, trans. Jon Rothschild (1984). The European Crusaders as seen by the Muslim world.

Marcus, Harold G., *A History of Ethiopia* (2002). An authoritative overview of the history of this great culture.

Mass, Jeffrey, *Yoritomo and the Founding of the First Bakufu: The Origins of Dual Government in Japan* (1999). A revisionist account of how the Kamakura military leader Minamoto Yoritomo established the "dual polity" of court and warrior government in Japan.

McDermott, Joseph, *A Social History of the Chinese Book: Books and Literati Culture in Late Imperial China* (2006). The history of the book in China since the Song dynasty, with comparisons to the book's role in other civilizations, particularly the European.

McEvitt, Christopher, *The Crusaders and the Christian World of the East: Rough Tolerance* (2008). Excellent work on the relations of religious groups in the Crusader kingdoms.

McIntosh, Roderik, *The Peoples of the Middle Niger: The Island of Gold* (1988). A historical survey of an area often omitted from other textbooks.

Moore, Jerry D., *Cultural Landscapes in the Ancient Andes: Archaeologies of Place* (2005). The most recent and up-to-date analysis of findings based on recent archaeological evidence, emphasizing the importance of local cultures and diversity in the Andes.

Mote, Frederick W., *Imperial China, 900–1800* (1999). Still the best work on this period, written by an expert on the full scope of Chinese history. The chapter on the Mongols is superb.

Niane, D. T. (ed.), *Africa from the Twelfth to the Sixteenth Century*, vol. 4 of *General History of Africa* (1984). The fourth volume of UNESCO's history of Africa covers four centuries of African history. This work features the scholarship of Africans.

Oliver, Roland (ed.), *From c. 1050 to c. 1600*, vol. 3 of *The Cambridge History of Africa*, ed. J. D. Fage and Roland Oliver (1977). Another general survey of African history. This volume draws heavily on the work of British scholars.

Peters, Edward, *The First Crusade* (1971). The Crusaders as seen through their own eyes.

Petry, Carl F. (ed.), *Islamic Egypt, 640–1517*, vol. 1 of *The Cambridge History of Egypt* (1998). A solid overview of the history of Islamic Egypt up to the Ottoman conquest.

Polo, Marco, *The Travels of Marco Polo*, ed. Manuel Komroff (1926). A solid translation of Marco Polo's famous account.

Popovic, Alexandre, *The Revolt of African Slaves in Iraq in the 3rd/9th Century*, trans. Leon King (1999). The account of a massive revolt against their enslavers by enslaved Africans taken to labor in Iraq's mines and fields.

Rossabi, Morris, *A History of China* (2014). Part of the Blackwell History of the World series and an excellent overview of Chinese history.

———, *Voyager from Xanadu: Rabban Sauma and the First Journey from China to the West* (2010). Rossabi's exploration in this second/revised edition uses additional historical sources and speculation to imaginatively expand on E. A. Wallis Budge's 1920s translation of Bar Sāwmā's late thirteenth-century account of his westward travels from Mongol territories to European cities like Rome and Paris.

Scott, Robert, *Gothic Enterprise: A Guide to Understanding the Medieval Cathedral* (2003). The meaning and social function of religious building in medieval cities in northern Europe.

Shaffer, Lynda Norene, *Maritime Southeast Asia to 1500* (1996). A history of the peoples of the southeast fringe of the Eastern Hemisphere, up to the time that they became connected to the global commercial networks of the world.

Shimada, Izumi, "Evolution of Andean Diversity: Regional Formations (500 BCE–CE 600)," in Frank Salomon and Stuart Schwartz (eds.), *South America*, vol. 3 of *The Cambridge History of the Native Peoples of the Americas* (1999), pt. 1, pp. 350–517. A splendid overview that contrasts the varieties of lowland and highland cultures.

Steinberg, David Joel, et al., *In Search of Southeast Asia: A Modern History*, rev. ed. (1987). An account of the emergence of the modern Southeast Asian polities of Cambodia, Burma, Thailand, and Indonesia.

Tanner, Harold M., *China: A History* (2009). Along with Rossabi

(2014), an excellent overview of the full history of China.

Tyerman, Christopher, *God's War: A New History of the Crusades* (2006). The balance of religious and nonreligious motivations in the Crusades.

Waley, Daniel, *The Italian City-Republics*, 3rd ed. (1988). The structures and culture of the new cities of medieval Italy.

Watson, Andrew, *Agricultural Innovation in the Early Islamic World: The Diffusion of Crops and Farming Techniques, 700–1100* (1983). An impressive study of the spread of new crops throughout the Muslim world.

West, Charles, *Reframing the Feudal Revolution: Political and Social Transformation between Marne and Moselle, c. 800–c. 1100* (2013). Big change seen through an intensely studied region.

Wickham, Chris, *Sleepwalking into a New World: The Emergence of Italian City Communes in the Twelfth Century* (2015). Origins of the city democracies of medieval Italy.

Chapter 11: Crises and Recovery in Afro-Eurasia, 1300–1500

Barkey, Karen, *Empire of Difference: The Ottomans in Comparative Perspective* (2008). A revisionist view of the rise and flourishing of the Ottoman Empire.

Bois, Guy, *The Crisis of Feudalism: Economy and Society in Eastern Normandy, c. 1300–1550* (1984). A good case study of a French region that illustrates the turmoil in fourteenth-century Europe.

Brook, Timothy, *Praying for Power: Buddhism and the Formation of Gentry Society in Late Ming China* (1994). An analysis of the role of a significant religious force in the

political and social developments of the Ming.

Clunas, Craig, and Jessica Harrison-Hall (eds.), *Ming: 50 Years That Changed China* (2014). Developed to accompany an exhibition at the British Museum, this catalog includes richly illustrated scholarly essays that explore clothing, jewelry, courtly objects, and commerce during the Ming dynasty.

Dardess, John, *A Ming Society: T'ai-ho County, Kiangsi, Fourteenth to Seventeenth Centuries* (1996). A work that covers the different changes and developments of a single locality in China through the centuries.

Dols, Michael Walter, *The Black Death in the Middle East* (1977). One of the few scholarly works to examine the Black Death outside Europe.

Dreyer, Edward, *Early Ming China: A Political History, 1355–1435* (1982). A useful account of the early years of the Ming dynasty.

Faroqhi, Suraiya N., and Kate Fleet (eds.), *The Cambridge History of Turkey*, vol. 2, *The Ottoman Empire as a World Power, 1453–1603* (2013). An overview of this crucial period in Ottoman history, written by experts in the field.

Finkel, Caroline, *Osman's Dream: The Story of the Ottoman Empire, 1300–1923* (2005). The most authoritative overview of Ottoman history.

Finnane, Antonia, *Changing Clothes in China: Fashion, History, Nation* (2008). An exploration of changing Chinese identities from the perspective of clothing.

Hale, John, *The Civilization of Europe in the Renaissance* (1994). A beautifully crafted account of the politics, economics, and culture of the Renaissance period in western Europe.

He, Yuming, *Home and the World: Editing the "Glorious Ming" in Woodblock-Printed Books of the Sixteenth and Seventeenth Centuries* (2013). An insightful exploration of Ming society through a close look at its vibrant print culture and market for books.

Hodgson, Marshall, *The Venture of Islam: Conscience and History in a World Civilization,* vol. 3 (1974). A good volume on the workings of the Ottoman state.

Hoffman, Philip T., *Why Did Europe Conquer the World?* (2015). Makes an interesting case for the importance of Europe's use of gunpowder technologies.

Itzkowitz, Norman, *Ottoman Empire and Islamic Tradition* (1972). Another good book on the Ottoman state.

Jackson, Peter, *The Delhi Sultanate* (1999). A meticulous, highly specialized political and military history.

Jackson, Peter, and Lawrence Lockhart (eds.), *The Cambridge History of Iran,* vol. 6 (1986). A volume that deals with the Timurid and Safavid periods in Iran.

Jones, E. L., *The European Miracle* (1981). A provocative work on the economic and social recovery from the Black Death.

Kafadar, Cemal, *Between Two Worlds: The Construction of the Ottoman State* (1995). A thorough reconsideration of the origins of one of the world's great land empires.

Karamustafa, Ahmed, *God's Unruly Friends: Dervish Groups in the Islamic Later Middle Period, 1200–1550* (1994). A book that describes the unorthodox Islamic activities that were occurring in the Islamic world prior to and alongside the establishment of the Ottoman and Safavid Empires.

Levathes, Louise, *When China Ruled the Seas: The Treasure Fleet of the Dragon Throne, 1405–33* (1994). A book that provides a lively account of the Zheng He expeditions.

Lowry, Heath W., *The Nature of the Early Ottoman State* (2003). New perspectives on the rise of the Ottomans to prominence.

McNeill, William, *Plagues and Peoples* (1976). A pathbreaking work with a highly useful chapter on the spread of the Black Death throughout the Afro-Eurasian landmass.

Morgan, David, *Medieval Persia, 1040–1797* (1988). Contains an informative discussion of the Safavid state.

Peirce, Leslie, *The Imperial Harem: Women and Sovereignty in the Ottoman Empire* (1993). A work that describes the powerful place that imperial women had in political affairs.

Pirenne, Henri, *Economic and Social History of Medieval Europe* (1937). A classic study of the economic and social recovery from the Black Death.

Reid, James J., *Tribalism and Society in Islamic Iran, 1500–1629* (1983). A useful account of how the Mongols and other nomadic steppe peoples influenced Iran in the era when the Safavids were establishing their authority.

Savory, Roger. *Iran under the Safavids* (1980). A standard and still-useful work on Safavid history.

Schäfer, Dagmar, *The Crafting of the 10,000 Things: Knowledge and Technology in Seventeenth-Century China* (2011). An innovative study of the philosophy of technology and crafts in the late Ming period with important implications for the global history of science.

Singman, Jeffrey L. (ed.), *Daily Life in Medieval Europe* (1999). An introductory description of the social and material world experienced by Europeans of different walks of life.

Tuchman, Barbara W., *A Distant Mirror: The Calamitous Fourteenth Century* (1978). A book that shows, in a vigorous way, how war, famine, and pestilence devastated Europeans in the fourteenth century.

Wittek, Paul, *The Rise of the Ottoman Empire* (1958). A work that contains vital insights on the emergence of the Ottoman state amid the political chaos in Anatolia.

Glossary

Abd al-Rahman III Islamic ruler in Spain who held a countercaliphate and reigned from 912 to 961 CE.

aboriginals Original, native inhabitants of a region, as opposed to invaders, colonizers, or later peoples of mixed ancestry.

absolute monarchy Form of government in which one body, usually the monarch, controls the right to tax, judge, make war, and coin money. The term *enlightened absolutist* was often used to refer to state monarchies in seventeenth- and eighteenth-century Europe.

acid rain Precipitation containing large amounts of sulfur, which comes mainly from coal-fired power plants.

adaptation Ability to alter behavior and to innovate, finding new ways of doing things.

African National Congress (ANC) Multiracial organization founded in 1912 in an effort to end racial discrimination in South Africa.

Afrikaners Descendants of the original Dutch settlers of South Africa; formerly referred to as Boers.

Agones Athletic contests in ancient Greece.

Ahmosis Egyptian ruler in the southern part of the country who ruled from 1550 to 1525 BCE; Ahmosis used Hyksos weaponry—chariots in particular—to defeat the Hyksos themselves.

Ahura Mazda Supreme God of the Persians, believed to have created the world and all that is good and to have appointed earthly kings.

AIDS *See* HIV/AIDS.

Akbarnamah Mughal intellectual Abulfazl's *Book of Akbar*, which attempted to reconcile the traditional Sufi interest in the inner life within the worldly context of a great empire.

Alaric II Visigothic king who issued a simplified code of innovative imperial law.

Alexander the Great (356–323 BCE) Leader who used novel tactics and new kinds of armed forces to conquer the Persian Empire, which extended from Egypt and the Mediterranean Sea to the interior of what is now Afghanistan and as far as the Indus River valley. Alexander's conquests broke down barriers between the Mediterranean world and Southwest Asia and transferred massive amounts of wealth and power to the Mediterranean, transforming it into a more unified world of economic and cultural exchange.

Alexandria Port city in Egypt named after Alexander the Great. Alexandria was a model city in the Hellenistic world. It was built up by a multiethnic population from around the Mediterranean world.

al-Khwarizmi Scientist and mathematician who lived from 780 to 850 CE and is known for having modified Indian digits into Arabic numerals.

Allied Powers Name given to the alliance between Britain, France, Russia, and Italy, all of which fought against Germany and Austria-Hungary (the Central Powers) in World War I. In World War II, the name was used for the alliance between Britain, France, and the United States, all of which fought against the Axis powers (Germany, Italy, and Japan).

allomothering System in which mothers relied on other women, including their own mothers, daughters, sisters, and friends, to help in the nurturing and protecting of their children.

alluvium Area of land created by river deposits.

alphabet A mid-second-millennium BCE Phoenician system of writing based on relatively few letters (twenty-two) that combined to make sounds and words. Adaptable to many languages, the alphabet was simpler and more flexible than writing based on symbols for syllables and ideas.

American Railway Union Workers' union that initiated the Pullman strike of 1894, which led to violence and ended in the leaders' arrest.

Amnesty International Nongovernmental organization formed to defend "prisoners of conscience"—those detained for their beliefs, race, sex, ethnic origin, language, or religion.

Amorites Name, which means "westerners," used by Mesopotamian urbanites to describe the transhumant herders who began to migrate into their cities in the late third millennium BCE.

Amun Once-insignificant Egyptian god elevated to higher status by Amenemhet I (1985–1955 BCE).

Amun means "hidden" in Ancient Egyptian; the name was meant to convey the god's omnipresence.

Analects, The Texts that included the teachings and cultural ideals of Confucius.

anarchists Advocates of anarchism, the belief that society should be a free association of its members, not subject to government, laws, or police.

Anatolia The area now mainly known as modern Turkey. In the sixth millennium BCE, people from Anatolia, Greece, and the Levant took to boats and populated the Aegean. Their small villages endured almost unchanged for two millennia.

Angkor Wat Magnificent temple complex that crowned the royal palace of the Khmer Empire in Angkor, adorned with statues representing the Hindu pantheon of gods.

Anglo-Boer War (1899–1902) Anti-colonial struggle in South Africa between the British and the Afrikaners over the gold-rich Transvaal. In response to the Afrikaners' guerrilla tactics and in order to contain the local population, the British instituted the first concentration camps. Ultimately, Britain won the conflict.

animal domestication Gradual process that occurred simultaneously with or just before the domestication of plants, depending on the region.

annals Historical records. Notable annals are the cuneiform inscriptions that record successful Neo-Assyrian military campaigns.

Anti-Federalists Critics of the U.S. Constitution who sought to defend the people against the power of the federal government and insisted on a Bill of Rights to protect individual liberties from government intrusion.

apartheid Racial segregation policy of the Afrikaner-dominated South African government. Legislated in 1948 by the Afrikaner National Party, it had existed in South Africa for many years.

Arab-Israeli War of 1948–1949 Conflict between Israeli and Arab armies that arose in the wake of a U.N. vote to partition Palestine into Arab and Jewish territories. The war shattered the legitimacy of Arab ruling elites.

Aramaic Dialect of a Semitic language spoken in Southwest Asia; it became the lingua franca of the Persian Empire.

Aristotle (384–322 BCE) Philosopher who studied under Plato but came to different conclusions about nature and politics. Aristotle believed in collecting observations about nature and discerning patterns to ascertain how things worked.

Aryans Nomadic charioteers who spoke Indo-European languages and entered South Asia in 1500 BCE. The early Aryan settlers were herders.

Asante state State located in present-day Ghana, founded by the Asantes at the end of the seventeenth century. It grew in power in the next century because of its access to gold and its involvement in the slave trade.

ascetic One who rejects material possessions and physical pleasures.

Asiatic Society Cultural organization founded by British Orientalists who supported native culture but still believed in colonial rule.

Aśoka Emperor of the Mauryan dynasty from 268 to 231 BCE; he was a great conqueror and unifier of India. He is said to have embraced Buddhism toward the end of his life.

Assur One of two cities on the upper reaches of the Tigris River that were the heart of Assyria proper (the other was Nineveh).

Aśvaghosa First known Sanskrit writer. It is believed that he lived from 80 to 150 CE and composed a biography of the Buddha.

Ataturk, Mustafa Kemal (1881–1938) Ottoman army officer and military hero who helped forge the modern Turkish nation-state. He and his followers deposed the sultan, declared Turkey a republic, and constructed a European-like secular state, eliminating Islam's hold over civil and political affairs.

Atlantic system New system of trade and expansion that linked Europe, Africa, and the Americas. It emerged in the wake of European voyages across the Atlantic Ocean.

atma Vedic term signifying the eternal self, represented by the trinity of deities.

atman In the Upanishads, an eternal being who exists everywhere. The atman never perishes, but is reborn or transmigrates into another life.

Attila Sole ruler of all Hunnish tribes from 434 to 453 CE. Harsh and much feared, he formed the first empire to oppose Rome in northern Europe.

Augustus Latin term meaning "the Revered One"; title granted by the Senate to the Roman ruler Octavian in 27 BCE to signify his unique political position. Along with his adopted family name, *Caesar*, the military honorific *imperator*, and the senatorial term *princeps*, *Augustus* became a generic term for a leader of the Roman Empire.

australopithecines Hominin species, including *anamensis*, *afarensis* (Lucy), and *africanus*, that appeared in Africa beginning around 4 million years ago and, unlike other animals, sometimes walked on two legs. Their brain capacity was a little less than one-third of a modern human's. Although not humans, they carried the genetic and biological material out of which modern humans would later emerge.

Austro-Hungarian Empire Dual monarchy established by the Habsburg family in 1867; it collapsed at the end of World War I.

authoritarianism Centralized and dictatorial form of government, proclaimed by its adherents to be superior to parliamentary democracy and especially effective at mobilizing the masses. This idea was widely accepted in parts of the world during the 1930s.

Avesta Compilation of Zoroastrian holy works transmitted orally by priests for millennia and eventually recorded in the sixth century BCE.

Awadh Kingdom in northern India; one of the first successor states to have gained a measure of independence from the Mughal ruler in Delhi, and the most prized object for annexation by the East India Company.

Axial Age Pivotal period in the mid-first millennium BCE when radical thinkers, such as Zoroaster in Persia, Confucius and Master Lao in East Asia, Siddhartha Gautama (the Buddha) in South Asia, and Socrates in the Mediterranean, offered dramatically new ideas that challenged their times.

Axis Powers The three aggressor states in World War II: Germany, Japan, and Italy.

Aztec Empire Mesoamerican empire that originated with a league of three Mexica cities in 1430 and gradually expanded through the Central Valley of Mexico, uniting numerous small, independent states under a single monarch who ruled with the help of counselors, military leaders, and priests. By the late fifteenth century, the Aztec realm may have embraced 25 million people. In 1521, the Aztecs were defeated by the conquistador Hernán Cortés.

baby boom Post–World War II upswing in U.S. birthrates, which reversed a century of decline.

Bactria (c. 250–50 BCE) Hellenistic kingdom in Gandhara region (modern Pakistan) that became an independent state around 200 BCE, with a major city at Aï Khanoum. Its people and culture are sometimes called "Indo-Greek" because of the blending of Indian and Greek populations and ideas.

Bactrian camel Two-humped animal domesticated in central Asia around 2500 BCE. The Bactrian camel was heartier than the one-humped dromedary and became the animal of choice for the harsh and varied climates typical of Silk Road trade.

Baghdad Capital of the Islamic empire under the Abbasid dynasty, founded in 762 CE (located in modern-day Iraq). In the medieval period, it was a center of administration, scholarship, and cultural growth for what came to be known as the Golden Age of Islamic science.

Baghdad Pact (1955) Middle Eastern military alliance between countries friendly with America that were also willing to align themselves with the western countries against the Soviet Union.

Balam Na Stone temple and place of pilgrimage for the Maya people of Mexico's Yucatán Peninsula.

Balfour Declaration Letter (November 2, 1917) written by Lord Arthur J. Balfour, British foreign secretary, that promised a homeland for the Jews in Palestine.

Bamboo Annals Shang stories and foundation myths that were written on bamboo strips and later collected.

Bantu Language first spoken by people who lived in the southeastern region of modern Nigeria around 1000 CE.

Bantu migrations Waves of population movement from West Africa into eastern and southern Africa during the first millennium CE, bringing new agricultural practices to these regions and absorbing much of the hunting and gathering population.

barbarian Derogatory term used to describe pastoral nomads, painting them as enemies of civilization; the term *barbarian* used to have a more neutral meaning than it does today.

barbarian invasions Violent migration of people in the late fourth and fifth centuries CE from the frontiers of the Roman Empire into its western provinces. These migrants had long been used as non-Roman soldiers.

basilicas Early Christian churches modeled on Roman law-court buildings that could accommodate over a thousand worshippers.

Battle of Adwa (1896) Battle in which the Ethiopians defeated Italian colonial forces; it inspired many of Africa's later national leaders.

Battle of Wounded Knee (1890) Bloody massacre of Sioux Ghost Dancers by U.S. armed forces.

Bay of Pigs (1961) Unsuccessful invasion of Cuba by Cuban exiles supported by the U.S. government. The invaders intended to incite an insurrection in Cuba and overthrow the communist regime of Fidel Castro.

Bedouins Nomadic pastoralists in the deserts of Southwest Asia.

Beer Hall Putsch (1923) Nazi intrusion into a meeting of Bavarian leaders in a Munich beer hall in an attempt to force support for their cause; Adolf Hitler was imprisoned for a year after the incident.

Beghards Eccentric sixteenth-century European group whose members claimed to be in a state of grace that allowed them to do what they pleased—ranging from adultery, free love, and nudity to murder; also called Brethren of Free Speech.

bell beaker Ancient drinking vessel, an artifact from Europe, so named because its shape resembles an inverted bell.

Berenice of Egypt Egyptian queen who helped rule over the kingdom of the Nile from around 320 to 280 BCE.

Beringia Prehistoric thousand-mile-long land bridge that linked Siberia and North America (which had not been populated by hominins). About 30,000 years ago, *Homo sapiens* edged into this landmass.

Berlin Airlift (1948) Supply of vital necessities to West Berlin by air transport, primarily under U.S. auspices, initiated in response to a land and water blockade of the city instituted by the Soviet Union in the hope that the Allies would be forced to abandon West Berlin.

Berlin Wall Wall dividing the city of Berlin, built in 1961 by communist East Germany to prevent its citizens from fleeing to West Germany; torn down in 1989.

bhakti Religious practice that grew out of Hinduism and emphasizes personal devotion to gods.

big men Leaders of the extended household communities that formed village settlements in African rain forests.

big whites Literal translation of *grands blancs;* French plantation owners in Saint-Domingue (present-day Haiti) who created one of the wealthiest enslaver societies.

Bilad al-Sudan Arabic for "the land of the Blacks"; it consisted of the land lying south of the Sahara.

bilharzia Debilitating waterborne illness that was widespread in Egypt, where it infected peasants who worked in the irrigation canals.

Bill of Rights First ten amendments to the U.S. Constitution; ratified in 1791.

biomes Distinct biological systems, including humans, that have formed in response to shared physical conditions.

bioprospecting Transferring knowledge about biological, chemical, and botanical resources from one location on the planet to another with commercial aims, especially in agriculture and pharmaceuticals. Often, this involves the exploitation of indigenous forms of knowledge. In the modern age, it frequently leads to patents, which reward the owner of the patent and not necessarily the discoverer of the knowledge.

bipedalism Walking on two legs, thereby freeing hands and arms to carry objects such as weapons and tools; one of several traits that distinguished hominins.

Black Death Plague pandemic that ravaged Europe, East Asia, and North Africa in the fourteenth century, killing large numbers of people, including perhaps as much as one-third of the European population.

Black Jacobins Nickname for the rebels in Saint-Domingue, including Toussaint L'Ouverture, a formerly enslaved man who led the enslaved people of this French colony in the world's largest and most successful insurrection of its kind.

Black Lives Matter A decentralized and eventually global movement founded in 2013 that champions nonviolent civil disobedience in resistance to police brutality and violence against Black people.

Black Panthers Radical African American group in the 1960s and 1970s that advocated Black separatism and pan-Africanism.

black shirts Fascist troops of Mussolini's regime; these squads received money from Italian landowners to attack socialist leaders.

Black Tuesday (October 29, 1929) Historic day when the U.S. stock market crashed, plunging the United States and international trading systems into crisis and leading the world into the Great Depression.

blitzkrieg "Lightning war"; type of warfare waged by the Germans during World War II, using coordinated aerial bombing campaigns along with tanks and infantry in motorized vehicles.

bodhisattvas In Mahayana Buddhism, enlightened beings who have earned nirvana but remain in this world to help others reach it.

Bolívar, Simón (1783–1830) Venezuelan leader who urged his followers to overcome their local identities and become "American." He wanted the liberated South American countries to form a Latin American confederation, urging Peru and Bolivia to join Venezuela, Ecuador, and Colombia in the "Gran Colombia."

Bolsheviks Former members of the Russian Social Democratic Party who advocated the destruction of capitalist political and economic institutions and seized power in Russia in 1917 when the Russian Empire collapsed. In 1918, the Bolsheviks changed their name to the Russian Communist Party.

Book of the Dead Ancient Egyptian funerary text that contains drawings and paintings as well as spells describing how to prepare the jewelry and amulets that were buried with a person in preparation for the afterlife.

bourgeoisie A French term originally designating non-noble city dwellers (*Bürger* in German). They sought to be recognized not by birth or aristocratic title but by property and ability. In the nineteenth century, *bourgeois* came to refer to non-noble property owners, especially those who controlled modern industry. A bourgeois was an individual. We can refer to "bourgeois values." *Bourgeoisie* refers to the entire class, as in the French bourgeoisie as a whole.

Boxer Protocol Written agreement between the victors of the Boxer Uprising and the Qing Empire in 1901 that placed western troops in Beijing and required the regime to pay exorbitant damages for foreign life and property.

Boxer Uprising (1899–1900) Chinese peasant movement that opposed foreign influence, especially that of Christian missionaries; it was put down after the Boxers were defeated by an army composed mostly of Japanese, Russians, British, French, and Americans.

Brahma One of three major deities that form a trinity in Vedic religion. Brahma signifies birth. *See also* Vishnu *and* Shiva.

Brahmans Vedic priests who performed rituals and communicated with the gods. Brahmans provided guidance on how to live in balance with the forces of nature as represented by the various deities. Brahmanism was reborn as Hinduism sometime during the first half of the first millennium CE.

British Commonwealth of Nations Union formed in 1926 that conferred "dominion status" on Britain's White settler colonies in Canada, Australia, and New Zealand.

British East India Company *See* East India Company.

bronze Alloy of copper and tin brought into Europe from Anatolia; used to make hard-edged weapons.

brown shirts Troops of German men who advanced the Nazi cause by holding street marches, mass rallies, and confrontations and by beating Jews and anyone who opposed the Nazis.

Buddha "Enlightened One." The term was applied to Kshatriya-born Siddhartha Gautama (c. 563–483 BCE), whose ideas—about the relationship between desire and suffering and how to eliminate both through wisdom, ethical behavior, and mental discipline in order to achieve contentment (nirvana)—offered a radical challenge to Brahmanism.

Buddhism Major South Asian religion that aims to end human suffering through the renunciation of desire. Buddhists believe that removing the illusion of a separate identity would lead to a state of contentment (nirvana). These beliefs challenged the traditional Brahmanic teachings of the time and provided the peoples of South Asia with an alternative to established traditions.

bullion Uncoined gold or silver.

Byzantium Modern term for the Eastern Roman Empire (which would last until 1453), centered at its "New Rome," Constantinople, which was founded in 324 CE by Constantine on the site of the Greek city Byzantium.

Cahokia Commercial city on the Mississippi for regional and long-distance trade of commodities such as salt, shells, and skins and of manufactured goods such as pottery, textiles, and jewelry; marked by massive artificial hills, akin to earthen pyramids, used to honor spiritual forces.

calaveras Allegorical skeleton drawings by the Mexican printmaker and artist José Guadalupe Posada. The works drew on popular themes of betrayal, death, and festivity.

caliphate Islamic state, headed by a caliph—chosen either by election from the community (Sunni) or from the lineage of Muhammad (Shiite)—with political authority over the Muslim community.

Calvin, Jean (1509–1564) A French theologian during the Protestant Reformation. Calvin developed a Christianity that emphasized moral regeneration through church teachings and laid out a doctrine of predestination.

candomblé Yoruba-based religion in northern Brazil; it interwove African practices and beliefs with Christianity.

Canton system System officially established by imperial decree in 1759 that required European traders to have Chinese guild merchants act as guarantors for their good behavior and payment of fees.

caravan cities Cities (like Petra and Palmyra) that were located along land routes of the Silk Roads and served as hubs of commerce and cultural exchange between travelers and merchants participating in long-distance trade.

caravans Companies of men who transported and traded goods along overland routes in North Africa and central Asia; large caravans consisted of 600–1,000 camels and as many as 400 men.

caravanserais Inns along major trade routes that accommodated large numbers of traders, their animals, and their wares.

caravel Sailing vessel suited for nosing in and out of estuaries and navigating in waters with unpredictable currents and winds.

carrack Ship used on open bodies of water, such as the Mediterranean.

Carthage City in what is modern-day Tunisia; emblematic of the trading aspirations and activities of merchants in the Mediterranean. Pottery and other archaeological remains demonstrate that trading contacts with Carthage were as far-flung as Italy, Greece, France, Iberia, and West Africa.

cartography Mapmaking.

caste system Hierarchical system of organizing people and distributing labor.

Caste War of Yucatán (1847–1901) Conflict between Maya Indians and the Mexican state over Indian autonomy and legal equality, which resulted in the Mexican takeover of the Yucatán Peninsula.

Castro, Fidel (1926–2016) Cuban communist leader who seized power in January 1959. Castro became increasingly radical as he consolidated power, announcing a massive redistribution of land and the nationalization of foreign oil refineries; he declared himself a socialist and aligned himself with the Soviet Union in the wake of the 1961 CIA-backed Bay of Pigs invasion.

Çatal Hüyük Site in Anatolia discovered in 1958. It was a dense honeycomb of settlements filled with rooms whose walls were covered with paintings of wild bulls, hunters, and pregnant women. Çatal Hüyük symbolizes an early transition to urban dwelling and dates to the eighth millennium BCE.

cathedra Bishop's seat, or throne, in a church.

Catholic Church *See* Roman Catholicism.

Cato the Elder (234–149 BCE) Roman statesman, often seen as emblematic of the transition from a Greek to a Roman world. He wrote a manual for the new economy of plantation slavery in agriculture, invested in shipping and trading, learned Greek rhetoric, and added the genre of history to Latin literature.

caudillos South American local military chieftains.

cave drawings Images on cave walls. The subjects are most often large game, although a few are images of humans. Other elements are impressions made by hands dipped in paint and pressed on a wall as well as abstract symbols and shapes.

Celali revolts (1595–1610) Peasant and artisan uprisings against the Ottoman state.

Central Powers Alliance of Germany and Austria-Hungary in World War I.

Chan Chan City founded around 900 CE by the Moche people in what is now modern-day Peru. It became the largest city of the Chimú Empire with a core population of 30,000 inhabitants.

Chan Santa Cruz Separate Maya community formed as part of a crusade for spiritual salvation and the complete cultural separation of the Maya Indians; means "little holy cross."

Chandragupta Maurya (r. 321–297 BCE) Also called Chandragupta Mori (and mentioned, though not by name, in many contemporary Greek sources); founder of South Asia's first empire, as the Mauryan dynasty of India, in the power vacuum left by the withdrawal of Alexander of Macedon's Greek forces from the region.

Chandragupta I (R. C. 320–335 CE) Founder of the Gupta dynasty of India who took the title "King of Kings" and significantly expanded the territory of his empire to include all of the northern plain of India.

Chandragupta II (R. C. 380–415 CE) Grandson of Chandragupta I who further expanded Gupta territories and was a literary patron. During his reign the renowned Sanskrit author Kalidasa is thought to have flourished.

Chandravansha One of two main lineages (the lunar one) of Vedic society, each with its own creation myth, ancestors, language, and rituals. Each lineage included many clans. *See also* Suryavansha.

chapatis Flat, unleavened Indian bread.

chariot Horse-drawn vehicle with two spoked and metal-rimmed wheels. Made possible by the interaction of pastoralists and settled communities, the chariot revolutionized warfare in the second millennium BCE.

charismatic Person who uses personal strengths or virtues, often laced with a divine aura, to command followers.

Charlemagne Emperor of the west and heir to Rome from 768 to 814 CE.

chartered companies Firms that were awarded monopoly trading rights over vast areas by European monarchs (for example, the Virginia Company and the Dutch East India Company).

Chartism (1834–1848) Mass democratic movement to pass the Peoples' Charter in Britain, granting male suffrage, secret ballot, equal electoral districts, and annual parliaments and absolving the requirement of property ownership for members of the parliament.

chattel slavery Form of slavery in which people were sold as property, the rise of which coincided with the expansion of city-states. Chattel slavery was eschewed by the Spartans, who also rejected the innovation of coin money.

Chavín Agrarian people living from 1400 to 200 BCE in complex societies in what is now Peru. They manufactured goods (ceramics, textiles, and precious metals), conducted limited long-distance trade, and shared an artistic and religious tradition, most notably at Chavín de Huántar.

Chernobyl (1986) Site in the Soviet Union (in present-day Ukraine) of the meltdown of a nuclear reactor.

Chiang Kai-shek (1887–1975) Leader of the Guomindang following Sun Yat-sen's death who mobilized the Chinese masses through the New Life movement. In 1949, he lost the Chinese Revolution to the communists and moved his regime to Taiwan.

Chimú Empire South America's first empire, centered at Chan Chan, in the Moche Valley on the Pacific coast from 1000 through 1470 CE, whose development was fueled by agriculture and commercial exchange.

chinampas Floating gardens used by Aztecs in the 1300s and 1400s to grow crops.

China's Sorrow Name for the Yellow River, which, when it changed course or flooded, could cause mass death and waves of migration.

chinoiserie Chinese silks, teas, tableware, jewelry, and paper; popular among Europeans in the seventeenth and eighteenth centuries.

Christendom Entire portion of the world in which Christianity prevailed.

Christianity New religious movement originating in the Eastern Roman Empire in the first century CE, with roots in Judaism and resonance with various Greco-Roman religious traditions. The central figure, Jesus,

was tried and executed by Roman authorities, and his followers believed he rose from the dead. The tradition was spread across the Mediterranean by his followers, and Christians were initially persecuted—to varying degrees—by Roman authorities. The religion was eventually legalized in 312 CE, and by the late fourth century CE it became the official state religion of the Roman Empire.

Church of England Established form of Christianity in England dating from the sixteenth century.

city Highly populated concentration of economic, religious, and political power. The first cities appeared in river basins, which could produce a surplus of agriculture. The abundance of food freed most city inhabitants from the need to produce their own food, which allowed them to work in specialized professions.

city-state Political organization based on the authority of a single, large city that controls outlying territories.

Civil Rights Act (1964) U.S. legislation that banned racial segregation in public facilities, outlawed racial discrimination in employment, and marked an important step in correcting legal inequality.

civil rights movement Powerful movement for equal rights and the end of racial segregation in the United States that began in the 1950s with court victories against school segregation and nonviolent boycotts.

civil service examinations Set of challenging exams instituted by the Tang to help assess potential bureaucrats' literary skill and knowledge of the Confucian classics.

Civil War, American (1861–1865) Conflict between the northern and southern states of America that led

to the abolition of slavery in the United States.

clan A social group comprising many households, claiming descent from a common ancestor.

clandestine presses Small printing operations that published banned texts in the early modern era, especially in Switzerland and the Netherlands.

closing of the frontier In 1893, responding to the recent U.S. Census, the historian Frederick Jackson Turner popularized the idea that the western frontier—so long crucial to the making of American identity—had closed. His announcement spurred many to worry that having lost the manliness and self-reliance nurtured by the hard life on the frontier, Americans would grow soft and weak.

Clovis people Early humans in America who used basic chipped blades and pointed spears in pursuing prey. They extended the hunting traditions they had learned in Afro-Eurasia, such as establishing campsites and moving with the herds. They were known as "Clovis people" because the type of arrowhead point that they used was first found by archaeologists at a site near Clovis, New Mexico.

Code of Manu Brahmanic code of law that took shape in the third to fifth centuries CE and expressed ideas going back to Vedic times. Framed as a conversation between Manu (the first human and an ancient lawgiver) and a group of wise men, it articulated the rules of the hierarchical *varna* system.

codex Early form of book, with separate pages bound together; it replaced the scroll as the main medium for written texts. The codex emerged around 300 CE.

cognitive skills Skills such as thought, memory, problem solving, and—ultimately—language.

Hominins were able to use these skills and their hands to create new adaptations, like tools, which helped them obtain food and avoid predators.

Cohong Chinese merchant guild that traded with Europeans under the Qing dynasty.

coins Form of money that replaced goods, which previously had been bartered for services and other products. Originally used mainly to hire mercenary soldiers, coins became the commonplace method of payment linking buyers and producers throughout the Mediterranean.

Cold War (1945–1990) Ideological rivalry in which the Soviet Union and eastern Europe opposed the United States and western Europe, but no direct military conflict occurred between the two rival blocs.

colonies Regions under the political control of another country.

colons French settlers in Algeria.

Colosseum Huge amphitheater in Rome completed by Titus and dedicated in 80 CE. Originally begun by Flavian, the structure is named after a colossal statue of Nero that formerly stood beside it.

Columbian exchange Movements between Afro-Eurasia and the Americas of previously unknown plants, animals, people, diseases, and products that followed in the wake of Columbus's voyages.

commanderies The thirty-six provinces (*jun*) into which Shi Huangdi divided territories. Each commandery had a civil governor, a military governor, and an imperial inspector.

Communist Manifesto, The Pamphlet published by Karl Marx and Friedrich Engels in 1848 at a time when political revolutions were sweeping Europe. It called on the workers of all nations to unite in overthrowing capitalism.

Compromise of 1867 Agreement between the Habsburg state and the peoples living in Hungarian parts of the empire that the state would be officially known as the Austro-Hungarian Empire.

concession areas Territories, usually ports, where Chinese emperors allowed European merchants to trade and European people to settle.

Confucian ideals The ideals of honoring tradition, emphasizing the responsibility of the emperor, and respecting the lessons of history, promoted by Confucius, which the Han dynasty made the official doctrine of the empire by 50 BCE.

Confucianism Ethics, beliefs, and practices stipulated by the Chinese philosopher Kong Qiu, or Confucius, which served as a guide for Chinese society up to modern times.

Confucius (551–479 BCE) Radical thinker whose ideas—especially about how ethical living that was centered on *ren* (benevolence), *li* (proper ritual), and *xiao* (filial piety toward ancestors living and dead) shaped the politically engaged superior gentleman—transformed society and government in East Asia.

cong tube Ritual object crafted by the Liangzhu, made of jade and used in divination practices.

Congo Free State Large colonial state in Africa created by Leopold II, king of Belgium, during the 1880s and ruled by him alone. After rumors of mass slaughter and enslavement, the Belgian parliament took possession of the colony.

Congress of Vienna (1814–1815) International conference to reorganize Europe after the downfall of Napoleon. European monarchies agreed to respect one another's borders and to cooperate in guarding against future revolutions and war.

conquistadors Spanish military leaders who led the conquest of the New World in the sixteenth century.

Constantine Roman emperor who converted to Christianity in 312 CE. In 313, he issued a proclamation that gave Christians new freedoms in the empire. He also founded Constantinople (at first called "New Rome").

Constantinople Capital city of Byzantium, which was founded as the New Rome by the emperor Constantine.

Constitutional Convention (1787) Meeting to formulate the Constitution of the United States of America.

Contra rebels Opponents of the Sandinistas in Nicaragua; they were armed and financed by the United States and other anticommunist countries (1980).

conversos Jewish and Muslim converts to Christianity in the Iberian Peninsula and the New World.

Coptic Form of Christianity practiced in Egypt. It was doctrinally different from Christianity elsewhere, and Coptic Christians had their own views of the nature of Christ.

Corn Laws Laws that imposed tariffs on grain imported to Great Britain, intended to protect British farming interests. The Corn Laws were abolished in 1846 as part of a British movement in favor of free trade.

cosmology Branch of metaphysics devoted to understanding the order of the universe.

cosmopolitans Meaning "citizens of the world," as opposed to a city-state, this term refers particularly to inhabitants of the large, multiethnic cities that were nodes of exchange in the Hellenistic world.

Council of Nicaea Church council convened in 325 CE by Constantine and presided over by him as well. At this council, a Christian creed was articulated and made into a formula that expressed the philosophical and technical elements of Christian belief.

Counter-Reformation Movement to counter the spread of the Reformation; initiated by the Catholic Church at the Council of Trent in 1545. The Catholic Church enacted reforms to attack clerical corruption and placed a greater emphasis on individual spirituality. During this time, the Jesuits were founded to help revive the Catholic Church.

coup d'état Overthrow of an established state by a group of conspirators, usually from the military.

creation narratives Narratives constructed by different cultures that draw on their belief systems and available evidence to explain the origins of the world and humanity.

creed From the Latin *credo*, meaning "I believe," an authoritative statement of belief. The Nicene Creed, formulated by Christian bishops at the Council of Nicaea in 325 CE, is an example of one such formal belief statement.

creoles Persons of mixed European and African (or other) descent who were born in the Americas.

Crimean War (1853–1856) War waged by Russia against Great Britain and France. Spurred by Russia's encroachment on Ottoman territories, the conflict revealed Russia's military weakness when Russian forces fell to British and French troops.

crossbow Innovative weapon used at the end of China's Warring States period that allowed archers to shoot their enemies with accuracy, even from a distance.

Crusades Wave of attacks launched in the late eleventh century by western European Christians against Muslims. The First Crusade began in 1095, when Pope Urban II appealed to the warrior nobility of France to free Jerusalem from Muslim rule. Four subsequent Crusades were fought over the next two centuries.

Cuban Missile Crisis (1962) Diplomatic standoff between the United States and the Soviet Union that was provoked by the Soviet Union's attempt to base nuclear missiles in Cuba; it brought the world close to a nuclear war.

cult Religious movement, often based on the worship of a particular god or goddess.

cultigen Organism that has diverged from its ancestors through domestication or cultivation.

cuneiform Wedge-shaped form of writing. As people combined rebus symbols with other visual marks that contained meaning, they became able to record and transmit messages over long distances by using abstract symbols or signs to denote concepts; such signs later came to represent syllables, which could be joined into words. By impressing these signs into wet clay with the cut end of a reed, scribes engaged in cuneiform.

Cyrus the Great Founder of the Persian Empire. This sixth-century ruler (559–529 BCE) conquered the Medes and unified the Iranian kingdoms.

czar *See* tsar.

daimyo Ruling lord who commanded a private army in pre-Meiji Japan.

dan Fodio, Usman (1754–1817) Fulani Muslim cleric whose visions led him to challenge the Hausa ruling classes, who he believed were insufficiently faithful to Islamic beliefs and practices. His ideas

gained support among those who had suffered under the Hausa landlords. In 1804, his supporters and allies overthrew the Hausa in what is today northern Nigeria.

Daoism East Asian philosophy of the Axial Age introduced by Master Lao and expanded by his student Zhuangzi. It was remarkable for its emphasis on following the *dao* (the natural way of the cosmos) and held that the best way to do that was through *wuwei* (doing nothing).

dar al-Islam Arabic for "the House of Islam"; describes a sense of common identity.

Darius I (r. 522–486 BCE) Leader who put the emerging unified Persian Empire onto solid footing after Cyrus the Great's death.

Darwin, Charles (1809–1882) British scientist who became convinced that the species of organic life had evolved under the uniform pressure of natural laws, not by means of a special, one-time creation as described in the Bible.

D-Day (June 6, 1944) Day of the Allied invasion of Normandy under General Dwight Eisenhower to liberate western Europe from German occupation.

Dear Boy Nickname of an early human skull discovered in 1931 by a team of archaeologists named the Leakeys. Other objects discovered with Dear Boy demonstrated that by his time, early humans had begun to fashion tools and to use them for butchering animals and possibly for hunting and killing smaller animals.

Decembrists Russian army officers who were influenced by events in revolutionary France and formed secret societies that espoused liberal governance. They launched a revolt that was put down by Nicholas I in December 1825.

Declaration of Independence U.S. document stating the theory of government on which America was founded.

Declaration of the Rights of Man and of the Citizen (1789) French charter of liberties formulated by the National Assembly that marked the end of dynastic and aristocratic rule. The seventeen articles later became the preamble to the new constitution, which the assembly finished in 1791.

decolonization End of empire and emergence of new independent nation-states in Asia and Africa as a result of the defeat of Japan in World War II and weakened European influence after the war.

degeneration In the later nineteenth century, many Europeans began to fear that Darwin had been wrong: urbanization, technology, racial hybridity, the emergence of the "modern" woman, and over-refinement were causing Europeans not to progress as a species but to degenerate. This fear was often combined with anxieties about colonialism, homosexuality, emigration, and/or the advancement of women.

Delhi Sultanate (1206–1526) A Turkish Muslim regime in northern India that, through its tolerance for cultural diversity, brought political integration without enforcing cultural homogeneity.

democracy The idea that people, through membership in a nation, should choose their own representatives and be governed by them.

Democritus Thinker in ancient Greece who lived from around 460 to 370 BCE; he deduced the existence of the atom and postulated that there was such a thing as an indivisible particle.

demotic writing The second of two basic forms of ancient Egyptian writing. Demotic was a cursive script written with ink on papyrus, on pottery, or on other absorbent objects. It was the most common and practical form of writing in Egypt and was used for administrative record keeping and in private or pseudo-private forms like letters and works of literature. *See also* hieroglyphs.

developing world Term applied to poor countries of the Third World and the former eastern communist bloc seeking to develop viable nation-states and prosperous economies. The term has come under sustained criticism for suggesting that there is a single path of economic growth that countries everywhere follow. It has been replaced by equally problematic terms like "advanced economy" and "emerging markets."

devshirme The Ottoman system of taking non-Muslim children in place of taxes in order to educate them in Muslim ways and prepare them for service in the sultan's bureaucracy.

dhamma Moral code espoused by Aśoka in the Kalinga edict, which was meant to apply to all—Buddhists, Brahmans, and Greeks alike.

dhimma system Ottoman law that permitted followers of religions other than Islam, such as Armenian Christians, Greek Orthodox Christians, and Jews, to choose their own religious leaders and to settle internal disputes within their religious communities as long as they accepted Islam's political dominion.

dhows Ships used by Arab seafarers whose large sails were rigged to maximize the capture of wind.

Dien Bien Phu (1954) Site of a defining battle in the war between French colonialists and the Viet Minh that secured North Vietnam for Ho Chi Minh and his army and left the south to form its own government with French and American support.

Diogenes Greek philosopher who lived from around 412 to 323 BCE and who espoused a doctrine of self-sufficiency and freedom from social laws and customs. He rejected cultural norms as out of tune with nature and therefore false.

Directory Temporary military committee in France that took over affairs of the state from the radicals in 1795 and held control until the coup of Napoleon Bonaparte.

divination Rituals used to communicate with gods or royal ancestors and to foretell future events. Divination was used to legitimize royal authority and demand tribute.

Djoser Ancient Egyptian king who reigned from 2630 to 2611 BCE. He was the second king of the Third Dynasty and celebrated the Sed festival in his tomb complex at Saqqara.

domestication Bringing a wild animal or plant under human control.

Dominion in the British Commonwealth Canadian promise to keep up the country's fealty to the British crown, even after its independence in 1867. Later applied to Australia and New Zealand.

Dong Zhongshu Emperor Wu's chief minister, who advocated a more powerful view of Confucius by promoting texts that focused on Confucius as a man who possessed aspects of divinity.

double-outrigger canoes Vessels used by early Austronesians to cross the Taiwan Straits and colonize islands in the Pacific. These sturdy canoes could cover over 120 miles per day.

Duma Russian parliament.

Dutch learning Broad term for European teachings that were strictly regulated by the shoguns inside Japan.

dynastic cycle Political narrative in which influential families vied for supremacy. Upon gaining power, they legitimated their authority by claiming to be the heirs of previous grand dynasts and by preserving or revitalizing the ancestors' virtuous governing ways. This continuity conferred divine support.

dynasty Hereditary ruling family that passed control from one generation to the next.

Earth Summit (1992) Meeting in Rio de Janeiro between many of the world's governments in an effort to address international environmental problems.

East India Company (1600–1858) British charter company created to outperform Portuguese and Spanish traders in Asia; in the eighteenth century the company became, in effect, the ruler of a large part of India.

Eastern Front Battlefront between Berlin and Moscow during World War I and World War II.

economic inequality Systematically uneven distribution of both income and opportunity among different groups of people or different nations.

economic nationalism An ideology that supports state interventionism over other means of regulating a nation's market, often involving restrictions on the movement of capital, labor, and goods.

Edict of Nantes (1598) Edict issued by Henry IV to end the French Wars of Religion. The edict declared France a Catholic country but tolerated some Protestant worship.

Eiffel Tower Steel monument completed in 1889 for the Paris Exposition. It was twice the height of any other building at the time.

eight-legged essay Highly structured essay form with eight parts, required on Chinese civil service examinations.

Ekklesia Church or early gathering committed to leaders chosen by God and fellow believers.

Ekpe Powerful slave trade institution that organized the supply and purchase of enslaved people inland from the Gulf of Guinea in West Africa.

Elamites A people with their capital in the upland valley of modern Fars who became a cohesive polity that incorporated transhumant people of the Zagros Mountains. A group of Elamites who migrated south and west into Mesopotamia helped conquer the Third Dynasty of Ur in 2400 BCE.

empire Group of states or ethnic groups governed by a single sovereign power with varying degrees of centralization using a range of methods, including common language, shared religious beliefs, trade, political systems, and military might.

Enabling Act (1933) Emergency act passed by the Reichstag (German parliament) that helped transform Hitler from Germany's chancellor, or prime minister, into a dictator following the suspicious burning of the Reichstag building and a suspension of civil liberties.

enclosure A movement in which landowners took control of lands that traditionally had been common property serving local needs.

encomenderos Commanders of the labor services of the colonized peoples in Spanish America.

encomiendas Grants from European Spanish governors to control the labor services of colonized peoples.

Endeavor Ship of Captain James Cook, whose celebrated voyages to the South Pacific in the late eighteenth century supplied Europe with information about the plants, birds, landscapes, and people of this uncharted territory.

Engels, Friedrich (1820–1895) German social and political philosopher who collaborated with Karl Marx on many publications, including *The Communist Manifesto*.

English Navigation Act of 1651 Act stipulating that only English ships could carry goods between the mother country and its colonies.

English Peasants' Revolt (1381) Uprising of serfs and free farm workers that began as a protest against a tax levied to raise money for a war on France. The revolt was suppressed, but led to the gradual emergence of a free peasantry as labor shortages made it impossible to keep peasants bound to the soil.

enlightened absolutists Seventeenth- and eighteenth-century monarchs who claimed to rule rationally and in the best interests of their subjects and who hired loyal bureaucrats to implement the knowledge of the new age.

Enlightenment Intellectual movement in eighteenth-century Europe, which extended the methods of the natural sciences, especially physics, to society, stressing natural laws and reason as the basis of authority.

entrepôts Multiethnic trading stations, often supported and protected by regional leaders, where traders exchanged commodities and replenished supplies in order to facilitate long-distance trade.

Epicurus Greek philosopher who espoused emphasis on the self. He lived from 341 to 279 BCE and founded a school in Athens called The Garden. He stressed the importance of sensation, teaching that pleasurable sensations were good and painful sensations bad. Members of his school sought to find peace and relaxation by avoiding unpleasantness or suffering.

Estates-General French quasi-parliamentary body called in 1789 to deal with the financial problems that afflicted France. It had not met since 1614.

Etruscans A dominant people on the Italian Peninsula until the fourth century BCE. The Etruscan states were part of the foundation of the Roman Empire.

eunuchs Surgically castrated men who rose to high levels of military, political, and personal power in several empires (for instance, the Tang and the Ming Empires in China; the Abbasid and Ottoman Empires; and the Byzantine Empire).

Eurasia The combined area of Europe and Asia.

European Union (EU) Supranational body organized in the 1950s as an attempt at reconciliation between Germany and the rest of Europe. It emerged from the European Coal and Steel Community and initially aimed to forge closer industrial cooperation. By 1993, through various treaties, many European states had relinquished important elements of their sovereignty, and the cooperation became a full-fledged union with a common parliament and a common currency. By 2020, all twenty-seven member states of the EU except Denmark had adopted, or pledged to adopt, the euro as their currency.

evolution Process by which species of plants and animals change over time, as a result of the favoring, through reproduction, of certain traits that are useful in that species' environment.

Exclusion Act of 1882 U.S. congressional act prohibiting nearly all immigration from China to the United States; fueled by animosity toward Chinese workers in the American West.

Ezo Present-day Hokkaido, Japan's fourth main island.

Farang Persian word meaning "Frank," which was used to describe Crusaders.

fascism Form of hypernationalism that emerged in Europe after the Great War (World War I), in which a charismatic leader was followed by a mass party and supported by established elites and churches and existing government institutions. Fascist movements were widespread but came to power only in Italy and Germany.

Fatehpur Sikri Mughal emperor Akbar's temporary capital near Agra.

Fatimids Shiite dynasty that ruled parts of the Islamic empire beginning in the tenth century CE. They were based in Egypt and founded the city of Cairo.

February Revolution (1917) The first of two uprisings of the Russian Revolution, which led to the end of the Romanov dynasty.

Federal Deposit Insurance Corporation (FDIC) Organization created in 1933 to guarantee all bank deposits up to $5,000 as part of the New Deal in the United States.

Federal Republic of Germany (1949–1990) Country formed from the areas of Germany occupied by the Allies after World War II. Also known as West Germany, this country experienced rapid demilitarization, democratization, and integration into the world economy.

Federal Reserve Act (1913) U.S. legislation that created a series of boards to monitor the supply and demand of the nation's money.

Federalists Supporters of the ratification of the U.S. Constitution, which was written to replace the Articles of Confederation.

feminist movements Movements that call for equal treatment for men and women—equal pay and equal opportunities for obtaining jobs and advancement. Feminism arose mainly in Europe and in North America in the 1960s and then became global in the 1970s.

Fertile Crescent An area in Southwest Asia, bounded by the Mediterranean Sea in the west and the Zagros Mountains in the east; site of the world's first agricultural revolution.

feudalism System instituted in medieval Europe after the collapse of the Carolingian Empire (814 CE) whereby each peasant was under the authority of a lord. *See also* manorialism.

fiefdoms Medieval economic and political units.

First World Term invented during the Cold War to refer to western Europe and North America (also known as the "free world" or the west); Japan later joined this group. Following the principles of liberal modernism, First World states sought to organize the world on the basis of capitalism and democracy.

five pillars of Islam Five practices that unite all Muslims: (1) proclaiming that "there is no God but God and Muhammad is His Prophet"; (2) praying five times a day; (3) fasting during the daylight hours of the holy month of Ramadan; (4) traveling on pilgrimage to Mecca; and (5) paying alms to support the poor.

Five-Year Plan Soviet effort launched under Stalin in 1928 to replace the market with a state-owned and state-managed economy in order to promote rapid economic development over a five-year period and thereby "catch and overtake" the leading capitalist countries. The First Five-Year Plan was followed by the Second Five-Year Plan (1933–1937), and so on, until the collapse of the Soviet Union in 1991.

Flagellants European social group that came into existence during the Black Death in the fourteenth century; they believed that the plague was the wrath of God.

floating population Poor migrant workers in China who supplied labor under Emperor Wu.

fluitschips Dutch shipping vessels that could carry heavy, bulky cargo with relatively small crews.

flying cash Letters of exchange— early predecessors of paper money— first developed by guilds in the northern Song province Shanxi that eclipsed coins by the thirteenth century.

fondûqs Complexes in caravan cities that included hostels, storage houses, offices, and temples; from the Arabic word for "hotel."

Forbidden City of Beijing Palace city of the Ming and Qing dynasties.

Force Publique Colonial army used to maintain order in the Belgian Congo; during the early stages of King Leopold's rule, it was responsible for bullying local communities.

Fourierism Form of utopian socialism based on the ideas of Charles Fourier (1772–1837), who envisioned communes where work was made enjoyable and systems of production and distribution were run without merchants. His ideas appealed to the middle class, especially women, as a higher form of Christian communalism.

free labor Wage-paying rather than enslaved labor.

free markets Unregulated markets.

Free Officers Movement Secret organization of Egyptian junior military officers who came to power in a coup d'état in 1952, forced King Faruq to abdicate, and consolidated their own control through dissolving the parliament, banning opposing parties, and rewriting the constitution.

free trade (laissez-faire) Domestic and international trade unencumbered by tariff barriers, quotas, and fees.

Front de Libération Nationale (FLN) Algerian anticolonial, nationalist party that waged an eight-year war against French troops, beginning in 1954, that forced nearly all of the 1 million European colonists to leave.

Fulani Muslim group in West Africa that carried out religious revolts at the end of the eighteenth and the beginning of the nineteenth centuries in an effort to return to the pure Islam of the past.

fur trade Trading of animal pelts (especially beaver skins) by Indians for European goods in North America.

Gandharan style Style of artwork, especially statuary, originating in the Gandharan region of modern Pakistan, that blends Hellenistic artistic influences with Buddhist stylistic features and subjects.

Gandhi, Mohandas Karamchand (Mahatma) (1869–1948) Indian leader who led a nonviolent struggle for India's independence from Britain.

garrison towns Stations for soldiers originally established in strategic locations to protect territorial acquisitions. Eventually, they became towns. Alexander the Great's garrison towns evolved into cities that served as centers from which

Hellenistic culture was spread to his easternmost territories.

garrisons Military bases inside cities; often used for political purposes, such as protecting rulers, putting down domestic revolts, or enforcing colonial rule.

gauchos Argentine, Brazilian, and Uruguayan cowboys who wanted a decentralized federation, with autonomy for their provinces and respect for their way of life.

Gdańsk shipyard Site of mass strikes in Poland that led in 1980 to the formation of the first independent trade union, Solidarity, in the Soviet bloc.

gender relations A relatively recent development that implies roles emerged only with the appearance of modern humans and perhaps Neanderthals. When humans began to think imaginatively and in complex symbolic ways and give voice to their insights, perhaps around 150,000 years ago, gender categories began to crystallize.

genealogy History of the descent of a person or family from a distant ancestor.

Geneva Peace Conference (1954) International conference to restore peace in Korea and Indochina. The chief participants were the United States, the Soviet Union, Great Britain, France, the People's Republic of China, North Korea, South Korea, Vietnam, the Viet Minh party, Laos, and Cambodia. The conference resulted in the division of North and South Vietnam.

Genoa One of two Italian cities (the other was Venice) that linked Europe, Africa, and Asia as nodes of commerce in 1300. Genoese ships linked the Mediterranean to the coast of Flanders through consistent routes along the Atlantic coasts of Spain, Portugal, and France.

German Democratic Republic (1949–1990) Country formed from the areas of Germany occupied by the Soviet Union after World War II. Also known as East Germany.

German Social Democratic Party Founded in 1875, the most powerful socialist party in Europe before 1917.

Ghana The most celebrated medieval political kingdom in West Africa.

Ghost Dance American Indian ritual performed in the nineteenth century in the hope of restoring the world to precolonial conditions.

Gilgamesh, Epic of Heroic narrative written in the Babylonian dialect of Semitic Akkadian. This story and others like it were meant to circulate and unify the kingdom.

Girondins Liberal revolutionary group that supported the creation of a constitutional monarchy during the early stages of the French Revolution.

global climate change A wide range of phenomena caused by global warming. These changes encompass not only rising temperatures, but also changes in precipitation patterns; ice mass loss on mountain glaciers around the world; shifts in the life cycles and migration patterns of flora and fauna; extreme weather events; and sea level rise.

global war on terror Global crusade to root out anti-American, anti-western Islamist terrorist cells; launched by President George W. Bush as a response to the 9/11 attacks.

global warming Upward temperature trends worldwide due to the release of carbon into the air, mainly by the burning of fossil fuels and other human activities.

globalization Development of integrated worldwide cultural and economic structures.

globalizing empires Empires that cover immense territory; exert significant influence beyond their borders; include large, diverse populations; and work to integrate conquered peoples.

Gold Coast Name that European mariners and merchants gave to the part of West Africa from which gold was exported. This area was conquered by the British in the nineteenth century and became a British colony; upon independence, it became Ghana.

Goths One of the groups of "barbarian" migrants into Roman territory in the fourth century CE.

government schools Schools founded by the Han dynasty to provide an adequate number of officials to fill positions in the administrative bureaucracy. The Imperial University had 30,000 members by the second century BCE.

Gracchus brothers Two tribunes, the brothers Tiberius and Gaius Gracchus, who in 133 and 123–121 BCE attempted to institute land reforms that would guarantee all of Rome's poor citizens a basic amount of land that would qualify them for army service. Both men were assassinated.

Grand Canal A thousand-mile-long connector between the Yellow and Yangzi Rivers created in 486 BCE to link the north and south of China.

grand unity Guiding political idea embraced by Qin rulers and ministers with an eye toward joining the states of the Central Plains into one empire and centralizing administration.

"greased cartridge" controversy Controversy spawned by the rumor that cow and pig fat had been used to grease the shotguns of the sepoys in the British army in India. Believing that this was a British attempt to defile their religions and speed their conversion to Christianity, the sepoys mutinied against the British officers.

Great Depression Worldwide depression following the U.S. stock market crash on October 29, 1929.

great divide The division between economically developed nations and less developed nations.

Great East Asia Co-Prosperity Sphere Term used by the Japanese during the 1930s and 1940s to refer to Hong Kong, Singapore, Malaya, Burma, and other states that they seized during their attempt to dominate Asia.

Great Flood One of many traditional Mesopotamian stories that were transmitted orally from one generation to another before being recorded. The Sumerian King List refers to this crucial event in Sumerian memory and identity. The Great Flood narrative assigned responsibility for Uruk's demise to the gods.

Great Game Competition over areas such as Turkistan, Persia (present-day Iran), and Afghanistan. The British (in India) and the Russians believed that controlling these areas was crucial to preventing their enemies' expansion.

Great League of Peace and Power Iroquois Indian alliance that united previously warring communities.

Great Leap Forward (1958–1961) Plan devised by Mao Zedong to achieve rapid agricultural and industrial growth in China. The plan, which failed miserably, may have led to the deaths of as many as 45 million people from famine and malnutrition.

great plaza at Isfahan The center of Safavid power in the seventeenth century created by Shah Abbas (r. 1587–1629) to represent the unification of trade, government, and religion under one supreme political authority.

Great Proletarian Cultural Revolution (1966–1976) Mass mobilization of urban Chinese youth inaugurated by Mao Zedong in an attempt to reinvigorate the Chinese Revolution and to prevent the development of a bureaucratized Soviet style of communism; with this movement, Mao turned against his longtime associates in the Communist Party.

Great Recession The economic downturn, with global reverberations, provoked by the financial crash of 2008.

Great Trek Afrikaner migration to the interior of Africa after the British Empire abolished slavery in 1833.

Great War (World War I) (August 1914–November 1918) A total global war involving the armies of Britain, France, and Russia (the Allies) against those of Germany, Austria-Hungary, and the Ottoman Empire (the Central Powers). Italy joined the Allies in 1915, and the United States joined them in 1917, helping tip the balance in favor of the Allies, who also drew upon the populations and material of their colonial possessions.

Greek Orthodoxy Branch of eastern Christianity, originally centered in Constantinople, that emphasizes the role of Jesus in helping humans achieve union with God.

Greek philosophers "Wisdom lovers" of the ancient Greek city-states, including Socrates, Plato, Aristotle, and others, who pondered such issues as self-knowledge, political engagement and withdrawal, and evidence-based inquiry to understand the order of the cosmos.

Greenbacks An American political party of the late nineteenth century that worked to advance the interests of farmers by promoting cheap money.

griots Counselors and other officials serving the royal family in African kingships. They were also responsible for the preservation and transmission of oral histories and repositories of knowledge.

Group Areas Act (1950) Act that divided South Africa into separate racial and tribal areas and required Africans to live in their own separate communities, including the "homelands."

guerrillas Portuguese and Spanish peasant bands who resisted the revolutionary and expansionist efforts of Napoleon; after the French word *guerre.*

guest workers Migrants seeking temporary employment abroad.

Gulag Administrative name for the vast system of forced labor camps under the Soviet regime; it originated in a small monastery near the Arctic Circle and spread throughout the Soviet Union and to other Soviet-style socialist countries. Penal labor was required of both ordinary criminals (rapists, murderers, thieves) and those accused of political crimes (counterrevolution, anti-Soviet agitation).

Gulf War (1991) Armed conflict between Iraq and a coalition of thirty-two nations, including the United States, Britain, Egypt, France, and Saudi Arabia. It was started by Iraq's invasion of Kuwait, which it had long claimed, on August 2, 1990.

gunpowder Explosive powder. By 1040, the first gunpowder recipes were being written down. Over the next 200 years, Song entrepreneurs invented several incendiary devices and techniques for controlling explosions.

gunpowder empires Muslim empires of the Ottomans, Safavids, and Mughals that used cannonry and gunpowder to advance their military causes.

Guomindang Nationalist Party of China, founded just before World War I by Sun Yat-sen and later led by Chiang Kai-shek.

Habsburg Empire Ruling house of Austria, which once ruled both Spain and central Europe but came to settle in lands along the Danube River; it played a prominent role in European affairs for many centuries. In 1867, the Habsburg Empire was reorganized into the Austro-Hungarian Empire, and in 1918 it collapsed.

hadith Sayings, attributed to the Prophet Muhammad and his early converts, used to guide the behavior of Muslim peoples.

Hagia Sophia Enormous and impressive church sponsored by Justinian and built starting in 532 CE. At the time, it was the largest church in the world.

hajj Pilgrimage to Mecca; an obligation for Muslims.

Hammurabi's Code Legal code created by Hammurabi (r. 1792–1750 BCE). The code divided society into three classes—free, dependent, and enslaved—each with distinct rights and responsibilities.

Han agrarian ideal Guiding principle for the free peasantry that made up the base of Han society. In this system, peasants were honored for their labors, while merchants were subjected to a range of controls, including regulations on luxury consumption, and were belittled for not engaging in physical labor.

Han Chinese Inhabitants of China proper who considered others to be outsiders and felt that they were the only authentic Chinese.

Han Fei Chinese state minister who lived from 280 to 233 BCE; a proponent and follower of Xunzi.

Han military Like its Roman counterpart, a ruthless military machine that expanded the Han Empire and created stable conditions that permitted the safe transit of goods by caravans. Emperor Wu heavily influenced the transformation of the military forces and reinstituted a policy that made military service compulsory.

Hangzhou City and former provincial seaport that became the political center of the Chinese people in their ongoing struggles with northern steppe nomads. It was also one of China's gateways to the rest of the world by way of the South China Sea.

Hannibal Great general from Carthage whose campaigns in the third century BCE swept from Spain toward the Italian Peninsula. He crossed the Pyrenees and the Alps with war elephants. He was unable, however, to defeat the Romans in 217 BCE.

Harappa One of the two largest of the cities that, by 2500 BCE, began to take the place of villages throughout the Indus River valley (the other was Mohenjo Daro). Each covered an area of about 250 acres and probably housed 35,000 residents.

harem Secluded women's quarters in a Muslim household.

Harlem Renaissance Cultural movement in the 1920s that was based in Harlem, a part of New York City with a large African American population. The movement gave voice to Black novelists, poets, painters, and musicians, many of whom used their art to protest racism; also referred to as the "New Negro movement."

harnesses Tools made from wood, bone, bronze, and iron for steering and controlling chariot horses. Harnesses discovered by archaeologists reveal the evolution of headgear from simple mouth bits to full bridles with headpiece, mouthpiece, and reins.

Hatshepsut Leader known as ancient Egypt's most powerful woman ruler. Hatshepsut served as regent for her young son, Thutmosis III, whose reign began in 1479 BCE. She remained co-regent until her death.

Haussmannization Redevelopment and beautification of urban centers; named after the city planner who "modernized" mid-nineteenth century Paris.

Heian period Period from 794 to 1185 CE during which the pattern of regents ruling Japan in the name of the sacred emperor began.

Hellenism Process by which the individuality of the cultures of the earlier Greek city-states gave way to a uniform culture that stressed the common identity of all who embraced Greek ways. This culture emphasized the common denominators of language, style, and politics to which anyone, anywhere in the Afro-Eurasian world, could have access.

hieroglyphs One of two basic forms of Egyptian writing that were used in conjunction throughout antiquity. Hieroglyphs are pictorial symbols; the term derives from a Greek word meaning "sacred carving." They were employed exclusively in temple, royal, and divine contexts. *See also* demotic writing.

hijra Tradition of Islam whereby one withdraws from one's community to create another, holier, one. The practice is based on the Prophet Muhammad's withdrawal from the city of Mecca to Medina in 622 CE.

Hinayana Buddhism (termed "Lesser Vehicle" Buddhism by the Mahayana/"Greater Vehicle" school; also called Theraveda Buddhism) A more traditional, conservative branch of Buddhism that accepted the divinity of the Buddha but not of bodhisattvas.

Hindu revivalism Movement to reconfigure traditional Hinduism to be less diverse and more amenable to producing a narrowed version of Indian tradition.

Hinduism Ancient Brahmanic Vedic religion that emerged as the dominant faith in India in the third century CE. It reflected rural and agrarian values and focused on the trinity of Brahma (birth), Vishnu (existence), and Shiva (destruction).

Hiroshima Japanese port devastated by an atomic bomb on August 6, 1945.

Hitler, Adolf (1889–1945) German dictator and leader of the Nazi Party who seized power in Germany after its economic collapse in the Great Depression. Hitler and his Nazi regime started World War II in Europe and systematically murdered Jews and other non-Aryan groups in the name of racial purity.

Hittites An Anatolian chariot warrior group that spread east to northern Syria, though they eventually faced weaknesses in their own homeland. Rooted in their capital at Hattusa, they interacted with contemporary states both violently (as at the Battle of Qadesh against Egypt) and peacefully (as in the correspondence of the Amarna letters).

HIV/AIDS An epidemic of acquired immunodeficiency syndrome (AIDS) caused by the human immunodeficiency virus (HIV), which compromises the ability of the infected person's immune system to ward off other diseases. First detected in 1981, AIDS killed 12 million people in the two decades that followed.

Holocaust Deliberate racial extermination by the Nazis of Jews, along with some other groups the Nazis considered "inferior" (including Sinta and Roma [gypsies], Jehovah's Witnesses, homosexuals, and people with mental illness), which claimed the lives of around 6 million European Jews.

Holy Roman Empire Enormous realm that encompassed much of Europe and aspired to be the Christian successor state to the Roman Empire. In the time of the Habsburg dynasts, the empire was a loose confederation of principalities that obeyed an emperor elected by elite lower-level sovereigns. Despite its size, the empire never effectively centralized power; it was split into Austrian and Spanish factions when Charles V abdicated to his sons in 1556.

Holy Russia Name applied to Muscovy and then to the Russian Empire by Slavic Eastern Orthodox clerics who were appalled by the Muslim conquest in 1453 of Constantinople (the capital of Byzantium and of eastern Christianity) and who were hopeful that Russia would become the new protector of the faith.

home charges Fees India was forced to pay to Britain as its colonial master; these fees included interest on railroad loans, salaries to colonial officers, and the maintenance of imperial troops outside India.

hominids The family, in scientific classification, that includes gorillas, chimpanzees, and humans (that is, *Homo sapiens*, in addition to our now-extinct hominin ancestors such as the various australopithecines as well as *Homo habilis*, *Homo erectus*, and *Homo neanderthalensis*).

hominins A scientific classification for modern humans and our now-extinct ancestors, including australopithecines and others in the genus *Homo*, such as *Homo habilis* and *Homo erectus*. Researchers once used the term *hominid* to refer to *Homo sapiens* and extinct hominin species, but the meaning of *hominid* has been expanded to include great apes (humans, gorillas, chimpanzees, and orangutans).

Homo The genus, in scientific classification, that contains only "true human" species.

Homo caudatus "Tailed man," believed by some European Enlightenment thinkers to be an early human species.

Homo erectus Species that emerged about 1.8 million years ago, had a large brain, walked truly upright, migrated out of Africa, and likely mastered fire. *Homo erectus* means "standing human."

Homo habilis Species, confined to Africa, that emerged about 2.5 million years ago and whose toolmaking ability truly made it the forerunner, though a very distant one, of modern humans. *Homo habilis* means "skillful human."

Homo sapiens The first humans; emerged in Africa as early as 300,000 years ago and migrated out of Africa beginning about 180,000 years ago. They had bigger brains and greater dexterity than previous hominin species, whom they eventually eclipsed.

homogeneity Uniformity of the languages, customs, and religion of a particular people or place. It can also be demonstrated by a consistent calendar, set of laws, administrative practices, and rituals.

horses Animals used by full-scale nomadic communities to dominate the steppe lands in western Afro-Eurasia by the second millennium BCE. Horse-riding nomads moved their large herds across immense tracts of land within zones defined by rivers, mountains, and other natural geographic features. In the arid zones of central Eurasia, the nomadic economies made horses a crucial component of survival.

Huguenots French Protestants who endured severe persecution in the sixteenth and seventeenth centuries.

humanism The Renaissance aspiration to develop a greater understanding of the human experience than the Christian scriptures offered by reaching back into ancient Greek and Roman texts.

Hundred Days' Reform (1898) Abortive modernizing reform program of the Qing government of China.

hunting and gathering Lifestyle in which food is acquired through hunting animals, fishing, and foraging for wild berries, nuts, fruit, and grains, rather than planting crops, vines, or trees. As late as 1500 CE, as much as 15 percent of the world's population still lived by this method.

Hyksos Chariot-driving, axe- and composite-bow-wielding, Semitic-speaking people (their name means "rulers of foreign lands") who invaded Egypt, overthrew the Thirteenth Dynasty, set up their own rule over Egypt, and were expelled by Ahmosis to begin the period known as New Kingdom Egypt.

Ibadat Khana "House of Worship" in which the Mughal emperor Akbar engaged in religious debate with Hindu, Muslim, Jain, Parsi, and Christian theologians.

Ibn Sina Philosopher and physician who lived from 980 to 1037 CE. He was also schooled in the Quran, geometry, literature, and Indian and Euclidian mathematics.

ideology Dominant set of ideas of a widespread culture or movement.

Il Duce (leader) Name used by the fascist Italian leader Benito Mussolini.

Iliad Epic Greek poem about the Trojan War, composed several centuries after the events it describes. It was based on oral tales passed down for generations.

Il-Khanate Mongol-founded dynasty in thirteenth-century Persia.

imam Muslim religious leader and politico-religious descendant of Ali; believed by some to have a special relationship with Allah.

Imperial University Institution founded in 136 BCE by Emperor Wu (Han Wudi) not only to train future bureaucrats in the Confucian classics but also to foster scientific advances in other fields.

imperialism Acquisition of new territories by a state and the incorporation of these territories into a political system as subordinate colonies.

Imperium Latin word used to express Romans' power and command over their subjects. It is the basis of the English words *empire* and *imperialism*.

Inca Empire Empire of Quechua-speaking rulers in the Andean valley of Cuzco that encompassed a population of 4 to 6 million. The Incas lacked a clear inheritance system, causing an internal split that Pizarro's forces exploited in 1533.

Indian Institutes of Technology (IIT) Institutions originally designed as engineering schools to expand knowledge and to modernize India, which produced a generation of pioneering computer engineers, many of whom moved to the United States.

Indian National Congress Formed in 1885, a political party deeply committed to constitutional methods, industrialization, and cultural nationalism.

Indian National Muslim League Founded in 1906, an organization dedicated to advancing the political interests of Muslims in India.

Indo-European migrations The migrations, tracked linguistically and culturally, of the peoples of a distinct language group (including Sanskrit, Persian, Greek, Latin, and German) from central Eurasian steppe lands into Europe, Southwest Asia, and South Asia.

Indo-Greek Of or relating to the fusion of Indian and Greek culture in the area under the control of the Bactrians, in the northwestern region of India, around 200 BCE.

Indu Name used for what we would today call India by Xuanzang, a Chinese Buddhist pilgrim who visited the area in the 630s and 640s CE.

indulgences Church-sponsored fund-raising mechanism that gave certification that one's sins had been forgiven in return for money.

industrial revolution Gradual accumulation and diffusion of old and new technical knowledge that led to major economic changes in Britain, northwestern Europe, and North America. It resulted in large-scale industry and the harnessing of fossil fuels, which allowed economic growth to outpace the rate of population increase.

innovation Creation of new methods that allowed humans to make better adaptations to their environment, such as the making of new tools.

Inquisition General term for a tribunal of the Roman Catholic Church that enforced religious orthodoxy. Several inquisitions took place over centuries, seeking to punish heretics, witches, Jews, and those whose conversion to Christianity was called into doubt.

internal and external alchemy In Daoist ritual, use of trance and meditation or chemicals and drugs, respectively, to cause transformations in the self.

International Monetary Fund (IMF) Agency founded in 1944 to help restore financial order in Europe and the rest of the world, to revive international trade, and to offer financial support to Third World governments.

invisible hand As described in Adam Smith's *The Wealth of Nations*, the idea that the operations of a free market produce economic efficiency and economic benefits for all.

iron Malleable metal found in combined forms almost everywhere in the world; it became the most important and widely used metal in world history after the Bronze Age.

Iron Curtain Term popularized by Winston Churchill after World War II to refer to a rift that divided western Europe, under American influence, from eastern Europe, under the domination of the Soviet Union.

irrigation Technological advance whereby water delivery systems and water sluices in floodplains or river-basin areas were channeled or redirected and used to nourish soil.

Islam A religion that dates to 610 CE, when the Prophet Muhammad believed God came to him in a vision. Islam (which means submission—in this case, to the will of God) requires its followers to act righteously, to submit themselves to the one and only true God, and to care for the less fortunate. Muhammad's most insistent message was the oneness of God, a belief that has remained central to the Islamic faith ever since.

Jacobins Radical French political group that came into existence during the French Revolution; executed the French king and sought to remake French culture.

Jacquerie (1358) French peasant revolt in defiance of feudal restrictions.

jade The most important precious substance in East Asia; associated with goodness, purity, luck, and virtue. Jade was carved into such items as ceremonial knives, blade handles, religious objects, and elaborate jewelry.

Jagat Seths Enormous trading and banking empire in eastern India during the first half of the eighteenth century.

Jainism System of thought, originating in the seventh century BCE, that challenged Brahmanism. Spread by Vardhamana Mahavira, Jainism encouraged purifying the soul through self-denial and nonviolence.

Jaja (1821–1891) A merchant prince who founded the Opobo city-state, in what is known in modern times as the Rivers state of Nigeria.

janissaries Corps of infantry soldiers conscripted as children under the *devshirme* system of the Ottoman Empire and brought up with intense loyalty to the Ottoman state and its sultan. The sultan used these forces to clip local autonomy and to serve as his personal bodyguards.

jatis Social groups as defined by Hinduism's *varna* (caste) system.

Jesuits Religious order founded by Ignatius Loyola to counter the inroads of the Protestant Reformation; the Jesuits, or the Society of Jesus, were active in politics, education, and missionary work.

jihad Literally, "striving" or "struggle." This word also connotes military efforts, or "striving in the way of God." In addition, it came to mean spiritual struggles against temptation or inner demons, especially in Sufi, or mystical, usage.

Jih-pen Chinese for "Japan."

Jim Crow laws Laws that codified racial segregation and inequality in the southern part of the United States after the Civil War.

jizya Special tax that non-Muslims were forced to pay to their Islamic rulers in return for which they were given security and property and granted cultural autonomy.

jongs Large oceangoing vessels built by Southeast Asians that plied the regional trade routes from the fifteenth century to the early sixteenth century.

Judah The southern kingdom of David, which had been a Neo-Assyrian vassal until 612 BCE, when it became a vassal of Neo-Assyria's successor, Babylon, against whom the people of Judah rebelled, resulting in the destruction of Jerusalem in the sixth century BCE.

Julius Caesar Formidable Roman general who lived from 100 to 44 BCE. He was also a man of letters, a great orator, and a ruthless military man who boasted that his campaigns had led to the deaths of over a million people.

junks Large seafaring vessels used in the South China Sea after 1000 CE,

which helped make shipping by sea less dangerous.

Justinian Roman or Byzantine emperor who ascended to the throne in 527 CE. In addition to his many building projects and military expeditions, he issued a new law code.

kabuki Theater performance that combined song, dance, and skillful staging to dramatize conflicts between duty and passion in Tokugawa Japan.

kamikaze Japanese for "divine winds," or typhoons; such a storm saved Japan from a Mongol attack.

kanun Highly detailed system of Ottoman administrative law that jurists developed to deal with matters not treated in the religious law of Islam.

karim Loose confederation of shippers banding together to protect convoys.

karma Literally, "fate" or "action"; in Confucian thought, a universal principle of cause and effect.

Kassites Nomads who entered Mesopotamia from the eastern Zagros Mountains and the Iranian plateau as early as 2000 BCE. They gradually integrated into Babylonian society by officiating at temples. By 1745 BCE, they had asserted order over the region, and they controlled southern Mesopotamia for the next 350 years, creating one of the territorial states.

Keynesian Revolution Post-Depression economic ideas developed by the British economist John Maynard Keynes, wherein the state took a greater role in managing the economy, stimulating it by increasing the money supply and creating jobs.

KGB Soviet political police and spy agency, formed as the Cheka not long after the Bolshevik coup in October 1917. Grew to more than

750,000 operatives with military rank by the 1980s.

khan Mongol ruler acclaimed at an assembly of elites, who was supposedly descended from Chinggis Khan on the male line; those not descended from Chinggis continually faced challenges to their legitimacy.

khanate Major political unit of the vast Mongol Empire. There were four khanates, including the Yuan Empire in China, forged by Chinggis Khan's grandson Kublai.

Kharijites Radical sect from the early days of Islam. The Kharijites seceded from the "party of Ali" (who themselves came to be known as the Shiites) because of disagreements over succession to the role of the caliph. They were known for their strict militant piety.

Khmer A people who created the most powerful empire in Southwest Asia between the tenth and thirteenth centuries in what is modern-day Cambodia.

Khomeini, Ayatollah Ruhollah (1902–1989) Iranian religious leader who used his traditional Islamic education and his training in Muslim ethics to accuse Shah Reza Pahlavi's government of gross violations of Islamic norms. He also identified the shah's ally, America, as the great Satan. The shah fled the country in 1979; in his wake, Khomeini established a theocratic state ruled by a council of Islamic clerics.

Khufu A pyramid, among those put up in the Fourth Dynasty in ancient Egypt (c. 2613–2494 BCE), which is the largest stone structure in the world. It is in an area called Giza, just outside modern-day Cairo.

Khusro I Anoshirwan Sasanian emperor who reigned from 531 to 579 CE. He was a model ruler and

was seen as the personification of justice.

Kiev City that became one of the greatest cities of Europe after the eleventh century. It was built to be a small-scale Constantinople on the Dnieper.

Kikuyu Kenya's largest ethnic group; organizers of a revolt against the British in the 1950s.

King, Martin Luther, Jr. (1929–1968) Civil rights leader who borrowed his most effective weapon—the commitment to nonviolent protest and the appeal to conscience—from Gandhi.

Kingdom of Jerusalem What Crusaders set out to liberate from Muslim rule when they launched their attacks.

Kizilbash Mystical, Turkish-speaking tribesmen who facilitated the Safavid rise to power.

Knossos Area in Crete where, during the second millennium BCE, a primary palace town existed.

Koine **Greek** Simpler than regional versions of Greek such as Attic or Ionic, this "common Greek" dialect became an international language across the regions influenced by Hellenism and facilitated trade of goods and ideas.

Köprülü reforms Reforms named after two grand viziers who revitalized the Ottoman Empire in the seventeenth century through administrative and budget trimming as well as by rebuilding the military.

Korean War (1950–1953) Cold War conflict between Soviet-backed North Korea and U.S.- and U.N.-backed South Korea. The two sides seesawed back and forth over the same boundaries until 1953, when an armistice divided the country at roughly the same spot as at the start of the war. Casualties included

33,000 Americans, at least 250,000 Chinese, and up to 3 million Koreans.

Koryo dynasty Leading dynasty of the northern-based Koryo kingdom in Korea. It is from this dynasty that the name "Korea" derives.

Kremlin Moscow's walled city center, whose name was once synonymous with the Soviet government.

Kshatriyas Originally the warrior *varna* (caste) in Vedic society, the dominant clan members and ruling *varna* who controlled the land.

Ku Klux Klan Racist organization that first emerged in the U.S. South after the Civil War and then gained national strength as a radically traditionalist movement during the 1920s.

Kublai Khan (1215–1294) Mongol leader who seized southern China after 1260 and founded the Yuan dynasty.

kulak Originally a pejorative word used to designate better-off peasants, a term used in the late 1920s and early 1930s to refer to any peasant, rich or poor, perceived as an opponent of the Soviet regime. Russian for "fist."

Kumarajiva Renowned Buddhist scholar and missionary who lived from 344 to 413 CE. He was brought to China by Chinese regional forces from Kucha, modern-day Xinjiang.

Kushans Northern nomadic group that migrated into South Asia around 50 CE. They unified the tribes of the region and set up the Kushan Empire, which embraced a large and diverse territory and played a critical role in the formation of the Silk Roads.

Labour Party Political party founded in Britain in 1900 that represented workers and was based on socialist principles.

laissez-faire The concept that the economy works best when it is left alone—that is, when the state does not regulate or interfere with the workings of the market.

"Land under the Yoke of Ashur" Lands not in Neo-Assyria proper, but under its authority, which had to pay the Neo-Assyrian Empire exorbitant amounts of tribute.

language System of communication reflecting cognitive abilities. Natural language is generally defined as words arranged in particular sequences to convey meaning and is unique to modern humans.

language families Related tongues with a common ancestral origin; language families contain languages that diverged from one another but share grammatical features and root vocabularies. More than a hundred language families exist.

Laozi Also known as Master Lao; perhaps a contemporary of Confucius, and the person after whom Daoism is named. His thought was elaborated upon by generations of thinkers.

latifundia Broad estates that produced goods for big urban markets, including wheat, grapes, olives, cattle, and sheep.

League of Nations Organization founded after World War I to solve international disputes through arbitration; it was dissolved in 1946 and its assets were transferred to the United Nations.

Legalism Also called Statism, a system of thought about how to live an ordered life. Developed by Master Xun, or Xunzi (310–237 BCE), it is based on the principle that people, being inherently inclined toward evil, require authoritarian control to regulate their behavior.

Lenin, Vladimir (1870–1924) Leader of the Bolshevik Revolution in Russia and the first leader of the Soviet Union.

LGBTQ Acronym for people who identify as lesbian, gay, bisexual, transgender, or queer.

Liangzhu Culture spanning centuries from the fourth to the third millennium BCE that represented the last new Stone Age culture in the Yangzi River delta. One of the Ten Thousand States, it was highly stratified and is known for its jade objects.

liberalism Political and social theory that advocates representative government, free trade, and freedom of speech and religion.

limited-liability joint-stock company Company that mobilized capital from a large number of investors, called shareholders, who were not to be held personally liable for financial losses incurred by the company.

Linear A and B Two linear scripts first discovered on Crete in 1900. On the island of Crete and on the mainland areas of Greece, documents of the palace-centered societies were written on clay tablets in these two scripts. Linear A script, apparently written in Minoan, has not yet been deciphered. Linear B was first deciphered in the early 1950s.

"Little Europes" Urban landscapes between 1100 and 1200 composed of castles, churches, and towns in what are today Poland, the Czech Republic, Hungary, and the Baltic States.

Little Ice Age A period of global cooling—not a true ice age—that extended roughly from the sixteenth to the nineteenth century. The dates, especially for the start of the period, remain the subject of scientific controversy.

Liu Bang Chinese emperor from 206 to 195 BCE; after declaring himself the prince of his home area of Han, in 202 BCE, Liu declared himself the first Han emperor.

llamas Animals domesticated in the Americas that are similar in utility and function to camels in Afro-Eurasia. Llamas can carry heavy loads for long distances.

Long March (1934–1935) Trek of over 6,000 miles (or 10,000 kilometers) by Mao Zedong and his communist followers to establish a new base of operations in northwestern China.

Longshan peoples Peoples who lived in small agricultural and river-basin villages in East Asia during the third millennium BCE. They set the stage for the Shang dynasty in terms of a centralized state, urban life, and a cohesive culture.

lord Privileged landowner who exercised authority over the people who lived on his land.

lost generation The 17 million former members of the Red Guard and other Chinese youth who were denied education from the late 1960s to the mid-1970s as part of the Chinese government's attempt to prevent political disruptions.

Louisiana Purchase (1803) American purchase of French territory from Napoleon that included much of the present-day United States between the Mississippi River and the Rocky Mountains.

Lucy Relatively intact skeleton of a young adult female australopithecine unearthed in the valley of the Awash River in 1974 by an archaeological team working at a site in present-day Hadar, Ethiopia. The researchers nicknamed the skeleton Lucy. She stood just over 3 feet tall and walked upright at least some of the time.

Her skull contained a brain within the ape size range, but her jaw and teeth were humanlike. Lucy's skeleton was relatively complete and at the time was the oldest hominin skeleton ever discovered.

Luftwaffe German air force.

Luther, Martin (1483–1546) A German monk and theologian who sought to reform the Catholic Church; he believed in salvation through faith alone, the importance of reading scripture, and the priesthood of all believers. His Ninety-Five Theses, which enumerated the abuses by the Catholic Church as well as his reforms, started the Protestant Reformation.

Maastricht Treaty (1993) Treaty that formed the European Union, a fully integrated trading and financial bloc with its own bureaucracy and elected representatives.

ma'at Term used in ancient Egypt to refer to stability or order, the achievement of which was the primary task of Egypt's ruling kings, the pharaohs.

Maccabees Leaders of a riot in Jerusalem in 167 BCE that was a response to a Seleucid edict outlawing the practice of Judaism. 1000 CE.

Madhyamika (Middle Way) Buddhism Chinese branch of Mahayana Buddhism established by Kumarajiva (344–413 CE) that used irony and paradox to show that reason is limited.

madrasas Higher schools of Muslim education that taught law, the Quran, religious sciences, and the regular sciences.

magnetic needle compass A navigational instrument invented by the Chinese that helped guide sailors on the high seas after.

Mahayana Buddhism "Great Vehicle" Buddhism; an accessible form of Buddhism that spread along the Silk Roads and included in its theology a divine Buddha as well as bodhisattvas.

Mahdi The "chosen one" in Islam whose appearance was believed to foretell the end of the world and the final day of reckoning for all people.

maize Grains, the crops that the settled agrarian communities across the Americas cultivated, along with legumes (beans) and tubers (potatoes).

Maji Maji Revolt (1905–1907) Swahili insurrection against German colonialists; inspired by the belief that those who were anointed with specially blessed water (*maji*) would be immune to bullets. It resulted in 200,000 to 300,000 African deaths.

Mali Empire West African empire, founded by the legendary king Sundiata in the early thirteenth century. It facilitated thriving commerce along routes linking the Atlantic Ocean, the Sahara, and beyond.

Mamluks (Arabic for "owned" or "possessed") Military men who ruled Egypt as an independent regime from 1250 until the Ottoman conquest in 1517.

Manaus Opera House Opera house built in the interior of Brazil in a lucrative rubber-growing area at the turn of the twentieth century.

Manchukuo Japanese puppet state in Manchuria in the 1930s.

Manchus Descendants of the Jurchens who helped the Ming army recapture Beijing in 1644 after its seizure by the outlaw Li Zicheng. The Manchus numbered around 1 million but controlled a domain that included perhaps 250 million people. Their rule lasted more than 250 years and became known as the Qing dynasty.

mandate of heaven Religious ideology established by Zhou leaders to communicate legitimate transfer and retention of royal power as the will of their supreme god. The mandate later became Chinese political doctrine.

Mande A people who lived in the area between the bend in the Senegal River to the west and the bend in the Niger River to the east and between the Senegal River to the north and the Bandama River to the south. Also known as the Mandinka. Their civilization emerged around 1100.

Mandela, Nelson (1918–2013) Leader of the African National Congress (ANC) who was imprisoned for more than two decades by the apartheid regime in South Africa for his political activities, until worldwide protests led to his release in 1990. In 1994, Mandela won the presidency in South Africa's first free mass elections.

Manifest Destiny Belief that it was God's will for the American people to expand their territory and political processes across the North American continent.

manorialism System in which the manor (a lord's home, its associated industry, and surrounding fields) served as the basic unit of economic power; an alternative to the concept of feudalism (the hierarchical relationships of king, lords, and peasantry) for thinking about the nature of power in western Europe from 1000 to 1300 CE.

Mao Zedong (1893–1976) Chinese communist leader who rose to power during the Long March (1934–1935). In 1949, Mao and his followers defeated the Nationalists and established a communist regime in China.

maroon community Sanctuary for formerly enslaved freedom seekers in the Americas.

Marshall Plan Economic aid package given by the United States to Europe after World War II in hopes of a rapid period of reconstruction and economic gain that would protect the countries that received the aid from a communist takeover.

martyr Literally meaning "witness," a person executed by Roman authorities for maintaining his or her Christian beliefs rather than worshipping the emperor.

Marx, Karl (1818–1883) German philosopher and economist who created Marxism and believed that a revolution of the working classes would overthrow the capitalist order and create a classless society.

Marxism A current of socialism created by Karl Marx and Friedrich Engels. It stressed the primacy of economics and technology—and, above all, class conflict—in shaping human history. Economic production provided the foundation, the "base" for society, which shaped politics, values, art, and culture (the superstructure). In the modern, industrial era, they believed class conflict boiled down to a two-way struggle between the bourgeoisie (who controlled the means of industrial production) and the proletariat (workers who had only their labor power to sell).

mass consumption Increased purchasing power and appetite for goods in the prosperous and mainly middle-class societies of the early twentieth century, stemming from mass production.

mass culture Distinctive form of popular culture that arose in the wake of World War I. It reflected the tastes of the working and middle classes, who now had more time and money to spend on entertainment, and relied on new technologies, especially film and radio, that could reach an entire nation's population and consolidate their sense of being a single state.

mass production System in which factories were set up to produce huge quantities of identical products, reflecting the early twentieth-century world's demands for greater volume, faster speed, reduced cost, and standardized output.

mastaba Word meaning "bench" in Arabic; it refers to a huge flat structure identical to earlier royal tombs of ancient Egypt.

Mau Mau Uprising (1952–1957) Uprising orchestrated by a Kenyan guerrilla movement; this conflict forced the British to grant independence to the Black majority in Kenya.

Mauryan Empire (321–184 BCE) The first large-scale empire in South Asia, stretching from the Indus in the west to the mouth of the Ganges in the east and nearly to the southern tip of the Indian subcontinent; begun by Chandragupta Maurya, in the aftermath of Alexander's time in India, and expanded to its greatest extent by his grandson Aśoka.

Mawali Non-Arab "clients" to Arab tribes in the early Islamic empire. Because tribal patronage was so much a part of the Arabian cultural system, non-Arabs who converted to Islam affiliated themselves with a tribe and became clients of that tribe.

Maxim gun European weapon that was capable of firing many bullets per second; it was used against Africans in the conquest of the continent.

Maya Civilization that ruled over large stretches of Mesoamerica; it was composed of a series of kingdoms, each built around ritual centers rather than cities. The Maya engaged neighboring peoples in warfare and trade and expanded borders through tributary relationships. They were not defined by a great ruler or one capital city, but by their shared religious beliefs.

McCarthyism Campaign by U.S. Republican senator Joseph McCarthy in the late 1940s and early 1950s to uncover closet communists, particularly in the State Department and in Hollywood.

Meat Inspection Act (1906) Legislation that provided for government supervision of meatpacking operations; it was part of a broader progressive reform movement dedicated to correcting the negative consequences of urbanization and industrialization in the United States.

Mecca Arabian city in which the Prophet Muhammad was born. Mecca was a trading center and pilgrimage destination in the pre-Islamic and Islamic periods. Exiled in 622 CE because of resistance to his message, Muhammad returned to Mecca in 630 CE and claimed the city for Islam.

Medes Rivals of the Neo-Assyrians and the Persians. The Medes inhabited the area from the Zagros Mountains to the modern city of Tehran; known as expert horsemen and archers, they were eventually defeated by the Persians.

megalith Literally, "great stone"; the word *megalith* is used when describing structures such as Stonehenge. These massive structures are the result of cooperative planning and work.

megarons Large buildings found in Troy (level II) that are the predecessors of the classic Greek temple.

Meiji Empire Empire created under the leadership of Mutsuhito, emperor of Japan from 1868 until 1912.

During the Meiji period Japan became a world industrial and naval power.

Meiji Restoration (1868–1912) Reign of the Meiji Emperor, which was characterized by a new nationalist identity, economic advances, and political transformation.

Mencius Disciple of Confucius who lived from 372 to 289 BCE.

mercantilism Economic theory that drove European empire builders. In this economic system, the world had a fixed amount of wealth, which meant one country's wealth came at the expense of another's. Mercantilism assumed that colonies existed for the sole purpose of enriching the country that controlled the colony.

Mercosur Free-trade pact between the governments of Argentina, Brazil, Paraguay, and Uruguay.

meritocracy Rule by persons of talent.

Meroitic kingdom Thriving kingdom from the fourth century BCE to 300 CE. A successor to Kush, it was influenced by both Egyptian and Sudanic cultures.

Mestizos Mixed-blood offspring of Spanish settlers and Amerindians.

Métis Mixed-blood offspring of French settlers and Amerindians.

Mexican Revolution (1910–1920) Conflict fueled by the unequal distribution of land and by disgruntled workers; it erupted when political elites split over the succession of General Porfirio Díaz after decades of his rule. The fight lasted over ten years and cost 1 million lives, but it resulted in widespread reform and a new constitution.

Mfecane movement African political revolts in the first half of the nineteenth century that were caused by the expansionist methods of King Shaka of the Zulu people.

microsocieties Small-scale, fragmented communities that had little interaction with others. These communities were the norm for peoples living in the Americas and islanders in the Pacific and Aegean from 2000 to 1200 BCE.

Middle Kingdom Period of Egyptian history lasting from about 2055 to 1650 BCE, characterized by a consolidation of power and building activity in Upper Egypt.

migration Long-distance travel for the purpose of resettlement. In the case of early humans, the need to move was usually a response to an environmental shift, such as climate change during the Ice Age.

millenarian Believer (usually religious) in the cataclysmic destruction of a corrupt, fallen society and its replacement by an ideal, utopian future.

millenarian movement Believer (usually religious) in the cataclysmic destruction of a corrupt, fallen society and its replacement by an ideal, utopian future.

millets Minority religious communities of the Ottoman Empire.

minaret Slender tower within a mosque from which Muslims are called to prayer.

minbar Pulpit inside a mosque from which Muslim religious speakers broadcast their message to the faithful.

Ming dynasty Successor to the Mongol Yuan dynasty that reinstituted and reinforced Han Chinese ceremonies and ideals, including rule by an ethnically Han bureaucracy.

Minoans A people who built a large number of elaborate, independent palace centers on Crete, at Knossos, and elsewhere around 2000 BCE. Named after the legendary King Minos, said to have ruled Crete at

the time, they sailed throughout the Mediterranean and by 1600 BCE had planted colonies on many Aegean islands, which in turn became trading and mining centers.

mission civilisatrice Term French colonizers used to refer to France's form of "rationalized" colonial rule, which attempted to bring "civilization" to the "uncivilized."

mitochondrial DNA Form of DNA found in mitochondria, structures located outside the nuclei of cells. Examining mitochondrial DNA enables researchers to measure the genetic variation among living organisms, including human beings. Only females pass mitochondrial DNA to their offspring.

Moche A people who extended their power and increased their wealth at the height of the Chimú Empire over several valleys in what is now Peru.

Model T Automobile manufactured by the Ford Motor Company, which was the first to be priced reasonably enough to be sold to the masses.

modernism In the arts, modernism refers to the effort to break with older conventions and seek new ways of seeing and describing the world.

Mohism School of thought in ancient China, named after Mo Di, or Mozi (c. 479–381 BCE). It emphasized one's obligation to society as a whole, not just to one's immediate family or social circle.

monarchy Political system in which one individual holds supreme power and passes that power on to his or her next of kin.

monasticism From the Greek word *monos* (meaning "alone"), the practice of living without the ties of marriage or family, forsaking earthly luxuries for a life of prayer and study. While Christian monasticism originated in Egypt, a variant of ascetic life had long been practiced in Buddhism.

monetization An economic shift from a barter-based economy to one dependent on currency.

Mongols Combination of nomadic forest and steppe peoples who lived by hunting and livestock herding and were expert horsemen. Beginning in 1206, the Mongols launched a series of conquests that brought far-flung parts of the world together under their rule. By incorporating conquered peoples and adapting some of their customs, the Mongols created a unified empire that stretched from the Pacific Ocean to the shores of the eastern Mediterranean and the southern steppes of Eurasia.

monotheism The belief in only one god; to be distinguished from polytheism (the belief in many gods) and henotheism (the belief that there may be many gods but one is superior to the others).

Moors Term employed by Europeans in the medieval period to refer to Muslim occupants of North Africa, the western Sahara, and the Iberian Peninsula.

mosque Place of worship for the people of Islam.

mound people Name for the people of Cahokia, since its landscape was dominated by earthen monuments in the shapes of mounds. The mounds were carefully maintained and were the loci from which Cahokians paid respect to spiritual forces. *See also* Cahokia.

Mu Chinese ruler (956–918 BCE) who put forth a formal bureaucratic system of governance, appointing officials, supervisors, and military captains to whom he was not related. He also instituted a formal legal code.

muckrakers Journalists who aimed to expose political and commercial corruption in late nineteenth- and early twentieth-century America.

Muftis Experts on Muslim religious law.

Mughal Empire One of Islam's greatest regimes. Established in 1526, it was a vigorous, centralized state whose political authority encompassed most of modern-day India. During the sixteenth century, it had a population of between 100 and 150 million.

Muhammad (570–632 CE) Prophet and founder of the Islamic faith. Born in Mecca in Saudi Arabia and orphaned when young, Muhammad lived under the protection of his uncle. His career as a prophet began around 610 CE, with his first experience of spiritual revelation.

Muhammad Ali (r. 1805–1848) Ruler of Egypt who initiated a set of modernizing reforms that sought to make it competitive with the great powers.

mullahs Religious leaders in Iran who in the 1970s led a movement opposing Shah Mohammad Reza Pahlavi and denounced American materialism and secularism.

multinational corporations Corporations based in many different countries that have global investment, trading, and distribution goals.

Muscovy The principality of Moscow. Originally a mixture of Slavs, Finnish tribes, Turkic speakers, and many others, Muscovy used territorial expansion and commercial networks to consolidate a powerful state and expanded to become the Russian Empire, a huge realm that spanned parts of Europe, much of northern Asia, numerous North Pacific islands, and even—for a time—a corner of North America (Alaska).

Muslim Brotherhood Egyptian organization founded in 1928 by Hassan al-Banna. It attacked liberal democracy as a cover for middle-class, business, and landowning interests and fought for a return to a purified Islam.

Muslim League National Muslim party of India.

Mussolini, Benito (1883–1945) Italian dictator and founder of the fascist movement in Italy. During World War II, he allied Italy with Germany and Japan.

Muwahhidin Literally, "unitarians"; followers of the Wahhabi movement that emerged in the Arabian Peninsula in the eighteenth century.

Mycenaeans Mainland competitors of the Minoans who took over Crete around 1400 BCE. Migrating to Greece from central Europe, they brought their Indo-European language, chariots, and metalworking skills, which they used to dominate until 1200 BCE.

Nagasaki Second Japanese city to be hit by an atomic bomb near the end of World War II.

Napoleon Bonaparte (1769–1821) General who rose to power in a postrevolutionary coup d'état, eventually proclaiming himself emperor of France. He placed security and order ahead of social reform and created a civil legal code. Napoleon expanded his empire through military action, but after his disastrous Russian campaign, the united European powers defeated Napoleon and forced him into exile. He escaped and reassumed command of his army but was later defeated at the Battle of Waterloo.

Napoleonic Code Legal code drafted by Napoleon in 1804; it distilled different legal traditions to create one uniform law. The code confirmed the abolition of feudal privileges of all kinds and set the conditions for exercising property rights.

National Assembly of France Governing body of France that succeeded the Estates-General in 1789 during the French Revolution. It was composed of, and defined by, the delegates of the Third Estate.

National Association for the Advancement of Colored People (NAACP) A U.S. civil rights organization, founded in 1910, dedicated to ending inequality and segregation for Black Americans.

National Recovery Administration (NRA) U.S. New Deal agency created in 1933 to prepare codes of fair administration and to plan for public works. It was later declared unconstitutional.

nationalism The idea that members of a shared community called a nation should have sovereignty within the borders of their state.

nation-state Form of political organization that derived legitimacy from its inhabitants, often referred to as citizens, who in theory, if not always in practice, shared a common language, common culture, and common history.

native learning Japanese movement to promote nativist intellectual traditions and the celebration of Japanese texts.

native paramountcy British form of "rationalized" colonial rule, which attempted to bring "civilization" to the "uncivilized" by proclaiming that when the interests of European settlers in Africa clashed with those of the African population, the latter should take precedence.

natural rights Belief that emerged in eighteenth-century western Europe and North America that

rights fundamental to human nature were discernible to reason and should be affirmed in human-made law.

natural selection Charles Darwin's theory that populations grew faster than the food supply, creating a "struggle for existence" among species. In later work he showed how the passing on of individual traits was also determined by what he called sexual selection—according to which the "best" mates are chosen for their strength, beauty, or talents. The outcome: the "fittest" survived to reproduce, while the less adaptable did not.

Nazis (National Socialist German Workers' Party) German organization dedicated to winning workers over from socialism to nationalism; the first Nazi Party platform combined nationalism with anticapitalism and anti-Semitism.

Neanderthals Members of an early wave of hominins from Africa who settled in western Afro-Eurasia, in an area reaching from present-day Uzbekistan and Iraq to Spain, approximately 150,000 years ago.

Negritos Hunting and gathering inhabitants of the East Asian coastal islands who migrated there around 28,000 BCE but by 2000 BCE had been replaced by new migrants.

Negritude The idea of a Black identity and culture different from, but not inferior to, European cultural forms; shaped by African and African American intellectuals like Senegal's first president, Léopold Sédar Senghor.

Nehemiah Jewish eunuch of the Persian court who was given permission to rebuild the fortification walls around the city of Jerusalem from 440 to 437 BCE.

Neo Assyrian Empire Afro-Eurasian empire that dominated

from 911 to 612 BCE. The Neo-Assyrians extended their control over resources and people beyond their own borders, and their empire lasted for three centuries.

neocolonialism Contemporary geopolitical policy or practice in which a politically, economically, and often militarily superior nation asserts control over a country that remains nominally sovereign.

Nestorian Christians Denomination of Christians whose beliefs about Christ differed from those of the official Byzantine church. Named after Nestorius, former bishop of Constantinople, they emphasized the human aspects of Jesus.

New Deal President Franklin Delano Roosevelt's package of government reforms that were enacted during the 1930s to provide jobs for the unemployed, social welfare programs for the poor, and security to the financial markets.

New Economic Policy Enacted decrees of the Bolsheviks between 1921 and 1927 that grudgingly sanctioned private trade and private property.

New Negro movement *See* Harlem Renaissance.

New World Term applied to the Americas that reflected the Europeans' view that anything previously unknown to them was "new," even if it had existed and supported societies long before European explorers arrived on its shores.

nirvana Literally, "nonexistence"; nirvana is the state of complete liberation from the concerns of worldly life, as in Buddhist thought.

Noble Eightfold Path Buddhist concept of a way of life by which people may rid themselves of individual desire to achieve nirvana.

The path consists of wisdom, ethical behavior, and mental discipline.

Noh drama Masked theater favored by Japanese bureaucrats and regional lords during the Tokugawa period.

Nok culture Spectacular culture that arose in present-day Nigeria in the sixth century BCE. Iron smelting occurred there around 600 BCE. Thus the Nok people made the transition from stone to iron materials.

nomads People who move across vast distances without settling permanently in a particular place. Often pastoralists, nomads and transhumant herders introduced new forms of chariot-based warfare that transformed the Afro-Eurasian world.

nongovernmental organizations (NGOs) Term used to refer to private organizations like the Red Cross that play a large role in international affairs. *See also* supranational organizations.

nonviolent resistance Moral and political philosophy of resistance developed by Indian National Congress leader Mohandas Gandhi. Gandhi believed that if Indians pursued self-reliance and self-control in a nonviolent way, the British would eventually have to leave.

North American Free Trade Agreement (NAFTA) Treaty negotiated in the early 1990s to promote free trade between Canada, the United States, and Mexico.

North Atlantic Treaty Organization (NATO) International organization set up in 1949 to provide for the defense of western European countries and the United States from the perceived Soviet threat.

Northern Wei dynasty Regime founded in 386 CE by the Tuoba, a people originally from Inner Mongolia, that lasted one and a half centuries. The rulers of this dynasty adopted many practices of the earlier Chinese Han regime. At the same time, they struggled to consolidate authority over their own nomadic people. Ultimately, several decades of intense internal conflict led to the dynasty's downfall.

Northwest Passage Long-sought marine passageway between the Atlantic and Pacific Oceans along the northern coast of North America.

Oceania Collective name for Australia, New Zealand, and the islands of the southwest Pacific Ocean.

Odyssey An epic tale, composed in the eighth century BCE, of the journey of Odysseus, who traveled the Mediterranean back to his home in Ithaca after the siege of Troy.

oikos The word for "small family unit" in ancient Greece, similar to the *familia* in Rome. Its structure, with men as heads of household over women and children, embodied the fundamental power structure in Greek city-states.

oligarchy Clique of privileged rulers.

Olmecs Mesoamerican people, emerging around 1500 BCE, whose name means "inhabitants in the land of rubber," one of their major trade goods. Living in decentralized agrarian villages, this complex, stratified society shared language and religious ideas that were practiced at sacred ritual centers.

open-door policy Policy proposed by U.S. secretary of state John Hay that would give all foreign nations equal access to trade with China. As European imperial powers carved out spheres of influence in late nineteenth-century China, American leaders worried that the United States would be excluded from trade with China.

Opium Wars (1839–1842, 1856–1860) Wars fought between the British and Qing China over British trade in opium; the result was that China granted to the British the right to trade in five different ports and ceded Hong Kong to the British.

oracle bones Animal bones inscribed, heated, and interpreted by Shang ritual specialists to determine the will of the ancestors.

Organization of the Petroleum Exporting Countries (OPEC) International association established in 1960 to coordinate price and supply policies of oil-producing states.

Orientalism Genre of literature and painting that portrayed the nonwestern peoples of North Africa and Asia as exotic, sensuous, and economically backward with respect to Europeans.

Orientalists Western scholars who specialized in the study of Asia when Orientalism was at its peak.

Orrorin tugenensis Early hominid that first appeared 6 million years ago.

Ottoman Empire A Turkish warrior band that transformed itself into a vast, multicultural, bureaucratic empire that lasted from the early fourteenth century through the early twentieth century and encompassed Anatolia, the Arab world, and large swaths of southern and eastern Europe.

Pacific War (1879–1883) War between Chile and the alliance of Bolivia and Peru.

pagani Pejorative word used by Christians to designate pagans.

palace Official residence of the ruler, his family, and his entourage. The palace was both a social institution and a set of buildings. It first appeared around 2500 BCE, about a millennium later than the

Mesopotamian temple, and quickly joined the temple as a defining landmark of city life. Eventually, it became a source of power rivaling the temple, and palace and temple life often blurred, as did the boundary between the sacred and the secular.

Palace of Versailles The palace complex, 11 miles away from the French capital of Paris, built by Louis XIV in the 1670s and 1680s to house and entertain his leading clergymen and nobles, with the hopes of diverting them from plotting against him.

Palmyra Roman trading depot located in modern-day Syria; part of a network of trading cities that connected various regions of Afro-Eurasia.

pan movements Groups that sought to link people across state boundaries in new communities based on ethnicity or, in some cases, religion (for example, pan-Germanism, pan-Islamism, and pan-Slavism).

pandemic An outbreak of disease occurring worldwide or over a great area spanning international boundaries and affecting a large number of people.

Pansophia Ideal republic of inquisitive Christians united in the search for knowledge of nature as a means of loving God.

papacy The institution of the pope, the Catholic spiritual leader in Rome.

papal Of, relating to, or issued by a pope.

Parthians Horse-riding people who pushed southward around the middle of the second century BCE and wiped out the Greek kingdoms in Iran. They then extended their power all the way to the Mediterranean, where they ran up against

the Roman Empire in Anatolia and Mesopotamia.

pastoral nomads Peoples who move with their herds in perpetual motion across large areas, like the steppe lands of Inner Eurasia, and facilitate long-distance trade.

pastoralism A way of life in which humans herd domesticated animals and exploit their products (hides/fur, meat, and milk). Pastoralists include nomadic groups that range across vast distances, as well as transhumant herders who migrate seasonally in a more limited range.

paterfamilias Latin for "father of the family," the foundation of the Roman social order.

patria Latin, meaning "fatherland."

patrons In the Roman system of patronage, men and women of wealth and high social status who protected dependents or "clients" of a lower class.

Pax Mongolica The political and especially the commercial stability that the vast Mongol Empire provided for the travelers and merchants of Eurasia during the thirteenth and fourteenth centuries.

Pax Romana Latin term for "Roman Peace," referring to the period from 25 BCE to 235 CE, when conditions in the Roman Empire were relatively settled and peaceful, allowing trade and the economy to thrive.

Pax Sinica Modern term (paralleling the term *Pax Romana)* for the "Chinese Peace" that lasted from 149 to 87 BCE, a period when agriculture and commerce flourished, fueling the expansion of cities and the growth of the population of Han China.

Peace Preservation Law (1925) Act instituted in Japan that specified up to ten years' hard labor for any

member of an organization advocating a basic change in the political system or the abolition of private property.

Pearl Harbor American naval base in Hawaii on which the Japanese launched a surprise attack on December 7, 1941, bringing the United States into World War II.

Peloponnesian War War fought between 431 and 404 BCE between two of Greece's most powerful city-states, Athens and Sparta.

Peninsular War (1808–1813) Conflict in which the Portuguese and Spanish populations, supported by the British, resisted an invasion of the Iberian Peninsula by the French under Napoleon.

peninsulares Men and women born in Spain or Portugal who resided in the Americas. They regarded themselves as superior to Spaniards or Portuguese born in the colonies (creoles).

People's Charter Document calling for universal suffrage for adult males, the secret ballot, electoral districts, and annual parliamentary elections. It was signed by over 3 million British between 1839 and 1842.

periplus "Sailing around" manual that preserved firsthand knowledge of navigation strategies and trading advice.

Persepolis Darius I's capital city in the highlands of Fars; a ceremonial center and expression of imperial identity as well as an important administrative hub of the Persian Empire.

Peterloo Massacre (1819) The killing of 11 and wounding of 460 following a peaceful demonstration for political reform by workers in Manchester, England.

Petra Literally, "rock"; city in modern-day Jordan that was the

Nabatean capital. It profited greatly by supplying provisions and water to travelers and traders. Many of its houses and shrines were cut into the rocky mountains.

phalanx Military formation used by Philip II of Macedon, whereby heavily armored infantry were closely arrayed in battle.

Philip II of Macedon Father of Alexander the Great, under whose rule Macedonia developed into a large ethnic and territorial state. After unifying Macedonia, Philip went on to conquer neighboring states.

philosophes Enlightenment thinkers who applied scientific reasoning to human interaction and society as opposed to nature.

philosophia Literally, "love of wisdom"; a system of thought that originally included speculation on the nature of the cosmos, the environment, and human existence. It eventually came to include thought about the nature of humans and life in society.

Phoenicians An ethnic group in the Levant known for their ships, trading, and alphabet, and referred to in Hebrew scripture as the Canaanites. The term *Phoenician* (Greek for "purple people") derives from the major trade good they manufactured, a rare and expensive purple dye.

phonemes Primary and distinctive sounds that are characteristic of human language.

piety Strong sense of religious duty and devoutness, often inspiring extraordinary actions.

plant domestication The practice of growing plants, harvesting their seeds, and saving some of the seeds for planting in subsequent growing cycles, resulting in a steady food supply. Plant domestication was practiced as far back as 9000 BCE in the southern Levant and spread from there into the rest of Southwest Asia.

plantation slavery System whereby enslaved labor was used for the cultivation of crops wholly for the sake of producing surplus that was then used for profit; such plantations were a crucial part of the growth of the Mediterranean economy.

Plato (427–347 BCE) Disciple of the great philosopher Socrates; his works are the only record we have of Socrates's teaching. He was also the author of formative philosophical works on ethics and politics.

plebs The "common people" of Rome, whose interests were protected by officials called tribunes.

pochteca Archaic term for merchants of the Mexica.

polities Politically organized communities or states.

polyglot communities Societies composed of diverse linguistic and ethnic groups.

popular culture Affordable and accessible forms of art and entertainment available to people at all levels of society.

popular sovereignty The idea that the power of the state resides in the people.

populists Members of a political movement that supported U.S. farmers in late nineteenth-century America. The term is often used generically to refer to political groups who appeal to the majority of the population.

potassium-argon dating Major dating technique based on the decay of potassium into argon over time. This method makes possible the dating of objects up to a million years old.

potato famine (1840s) Severe famine in Ireland that led to the rise of radical political movements and the migration of large numbers of Irish to the United States.

potter's wheel Fast wheel that enabled people to mass-produce vessels in many different shapes. This advance, invented at the city of Uruk, enabled potters to make significant technical breakthroughs.

pottery Vessels made of mud and, later, clay used for storing and transporting food.

Prague Spring (1968) Program of liberalization by which communist authorities in Czechoslovakia strove to create a democratic and pluralist socialism; crushed by the Soviets, who branded it a "counterrevolutionary" movement.

predestination Belief of many sixteenth- and seventeenth-century Protestant groups that God had foreordained the lives of individuals, including their bad and good deeds.

primitivism Western art movement of the late nineteenth and early twentieth centuries that drew upon the so-called primitive art forms of Africa, Oceania, and pre-Columbian America.

printing press A machine used to print text or pictures from type or plates, dramatically increasing the speed at which information could be copied and disseminated. The spread of printing press technology in the 1450s created a revolution in communication around the world.

progressive reformers Members of the U.S. reform movement in the early twentieth century that aimed to eliminate political corruption, improve working conditions, and regulate the power of large industrial and financial enterprises.

proletarians Industrial wage workers.

prophets Charismatic freelance religious men of power who found themselves in opposition to the formal power of kings, bureaucrats, and priests.

Prophet's Town Indian village in present-day Indiana that was burned down by American forces in the early nineteenth century.

Protestant Reformation Religious movement initiated by sixteenth-century monk Martin Luther, who openly criticized the corruption in the Catholic Church and voiced his belief that Christians could speak directly to God. His doctrines gained wide support, and those who followed this new view of Christianity rejected the authority of the papacy and the Catholic clergy, broke away from the Catholic Church, and called themselves "Protestants."

Protestantism Division of Christianity that emerged in western Europe from the Protestant Reformation.

Proto-Indo-European The parent of all the languages in the Indo-European family, which includes, among many others, English, German, Norwegian, Portuguese, French, Russian, Persian, Hindi, and Bengali.

Pullman Strike (1894) American Railway Union strike in response to wage cuts and firings.

Punic Wars Series of three wars fought between Rome and Carthage from 264 to 146 BCE that resulted in the end of Carthaginian hegemony in the western Mediterranean, the growth of Roman military might (army and navy), and the beginning of Rome's aggressive foreign imperialism.

puppet states Governments with little power in the international arena that follow the dictates of their more powerful neighbors or patrons.

Puritans Seventeenth-century reform group of the Church of England; also known as dissenters or nonconformists.

Qadiriyya Sufi order that facilitated the spread of Islam into West Africa.

qadis Judges in the Ottoman Empire.

qanats Underground water channels, vital for irrigation, that were used in Persia. Little evaporation occurred when water was being moved through *qanats*.

Qing dynasty (1644–1911) Minority Manchu rule over China that incorporated new territories, experienced substantial population growth, and sustained significant economic growth.

Questions of King Milinda (Milinda-punha) Name of a second-century BCE text espousing the teachings of Buddhism as set forth by Menander, a Yavana king. It featured a discussion between the king and a sophisticated Buddhist sage named Nagasena.

Quetzalcoatl Ancient deity and legendary ruler of Native American peoples living in Mexico.

Quran The scripture of the Islamic faith. Originally a verbal recitation, the Quran was eventually compiled into a book with its verses in the order in which we have them today. According to traditional Islamic interpretation, the Quran was revealed to Muhammad by the angel Gabriel over a period of twenty-three years.

radicalism The conviction that real change is possible only by going to the root (in Latin, *radix*) of the problem and promoting complete political and social reform. Tendencies toward radicalism can be found in every culture that develops a complex set of institutions and hierarchies, but have been found most frequently in the west since 1789.

radicals Widely used term in nineteenth-century Europe that referred to those individuals and political organizations that favored the total reconfiguration of Europe's old state system.

radiocarbon dating Dating technique using the isotope C^{14}, contained by all living organisms, which plants acquire directly from the atmosphere and animals acquire indirectly when they consume plants or other animals. When organisms die, the C^{14} they contain begins to decay into a stable nonradioactive isotope, C^{12}. The rate of decay is regular and measurable, making it possible to ascertain the ages of fossils that leave organic remains up to 40,000 years.

Raj British crown's administration of India following the end of the East India Company's rule after the Rebellion of 1857.

raja "King" in the Kshatriya period in South Asia; could also refer to the head of a family, but indicated the person who had control of land and resources in South Asian city-states.

Ramadan Ninth month of the Muslim year, during which all Muslims must fast during daylight hours.

rape of Nanjing Attack against the Chinese in which the Japanese slaughtered at least 100,000 civilians and raped thousands of women between December 1937 and February 1938.

Rashtriya Swayamsevak Sangh (RSS) (1925) Campaign to organize Hindus as a militant, modern community in India; translated in English as "National Volunteer Organization."

Rebellion of 1857 Indian uprising against the East India Company whose aims were religious purification, an egalitarian society, and local and communal solidarity without the interference of British rule.

rebus Probably originating in Uruk, a representation that transfers meaning from the name of a thing to the sound of that name. For example, a picture of a bee can represent the sound "b." Such pictures opened the door to writing: a technology of symbols that uses marks to represent specific discrete sounds.

Reconquista Spanish reconquest of territories lost to the Islamic empire, beginning with Toledo in 1061.

Red Guards Chinese students who were the shock troopers in the early phases of Mao Zedong's Great Proletarian Cultural Revolution in 1966–1976.

Red Lanterns Female supporters of the Chinese Boxers who dressed in red garments. Most were teenage girls and unmarried women.

Red Turban movement Diverse religious movement in China during the fourteenth century that spread the belief that the world was drawing to an end as Mongol rule was collapsing.

Reds Bolsheviks.

Reich German empire composed of Denmark, Austria, and parts of western France (1933–1945).

Reichstag The German parliament.

Reign of Terror Campaign at the height of the French Revolution in the early 1790s that used violence, including systematic execution of opponents of the revolution, to purge France of its enemies and to extend the revolution beyond its borders; radicals executed as many as 40,000 persons who were judged enemies of the state.

Renaissance Term meaning "rebirth" used by historians to characterize the cultural flourishing of European nations between 1430 and 1550, which emphasized a break from the church-centered medieval world and a new concept of humankind as the center of the world.

republican government Government in which power and rulership rest with representatives of the people, not with a king.

res publica Term (meaning "public thing") used by Romans to describe their Republic, which was advised by a Senate and was governed by popular assemblies of free adult males, who were arranged into voting units, based on wealth and social status, to elect officers and legislate.

Restoration (1815–1848) European movement after the defeat of Napoleon to restore Europe to its pre-French-revolutionary status and to quash radical movements.

Rift Valley Area of northeastern Africa where some of the most important early human archaeological discoveries of fossils were made, especially one of an intact skull that is 1.8 million years old.

river basin Area drained by a river, including all its tributaries. River basins were rich in fertile soil, water for irrigation, and plant and animal life, which made them attractive for human habitation. Cultivators were able to produce surplus agriculture to support the first cities.

Roman army Military force of the Roman Empire. The Romans devised a military draft that could draw from a huge population. In their encounter with Hannibal, they lost up to 80,000 men in three separate encounters and still won the war.

Roman Catholicism Western European Christianity, centered on the papacy in Rome, that emphasizes the atoning power of Jesus's death and aims to expand as far as possible.

Roman law The legal system of Rome, under which disputes were brought to public courts and decisions were made by judges and sometimes by large juries. Rome's legal system featured written law and institutions for settling legal disputes.

roving bandits Large bands of dispossessed and marginalized peasants who vented their anger at tax collectors in the waning years of the Ming dynasty.

Royal Road A 1,600-mile road from Sardis in Anatolia to Susa in Iran; used by messengers, traders, the army, and those taking tribute to the king in the fifth century BCE.

Russification Programs to assimilate people of over 146 dialects into the Russian Empire.

Sack of Constantinople Rampage in 1204 by the Frankish armies on the capital city of Constantinople.

sacred kingships Institutions that marked the centralized politics of West Africa. The inhabitants of these kingships believed that their kings were descendants of the gods.

Sahel The area of sub-Saharan Africa spanning the continent just south of the Sahara Desert.

St. Bartholomew's Day Massacre (1572) Roman Catholic massacre of French Protestants in Paris.

St. Patrick A formerly enslaved man brought to Ireland from Britain who later became a missionary, also called the "Apostle of Ireland." He died in 461 CE.

Salt March (1930) A 240-mile trek to the sea in India, led by Mohandas Gandhi, to gather salt for free, thus breaking the British colonial monopoly on salt.

samurai Japanese warriors who made up the private armies of Japanese daimyos.

Sandinista coalition Left-leaning Nicaraguan coalition of the 1970s and 1980s.

Sanskrit cosmopolis Cultural synthesis based on Hindu spiritual beliefs expressed in the Sanskrit language that unified South Asia in place of a centralized empire.

Santería African-based religion, blended with Christian influences, that was first practiced by enslaved people in Cuba.

Sargon the Great King of Akkad, a city-state located near present-day Baghdad. Reigning from 2334 to 2279 BCE, Sargon helped bring the competitive era of city-states to an end and sponsored monumental works of architecture, art, and literature.

Sasanian Empire Empire that succeeded the Parthians in the mid-220s CE in Inner Eurasia. The Sasanian Empire controlled the trade crossroads of Afro-Eurasia and possessed a strong armored cavalry, which made it a powerful rival to Rome. The Sasanians were also tolerant of Judaism and Christianity, which allowed Christians to flourish.

sati Hindu practice whereby a widow was burned to death on the pyre of her dead husband.

satrap Governor of a province in the Persian Empire. Each satrap was a relative or intimate associate of the king.

satrapy Province in the Persian empire, ruled over by a governor, called a satrap, who was usually a relative or associate of the king.

satyagraha See nonviolent resistance.

scientific method Method of inquiry based on experimentation in nature. Many of its principles were first laid out by the philosopher Sir Francis Bacon (1561–1626), who claimed that real science entailed the formulation of hypotheses that could be tested in carefully controlled experiments.

Scramble for Africa European rush to colonize parts of Africa at the end of the nineteenth century.

scribes Those who wield writing tools; from the very beginning they were at the top of the social ladder, under the major power brokers.

Scythian ethos Warrior ethos that embodied the extremes of aggressive horse-mounted culture. In part, the Scythian ethos was the result of the constant struggle between settlers, hunters and gatherers, and nomads on the northern frontier of Europe around 1000 BCE.

Sea Peoples Migrants from north of the Mediterranean who invaded cities of Egypt, Asia Minor, and the Levant in the second millennium BCE.

SEATO (Southeast Asia Treaty Organization) Military alliance of pro-American, anticommunist states in Southeast Asia from 1954 to 1977.

Second World Term invented during the Cold War to refer to the communist countries, as opposed to the west (or First World) and the former colonies (or Third World).

second-generation societies First-millennium BCE societies that innovated on their older political, religious, and cultural ideas by incorporating new aspects of cultures they encountered to reshape their way of life.

Seleucus Nikator Successor of Alexander the Great who lived from 358 to 281 BCE. He controlled Mesopotamia, Syria, Persia, and parts of the Punjab.

Self-Strengthening movement A movement of reformist Chinese bureaucrats in the latter half of the nineteenth century that attempted to adopt western elements of learning and technological skill while retaining their core Chinese culture.

Semu Term meaning "outsiders," or non-Chinese people—Mongols, Tanguts, Khitan, Jurchen, Muslims, Tibetans, Persians, Turks, Nestorians, Jews, and Armenians—who became a new ruling elite over a Han majority population in the late thirteenth century.

sepoys Hindu and Muslim recruits of the East India Company's military force.

serfs Peasants who farmed the land and paid fees to be protected and governed by lords under a system of rule called manorialism.

settled agriculture Humans' use of tools, animals, and their own labor to work the same plot of land for more than one growing cycle. It involves switching from a hunting and gathering lifestyle to one based on farming.

Seven Years' War (1756–1763) Also known as the French and Indian War; worldwide war that ended when Prussia defeated Austria, establishing itself as a European power, and when Britain gained control of India and many of France's colonies through the Treaty of Paris.

sexual revolution Increased freedom in sexual behavior, resulting in part from advances in contraception, notably the introduction of oral contraception in 1960, that allowed men and women to limit childbearing and to have sex with less fear of pregnancy.

shah Traditional title of Persian rulers.

shamans Certain humans whose powers supposedly enabled them to commune with the supernatural and to transform themselves wholly or partly into beasts.

shamisen Three-stringed instrument, often played by Japanese geisha.

Shandingdong Man A *Homo sapiens* whose fossil remains and relics can be dated to about 18,000 years ago. His physical characteristics were close to those of modern humans, and he had a similar brain size.

Shang state Dynasty in northeastern China that ruled from 1600 to 1046 BCE. Though not as well defined by borders as the territorial states in the southwest of Asia, it did have a ruling lineage. Four fundamental elements of the Shang state were a metal industry based on copper, pottery making, standardized architectural forms and walled towns, and divination using animal bones.

Shanghai School Late nineteenth-century style of painting characterized by an emphasis on spontaneous brushwork, feeling, and the incorporation of western influences into classical Chinese pieces.

sharecropping System of farming in which tenant farmers rented land and gave over a share of their crops to the land's owners. Sometimes seen as a cheap way for the state to conduct agricultural affairs, sharecropping often resulted in the impoverishment and marginalization of the underclass.

sharia Body of Islamic law that has developed over centuries, based on the Quran, the sayings of Muhammad (hadith), and the legal opinions of Muslim scholars (*ulama*).

Sharpeville Massacre (1960) Massacre of sixty-nine Black Africans when police fired upon a rally against the recently passed laws requiring non-White South Africans to carry identity papers.

Shawnees Native American tribe that inhabited the Ohio Valley during the eighteenth century.

Shays's Rebellion (1786) Uprising of armed farmers that broke out when the Massachusetts state government refused to offer them economic relief.

Shi Huangdi Title taken by King Zheng in 221 BCE when he claimed the mandate of heaven and consolidated the Qin dynasty. He is known for his tight centralization of power, including standardizing weights, measures, and writing; constructing roads, canals, and the beginnings of the Great Wall; and preparing a massive tomb for himself filled with an army of terra-cotta warriors.

Shiism One of the two main branches of Islam, practiced in the Safavid Empire. Although always a minority sect in the Islamic world, Shiism contains several subsects, each of which has slightly different interpretations of theology and politics.

Shiites Minority tradition within modern Islam that traces political succession through the lineage of Muhammad and breaks with Sunni understandings of succession at the death of Ali (cousin and son-in-law of Muhammad and fourth caliph) in 661 CE.

Shinto Literally, "the way of the gods"; Japan's official religion, which promoted the state and the emperor's divinity.

Shiva The third of three Vedic deities, signifying destruction. *See also* Brahma *and* Vishnu.

shoguns Japanese military commanders. From 1185 to 1333, the Kamakura shoguns served as military "protectors" of the ruler in the city of Heian.

Shotoku (574–622 CE) Prince in the early Japanese Yamoto state who is credited with having introduced Buddhism to Japan.

Shudras Literally, "small ones"; workers and enslaved people from outside the Vedic lineage.

Siddhartha Gautama *See* Buddha.

Sikhism Islamic-inspired religion that calls on its followers to renounce the *varna* (caste) system and to treat all believers as equal before God.

Silicon Valley Valley between the California cities of San Francisco and San Jose, known for its innovative computer and high-technology industries.

silk Luxury textile that became a vastly popular export from China (via the Silk Roads) to the cities of the Roman world.

Silk Roads More than 5,000 miles of trade routes linking China, central Asia, and the Mediterranean. They were named for the silk famously traded along their land and sea routes, although ideas, people, and many other high-value commodities also moved along their lengths.

Silla One of three independent Korean states that may have emerged as early as the third century BCE. These states lasted until 668 CE, when Silla took control over the entire peninsula.

Silver Islands Term used by European merchants in the sixteenth century to refer to Japan because of its substantial trade in silver with China.

Sino-Japanese War (1894–1895) Conflict over the control of Korea in which China was forced to cede the province of Taiwan to Japan.

sipahi Urdu for "soldier."

small seal script Unified script that was used to the exclusion of other scripts under the Qin with the aim of centralizing administration; its use led to a less complicated style of clerical writing than had been in use under the Han.

social Darwinism Belief that Charles Darwin's theory of evolution was applicable to humans and justified the right of the ruling classes or countries to dominate the weak.

social hierarchies Distinctions between the privileged and the less privileged.

Social Security Act (1935) New Deal act that instituted old-age pensions and insurance for the unemployed.

socialism Political ideology that calls for a classless society with collective ownership of all property.

Socrates (469–399 BCE) Philosopher of Athens who encouraged people to reflect on ethics and morality. He stressed the importance of honor and integrity as opposed to wealth and power. Plato was his student.

Sogdians A people who lived in central Asia's commercial centers and maintained the stability and accessibility of the Silk Roads. They were crucial to the interconnectedness of the Afro-Eurasian landmass.

Solidarity The Soviet bloc's first independent trade union, established in Poland at the Gdańsk shipyard.

Song dynasty Chinese dynasty that took over the mandate of heaven for three centuries starting in 960 CE. It ruled in an era of many economic and political successes, but it eventually lost northern China to nomadic tribes.

Song porcelain Type of porcelain perfected during the Song dynasty

that was light, durable, and quite beautiful.

South African War (1899–1902) *See* Anglo-Boer War.

Soviet bloc International alliance that included the eastern European countries of the Warsaw Pact as well as the Soviet Union, but also came to include Cuba.

Spanish-American War (1898) War between the United States and Spain in Cuba, Puerto Rico, and the Philippines. It ended with a treaty in which the United States took over the Philippines, Guam, and Puerto Rico; Cuba won partial independence.

speciation The formation of species.

specie Money in coin.

species A group of animals or plants sharing one or more distinctive characteristics.

spiritual ferment Process that occurred after 300 CE in which religion touched more areas of society and culture than before and in different, more demanding ways.

Spring and Autumn period Period between the eighth and fifth centuries BCE during which China was ruled by the feudal system. In this anarchic and turbulent time, there were 148 different tributary states.

SS (*Schutzstaffel*) Hitler's security police force.

Stalin, Joseph (1878–1953) Leader of the Communist Party and the Soviet Union; sought to create "socialism in one country." The name Stalin means "man of steel."

steel An alloy more malleable and stronger than iron that became essential for industries like shipbuilding and railways.

Stoicism Widespread philosophical movement initiated by Zeno

(334–262 BCE). Zeno and his followers sought to understand the role of people in relation to the cosmos. For the Stoics, everything was grounded in nature. Being in love with nature and living a good life required being in control of one's passions and thus indifferent to pleasure or pain.

Strait of Malacca Seagoing gateway to Southeast and East Asia.

Strategic Defense Initiative Master plan, championed by U.S. president Ronald Reagan in the 1980s, that envisioned the deployment of satellites and space missiles to protect the United States from incoming nuclear bombs; nicknamed "Star Wars."

stupa Dome monument marking the burial site of relics of the Buddha.

Suez Canal Channel built in 1869 across the Isthmus of Suez to connect the Mediterranean Sea with the Red Sea in order to lower the costs of international trade.

Sufi brotherhoods Sufi religious orders that were responsible for the expansion of Islam into many regions of the world.

Sufis Islamic mystics who stressed contemplation and ecstasy through poetry, music, and dance.

Sufism Emotional and mystical form of Islam that appealed to the common people.

sultan Islamic political leader. In the Ottoman Empire, the sultan combined a warrior ethos with an unwavering devotion to Islam.

Sumerian King List Text that recounts the making of political dynasties. Recorded around 2000 BCE, it organizes the reigns of kings by dynasty, one city at a time.

Sumerian pantheon The Sumerian gods, each of whom had a home in a particular floodplain city. In the

Sumerian belief system, both gods and the natural forces they controlled had to be revered.

Sumerian temples Homes of the gods and symbols of Sumerian imperial identity. Sumerian temples also represented the gods' ability to hoard wealth at sites where people exchanged goods and services. In addition, temples distinguished the urban from the rural world.

Sun Yat-sen (1866–1925) Chinese revolutionary and first provisional president of the Republic of China. Sun played an important role in the overthrow of the Qing dynasty and later founded the Guomindang, the Nationalist Party of China.

Sunnis Majority sect within modern Islam that follows a line of political succession from Muhammad, through the first four caliphs (Abu Bakr, Umar, Uthman, and Ali), to the Umayyads and beyond, with caliphs chosen by election from the *umma* (not from Muhammad's direct lineage).

superior man In the Confucian view, a person of perfected moral character, fit to be a leader.

superpowers Label applied to the United States and the Soviet Union after World War II because of their size, their possession of the atomic bomb, and the fact that each embodied a model of civilization (capitalism and communism, respectively) applicable to the whole world.

supranational organizations Organizations that transcend national boundaries, such as nongovernmental organizations (NGOs), the World Bank, and the International Monetary Fund (IMF). These can be distinguished from international organizations, which are intergovernmental projects in which national governments cooperate for common goals—for example, the United Nations, the World Health Organization, and NATO.

survival of the fittest Charles Darwin's belief that as animal populations grew and resources became scarce, a struggle for existence arose, the outcome of which was that only the "fittest" survived to reproduce.

Suryavansha The second lineage of two (the solar) in Vedic society. *See also* Chandravansha.

Swadeshi movement Voluntary organizations in India that championed the creation of indigenous manufacturing enterprises and schools of nationalist thought in order to gain autonomy from Britain.

syndicalists Advocates of syndicalism, a movement of workplace associations that included unskilled labor and sought a replacement for capitalism led by workers. They believed those associations, rather than traditional political parties and parliaments, should make basic decisions.

tabula rasa Term used by John Locke to describe the human mind before it begins to acquire ideas from experience; Latin for "clean slate."

Taiping Heavenly Kingdom (Heavenly Kingdom of Great Peace) Religious sect established by the Chinese prophet Hong Xiuquan in the mid-nineteenth century. Hong Xiuquan believed that he was Jesus's younger brother. The group struggled to rid the world of evil and "restore" the heavenly kingdom, imagined as a just and egalitarian order.

Taiping Rebellion (1850–1864) Rebellion by followers of Hong Xiuquan and the Taiping Heavenly Kingdom against the Qing government over the economic and social turmoil caused by the Opium Wars. Despite raising an army of 100,000 rebels, the rebellion was crushed.

Taj Mahal Royal palace of the Mughal Empire, built by Shah Jahan in the seventeenth century in homage to his wife, Mumtaz.

Tale of Genji Japanese work written in the early eleventh century by Lady Murasaki that gives vivid accounts of Heian court life; Japan's first novel.

talking cure Psychological practice developed by Sigmund Freud whereby the symptoms of neurotic and traumatized patients would decrease after regular periods of thoughtful discussion.

Talmud Huge volumes of oral commentary on Jewish law eventually compiled in two versions, the Palestinian and the Babylonian, in the fifth and sixth centuries BCE.

Talmud of Jerusalem Codified written volumes of the traditions of Judaism; produced by the rabbis of Galilee around 400 CE.

Tang dynasty (618–907 CE) Regime that promoted a cosmopolitan culture, turning China into the hub of East Asian cultural integration, while expanding the borders of its empire. In order to govern such a diverse empire, the Tang established a political culture and civil service based on Confucian teachings. Candidates for the civil service were required to take examinations, the first of their kind in the world.

Tanzimat Reorganization period of the Ottoman Empire in the mid-nineteenth century; its modernizing reforms affected the military, trade, foreign relations, and civilian life.

tappers Rubber harvesters in Brazil, most of whom were either Indian or mixed-blood people.

Tarascans Mesoamerican society of the fifteenth century; rivals to and sometimes subjects of the Aztecs.

Tecumseh (1768–1813) Shawnee who circulated Tenskwatawa's message of Indian renaissance among Indian villages from the Great Lakes to the Gulf Coast. He preached the need for Indian unity, insisting that Indians resist any American attempts to get them to sell more land. In response, thousands of followers renounced their ties to colonial ways and prepared to combat the expansion of the United States.

tekkes Schools that taught the devotional strategies and religious knowledge needed for students to enter Sufi orders and become masters of the brotherhood.

temple Building where believers worshipped their gods and goddesses and where some peoples believed the deities had their earthly residence.

Tenskwatawa (1775–1836) Shawnee prophet who urged disciples to abstain from alcohol and return to traditional customs, reducing dependence on European trade goods and severing connections to Christian missionaries. His message spread to other tribes, raising the specter of a pan-Indian confederacy.

Teotihuacán City-state in a large, mountainous valley in present-day Mexico; the first major community to emerge after the Olmecs.

territorial state A kingdom made up of city-states and hinterlands joined together by a shared identity, controlled through the centralized rule of a charismatic leader, and supported by a large bureaucracy, legal codes, and military expansion.

Third Estate The French people minus the clergy and the aristocracy; this term was popularized in the late eighteenth century and used to exalt the power of the bourgeoisie during the French Revolution.

Third Reich The German state from 1933 to 1945 under Adolf Hitler.

Third World A collective term used for nations of the world, mostly in Asia, Latin America, and Africa, that were not highly industrialized like First World nations or tied to the Soviet bloc (the Second World); it implies a revolutionary challenge to the existing (liberal, capitalist) order. Debate surrounding the best terminology to describe these nations is ongoing.

Thirty Years' War (1618–1648) Conflict begun between Protestants and Catholics in Germany that escalated into a general European war fought against the unity and power of the Holy Roman Empire.

Tiahuanaco Also called Tiwanaku; the first great Andean polity, on the shores of Lake Titicaca.

Tiananmen Square Largest public square in the world and site of the pro-democracy demonstrations in 1989 that ended with the killing of thousands of protesters by the Chinese army.

tiers monde Term meaning "Third World," coined by French intellectuals to describe countries seeking a "third way" between Soviet communism and western capitalism.

Tiglath Pileser III Neo-Assyrian ruler from 745 to 728 BCE who instituted reforms that changed the administrative and social structure of the empire to make it more efficient, and who introduced a standing army.

Tlaxcalans Mesoamerican society of the fifteenth century; these people were enemies of the powerful Aztec Empire.

Tokugawa shogunate Hereditary military administration founded in 1603 that ruled Japan while keeping the emperor as a figurehead; it was toppled in 1868 by reformers who felt that Japan should adopt, not reject, western influences.

Toltecs Mesoamerican peoples who filled the political vacuum left by Teotihuacán's decline; established a temple-filled capital and commercial hub at Tula.

Tomb Culture Warlike group from Northeast Asia who arrived by sea in the middle of the third century CE and imposed their military and social power on southern Japan. These conquerors are known today as the Tomb Culture because of their elevated necropolises near present-day Osaka.

Topkapi Palace Palace complex located in Istanbul that served as both the residence of the sultan, along with his harem and larger household, and the political headquarters of the Ottoman Empire.

total war All-out war involving civilian populations as well as military forces, often used in reference to World War II.

transhumant herders Pastoral peoples who move seasonally from lowlands to highlands in proximity to city-states, with which they trade the products of their flocks (milk, fur, hides) for urban products (manufactured goods, such as metals).

Trans-Siberian Railroad Railroad built over very difficult terrain between 1891 and 1904 and subsequently expanded; it created an overland bridge for troops, peasant settlers, and commodities to move between Europe and the Pacific.

Treaty of Brest-Litovsk (1918) Separate peace between imperial Germany and the new Bolshevik regime in Russia. The treaty acknowledged the German victory on the Eastern Front and withdrew Russia from the war.

Treaty of Nanjing (1842) Treaty between China and Britain following the Opium Wars; it called for indemnities, the opening of new ports, and the cession of Hong Kong to the British.

Treaty of Tordesillas (1494) Treaty in which the pope decreed that the non-European world would be divided into spheres of trade and missionary responsibility between Spain and Portugal.

trickle trade Method by which a good is passed from one village to another, as in the case of obsidian among farming villages; the practice began around 7000 BCE. Also called "down-the-line trade."

Tripartite Pact (1940) Pact that stated that Germany, Italy, and Japan would act together in all future military ventures.

Triple Entente Alliance developed before World War I that included Britain, France, and Russia.

Troy City founded around 3000 BCE in the far west of Anatolia. Troy is legendary as the site of the war that was launched by the Greeks (the Achaeans) and that was recounted by Homer in the *Iliad*.

Truman Doctrine (1947) Declaration promising U.S. economic and military intervention, whenever and wherever needed, for the sake of preventing communist expansion.

Truth and Reconciliation Commission Quasi-judicial body established after the overthrow of the apartheid system in South Africa and the election of Nelson Mandela as the country's first Black president in 1994. The commission was to gather evidence about crimes committed during the apartheid years.

Those who showed remorse for their actions could appeal for clemency. The South African leaders believed that an airing of the grievances from this period would promote racial harmony and reconciliation.

truth commissions Commissions established to inquire into human rights abuses by previous regimes. In Argentina, El Salvador, Guatemala, and South Africa, these commissions were vital for creating a new aura of legitimacy for democracies and for promising to uphold the rights of individuals.

tsar Russian word derived from the Latin *Caesar* to refer to the Russian ruler of Kiev, and eventually to all rulers in Russia. Also spelled as *czar*.

Tula Toltec capital city; a commercial hub and political and ceremonial center.

Uitlanders Literally, "outsiders"; British populations living in Afrikaner republics, who were denied voting rights and subjected to other forms of discrimination in the late nineteenth century.

ulama Arabic word that means "learned ones" or "scholars"; used for those who devoted themselves to knowledge of Islamic sciences.

Umayyads Family who founded the first dynasty in Islam. They established family rule and dynastic succession to the role of caliph. The first Umayyad caliph established Damascus as his capital and was named Mu'awiya Ibn Abi Sufyan.

umma Arabic word for "community"; used to refer to the Islamic polity or Islamic community.

Universal Declaration of Human Rights (1948) U.N. declaration that laid out the rights to which all human beings are entitled.

universalizing religions Religions that appeal to diverse populations; are

adaptable to new cultures and places; promote universal rules and principles; proselytize new believers, often through missionaries; foster community; and, in some cases, do all of this through the support of an empire.

universitas Term used from the end of the twelfth century to denote scholars who came together, first in Paris. The term is borrowed from the merchant communities, where it denoted the equivalent of the modern union.

untouchables People in the Indian *varna* (caste) system whose jobs, usually in the more unsanitary aspects of urban life, rendered them "ritually and spiritually" impure.

Upanishads First-millennium BCE Vedic wisdom literature, in the form of a dialogue between students and teacher; together with the Vedas, they brought a cultural and spiritual unity to much of South Asia.

urban-rural divide Division between those living in cities and those living in rural areas. One of history's most durable worldwide distinctions, the urban-rural divide eventually encompassed the globe. Where cities arose, communities adopted lifestyles based on the mass production of goods and on specialized labor. Those living in the countryside remained close to nature, cultivating the land or tending livestock. They diversified their labor and exchanged their grains and animal products for necessities available in urban centers.

utopian socialism The most visionary of all Restoration-era movements. Utopian socialists like Charles Fourier dreamed of transforming states, workplaces, and human relations and proposed plans to do so.

Vaishyas Householders or lesser clan members in Vedic society who worked the land and tended livestock.

Vardhamana Mahavira Advocate of Jainism who lived from around 540 to 468 BCE; he emphasized interpretation of the Upanishads to govern and guide daily life.

varna Sanskrit for "color"; refers to the four ranked social groups within early Vedic society (priests, warriors, commoners, and laborers). The term *caste*, which derives from the term *casta* ("race/breed" in Spanish and Portuguese) is a later, anachronistic term often used for these divisions.

vassal states Subordinate states that had to pay tribute in luxury goods, raw materials, and manpower as part of a broad confederation of polities under a king's protection.

Vedas Rhymes, hymns, and explanatory texts composed and orally transmitted in Sanskrit by Brahman priests. They shaped the society and religious rituals of Vedic peoples and became central texts in Hinduism.

Vedic peoples Indo-European nomadic group who migrated from the steppes of Inner Asia around 1500 BCE into the Indus basin, on to the Ganges River valley, and then as far south as the Deccan plateau, bringing with them their distinctive religious ideas (Vedas), Sanskrit, and domesticated horses.

veiling Practice of modest dress required of respectable women in the Neo-Assyrian Empire, introduced by Middle Assyrian authorities in the thirteenth century BCE.

Venus figures Representations of the goddess of fertility drawn on the Chauvet Cave in southeastern France. Discovered in 1994, they are probably about 35,000 years old.

Versailles Conference (1919) Peace conference among the victors of World War I; resulted in the Treaty of Versailles, which forced Germany to pay reparations and to give up its colonies to the victors.

Viet Cong Vietnamese communist group committed to overthrowing the government of South Vietnam and reunifying North and South Vietnam.

Viet Minh (League for the Independence of Vietnam) Group founded in 1941 by Ho Chi Minh to oppose the Japanese occupation of Indochina; it later fought the French colonial forces for independence.

Vietnam War (1965–1975) Conflict that resulted from U.S. concern over the spread of communism in Southeast Asia. The United States intervened on the side of South Vietnam in its struggle against peasant-supported Viet Cong guerrilla forces, who wanted to reunite Vietnam under a communist regime. Faced with antiwar opposition at home and ferocious resistance from the Vietnamese, American troops withdrew in 1973; the puppet South Vietnamese government collapsed two years later.

Vikings Warrior group from Scandinavia that used its fighting skills and sophisticated ships to raid and trade deep into eastern Europe, southward into the Mediterranean, and westward to Iceland, Greenland, and North America.

Vishnu The second of three Vedic deities, signifying existence. *See also* Brahma *and* Shiva.

viziers Bureaucrats of the Ottoman Empire.

vodun Mixed religion of African and Christian customs practiced by enslaved and free Blacks in the colony of Saint-Domingue.

Voting Rights Act (1965) Law that granted universal suffrage in the United States.

Wafd Nationalist party that came into existence during a rebellion in Egypt in 1919 and held power sporadically after Egypt was granted limited independence from Britain in 1922.

Wahhabism Early eighteenth-century reform movement organized by Muhammad Ibn Abd al-Wahhab, who preached the absolute oneness of Allah and a return to the pure Islam of Muhammad.

Wang Mang Han minister who usurped the throne in 9 CE because he believed that the Han had lost the mandate of heaven. He ruled until 23 CE.

war ethos Strong social commitment to a continuous state of war. The Roman army constantly drafted men and engaged in annual spring military campaigns. Soldiers were taught to embrace a sense of honor that did not allow them to accept defeat, and those who repeatedly threw themselves into battle were commended.

War of 1812 Conflict between Britain and the United States arising from U.S. grievances over oppressive British maritime practices in the Napoleonic wars.

War on Poverty U.S. president Lyndon Johnson's push for an increased range of social programs and increased spending on social security, health, education, and assistance for the disabled.

Warring States period Period extending from the late fifth century to 221 BCE, when China's regional warring states were unified by the Qin dynasty.

Warsaw Pact (1955–1991) Military alliance between the Soviet Union and other communist states that was established in response to the creation of the North Atlantic Treaty Organization (NATO).

Weimar Republic (1919–1933)
Constitutional republic of Germany
that was subverted by Hitler soon
after he became chancellor.

Western Front Battlefront that
stretched from the English Channel
through Belgium and France to the
Alps during World War I.

White and Blue Niles The two
main branches of the Nile, rising
out of central Africa and Ethiopia,
respectively. They come together at
the present-day capital city of Sudan,
Khartoum.

White Lotus Rebellion Series of
uprisings in northern China (1790–
1800s) inspired by mystical beliefs
in folk Buddhism and, at times, the
idea of restoring the Ming dynasty.

White Wolf Mysterious militia
leader, depicted in popular myth as a
Chinese Robin Hood whose mission
was to rid the country of the injus-
tices of Yuan Shikai's government in
the early years of the Chinese republic (1910s).

Whites "Counterrevolutionaries"
of the Bolshevik Revolution (1917)
who fought the Bolsheviks (the
Reds); included former supporters of
the tsar, Social Democrats, and large
independent peasant armies.

witnessing Dying for one's faith, or
becoming a martyr.

wokou Supposedly Japanese pirates,
many of whom were actually Chinese subjects of the Ming dynasty.

**Works Progress Administration
(WPA)** New Deal program instituted
in 1935 that put nearly 3 million
people to work building roads,
bridges, airports, and post offices.

World Bank International agency
established in 1944 to provide economic assistance to war-torn and
poor countries. Its formal title is the
International Bank for Reconstruction and Development.

World War I *See* Great War.

World War II (1939–1945) Worldwide war that began in September
1939 in Europe, and even earlier in
Asia, and pitted Britain, the United
States, and the Soviet Union (the
Allies) against Nazi Germany, Japan,
and Italy (the Axis).

Wu, Emperor (r. 141–87 BCE) Also
known as Emperor Han Wudi, or
the "Martial Emperor"; the ruler of
the Han dynasty for more than fifty
years, during which he expanded the
empire through his extensive military campaigns.

Wu Zhao Chinese empress who
reigned from 684 to 705 CE. She
began as a concubine in the court of
Li Shimin and became the mother of
his son's child. She eventually gained
power equal to that of the emperor,
and she named herself regent when
she finagled a place for one of her
own sons after their father's death.

Xiongnu The most powerful and
intrusive of the nomadic peoples of
Inner Asia; originally pastoralists from
the eastern part of the Asian steppe in
what is modern-day Mongolia. They
appeared along the frontier with
China in the late Zhou dynasty and
by the third century BCE had become
the most powerful of all the pastoral
communities in that area.

Xunzi (310–237 BCE) Confucian
moralist whose ideas were influential
to Qin rulers. He believed that rational statecraft was more reliable than
fickle human nature and that strict
laws and severe punishments could
create stability in society.

Yalta Accords Results of a meeting
between President Roosevelt, Prime
Minister Churchill, and Premier
Stalin held in the Crimea in 1945
to plan for the post–World War II
order.

Yavana kings Sanskrit name for
Greek rulers, derived from the

Greek name for the area of western
Asia Minor called Ionia, a term
that was then extended to anyone
who spoke Greek or came from the
Mediterranean.

yellow press Newspapers that
sought mass circulation by featuring
sensationalist reporting.

Yellow Turbans Daoist millenarian
Chinese religious movement that
emerged during the Later (Eastern)
Han period. The group was named
for the yellow scarves adherents
wore around their heads.

Yin City that became the capital
of the Shang dynasty in 1350 BCE,
ushering in a golden age.

Young Egypt Antiliberal, fascist
group that gained a large following
in Egypt during the 1930s.

Young Italy Nationalist organization
founded in 1832, made up of young
students and intellectuals devoted
to the unification and renewal of the
Italian state.

Yuan dynasty Dynasty established
by the Mongols after the defeat of
the Song. The Yuan dynasty was
strong from 1279 to 1368; its capital
was at Dadu, or modern-day Beijing.

Yuan Mongols Mongol rulers of
China who were overthrown by the
Ming dynasty in 1368.

Yuezhi A Turkic nomadic people
who roamed pastoral lands to the
west of the Xiongnu territory of
central Mongolia. They had friendly
relationships with the farming societies in China, but detested the
Xiongnu and had frequent armed
clashes with them.

zaibatsu Large-scale, family-owned
corporations in Japan, consisting of
factories, import-export businesses,
and banks, that dominated the
Japanese economy until 1945.

zamindars Archaic tax system
of the Mughal Empire in which

decentralized lords collected tribute for the emperor.

Zapatistas Group of indigenous rebels that rose up against the Mexican government in 1994 and drew inspiration from an earlier Mexican rebel, Emiliano Zapata.

Zheng *See* Shi Huangdi.

Zheng He Ming naval commander who, from 1405 to 1433, led seven massive naval expeditions to impress other peoples with Ming might and to establish tributary relations with Southeast Asia, Indian Ocean ports, the Persian Gulf, and the east coast of Africa.

Zhong Shang Administrative central complex of the Shang.

Zhongguo Term originating in the ancient period and subsequently used to emphasize the central cultural and geographic location of China in the world; means "the middle kingdom."

ziggurat Stepped platform that served as the base of a Sumerian temple, which had evolved from the earlier elevated platform base by the end of the third millennium BCE.

Zionism Political movement advocating the reestablishment of a Jewish homeland in Palestine.

Zoroaster Sometimes known as Zarathustra; thought to have been a teacher around 1000 BCE in eastern Iran and credited with having solidified the region's religious beliefs into a unified system that moved away from animistic nomadic beliefs. The main source for his teachings is a compilation called the Avesta.

Zoroastrianism Dualistic Persian religion, based on the teaching of Zoroaster, in which forces of light and truth battle with those of darkness and falsehood.

Zulus African tribe that, under Shaka, created a ruthless warrior state in southern Africa in the early nineteenth century.

Credits

Front Matter

Photos Front endpaper: ixstudio/Alamy Stock Photo; rear endpaper: Arunas Gabalis/Alamy Stock Photo; frontispiece: Photo Josse/Bridgeman Images; p. vii: Eric Lafforgue/age fotostock; p. viii: www.BibleLandPictures.com/Alamy Stock Photo; p. ix: Album/Alamy Stock Photo; p. x: Dagli Orti/Louvre/Bridgeman Images; p. xi: (left) Lou-Foto/Alamy Stock Photo; (middle) age fotostock; (right) Erich Lessing/Art Resource; p. xii: The Cleveland Museum of Art; p. xiii: Bert Hoferichter/Alamy Stock Photo; p. xiv: Zhang Peng/LightRocket via Getty Images; p. xv: Patrick Ward/Getty Images; p. xvi: The Picture Art Collection/Alamy Stock Photo; p. xvii: The Picture Art Collection/Alamy Stock Photo.

Chapter 1

Photos Page 2: Eric Lafforgue/age fotostock; p. 9: Jan Michael Hosan/Fotogloria/Universal Images Group via Getty Images; 12: Robert Preston/Alamy; p. 15: John Reader/Science Source; p. 16: Sabena Jane Blackbird/Alamy Stock Photo; p. 18: Pascal Goetgheluck/Science Source; p. 19: Lionel Bret/Science Source; p. 27: Alamy Stock Photo; p. 28: Prisma by Dukas Presseagentur GmbH/Alamy Stock Photo; p. 30: Erich Lessing/Art Resource; p. 35: Kimbell Art Museum Fort Worth Texas/Art Resource; p. 43: De Agostini Picture Library/Getty Images; p. 54: (left) Album/Alamy Stock Photo; (right) age fotostock/Alamy Stock Photo; p. 55: (top right) Ganesh Krishnan/Alamy Stock Photo; (top left) RONALD WITTEK/EPA/REX/Shutterstock; (bottom left) Jon Arnold Images Ltd /Alamy Stock Photo; (bottom right) Subhendu Sarkar/LightRocket via Getty Images.

Primary Sources 1.1: "From Rg-Veda 10.90," in *Sources of Indian Tradition 2nd Ed., Vol. 1, From the Beginning to 1800*, edited and revised by Ainslie T. Embree. pp. 18–19. Copyright © 1988 Columbia University Press. Reprinted with permission of the publisher. **1.2**: Genesis 1:1–31. Scripture quotations are from the New Revised Standard Version Bible, copyright © 1989 National Council of the Churches of Christ in the United States of America. Used by permission. All rights reserved. **1.3**: "The Creation of the Universe" from the *Huainanzi* in *Sources of Chinese Tradition, 2nd Ed., Vol. 1: From Earliest Times to 1600*, compiled by Wm. Theodore de Bary and Irene Bloom, pp. 346–347. Copyright © 1999 Columbia University Press. Reprinted with permission of the publisher. **1.4**: Excerpts from *Popol Vuh: The Sacred Book of the Ancient Quiché Maya*, pp. 165–168. English version by Delia Goetz & Sylvanus G. Morley, from the Spanish translation by Adrián Recinos. Copyright © 1950 The University of Oklahoma Press. Reproduced with permission. All rights reserved. **1.5**: "Yoruba Creation Narrative" as translated by P.J. Criss. Reprinted by permission of the Estate of P.J. Criss.

Chapter 2

Photos Page 56: www.BibleLandPictures.com/Alamy Stock Photo; p. 58: © artefacts-berlin.de/German Archaeological Institute; p. 65: Granger; p. 67: Peter Bull Art Studio; p. 68: World Religions Photo Library/Alamy Stock Photo; p. 69: Penn Museum, image #141592; p. 71: (top left) Alamy Stock Photo; (top right) Erich Lessing/Art Resource; (bottom left) Ancient Art and Architecture/Alamy Stock Photo; (bottom right) © The Trustees of the British Museum/Art Resource; p. 78: National Geographic Image Collection/Alamy Stock Photo; p. 79: The Picture Art Collection/Alamy Stock Photo; p. 80: (left) World History Archive/Alamy Stock Photo; (right) Heritage Image Partnership Ltd/Alamy Stock Photo; p. 83: Dinodia Photos/Alamy Stock Photo; p. 86: robertharding/Alamy Stock Photo; p. 90: Asian Art & Archaeology Inc./CORBIS/via Getty Images; p. 91: HIP/Art Resource; p. 95: Image Hans Elbers/Getty Images; p. 103: (top) Bygone Collection/Alamy Stock Photo; (bottom, all) Borromeo/Art Resource; p. 104: Zens photo/Getty Images; p. 105: DEA/G. DAGLI ORTI/Getty Images; p. 106: (left) Egyptian National Museum Cairo Egypt/Bridgeman Images; (right) HIP/Art Resource; p. 107: (top) Alamy Stock Photo; (bottom) Réunion des Musées Nationaux/Art Resource.

Primary Sources 2.1: Inscription translation for Item #18390 (Tablet from 3rd Dynasty of Ur) from British Museum, Collection Online. Copyright © The Trustees of the British Museum, 2018. Reprinted by permission of the British Museum. **2.2**: Excerpts from "The Offering Ritual," from *Writings of the Ancient World: The Ancient Egyptian Pyramid Texts* 2nd Ed., translated by James P. Allen. Copyright © 2015 by SBL Press. Reprinted with permission. **2.5**: Doc. 116 from *Documents in Mycenaean Greek*, 2nd ed. by M. Ventris and J. Chadwick (Cambridge: Cambridge University Press, 1973), p. 245. Reprinted by permission of Cambridge University Press.

Chapter 3

Page 108: Album/Alamy Stock Photo; p. 114: (top left) Art Resource; (top right) Scala/Art Resource; (bottom) Imaginechina Limited/Alamy Stock Photo; p. 117: John Beasley/Alamy Stock Photo; p. 120: Jose Lucas/Alamy Stock Photo; p. 123: Album/Alamy Stock Photo; p. 124: (right) DEA/S. VANNINI/De Agostini/Getty Images; (left) Peter Horree/Alamy Stock Photo; p. 126: Eric Lessing/Art Resource; p. 127: (left) bpk Bildagentur/Vorderasiatisches Museum, Staatliche Museen/Art Resource; (right) De Agostini Picture Library/Bridgeman Images; p. 129: PRISMA ARCHIVO/Alamy Stock Photo; p. 132: Hobart and Edward Small Moore Memorial Collection Gift of Mrs. William H. Moore. Yale University Art Gallery; p. 132: ephotocorp/Alamy Stock Photo; p. 139: Lyndon Giffard Images/Alamy Stock Photo; p. 143: WaterFrame/Alamy Stock Photo; p. 145: Erich Lessing/Art

Resource; p. 160: Granger Collection; p. 161: (left) Granger Collection; (right) Vanni Archive/ Art Resource.

Primary Sources 3.3: Exodus 20:1–17 and Leviticus 26:14–26. Scripture quotations are from the New Revised Standard Version Bible, copyright © 1989 National Council of the Churches of Christ in the United States of America. Used by permission. All rights reserved. **3.5**: Zuo zhuan translated by Earnest Caldwell in "Social Change and Written law in Early Chinese Legal Thought," *Law and History Review* 32(1), p. 15. Reprinted by permission of Cambridge University Press.

Chapter 4

Photos Page 162: Dagli Orti/Louvre/ Bridgeman Images; p. 169: (left) A. Paul Jenkin/Animals Animals; (right) Alexander Frolov/Alamy Stock Photo; p. 170: World History Archive/Alamy Stock Photo; p. 174: The Trustees of the British Museum/Art Resource; p. 175: British Museum/Bridgeman Images; p. 176: Heritage Image Partnership Ltd/Alamy Stock Photo; p. 180: EmmePi Travel/Alamy Stock Photo; p. 181: Lloyd Cluff/Getty Images; p. 183: Scala/Art Resource; p. 184: Courtesy of the Metropolitan Museum of Art; p. 187: (left) Dagli Orti/Shutterstock (right) North Wind Picture Archives; p. 191: Dinodia Photos/Alamy Stock Photo; p. 192: (both) The Trustees of the British Museum/Art Resource; p. 195: Giraudon/ Art Resource; p. 197: Freer Gallery of Art, Smithsonian Institution/Bridgeman Images; p. 210: (right) Bridgeman Images; (left) Granger Collection; p. 211: Courtesy of the Metropolitan Museum of Art.

Primary Sources 4.1: "Featured Object Number 8, May 1990, Human-Headed Winged Bull from Khorsabad (OIM A7369)," translated by John A. Brinkman, Oriental Institute Museum, 1990, pp. 3–4, https://oi.uchicago.edu/sites/ oi.uchicago.edu/files/uploads/Lamassu_ A7369_1990_factsheet.pdf. Courtesy of the Oriental Institute of the University of Chicago. **4.2**: Behistun Inscription, translated by Roland G. Kent in *Old Persian: Grammar, Texts, Lexicon*, 2nd Revised Ed. pp. 131–32. Copyright © 1953 American Oriental Society. Reprinted with permission. **4.3**: "Zhou Succession Story," from

Early Chinese Literature, edited by Burton Watson, pp. 35–36. Copyright © 1962 Columbia University Press. Reprinted with permission of the publisher.

Chapter 5

Photos Page 212: (left) Lou-Foto/ Alamy Stock Photo; (middle) age fotostock (right) Erich Lessing/Art Resource; p. 219: Artokoloro Quint Lox Limited/Alamy Stock Photo; p. 221: Pictures from History/Bridgeman Images; p. 223: Courtesy of the Hunan Provincial Museum; p. 224: SSPL/Getty Images; p. 227: (left) Paul Almasy/Corbis/VCG via Getty Images; (right) Corbis/VCG/Getty; p. 229: Borromeo/Art Resource; p. 232: gameover/ Alamy Stock Photo; p. 233: World History Archive/Ann Ronan Collection/age fotostock; p. 234: Francis Farquhar/Bridgeman Images; p. 235: Album/Alamy Stock Photo; p. 237: Scala/Art Resource; p. 239: (left) Insights Images/Peter Langer/Media Bakery; (right) Jess Kraft/Shutterstock; p. 245: Eric Lafforgue /age fotostock; p. 246: (left) Lou-Foto/Alamy Stock Photo; (middle) age fotostock (right) Erich Lessing/Art Resource; p. 260: (left) Erich Lessing/Art Resource; (right) G. Dagli Orti /De Agostini Picture Library/Bridgeman Images; p. 261: (top) Boltin Picture Library/ Bridgeman Images; (bottom) Bridgeman Images.

Primary Sources 5.1: Ahunuvaiti Gatha, Yasna 33:1–14 from *The Gathas: The Hymns of Zarathushtra* (1999), translated by D.J. Irani, edited by K.D. Irani. Reprinted by permission of the Estate of K.D. Irani. **5.2**: Confucius, from *The Analects (Norton Critical Editions),* edited by Michael Nylan, translated by Simon Leys. Copyright © 2014 by W.W. Norton & Company, Inc. *The Analects of Confucius* translation copyright © 1997 by Pierre Ryckmans. Used by permission of W. W. Norton & Company, Inc. **5.4**: Plato, excerpts from *The Apology of Socrates*. Translated by Cathal Woods and Ryan Pack. Reprinted with permission.

Chapter 6

Photos Page 262: Courtesy of The Cleveland Museum of Art; p. 268: Luisa Ricciarini/Bridgeman Images; p. 269: Erich Lessing/Art Resource; p. 270: (left) Bridgeman Images; (right) A. Dagli Orti/

De Agostini Picture Library/Bridgeman Images; p. 273: Vanni/Art Resource; p. 275: William Francis Warden Fund/ Bridgeman Images; p. 276: DeA Picture Library/Art Resource, NY; p. 278: Werner Forman Archive/Bridgeman Images; p. 282: (left) Brian A. Vikander/ Getty Images; (right) Bridgeman Images; p. 284: (top row) The Granger Collection; (middle row) Dilip Rajgor/Dinodia Photo/ age fotostock; (bottom left) MCLA Collection/Alamy Stock Photo; (bottom right) Jonathan O'Rourke/Alamy Stock Photo; p. 286: Igor Dymov/Alamy Stock Photo; p. 287: Courtesy of The Cleveland Museum of Art; p. 288: (both) Courtesy of The Metropolitan Museum of Art; p. 292: (top row) Heritage Image Partnership Ltd/Alamy Stock Photo; (middle row) The History Collection/Alamy Stock Photo; (bottom row) PjrStudio/Alamy Stock Photo; p. 294: DEA/G. DAGLI ORTI/Getty Images; p. 296: robertharding/Alamy Stock Photo; p. 298: NASA/JPL; p. 313: (top row) Birmingham Museums and Art Gallery/ Bridgeman Images; (middle row) Dilip Rajgor/Dinodia Photo/agefotostock; (bottom) HIP/Art Resource; (right) Lou-Foto/ Alamy Stock Photo.

Primary Sources 6.1: Arrian, from *The Campaigns of Alexander*, translated by Aubrey de Sélincourt, revised with an introduction and notes by J. R. Hamilton (Penguin Classics 1958, Revised edition 1971). Copyright © the Estate of Aubrey de Sélincourt, 1958. Introduction and Notes copyright © J. R. Hamilton, 1971. Reproduced by permission of Penguin Books Ltd. **6.2**: Aśoka, "The Kalinga Edict," from *Inscriptions of Aśoka*, translated by D.C. Sircar. Reprinted by permission of the Publications Division of the Ministry of Information and Broadcasting of India, 1967. **6.4**: Excerpts from *The Perfection of Wisdom in Eight Thousand Lines & Its Verse Summary,* translated by Edward Conze. Copyright © 1973 by Edward Conze. Reprinted with the permission of The Permissions Company, Inc., on behalf of City Lights Books, www.citylights.com.

Chapter 7

Photos Page 315: Bert Hoferichter/ Alamy Stock Photo; p. 318: The Art Institute of Chicago; p. 322: Snark/Art Resource; p. 323: (top) Patrick AVENTURIER/

Gamma-Rapho via Getty Images; (bottom) Bridgeman Images; p. 324: British Museum/Art Resource; p. 325: DeAgostini/Getty Images; p. 326: (left) Artokoloro Quint Lox Limited/: Alamy Stock Photo; (middle and right) Asian Art & Archaeology Inc./Getty Images; p. 333: Museum of Fine Arts Boston; Museum purchase with funds donated by Mrs. Gardner Brewer and by contribution and the Benjamin Pierce Cheney Donation; p. 337: Vanni/Art Resource; p. 339: Atlantide Phototravel/Getty Images; p. 340: Album/Alamy Stock Photo; p. 341: (left) Cultura RM/Alamy Stock Photo; (right) Scala/Art Resource; p. 342: (left) Toño Labra/age fotostock; (right) The Print Collector/Alamy Stock Photo; p. 344: HIP/Art Resource; p. 346: Arterra Picture Library/Alamy Stock Photo; p. 50: Erich Lessing/Art Resource; p. 362: (left) robertharding/Alamy Stock Photo; (top right) Universal Images Group North America LLC/DeAgostini/Alamy Stock Photo; (bottom right) Werner Otto/Alamy Stock Photo; p. 363: (left) robertharding/Alamy Stock Photo; (right) Getty Images.

Primary Sources 7.1: Dong Zhongshu, "Responsibilities of Han Rulership" in *Sources of Chinese Tradition, 2nd Ed., Vol. 1: From Earliest Times to 1600*, compiled by Wm. Theodore de Bary and Irene Bloom, pp. 298–300. Copyright © 1999 Columbia University Press. Reprinted with permission of the publisher. 7.3: Pan Chao, excerpts from "Lessons for Women," *Pan Chao: Foremost Woman Scholar of China*. Translated by Nancy Lee Swann. Reprinted by permission of the East Asian Library and Gest Collection at Princeton University. 7.4: Musonius Rufus, in Mary R. Lefkowitz & Maureen B. Fant, eds. *Women's Life in Greece and Rome: A Source Book in Translation*. Second Edition. pp. 50–54. © 1982, 1992 Mary F. Lefkowitz and Maureen B. Fant. Reprinted with permission of Johns Hopkins University Press and Bristol Classical Press, an imprint of Bloomsbury Publishing Plc.

Chapter 8

Photos Page 365: Zhang Peng/LightRocket via Getty Images; p. 372: (right) Granger Collection; (left) Nir Alon/Alamy Stock Photo; p. 373: (right) INTERFOTO/Alamy Stock Photo; (left) Bettmann/Getty Images; p. 374: Scala/Art Resource; p. 376: The State Hermitage Museum, St. Petersburg/photo by Vladimir Terebenin; p. 380: Getty Images; p. 384: INTERFOTO/Alamy Stock Photo; p. 385: (left) Art Resource; (right) Martin Lindsay/Alamy Stock Photo; p. 387: akg-images; p. 388: Heritage Image Partnership Ltd/Alamy Stock Photo; p. 390: ephotocorp/Alamy Stock Photo; p. 392: Historical Views/age fotostock; p. 393: Zhang Peng/LightRocket via Getty Images; p. 394: Art Collection 3/Alamy Stock Photo; p. 400: EDU Vision/Alamy Stock Photo; p. 401: Angelo Hornak/Alamy Stock Photo; p. 403: Werner Forman/Art Resource; p. 404: Kumar Sriskandan/Alamy Stock Photo; p. 418: (left) Eric BRISSAUD/Gamma-Rapho via Getty Images; (right) Public Domain; p. 419: (both) Art Resource.

Primary Sources 8.2: Excerpts from *Egeria: Diary of a Pilgrimage*, translated and annotated by George E. Gingras, Copyright © 1970 by Rev. Johannes Quasten and Rev. Walter J. Burghardt, S.J. and Thomas Comerford Lawler. Paulist Press, Inc., New York/Mahwah, NJ. Reprinted by permission of Paulist Press, Inc. www.paulistpress.com. 8.5. From *Srimad Bhagavatam: Third Canto*, translated by A.C. Bhaktivedanta Swami Prabhupāda (Bhaktivedanta Book Trust, 1974), p. 16. Quoted text courtesy of The Bhaktivedanta Book Trust International, Inc. www.Krishna.com.

Chapter 9

Photos Page 420: Patrick Ward/Getty Images; p. 424: SUHAIB SALEM/REUTERS/Newscom; p. 435: (right) Patrick Ward/Getty Images; (left) geogPhotos/Alamy Stock Photo; p. 440: (left) Michel Piccaya/Shutterstock; (right) B.O'Kane/Alamy Stock Photo; p. 444: (left) De Agostini Picture Library/Bridgeman Images; (right) CPA Media Pte Ltd/Alamy Stock Photo; p. 445: (left) Werner Forman/Art Resource; (right) Kurt Scholz/SuperStock; p. 447: Eye Ubiquitous/Alamy Stock Photo; p. 450: (left) CulturalEyes-AusGS/Alamy Stock Photo; (right) Paul Fearn/Alamy Stock Photo; p. 454: GoFrance/Neil Sutherland/Alamy Stock Photo; p. 455: Giraudon/Bridgeman Images; p. 456: (left) imageBROKER/Alamy Stock Photo; (right) robertharding/Alamy Stock Photo; p. 459: Heritage Image Partnership Ltd/Alamy Stock Photo; p. 460: INTERFOTO/Alamy Stock Photo; p. 470: (left) Leemage/Corbis via Getty Images; (right) © British Library Board. All Rights Reserved/Bridgeman Images; p. 471: (top) British Library Board. All Rights Reserved/Bridgeman Images; (second row, left) Bridgeman-Giraudon/Art Resource; (second row, right) V&A Images London/Art Resource; (third row) EITAN ABRAMOVICH/AFP via Getty Images; (bottom) Edwin Binney 3rd Collection/Bridgeman Images.

Primary Sources 9.1: "Sura 4:1–14 (Women) from The Qur'an", edited by Jane Dammen McAuliffe, Jack Miles, translated by Marmaduke Pickthall, from *The Norton Anthology of World Religions*, edited by Jack Miles, et. al.. Copyright © 2015 by W.W. Norton & Company, Inc. Used by permission of W.W. Norton & Company, Inc. 9.3: "The Book of Analects for Women: Consort Song," translated by Heying Jenny Zhan and Robert Bradshaw in *Journal of Historical Sociology* 9(3), pp. 261–269. Copyright © 1996 Blackwell Publishers Ltd. Reprinted by permission of John Wiley & Sons, Inc.

Chapter 10

Photos Page 472: The Picture Art Collection/Alamy Stock Photo; p. 475: Godong/Alamy Stock Photo; p. 478: Granger; p. 479: Lao Ma/Shutterstock; p. 482: British Library Board. All Rights Reserved/Bridgeman Images; p. 486: Keren Su/China Span/Alamy Stock Photo; p. 490: FLHC 16/Alamy Stock Photo; p. 491: Hemis/Alamy Stock Photo; p. 492: Granger; p. 496: GL Archive/Alamy Stock Photo; p. 497: © British Library Board/Robana/Art Resource; p. 501: The Picture Art Collection/Alamy Stock Photo; p. 502: Hemis/Alamy Stock Photo; p. 503: Bridgeman Art Library/Getty Images; p. 505: Beren Patterson/Alamy Stock Photo; p. 507: INTERFOTO/Alamy Stock Photo; p. 513: akg-images; p. 528: Giraudon/Art Resource; p. 529: (top) Art Resource; (bottom) Pictorial Press Ltd/Alamy Stock Photo.

Primary Sources 10.1: Rabban Bar Sāwmā, from *The Monks of Kublai Khan, Emperor of China: Medieval Travels from*

China through Central Asia to Persia and Beyond, translated by Sir E.A. Wallis Budge. Originally published by Harrison & Sons, Ltd. in 1928 for the Religious Tract Society. Reprinted by permission of Lutterworth Press. **10.3**: From *Ibn Battuta*: *Travels in Asia & Africa,1325–1354* translated by H. A. R. Gibb, pp. 55–57. Copyright © 1929 George Routledge & Sons. Reprinted by permission of Taylor & Francis Books (UK). **10.4**: Al-'Umarī, from *Corpus of Early Arabic Sources for West African History*, translated by J.F.P. Hopkins, edited and annotated by N. Levtzion and J.F.P. Hopkins (Cambridge: Cambridge University Press, 1981). © University of Ghana, International Academic Union, Cambridge University Press 1991. Reprinted with the permission of Cambridge University Press.

Chapter 11

Photos Page 530: The Picture Art Collection/Alamy Stock Photo; p. 534: Sarin Images/Granger; p. 538: DeAgostini/Getty Images; p. 542: Album/Art Resource; p. 542: Sonia Halliday Photo Library/Alamy Stock Photo; p. 543: Muhammed Enes Yldrm/Anadolu Agency/Getty Images; p. 545: The Stapleton Collection/Bridgeman Images; p. 547: volkerpreusser/Alamy Stock Photo; p. 550: incamerastock/Alamy Stock Photo; p. 552: Granger; p. 554: (left) Ian Dagnall/Alamy Stock Photo; (right) Classic Image/Alamy Stock Photo; p. 555: Everett Collection Historical/Alamy Stock Photo; p. 558: RMN-Grand Palais/Art Resource; p. 559: Pictures from History/Bridgeman Images; p. 560: Granger; p. 561: RMN-Grand Palais/Art Resource; p. 564: (left) The Picture Art Collection/Alamy Stock Photo; (right) Gregory A. Harlin/National Geographic Image Collection/Bridgeman Images; p. 578: (both) Bridgeman Images; p. 579: Granger.

Primary Sources 11.1: Michael Dols, "Ibn al-Wardi's Risalah al-Naba' 'an al-Waba', a Translation of a Major Source for the History of the Black Death in the Middle East" in *Near Eastern Numismatics, Iconography, Epigraphy and History*: *Studies in Honor of George C. Miles*, ed. Dickran K. Kouymjian (Beirut: American University of Beirut, 1974), 447–454. Reprinted by permission of the American University of Beirut Press. **11.2**: Marchione di Coppo Stefani, Cronaca Fiorentina, edited by Niccolo Rodolico, Vol. 30 of Rerum Italicarum Scriptores (Citta di Castello: S. Lapi, 1903–1913), as translated by Duane Osheim at http://www2.iath.virginia.edu/osheim/marchione.html. Reprinted by permission of Duane Osheim. **11.3**: Ibn Khaldûn, excerpts from *The Muqaddimah*: *An Introduction to History Vol. 1*, translated by Franz Rosenthal (New York: Pantheon Books, 1958). © 1958 by Bollingen Foundation, Inc. Reprinted by permission of Princeton University Press. **11.4**: al-Maqrizi, "The Guide to the Knowledge of Dynasties and Kings," translated by Hamid Irbouh and excerpted in *The Middle East and Islamic World Reader*, copyright © 2003, Revised edition copyright © 2012 by Marvin Gettleman and Stuart Schaar. Used by permission of Grove/Atlantic, Inc. Any third party use of this material, outside of this publication, is prohibited.

Index

Italic page references indicate maps, illustrations, or chronology entries.

Greece, Greeks, 141
    art and architecture of, 92, *114,*
        145, 236–237, *237,* 284, 285,
        287, *288,* 294
    central marketplace of, 234, *234,*
        283, 293–294
    city-states of, 184, 230–238, *231,*
        251, 265, 269, 272–279
    colonies of, *186, 201, 234, 244,*
        275–276
    competition in, 233, 237–238,
        271
    confederations of, 271
    economy of, 234–236
    emigrants in Aegean, 92
    enslaved people, 232, 233, 235,
        265, 275–276, *276*
    entertainment in, 272–273
    garrison towns of, 282–283, 293
    Hellenism spread by, 264,
        266–267, 271–279, 282–285,
        300–301
    and Islam, 433
    language as part of Indo-
        European family, 111
    language of, *187,* 272, 278, 283,
        292, 301, 351, 374, 433
    learning in, 435, 553–554
    metallurgy of, 92, 142, 160, *161*
    and Persians, 176, *177,* 184, *186,*
        201, 230
    philosophy of, 237–238, 273–274
    self-government of, 232
    and war, 183, *183, 184,* 232,
        233–234, 265, 268
    weapons and military
        organization, 171
    writing of, 104–105, *105*
"Greek-based" culture. *see* Hellenism
Greek Orthodox Church, 452, 459–460
green obsidian, 400
"Green Revolution"
    in Tang China, 446
    and Vietnam, 446
Greenland, 459
Guangzhou, China, *477,* 563. *see also*
    Canton, China
Gujarat Peninsula, 83
Gulf of Mexico, 505, 507
gunpowder, 488
Guorún, 468
Gupta dynasty, 385–387, 388, *390*
Gupta period, *407*

Gutenberg, Johannes, 555, *555, 569*
gymnasiums, Greek-style, 271, 277,
    283, 284

H

Habsburgs, 547, 551
    and Holy Roman Empire, 378
hadith, 432
Hadza (tribe), 25
Hagia Sophia (Constantinople), 380,
    380, 383, *454,* 459, 496, *543*
Hamath, 183
Hammurapi (Hammurabi), 126, 151
Hammurapi's Code, 126, *126,*
    151–154
Han Chinese, *348*
    global themes and sources,
        355–361
Han Empire, 315, 317–319, *320,*
    322–321, *329,* 350–351, *352–353,*
    391–392, 492, 539–540, 552
    administration of, 323–324
    ancient burials, *318*
    armies of, 323, 327–328
    collapse of, 404, 446
    comparison with Roman Empire,
        378–379
    comparisons with other large
        empires, 362–363
    Confucianism in, 317, 324, 327
    decline and fall of, 378–379
    economy of, *224,* 324–325,
        327–330
    entertainment in, 326, *326,*
        341
    expansionism of, 327–330
    images of power in, *362,*
        362–363, *363*
    Later Han dynasty, 331–332,
        350–351
    political and domestic order in,
        355–361
    and politics, 355–357
    rebellions in, 332
    religion of, 327
    and Silk Road, 346–347, *348*
    social order of, 317, 324–327,
        331–332
    women in, 355, 358–359
Han Fei, 222
Han Yu, 447
Hangzhou, China, 513, 563
Hannibal, 336

Harappan culture, 82–87, 97
    city life in, 86–87
    climate change at the end of the
        third millennium BCE, *118,*
        118–119
    dearth of knowledge about, 85
    and gemstones, 87, 106–107, *107*
    lack of monumental architecture
        of, 86
    trade by, *84,* 87
    writing by, 86, 103–104
Harun al-Rashid, 433, 452–453, 457
Hathor (Egyptian goddess), 79
Hatshepsut, ruler of Egypt, 123–124,
    124
Hattusa, Anatolia, 129
Hattusilis I, Hittite ruler, 128
Hawaii, 139
Hazda tribe, *27*
health care. *see also* disease
Hebrews, 156–157
Heka, 79
Helena, 409–411
Heliopolis, 117
Helios (Greek sun god), *292*
Hellenism, 264, *266–267,* 271–279,
    282–285, 294, 299, 301, 312
henotheism, 187
Henrique, Prince, 550
Heracles (Greek demigod), 284
Hermes (Greek god), *237*
Herodotus, 74, 179
Hetepheres I, Queen of Egypt, *78,* 106,
    106
hieratic writing, *80,* 80–81
hieroglyphics, *80,* 80–81, 101, 102–103,
    124, 374
Hijaz, 423
hijra (withdrawal), 424
Himalayas
    Buddha from, 229
    East Asia isolated by, 88, 289
    Indus Valley shaped by, 85
Hinayana Buddhism, 388–389
Hindi language, 111
Hindu Kush Mountains, 188, 384
Hindus, Hinduism, *370,* 387–388, 485,
    486, 487
    artistic representations of, 418,
        419
    Brahmanic origin of, 365,
        387–388, 389–390, 404, *406,*
        486–487

metallurgy
    Afro-Eurasian, 115, 160, *160–161*
    Egyptian, 78
    Greek, 92, 142, 160, *161*
    Shang and Zhou, 134, *197*
Mexica society. *see also* Aztecs
Mexico
    "first-generation" society of, 240–243
    maize cultivation in, 39
    Teotihuacán in, 398–400, *407*
Michelangelo, 553, *554*
micro-states, societies, 110, 141–144
    in Aegean, 141–146
    of Israel and Judah, 185, 187
    in South Pacific, 138–141, *140*
microbes, nomads and, 292
Middle Assyrians, *121*, 175
Middle East. *see also* Southwest Asia
Middle Kingdom, of Egypt, 76, *76*, 81, 116–117, *117*, 122, 126, *148–149*, 160
migration, immigration. *see also* nomads; pastoralism
    Austronesian, 138–140, *140*
    Bantu, *396*, 396–398
    c. 1200 BCE, 165, *166–167*, 168, 182–183
    and climate change, 480–481
    economic discord caused by, 480–481
    forced, 165, 168, 172, 174, 281
    of Gauls, 333
    of *Homo erectus*, 17–19, *20–21*, 44–45
    of *Homo sapiens*, *17*, 19–24, *20–21*
    Indo-European, 111, *131*
    into late Roman Empire, 374–377, *375*
    of nomads and herders, 111–116, *112–113*, 130, 146, 292
    political discord caused by, 480–481
    Vedic, 130–133
Miletus, 237
military
    in early empires, 170–171, 362–363
    of Mongol states, 514–515
millet, *48*, 83, *83*, 436
    as East Asian staple crop, 35–37
Ming dynasty, 556–565, *562, 568*

Black Death in, 556
bureaucracy of, 557–560, 561, 563, 566, 579
and commerce and trade, 563–565
economy in, 563
fashion of, 558–559, *558–559*
fleet of, *564*
gender in, 561
"mandate of heaven" claimed by, 539
population of, 563
rebellions in, 561
religion of, 560, *561*
rulership in, 561–563
trade under, 563–565
mining
    and Roman Empire, 342, 344
Minoan culture, *114, 121*, 143–144, 145, *145, 149*, 183
Minos, King, 143
Mississippi River Valley
    Cahokia in, 507
mitochondrial DNA (mDNA), 8
Mo Di, 378
Moche people, 503–505, *518*
Mogao Caves, *393*
Mohammed. *see* Muhammad, prophet of Islam
Mohenjo Daro, 82–83, 85, 86, *86*
Moldavia (Moldova), 542
monarchies, *547*, 548, 555
monasticism, 455
    Buddhist, 285, 390, 394–395, *447*
    European, 395, *456*
money, monetary system. *see also* coins
    in Mediterranean region, 234
    simultaneous development of, 234
    transition to economy of, 275–276, *302–303*, 344
Mongke Khan, 512
Mongol conquests, legacy of, 515–516
Mongol states (khanates), 514–515
    assimilation of conquered people in, 514–515
    conquered peoples of, 514–515
    divisions of, 514–515
Mongolia, Mongols, 88, *519*
    in Afro-Eurasia, 508–516, *510 511,* 531–532
    Afro-Eurasian interconnectedness and, 516

Baghdad sacked by, 512, 540
Black Death brought by, 531–532, 540
Caffa besieged by, 531
China conquered by, 512–514, *513*, 534
and gender, 508–509
geographical origins of, 514–515
in Islamic world, 540
Korea invaded by, 512
military prowess of, 514–515
as nomadic pastoralists, 514–515
Persia ruled by, 515
and sedentary peoples, 514–515
spread of disease by, 540
waning power of, 536–540
Mongolian steppes, China and, 88
monogamy, 224
monotheism, 187–188, 199
monsoon trade winds, 285, 300
Moors, 550, 551
morals. *see also* ethics; values
    Axial Age code of, 247
    Confucian, 213, 219–220, 326
    and gender, 219–220, 224
    Greek, 249
    of Israelites, 188
Morocco, 550
    and agriculture, 436
    hominids discovered in, 3
Moses, 423
Mosul, 296
Mount Vesuvius, *339*
Mu Wang, Zhou king, *195*
Mughal Empire
    agrarian resources of, 540
    Turkish warriors in, 540
Muhammad, prophet of Islam, 422, 432, 440
    and Christian texts, 425–426
    and conflicting biographical data, 425–429
    early biographies of, 427–428
    and Jewish texts, 425–426
    and lack of 7th-century Arabic-Muslim sources, 425–429
    life of, 423–425, 427–428, *462*
    in Medina, 423–424
    and recent scholarship, 426–427
Mumbai, India, *388*, 418

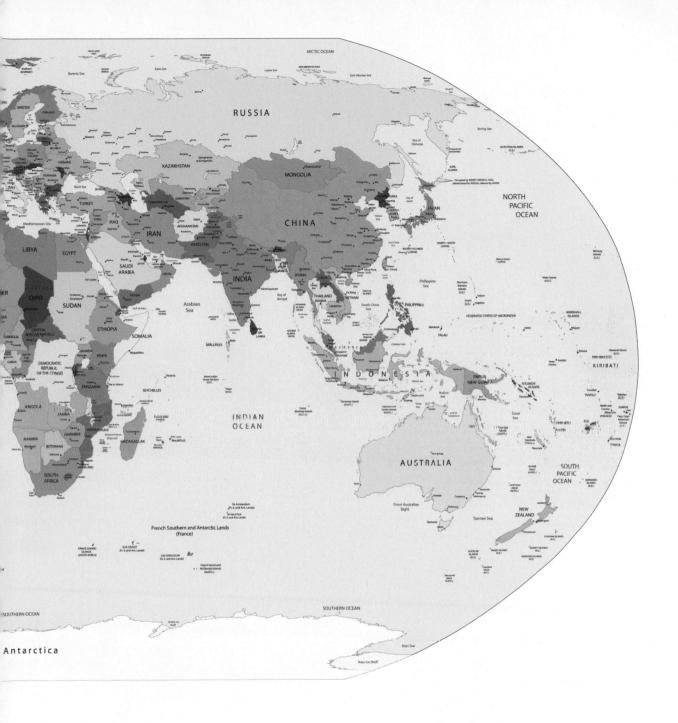